Human Rights in Global Health

Human Rights in Global Health

Rights-Based Governance for a Globalizing World

Edited by Benjamin Mason Meier

and

Lawrence O. Gostin

OXFORD
UNIVERSITY PRESS

Oxford University Press is a department of the University of Oxford. It furthers the University's
objective of excellence in research, scholarship, and education by publishing worldwide. Oxford is a
registered trademark of Oxford University Press in the UK and certain other countries.

Published in the United States of America by Oxford University Press
198 Madison Avenue, New York, NY 10016, United States of America.

Library of Congress Cataloging-in-Publication Data
Names: Meier, Benjamin Mason. | Gostin, Lawrence O. (Lawrence Ogalthorpe), editor.
Title: Human rights in global health : rights-based governance for a globalizing world /
    edited by Benjamin Mason Meier and Lawrence O. Gostin.
Description: Oxford [UK] ; New York, NY : Oxford University Press, [2018] | Includes
    bibliographical references and index.
Identifiers: LCCN 2017046074 | ISBN 9780190672676 ((hardback) : alk. paper) |
    ISBN 9780190672683 ((pbk.) : alk. paper)
Subjects: LCSH: Right to health. | Public health—International cooperation. | Human rights. |
    World health. | Globalization—Health aspects
Classification: LCC K3260.3 .H89 2018 | DDC 362.1—dc23
LC record available at https://lccn.loc.gov/2017046074

9 8 7 6 5 4 3 2 1

Paperback printed by Webcom Inc., Canada
Hardback printed by Bridgeport National Bindery, Inc., United States of America

Note to Readers

This publication is designed to provide accurate and authoritative information in regard to the subject
matter covered. It is based upon sources believed to be accurate and reliable and is intended to be current
as of the time it was written. It is sold with the understanding that the publisher is not engaged in rendering
legal, accounting, or other professional services. If legal advice or other expert assistance is required, the
services of a competent professional person should be sought. Also, to confirm that the information has
not been affected or changed by recent developments, traditional legal research techniques should be
used, including checking primary sources where appropriate.

*(Based on the Declaration of Principles jointly adopted by a Committee of the
American Bar Association and a Committee of Publishers and Associations.)*

You may order this or any other Oxford University Press publication
by visiting the Oxford University Press website at www.oup.com.

To our students

In this uncertain present, you give us hope for the future of human rights in global health …

CONTENTS

CONTRIBUTORS

Carolin Anthes is a Research Associate at the Peace Research Institute Frankfurt (PRIF), examining institutional roadblocks to human rights mainstreaming in FAO. Previously, she served as a consultant in FAO's Right to Food Team on mainstreaming the right to food and a human rights-based approach within the Organization, and she advised the Office of the UN High Commissioner for Human Rights (OHCHR) on the nexus between land and human rights.

Thirukumaran Balasubramaniam is the Geneva Representative of Knowledge Ecology International (KEI). Mr. Balasubramaniam has represented KEI in various multilateral fora, including the Human Rights Council, World Health Organization, the World Intellectual Property Organization, and the World Trade Organization. Previously, Mr. Balasubramaniam served at the World Health Organization in Geneva, dealing with issues related to access to medicines and intellectual property. Mr. Balasubramaniam holds a BA in Economics from the University of Pennsylvania.

Judith R. Bueno de Mesquita is a Lecturer in the School of Law and Human Rights Centre, and Deputy Director of the Human Rights Centre Clinic at the University of Essex. Her research and teaching focus on health and human rights; economic, social, and cultural rights; and development and rights. She also has extensive experience working as a consultant for international organizations, including the World Health Organization and United Nations Population Fund.

Kent Buse serves as Chief, Strategic Policy Directions at UNAIDS. He is a political economist who has taught at Yale University and at the London School of Hygiene and Tropical Medicine. He is an author/editor of five books, including *Making Health Policy, Making Sense of Global Health Governance*, and *Thinking Politically about HIV*. His peer-reviewed papers cover the politics of health policy, global public-private health partnerships, sexual and reproductive health and rights, accountability, and human rights.

Flavia Bustreo is the former Assistant Director-General for Family, Women's and Children's Health at the World Health Organization. A trained clinician, Dr. Bustreo's experience spans global policy leadership, including as Vice-Chair of the GAVI Vaccine Alliance Board, Executive Director of the Partnership for Maternal, Newborn and Child Health, and Interim Deputy Director of the Child

Survival Partnership. In September 2016, Dr. Bustreo was Italy's candidate for Director-General of the World Health Organization.

Audrey R. Chapman is Professor of Community Medicine and Healthcare and holds the Healey Memorial Chair in Medical Ethics and Humanities at the University of Connecticut School of Medicine. Dr. Chapman concurrently holds an adjunct appointment at the UConn School of Law and is an affiliate of the UConn Human Rights Institute. She has published extensively on ethical, legal, human rights, theological, and regulatory issues related to health, genetic developments, and pharmaceuticals.

Andrés Constantin is an Abogado—JD equivalent—from Universidad Torcuato Di Tella in Buenos Aires, Argentina. He is a Global Health Law Scholar at Georgetown University and an LLM Candidate in Global Health Law from the Georgetown University Law Center. He has served as Adjunct Professor of Law at Universidad Torcuato Di Tella Law School.

Joanne Csete teaches health and human rights at the Columbia University Mailman School of Public Health. She was the founding director of the HIV Program at Human Rights Watch and was executive director of the Canadian HIV/AIDS Legal Network. She worked on health programs in Africa for over ten years, including in the UNICEF regional office in Nairobi, and also taught at the University of Wisconsin–Madison. She holds degrees from Princeton, Columbia, and Cornell Universities.

Olivier De Schutter teaches human rights law at the University of Louvain (UCL). He was the United Nations Special Rapporteur on the right to food between 2008 and 2014 and since 2015 is a member of the UN Committee on Economic, Social and Cultural Rights. He co-chairs the International Panel of Experts on Sustainable Food Systems (IPES-Food).

Dabney P. Evans is an Assistant Professor of Global Health in the Rollins School of Public Health at Emory University. She is a mixed-methods researcher of issues affecting vulnerable populations at the intersection of public health and human rights. She is architect and Director of the Emory University Institute of Human Rights and was among the first faculty in the United States to include health and human rights in the public health curriculum.

Emilie Filmer-Wilson is the Human Rights Adviser at the United Nations Population Fund (UNFPA). She has over twelve years of experience working within the UN development system on human rights, including supporting the UN Development Group to strengthen human rights policy coherence and field leadership; managing the human rights-based training for the UN at the UN System Staff College; and providing knowledge management and practical guidance on human rights for UNDP.

Connor Fuchs is a graduate student at Emory University, pursuing JD and MPH degrees. His interests center around how the law can be used to improve health access and outcomes globally. He has previously conducted research in Bangladesh and Cambodia, in addition to providing legal technical assistance to state and local governments in the United States on tobacco control and nutrition initiatives.

Virgínia Brás Gomes currently serves as the Chair of the UN Committee on Economic, Social and Cultural Rights, as well as the senior social policy adviser in the Ministry of Employment, Solidarity and Social Security of Portugal. In addition, Ms. Brás Gomes serves as a member of the International Board of the Programme for Women's Economic, Social and Cultural Rights; the UNRISD Advisory Group for the project on *Linking Social Protection and Human Rights*; the Board of the Portuguese UNICEF Committee; and the National Committee for Human Rights.

Lawrence O. Gostin is University Professor (Georgetown University's highest academic rank), Founding O'Neill Chair in Global Health Law, and Director of the O'Neill Institute for National and Global Health Law. Professor Gostin is the Director of the World Health Organization Collaborating Center on Public Health Law & Human Rights, and serves on expert WHO advisory committees. He is a Member of the Institute of Medicine/National Academy of Sciences, Council of Foreign Relations, and Hastings Center.

Rachel Hammonds is a postdoctoral researcher in the Law and Development Research Group at the University of Antwerp's Law Faculty, where she leads a team of researchers examining efforts to localize human rights. Her work focuses on the intersection of development policy, health, and human rights.

Sarah Hawkes is Professor of Global Public Health at University College London (UCL), where she leads a research theme analyzing the use of evidence in policy processes, particularly in relation to gender and health, and sexual health. Professor Hawkes is the Founding Director of the UCL Centre for Gender and Global Health. She has lived and worked over the past twenty years in Asia, where she has gathered evidence, built capacity, and helped develop programs on gender, sexual health, and human rights.

Ralf Jürgens joined the Global Fund to Fight AIDS, Tuberculosis and Malaria as Senior Coordinator, Human Rights, in May 2015. Prior to his current role, he was director of programs for the Open Society Public Health Program in New York City. Mr. Jürgens also co-founded and served as executive director of the Canadian HIV/AIDS Legal Network. He has a master's degree in law from McGill University and a doctorate in law from the University of Munich.

Florian Kastler is an associate member of the Health and Law Institute of Paris Descartes University, Sorbonne Paris Cité. His joint PhD in international public law, received from Paris Descartes University and Neuchâtel University, focuses on the normative role of the World Health Organization. He currently teaches Global Health Law at Sciences Po, Paris, as well as at Paris Descartes University.

Rajat Khosla works as Human Rights Adviser in the Department of Reproductive Health Research at the World Health Organization. A lawyer by training, Mr. Khosla specializes on issues related to sexual and reproductive health and human rights, and was previously health policy adviser with Amnesty International, where he provided research guidance and policy support on a variety of health and human right issues, in particular around maternal health and sexual and reproductive rights and HIV.

Julia Kreienkamp is a Research Assistant at the Global Governance Institute (GGI) at University College London. Her research interests include global governance, climate change, and human rights. She holds an MSc in International Relations from the London School of Economics and Political Science (LSE) and a BA in Politics and Economics from the University of Münster, Germany.

Hyeyoung Lim currently works as a Human Rights Adviser at the Global Fund to Fight AIDS, Tuberculosis, and Malaria. Previously, Dr. Lim worked as a Human Rights Officer at the Office of the UN High Commissioner for Human Rights, focusing on a number of mandates, including human rights advocacy around the Post-2015 Development Framework and support for the UN Human Rights Treaty Bodies and Special Procedures Mechanism.

Gillian MacNaughton is an assistant professor in the School for Global Inclusion and Social Development at the University of Massachusetts Boston. Her research focuses on economic and social rights and rights-based approaches to social justice, and has been published recently in the *Health and Human Rights Journal*, the *Journal of Human Rights*, and the *Georgetown Journal of International Law*. She has consulted for WHO, UNICEF, UNDP, and the UN Special Rapporteur on the right to health.

Veronica Magar is Team Leader for Gender, Equity and Human Rights at the World Health Organization. She was formerly Executive Director of the Delhi-based NGO *reach—research and action for change*, leading community-based research and policy analysis. Dr. Magar has worked with UN agencies, NGOs, and governments in more than thirty countries across Asia, Africa, and the Middle East, addressing gender inequality and human rights. Dr. Magar has a master's degree and doctorate in public health.

Stephen P. Marks is the François-Xavier Bagnoud Professor of Health and Human Rights at the Harvard T. H. Chan School of Public Health, where he directs the Program on Human Rights in Development. He has served as Expert Member of the UN High-Level Task Force on the Implementation of the Right to Development (2004–2010, chair from 2005–2010), has worked for various UN agencies, and has published widely on human rights, development, and public health.

Bronwyn McBride is a doctoral student at the University of British Columbia and research assistant at the British Columbia Centre for Excellence in HIV/AIDS, where she contributes to research on sex work. Ms. McBride completed her Master's of Public Health–Global Health in 2017 at Simon Fraser University. She has also worked in the policy and strategy division at UNAIDS Secretariat in Geneva, with the International Development Research Centre in Vietnam on a maternal health intervention, and on health and education projects in India.

Mariah McGill is a Senior Fellow with the Program on Human Rights and the Global Economy at Northeastern University School of Law. She is a human rights lawyer, exploring human rights-based approaches to health and other rights. Her recent research has been published in the *Southern California Journal of Interdisciplinary Law*, the *Health and Human Rights Journal*, and the *Northeastern University Law Journal*.

Benjamin Mason Meier is an Associate Professor of Global Health Policy at the University of North Carolina at Chapel Hill, a Scholar at Georgetown Law School's O'Neill Institute for National and Global Health Law, and a consultant to international organizations, national governments, and non-governmental organizations. Dr. Meier's interdisciplinary research—at the intersection of public health, international law, and public policy—examines the development, evolution, and application of human rights in global health.

Suerie Moon is Director of Research at the Global Health Centre, Graduate Institute of International and Development Studies, Geneva. Her research examines the health implications of global governance processes and the political economy of global health, with a focus on innovation and access to medicines; trade, investment, and intellectual property rules; outbreak preparedness and response; and development assistance for health. Dr. Moon teaches at the Graduate Institute and Harvard T. H. Chan School of Public Health.

Luis Mora is Chief of the Gender, Human Rights and Culture Branch at the United Nations Population Fund (UNFPA). He has also served as UNFPA Deputy Regional Director for Latin America and the Caribbean; UNFPA Senior Programme Adviser; UNFPA/UNIFEM Adviser on Gender and Development; UNDP/ UNIFEM Specialist for the Global Initiative on Gender Mainstreaming; UNDP Head of Information in Haiti; and legal assistant at the UN High Commissioner for Refugees for Central and Western Africa.

Mitra Motlagh works for the human rights unit at UNICEF and has fourteen years of experience in international law and development. Prior to joining UNICEF, she worked for the United Nations Development Programme and the World Health Organization at regional and national levels, collaborated with the International Criminal Court, and worked as a lawyer in the area of European Competition law.

Amrei Müller is a Leverhulme Trust Early Career researcher in the Health and Human Rights Unit at Queen's University Belfast. Her research interests lie in the areas of human rights law, in particular the right to health, the European Convention on Human Rights, and international humanitarian law. At present, Dr. Müller is conducting research for the project "Healthcare in conflict: Do armed groups have obligations and responsibilities?"

Thérèse Murphy is Professor of Law and Director of the Health and Human Rights Unit at Queen's University Belfast. She is a long-standing member of the editorial board of the *Human Rights Law Review*, and her books include *Health and Human Rights* (2013) and edited collections on *New Technologies and Human Rights* (2009), *European Law and New Health Technologies* (2013), and *The United Nations Special Procedures System* (2017).

Helena Nygren-Krug joined UNAIDS in 2013, and she is currently Senior Advisor in the Executive Office. From 1999 to 2013, she led the World Health Organization's work on health and human rights. Prior to that, she worked at the Carter Center, the United Nations Office of the High Commissioner for Human Rights, the Red Cross, and the UN Centre for Human Rights.

Gorik J. Ooms is a human rights lawyer and a global health scholar, Professor of Global Health Law & Governance at the London School of Hygiene and Tropical Medicine, Adjunct Professor at the Law Faculty of Georgetown University, and Visiting Professor at the Faculty of Medicine and Health Sciences of Ghent University. Between 1990 and 2008, he worked with Médecins Sans Frontières Belgium in different positions, and as Executive Director from August 2004 to June 2008.

Kumanan Rasanathan is a public health physician with almost twenty years of experience in health and related sectors and is currently Chief of the UNICEF Implementation Research and Delivery Science Unit and Senior Adviser in UNICEF's Health Section. Dr. Rasanathan previously worked at the World Health Organization (on primary health care and the social determinants of health) and in a number of different countries as a clinician, researcher, policymaker, program manager, and advocate.

Mary Robinson is President of the Mary Robinson Foundation–Climate Justice. She served as President of Ireland (1990–1997) and United Nations High Commissioner for Human Rights (1997–2002). A former President of the International Commission of Jurists, she was President and founder of "Realizing Rights: The Ethical Globalization Initiative" (2002–2010). She is a member of the Elders and the recipient of numerous honors and awards, including the Presidential Medal of Freedom from US President Barack Obama.

Jennifer Prah Ruger is the Amartya Sen Professor of Health Equity, Economics, and Policy in the School of Social Policy & Practice and the inaugural Associate Dean for Global Studies and Faculty Chair at the Center for High Impact Philanthropy at the University of Pennsylvania. As a leading scholar of global and domestic health, Dr. Ruger has authored over 100 publications and is internationally recognized for her leadership and work on global and national health inequities.

Yusra Ribhi Shawar has undertaken research on global health governance and the politics of health policy in low-income countries. Her work has appeared in journals including the *Lancet, Lancet Global Health*, and *Health Policy and Planning* and has been funded by Save the Children, the Conrad N Hilton Foundation, the Gates Foundation, Novartis, and USAID. She completed a postdoctoral fellowship at the University of Pennsylvania and has received her PhD from American University and master's degree from the University of Virginia.

Michel Sidibé currently serves as the Executive Director of UNAIDS, holding the rank of Under-Secretary-General of the United Nations. A long-standing champion of a people-centered approach to health and development, Mr. Sidibé leads UNAIDS contributions to regional and country responses, as well as UNAIDS efforts in global policies, evidence, and monitoring and evaluation. Prior to his work at UNAIDS, Mr. Sidibé spent fourteen years at UNICEF, where he oversaw programs across ten francophone African countries.

Matthew Smith is a former consultant with the Global Fund's Human Rights Team. A Geneva native, he holds an MA in Applied Human Rights from the University of York. He is currently based in Mauritius, where he supports the International Organisation for Migration's implementation of the Partnership on Health and Mobility in East and Southern Africa as it aims to redress health vulnerabilities among migrants and migration-affected communities in the island states of the southwest Indian Ocean.

Marcus Stahlhofer is Technical Officer in the Department for Maternal, Newborn, Child and Adolescent Health and the Department of Nutrition of the World Health Organization. He leads the integration of human rights standards into newborn, child, and adolescent health, including through the development of rights-based guidelines and tools to strengthen national legal and policy frameworks, as well as quality-of-care standards. He holds degrees in International Relations, International Politics, and International Human Rights Protection.

Lee Swepston is the former Senior Adviser on Human Rights and Human Rights Coordinator for the International Labor Organization (ILO). Since 1973, Mr. Swepston has published widely on human rights and work, forced labor, child labor, and related issues. He is a visiting professor with the Raoul Wallenberg Institute and the Law School of the University of Lund (Sweden), where he teaches a master's course on human rights and international labor law.

Konstantinos Tararas has worked since 2001 for UNESCO's Social and Human Sciences Sector. Mr. Tararas has contributed—as coordinator, researcher, resource person, and trainer—to a diverse range of activities, including on human rights mainstreaming, the clarification of the right to enjoy the benefits of scientific progress and its applications, and HIV/AIDS-related discrimination. In addition, he has participated in the development of a number of UNESCO publications and in relevant UN inter-agency platforms.

Rebekah Thomas is Technical Officer for Human Rights in the Gender, Equity and Human Rights Team at the World Health Organization. Ms. Thomas has a master's degree in International Law and has worked for over ten years in migration, HIV, and health, promoting the practical application of human rights. She sits on the WHO Guideline Review Committee and the WHO Ethics Review Committee and is an Associate Editor for *BMC International Health and Human Rights*.

Susan Timberlake received a BA in Anthropology from Stanford University, a JD from the University of Georgia School of Law, and an LLM in International Law from Cambridge University. She joined the UN High Commissioner for Refugees in 1984, moved to the World Health Organization in 1994, and moved to UNAIDS in 1996, where she worked as Human Rights Advisor until she retired in 2014 as Chief of the UNAIDS Human Rights and Law Division.

Alicia Ely Yamin is a Visiting Professor of Law at Georgetown University Law Center and the Director of the Health and Human Rights Initiative at the O'Neill Institute for National and Global Health Law; an Adjunct Lecturer on Law and Global Health at the Harvard T. H. Chan School of Public Health; and a Global Fellow at the Centre on Law and Social Transformation.

FOREWORD

Human Rights in Global Health Governance

MARY ROBINSON
Former President of Ireland (1990–1997) and United Nations High Commissioner for Human Rights (1997–2002).

Out of the ashes of World War II, the birth of the United Nations gave rise to the international legal system of human rights that exists today. Over the decades that followed, a system of global governance was formed upon this foundation of human rights, including the human right to health and a wide range of health-related human rights. I am delighted to welcome this comprehensive compilation on *Human Rights in Global Health*, exploring the operationalization of these human rights in global health governance. Having planted the seeds of the human rights-based approach in my role as United Nations High Commissioner for Human Rights, I am delighted to see these contributing chapters sharing the enduring results of these efforts to advance global health. This volume will be vital to the continuing advancement of rights-based global governance to safeguard the health of the world's most vulnerable peoples.

Human rights have evolved dramatically in guiding political cooperation through international organizations. Those campaigning for human rights in the mid-twentieth century would surely have found it hard to fathom a world in which human rights are protected and promoted by a supranational body of international bureaucrats. What began in 1948 with a non-binding declaration that all humans have rights has gradually developed into a bold and complex arrangement of human rights standards, practices, and institutions. A broad coalition has helped to bring this rights-based reality to fruition. States have led this effort, elaborating human rights standards through the progressive development of international treaties. Bringing states together anew following the Cold War, all categories of rights—civil, cultural, economic, social, and political—are now seen as indivisible and of equal importance, particularly in a rapidly globalizing world. These formal developments in international law, alongside national legal reforms and civil society advocacy, have placed human rights at the center of governance.

I have long maintained that placing human rights standards at the heart of global governance, "mainstreaming" rights in international organizations, is the best means through which the voices of the poorest and most vulnerable can be heard on the global stage. Recent years have revealed the extent to which this is true—particularly for indigenous peoples, women and children, persons with disabilities, and those already suffering the devastating effects of climate change. Instilling this ethos of human rights into the culture of international organizations—in their work at the global, regional, and country levels—must be a cornerstone of practical efforts to prevent rights violations and facilitate accountability for the progressive realization of rights.

As I saw as High Commissioner, the United Nations human rights system cannot do this alone, requiring the support of organizations with the field presence, technical mandate, and government relationships necessary to mainstream rights within their respective areas of competence. In recent years, the United Nations human rights system has continued to support human rights mainstreaming across this larger set of organizations, tasking the Office of the High Commissioner for Human Rights with efforts to build human rights capacity among United Nations agencies and programs and to provide technical assistance to institutions in translating a commitment to human rights into programmatic guidance for rights-based activities.

This volume makes clear the importance of translating human rights into institutional programming for public health.

I first recognized the potential for human rights to contribute to the practice of public health in responding to the unprecedented global health threat of HIV/AIDS. Addressing AIDS-related stigma and discrimination through human rights protections was central to the public health response. Under my direction, the Office of the High Commissioner for Human Rights published guidance for governments, United Nations agencies, and civil society in developing rights-based HIV/AIDS policy. These 1998 *International Guidelines on HIV/AIDS and Human Rights* led to a flurry of activity to establish the right to health as a framework for the global HIV/AIDS response. Supported by the new Joint United Nations Programme on HIV/AIDS, the Commission on Human Rights adopted for the first time a 2001 resolution recognizing that access to medication in the context of pandemics such as HIV/AIDS is "one fundamental element for achieving progressively the full realization of the right of everyone to the enjoyment of the highest attainable standard of health."

Ensuring human rights for people living with HIV/AIDS would require cooperation across human rights and global health institutions—bringing together the Office of the High Commissioner for Human Rights with the Joint United Nations Programme on HIV/AIDS and the World Health Organization. Supported by global economic governance and public-private partnerships, the Global Fund to Fight AIDS, Tuberculosis and Malaria emerged in 2002, founded upon human rights principles of participation, equity, accountability, and transparency and supporting countries in responding to the challenges imposed by infectious disease. This rights-based approach to health required coordination across governments, collaboration with civil society, and participation from the most vulnerable, including those living with the burden of the disease itself. As public health practice for HIV/AIDS shifted to embrace human rights, so did governance efforts to erase the inequities of the disease.

However, at the end of my term as High Commissioner in September 2002, I felt some frustration at the fact that economic and social rights were not taken seriously enough by many developed countries, and tended to be regarded more as political aspirations. There were no non-governmental organizations working on economic and social rights, so I founded Realizing Rights: The Ethical Globalization Initiative to pioneer work in African countries on issues such as the right to health. I had been invited by Nelson Mandela to join him on the Gavi Fund Board, and subsequently followed Graça Machel as Chair of the Board during the amalgamation of the boards of the Gavi Fund and Alliance. This gave me particular insights into the role a global partnership can play in furthering the right to health.

As these global health and human rights efforts make clear, across public health challenges in a globalizing world, international organizations have operationalized human rights in distinct ways. The emergence of human rights-based approaches has sought to shift organizations through human rights mainstreaming, yet distinct institutional structures have presented organizations with unique obstacles to human rights implementation. This is particularly true, as explored in this volume's contributing chapters, for health-related human rights and the institutions tasked with mainstreaming them in organizational policies, programs, and practices.

The mainstreaming of human rights in institutions of global health governance can be seen as a measure of success for the implementation of health-related human rights. With the human rights system "demystifying" legal standards for technical officers, global health institutions can operationalize human rights through organizational actions. As international organizations take actions grounded in human rights, global health governance can emphasize not only the availability, accessibility, acceptability, and quality of health services, but also the economic, social, and political inequalities that underpin disability and death. Human rights can provide a path to realize the highest attainable standard of health. At this moment in history, as many nations turn inward—often to the detriment of the most vulnerable and marginalized members of society—global governance must act to reinforce rights-based policy frameworks to promote public health. This volume, providing the first systematic account of the implementation of health-related human rights through global governance, will serve as a model for future research, practice, and advocacy to advance human rights in global health.

PREFACE

No understanding of global health and human rights is complete without addressing the global institutions responsible for implementing human rights law to promote global public health. As globalization transforms threats to global public health, it has also upended national human rights implementation, shifting the protection and promotion of human rights from national governments to global institutions. The study of these institutions is relatively new, but it holds promise for understanding how human rights are implemented for health in a rapidly globalizing world. Where international organizations have adopted divergent approaches to human rights implementation, this heterogeneity in human rights-based approaches has raised an imperative for scholars and advocates to study, analyze, and compare institutional strategies to advance human rights in global health.

This edited volume is the first to examine systematically the role of global institutions in operationalizing human rights for global health, focusing on those international organizations that (1) explicitly or implicitly apply human rights as a means to (2) directly or indirectly influence public health. Following from a description of the field of global health and human rights—including the theoretical background of human rights, political evolution of health-related human rights under international law, and institutional role of human rights in global governance—this edited volume examines the diverse experiences of institutions that operate in the global health sphere, with sections devoted to:

- The World Health Organization—examining the evolution of the World Health Organization's (WHO's) work to develop human rights for public health, current efforts to mainstream human rights in the Geneva Secretariat, and the future of WHO's rights-based role in an expanding global health governance landscape.
- Inter-Governmental Organizations—exploring the distinct ways in which United Nations (UN) specialized agencies and ancillary organizations have mainstreamed human rights to promote an expansive set of underlying determinants of health through the United Nations Children's Fund (UNICEF), the International Labor Organization (ILO), the United Nations Educational, Scientific and Cultural Organization (UNESCO), the United Nations Population Fund (UNFPA), the Food

and Agriculture Organization of the United Nations (FAO), and the Joint
United Nations Programme on HIV/AIDS (UNAIDS).
- Global Economic Governance and Global Health Funding Agencies—
  recognizing the influence of a human right to development and a rights-
  based approach to development on global health through the World Bank,
  the World Trade Organization, national foreign assistance programs, and
  the Global Fund to Fight AIDS, Tuberculosis and Malaria.
- Global Health in Human Rights Governance—considering how global
  health has been advanced by the UN human rights system through the
  Office of the UN High Commissioner for Human Rights (OHCHR),
  the UN special procedures mandate holders, the UN human rights
  treaty bodies, and the UN Human Rights Council's Universal Periodic
  Review (UPR).

For some of these institutions, there has never before been a study of either the
institution's human rights or global health mandate, and the groundbreaking
chapters in this edited volume often present the first effort to examine an organization's unique approach to human rights in global health.

While seeking to develop a comprehensive survey of the intersection of human
rights and public health through global governance, this volume focuses primarily
on member state international organizations that engage with human rights as a
basis for global health. Global health governance has come to include both state-
and non-state-based governance, yet the editors chose to limit this examination to
state-based organizations bound by human rights law—excluding contributions on
non-governmental organizations or transnational corporations and only analyzing
public-private partnerships to the extent that they implicate global governance
institutions already addressed in this volume. Further constraining the norms
addressed in this volume, the contributing chapters explicitly focus on human rights
law, excluding, among other norms, humanitarian law principles that guide governance in conflict situations. Where institutions of global health governance were
known not to consider human rights in their work, these organizations have been
excluded from this analysis, and additional research will be necessary to understand
why these institutions have yet to assume their human rights responsibilities.

The contributing authors who came together in this edited volume represent an
unprecedented collection of experts on a range of global governance institutions
that operationalize human rights to promote global health. While many of the organizations analyzed in this volume do not envision themselves as "doing global
health" or "doing human rights," the contributors recognize the ways in which each
organization influences both determinants of health and norms of human rights
throughout the world. With institution-specific chapters developed by those who
know the institutions best, these chapters have brought together practitioners
within institutions and scholars in academia, combining secondary analysis of institutional documents alongside interview-based research with organizational
insiders. To facilitate comparative analysis, the authors structured their respective
chapters in a consistent way, with aspects of each chapter covering the historical evolution, contemporary practice, and future opportunities for human rights, thereby

providing a basis to assess generalizable themes across institutions of global govern-ance and analyze structural determinants of human rights in global health.

The editors are grateful to Oxford University Press, which saw the promise of comparative institutional analysis of human rights in global health, and especially to our editor, Blake Ratcliff, who shepherded this process from conceptualization to completion. With the chapters in this edited volume assembled during an April 2017 residency at the Brocher Foundation—which encourages research on the ethical, legal, and social implications of new medical technologies—the editors expect to return to the Brocher Foundation in December 2018, hosting a work-shop that will bring together the contributing authors to discuss good institutional practices to advance human rights for global health. In both the administration of these contributing chapters and the editing of individual chapters, the editors are indebted to Hanna Huffstetler, Edith Lee, Max Seunik, and Yayoi Shionoiri for their dedicated support throughout the development of this edited volume. Finally, as educators, we are thankful for our students at the University of North Carolina at Chapel Hill and Georgetown University, whose commitment to global health and human rights gives us hope in these uncertain times for a promising future of human rights in global health governance.

The past year has brought unprecedented challenges to the world's institutions for global health and human rights, but as seen in the chapters that follow, human rights have strengthened global governance for health, endowing organizations with the enduring rights-based structures necessary to realize justice in global health through the difficult years to come.

Introduction

Responding to the Public Health Harms of a Globalizing World through Human Rights in Global Governance

BENJAMIN MASON MEIER AND LAWRENCE O. GOSTIN

Institutions matter for the advancement of human rights in global health. Where academics long shunned scholarship on the right to health and other health-related human rights, the end of the Cold War and advent of neoliberal globalization has brought with it new interest in studies at the intersection of public health and human rights. Yet despite a burgeoning stream of analysis on the scope and content of human rights in global health, this scholarship has focused largely on national governments, neglecting research on the global governance institutions that structure the realization of human rights for global health. Given the dramatic development of human rights under international law and the parallel proliferation of global institutions for public health, there arises an imperative to understand the implementation of human rights law through global health governance.

Human rights are now understood to be central to global health, offering universal frameworks for the advancement of justice in public health. "Health and human rights" has become a discipline in its own right, finding broad acceptance and proving highly influential in local, national, and global contexts. Academics teach the subject in schools of law, medicine, public health, international relations, public policy, and global studies. Non-governmental organizations apply human rights norms and principles in public health practice, advocating for a rights-based approach to public health. Governments are often called upon to find ways to conform health policy to evolving human rights standards. Global governance institutions develop policies, programs, and practices to operationalize human rights in efforts to promote health.

This edited volume focuses on the influence of human rights in global health. In approaching governance for global health, this volume examines the relationship

Human Rights in Global Health. Benjamin Mason Meier and Lawrence O. Gostin.
© Oxford University Press 2018. Published 2018 by Oxford University Press.

between human rights, global governance, and public health—focusing broadly on the health of populations, societies, nations, and the world through underlying social, political, and economic determinants of health. This expansive definition of health determinants implicates an array of global organizations. As an institutional analysis that focuses on organizations, the organizations in this volume include those international bureaucracies that exercise their institutional mandate in ways that influence public health. Through the comparative institutional analysis in this volume, the contributing authors are able to examine evolving institutional dynamics to mainstream human rights in organizational practices and analyze distinct institutional factors that facilitate or inhibit human rights mainstreaming for public health advancement. Based upon these comparative experiences, this edited volume provides a research base for institutionalizing human rights in global health.

This introductory chapter frames the comparative examination of human rights in global health governance. Part I defines the broader field of global health governance, examining the institutions that address public health challenges in a globalizing world. With these institutions providing a basis to implement human rights for global health, Part II examines the development of health-related human rights under international law and the need to implement these rights through global governance. Framing human rights in global governance, Part III outlines the wide array of institutions of global health governance that bear human rights implementation responsibilities, detailing the evolving standards by which institutions have sought to mainstream human rights in organizational policies, programs, and practices. To compare these rights-based efforts, Part IV outlines the research methods by which the contributing authors have studied individual institutions of global governance for health. Part V outlines the structure of this edited volume, delineating the sections and chapters that identify distinct organizational approaches to (and determinants of) human rights in global health governance. This introduction concludes by recognizing the importance of comparative analysis in understanding institutional approaches to human rights in global health, framing this new field of inquiry and calling on scholars, practitioners, and advocates to work together to advance rights-based governance in a globalizing world.

I. GLOBAL HEALTH GOVERNANCE

Global health governance has become a basis to realize a more just world through public health. Through an appreciation of the broader social, economic, and political conditions that underlie global health (McMichael 1999), public health "implicates our collective responsibility for unhealthy behavior," with public health practitioners examining structural determinants of health, including "the causes of disease in the way society organizes itself, produces and distributes wealth, and interacts with the natural environment" (Gostin, Burris, and Lazzarini 1999, 64). As "international health" efforts lost the capacity to act through national governments alone to influence public health, "global health" has become the dominant terminology to describe the ideas of collective action and the needs of all peoples, rather than those of particular countries (Brown, Cueto, and Fee 2006). Shifting from medical care to public health, global health has come to define the determinants of public health that affect the entire world (Fried et al. 2010), with global health governance reflecting the institutions that structure these global determinants of public health (Birn, Pillay, and Holtz 2017).

This focus on global health has required measures beyond the purview of national governments, allowing for both state and non-state actors to integrate their varying functions to better respond to threats of global concern. Global health governance institutions encompass a range of inter-governmental organizations, funding agencies, and international bureaucracies that work across a range of economic, social, and cultural fields that underlie public health in a globalizing world (Youde 2013). These institutions provide expert policy guidance, financial and technical assistance, normative standards, and accountability mechanisms (Clinton and Sridhar 2017). Given the rise of public health on the global policy agenda and the political spotlight on global health inequalities, states and international organizations are partnering with non-governmental organizations (e.g., civil society organizations and philanthropic foundations) to address determinants of global health (Silberschmidt, Matheson, and Kickbusch 2008). Addressing these global determinants of health, global institutions have proliferated, forming governance structures through multi-level and multi-sectoral approaches to governance (Moon et al. 2010).

In seeking to integrate a wide range of actors to progressively realize health, global health governance offers institutional leadership in a more fragmented landscape of organizations. Increasingly influential in global health governance, these proliferating governance institutions are playing crucial roles in developing normative frameworks for global health policy (Hein and Kohlmorgen 2009) and implementing normative frameworks through humanitarian initiatives and development assistance (Pfeiffer et al. 2008). These institutions have become essential to achieving public health in a globalizing world, acting in a supervisory role to address social inequities, health security threats, and regulatory norms (Harman 2012). While not party to human rights treaties (Brabandere 2009), such institutions have a vital role in ensuring global commitment to realize health-related human rights, with these evolving institutional responsibilities leading the global health governance landscape to become central to developing and implementing human rights for global health.

II. HUMAN RIGHTS

Human rights law offers universal frameworks for the advancement of justice in global health. Instrumental to human dignity, human rights seek to address basic needs and frame necessary entitlements to uphold a universal moral vision (Donnelly 2003). As a basis for global justice under international law, human rights stand as a foundational normative framework for global health, offering universal standards by which to frame government responsibilities and facilitate legal accountability (Gruskin et al. 2012). Yet political obstacles long hampered the development of international legal obligations to realize health-related human rights (Meier 2010). Where health-related human rights have come to be codified under international law, this international legal framework has provided a basis for advancing health and safety (Gostin 2014). By framing public health threats as "rights violations," international law now offers global standards by which to articulate duties and evaluate policies and outcomes under law, shifting the policy debate from political aspiration to legal accountability (Yamin 2008). Empowering individuals to seek redress for rights violations rather than serving as passive recipients of government benevolence, human rights law identifies individual rights-holders and their entitlements, and corresponding duty-bearers and their obligations (Steiner, Alston, and Goodman 2008). This "health and human rights movement"—spanning interconnected legal and public health analyses over the past few decades—has been a powerful force for promoting those human rights that underlie global health.

With the 1946 Constitution of the World Health Organization (WHO) serving as the first international treaty to conceptualize a human right to health, states declared that "the enjoyment of the highest attainable standard of health is one of the funda-mental rights of every human being," defining health positively to include "a state of complete physical, mental, and social well-being and not merely the absence of disease or infirmity" (WHO 1946, preamble). Drawing on the WHO Constitution, the nascent United Nations (UN) proclaimed the 1948 Universal Declaration of Human Rights (UDHR) as a "a common standard of achievement for all peoples and all nations" (UN General Assembly 1948, preamble), including in it a set of interrelated rights to medical care and underlying determinants of health:

> Everyone has the right to a standard of living adequate for the health and well-being of himself and of his family, including food, clothing, housing and med-ical care and necessary social services . . . (Ibid., art. 25).

From this birth of human rights for global health, the UN human rights system has sought—through treaties, resolutions, declarations, and interpretations—to de-velop health-related human rights under international law, with human rights now advancing public health through an expansive and reinforcing set of international standards (Gostin 2014). With each government duty-bearer accepting resource-dependent legal obligations to realize health-related rights "to the maximum of its available resources, with a view to achieving progressively the full realization of the rights," states have been pressed to progressively realize rights under international law (UN General Assembly 1966, art. 2).

Health-related human rights have now been firmly established under interna-tional law, evolving since the birth of the UN to codify norms and principles over a wide range of determinants of health. With the end of the Cold War, a political space opened in international relations to advance economic, social, and cultural rights, including the right to health and rights to wide-ranging entitlements that un-derlie health (Moyn 2010). Yet, despite the dramatic development of state support for the obligations of health-related human rights under international law, studies have continued to show an ambiguous relationship between human rights treaty ratification and public health promotion (Palmer et al. 2009). Human rights are not realized automatically upon ratification, requiring attention to the processes by which human rights are implemented. This implementation process, from the acceptance of international norms to the improvement of individual lives, is con-tingent on a long chain of programmatic steps, necessitating efforts to address the pathways of human rights implementation (Getgen and Meier 2009). Where human rights require commitment and resources—through national policies and international cooperation—to assure their realization, duty-bearers seek to implement human rights in policies, programs, and practices (Backman et al. 2008).

Following from the evolving codification of the right to health over the past seventy years, the UN human rights system has shifted from the development of human rights under international law to the implementation of those rights through public policy. When UN Secretary-General Kofi Annan spoke for the last time to the UN Commission on Human Rights, his 2005 address sought to acknowledge this shift toward an "era of implementation":

> The cause of human rights has entered a new era. For much of the past 60 years, our focus has been on articulating, codifying and enshrining rights. That effort produced a remarkable framework of laws, standards and mechanisms—the Universal Declaration, the international covenants, and much else. Such work needs to continue in some areas. But the era of declaration is now giving way, as it should, to an era of implementation (UN Secretary-General 2005).

With the preceding decades leading to the unprecedented development of human rights through international treaties, declarations, and conferences, the implementation of these human rights now requires global institutions.

This rise of global governance for health has raised a need to look beyond state duty-bearers to assess the implementation of human rights for global health. Although international law speaks most directly to states, such legal frameworks have limited effect on the globalizing forces that increasingly underlie public health, necessitating a focus on human rights implementation through institutions of global governance (Meier 2011). These global governance institutions assist states in implementing human rights, thereby providing governments with the international norms, technical assistance, and accountability mechanisms to oversee the realization of rights (Baehr and Gordenker 2005). Beyond support for state duty-bearers, these organizations have independent responsibilities—as manifestations of the global community—to implement human rights through their institutional policies, programs, and practices (Hunt 2017). These global institutions bear human rights responsibilities in both the mission they pursue and the ways in which that mission is carried out. Yet, while institutions of global governance are essential to implement human rights for global health, human rights scholarship has long neglected institutional theory and organizational practice (Sano and Martin 2017).

III. HUMAN RIGHTS IN GLOBAL GOVERNANCE FOR HEALTH

The focus of this volume—on the human rights responsibilities of global institutions—expressly includes human rights governance, but it must look beyond the UN human rights system to encompass an array of organizations of global governance for health. While the UN human rights system has a mandate to implement human rights, it does not have the exclusive institutional competence, expertise, or capacity to implement human rights for global health advancement (UNDG 2015).

Where states did not originally envision that human rights would be implemented by international organizations, it is now clear that the operationalization of human rights in global health requires a wide range of institutions, including the:

- World Health Organization—drawing from the evolution of WHO's efforts to develop human rights for global health, the current processes to mainstream human rights in the Geneva Secretariat, and the future of WHO's rights-based role in an expanding global health governance landscape.
- United Nations System—expanding the ways in which health-related UN specialized agencies, joint programs, and ancillary organizations have mainstreamed human rights to promote an expansive set of underlying determinants of health.
- International Systems for Economic Governance—recognizing the influence of rights-based economic governance on global health through international financial institutions, the international trade system, and national foreign assistance programs.
- Global Human Rights System—considering how global health has been advanced in human rights governance through the UN's human rights bureaucracies, special procedures mandate-holders, human rights treaty bodies, and inter-governmental reviews of human rights.

Complementing each other through interconnected collaborations and public-private partnerships, these international institutions are necessary to translate human rights law into organizational policies, programs, and practices, implementing human rights through global governance for health.

Global health governance has been central to developing human rights under international law, and these institutions are now seen as essential to implementing human rights in organizational actions. Sometimes these human rights implementation responsibilities are explicit in the constitutive framework of the organization; sometimes they are implicit in the organization's rights-based practices, as seen in, among other things:

- organizational policies and programs to realize normative attributes of health-related human rights, assuring the availability, accessibility, acceptability, and quality of public health programs; and
- public health practices that meet cross-cutting human rights principles, engaging in efforts that assure non-discrimination and equality, participation, and accountability (CESCR 2000).

In examining these policies, programs, and practices, it becomes clear that global health governance is constituted by health-related human rights, and organizational actions are framed by human rights-based approaches to health.

Codifying these human rights implementation responsibilities, the 1993 World Conference on Human Rights declared a groundbreaking post–Cold War consensus on human rights, articulating organizational responsibilities for human rights

(World Conference on Human Rights 1993). The resulting Vienna Declaration and Programme of Action took human rights out from under the exclusive purview of specialized human rights officials, establishing "the foundation for a holistic and integrated approach to human rights not only by the human rights machinery but also by the entire United Nations system" (Robinson 1998, para. 23). UN Secretary-General Kofi Annan sought to follow up on this new international consensus for human rights promotion, calling for the "mainstreaming" of human rights across all of the UN's principal policies, programs, and practices (UN Secretary-General 1997). To implement this cross-cutting approach to human rights, UN agencies worked together to operationalize a human rights-based approach to development cooperation, coordinating organizational activities to implement economic and social rights and recognizing good practices for human rights mainstreaming (UNDG 2003).

Mainstreaming human rights in global health governance has required institutions to translate state legal obligations under international human rights law into organizational policies and programs throughout global health governance. However, many organizations—including many that had long supported human rights as central to their work—did not initially understand the implications of mainstreaming and did little to change their practices (O'Neill and Bye 2002). Where these institutions were thought to be a necessary part of the human rights system, scholars lamented the inconsistent commitment of health-related organizations to their human rights responsibilities (Oberleitner 2008). Despite a clear *raison d'être* for human rights in global governance, these rights-based norms remained neglected in institutional policies and practices (Darrow and Arbour 2009). This neglect of institutional implementation has begun to change, with institutions tentatively taking steps toward a rights-based approach to health. Through the UN Development Group's (UNDG's) Human Rights Working Group, institutions have come together regularly to examine the application of human rights to practical programmatic issues, shifting the UN from the coordination of independent approaches to human rights to the mainstreaming of integrated practices for human rights. While these autonomous organizations continue to operate independently, such consultative processes have given hope for a shared approach to human rights mainstreaming in the UN system (UNDG 2015). These evolving developments in the institutional implementation of human rights have raised a research imperative to understand organizational approaches to human rights in global health governance.

IV. STUDYING HUMAN RIGHTS IMPLEMENTATION THROUGH COMPARATIVE ANALYSIS

Comparative analysis is necessary to understand the diverse approaches to mainstreaming human rights in global governance for health. Although global health governance institutions have begun to pursue human rights mainstreaming initiatives as a basis to implement human rights law, the lack of clarity in the meaning of mainstreaming has raised disparate notions of necessary rights-based activities (Hunt 2017). Even as principles of equity pervaded the development of the UN's 2030 Agenda for Sustainable Development, health-related human rights were found to be too difficult to implement in the resulting Sustainable Development Goals (SDGs), with global health governance institutions seen to place normative frameworks, including human rights, "at arm's length" (Brolan, Hill, and Ooms 2015, 8). However, where SDG 3 seeks to "ensure healthy lives and promote well-being for all at all ages," international organizations require a rights-based approach to health to facilitate accountability for achieving SDG targets for "universal health coverage" (Williams and Hunt 2017; Ghebreyesus 2017). To provide conceptual clarity of the complex global governance systems through which human rights are implemented for global health, recognizing that institutional structures can facilitate or impede mainstreaming efforts, it is essential to explore the practical ways that human rights are operationalized in global health governance—translating human rights into institutional activities through policies, programs, and practices to assure the realization of human rights.

This edited volume maps the range of human rights activities in institutions of global governance for health. Looking beyond formal institutional structures—which can overlook the actual policies, programs, and practices of an organization—previous surveys of human rights in global governance have sought to categorize UN agencies into "circles of willingness" to mainstream human rights in institutional practices (Oberleitner 2008, 364). These studies have examined the diverse practices through which organizations express their willingness to mainstream human rights through, among other things:

- making rhetorical commitments,
- working with the human rights system,
- engaging with non-state advocates,
- providing technical assistance to states,
- assessing staff activities, and
- reforming policies, budgets, and programs.

Across this continuum and over time, it is necessary to study the actions of global institutions to implement human rights for global health.

Comparative research can provide rich description of the distinct contextual activities of each institution, recognizing where an organization's human rights rhetoric does not extend to institutional rights-based policies, programs, and practices and identifying institutional actions that can be thought of as "authentically human rights-conscious" (Alston 1992, 1). Such qualitative research can provide a basis to understand the causal pathways linking international human rights law to rights-based policy implementation through organizational practice (Sano and Martin 2017). Through detailed description of human rights activities and organizational dynamics, it is possible to compare how global governance institutions seek varied approaches to implement human rights to advance global health—mainstreaming rights in the organizational policies, programs, and practices that influence public health.

Through comparative institutional analysis, it becomes clear that organizational commitment to mainstreaming human rights is based upon specific underlying structural factors. In examining these underlying determinants of human rights commitment within an organization, previous institutional analyses across disciplines have examined both endogenous dynamics and exogenous shocks that influence organizational approaches to mainstreaming human rights. With scholars looking inside the organization, they have examined, among other issues, institutional culture, organizational leadership, and bureaucratic processes (Oestreich 2007). Beyond the institution itself, human rights commitments in many institutions can be shaped by member state oversight, NGO advocacy, and even academic research (Hafner-Burton 2013). Out of this understanding of institutional actions and structural determinants arose the research imperative to develop this volume, with chapters devoted to the determinants of human rights implementation in specific institutions of global health governance.

V. STRUCTURE OF THIS VOLUME

Building from this institution-specific research agenda, this volume provides a comparative basis to see the range of distinct operational approaches to (and determinants of) human rights mainstreaming across international organizations, offering proof of results and obstacles to the implementation of human rights in global health governance. This volume is organized in five main sections—(1) Global Health and Human Rights, (2) the World Health Organization, (3) Inter-Governmental Organizations, (4) Global Economic Governance and Global Health Funding Agencies, and (5) Global Health in Human Rights Governance—concluding each section with a forward-looking chapter that assesses future prospects for institutional operationalization of human rights in global health:

Section I. Global Health and Human Rights

Section I introduces the reader to the central importance of human rights for global health. By addressing threats to public health as human rights violations, international law has offered global standards by which to frame government responsibilities and evaluate health policies (Gostin 2014). Spanning interdisciplinary legal and public health scholarship throughout the last thirty years, the discipline of "Health and Human Rights" has created a long-sought normative framework to promote those human rights that underlie the public's health (Gruskin et al. 2012). Chapter 1 provides a theoretical basis for this volume by laying out the role of human rights under international law as a basis for public health, introducing the human right to health and defining the "rights-based approach" to health. With chapter 2 discussing the evolution of human rights for public health, this chapter chronicles the expansion of the "health and human rights" movement following the Cold War—from a movement that once focused on negative human freedoms but, through sexual and reproductive rights advocacy, now addresses the interconnected civil, cultural, economic, political, and social rights that impact public health. From this foundation in the right to health and health-related human rights, chapter 3 conceptualizes human rights as a framework for global health governance, focusing on governments and inter-governmental organizations that define global governance for health—rather than the corporate entities, individual philanthropists, non-governmental organizations, and other actors that are not bound by human rights law. This focus on global health governance has re-energized advocacy networks at the intersection of global health and human rights, and Part I concludes in chapter 4 by analyzing how global health governance must be reformed to realize human rights through sustainable development.

Section II. The World Health Organization

As the UN's principal specialized agency for global health, WHO possesses a unique institutional mandate to implement the right to health, with the 1946 WHO Constitution declaring for the first time that "the enjoyment of the highest attainable standard of health is one of the fundamental rights of every human being" (WHO 1946, preamble). Section II explores the evolving role of WHO in the development and implementation of human rights for global health, reviews the current state of gender, equity, and human rights mainstreaming in the WHO Secretariat, and looks to the future of WHO's human rights leadership in global health. WHO is seeking to hold human rights as essential to its organizational mission, employing human rights to advance global health in a globalizing world and position itself as a leader in global health governance, but the Organization has long faced obstacles to human rights in global health (Meier and Onzivu 2014).

States intended WHO to serve at the forefront of efforts to realize human rights to advance global health, and yet, as detailed in chapter 5, this promise of a rights-based approach to health has long been threatened by political constraints in international relations, organizational resistance to legal discourses, and medical ambivalence toward human rights. Where the WHO Secretariat in Geneva has faced obstacles in past efforts to mainstream human rights, chapter 6 reviews how WHO has sought to revitalize the rights-based approach to health under its current "gender, equity, and human rights" mainstreaming process, which seeks, as described by the WHO Director-General, "to achieve a WHO in which each staff member has the core value of gender, equity and human right in his/her DNA." As WHO seeks anew to mainstream human rights efforts across the Geneva Secretariat—emphasizing enabling legal environments, marginalized populations, and accountability as rights-based pillars of WHO's work—chapter 7 discusses what role these WHO efforts will play in advancing human rights into the future in an expanding global health governance landscape.

Examining institutions of global governance beyond WHO, the chapters in Sections III through V—developed by scholars and practitioners—each focus on a specific institution, assuring comparability across organizations through a similar chapter structure, framed by:

- describing the origins of the institution,
- reviewing the birth and historical evolution of global health and human rights within the institution,
- describing current efforts to mainstream human rights in global health through institutional policies, programs, and practices,

- analyzing the distinct institutional factors that facilitate or inhibit human rights mainstreaming in global governance for health, and
- concluding with future institutional efforts to mainstream human rights in global health governance.

Section III. Inter-Governmental Organizations

In this expanding global health governance landscape, Section III reviews how the UN system has come together to mainstream human rights in a multi-sectoral approach to global health. The 1945 UN Charter elevated human rights as one of the principal purposes of the postwar international system while providing that "various specialized agencies, established by inter-governmental agreement and having wide international responsibilities, as defined in their basic instruments, in economic, social, cultural, educational, health and related fields, shall be brought into relationship with the United Nations" (UN 1945, art. 57). Grounded in the "functional decentralization" of the UN system, each agency would have autonomy to develop distinct institutional policies and programs to implement human rights within its respective sphere of influence (Samson 1992). This decentralization across the UN's global health "fiefdoms" led to independence in organizational initiatives and heterogeneity in organizational processes (Baehr and Gordenker 2005, 157). Mandating a cross-cutting approach to human rights, UN Secretary-General Kofi Annan called on all UN programs, funds, and specialized agencies in 1997 to mainstream human rights in all their activities (UN Secretary-General 1997). Various agencies have taken up this call, and Section III explores how inter-governmental organizations through the UN have played a critical role in implementing human rights under their health-related mandates in global governance.

The UN Children's Fund (UNICEF) revitalized its mandate under the 1989 Convention on the Rights of the Child, and chapter 8 addresses UNICEF's evolving work to implement the child's right to health. With the longest human rights record (predating the UN system), chapter 9 examines the standards of the International Labor Organization (ILO), which over its ninety-nine-year history has been a forceful advocate for obligations to protect occupational safety and health. Chapter 10 focuses on the ways in which the human rights to education and science underlie global health, exploring the health-related efforts of the UN Educational, Scientific and Cultural Organization (UNESCO). Where sexual and reproductive health is dependent on human rights, chapter 11 explores the role of the United Nations Population Fund (UNFPA) in advancing sexual and reproductive health and rights. The Food and Agriculture Organization of the United Nations (FAO), as the UN's largest agency, seeks to eradicate hunger, food insecurity, and malnutrition, and chapter 12 examines its efforts to operationalize the right to food to support global health. Given its relatively recent birth in the midst of an exploding AIDS epidemic, chapter 13 discusses the Joint United Nations Programme on HIV/AIDS (UNAIDS), reviewing the human rights concerns that led to its creation, examining its specific mandate to engage a rights-based approach to health, and analyzing the human rights protections that UNAIDS has developed through community participation. With states coming together to develop the 2030 Agenda for Sustainable Development, Section III ends in chapter 14 by addressing the future influence of the SDGs in advancing rights-based partnerships for health across the UN system.

Section IV. Global Economic Governance and Global Health Funding Agencies

As human rights mainstreaming is often presented in the context of "development cooperation" (UNDG 2015), Section IV explores the bilateral and multilateral economic governance agencies that have sought to address development for health, breaking the vicious cycle linking economic poverty with morbidity and mortality. Increasingly relevant in global health governance, these institutions have been driven either (1) to address public health as a means to economic development or (2) to address economic development as a means to realize health (Meier and Fox 2008). With the latter approach aligned with a rights-based approach to health, Section IV highlights the role of human rights in global economic governance and international funding for global health. While these institutions do not universally view human rights as part of their organizational mission, they have an oversized influence on the ways in which states raise and spend resources for health promotion (Smith 2010), and as a consequence of their influence on states, these international financial institutions have been central to the drive to mainstream the rights-based approach, often welcoming human rights impact assessments of their economic development and poverty reduction efforts (Vandenhole and Gready 2014).

In framing human rights in global economic governance for health, chapter 15 analyzes the rights-based approach to development and the collective human right to development as a means to spur salubrious development conditions. Turning from the tarnished past of the neoliberal development agenda, chapter 16 examines how the World Bank has taken a renewed interest in health-related development financing (through such programs as the Health, Nutrition, and Population initiative and the Multi-Country HIV/AIDS Program), operationalizing rights-based principles in health programming even as it rejects a formal legal obligation for human rights. Chapter 17 examines the role of international trade governance as a determinant of health, exploring the rise of the World Trade Organization (WTO), the WTO agreements that influence health, and the conflict between trade-related intellectual property rights and the human right to health. From international institutions to national assistance, chapter 18 seeks to understand the role of human rights in bilateral foreign assistance programs (with case studies on various foreign health assistance efforts), conceptualizing international development assistance not as a voluntary, charitable gesture, but rather as an international obligation on donor states to reduce global health inequalities. As state and non-state actors have come together to facilitate "mutual accountability" between donor and recipient states for global health funding, chapter 19 examines how donor states have coalesced around a shared policy agenda for infectious disease prevention, treatment, and control, employing human rights to structure health financing through the Global Fund to Fight AIDS, Tuberculosis and Malaria (Global Fund). Viewing the Global Fund as a partnership model to bring together state and non-state actors in global health through the normative frameworks of human rights, chapter 20 concludes with future considerations for multilateral funding to realize the right to health.

Section V. Global Health in Human Rights Governance

Where human rights have been instrumental in global health governance, the rights-based approach to health is also advanced where global health is incorporated in human rights governance. Institutions of human rights governance have a central role in the "era of implementation" for human rights, collaborating with global health institutions to "welcome, encourage, foster, support and scrutinize" human rights mainstreaming efforts (Hunt 2017, 529). Beyond human rights system support for institutions of global health governance, institutions of human rights governance can mainstream public health in their human rights efforts, independently implementing human rights in global health (O'Neill and Bye 2002). Focused on the UN human rights system, Section V identifies the ways in which various human rights institutions have proven relevant to advancing human rights for global health.

Chapter 21 examines the evolving approach taken by the Office of the UN High Commissioner for Human Rights (OHCHR) to address public health threats under its human rights mandate, working with institutions to go beyond rhetorical invocation of human rights and recognizing the programmatic implications of a right to health. The Human Rights Council (HRC) has given thematic mandates to over forty special procedures mandate-holders to develop human rights and assess implementation in individual states, and chapter 22 analyzes the role of these independent experts and special rapporteurs in addressing the human rights implications of a range of determinants of health. Looking to human rights treaty bodies as an institution of global governance, chapter 23 assesses how the ten core human rights treaty bodies have advanced public health by monitoring, interpreting, and adjudicating health-related human rights. With the HRC's Universal Periodic Review (UPR) process established in 2006 to facilitate accountability across all states and human rights treaties, chapter 24 analyzes the promise of this accountability mechanism for global health advancement, addressing how the first cycle of state reviews has assessed public health information under a wide range of health-related human rights and assessing the future of international human rights accountability for global health.

Through this systematic survey of human rights in global governance for public health, it is possible to recognize the varied approaches to human rights mainstreaming, analyze the underlying determinants of human rights implementation, and develop an empirical basis to assess the role of human rights in institutions of global health governance. By qualitatively assessing both an institution's actions and the structural determinants of those actions, lessons can be learned: some of these institutions are unique in their approach to human rights; others have developed approaches that can be applied across institutions. Such an assessment, identifying "good practices" across institutions in the operationalization of human rights, can support the development of a practical framework for human rights mainstreaming and facilitate consistent application of international human rights in global health governance. In understanding the "practical interoperability" of human rights across decentralized institutions, harmonizing institutional approaches to mainstreaming universal rights where possible, such inter-institutional understanding can facilitate shared practices without infringing institutional autonomy (Hunt 2017). These shared practices, analyzed in the conclusion of this volume, can provide a basis to facilitate accountability for the efficacy of institutional efforts to implement human rights through organizational policies, programs, and practices, moving institutions toward "authentic" human rights initiatives to promote global health.

With this understanding of human rights in global health governance, it then becomes possible to examine the influence of rights-based governance in promoting justice in global health. Human rights advocates have long championed the benefits of human rights mainstreaming for institutional practice, but "this judgement rests to a large extent on the self-assessment of a small number of organisations rather than on a thorough external review based on sound empirical methodology" (Oberleitner 2008, 387). Raising an imperative for empirical assessments of human rights in global health governance, "the mainstreaming of human rights throughout the UN system has created demand for tools that might help with that endeavour and, crucially, offer proof of results" (Murphy 2013, 129). By identifying the public health results associated with human rights implementation, a research agenda has arisen to identify the ways in which mainstreaming human rights in institutional policies and programs has proven instrumental to improving public health indicators (Bustreo and Hunt et al. 2013). While human rights have intrinsic value in global health, human rights practitioners have come to recognize the importance of establishing an instrumental justification for human rights implementation in global health governance—improving public health (Hunt, Yamin, and Bustreo 2015). It is necessary to carry this research agenda forward, examining the influence of human rights implementation across institutions of global health governance through an analysis of correlative impacts on core institutional activities and public health outcomes. The chapters in this volume provide a comparative basis for future empirical studies to analyze the impact of human rights mainstreaming on global health promotion.

CONCLUSION

Human rights are not an abstract set of aspirational principles but rather a normative framework for governance. With the paradigm for human rights implementation shifting to reflect the rise of institutions of global health governance, it is necessary to examine these institutions that advance public health and human rights, analyzing the disparate pathways by which human rights are mainstreamed in organizational policies, programs, and practices. The process of translating human rights—from the language of revolutions to the practice of institutions—has required international organizations to embark on major shifts to both their missions and the activities necessary to carry out those missions. Building from the institution-specific research in this edited volume, with contributing chapters providing a basis to understand the range of distinct organizational approaches to human rights mainstreaming, comparative research across these institutions can examine generalizable institutional factors that facilitate or impede the operationalization of human rights in global health. As seen throughout the chapters in this volume, these institutional factors provide evidence of institutional strength for human rights implementation as a basis for global health advancement, renewing the promise of global governance in the face of unprecedented challenges to global health and human rights.

REFERENCES

Alston, Philip. 1992. *The United Nations and Human Rights: A Critical Appraisal.* New York: Oxford University Press.

Backman, Gunilla, Paul Hunt, Rajat Khosla, Camila Jaramilo-Strouss, Belachew Mekuria Fikre, Caroline Rumble, David Pevalin [et al.]. 2008. "Health Systems and the Right to Health: An Assessment of 194 Countries." *The Lancet* 372: 2047–2085.

Baehr, Peter R. and Leon Gordenker, eds. 2005. *The United Nations: Reality and Ideal.* London: Palgrave MacMillan UK.

Birn, Anne-Emanuelle, Yogan Pillay, and Timothy Holtz, eds. 2017. *Textbook of Global Health.* New York: Oxford University Press.

Brabandere, Eric De. 2009. "Non-State Actors, State-Centrism and Human Rights Obligations." *Leiden Journal of International Law* 22(1): 191–209.

Brolan, Claire E., Peter S. Hill, and Gorik Ooms. 2015. "'Everywhere but Not Specifically Somewhere': A Qualitative Study on Why the Right to Health Is Not Explicit in the Post-2015 Negotiations." *BMC International Health and Human Rights* 15(1): 22.

Brown, Theodore M., Marcos Cueto, and Elizabeth Fee. 2006. "The World Health Organization and the Transition from 'International' to 'Global' Public Health." *American Journal of Public Health* 96(1): 62–72.

Bustreo, Flavia and Paul Hunt [et al.]. 2013. *Women's and Children's Health: Evidence of Impact of Human Rights.* Geneva: World Health Organization.

CESCR (Committee on Economic, Social and Cultural Rights). 2000. "General Comment No. 14: The Right to the Highest Attainable Standard of Health (Art. 12)." 11 August. UN Doc. E/C.12/2000/4.

Clinton, Chelsea and Devi Lalita Sridhar. 2017. *Governing Global Health: Who Runs the World and Why?* New York: Oxford University Press.

Darrow, Mac and Louise Arbour. 2009. "The Pillar of Glass: Human Rights in the Development Operations of the United Nations." *American Journal of International Law* 103(3): 446–501.

Donnelly, Jack, 2nd ed. 2003. *Universal Human Rights in Theory and Practice.* Ithaca: Cornell University Press.

Fried Linda P., Margaret E. Bentley, Pierre Buekens, Donald S. Burke, Julio J. Frenk, Michael J. Klag, and Harrison Spencer. 2010. "Global Health Is Public Health." *The Lancet* 375: 535–537.

Getgen, Jocelyn E. and Benjamin Mason Meier. 2009. "Ratification of Human Rights Treaties: The Beginning, Not the End." *The Lancet* 373(9679): 1987–1992.

Ghebreyesus, Tedros Adhanom. 2017. "All Roads Lead to Universal Health Coverage." *Lancet Global Health* 5(9): e839–e840.

Gostin, Lawrence O. 2014. *Global Health Law.* Cambridge: Harvard University Press.

Gostin, Lawrence O., Scott Burris, and Zita Lazzarini. 1999. "The Law and the Public's Health: A Study of Infectious Disease Law in the United States." *Columbia Law Review* 99(1): 59–128.

Gruskin, Sofia, Shahira Ahmed, Dina Bogecho, Laura Ferguson, Johanna Hanefeld, Sarah MacCarthy, Zyde Raad, and Riley Steiner. 2012. "Human Rights in Health Systems Frameworks: What Is There, What Is Missing and Why Does It Matter?" *Global Public Health* 7: 337–351.

Hafner-Burton, Emilie M. 2013. *Making Human Rights a Reality*. Princeton: Princeton University Press.

Harman, Sophie. 2012. *Global Health Governance*. London: Routledge.

Hein, Wolfgang and Lars Kohlmorgen, eds. 2009. "Transnational Norm-Building in Global Health: The Important Role of Non-State Actors in Post-Westphalian Politics." In *Health for Some: The Political Economy of Global Health Governance*, edited by Sandra J. MacLean, Sherrie A. Brown, and Pieter Fourie. London: Palgrave Macmillan.

Hunt, Paul. 2017. "Configuring the UN Human Rights System in the 'Era of Implementation': Mainland and Archipelago." *Human Rights Quarterly* 39(3): 489–538.

Hunt, Paul, Alicia Ely Yamin, and Flavia Bustreo. 2015. "Making the Case: What Is the Evidence of Impact of Applying Human Rights-Based Approaches to Health?" *Health and Human Rights* 17(2): 1–9.

McMichael, Anthony J. 1999. "Prisoners of the Proximate: Loosening the Constraints on Epidemiology in an Age of Change." *American Journal of Epidemiology* 149(10): 887–897.

Meier, Benjamin Mason. 2010. "Global Health Governance and the Contentious Politics of Human Rights: Mainstreaming the Right to Health for Public Health Advancement." *Stanford Journal of International Law* 46: 1–50.

Meier, Benjamin Mason. 2011. "Global Health Takes a Normative Turn: The Expanding Purview of International Health Law and Global Health Policy to Meet the Public Health Challenges of the 21st Century." *The Global Community: Yearbook of International Law and Jurisprudence* 1: 69–108.

Meier, Benjamin Mason and Ashley M. Fox. 2008. "Development as Health: Employing the Collective Right to Development to Achieve the Goals of the Individual Right to Health." *Human Rights Quarterly* 30: 259–355.

Meier, Benjamin Mason and William Onzivu. 2014. "The Evolution of Human Rights in World Health Organization Policy and the Future of Human Rights through Global Health Governance." *Public Health* 128(2): 179–187.

Moon, Suerie, Nicole A. Szlezák, Catherine M. Michaud, Dean T. Jaminson, Gerald T. Keusch, William C. Clark, and Barry R. Bloom. 2010. "The Global Health System: Lessons for a Stronger Institutional Framework." *PLoS Medicine* 7(1): e1000193.

Moyn, Samuel. 2010. *The Last Utopia: Human Rights in History*. Cambridge: Harvard University Press.

Murphy, Thérèse. 2013. *Health and Human Rights*. Oxford: Hart.

Oberleitner, Gerd. 2008. "A Decade of Mainstreaming Human Rights in the UN: Achievements, Failures, Challenges." *Netherlands Quarterly of Human Rights* 26(3): 359–390.

Oestreich, Joel E. 2007. *Power and Principle: Human Rights Programming in International Organizations*. Washington: Georgetown University Press.

O'Neill, William and Vegard Bye. 2002. *From High Principles to Operational Practice: Strengthening OHCHR Capacity to Support UN Country Teams to Integrate Human Rights in Development Programming*. Geneva: OHCHR.

Palmer, Alexis, Jocelyn Tomkinson, Charlene Phung, Nathan Ford, Michel Joffres, Kimberly A. Fernandes, Leilei Zeng, Viviane Lima, Julio S. G. Montaner, Gordon H. Guyatt, and Edward J. Mills. 2009. "Does ratification of human-rights treaties have effects on population health?" *Lancet* 373: 1987–1992.

Pfeiffer, James, Wendy Johnson, Meredith Fort, Aaron Shakow, Amy Hagopian, Steve Gloyd, and Kenneth Gimbel-Sherr. 2008. "Strengthening Health Systems in Poor Countries: A Code of Conduct for Nongovernmental Organizations." *American Journal of Public Health* 98(12): 2134–2140.

Robinson, Mary. 1998. "Five-year Review of the Implementation of the Vienna Declaration and Programme of Action: Interim report of the United Nations High Commissioner for Human Rights." 20 February. UN Doc. E/CN.4/1998/104.

Samson, Klaus 1992. "Human Rights Co-ordination within the UN System." In *The United Nations and Human Rights: A Critical Appraisal*, edited by Philip Alston. New York: Oxford University Press.

Sano, Hans-Otto and Tomas Max Martin. 2017. "Inside the Organization. Methods of Researching Human Rights and Organizational Dynamics." In *Research Methods in Human Rights: A Handbook*, edited by Bård A. Andreassen, Hans-Otto Sano, and Siobhán McInerney-Lankford. Cambridge: Edward Elgar.

Silberschmidt, Gaudenz, Don Matheson, and Ilona Kickbusch. 2008. "Creating a Committee C of the World Health Assembly." *The Lancet* 371(9623): 1483–1486.

Smith, Richard D. 2010. "The Role of Economic Power in Influencing the Development of Global Health Governance." *Global Health Governance* 3(2): 1–12.

Steiner, Henry J., Philip Alston, and Ryan Goodman, eds. 2008. *International Human Rights in Context: Law, Politics, Morals*. Oxford: Oxford University Press.

UN (United Nations). 1945. "Charter of the United Nations." 24 October. UN Doc. 1 UNTS XVI.

UN General Assembly. 1948. "Universal Declaration of Human Rights." 10 December. Res. 217 A (III).

UN General Assembly. 1966. "International Covenant on Economic, Social and Cultural Rights." 16 December. Res. 2200A (XXI).

UN Secretary-General. 1997. "Renewing the United Nations: A Programme for Reform." 14 July. UN Doc. A/51/950.

UN Secretary-General. 2005. "Address to the UN Commission on Human Rights." 7 April. Available at: http://www.un.org/sg/STATEMENTS/index.asp?nid=1388.

UNDG (United Nations Development Group). 2003. *The Human Rights Based Approach to Development Cooperation: Towards a Common Understanding Among UN Agencies*. Available at https://undg.org/document/the-human-rights-based-approach-to-development-cooperation-towards-a-common-understanding-among-un-agencies/.

UNDG (UN Development Group). 2015. "Guidance Note on Human Rights for Resident Coordinators and Country Teams." *United Nations Development Group*.

Vandenhole, Wouter and Paul Gready. 2014 "Failures and Successes of Human Rights-Based Approaches to Development: Towards a Change Perspective." *Nordic Journal of Human Rights* 32(4): 291–311.

WHO (World Health Organization). 1946. *Constitution of the World Health Organization*. Available at: http://www.who.int/governance/eb/who_constitution_en.pdf.

Williams, Carmel and Paul Hunt. 2017. "Neglecting Human Rights: Accountability, Data and Sustainable Development Goal 3." *International Journal of Human Rights* 21(8): 1114–1143.

World Conference on Human Rights. 1993. "Vienna Declaration and Programme of Action." 25 June. UN Doc. A/CONF.157/23.

Yamin, Alicia. 2008. "Will We Take Suffering Seriously? Reflections on What Applying a Human Rights Framework to Health Means and Why We Should Care." *Health and Human Rights* 10(1): 45–63.

Youde, Jeremy. 2013. *Global Health Governance*. Oxford: Wiley.

Global Health and Human Rights

1

The Origins of Human Rights
in Global Health

LAWRENCE O. GOSTIN AND BENJAMIN MASON MEIER

Celebrated by health advocates throughout the world, human rights have become a cornerstone of global health governance, foundational to contemporary policy discourses, programmatic interventions, and public health advancements. This chapter explores the central importance of human rights for global health, laying out the role of human rights under international law as a normative basis for public health. By addressing public health harms as human rights violations, international law has offered global standards by which to frame government responsibilities and evaluate health policies, shifting the global health debate from political aspiration to legal accountability under the "rights-based approach" to health. Yet despite a burgeoning stream of analysis on the scope and content of human rights for global health, there has been little examination of the historical origins of the health and human rights movement.

This chapter offers an account of the development of human rights and their role in protecting and promoting public health since the end of World War II and birth of the United Nations (UN). Part I conceptualizes the theoretical foundations of human rights in global health, exploring the underpinnings of the health and human rights movement in social medicine discourses, outlining the codification of human rights under international law, and examining the right to health and the rights-based approach to health. Recognizing the context for the development of these rights under the UN system, Part II discusses the health-related atrocities of World War II and the postwar proclamation of health-related human rights through the creation of the World Health Organization (WHO) and the development of the Universal Declaration of Human Rights (UDHR). Part III chronicles the evolution of health-related human rights through the UN and WHO—from the repudiation of public

Human Rights in Global Health. Benjamin Mason Meier and Lawrence O. Gostin.
© Oxford University Press 2018. Published 2018 by Oxford University Press.

health under international law, to the revitalization of human rights in global health policy, to the operationalization of rights through the HIV/AIDS response. This chapter concludes that the historical development of human rights under international law continues to influence the contemporary implementation of human rights in global health governance.

I. HUMAN RIGHTS IN GLOBAL HEALTH

Human rights offer universal frameworks to advance justice in health, standing as the most developed and accepted international framework for global health. Setting global norms for the essential needs required to realize the "inherent dignity" of all individuals (Donnelly 2003), human rights standards transform harms into injustices by recognizing health and human rights as interdependent approaches to defining and advancing human well-being (Mann et al. 1999). Through the normative frameworks of human rights, the conceptualization of health disparities as "rights violations" offers international standards by which to frame legal accountability for the progressive realization of human dignity (Gostin and Mann 1994). By empowering individuals to seek redress for rights violations rather than serving as passive recipients of government benevolence, international human rights law identifies individual rights-holders and their entitlements and corresponding duty-bearers and their obligations (Gostin 2014).

A. Social Medicine Origins of Human Rights in Public Health

Arising out of the industrial revolution and reimagined during World War II, social medicine came to view medicine as an interdisciplinary social science necessary to examine how social inequalities shape the experience of disease. A social medicine movement was borne of the revolutionary discourses of 1848, with health examinations concluding that "medicine is a social science, and politics nothing but medicine at a larger scale" (Virchow 1848) and with widespread deprivations leading to a wave of leftist revolutions across European states (Krieger and Birn 1998). While largely failing to overthrow political regimes, these revolutionary demands resulted in vast changes in national social policies to improve public health (Rosen 1974). From the failed uprisings of 1848 to the UDHR in 1948, a century of research and advocacy in social medicine would establish a normative basis for the postwar development of health-related human rights under international law (Oppenheimer, Bayer, and Colgrove 2002). Over this century of progress, illness was seen to have multiple social causes, and social medicine scholars looked to social and political reform, rather than medicine, as a means of health promotion (Coleman 1982). Social medicine, as a distinct academic discipline, came to be defined as "the preventive and curative art considered, both in scientific foundations as well as in its individual and collective applications, from the point of view of the reciprocal relations which link the health of man to his environment" (Sand 1934). Rediscovered through an increased understanding of underlying determinants of health, social medicine found focus after World War II in conceptualizations of "multi-causal" determinants of health and examinations of health through the lens of social class and other inequalities (Ryle 1948).[1]

Instead of viewing improved health as the result of scientific advancements and medical interventions for the elimination of specific diseases (e.g., through vaccines and pharmacotherapies), scholars concluded that changes in the social and environmental conditions brought about by economic development (e.g., improved nutrition and sanitation) are the underlying source of the public's health (McKeown 1979). Through these advocate demands and academic analyses, correlating health and disease with social circumstances, the field of "public health" came to frame structural interventions to correct for societal deficiencies in underlying social determinants of health (Porter and Porter 1988). This understanding of public health would be developed under international law through human rights.

B. Human Rights under International Law as a Basis for Public Health

The codification of human rights became a foundation for global governance in the aftermath of World War II. To assess and adjudicate principles of justice, states worked under the auspices of the nascent UN to enumerate cultural, civil, economic, political, and social rights under international law (Alston 1984), proclaiming the UDHR on December 10, 1948 to create "a common standard of achievement for all peoples and all nations" (UN General Assembly 1948, preamble). Building from this nonbinding Declaration, states continued to negotiate international human rights law in the ensuing years—and against the political divisions of the Cold War—developing specific legal obligations under two separate human rights covenants, adopting on December 16, 1966 the International Covenant on Civil and Political Rights (ICCPR) and the International Covenant on Economic, Social and Cultural Rights (ICESCR). These three documents—the UDHR, ICCPR, and ICESCR, adopted separately by the UN General Assembly and referred to collectively as the "International Bill of Human Rights"—form the normative basis of the human rights system, from which rights would evolve to protect health under international law.

The health and human rights movement seeks, as depicted in Figure 1.1, to apply human rights under international law to advance the public's health. Differing from professional, ethical, or religious values, international legal norms are enabled through state authority and thus distinctively influence state behavior (Finnemore 1999). While these formalistic legal obligations of human rights are distinct from

---

1. Eschewing personal medicine for "state medicine," John Ryle, the first academic chair in social medicine, argued in the aftermath of World War II:

> Among the more potent measures of protection may be included a national food policy, a national housing policy, improved working conditions, an improved and co-ordinated medical and health service, and social security legislation; and last but not least, a national education policy in which education for health—physical, mental, and moral—should come to play a far more significant part. These, rather than new hospitals and new specific remedies and surgical skills (much as we shall continue to need them), are among the true insurance policies for the advancement alike of human health and equity (Ryle 1948, 100).

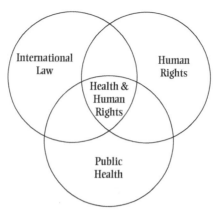

Figure 1.1 Situating the Health and Human Rights Movement.

parallel normative discourses of ethics, bioethics, and social justice, they often share overlapping:

- histories (as discussed above);
- aims (e.g., identifying rights and assigning responsibility for respecting and promoting well-being); and
- outcomes (e.g., achieving dignity of the person and fairness across groups).

While human rights law is often complementary to these other normative frameworks, the principles of human rights remain uniquely necessary, establishing under law the basic rights and freedoms to which all human beings are entitled and binding states parties to realize these rights (Shelton 2013). Human rights are now seen to impact health through an expansive and reinforcing set of (1) international conventions or treaties; (2) customary international laws; (3) "general principles" of law; and (4) judicial decisions, along with the teachings of legal scholars (Murphy 2014).

The human right to health—codified under international human rights law through the ICESCR, providing for "the right of everyone to the enjoyment of the highest attainable standard of physical and mental health" (UN General Assembly 1966, art. 12)—has evolved under international law to offer normative guidance for public health (Toebes 1999). Structuring accountability for these human rights and correlative governmental duties, the UN Committee on Economic, Social and Cultural Rights, charged with overseeing the implementation of the ICESCR, issued General Comment 14 in 2000 to provide authoritative interpretation of state obligations pursuant to the right to health (CESCR 2000). Where all human rights are seen to be indivisible, interdependent, and interrelated (UN General Assembly 1993), the Committee's General Comment sought to elaborate the interconnected rights that influence health. Holding that there exist legal obligations to address "underlying determinants of health" (CESCR 2000, para. 11), the Committee clarified in General Comment 14 that the right to health depends on a wide variety of interconnected rights for the public's health—beginning in preventive and curative health care and expansively encompassing underlying rights to food, housing, work, education, human dignity, life, non-discrimination, equality, prohibitions against torture, privacy, access to information, and the freedoms of association, assembly, and movement (Meier and Mori 2005). Through these "health-related human rights" that underlie public health, UN agencies, development organizations, and advocacy groups have increasingly invoked a "rights-based approach to health" (Gruskin 2004).

C. The Rights-Based Approach to Health

As a framework for governance, policymakers have increasingly operationalized this human rights-based approach to health, grounded in the right to health and in rights to various underlying determinants of health. Many states have incorporated these human rights into their domestic health systems, establishing the right to health and other health-related human rights under a national constitution or statutory law to safeguard the highest attainable standard of health (Gostin 2014). These health-related human rights frame the policy environment, integrate core principles into programming, and facilitate accountability under international law (Alston and Robinson 2005).

As duty-bearers, states assume a legal obligation to respect, protect, and fulfill specific human rights, with international legal mechanisms to facilitate state accountability for human rights realization. International human rights law has sought to identify individual rights-holders and their entitlements and corresponding state duty-bearers and their obligations (Robinson 2005), empowering individuals to seek legal redress for health violations (Yamin 2008). With a state duty-bearer accepting resource-dependent obligations to realize rights "to the maximum of its available resources, with a view to achieving progressively the full realization of the rights" (UN General Assembly 1966, art. 2), states have been pressed to realize rights progressively through policies to assure that health is available, accessible, acceptable, and of sufficient quality (Felner 2009). Beyond these health-related human rights, the rights-based approach to health also encompasses specific cross-cutting human rights principles, including:

- *Non-discrimination and Equality*—eliminating discrimination in any form, providing for those who are not able to provide for themselves, for excluded individuals, and for vulnerable populations;
- *Participation*—providing meaningful opportunities for engagement in all health-related decision making, thereby allowing for sustainable health services that more effectively address local needs; and
- *Accountability*—ensuring access to effective and appropriate remedies (CESCR 2000).

Through the application of this rights-based approach, governments bear specific obligations to realize the highest attainable standard of health for all those within their borders, with social mobilization and civil society action spurring states to uphold their international obligations (London 2008).

II. DEVELOPING HUMAN RIGHTS THROUGH GLOBAL GOVERNANCE

In concretizing norms as a basis of global health policy, the postwar birth of the UN brought with it an understanding that these universal norms must be codified, enforcing global justice under international human rights law (UN 1950). Responding to the deprivations and harms of World War II, states developed these postwar institutions to advance public health and human rights.

A. Human Rights out of the Cauldron of War

The codification of human rights for global health begins, as with all contemporary human rights, in the context of World War II. The failure of the League of Nations to prevent rapidly escalating Nazi atrocities through its Minority Treaties System gave strength to a growing call for the creation of a new system to protect individual freedom from the tyranny of the state. Heeding this call on January 6, 1941, US President Franklin Delano Roosevelt announced to the world that the postwar era would be founded upon four "essential human freedoms": freedom of speech, freedom of religion, freedom from fear, and freedom from want (Congressional Record 1941). It is the final of these "Four Freedoms"—freedom from want—that heralded a state obligation to provide for the health of its peoples. As Roosevelt conceived it, this freedom from want would be couched in the language of liberty, with the understanding that "a necessitous man is not a free man" (Roosevelt 1944). In this wartime context, the "Four Freedoms" speech was initially derided as American propaganda but quickly deepened its impact as it came to form an ideological basis of the alliance between the Allied Powers.

Beyond the establishment of health as an international priority, World War II showed the world the harm that could be caused through "health policy," and such rights would also seek to prevent harm caused under the auspices of public health. The Nazi atrocities committed during World War II, enabled by German public health theory and human research programs, constituted a complete disregard for the value of human life and the inherent rights of research subjects (Barondess 1996). During the war, with eugenics and euthanasia receiving widespread acceptance in the state medical establishment, German physicians— drawing on debased Darwinian notions of public health and welfare—voluntarily aided in theorizing, planning, and operating the genocidal campaign of the Holocaust (Bachrach and Kuntz 2004). In addition to the wholesale extermination of millions, German doctors also performed fatal experiments on otherwise healthy patients, taking part in "medical experiments without the subjects' consent, upon civilians and members of the armed forces of nations then at war with the German Reich . . . in the course of which experiments the[y] committed murders, brutalities, cruelties, tortures, atrocities, and other inhuman acts" (United States v. Karl Brandt 1948). The silence of the German medical community and the breakdown of ethical protections in the face of such atrocities amounted to complicity by the entire profession, highlighting the lack of any meaningful legal or ethical regulation of physicians. The so-called Doctors' Trial of 1946–1947, in which US judges at Nuremberg passed judgment on Nazi physicians, would mark the first international criminal prosecution of physicians for war crimes and crimes against humanity, finding widespread patient and subject harms that would come to be seen as violations of human rights (Annas and Grodin 1992).

Rising out of the cauldron of war and drawing on social medicine debates of the late nineteenth and early twentieth centuries, health became enshrined in the lexicon of human rights, seeking state obligations that would serve to prevent public health harm, whether in the guise of the deprivations like those that had taken place during the Great Depression in the West or the atrocities like those that had been perpetrated during World War II.

B. The United Nations as a Beacon for Health and Human Rights

This freedom from want and prevention from harm took form in the development of human rights grounded in international law. Rather than simply appealing to informal notions of religious principle or individual morality, human rights were thought to provide a formal legal basis for assessing and adjudicating principles of justice. With the Allied States meeting in Dumbarton Oaks in 1944 to initiate postwar planning, the protection of human rights would develop out of proposals for a new international organization to replace the League of Nations:

> With a view to the creation of conditions of stability and well being which are necessary for peaceful and friendly relations among nations, the Organization should facilitate solutions of international economic, social and other humanitarian problems and *promote respect for human rights and fundamental freedoms* (U.S. Department of State 1944).

This proposed organization to promote respect for human rights would take shape in the UN.

The Charter of the United Nations (UN Charter), signed on June 26, 1945, would be the first international treaty to recognize the concept of human rights. With states seeking "to take joint and separate action in co-operation with the Organization [UN]" (UN 1945, art. 56), human rights became one of the four principal purposes of this new world body. Operating through its Economic and Social Council (ECOSOC), the UN would seek to "make recommendations for the purpose of promoting respect for, and observance of, human rights and fundamental freedoms for all" (Ibid., art. 62).

In drafting the UN Charter, however, states did not initially mention health, either as a goal of the organization or as a human right. In fact, the original October 1944 Dumbarton Oaks proposals, recognizing the importance of human rights to the organization of a postwar world, exclude any mention of health. But for the late efforts of the Brazilian and Chinese delegations to the 1945 San Francisco Conference on International Organization—jointly proposing the word "health" as a matter of study for the UN General Assembly (art. 13), finding international health cooperation to be among the purposes of ECOSOC (art. 55), and advocating for the establishment of an international health organization (art. 57)—health would have received no mention in the creation of the UN (American Journal of Public Health 1945).

Notwithstanding this invocation of human rights and international health in the UN Charter, it would fall to subsequent international negotiations to codify a distinct human right to health under international law. Pursuant to Article 55 of the UN Charter, by which states bound themselves to "promote . . . solutions of international economic, social, health, and related problems" (UN 1945, art. 55(b)), the UN established a Technical Preparatory Committee to prepare "proposals for the establishment of a single health organization of the United Nations" (WHO 1948, 39).

C. The World Health Organization Gives Birth to a Human Right to Health

The rapid drafting and adoption of the Constitution of the World Health Organization (WHO Constitution) would make it the first international treaty to find a unique human right to health. In establishing the contours of a human right to health under the WHO Constitution, a document far more substantively expansive than those of its institutional predecessors, the preamble declares that "the enjoyment of the highest attainable standard of health is one of the fundamental rights of every human being," defining health positively to include "a state of complete physical, mental, and social well-being and not merely the absence of disease or infirmity" (WHO 1946, preamble). To enable this positive vision of health, expanding the mandate of international public health far beyond the "absence of disease" originally envisioned by prewar "International Sanitary Conventions," the 1946 International Health Conference "extended [WHO] from the negative aspects of public health—vaccination and other specific means of combating infection—to positive aspects, i.e. the improvement of public health by better food, physical education, medical care, health insurance, etc" (Stampar 1949, 1).

In meeting this expansive, positive definition of health through a government focus on "social medicine" to address underlying determinants of health, states parties to WHO would declare that "governments have a responsibility for the health of their peoples which can be fulfilled only by the provision of adequate *health and social measures*" (WHO 1946, preamble, emphasis added). Among state delegations, it was held that these health and social measures, developed through national public health systems, would serve to create "a common front against poverty and disease" (Doull 1949, 329). As compared with the preamble of the UN Charter, which speaks in aspirational terms and introduces the text to follow, this preambular language of the WHO Constitution would codify far-reaching human rights norms commensurate with contemporary public health discourse (WHO 1958)—creating what would be referred to as a "Magna Carta of health" (Parran 1946), "represent[ing] the broadest and most liberal concept of international responsibility for health ever officially promulgated" (Allen 1950, 30), and encompassing the aspirations of WHO's mandate following the ravages of the Second World War (Bok 2014).

D. A Universal Declaration of Human Rights

Drawing on the WHO Constitution and working through the postwar UN, states proclaimed the UDHR on December 10, 1948, establishing through it "a common standard of achievement for all peoples and all nations" (UN General Assembly 1948, preamble). In defining a collective set of interrelated social welfare rights for the public's health, the UN Secretariat began by compiling multiple suggested provisions relevant to both medical care and underlying determinants of health, which the first session of ECOSOC's Commission on Human Rights Drafting Committee consolidated into two concise articles:

> Everyone has the right to medical care. The State shall promote public health and safety.
> Everyone has the right to good food and housing and to live in surroundings that are pleasant and healthy (UN Commission on Human Rights 1947).[2]

In considering this draft language, delegates on the Drafting Committee, led by Eleanor Roosevelt, widow of the late US President Roosevelt, were determined to include in the UDHR a recognition of the importance of "public health," with preliminary emphasis on the draft statement that "the state shall promote public health and safety." While this appeared as a collective responsibility rather than an individual right, this state obligation for the public's health, paired with a right to medical care, made comprehensive the public health understanding that state obligations for health would entail both individual health services and national health systems, the latter to include social measures for the public's health (Morsink 1999).

Thus, out of the first session of the Commission on Human Rights' Drafting Committee, this right was converted to:

> Everyone, without distinction as to economic or social conditions, has a right to the highest attainable standard of health.
> The Responsibility of the State and community for the health and safety of its people can be fulfilled only by provision of adequate health and social measures (UN Commission on Human Rights 1947).

2. While the UN Commission on Human Rights sought brevity in the final UDHR, the UN Secretariat's original draft compiled wide-ranging health-related rights, including in:

- Article 35—Everyone has the right to medical care. The State shall promote public health and safety.
- Article 39—Everyone has the right to such equitable share of the national income as the need for his work and the increment it makes to the common welfare may justify.
- Article 40—Everyone has the right to such help as may be necessary to make it possible for him to support his family.
- Article 41—Everyone has the right to social security. The State shall maintain effective arrangements for the prevention of unemployment and for insurance against the risks of unemployment, accident, disability, sickness, old age, and other involuntary or undeserved loss of livelihood.
- Article 42—Everyone has the right to good food and housing and to live in surroundings that are pleasant and healthy (UN Division on Human Rights 1947).

In language similar to the WHO Constitution, this expansive rights-based vision of "the highest attainable standard of health" was in accordance with (1) the expansion of postwar European welfare policy, founded on the notion that "social security cannot be fully developed unless health is cared for along comprehensive lines" (Beveridge 1942); (2) the early development of health-related rights in Latin America, encompassing "the right to the preservation of . . . health through sanitary and social measures relating to food, clothing, housing and medical care" (IACHR 1948); and (3) the recent amendments to the Soviet Constitution, which established protections of medical care and "maintenance in old age and also in case of sickness or disability" (Guins 1950). With draft UDHR language including both the fulfillment of "adequate health and social measures," this expansive vision reflected budding national welfare policies and prevailing social medicine discourses as a basis for public health systems (Jenks 1946).

As a result of this developing consensus on the importance of interconnected determinants of health, framed under the broad social medicine umbrella of "a standard of living," subsequent sessions of the Commission on Human Rights merged notions of social security into this draft UDHR article:

1. Everyone has the right to a standard of living, including food, clothing, housing and medical care, and to social services, adequate for the health and well-being of himself and his family and to security in the event of unemployment, sickness, disability, old age or other lack of livelihood in circumstances beyond his control.
2. Mother and child have the right to special care and assistance (ECOSOC 1948).

There was widespread international agreement that this "standard of living" included both the fulfillment of medical care and the realization of underlying determinants of health, including within this right public health obligations for food safety and nutrition, sanitary housing, disease prevention, and comprehensive social security (UN 1950).

When the debate moved to the UN General Assembly, there was little explicit discussion of the health issues in this draft article, with the nine proposed amendments focusing instead on defining a separate right to social security. While a desire for brevity led many state representatives to suggest the exclusion of those component rights essential to health and well-being, the Soviet Union's insistence on a circumscribed right to medical care forced the full elaboration of public health obligations for underlying determinants of health.

With only minor amendments in the final debates, the UN General Assembly voted unanimously (40–0, 2 abstentions) to adopt the UDHR, commemorated in figure 1.2, including the following text of Article 25:

(1) Everyone has the right to a standard of living adequate for the health and well-being of himself and of his family, including food, clothing, housing and medical care and necessary social services, and the right to security in the event of unemployment, sickness, disability, widowhood, old age or other lack of livelihood in circumstances beyond his control.

Figure 1.2 Eleanor Roosevelt, Chairperson of the Commission on Human Rights, holds a copy of the UDHR.
PHOTO CREDIT: UN Archives.

(2) Motherhood and childhood are entitled to special care and assistance. All children, whether born in or out of wedlock, shall enjoy the same social protection (UN General Assembly 1948, art. 25).

Buttressed by Article 22's "right to social security" and Article 27's right "to share in scientific advancement and in its benefits," there was widespread international agreement that a human right to health included both the fulfillment of necessary medical technologies and the realization of underlying determinants of health— explicitly including food, clothing, housing, and social services as part of this holistic encapsulation of health determinants.

III. EVOLUTION OF HUMAN RIGHTS FOR GLOBAL HEALTH

Despite the postwar promise of human rights in guiding international efforts to ameliorate health hazards worldwide, the rapidly ensuing Cold War brought with it a more power-driven model of global health cooperation, grounded in the international politics of infectious disease control. The dueling priorities of the Cold War Superpowers and a medical focus on scientific technologies made the elaboration of human rights for public health more rhetorical than real (Meier 2010). Yet, upon this realist foundation for international health institutions, states have come to build a rights-based approach to global health (Meier 2011). Beginning in the 1970s, there arose a renewed influence of human rights in the development of international health law—focusing on underlying determinants of health in the developing world, raising awareness through global efforts to advance primary health care, taking hold in response to the injustices of a deepening HIV/AIDS pandemic, and enduring as a feature of the public health response to the health inequities of globalization.

A. The Cold War Stymies the Development of Human Rights in International Health

As the UN Commission on Human Rights (now the UN Human Rights Council) moved to translate the hortatory rights of the UDHR into binding treaties under international law, health-related rights were transformed through the development of international legal obligations under the International Covenant on Economic, Social and Cultural Rights (ICESCR) (Green 1956). However, these efforts to codify human rights for health faced conceptual limitations through the political constraints of the Cold War, hobbling efforts to advance public health discourses in human rights law (Tobin 2012).

With the WHO Secretariat initially asserting leadership for developing human rights standards on health, WHO suggested wide-ranging legal language to support the efforts of the Commission on Human Rights in developing an International Covenant on Human Rights. Drawn from the WHO Constitution and language abandoned in the drafting of the UDHR, WHO's expansive proposal emphasized: (1) a positive definition of health; (2) the importance of social measures in realizing underlying determinants of health; (3) governmental responsibility for health provision; and (4) the role of public health systems in creating a wide-range of measures for what would become "primary health care" (WHO 1951). Despite support from European and Latin American states, this WHO proposal was challenged in the Commission on Human Rights, with dueling US and Soviet amendments seeking to eliminate the expansive WHO proposal in its entirety, replacing it with each nation's respective view of health rights, as shown in Table 1.1.

Rather than adopting either of these conflicting amendments—the United States' vague pronouncement of a right without corresponding obligations or the Soviet Union's limited obligations for medical care—states reached a compromise, by which the US proposal was added to the first paragraph of the WHO proposal

Table 1.1. US AND SOVIET PROPOSALS FOR A HUMAN RIGHT TO HEALTH (UN COMMISSION ON HUMAN RIGHTS 1951)

US Proposal	USSR Proposal
The States Parties to the Covenant recognize the right of everyone to the enjoyment of the highest standard of health obtainable.	Each State party hereto undertakes to combat disease and provide conditions which would assure the right of all its nationals to a medical service and medical attention in the event of sickness.

and the Soviet proposal on medical care was added as an additional obligation on state governments:

> The States parties to this Covenant recognize the right of everyone to the enjoyment of the highest standard of health obtainable. With a view to implementing and safeguarding this right, each State party hereto undertakes to provide legislative measures to promote and protect health and in particular:
> 1. to reduce infant mortality and to provide for healthy development of the child;
> 2. to improve nutrition, housing, sanitation, recreation, economic and working conditions and other aspects of environmental hygiene;
> 3. to control epidemic, endemic and other diseases;
> 4. to provide conditions which would assure the right of all its nationals to a medical service and medical attention in the event of sickness (UN Commission on Human Rights 1951).

Providing simultaneously for the general recognition of a right to health in an opening paragraph with an enumeration of state obligations in subsequent paragraphs, the revised draft of the right to health was initially the most detailed draft among the economic, social, and cultural rights, reflecting state obligations to progressively realize a wide range of health determinants (Toebes 1999).

With the Cold War Superpowers continuing to be divided on the very meaning of human rights, states were pressed to replace the unified International Covenant on Human Rights with two separate human rights covenants—one on civil and political rights and the other on economic, social, and cultural rights (UN General Assembly 1952). Indicative of the political debates of the Cold War, the comprehensive vision of rights laid out by states in the UDHR unraveled along ideological and economic lines, with the Superpowers (and their respective spheres of influence) split on both a belief in the universality of economic and social rights and the feasibility of realizing these rights (Alston 1979). With the United States seeking the advancement of international legal obligations for only civil and political rights (those classic civil liberties already protected by Western states' national constitutions), US representatives dismissed social and economic rights (including a right to health) as "aspirational" (UN 1952). Notwithstanding this enduring international intransigence on the nature of rights, dividing the UN framework into two separate covenants, states continued to meet together in the Commission on Human Rights, finalizing the drafting of health obligations for inclusion in what would become the ICESCR.

Following a six-year effort in the Commission on Human Rights to transform the UDHR into legally binding obligations, the debate then moved to the UN General Assembly to adopt the ICESCR's conceptualization of human rights for health. Through the 1957 debates of the General Assembly, state challenges to the ICESCR article on the right to health prevailed in eliminating from the opening paragraph both the definition of health and any reference to "social well-being," under the contradictory rationales that the definition was either unnecessarily verbose or irreconcilably incomplete. Narrowing state obligations in the second paragraph, state challenges also succeeded in substituting "the improvement of nutrition, housing, sanitation, recreation, economic and working conditions and other aspects of environmental hygiene" with the less-specific "improvement of all aspects of environmental and industrial hygiene" (UN General Assembly 1957). On January 30, 1957, the General Assembly voted in favor of an amended right to health (54–0, with 7 abstentions), with the right to health retaining the following legal language in the years leading up to the 1966 adoption of the ICESCR:

1. The States Parties to the present Covenant recognize the right of everyone to the enjoyment of the highest attainable standard of physical and mental health.
2. The steps to be taken by the States Parties to the present Covenant to achieve the full realization of this right shall include those necessary for:
   (a) The provision for the reduction of the stillbirth-rate and of infant mortality and for the healthy development of the child;
   (b) The improvement of all aspects of environmental and industrial hygiene;
   (c) The prevention, treatment and control of epidemic, endemic, occupational and other diseases;
   (d) The creation of conditions which would assure to all medical service and medical attention in the event of sickness (UN General Assembly 1966, art. 12).

Although Western states continued to avoid a rights-based approach to health, as human rights had become a basis for Soviet criticism of capitalist inequalities in health (Evang 1967), WHO noted as early as 1968 that "people are beginning to ask for health, and to regard it as a right," rediscovering the political promise of human rights as a means to galvanize international health cooperation (WHO 1968, ix).

B. Human Rights Rediscovered as a Basis for Addressing Underlying Determinants of Health

With public health discourse refocusing on underlying determinants of health, there was a return to the promise of human rights for global health policy through "primary health care"—addressing health care in addition to the underlying social, political, and economic determinants of health (Barton 1979). Conceptualizing this normative vision of global justice around underlying determinants of health, this framing of health would ask the most prosperous states to assume international obligations to benefit the least powerful in international relations, seeking national and international redistributions through salubrious development policies (Gunn 1983). At the intersection of an evolving right to health and right to development, extending a growing call in the developing world for a "New International Economic Order," this rights-based approach to global health sought to address the underlying determinants of health implicated by a lack of economic development (Litsios 2005). Concurrent with the expansion of the broader human rights movement and the promulgation of the human rights covenants (Morgan 2010), states came together to ensure the realization of human rights through global health policy (Cueto 2004). Rather than viewing health as instrumental to the economic development of the powerful through international trade, global health policy would come to advance public health as intrinsic to global justice, a right unto itself.

With growing agreement that WHO had the constitutional authority and normative legitimacy to elaborate international obligations for underlying determinants of health (Roscam Abbing 1979), WHO sought to structure the codification of health norms through the 1978 Declaration of Alma-Ata. WHO joined with UNICEF to convene the International Conference on Primary Health Care in Alma-Ata, USSR (now Almaty, Kazakhstan) as a means to bring together interdisciplinary public health and development actors from around the world—in a rare moment of Cold War détente—to memorialize the multi-sectoral norms of primary health care. This Conference, with representatives from 134 state governments, adopted the Declaration on Primary Health Care, a document that has come to be known as the Declaration of Alma-Ata. The Declaration of Alma-Ata recognized the necessity of broad-based socioeconomic development in order to build the sustainable, comprehensive primary health systems that would allow for the realization of human rights through health policy (Tarantola 2008). Finding that health inequalities are of "common concern to all countries" and recognizing that "all countries should cooperate in a spirit of partnership and service to ensure primary health care for all people" (WHO 1978, art. IX), the Conference's approach to primary health care would seek social justice in the distribution of global health resources, implicating government responsibility for individual health and subverting national self-interest to realize the vision of public health proclaimed by the WHO Constitution (Taylor and Jolly 1988).

Through the Declaration of Alma-Ata, delegates memorialized their normative agreement that inequity in underlying determinants of health was unjust and that primary health care was the key to realizing determinants of global health through multi-sectoral national policy and international development assistance (Fluss and Gutteridge 1990). Reaffirming the human rights principles of the WHO Constitution, Article I of the Declaration of Alma-Ata outlined that:

> health, which is a state of complete physical, mental and social well-being, and not merely the absence of disease or infirmity, is a fundamental human right and that the attainment of the highest level of health is a most important world-wide social goal whose realization requires the action of many other social and economic sectors in addition to the health sector (WHO 1978, art. I).

The Declaration of Alma-Ata sought to rectify inequalities in health status both within and between states, enumerating seven specific governmental duties for essential aspects of primary health care, including:

> education concerning prevailing health problems and the methods of preventing and controlling them; promotion of food supply and proper nutrition; an adequate supply of safe water and basic sanitation; maternal and

child health care, including family planning; immunization against the major infectious diseases; prevention and control of locally endemic diseases; appropriate treatment of common diseases and injuries; and the provision of essential drugs (Ibid., art. VII).

However, such rights-based efforts would not guarantee the survival of the Declaration of Alma-Ata as an international framework for global health.

In the absence of global health governance to promote WHO's Health for All strategy, international health cooperation was sharply curtailed in the early 1980s (Nakajima 1989), with many states moving away from their non-binding commitments under the Declaration of Alma-Ata and giving less attention to global health in foreign policy (WHO Executive Board 1983).[3] With the political rise of international economic institutions—which, as discussed in chapter 15, provided far greater power to the financial interests of the developed world in global health governance (Zacher and Keefe 2008)—there was no normative counterweight to support public health at the start of the modern era of neoliberal economic globalization (Meier and Fox 2008). Yet despite the failure of these specific human rights norms in changing global health policy, the process of developing the Declaration of Alma-Ata nevertheless ushered in a new basis for human rights in global health.

C. Human Rights Become Inextricably Linked to the HIV/AIDS Response

The unfolding of the HIV/AIDS pandemic and the evolving international response would operationalize human rights as an effective force for the creation of public health policy. With governments responding reflexively to the emergent threat of AIDS through traditional public health policies—including compulsory testing, named reporting, travel restrictions, and coercive isolation or quarantine—human rights became a basis to resist intrusive public health infringements on individual liberty and to create a normative bond for stigma-induced cohesion among HIV-positive activists (Bayer 1991). Through holistic examination of the determinants of vulnerability to HIV infection, legal analysis moved away from an early focus on the conflicts between public health goals and individual human rights (Gostin and Lazzarini 1997), with WHO recognizing an "inextricable linkage" between public health and human rights as a normative basis for global HIV/AIDS policy (Mann and Tarantola 1998).

Although WHO would not retain leadership authority for the global response to HIV, with states creating a separate global bureaucracy through the 1996 establishment of the Joint UN Programme on HIV/AIDS (UNAIDS) (Garrett 1994), UNAIDS, as chronicled in chapter 13, would become a forceful actor in

---

3. Lacking a binding normative basis for global health, WHO, as discussed in chapter 5, came again to be controlled by economically powerful states, retreating back to the technical development of medical care services, which would be implemented through a narrower focus on Selective Primary Health Care, and facing increasing criticism for "diminishing its role just at the time when the world is looking for health leadership" (Godlee 1994, 1494).

pressing human rights for global HIV/AIDS governance (Ruger 2004). Supporting UNAIDS's budding rights-based initiatives for non-discrimination, participation, and treatment, the UN High Commissioner for Human Rights joined this dialogue in 1996, as analyzed in chapter 22, advancing "International Guidelines on HIV/AIDS and Human Rights" to elaborate the rights-based norms implicated by vulnerability to HIV and access to treatment (OHCHR and UNAIDS 2006).

With scientific breakthroughs establishing an effective treatment for HIV in the mid-1990s, advocacy for access to HIV treatment would be driven by human rights norms, with social movements adopting a rights-based discourse to support universal access to treatment in global health policy (Petchesky 2003). Where scholars and practitioners had long debated the enforceability of accountability mechanisms for social and economic rights—with these debates grounded largely in the politics of the Cold War—the 1990s brought with it a global consensus that all human rights are universal, indivisible, interdependent, and interrelated (UN General Assembly 1993). States began to coalesce again around a shared rights-based policy agenda for infectious disease prevention, treatment, and control, which would be implemented, as discussed in chapter 19, by the Global Fund to Fight AIDS, Tuberculosis and Malaria (the Global Fund) (Youde 2008). Although the HIV/AIDS pandemic first highlighted the operationalization of human rights for global health, this approach would soon be extended to a wide range of communicable and noncommunicable disease threats—as academic centers, non-governmental organizations, and public policies have arisen at the intersection of public health and human rights.

Through the underlying determinants laid bare through economic globalization (Kim et al. 2000), effects examined through the rise of the "ecological model" in public health (Susser and Susser 1996), health norms have returned again to their social medicine foundations (Oppenheimer, Bayer, and Colgrove 2002) as the global community confronts the novel public health harms of an increasingly globalized world (Lee 2003). This global health collaboration, driven not entirely out of national interest but also out of normative concern for the sick and dying, would progressively expand to encompass the suffering caused by a wide range of underlying determinants of poor health (Kickbusch et al. 2007). Despite a fear that public health would struggle "to maintain respect, funding, and self-definition in the late twentieth century" (Garrett 2000, 9), as global attention turned to the health harms of the least powerful developing states, such a feared collapse of global health has not occurred. As underlying determinants of health have again become a leading concern in international relations (Fidler 2004)—leading to unprecedented increases in global health funding, initiatives, and institutions (Beaglehole and Bonita 2008)—global governance has come to focus on human rights in global health (Gostin and Taylor 2008).

CONCLUSION

In a crowded global health policy landscape, human rights now stand as the predominant normative framework for health policies, programs, and practices. The field of global health and human rights is more than simply the application of human rights to global health. It is about a shared vision of global health justice, where the global community is guided by human rights norms. Speaking to social, political, and economic determinants of health, rights-based frameworks are influencing health governance and structuring both health services and health systems. Through a process begun over seventy years ago, these contemporary efforts build upon a rich legal history of rights-based developments, progressively expanding throughout the years to seek the highest attainable standard of health for all. Where the population perspective of public health has evolved to influence the framing of human rights law, this "health and human rights" movement has become a driving force for fundamental change.

REFERENCES

Allen, Charles E. 1950. "World Health and World Politics." *International Organization* 4(1): 27–43.

Alston, Philip. 1979. "The United Nations' Specialized Agencies and Implementation of the International Covenant on Economic, Social and Cultural Rights." *Columbia Journal of Transnational Law* 18: 79–118.

Alston, Philip. 1984. "Conjuring Up New Human Rights: A Proposal for Quality Control." *American Journal of International Law* 78(3): 607–621.

Alston, Philip and Mary Robinson. 2005. "Introduction: The Challenges of Ensuring the Mutuality of Human Rights and Development Endeavours." In *Human Rights and Development: Towards Mutual Reinforcement*. Oxford: Oxford University Press.

American Journal of Public Health. 1945 "Summary of Actions Related to Public Health during United Nations Conference in San Francisco." *American Journal of Public Health* 35: 1106–1107.

Annas, George and Michael Grodin. 1992. *The Nazi Doctors and the Nuremberg Code: Human Rights in Human Experimentation*. New York: Oxford University Press.

Bachrach, Susan and Dieter Kuntz, eds. 2004. *Deadly Medicine: Creating the Master Race*. Washington, D.C.: United States Holocaust Memorial Museum.

Barondess, Jeremiah. 1996. "Medicine Against Society: Lessons from the Third Reich." *JAMA* 276(20): 1657–1661.

Barton, W. L. 1979. "Signpost to a New Health Era: Alma-Ata." *World Health* Aug.–Sept.: 6–9.

Bayer, Ronald. 1991. "Public Health Policy and the AIDS Epidemic. An End to HIV Exceptionalism?" *New England Journal of Medicine* 324(21): 1500–1504.

Beaglehole, Robert and Ruth Bonita. 2008. "Global Public Health: A Scorecard." *The Lancet* 372(9654): 1988–1996.

Beveridge, William. 1942. *Social Insurance and Allied Services: Report by Sir William Beveridge*. London: Her Majesty's Stationary Office (HMSO).

Bok, Sissela. 2004. "Rethinking the WHO Definition of Health." *Harvard Center for Population and Development Studies, Working Paper Series* 17(7): 1–14.

CESCR (Committee on Economic, Social and Cultural Rights). 2000. "General Comment No. 14: The Right to the Highest Attainable Standard of Health (Art. 12 of the Covenant)." 11 August. UN Doc. E/C.12/2000/4.

Coleman, William. 1982. *Death Is a Social Disease: Public Health and Political Economy in Early Industrial France*. Madison: University of Wisconsin Press.

Congressional Record. 1941. "Records of the United States Senate." 6 January. Doc. SEN 77A-H1, Record Group 46.

Cueto, Marcos. 2004. "The Origins of Primary Health Care and Selective Primary Health Care." *American Journal of Public Health* 94(11): 1864–1874.

Donnelly, Jack. 2003. *Universal Human Rights in Theory and Practice*. 2nd ed. Ithaca: Cornell University Press.

Doull, James A. 1949. "Nations United for Health." In *Public Health in the World Today*, edited by James Stevens Simmons, 317–332. Cambridge: Harvard University Press.

ECOSOC. 1947. "Report of the Second Session of the Commission on Human Rights." 10 December. Doc. E/600.

ECOSOC. 1948. "Report of the Third Session of the Commission on Human Rights." 28 June. Doc. E/800.

Evang, K. 1967. *Health of Mankind: Ciba Foundation*. London: Churchill.

Felner, Eitan. 2009. "Closing the 'Escape Hatch': A Toolkit to Monitor the Progressive Realization of Economic, Social, and Cultural Rights." *Journal of Human Rights Practice* 1(3): 402–435.

Fidler, David P. 2004. "Caught Between Paradise and Power: Public Health, Pathogenic Threats, and the Axis of Illness." *McGeorge Law Review* 35(1): 45–104.

Finnemore Martha. 1999. "Are Legal Norms Distinctive?" *New York University Journal of International Law and Politics* 32(3): 699–1175.

Fluss, Sev and Frank Gutteridge. 1990. "Some Contributions of the World Health Organization to Legislation." In *Issues in Contemporary International Health*, edited by Thomas A. Lambo and Stacey B. Day, 35–54. New York: Plenum Medical Book Co.

Garrett, Laurie. 1994. *The Coming Plague: Newly Emerging Diseases in a World Out of Balance*. New York: Farrar, Straus and Giroux.

Garrett, Laurie. 2000. *Betrayal of Trust: The Collapse of Global Public Health*. 1st ed. New York: Hyperion.

Godlee, Fiona. 1994. "WHO in Retreat: Is It Losing Its Influence?" *British Medical Journal* 309(6967): 1491–1495.

Gostin, Lawrence O. 2014. *Global Health Law*. Cambridge: Harvard University Press.

Gostin, Lawrence O. and Zita Lazzarini. 1997. *Human Rights and Public Health in the AIDS Pandemic*. New York: Oxford University Press.

Gostin, Lawrence O. and Johnathan Mann. 1994. "Towards the Development of a Human Rights Impact Assessment for the Formulation and Evaluation of Public Health Policies." *Health and Human Rights* 1(1): 59–80.

Gostin, Lawrence O. and Allyn Taylor. 2008. "Global Health Law: A Definition and Grand Challenges." *Public Health Ethics* 1(1): 53–63.

Green, James F. 1956. *The United Nations and Human Rights*. Washington: Brookings.

Gruskin, Sofia. 2004. "Is There a Government in the Cockpit: A Passenger's Perspective on Global Public Health: The Role of Human Rights." *Temple Law Review* 77: 313–333.

Guins, George C. 1950. "Soviet Law—Terra Incognita." *The Russian Review* 9(1): 16–29.

Gunn, S. William A. 1983. "The Right to Health through International Cooperation." In *Il Diritto alla Tutela della Salute: Acts of the International Colloquium on the Right to Health Protection*. Torino, Italy.

IACHR (Inter-American Commission on Human Rights). 1948. "American Declaration of the Rights and Duties of Man." 2 May.

Jenks, C. W. 1946. "The Five Economic and Social Rights." *Annals of the American Academy of Political and Social Science* 243: 40–46.

Kickbusch, Ilona, Thomas Novotny, Nico Drager, Gaudenz Silberschmidt, and Santiago Alcazar. 2007. "Global Health Diplomacy: Training Across Disciplines." *Bulletin of the World Health Organization* 82(12): 971–973.

Kim, Jim Yong, Joyce V. Millen, Alec Irwin, and John Gershman. 2000. *Dying for Growth: Global Inequality and the Health of the Poor.* Monroe, Me.: Common Courage Press.

Krieger, Nancy and Anne-Emanuelle Birn. 1998. "A Vision of Social Justice as the Foundation of Public Health: Commemorating 150 Years of the Spirit of 1848." *American Journal of Public Health* 88(11): 1603–1606.

Lee, Kelley. 2003. *Health Impacts of Globalization: Towards Global Governance.* New York: Palgrave Macmillan.

Litsios, Socrates. 2005. "The Health, Poverty, and Development Merry-Go-Round: The Tribulations of WHO." In *Understanding the Global Dimensions of Health,* edited by S. William A. Gunn, P. B. Mansourian, A. M. Davies, Anthony Piel, and B. McA. Sayers. La Panetiere, Switzerland: International Association for Humanitarian Medicine Brock Chisholm.

London, Leslie. 2008. "What Is a Human-Rights Based Approach to Health and Does It Matter?" *Health and Human Rights* 10(1): 65–80.

Mann, Johnathan and Daniel Tarantola. 1998. "Responding to HIV/AIDS: A Historical Perspective." *Health and Human Rights* 2(4): 5–8.

Mann, Johnathan, Lawrence O. Gostin, Sofia Gruskin, Troyen Brennan, Zita Lazzarini, and Harvey Fineberg. 1999. "Health and Human Rights." In *Health and Human Rights: A Reader,* edited by Johnathan Mann, Sofia Gruskin, Michael A. Grodin, and George G. Annas. New York: Routledge.

McKeown, Thomas. 1979. *The Role of Medicine: Dream, Mirage, or Nemesis?* Princeton, N.J.: Princeton University Press.

Meier, Benjamin Mason. 2010. "Global Health Governance and the Contentious Politics of Human Rights: Mainstreaming the Right to Health for Public Health Advancement." *Stanford Journal of International Law* 46(1): 1–50.

Meier, Benjamin Mason. 2011. "Global Health Takes a Normative Turn: The Expanding Purview of International Health Law and Global Health Policy to Meet the Public Health Challenges of the 21st Century." *The Global Community: Yearbook of International Law and Jurisprudence* 1: 69–108.

Meier, Benjamin Mason and Ashley Fox. 2008. "Development as Health: Employing the Collective Right to Development to Achieve the Goals of the Individual Right to Health." *Human Rights Quarterly* 30: 259–355.

Meier, Benjamin Mason and Larisa M. Mori. 2005. "The Highest Attainable Standard: Advancing a Collective Human Right to Public Health." *Columbia Human Rights Law Review* 37: 101–147.

Morgan, Michael Cotey. 2010. "The Seventies and the Rebirth of Human Rights." In *The Shock of Global: The 1970s in Perspective,* edited by Niall Ferguson, Charles S. Maier, Erez Manela, and Daniel J. Sargent. Cambridge, Mass.: Belknap Press of Harvard University Press.

Morsink, Johannes. 1999. *The Universal Declaration of Human Rights: Origins, Drafting, and Intent.* Philadelphia: University of Pennsylvania Press.

Murphy, Thérèse. 2013. *Health and Human Rights.* Oxford: Hart Publishing.

Nakajima, Hiroshi. 1989. "Priorities and Opportunities for International Cooperation: Experiences in the WHO Western Pacific Region." In *International Cooperation for Health: Problems, Prospects, and Priorities,* edited Michael R. Reich and Eiji Marui, 317–331. Dover, Mass.: Auburn House Publishing Co.

OHCHR and UNAIDS. 2006. *International Guidelines on HIV/AIDS and Human Rights: 2006 Consolidated Version.* Available at: http://www.ohchr.org/Documents/Publications/HIVAIDSGuidelinesen.pdf.

Oppenheimer, Gerald, Ronald Bayer, and James Colgrove. 2002 "Health and Human Rights: Old Wine in New Bottles?" *Journal of Law, Medicine and Ethics* 30(4): 522–532.

Parran, Thomas. 1946. "Remarks at concluding meeting of International Health Conference." UN Doc. E/H/VP/18. 2. Reprinted in Parran, Thomas. 1946. "Chapter for World Health." *Public Health Reports* 61: 1265–1268.

Petchesky, Rosalind P. 2003. *Global Prescriptions: Gendering Health and Human Rights.* New York: Palgrave.

Porter, Dorothy and Roy Porter. 1988. "What Was Social Medicine? An Historiographical Essay." *Journal of Historical Sociology* 1(1): 90–106.

Robinson, Mary. 2005. "What Rights Can Add to Good Development Practice." In *Human Rights and Development: Towards Mutual Enforcement,* edited by Philip Alston and Mary Robinson, 25–43. Oxford: Oxford University Press.

Roosevelt, Franklin D. 1944. "Second Bill of Rights (or Economic Bill of Rights)." *1944 State of the Union Address.* Speech, 11 January.

Roscam Abbing, H. D. C. 1979. *International Organizations in Europe and the Right to Health Care.* Antwerp: Kluwer-Deventer.

Rosen, George. 1974. *From Medical Police to Social Medicine: Essays on the History of Health Care.* New York: Science History Publications.

Ruger, Jennifer Prah. 2004. "Combating HIV/AIDS in Developing Countries." *British Medical Journal* 329(7458): 121–122.

Ryle, John A. 1948. *Changing Disciplines, Lectures on the History, Method and Motives of Social Pathology.* London: G. Cumberlege, Oxford University Press.

Sand, René. 1934. *L'économie humaine par la médecine sociale.* Paris: Éd. Rieder.

Shelton, Dinah. 2013. *The Oxford Handbook of International Human Rights Law, First Edition.* Oxford: Oxford University Press.

Stampar Andrija. 1949. "Suggestions Relating to the Constitution of an International Health Organization." *WHO Official Records* 1(Annex 9).

Susser, Mervyn and Ezra Susser. 1996. "Choosing a Future for Epidemiology: II. From Black Box to Chinese Boxes and Eco-Epidemiology." *American Journal of Public Health* 86(5): 674–677.

Tarantola, Daniel. 2008. "A Perspective on the History of Health and Human Rights: from the Cold War to the Gold War." *Journal of Public Health Policy* 29(1): 42–53.

Taylor, Carl and Richard Jolly. 1988. "The Straw Men of Primary Health Care." *Social Science and Medicine* 26(9): 971–977.

Tobin, John. 2012. *The Right to Health in International Law.* New York: Oxford University Press.

Toebes, Bridgit C. A. 1999. *The Right to Health as a Human Right in International Law.* Antwerp: Intersentia.

UN (United Nations). 1945. "Charter of the United Nations." 24 October. UN Doc. 1 UNTS XVI.

UN. 1950. *These Rights and Freedoms.* UN Department of Public Information.

UN. 1952. "Letter from UN Division of Human Rights Director John Humphrey to UN Division of Human Rights Lin Mousheng." 3 January (on file with authors).

UN Commission on Human Rights. 1947. "Secretariat Draft Outline to Economic and Social Council. Commission on Human Rights Drafting Committee." 1 July. UN Doc. E/CN.4/21, Annex A.

UN Commission on Human Rights. 1951. "Summary Record of the 223rd Meeting." 13 June. UN Doc. E/CN.4/SR.223.

UN Division on Human Rights. 1947. "Draft Outline of the International Bill of Rights, prepared by the Division of Human Rights." 4 June. Doc. UN ESCOR. E/CN.4/AC.1/3/Add.1.

UN General Assembly. 1948. "*Universal Declaration of Human Rights.*" 10 December. Res. 217A(III).

UN General Assembly. 1952. "Resolution 3031 (XI)." 21 January. Res. 3031 (XI).

UN General Assembly. 1957. "Draft International Covenants on Human Rights." 28 January. UN Official Records.

UN General Assembly. 1966. "*International Covenant on Economic, Social and Cultural Rights.*" 16 December. Res. 2200A (XXI).

UN General Assembly. 1993. "Vienna Declaration and Programme of Action." 12 July UN Doc. A/CONF.157/23.

"United States v. Karl Brandt." 1948. In *Trials of War Criminals Before the Nuremberg Military Tribunals Under Control Council Law No. 10, Nuremberg, October 1946–April 1949.* Washington, D.C.: U.S. Government Printing Office.

U.S. Department of State. 1948. *The United Nations, Dumbarton Oaks Proposal for a General International Organization.* Department of State Publication 2297. Washington, D.C.: U.S. Government Printing Office.

Virchow, Rudolf Carl. 1848. "Report on the Typhus Epidemic in Upper Silesia." In *Archiv für pathologische Anatomie und Physiologie und für klinische Medicin, Volume 2,* 143–332. Berlin, Germany: George Reimer.

WHO (World Health Organization). 1948. 1 OFF. REC. WORLD HEALTH ORG. 39 (1948).

WHO. 1946. "Constitution of the World Health Organization." 22 July. Available at: http://www.who.int/governance/eb/who_constitution_en.pdf.

WHO. 1951. "Letter from WHO Director-General Brock Chisholm to UN Assistant Secretary-General H. Laugier." 12 January. WHO Doc. SOA 317/1/01(2) (on file with authors).

WHO. 1958. *The First Ten Years of the World Health Organization.* Geneva: World Health Organization.

WHO. 1968. *The Second Ten Years of the World Health Organization.* Geneva: World Health Organization.

WHO. 1978. *Declaration of Alma-Ata.* Geneva: World Health Organization.

WHO Executive Board, 71st Session. 1983. "Progress in Primary Health Care: A Situation Report." 10 January. WHO Doc. EB71/19.

Yamin, Alicia. 2008. "Beyond Compassion: The Central Role of Accountability in Applying a Human Rights Framework to Health." *Health and Human Rights* 10(2): 1–20.

Youde, Jeremy. 2008. "Is Universal Access to Antiretroviral Drugs an Emerging International Norm?" *Journal of International Relations and Development* 11(4): 415–440.

Zacher, Mark and Tania Keefe. 2008. *The Politics of Global Health Governance: United by Contagion, First Edition.* New York: Palgrave Macmillan.

2

The Evolution of Applying Human Rights Frameworks to Health

ALICIA ELY YAMIN AND ANDRÉS CONSTANTIN*

The history of how human rights have been applied to health is, as all histories are, deeply contested terrain. Any authors that pretend to tell this story objectively or comprehensively are either innocently unaware of the limitations of their own knowledge or cynically selective in their portrayal. This narrative makes no such pretense; it is largely based on the personal engagement of one author who lived through the history recounted (Yamin), as well as on the deeply shared ideological and normative commitments of both authors. Indeed, a central contention of this chapter is that "human rights" is invariably a site for struggle and contestation, both in normative and instrumental terms. Many of the authors who contribute to this volume disagree about fundamental issues of applying human rights frameworks to health, and readers should critically assess such disagreements.

The story of the evolution of applying human rights to health is on the one hand a promising tale about the expansion of understandings of rights and equality, which has everything to do with patterns of health and well-being, as well as the spaces in which rights are both exercised and violated. The populations actively claiming to be subjects of rights have grown to include persons with disabilities, sexual minorities, and other marginalized groups. And the way in which both violations and equal enjoyment of

* This chapter is based on a longer and more in-depth article by Yamin and Constantin, "A Long and Winding Road: The Evolution of Applying Human Rights Frameworks to Health" (forthcoming, 2018), as well as on previous work by Yamin. We are deeply grateful for the insights provided by Lynn Freedman in her peer-review of this chapter. All opinions expressed are those of Alicia Ely Yamin and Andrés Constantin, and do not necessarily reflect those of the UN Secretary-General's Independent Accountability Panel for the Global Strategy.

rights related to health are understood has evolved significantly. Actions in the private sphere, and in other sorts of institutions, including health care settings, are understood to lie within the domain of rights and state responsibility. Further, questions relating to access to entitlements, including health care, have begun to be regularly addressed in rights terms, and are increasingly enforced in courts across various regions.

On the other hand, the tremendous development of economic, social, and cultural rights (ESC rights), including the right to health itself, has not yet delivered on robustly egalitarian policies, and some have argued that it only fosters an anemic "sufficientarianism" that displaces more robust egalitarian projects. Indeed, the human rights architecture is based on an international Liberal order, which had been designed to address violations of civil and political rights (C/P rights), and has often sat too cozily with the global neoliberalism that has assumed a hegemonic grasp on the world order, where power is now exercised as often by private interests as by governments. This domination of networks and exchange—through, for example, the financialization of economies, transnational investment, and inter-country tax issues, coupled with the marketization of societies—while more diffuse and impersonal than the power exercised by the military rapist or torturer, is no less effective at degrading dignity. At the same time, the aspiration of universal standard-setting evolved into, on the one hand, the proliferation of human rights-based approaches (HRBAs) to health that are often untethered from the subversive potential of rights, and on the other, soft law interpretations that have grown increasingly fragmented and inconsistent.

This recounting breaks developments down into three periods. It begins in the 1990s, when connections between health and human rights were established conceptually as well as practically. The linkages among health, rights, and dignity were evident across the many issues that came together in the World Conference on Human Rights (Vienna Conference), the International Conference on Population and Development (ICPD), as well as the Fourth World Conference on Women (Beijing Conference). Part II examines the period between 2001 and 2010, focusing on the normative development of the human right to health, in both international law and domestic constitutional frameworks, together with the development of institutions and procedures to advance health-related human rights. At the same time, the world of global development adopted a significantly more technocratic approach in the 2000s, evidenced by the Millennium Development Goals (MDGs). Part III analyzes the last period, 2010–2017, taking stock of the transition from the MDGs to the Sustainable Development Goals (SDGs), with implications for health and human rights. This period has also brought about increasing attempts to "operationalize" or implement health-related human rights in practice, from policy guidance to national legal mobilization.

The chapter concludes that over twenty years after it began to take shape, the "health and human rights field" is a misnomer; it is not one field but many. This cluster of related work has achieved some extraordinary successes—from global standard-setting to national policies and legal judgments to successful social mobilization. However, applying human rights to health now faces new challenges of legitimacy. For example, a precariously constructed international normative scaffolding has grown increasingly reliant on a formalistic positivism (i.e., isolated from the realities of law's application, as well as tenuously tethered to normative theory), as well as fragmented. At the same time, the challenges of economic inequalities, eroding faith in internationalism, and the complexities of moving from legal norms to effective enjoyment in practice pose real questions for the democratic legitimacy and ultimate value of using HRBAs in health, or any social issue.

I. 1990S: BEGINNINGS OF THE "HEALTH AND HUMAN RIGHTS MOVEMENT"

In the wake of decolonization in the 1950s and 1960s, together with the undeniable brutality of military and other authoritarian regimes that were ravaging much of Latin America, among other regions, human rights became a leading model of emancipation in the 1970s. Yet human rights work at the time focused largely on C/P rights—negative rights protecting freedom of individuals primarily from infringement by governments—in the so-called "public sphere," a product of the binary construction of the traditional liberal state and the Cold War (Yamin and Gloppen 2011; Tobin 2012). The power that human rights were meant to regulate was largely envisioned as abuses stemming from state tyranny. These were violations by police and armed forces, violations of the right to bodily integrity, to political participation, and due process of law. International human rights law and practice had yet to evolve to address many other issues crucial to health, ranging from domestic violence in the so-called "private sphere" to affirmative access to entitlements from the state, including public health preconditions and health care, as well as broader social determinants (Charlesworth, Chinkin, and Wright 1991). These other issues required a different understanding of what exercises in power prevented people from living lives of dignity and a thorough understanding regarding how and when that power was exercised and might be regulated (Yamin 2016).

Following the collapse of the Berlin Wall and the end of the Cold War, the human rights field radically shifted. When human rights was no longer an arena for these heated political battles, it was possible to once again re-envision rights as interlocking building blocks to construct a life of dignity (Yamin and Gloppen 2011; Tobin 2012). In Vienna, in 1993, states not only recognized that all human rights are universal, indivisible, and interdependent and interrelated (UN General Assembly 1993), but it was also the Vienna Conference that made possible the two path-breaking conferences on sexual and reproductive rights that followed in the mid-1990s: the ICPD in 1994 and the Beijing Conference in 1995 were both critical to the construction of linkages between human rights and health.

During the early and mid-1990s, the nascent "health and human rights" movement was also being formally constructed as a theoretical field, with a pivotal role played by Jonathan Mann, former Director of the World Health Organization's (WHO) Global Programme on AIDS and subsequently the founding director of Harvard University's François-Xavier Bagnoud Center for Health and Human Rights. In a seminal 1994 article, Mann and colleagues characterized three linkages between health and human rights (Mann et al. 1994). The first dimension relates to the health consequences arising as a result of human rights violations—especially, in their discussion, C/P rights violations such as torture. The second dimension concerned the influence of health policies, programs, and practices on human rights—again, at its outset, with a focus in particular on C/P rights. The third and final dimension entailed the recognition of health and human rights as complementary dimensions of, and potentially complementary approaches to, understanding human dignity and well-being (Yamin 2016).

The first dimension speaks to the fact that torture and murder by agents of the state quite evidently impact the victims' health. Although those human rights violations were conducted by traditional security officers, the applicability of the state's obligation to prevent and sanction torture has subsequently been extended to include, *inter alia*, health care workers as agents of the state, as well as to the prevention, punishment, and eradication of torture and other human rights violations committed by private actors in the home or in other institutions, including intimate partner violence (UN Human Rights Council 2013; CAT 2004; HRC 2000; IACHR 2012; IACtHR 2016).

Expanding the arenas in which power was exercised to regulation, and in which standards over actions in the private sphere and in spaces beyond the public square, has been a long struggle and is still continually contested. Yet this expansion was and remains critical to making the application of human rights relevant to health, and this evolution demonstrates the link between "normativization" and making visible the political decisions, and human agency, behind the suffering of women and children, among others (Yamin 2016).

These shifts required new understandings of rights, equality, and the responsibilities of the state. The underlying idea in the traditional view—that the private sphere was a realm for personal morality and behavior—had to be adapted if rights could be deployed to protect women and children, who suffer most violations of their rights within the home (Ibid.). The 1979 UN Convention on the Elimination of All Forms of Discrimination against Women (CEDAW) and the 1989 UN Convention on the Rights of the Child (CRC) transcended these artificial public/private divides and called for states to take responsibility for changing social practices that affect women and children, respectively (UN General Assembly 1979; 1989). Yet it was not until the early 1990s, and the Vienna Conference, that these new understandings took hold in international law and in the proliferation of national legislation.

It was undoubtedly Mann's experience with the raging HIV/AIDS pandemic that influenced his profound concern with the second dimension of the connection between health and human rights: the violation of human rights as a result of health policies. Mann argued that health policies were so likely to be inadvertently discriminatory that an assumption should be made that all "health policies and programs should be considered discriminatory and burdensome on human rights until proven otherwise" (Mann et al. 1994, 16). The advent of effective antiretroviral therapy did not put an end to the need to assess laws and policies for their discriminatory effects on the basis of race, gender identity and sexual orientation, caste, ethnicity, and the like—in addition to HIV status. A 2015 case from the High Court of Kenya on the constitutionality of the so-called "Uhuru's HIV List" shows that Mann's insight remains important today. In that case, the Court found that the implementation of a directive issued by President Uhuru Kenyatta to all county commissioners to collect data on all schoolchildren living with HIV/AIDS violated their rights to privacy and the best interests of the child (eKLR 2016).

But it was the third dimension of the connection between health and human rights—what Mann and others called the "inextricable linkage" between health and human rights—that perhaps had the most profound implications for institutional change as well as public health practice because it captured the notion that having agency over one's life, one's dignity, is intrinsically connected to health. That agency required both freedoms from abuse and decisional autonomy in the private sphere, as well as access to endowments in the public sphere, and as a consequence, required both C/P rights and ESC rights. The "inextricable linkage" between health and human rights was perhaps best illustrated in women's health during the 1990s, where transformative paradigm shifts were occurring not just in human rights but also in public health. It was clear to women's health activists that patterns of reproductive health access and outcomes were an artifact of relations of power that restricted or enabled autonomy and access to endowments based on gender, class, and other axes of identity (Yamin 1997).

The 1994 Programme of Action adopted at the ICPD was the result of years of activism by women's groups from around the world (UNFPA 1994) and reflected a dramatic shift in public health from targeted policies based on demographic imperatives to policies based on reproductive rights—to personal reproductive autonomy and to collective gender equality. Further, issues that had previously been treated separately—such as family planning, sexually transmitted infections, and maternal health—were now joined together under the issue of "reproductive health" (Yamin 2013a).

The Beijing Conference enabled the sexual and reproductive health and rights (SRHR) movement to continue mobilizing around an expanded platform for women's health and human rights across the life course. In the year after the ICPD, the Beijing Conference positioned women's health within the broader sociopolitical context of women's empowerment that transcended public and private life, including poverty, sexuality, gender equality, employment, and political participation and decision-making (UN General Assembly 1995). The Platform for Action reiterated the paradigm of the ICPD: "[t]he human rights of women include their right to have control over and decide freely and responsibly on matters related to their sexuality, including sexual and reproductive health" (Ibid., para. 96).

A. Rights Paradigms and Changes in Public Health

Major paradigm shifts were occurring in public health as well as human rights during the 1990s. A year after the Beijing Conference, at the 1996 World AIDS Conference in Vancouver, Canada, combination therapy using protease inhibitors (now known as antiretroviral therapy, ART) had been revealed as effective treatment for HIV. Calls were immediately made to make ART available and affordable to all (Kallings and McClure 2008). The prevailing view in the global health field at the time was that ART was neither cost-effective nor practicable in low-resource settings (Wilkinson, Floyd, and Gilks 1998; Freedberg et al. 1998). Yet a critical mass of researchers, providers, and most importantly activists and patients rallied around the central premise that states had the power and the obligation to provide antiretrovirals (ARVs) (Forman 2013). From South Africa to Brazil, international human rights norms and constitutional frameworks enabled activists to appropriate their subjectivity and empowered them "to make claims for health benefits backed with the force of law" (Ibid., 61).

B. Setting Standards, Seeding Norms

During the late 1990s and early 2000s, the human rights community writ large worked to institutionalize this soft law—morally persuasive but nonbinding declarations from the UN conferences—of the 1990s into international treaties through the "general comments" and "concluding observations" of human rights treaty bodies. While these general comments are not binding, they formed part of a process of slowly accumulating a corpus of related norms and embedding health-related rights into international law (CESCR 2000; CEDAW 1999). The 1999 General Recommendation on Women and Health from the UN Committee on the Elimination of Discrimination against Women (CEDAW Committee), as well as the 2000 General Comment on the Right to Health from the Committee on Economic, Social and Cultural Rights (CESCR), exemplified this practice. Moreover, the UN Principles for the Protection of Persons with Mental Illness and the Improvement of Mental Health Care were also transformed into the 2006 UN Convention on the Rights of Persons with Disabilities (CRPD) (UN General Assembly 2006). Indeed, the rapid and inclusive process through which the landmark CRPD was negotiated, adopted, and entered into force also illustrates the opening in international arenas for accepting new realms of rights—as well as rights-holders.

At the regional level, new norms were also being rapidly developed. In the Americas, the Additional Protocol to the American Convention on Human Rights in the Area of Economic, Social and Cultural Rights (the Protocol of San Salvador), which entered into force in 1999, not only set out norms relating to health but also to a healthy environment (OAS 1999). The Inter-American Convention on the Prevention, Punishment and Eradication of Violence against Women (Convention of Belém do Pará), which entered into force in 1995, was equally important in advancing the conceptualization of violence as a matter of health, and in turn, of health as more than a matter of biological disease (OAS 1994).

At the same time as norms were being seeded and disseminated, advocacy groups were actively deploying these new norms for documentation, fact-finding, and supranational litigation. Many cases in the 1990s were brought up in supranational forums, arguing the futility of exhaustion of domestic remedies—either because SRHR issues had yet to be recognized as actionable in domestic legal systems or because such issues were not susceptible to reasoned public debate due to ideological or religious grounds, such as in the case of abortion (IACHR 2003).

Thus, international law and supranational (regional and international) forums came to be used in SRHR not only to demonstrate overlapping consensuses to shame governments but also to name rights long enshrined in international law through a gendered perspective. The right to bodily integrity, for example, took on a new meaning in the context of women having reproductive rights over their bodies. Although the struggle to use international forums to try to build normative consensuses is an ongoing struggle (ECHR 2007; 2010), the move to have international law interpreted in new ways—with an understanding of the law's differential effects on different groups of people—has proven critical to the application of human rights frameworks to health, in SRHR and beyond (Cook 1994; 1995).

C. At the Same Time, Backlash

In the years that immediately followed the ICPD and Beijing Conference, governments struggled to interpret the aspirational human rights norms set at those conferences into budgets, policies, and programs. The tools to operationalize these aspirational documents did not yet exist, nor did the necessary interdisciplinary and intersectional dialogues (Yamin 2005). It would be more than a decade before more systematic efforts were undertaken to translate these normative standards into government practice.

Moreover, the inability to translate broad emancipatory visions into practice led to a far narrower and more quantitative, pragmatic focus on SRHR in the Millennium Development Goals (MDGs) in 2001 (Fukuda-Parr and Yamin 2015). Despite the appearance of some commonalities with human rights commitments, the adoption of the MDGs as a blueprint for development created divisions between the development and human rights fields (Alston 2005). This was especially the case in SRHR, which became narrowed to a single goal regarding the reduction of maternal mortality ratios, and this global goal was then quickly turned into a national planning target, which was not only "an ineffective marker for monitoring progress at the national level" but also "too narrow for guiding policies, [as it omitted] critical aspects of SRHR" (Yamin and Boulanger 2014, 9). This inherent reductionism led to vertical, targeted programs not just in maternal mortality programs but across the goals, together with the marginalization of important human development and human rights concerns (Fukuda-Parr, Yamin, and Greenstein 2014).

II. 2001–2010: BUILDING NORMS AND INSTITUTIONS

If the 1990s had largely been about building bridges between the health and development fields and the human rights field conceptually, in the first decade of the millennium, the two largely developed along distinct paths, even as health-related human rights norms and institutions grew quickly. The 1999 CEDAW Committee's Recommendation on Women and Health and the 2000 CESCR General Comment on the Right to Health opened up new prospects for interpreting what the right to health required in terms of states' obligations. In particular, the CESCR spelled out interrelated human rights dimensions of availability, accessibility, acceptability, and quality and state obligations to *respect* by refraining from direct infringements; obligations to *protect* from third parties' violations; and obligations to progressively *fulfill* through legislative and other means.

As normative development of the right to health was proceeding apace, the UN was also creating institutions and procedures to support the elucidation and eventual enforcement of these new norms related to health and other ESC rights, in particular, as addressed in chapter 22, through the mandate of the Special Rapporteur on the

Right to the Highest Attainable Standard of Health (UN Commission on Human Rights 2002; Limon and Power 2014). In turn, the Special Rapporteur explicated aspects of the right to health that were critical to translate normative aspirations into policy-relevant guidelines for nonlawyers working in national health systems (Hunt 2004; 2016).

A. Health Systems as Core Social Institutions

One of the most fundamental advances during this decade was a reconceptualization of the role of health systems in promoting and protecting not just the right to health but also democratic governance (Freedman 2005). Furthered by the first Special Rapporteur on the Right to Health, this was a critical opening for human rights scholars and advocates working in this area, as it opened possibilities for operationalizing health-related human rights to a far greater extent (Yamin 2016).

This reconceptualization of health systems as core social institutions that reflect, encode, and embed patterns of inequality and discrimination was essential to transcending the rigid dichotomy in public health between progressive impulses to advance social determinants of health—which would be defined by a WHO Commission in 2008 as the conditions in which people are born, grow, live, work, and age (WHO CSDH 2008)—and approaches to health centering on access to care. Rather, if health systems are understood as part of democratic governance, "health claims, legitimate claims of entitlement to the services and other conditions necessary to promote health" can be seen as assets of social citizenship (Freedman 2005, 21).

B. HRBAs to Development and Health

Professors Lynn Freedman and Ronald Waldman co-led an MDG Task Force on MDG 4 and 5 (Freedman et al. 2004), and in a deliberate effort to incorporate human rights into the attainment of the MDGs, set out a view of health systems as core institutions aligned with human rights principles. This effort to raise awareness of HRBAs and development was notable for its far-reaching consequences and understanding of power relations in health, but not unique.

In 2003, the UN itself had set out the elements of an HRBA to development. This statement called for "a common understanding of [the human rights-based] approach and its implications for development programming," including human rights principles for universality and inalienability; indivisibility; interdependence and interrelatedness; non-discrimination and equality; participation and inclusion; accountability and the rule of law (UN Secretary-General 2003, 91). Nonetheless, the meaning of those principles was and continues to be contested, complicating attempts to "mainstream human rights in development and public health practice" (Yamin and Cantor 2014).

Throughout the first decade of the MDGs, a host of new players in human rights—from service delivery organizations to major international non-governmental human rights organizations—launched human rights campaigns around health issues, in some cases *explicitly* promoting government accountability for meeting programmatic and policy promises (Human Rights Watch 2012; Amnesty International 2013; CELS et al. 2013). These and other groups developed and deployed new forms of fact-finding and documentation, for example, linking budgetary expenditures with the realization of ESC rights. These awareness-raising and advocacy efforts were aimed at operationalizing and "making real" the growing body of normative standards that was continually being established (Díaz Echeverría 2006). They did not just focus on the right to health but on HRBAs to health, which were necessarily multi-sectoral and involved many different C/P and ESC rights in enabling diverse people to live healthy and flourishing lives (UN Human Rights Council 2012; UN Secretary-General 2003).

C. Judicialization: Health Rights as Legal Rights

These efforts at normative standard-setting, coupled with policy measurement and monitoring, coincided with a growing judicialization of health-related human rights, especially in middle-income countries (Gauri and Brinks 2008; Yamin and Gloppen 2011). The emergence of the global phenomenon of health-related human rights litigation generally coincided with the advent of effective ARVs to treat HIV/AIDS, although other factors relating to political and legal institutions played determinative roles (Yamin and Gloppen 2011). Some of the most well-known judicial decisions are from South Africa, where a string of cases relating to HIV/AIDS—from the *Hazel Tau* case (South Africa's National Competition Commission 2003) to *PMA and Another: In re Ex Parte President of the Republic of South Africa and Others* (SAFLII 2000) to the *Treatment Action Campaign* case (SAFLII 2002)—demonstrated how social movements coupled with favorable legal opportunity structures contributed to the recognition and enforcement of legal claims. However, South Africa is far from the only context in which judicialization transformed issues from government largesse into enforceable rights.

A wave of new or reformed constitutions in Latin America included robust enumerations of ESC rights and structural modifications that permitted easier access to courts. Social constitutionalism in Latin America and beyond embedded new understandings of the state that went beyond the traditional liberal state of the nineteenth century. Rights were no longer understood merely as shields from government interference; rather, across these countries, the social contract was understood to include a leveling of the background conditions that perpetuated inequalities and deprivation (Gargarella 2014; Uprinmy, Rodríguez Garavito, and García Villegas 2006). Structural modifications, including perhaps most importantly the introduction of protection writs (*amparos, tutelas*) to allow individuals to claim fundamental rights, created a new relationship between rights-holders and duty-bearers (Cepeda Espinosa 2008). In Latin America, more than any other region, the combination of expansive constitutional protections; perceptions of legislatures and executive branches as corrupt, ineffectual, and politicized; and extremely easy access to courts to resolve health claims led people to seek legal enforcement of a broad spectrum of health-related entitlements (Abramovich and Courtis 2004; Gargarella and Gonzalez-Bertomeu 2016). Over the years, the right to health and other health-related human rights continued to be enforced by courts around the world, including in some very low-income countries in sub-Saharan Africa.

Judicialization, however, has been subject to critiques. There is mixed evidence regarding the potential of individualized litigation to produce systemic pro-poor reforms where positive judgments do not lead to systemic changes or consider equity impacts adequately (Motta Ferraz 2009). During the last years of the decade, scholars increasingly recognized that for judicialization to play an equity-enhancing role in health systems, it was necessary for courts to purposively consider both formal and substantive equality and for the phenomenon of judicialization to be addressed in conjunction with the underlying political and regulatory failures that drive equality (Yamin and Lander 2015; Flood and Gross 2014; Yamin and Gloppen 2011).

As health-related human rights were increasingly being theorized in domestic constitutional theory, supranational institutions were ever more engaged in producing a proliferation of increasingly positivistic norms and standards for countries to follow in relation to health, among other issues (Kennedy 2002). Some of these norms, set out *inter alia* in general comments and special rapporteur reports, were inconsistent, as the number of procedures and institutions addressing some aspects of the same health issue grew exponentially (Gostin 2014). The dialectical construction of national and international law in relation to the right to health and other human rights, which had depended in large measure on democratization of political contexts at the national level, began to show fissures, although the full effects of this gap on social legitimacy would come to be felt in the next decade.

III. 2010–2017: WHERE ARE WE NOW?

Normative developments have continued apace in the last decade, expanding into areas previously not construed in terms of human rights, such as regulation of a variety of private actors. On the other hand, normative constructions have been sometimes untethered to social legitimacy. The idea of universal human rights has become inverted in some forums to mean the rights that states can universally agree upon—undermining the legitimacy of a purported global set of standards. Further, the effects of a global economic crisis in 2008, together with neoliberalism's hegemonic grasp upon the world's economies, has brought into question the very quest for ESC rights, including health-related human rights, in terms of whether it is genuinely subversive of power structures that leave vast sectors of humanity in drudgery and misery (Yamin 2016). And the rapid ascendance of conservative populist nationalism, which coincided with the beginning of the Sustainable Development Era, provides both cause and opportunity for profound self-reflection in the human rights community writ large (Yamin 2017a).

A. Tobacco Control Becomes a Human Rights Issue

By the end of the first decade of the millennium, tobacco control had become an issue not merely of health regulation but of health-related rights. For example, in 2010, Philip Morris International launched an arbitration under the 1998 Switzerland-Uruguay bilateral investment treaty against Uruguay's tobacco control measures (Koh 2016). On July 8, 2016, the International Centre for Settlement of Investment Disputes released its arbitration decision in favor of Uruguay with respect to all claims and recognized that regulatory authorities when making public policy determinations in contexts such as public health enjoy a "margin of appreciation" (ICSID 2016, para. 399).

B. Air Pollution, Mining, and Other Health Hazards

If efforts against tobacco face an uphill battle, controlling other private actors using rights frameworks may be an even greater challenge. For example, using rights to contain pollution and the health effects of extractive industries has proven of limited effectiveness (Yamin and Gloppen 2011). Policy reform efforts and cases involving air pollution and extraction activities on indigenous lands (Constitutional Court of Colombia 2016) have shown both the potential and limitations of approaches based upon legal enforcement of rights, which demand actions from multiple actors and invariably implicate complex institutional and social power relations. Making progress through rights, usually with legal enforcement as one dimension, is an iterative approach to transformation at best, and often remains palliative and "sufficientarian," or worse a paper victory only (Meyer 2009, 133).

C. Human Rights and Development Relinked

As the first decade of the MDG agenda came to a close, the sense among many scholars and activists in human development and human rights was that the highly reductionist approach of the MDGs narrowed targets and restricted a transformative development agenda based on rights (Fukuda-Parr, Yamin, and Greenstein 2014). As suggested above, the framing of MDG 5 (maternal health) sidelined the broader SRHR agenda articulated in the ICPD. Not only were some priorities neglected, but the cross-cutting human rights principles of participation, equality, democratic voice, transparency, and accountability did not count because they could not be counted (Yamin and Boulanger 2014).

The story of MDG 6, and especially in relation to HIV, is exceptional. Funding and awareness of HIV dramatically increased during this time period (Nattrass 2014). New institutions—including UNAIDS and the Global Fund to Fight AIDS, Tuberculosis and Malaria—provided leadership and organization in struggles to expand HIV treatment and prevention in low-resource settings (Ibid.). The stories of women's and children's health were more mixed.

In 2010, acknowledging inadequate progress and failures of accountability with respect to achieving MDG 4 (child survival) and MDG 5 (maternal health), the UN Secretary-General launched his "Global Strategy for Women's and Children's Health," which led to the creation of the Commission on Information and Accountability for Women's and Children's Health (CoIA) (UN Secretary-General 2010). CoIA in turn established an independent Expert Review Group (iERG), tasked with enhancing accountability at the global level for reducing maternal and child mortality (iERG 2012).

MDG? Millenium Development goal

At the same time as the UN development apparatus was reacting to the lack of rights provisions in the MDGs, so too were civil society advocates reengaging with rights-based advocacy in the development of a post-2015 development agenda. Beginning in 2010, civil society coalitions and campaigns struggled to expand the understanding of sexual and reproductive health that would be incorporated in the next global development framework (Yamin 2013b; Yamin and Boulanger 2014). More broadly, the resulting SDGs framework, in contrast to the MDGs, is universal in that it applies to poor and wealthy countries alike. It is also "interdependent," so that *inter alia* access to justice (SDG 16) must be considered in achieving SDG 3 (healthy lives) and SDG 5 (gender equality) (Ibid.).

After the SDGs were adopted, the UN Secretary-General launched in September 2015 the updated "Global Strategy for Women's, Children's and Adolescents' Health 2016–2030" and appointed an Independent Accountability Panel (IAP) (on which Yamin sits), with a more robust mandate than that of the prior iERG (IAP 2016). In its first report, released at the UN General Assembly in 2016, the IAP added judicial remedies to the global health accountability framework and explicitly rooted accountability in human rights frameworks, bringing this development discourse on health in line with international human rights law.

D. Operationalizing HRBAs

Toward the end of the first decade of the MDGs, the UN Human Rights Council, pushed by a concerted advocacy strategy by non-governmental organizations working with the Office of the UN High Commissioner for Human Rights (OHCHR), sought to define and clarify what an HRBA could add to maternal health. A series of resolutions by the UN Human Rights Council, which increasingly expanded upon an analytical framework connecting human rights approaches to maternal mortality, led to the Council's groundbreaking "UN Technical Guidance on the Application of a Human Rights-Based Approach to the Implementation of Policies and Programmes to Reduce Preventable Maternal Mortality and Morbidity" (UN Technical Guidance) (UN Human Rights Council 2012). This UN Technical Guidance represented a major advance in addressing the obligations of national ministries about what had largely been abstract legal concepts. It was then followed by UN Technical Guidance on the rights-based approach that would be applicable to policies and programs for children under five years of age (UN Human Rights Council 2014). These two Technical Guidance documents were then further operationalized through "Reflection Guides" directed at different actors with obligations, from health policy-makers to health service providers (OHCHR et al. 2015; 2016).

E. Converting HRBAs into Operational Tools

These inter-governmental Technical Guidance documents and their Reflection Guides, together with other tools being developed during that time (PMNCH 2015; African Union Commission 2013; PMNCH 2013; WHO 2014; UNICEF and UNFPA 2013), were a dramatic step forward in moving human rights frameworks and principles out of the ministries of justice and foreign affairs and into ministries of health, and, to lesser degrees, education, planning, and finance. But at the same time, the inherent challenges arising from the reliance on powerful institutions to implement HRBAs became clear. That is, in order to meet their promise to change the systems that perpetuate inequality, HRBAs to health must examine the dominant assumptions underlying the structural determinants of health—and serve as tools for subverting unjust structures (UN Human Rights Council 2012). Where they did not, such toolkits amounted to little more than technocratic formulas. Moreover, operationalizing HRBAs required budgeting and policy trade-offs, which was not only largely unfamiliar to the human rights community but also sometimes seen as anathema to brittle understandings of their deontologically based principles (Yamin and Cantor 2014).

F. Universal Health Coverage and the Right to Health

The potential for synergies as well as tensions in approaches to health and human rights is perhaps most acutely illustrated in the SDG target 3.8 on achieving universal health coverage (UHC) under SDG 3 (UN General Assembly 2015). WHO defines UHC as "all people receiving quality health services that meet their needs without exposing them to financial hardship in paying for" those services (WHO CGEUHC, 2014). Thus, progressively achieving UHC requires not a one-off decision, but a series of choices regarding: (1) expanding priority services; (2) including more people in coverage; and (3) reducing out-of-pocket payments (Yamin 2017b). The progressive realization of the right to health requires grappling with many of these same decisions, although it goes further to other dimensions of regulating power relations that shape health (Ibid.).

Given the universality, focus on inequalities, and interdependence of the SDGs, there is potential for synergistic approaches with human rights. However, taking seriously a right to health and an HRBA to health requires understanding health systems as social institutions and, thus, part of democratic governance (Ibid.). Thus, a legitimate, evidence-informed, and democratically deliberative (i.e., genuinely participatory) process—based on rational, public reasons that are not discriminatory or ideological—is vital to guaranteeing that efforts to achieve UHC are consistent with principles of human rights. But to see them as consistent requires the human rights community to recognize that progressively realizing the right to health invariably implies trade-offs, even if budgets are not taken as fixed (Ibid.).

G. Economic Injustice and Health-Related Rights

Many of the challenges noted above, such as the regulation of private actors, are derived from the implacable realities of neoliberalism. Indeed, in recent decades—as income inequality grew enormously, within and between countries and private actors have assumed ever-greater power to determine the parameters for people's well-being—rights-based approaches to health and development were justifiably critiqued as having little influence on, or even being a handmaiden to, neoliberalism (Moyn 2015). Reflecting on this limited influence, scholars noted that "[t]he tragedy of human rights is that they have occupied the global imagination but have so far contributed little of note, merely nipping at the heels of the neoliberal giant whose path goes unaltered and unresisted" (Ibid.). The human rights community today faces multiple simultaneous challenges in fighting old forms of tyranny and resurgent conservative ideologies that refuse to acknowledge diverse human beings as equal subjects of rights. However, scholars and advocates also face additional as-yet unmet challenges of devising ways to counter neoliberalism's rapacious tendency to market everything in its wake, from DNA to health care, which reduces people to consumers in marketized societies rather than agents capable of democratic change (Yamin 2017a; Yamin forthcoming 2018).

CONCLUSION

More than twenty years have passed since the "health and human rights field" began to take shape. If it ever really was one "field," it is no longer one, but many. Indeed, actors engaged across this field, including some of the authors to this collective volume, deeply disagree about fundamental issues. In retracing the origins and evolution of the so-called field, this chapter has implicitly argued for the importance of understanding the past in order to collectively reflect on the implications of divergent paths forward.

Further, this chapter has argued that human rights are, or should fundamentally be, about the regulation of power—as shields from tyranny in the public square and private bedroom and as curbs on public lassitude and private greed that undermine social justice but also as challenges to the structures of thought that drive patterns of suffering and indignity across the globe. Over the decades, human rights advocacy has extended the bounds of human and governmental agency; reinterpreted norms in light of gendered and other experiences; showed the porousness and arbitrariness of divides between the public and private, and between the political and economic realms in conventional conceptions of the liberal state; and created institutional frameworks and procedures. All of these have played critical roles in expanding application of human rights frameworks to health.

The recent rise in conservative populism threatens to undermine institutions of democratic governance and the very foundations of human rights, including pluralist constitutionalism and rules-based orders to democratic deliberation based on objective empirical truths. Further, the current global order assigns disproportionate and unquestioned qualities to the market as an allocator of goods and destinies, which is fundamentally incompatible with robustly inclusive democracies. The human rights community writ large faces many challenges ahead to recapture the subversive potential of human rights, including in relation to health. Future efforts would do well to acknowledge that throughout the history of health and human rights, the most important source of human rights consciousness and energy has come from the diverse people who have been affected by, and collectively struggled against, "pathologies of power" (Farmer 2003; Yamin 2017a).

REFERENCES

Abramovich, Victor and Christian Courtis. 2004. *Los derechos sociales como derechos exigibles*. Madrid: Trotta.

African Union Commission. 2013. Draft Policy Brief: Using Human Rights to Enhance Accountability for Women's and Children's Health." Available at: http://www.who.int/pmnch/media/events/2013/au_policy_brief_human_rights.pdf?ua=1.

Alston, Philip. 2005. "Ships Passing in the Night: The Current State of the Human Rights and Development Debate Seen through the Lens of the Millennium Development Goals." *Human Rights Quarterly* 27, No. 3: 755–829.

Amnesty International. 2013. *Building Ireland's Future: A Human Rights Handbook*. Available at: https://www.amnesty.org/en/documents/sec01/016/2009/en/.

CAT (UN Committee Against Torture). 2004. "UN Committee against Torture: Conclusions and Recommendations, Chile." 14 June. UN Doc. CAT/C/CR/32/5.

CEDAW (UN Committee on the Elimination of Discrimination Against Women). 1999. "CEDAW General Recommendation No. 24: Article 12 of the Convention (Women and Health)." UN Doc. A/54/38/Rev.1.

CELS (Centro de Estudios Legales y Sociales) et al. 2013. *Comments on the OHCHR Recommended Principles and Guidelines on Human Rights at International Borders*.

Cepeda Espinosa, Manuel José. 2008. *Polémicas constitucionales*. Bogotá: Legis Editores.

CESCR (UN Committee on Economic, Social, and Cultural Rights). 2000. "General Comment No. 14, The Right to the Highest Attainable Standard of Health." UN Doc. No. E/C.12/2000/4.

Charlesworth, Hilary, Christine Chinkin, and Shelley Wright. 1991. "Feminist Approaches to International Law." *The American Journal of International Law* 85(8): 613–645.

Constitutional Court of Colombia. 2016. "Sentencia C-389-16." 27 July.

Cook, Rebecca J. 1994. *Women's Health and Human Rights*. Geneva: World Health Organization.

Cook, Rebecca J. 1995. "Gender, Health and Human Rights." *Health and Human Rights* 1(4): 350–366.

Díaz Echeverría, Daniela Francisca. 2006. *Mortalidad Materna: Una tarea inconclusa*. Mexico: Fundar.

ECHR (European Court of Human Rights). 2007. "Tysiac v. Poland." 2007-I.

ECHR (European Court of Human Rights). 2010. "A, B & C v. Ir." 2010-VI.

eKLR (Kenya Law Reports). 2016. *Kenya Legal and Ethical Network on HIV & AIDS and Others v. Cabinet Secretary Ministry of Health and Others, Petition No. 250 of 2015*. Nairobi: Kenya Law Reports.

Farmer, Paul. 2003. *Pathologies of Power, Health, Human Rights and the New War on the Poor*. Berkeley: University of California Press.

Flood, Colleen M. and Aeyal Gross. 2014. *The Right to Health at the Public/Private Divide: A Global Comparative Study*. Cambridge: Cambridge University Press.

Forman, Lisa. 2013. "What Contributions Have Human Rights Approaches Made to Reducing AIDS-Related Vulnerability in Sub-Saharan Africa? Exploring the Case Study of Access to Antiretrovirals." *Global Health Promotion* 20(Suppl. 1): 57–63.

Freedberg, Kenneth, Julie Scharfstein, George Seage III, Elena Losina, Milton Weinstein, Donald Craven, and David Paltiel. 1998. "The Cost-Effectiveness of Preventing AIDS-Related Opportunistic Infections." *JAMA* 279(2): 130–136.

Freedman, Lynn. 2005. "Achieving the MDGs: Health Systems as Core Social Institutions." *Development* 48(1): 19–24.

Freedman, Lynn, Meg Wirth, Ronald Waldman, Mushtaque Chowdhury, and Allan Rosenfield. 2004. *Millennium Project: Interim Report of Task Force 4 on Child Health and Maternal Health.* United Nations Development Group.

Fukuda-Parr, Sakiko and Alicia Ely Yamin, eds. 2015. *The MDGs, Capabilities and Human Rights: The Power of Numbers to Shape Agendas.* London: Routledge.

Fukuda-Parr, Sakiko Alicia Ely Yamin, and Joshua Greenstein. 2014. "The Power of Numbers: A Critical Review of MDG Targets for Human Development and Human Rights." *Journal of Human Development and Human Capabilities* 15(2–3): 105–117.

Gargarella, Roberto. 2014. "Latin American Constitutionalism: Social Rights and the 'Engine Room' of the Constitution." *Notre Dame Journal of International & Comparative Law* 4(1): 9–18.

Gargarella, Roberto and Juan F. Gonzalez-Bertomeu. 2016. *The Latin American Casebook: Courts, Constitutions, and Rights.* London: Routledge.

Gauri, Varun and Daniel Brinks, eds. 2008. *Courting Social Justice: Judicial Enforcement of Social and Economic Rights in the Developing World.* New York: Cambridge University Press.

Gostin, Lawrence O. 2014. *Global Health Law.* Cambridge: Harvard University Press.

HRC (UN Human Rights Committee). 2000. "CCPR General Comment No. 28: Article 3 (The Equality of Rights Between Men and Women)." 29 March. UN Doc. CCPR/C/21/Rev.1/Add.10.

Human Rights Watch. 2012. "Discrimination, Inequality, and Poverty: A Human Rights Perspective." *Human Rights Watch.* January 11. Available at: https://www.hrw.org/news/2013/01/11/discrimination-inequality-and-poverty-human-rights-perspective.

Hunt, Paul. 2004. "Report on the right of everyone to the enjoyment of the highest attainable standard of physical and mental health." 8 October. UN Doc. A/59/422.

Hunt, Paul. 2016. "Interpreting the International Right to Health in a Human Rights-Based Approach to Health." *Health & Human Rights* 18(2): 109–130.

IACHR (Inter-American Commission on Human Rights). 2003. "María Mamérita Mestanza Chávez v. Perú, Case 12.191." 22 October.

IACHR (Inter-American Commission on Human Rights). 2012. "Precautionary Measure 370/12–334 Patients at the Federico Mora Hospital, Guatemala." 20 November.

IACtHR (Inter-American Court of Human Rights). 2016. "I.V. vs. Bolivia, Preliminary Objections, Merits, Reparations and Costs, Judgment, (ser. C) No. 329." 30 November.

IAP (Independent Accountability Panel). 2016. "2016: Old Challenges, New Hopes Accountability for the Global Strategy for Women's, Children's and Adolescents' Health." Available at: http://www.iapreport.org/downloads/IAP_Report_September2016.pdf.

ICSID. 2016. "Philip Morris Brands Sarl v. Uruguay, ICSID Case No. ARB/10/7, Award." 8 July.

iERG (independent Expert Review Group) on Information and Accountability for Women's and Children's Health, 2012. *Every woman, every child: from commitments to action: the first report of the independent Expert Review Group (iERG) on Information and Accountability for Women's and Children's Health.* Geneva: World Health Organization.

Kallings, Lars and Craig McClure. 2008. *20 Years of the International AIDS Society: HIV Professionals Working Together to Fight AIDS.* Geneva: International AIDS Society.

Kennedy, David W. 2002. "The International Human Rights Regime: Still Part of the Problem?" *Harvard Human Rights Journal* 15: 101–125.

Koh, Harold H. 2016. "Global Tobacco Control as a Health and Human Rights Imperative." *Harvard International Law Journal* 57(2): 433–453.

Limon, Marc and Hilary Power. 2014. *History of the United Nations Special Procedures Mechanism: Origins, Evolution and Reform.* Versoix: Universal Rights Group.

Mann, Jonathan, Lawrence Gostin, Sofia Gruskin, Troyen Brennan, Zita Lazzarini, and Harvey V. Fineberg. 1994. "Health and Human Rights." *Journal of Health and Human Rights* 1(1): 7–23.

Meyer, Lukas. 2009. "Sufficientarianism Both International and Intergenerational?" In *Absolute Poverty and Global Justice: Empirical Data, Moral Theories, Initiatives,* edited by Elke Mack, Michael Schramm, Stephan Klasen, and Thomas Pogge. Aldershot: Ashgate.

Motta Ferraz, Octavio Luiz. 2009. "The Right to Health in the Courts of Brazil: Worsening Health Inequities?" *Health and Human Rights* 11(2): 33–45.

Moyn, Samuel. 2015. "Do Human Rights Cause Inequality?" *Chronicle of Higher Education.* May 26. Available at: http://www.chronicle.com/article/Do-Human-Rights-Increase/230297/.

Nattrass, Nicoli. 2014. "Millennium Development Goal 6: AIDS and the International Health Agenda." *Journal of Human Development and Capabilities* 15 (2): 232–246.

OAS (Organization of American States). 1994. "Inter-American Convention on the Prevention, Punishment and Eradication of Violence against Women" ("Convention of Belém do Pará"). 9 June. 33 ILM 1534.

OAS (Organization of American States). 1999. "Additional Protocol to the American Convention on Human Rights in the Area of Economic, Social and Cultural Rights (Protocol of San Salvador)." 16 November. A-52.

OHCHR, Harvard FXB Center for Health and Human Rights, the Partnership for Maternal, Newborn and Child Health, UNFPA, and WHO. 2015. "Summary Reflection Guide on a Human Rights-Based Approach to Health: Application to sexual and reproductive health, maternal health and under-5 child health. Health Policy Makers." Available at: http://www.ohchr.org/Documents/Issues/Women/WRGS/Health/RGuide_HealthPolicyMakers.pdf.

OHCHR, Harvard FXB Center for Health and Human Rights, the Partnership for Maternal, Newborn and Child Health, UNFPA, and WHO. 2016. "Summary Reflection Guide on a Human Rights-Based Approach to Health: Application to sexual and reproductive health, maternal health and under-5 child health. Health Workers." Available at: http://www.ohchr.org/Documents/Issues/Women/WRGS/Health/HealthWorkers.pdf.

PMNCH (The Partnership for Maternal, Newborn and Child Health). 2013. "Knowledge Summary #23 Human Rights and Accountability." Available at: http://www.who.int/pmnch/knowledge/publications/summaries/ks23/en/.

PMNCH (The Partnership for Maternal, Newborn and Child Health). 2015. "Knowledge Summary #34 Operationalizing human rights in efforts to improve health." Available at: http://www.who.int/pmnch/knowledge/publications/summaries/ks34/en/.

SAFLII (Southern African Legal Information Institute). 2000. *Pharmaceutical Manufacturers Association of South Africa and Another: In re Ex Parte President of the Republic of South Africa and Others* (CCT31/99) [2000] ZACC 1 (25 February 2000).

SAFLII (Southern African Legal Information Institute). 2002. *Minister of Health and Others v Treatment Action Campaign and Others* (No. 1) (CCT9/02) [2002] ZACC 16 (5 July 2002).

South Africa's National Competition Commission. 2003. *Hazel Tau and Others v GlaxoSmithKline SA (Pty) Ltd and Others.* Available at: http://www.section27.org.za/wp-content/uploads/2010/10/TauvGSKevidenceAndLegalSubmissions.pdf.

Tobin, John. 2012. *The Right to Health in International Law*. Oxford: Oxford University Press.

UN Commission on Human Rights. 2002. "The right of everyone to the enjoyment of the highest attainable standard of physical and mental health." April 22. Res. 2002/31; UN Docs. E/2002/23-E/CN.4/2002/200.

UN General Assembly. 1979. "Convention on the Elimination of All Forms of Discrimination Against Women." 18 December. UN Doc. 1249 U.N.T.S. 13.

UN General Assembly. 1989. "Convention on the Rights of the Child." 20 November. UN Doc. 1577 U.N.T.S. 3.

UN General Assembly. 1993. "Vienna Declaration and Programme of Action." UN Doc. A/CONF.157/23.

UN General Assembly. 1995. "Beijing Declaration and Platform of Action," adopted at the Fourth World Conference on Women, 17 October. UN Doc. A/CONF.177/20.

UN General Assembly. 2006. "Convention on the Rights of Persons with Disabilities." 13 December. UN Doc. 2515 U.N.T.S. 3.

UN General Assembly. 2015. "Transforming Our World: The 2030 Agenda for Sustainable Development." 25 September. GA Res. 70/1.

UN Human Rights Council. 2012. "Technical guidance on the application of a human-rights based approach to the implementation of policies and programmes to reduce preventable maternal morbidity and mortality. Report of the Office of the United Nations High Commissioner for Human Rights." 2 July. UN Doc. A/HRC/21/22.

UN Human Rights Council. 2013. "Report of the Special Rapporteur on torture and other cruel, inhuman or degrading treatment or punishment, Juan E. Méndez." 1 February. UN Doc. A/HRC/22/53.

UN Human Rights Council. 2014. "Technical guidance on the application of a human rights-based approach to the implementation of policies and programmes to reduce and eliminate preventable mortality and morbidity of children under 5 years of age. Report of the Office of the United Nations High Commissioner for Human Rights." 30 June. UN Doc. A/HRC/27/31.

UN Secretary-General. 2003. "UN Statement of Common Understanding on Human Rights-Based Approaches to Development Cooperation and Programming, 2003." Available at: https://www.unicef.org/sowc04/files/AnnexB.pdf.

UN Secretary-General. 2010. *Global Strategy for Women's and Children's Health*. Geneva: The Partnership for Maternal, Newborn, and Child Health.

UNFPA (UN Population Fund). 1994. "Report of the International Conference on Population and Development, Cairo, September 5–13, 1994." UN Doc. No. A/CONF.171/13.

UNICEF and UNFPA. 2013. "CRC and CEDAW: Making the Connection between Women's and Children's Rights: Facilitator's Guide." Available at: https://www.unicef.org/gender/files/CRC_and_CEDAW_Facilitators_Guide-small.pdf.

Uprimny, Rodrigo, César A. Rodríguez Garavito and Mauricio García Villegas. 2006. *¿Justicia para todos?: sistema judicial, derechos sociales y democracia en Colombia*. Cali: Grupo Editorial Norma.

WHO (World Health Organization). 2014. *Reproductive, maternal, newborn and child health and human rights: a toolbox for examining laws, regulations and policies*. Geneva: World Health Organization.

WHO CGEUHC (World Health Organization Consultative Group on Equity and Universal Health Coverage). 2014. *Making fair choices on the path to universal health coverage: Final report of the WHO Consultative Group on Equity and Universal Health Coverage*. Geneva: World Health Organization.

WHO CSDH (Commission on Social Determinants of Health). 2008. *Closing the gap in a generation: health equity through action on the social determinants of health. Final Report of the Commission on Social Determinants of Health.* Geneva: World Health Organization.

Wilkinson, David, Katherine Floyd, and Charles Gilks. 1998. "Antiretroviral Drugs as a Public Health Intervention for Pregnant HIV-Infected Women in Rural South Africa: An Issue of Cost-Effectiveness and Capacity." *AIDS* 12: 1675–1682.

Yamin, Alicia Ely. 1997. "Transformative Combinations: Women's Health and Human Rights." *Journal of the American Medical Women's Association* 52: 169–173.

Yamin, Alicia Ely. 2005. "Learning to Dance: Bringing the Fields of Human Rights and Public Health Together to Promote Women's Well-Being." In *Learning to Dance: Case Studies on Advancing Women's Reproductive Health and Well-Being from the Perspectives of Public Health and Human Rights*, edited by Alicia Ely Yamin, 1–36. Francois-Xavier Bagnoud Center on Health and Human Rights Series: Harvard University Press.

Yamin, Alicia Ely. 2013a. "From Ideals to Tools: Applying Human Rights to Maternal Health." *PLoS Medicine* 10 No. 11: e1001546.

Yamin, Alicia Ely. 2013b. "Sexual and Reproductive Health, Rights, and MDG5: Taking Stock, Looking Forward." In *The Millennium Development Goals and Human Rights: Past, Present and Future*, edited by Malcolm Langford, Andrew Sumner, and Alicia Ely Yamin, 232–254. Cambridge: Cambridge University Press.

Yamin, Alicia Ely. 2016. *Power, Suffering and the Struggle for Dignity: Human Rights Frameworks for Health and Why They Matter.* Philadelphia: University of Pennsylvania Press.

Yamin, Alicia Ely. 2017a. "'Speaking Truth to Power': A Call for Praxis in Human Rights." *Open Democracy.* April 18. Available at: https://www.opendemocracy.net/openglobalrights/alicia-ely-yamin/speaking-truth-to-power-call-for-praxis-in-human-rights.

Yamin, Alicia Ely. 2017b. "Taking the Right to Health Seriously: Implications for Health Systems, Courts and Achieving Universal Health Coverage." *Human Rights Quarterly* 39 (2): 341–368.

Yamin, Alicia Ely. Forthcoming 2018. "Democracy, Health Systems and the Right to Health: Narratives of Charity, Markets and Citizenship." In *Human Rights, Democracy and Legitimacy in the Twenty-First Century*, edited by Silja Vonecky and Gerald Neuman. Cambridge University Press.

Yamin, Alicia Ely. Forthcoming. "The Right to Health: The Challenges of Constructing Fair Limits." In *Oxford Handbook of Comparative Constitutional Law in Latin America*, edited by Conrado Hubner Mendez and Roberto Gargarella. Oxford University Press.

Yamin, Alicia Ely and Vanessa M. Boulanger. 2014. "Why Global Goals and Indicators Matter: The Experience of Sexual and Reproductive Health and Rights in the Millennium Development Goals." *Journal of Human Development and Capabilities* 15 (2-3): 218–231.

Yamin, Alicia Ely and Rebecca Cantor. 2014. "Between Insurrectional Discourse and Operational Guidance: Challenges and Dilemmas in Implementing Human Rights-Based Approaches to Health." *Journal of Human Rights Practice* 6(3): 451–485.

Yamin, Alicia Ely and Siri Gloppen, eds. 2011. *Litigating Health Rights: Can Courts Bring More Justice to Health?* Cambridge: Harvard University Press.

Yamin, Alicia Ely and Fiona Lander. 2015. "Implementing a Circle of Accountability: A Framework for Judiciaries in Enforcing Health-related Rights." *Journal of Human Rights* 14(3): 312–331.

3

Framing Human Rights in Global Health Governance

BENJAMIN MASON MEIER AND LAWRENCE O. GOSTIN[*]

With globalization creating an imperative for globalized health institutions to meet an expanding set of global health challenges, human rights are increasingly guiding these institutions of global health governance. International, national, and non-governmental actors in this global health governance landscape are increasingly invoking a "rights-based approach to health," grounded in the right to health and rights to various underlying determinants of health, as a means to implement international legal norms and principles. As these human rights norms and principles increasingly provide legitimacy to institutions of global health governance, this chapter analyzes the shift from state obligations under international health law to institutional responsibilities under global health law, examining the mainstreaming of human rights in global governance for public health.

This chapter frames the implementation of human rights law through global health governance. Part I describes the birth and evolution of global health governance, defining global health and the global health governance landscape. With contemporary global governance for health framed by global health law, Part II looks to the shift from international health law (applicable to states) to global health law (applied to both state and non-state actors). Analyzing health-related human rights as part of global health law, Part III examines how human rights have become a framework for global health governance, with institutions of global governance seeking to

* The authors are grateful for the research assistance of Neha Acharya in the development of this analysis on global health governance, for the thoughtful support of Eric Friedman in the description of the Framework Convention on Global Health, and for the insightful comments of Gavin Yamey in the conceptualization of global health in early drafts of this chapter.

"mainstream" human rights in organizational practice. This chapter concludes that there is a need for institutional analysis to conceptualize organizational approaches to the implementation of health-related human rights.

I. FROM INTERNATIONAL HEALTH GOVERNANCE TO GLOBAL HEALTH GOVERNANCE

With international health governance originally conceived as a means to protect independent state interests against health threats, this paradigm of mutual self-interest among powerful states is being challenged by an increasingly globalizing world and a new normative reality—with global health governance pursued as a means to assure a more just world through public health.

A. From International Health to Global Health

"International health" long described the spread of disease across national borders, serving as a discipline of academic study, a term of art in public health practice, and a descriptor of the landscape for addressing health determinants (Basch 1978). However, as states lost the capacity to act alone to influence public health, "global health" became the dominant means to conceptualize the needs of all peoples, rather than those of particular nations (Brown, Cueto, and Fee 2006). Where assessments of "the global" remained limited through the 1980s, the rise of a rapidly globalizing world would necessitate a global approach to health (Roemer and Roemer 1990). Beyond the reach of national health protections, the threat to health was understood to be global (Garrett 1994) and would require the "globalization of public health" (Yach and Bettcher 1998).

This transition away from international health laid the foundations for a more holistic approach to global health through socioeconomic determinants, social justice, and preventative interventions (Birn, Pillay, and Holtz 2017). Global health came to include the "study, research, and practice that places a priority on improving health and achieving equity in health for all people worldwide" (Koplan et al. 2009, 1995). With the term "global" encompassing non-state actors beyond governmental or intergovernmental entities—including media agencies, foundations, and corporations— global health aims to integrate a multitude of actors with varying functions, all for the overarching goal of improving health across countries and throughout the world (Beaglehole and Bonita 2010). The interdisciplinary nature of global health has begun to address the systemic determinants that underlie global health threats (Lomazzi, Jenkins, and Borisch 2016). These contemporary health threats, from infectious disease epidemics to global climate change, are not confined by the borders of states, and, therefore, only through a joint commitment to interdependent systems can global health be fully realized (Frenk, Gómez-Dantés, and Moon 2014).

Such efforts to achieve an improved state of global health require an understanding of public health, focusing on the health of populations through multi-sectoral interventions to address underlying determinants of health (McMichael and Beaglehole 2003). As globalization began to transform health at the population level, the resulting health inequities of globalization would require a public health approach, examining the collective political, social, and economic determinants of health inequalities (Kickbusch and Buse 2001). Viewing global health as public health, global health efforts would entail an examination of public health as a public good (producing collective benefits that support society as a whole), incorporating a domestic medicine and clinical care focus with a broader, multi-sectoral approach to prevention-based methods (Fried et al. 2010). These multi-sectoral approaches to address societal and systemic health inequities across countries necessitate global governance (Ottersen et al. 2014).

B. Global Governance for Health

Global governance for health describes the structures and methods of governing public health through multi-level and multi-sectoral institutions, including the actors and norms that define global health in an increasingly globalized world. Where international health governance could address inter-governmental cooperation to control the spread of disease across national boundaries, the advent of "global health" has necessitated not only new terminology but also new forms of governance that encompass state and non-state actors (Buse, Hein, and Drager 2009). Drawing from a larger shift toward global governance in a globalizing world, global health governance aims to integrate state cooperation with non-state actors to address transnational health issues (Clinton and Sridhar 2017). These non-state actors—including non-governmental organizations (NGOs), philanthropic foundations, and private sector interests—have become leading partners in an enlarged global health policy landscape (Lee 2009). To facilitate responsibility for global health equity—including multi-sectoral participation among state and non-state actors and transparency of health policies and interventions—these partnerships allow for a more sustained application of global health governance by providing an active, accountable means to progressively meet health goals (Harman 2012). Incorporating a more comprehensive range of actors to shape the architecture for global health governance, an evolving debate has examined how health issues that cross borders are addressed, how to define and assess determinants of health, and how to involve a more wide-ranging set of actors and interests (Drager and Sunderland 2007).

1. THE RISE OF INTERNATIONAL HEALTH GOVERNANCE

From early efforts of international cooperation to prevent the spread of infectious disease along trade routes, international health governance developed historically to encompass a range of models that address an expanding set of public health challenges (Youde 2013). Public health was among the first fields to engage international cooperation. Although governments had employed local quarantine measures as early as the fourteenth century, these measures, when combined with patterns of trade, took on international dimensions, leading to the rise of an international public health order to protect port cities from the economic damage spawned by the spread of disease across borders (Barkhuus 1943).

Borne of an increasing understanding of disease transmission and the unsanitary conditions of industrialization, early international health councils and meetings concerning specific infectious disease threats transformed to become a standing international public health bureaucracy, governed by multilateral treaties and charged with maintaining and expanding the public health order (Jacobson 1979). Scientific consensus would frame this international cooperation by the end of the nineteenth century, and as health practitioners came to appreciate the permanence of infectious disease, states saw the need to establish a permanent international health bureaucracy to coordinate and govern a wide range of disease control efforts (Pannenborg 1979).

The notion of a permanent institution of international health governance originated in the 1902 organization of the International Sanitary Office of the American Republics, the predecessor to the Pan American Health Organization (Bustamante 1955). Beyond the Americas, European states in 1907 created the *Office International d'Hygiène Publique* (OIHP), which would soon expand to represent nearly sixty countries, with member states each sending "technicians" to Paris to disseminate epidemiological information and supervise international sanitary conventions (WHO 1958). The First World War, leading to the widespread displacement of populations and denigration of sanitary conditions, created new underlying threats to public health, and in response to these threats (and the concomitant devastation caused by the influenza pandemic of 1918–1919), the postwar establishment of the League of Nations increased the number of surveillance and reporting forums available for international cooperation to control the spread of disease, as depicted in Figure 3.1, leading in 1923 to the creation of the Health Organization of the League of Nations (Borowy 2009).

During the Second World War, with the League of Nations disbanded and OIHP activities crippled by the occupation of France, the UN Relief and Rehabilitation Administration (UNRRA) formally assumed governance over international health,

Figure 3.1 Health Committee of the League of Nations.
PHOTO CREDIT: UN Archives at Geneva.

exercising its provisional mandate to distribute medicines and epidemiologic information to combat disease in war-ravaged states that lacked a functioning public health authority (Sawyer 1947). As a temporary organization created to deal only with the emergency situations brought about by the war, UNRRA's activities retained the traditional decentralization of past international health governance, developing flexible, local responses to the disparate health effects of a world war.

2. POSTWAR SHIFTS FROM INTERNATIONAL TO GLOBAL HEALTH GOVERNANCE

In the aftermath of the Second World War, a new "functionalist" international system of governance would be created under the nascent United Nations (UN), with governance for specific health-related functions distributed among independent UN specialized agencies (Jenks 1950). The World Health Organization (WHO) would become the specialized agency responsible for disease prevention efforts and the leading postwar institution of international health governance, coordinating states to address transnational health issues (WHO 1958). However, other organizations would have authority over wide-ranging determinants of health, and these organizations would increasingly seek to exercise that authority over, *inter alia*, labor safety, health education, child development, nutrition assistance, and economic development (Ascher 1952). With each organization having autonomy through their own respective governing boards, organizational budgets, and programmatic initiatives, such functional decentralization within the UN system set in motion a fragmented international governance system for public health, with international organizations operating independently to address public health issues within the substantive scope of their respective organizational mandates (Koivusalo and Ollila 1997).

The limitations of international health coordination across overlapping organizational mandates have been exacerbated by the rise of non-state actors in the global health landscape. Where the international system of health governance no longer exerted the influence it once had on non-state determinants of the public's health, WHO recognized these global changes—with the end of the Cold War and the advent of neoliberal globalization—and increasingly examined public health as a global enterprise that necessitated new forms of "global governance" (Yach and Bettcher 1998). From international health governance through inter-governmental institutions, global governance at the turn of the twenty-first century required more than just multilateral negotiations among states (Moon et al. 2010). Taking on roles in global health governance, a multilevel proliferation of international, national, non-governmental, and corporate actors has arisen to address a multi-sectoral array of determinants of health (Szlezák et al. 2010). This new global health architecture has required actors to construct new normative frameworks for global governance, coordinating mechanisms for collective action, and accountability systems for policy implementation (Drager and Sunderland, 2007). Without institutional leadership or legal authority to govern this crowded landscape of actors—leading to what has been referred to generously as "open-source anarchy" (Fidler 2007), less generously as a "mosh pit" (Buse and Harmer 2009)—the functional decentralization and rising autonomy of actors in the global health landscape have complicated efforts to develop shared governance through global health law (Burci and Cassels 2016).

II. GLOBAL HEALTH LAW AS A BASIS FOR GLOBAL HEALTH GOVERNANCE

Global health law has become a basis to describe the new legal frameworks that govern this new set of public health threats, non-state actors, and regulatory norms that structure global health. These legal frameworks, placing public health obligations on the global community of state and non-state actors, are realized through global governance institutions that embrace transparency, engage multi-sectoral actors, monitor progress, and facilitate accountability. As a basis to frame institutions of global health governance, global health law includes legal obligations to realize human rights in global health.

A. From International Health Law to Global Health Law

Globalization has unleashed the spread of disease, connected societies in shared vulnerability, and highlighted the limitations of domestic legislation in addressing global determinants of health. Yet if globalization presented challenges to national disease prevention and health promotion efforts, international health law offered the promise of bridging national boundaries to alleviate these inequities (Taylor 2004). International law was seen as essential to developing the governance structures for "dealing with externalities that can take on global dimensions" and thus are outside the control of individual sovereign states (Slaughter 1997, 184). Although international health law has evolved to become a distinct approach to public health law, framing multilateral cooperation under international law to re-spond to global health security threats, such laws have remained incommensurate to the rising health threats of a rapidly globalizing world (Magnusson 2007). To address the health harms of globalization, including the rise of new actors in the global health landscape and new threats beyond the reach of the state, global health law has sought to "evolve beyond its traditional confines of formal sources and subjects of international law" to facilitate social justice in global health (Gostin and Taylor 2008, 55).

As such, global health law seeks to describe public international law that speaks to:

- New health threats—including non-communicable disease, injuries, mental health, dangerous products, and other globalized health risks,
- New health actors—including transnational corporations, private philanthropists, civil society, and other non-governmental organizations, and
- New health regulations—including "soft law" instruments, strategy documents, and other norms of global health policy (Gostin 2014).

Where these issues were beyond the reach of international health law, global health law could define, frame, and address the governance institutions necessary to re-spond to the public health challenges of the twenty-first century.

Global health law is built upon the foundations of international health law. International regulation of public health far predates any discussion of interna-tional health governance, with international law long viewed by states as necessary for collective action against infectious disease, coordinating national public health responses to protect international economic and security interests (Aginam 2005). Borne of a time when medicine was impotent to treat disease, the major trading powers of the Industrial Revolution were forced to acknowledge, with disease transmission flowing rapidly along trade routes, that infectious disease could no longer be construed as solely within the sovereign affairs of independent states, necessitating the development of international health law (Goodman 1952).

This early "sanitary period," marked by its emphasis on the prevention of epidemic disease, determined the course of international public health regulation through bilateral, regional, and multilateral treaties. The first International Sanitary Conference, held in Paris in 1851, sought to bring together physicians and diplomats to reach consensus among those states having trading interests in the Mediterranean basin. These states held a second conference in Paris in 1859, with subsequent conferences held in Constantinople (1866), Vienna (1874), Washington, D.C. (1881), Rome (1885), Venice (1892), Dresden (1893), Paris (1894), and again in Venice (1897). While international sanitary regulations were crafted at various points in this long march of successive International Sanitary Conferences, none of these early regulations mustered the widespread national ratification necessary for adoption (WHO 1958). This legislative inertia would not be broken until widespread scientific agreement was reached on health threats, theories, and technologies (Howard-Jones 1974). By the 1892 Venice Conference, technical experts had reached consensus on public health practice sufficient to draft and ratify a convention to prevent the spread of infectious disease. At the eleventh International Sanitary Conference in Paris in 1903, delegates drafted the first International Sanitary Convention of widespread applicability (Porter 1998). This Sanitary Convention set the stage for the International Health Regulations that followed and laid the groundwork for the development of international health law through WHO.

The WHO Constitution would be the first treaty to codify states' expansive postwar mandate for medical care and underlying determinants of health, with WHO's constitutional framework piercing the veil of national sovereignty to address public health, placing the relationship between government action and individual health "at the heart of international cooperation" (Fidler 2004, 61). Under the WHO Constitution, the WHO Secretariat would have authority to propose conventions, regulations, and recommendations on any matter of public health (WHO 1948). With this international legal authority to regulate public health, WHO's International Health Regulations (IHR) created a harmonized surveillance and reporting system for infectious disease control, setting both minimum mandatory controls and maximum permissible limitations on individual and commercial interests (Burci and Vignes 2004). However, beyond the IHR (last revised in 2005 to reflect contemporary health threats), states in the World Health Assembly (WHA) have employed WHO's legal authority, as described in chapter 5, to develop only two other treaties: the 1967 Nomenclature Regulations and the 2003 Framework Convention on Tobacco Control.

There are limits to international health law in creating universal legal standards to address the prevailing health inequities of a globalizing world. Where once public health was a central focus of international negotiation, international regulation of public health has waned in international relations as states eschewed voluntary limitations on their sovereign authority for public health (Pannenborg 1979). Because of the state-centric nature of international law, such international health agreements have remained: focused on infectious diseases (that threaten powerful interests), dependent on voluntary agreement (exclusively by sovereign states), and reliant on international consensus (resulting in vague norms). International health law is seen as inherently incapable of facilitating collective action to address contemporary global health priorities (Gostin 2005), creating an imperative to extend the influence of public health law as a basis for advancing global health, redressing health inequities within and across countries through global health law (Gostin 2008).

Global health law seeks to apply specific forms of "soft law" (including resolutions, global strategies, and codes of practice) to facilitate collective action across both state and non-state actors, including the public sector, private actors, and civil society. Even as "soft" norms for health were long relegated to the sidelines of international relations (Fidler 1999), global health law was seen as a basis to rediscover these norms for justice in global health (Ruger 2008). This expansion of international law to encompass global health law has provided a legal framework to structure efforts by the global community to advance global health (Gostin 2014). Although global health law would lack the formal legal enforceability of international health law, it would nonetheless build consensus to set priorities, mobilize constituencies, create incentives, coordinate actors, and facilitate accountability in an expanding global health governance landscape.

B. Applying Global Health Law to Global Health Governance

Where international health law traditionally applied to states, global health law has come to be seen as a framework to structure governance institutions, with the normative frameworks of global health law leading to many of the same political and pragmatic benefits as international law. As a legal basis for global health governance, global health law encompasses both international health law and "soft law" forms of global health policy (Gostin and Sridhar 2014). International health law continues to govern the actions of national governments, especially where binding obligations on states are necessary to prevent infectious disease through collective action (Davies 2008); however, these collective action problems across states do not encompass the entirety of global health governance (Meier 2011). With international law bearing most directly on states (which remain deeply relevant and important), such legal frameworks have limited effect on the global forces that increasingly underlie public health, with public international law appearing insufficient to understand contemporary changes in statehood, international relations, and global public goods for health (Skogly 2006). Filling these gaps in global health governance, a multilevel proliferation of international, national, non-governmental, and corporate actors has arisen to address a multi-sectoral array of determinants of health—complicating initiatives to develop international law for global health (Szlezák et al. 2010). In this context, global health law and global health governance can be seen as interrelated, with law a major aspect of governance and governance often taking the form of law (Gostin 2014).

As global health governance came to be seen as incapable of responding to globalized determinants of health through international health law, it became clear that new legal norms, processes, and institutions would be necessary to frame global health governance (Gostin and Taylor 2008). Grounded in practice, WHO has long sought to avoid exercising its formal legal authorities through "hard" legal treaties, focusing its normative role on adopting "soft," non-binding instruments through recommendations, including codes, strategies, guidelines, and other policies to influence states (Kastler 2016).

Contemporary global health governance partnerships are also seen to avoid discussions of international health law, leaving the international legal system impotent to respond to global health challenges (Fidler 2007). Where once international health law was the only option for states to address issues of international health, the new global health governance landscape now far more often looks to these "softer" international instruments, which have proven far easier to negotiate (without the need for formal ratification) and which have advanced issues of global health (often in ways indistinguishable from traditional multilateral treaties) (Gostin 2014). Looking beyond the regulation of states through international health law, global health law would apply these new sources of soft law to facilitate collective action across the state and non-state actors that can influence public health in a globalizing world.

Global health law provides a legal basis by which to structure global health governance. International organizations have become key lawmaking bodies, developing international legal norms to coordinate state and non-state actors (Alvarez 2005; White 2016). These new legal instruments and structures of global health law would provide actors with a basis to negotiate a shared vision for global health, coordinate with each other to realize institutional goals, and monitor benchmarks to facilitate accountability. Such negotiation can develop policies that either uphold or diminish global health goals; for example, the standards set under humanitarian law during times of armed conflict can either improve health conditions or cause detrimental effects, and understanding the interrelationship between global governance and domestic law is critical for aligning global health law in ways that are reinforced through national law (Gostin 2014). Negotiation therefore is crucial to the development of governance, with the negotiating process for non-binding norms still requiring partnerships with key stakeholders and consensus on shared principles (Klabbers 2015). Global health governance can provide an institutional platform to coordinate disparate state and non-state actors under global health law. Leading to accountability for global health goals, global health law can provide an institutional basis to develop benchmarks, monitor progress, and enhance compliance.

The application of global health law can thereby provide a normative framework for global health governance. In an increasingly globalized world, creating an imperative for globalized health institutions to meet an expanding set of global challenges to underlying determinants of health, normative frameworks can guide global health law beyond traditional forms of international law. As the limitations of international health law have moved global health law beyond the bastions of international legal diplomacy, stakeholders have engaged a diverse array of state and non-state actors through the rise of new policy institutions—institutions developed through their normative foundations (Meier 2011). Through such soft law norm-setting, applying non-formal sources of public international law to state and non-state actors, global health law seeks to create new policy institutions to alter behaviors, sustain funding, and coordinate partnerships for justice in global health (Gostin 2014). These norms can facilitate accountability for state and non-state actors in the absence of formal international law, with these norms of global health law structuring human rights in public health.

C. Global Health Law Necessitates Human Rights

Human rights have provided the leading normative frameworks for global health law, with rights serving as an ethical foundation for justice in global health governance. Established under international law, the UN Charter set out human rights as a central basis of postwar international relations, seeking to promote "universal respect for, and observance of, human rights and fundamental freedoms for all" and develop "international cooperation" to encourage collective respect for human rights (UN 1945, arts. 1, 55, 56). With human rights developed over the past seventy years under international law, as chronicled in chapters 1 and 2, these rights have provided a basis for norms, institutions, and processes to address global health (Yamin 2016). Human rights now stand as the most developed moral standard for promoting human dignity, social justice, and health equity through global governance (Gruskin, Mills, and Tarantola 2007). However, while almost all states have ratified core human rights treaties, state sovereignty and international politics stand as impediments to human rights implementation, even in liberal democracies, given that human rights place certain constraints on domestic policymakers (Brown and Paremoer 2014). Yet, even as states have continued to debate their accountability for human rights realization under international law, human rights have provided a moral foundation for global health law and framed an implementation framework through global health governance (Gostin 2014).

To solidify human rights in global health law, scholars have proposed a Framework Convention on Global Health (FCGH). This international treaty has been proposed "as a mechanism to channel more constructive and cooperative action to address ... the health of the world's population" (Gostin 2008, 383). Through a rights-based approach to global health funding, the FCGH seeks to codify mutual responsibilities between donor and recipient nations, coordinate the efforts of governmental and non-governmental actors, and enhance financial support for global health governance (Friedman and Gostin 2012). The FCGH Alliance has joined together civil society organizations, marginalized communities, academic researchers, and health practitioners to advocate for an FCGH as a basis to overcome an expanding array of governance challenges in enforcing health-related human rights through global health law (Gostin et al. 2016). Focusing on the shortcomings of weak accountability, inadequate funding, marginalization and discrimination, and national and global governance for health, the FCGH Alliance supports the FCGH as a model for reinforcing human rights, particularly the right to health, under WHO leadership (JALI 2016).

This FCGH effort seeks to create a human rights foundation for global governance of public health, developing an international legal framework to implement the human right to health under global health law, and thereby assuring that states live up to their mutual responsibilities for global health (Gable and Meier 2013). As a basis for realizing the right to health, the FCGH can assure under global health law that state and non-state actors respect the right to health by not interfering with individuals' realization of the right, protect individuals from violations of the right, and fulfill the right by ensuring global redistributions to improve public health (Gostin 2014).

Engaging human rights under international law as a basis for advancing public health, institutions of global health governance have come to assume responsibilities for implementing human rights. Although these global institutions are not party to human rights treaties or legally obligated to implement human rights under international law (Brabandere 2009), global health law has sought to move beyond this state-centric conception of human rights, operating across levels of governance to recognize the responsibilities borne by these coordinating institutions (Gable 2007). Some of these institutions have expressed this commitment to human rights as central to their mission—as seen in the WHO Constitution, which begins by proclaiming health as a "fundamental right"—whereas other institutions have embraced a "rights-based approach" to health, adopting human rights principles or methods as part of their public health practice (Gostin 2014). As global health governance institutions have been central to developing human rights under international law, they are now seen as necessary for implementing human rights in their institutional policies, programs, and practices.

III. MAINSTREAMING HUMAN RIGHTS IN GLOBAL GOVERNANCE FOR PUBLIC HEALTH

In seeking justice in an increasingly globalized world, human rights norms are progressively framing global governance for public health. Recognizing the need for global action to realize human rights, looking beyond the human rights system, these global governance institutions have long been seen as having a supervisory role in human rights implementation (Alston 1992). The establishment of rights-based global governance for health has required both the incorporation of public health considerations in human rights governance and the incorporation of human rights norms in global health governance. Overcoming the functional decentralization of global governance, this multi-sectoral effort has sought to shift global governance from the coordination of independent institutional approaches for human rights to the mainstreaming of integrated practices for global health and human rights (Hunt 2017).

A. Human Rights as a Basis for Global Governance

While the UN human rights system bears primary responsibility to promote human rights, decentralized authority for global governance has necessitated that human rights be "mainstreamed" across institutions. Decentralization was originally seen as a basis for complementary rights-based efforts across institutions, with scholars expecting that UN specialized agencies would shoulder "a major share of the responsibility" for the implementation of economic and social rights (Jenks 1969, 54); however, these institutions long neglected any responsibility to realize human rights (Alston 1979). After decades of neglect for the implementation of human rights through global governance, the end of the Cold War raised an opportunity to engage UN agencies, programs, and funds in the implementation of human rights, expanding the institutional avenues for human rights realization (Buergenthal 1997). The 1993 Vienna Declaration and Programme of Action would develop global consensus on the indivisibility of civil, political, economic, social, and cultural rights, requesting that all UN agencies and bodies assess the impact of their development policies on the realization of human rights (World Conference on Human Rights 1993). Where human rights had long been cloistered within the UN human rights system, the Vienna Declaration "established the foundation for a holistic and integrated approach to human rights not only by the human rights machinery but also by the entire United Nations system" (Robinson 1998, para. 23). This new post–Cold War consensus would expand institutional responsibilities for human rights throughout the global governance landscape. No longer the exclusive purview of a select group of human rights lawyers, human rights implementation would necessitate the entire UN system.

Given this new global consensus on the centrality of human rights, UN Secretary-General Kofi Annan followed up on the Vienna Declaration in 1997 by calling for the enhancement of human rights as a "cross-cutting" approach to all of the UN's principal activities and programs (UN Secretary-General 1997). This cross-cutting approach to human rights within the UN would seek to "fully integrate it [human rights] into the broad range of the Organization's activities" (Ibid., para. 79). Incorporating the Office of the UN High Commissioner for Human Rights (OHCHR) into the managerial structures of the UN—working across all areas and levels of UN governance, as discussed in chapter 21—OHCHR could support decentralized UN organizations to engage (some for the first time) with human rights norms and principles. With the UN Economic and Social Council (ECOSOC), the central UN member state forum for economic and social issues, lending political support for human rights in global governance (ECOSOC 1998), the UN system could come together to realize development objectives through human rights.

The Secretary-General's plan would call on the entire UN system to "mainstream" human rights in all policies, programs, and practices. Out of this mainstreaming mandate, UN institutions would begin to examine the implications of human rights to their development work, partnering with OHCHR and adopting human rights policy statements (O'Neill and Bye 2002). Select UN specialized agencies, programs, and funds would explicitly adopt a "rights-based approach," developing both internal documents and external publications to clarify the institution-specific application of this approach and guide the practical transformation of human rights into organizational actions (Pais 1998; UNDP 1998; World Bank 1998). With the Secretary-General reporting to the UN General Assembly on the promotion and protection of human rights, he would argue five years later that this UN mainstreaming effort should be extended from organizational secretariats to country offices, enhancing inter-agency cooperation with OHCHR country officers to strengthen national systems for human rights protection (UN 2002).

Seeking to harmonize these organizational mainstreaming efforts, the UN Development Group (UNDG), a coalition of thirty-two UN entities working together to coordinate UN development activities, adopted a "Statement of Common Understanding among United Nations Agencies on the Human Rights-Based Approach to Development Cooperation" (Common Understanding) (UNDG 2003). Led by OHCHR, UNDP, and UNICEF, UNDG's Human Rights Working Group advised that all programs, policies, and technical assistance should both extend the realization of international human rights to development practice and contribute to the development of capacities—for duty-bearers to meet their obligations and for rights-holders to claim their rights (Frankovits 2006). This rights-based Common Understanding would set forth that:

1. All programmes of development co-operation, policies and technical assistance should further the realisation of human rights as laid down in the Universal Declaration of Human Rights and other international human rights instruments.
2. Human rights standards contained in, and principles derived from, the Universal Declaration of Human Rights and other international human rights instruments guide all development cooperation and programming in all sectors and in all phases of the programming process.
3. Development cooperation contributes to the development of the capacities of "duty-bearers" to meet their obligations and/or of "rights-holders" to claim their rights (UNDG 2003, 1).

The application of this Common Understanding led to increased understanding of the practical implications of human rights mainstreaming for the sustainability of development programs (Nyamu-Musembi and Cornwall 2004). Through this practical framework for UN organizations, a larger set of institutions developed detailed and context-specific requirements for operationalizing a range of interdependent human rights (FAO 2005). Incorporating human rights principles in organizational practice, institutions would develop guidance documents on the application of principles for equality and non-discrimination, participation and inclusion, and accountability and the rule of law (UNDP 2006).

When Annan spoke for the last time to the UN Commission on Human Rights, his 2005 address to member states sought to acknowledge this shift toward an "era of implementation" for human rights in global governance:

The cause of human rights has entered a new era. For much of the past 60 years, our focus has been on articulating, codifying and enshrining rights. That effort produced a remarkable framework of laws, standards and mechanisms—the Universal Declaration, the international covenants, and much else. Such work needs to continue in some areas. But the era of declaration is now giving way, as it should, to an era of implementation (UN Secretary-General 2005).

Although Annan focused on necessary reforms to the UN human rights system—including, as addressed in Section V of this volume, the human rights treaty bodies, the OHCHR, and the "inter-governmental machinery" of human rights governance—this shift has forced a larger examination of those institutions outside of the traditional human rights system that play a central role in human rights implementation through global governance (Darrow and Arbour 2009).

All institutions of global governance are now seen as instrumental to the international human rights system, if not a part of that system itself, and as necessary to assure the "full implementation" of human rights. The implementation efforts of these global governance institutions seek to translate international law into organizational action—through their policies, programs, and practices (Hunt et al. 2014). In operationalizing human rights through global governance, these institutions employ international human rights law to pursue human rights objectives through a rights-based approach: setting standards, preventing violations, mainstreaming norms, and facilitating accountability (Clarke 2012; Mertus 2013). With these institutions encompassing what has been called the "archipelago" of human rights realization, they are seen to branch out from the "mainland" of the human rights system while maintaining autonomy in a decentralized global governance system (Hunt 2017). The complementarity of these institutions—within and beyond the human rights system—is crucial to human rights implementation, operationalizing the norms of human rights through the practicalities of global governance.

The implementation of human rights through global health governance seeks to translate international law into institutional practice for public health (Gable 2007), yet scholars have long noted that there remains no universally agreed definition of the rights-based approach, and as a consequence, institutions have manifested varying degrees of commitment to human rights implementation (Shelton 2014). This uneven commitment among institutions of global health governance, with technical officers either unwilling or unable to consider the institutional benefits of the rights-based approach to their core health mandates (Oestreich 2007), has led to additional human rights disparities across institutional headquarters and country offices (Elliott 2015). These disparities in institutional commitment to human rights have raised an imperative to mainstream human rights for global health.

B. Human Rights Mainstreaming for Global Health

In the full implementation of human rights in global health, it is essential to mainstream health-related human rights in global governance, operationalizing human rights in institutional policies, programs, and practices. Although the tension between individual negative rights and government public health measures dominated early human rights discourse in global health governance, particularly in the early years of the AIDS response (Gostin and Lazzarini 1997; Mann 1999), a positive human rights framework could acknowledge how organizations must act affirmatively as duty-bearers to implement economic, social, and cultural rights to assure global health (Marks 2001). The UN has sought through mainstreaming to bring human rights "from the periphery to the center of policymaking or programming," integrating human rights standards and methodologies into all the health-related activities of an organization (Darrow and Arbour 2009, 448). In creating a basis for institutional public health practice, "human rights norms, standards and principles must be incorporated in decision-making on policies, operational issues and budgets, be made part of an organisation's bureaucratic process, culture, and be internalised by staff" (Oberleitner 2008, 386). Moving beyond the declarations of governing bodies—encompassing planning and processes at the organization, department, and individual level—mainstreaming necessitates a wholesale repurposing of institutional operations (Kędzia 2009). Where human rights are mainstreamed in global health institutions, integrated centrally into the daily work of an organization, these institutions can serve an instrumental supervisory role in human rights implementation for global health advancement (Hunt 2015).

Mainstreaming entails the application of human rights norms and principles in concrete actions throughout institutional operations. Such human rights mainstreaming should entail reference to specific human rights obligations while recognizing both violations of the rights of rights-holders and breaches of obligations by duty-bearers (Coomans 2012). Facilitating accountability for rights-holders and duty-bearers in times of violations, mainstreaming can ensure the protection of certain inalienable rights and aim to reduce inequalities and discrimination in institutional policies. UNDG has developed tools for mainstreaming human rights norms within UN Country Teams, focusing, as illustrated in Figure 3.2, on integrating eight specific guidance areas in governance. While certain guidance areas must be initiated immediately, others require deeper levels of mainstreaming to occur over time. The order in which these areas are enforced requires different stages of "planning," "doing," and "assessing" (UNDG 2017). These efforts have concluded that institutional policies and programs must be grounded in specific human rights, with institutional practices guided by cross-cutting human rights principles (UNDG 2015).

Although institutions will continue to operate independently, these consultative UNDG processes have given hope for a shared approach to human rights mainstreaming in the UN system, harmonizing approaches to human rights across institutions through "sustained support, constructive scrutiny and quality control of their human rights content" (Hunt 2017, 490).

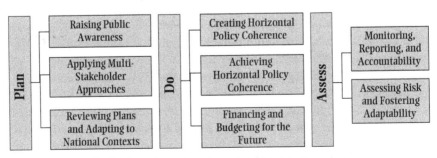

Figure 3.2 UNDG's Guidance Areas for Human Rights Mainstreaming.
NOTE: This figure was adapted from UNDG's "Mainstreaming the 2030 Agenda for Sustainable Development: Reference Guide for UN Country Teams."

Applied to global health governance, institutional mainstreaming policies should realize the attributes of a range of indivisible, interdependent, and interrelated health-related human rights, seeking to assure that health is available, accessible, acceptable, and of sufficient quality (CESCR 2000). Examining cross-cutting human rights principles in public health programming, institutional practices should assure that health is realized through processes that promote non-discrimination and equality, participation, and accountability (UNDG 2003). In pursuing human rights mainstreaming for public health promotion, these operations should seek to analyze the causes of health-related human rights violations, implicating an intersectoral and integrated response to addressing the human rights that underlie public health. While the human rights-based approach was long criticized for being too theoretically abstract for practical application (UNDP 2001), scholars and practitioners have come together to conceptualize the meaning of human rights mainstreaming to global health governance, developing organizational systems to assess mainstreaming effectiveness (Meier and Onzivu 2014).

Institutions have pursued distinct approaches to human rights mainstreaming in global health, creating a continuum of mainstreaming efforts and consequences across diverse institutions. At a minimum, institutions have been seen to invoke human rights in their rhetoric without changing organizational norms in their policies, programs, or practices (Coomans 2012). Recognizing the harm to human rights from these minimalist approaches to mainstreaming, scholars have long sought to distinguish "authentically human rights-conscious" organizations from those merely engaging in "epistemological misappropriation" of human rights discourse (Alston 2002, 842). Between these two extremes—between "talking the talk" and "walking the walk"—lies a range of actions indicative of the incorporation of human rights in global health governance, from human rights norms in policy statements to human rights methodologies in operational practices, with institutions seen to expand these rights-based initiatives progressively over time (Kędzia 2009). These policies, programs, and practices across the continuum of mainstreaming, viewed over time and across units, can indicate greater operationalization of human rights and more authentic human rights implementation.

In this progressive shift toward human rights in global health governance, institutions have faced challenges—both in their approach to human rights norms and in their application of rights-based principles. Where human rights champions within institutions are incorporated into bureaucratic procedures for human rights implementation, this approach risks co-opting rights advocates under administrative systems, suppressing their ability to challenge institutions from the outside (Koskenniemi 2006). Human rights mainstreaming has also proven challenging in its application, implicating shifts in organizational culture that have not always been welcomed by technical staff and requiring complex analyses that have proven challenging for those unacquainted with human rights norms and principles (Oberleitner 2008). Where global governance for health is structured by autonomous institutions with distinct practices (and country offices with self-directing coordinators), such a harmonized approach to human rights mainstreaming has been met with resistance by independent actors, leading to varied levels of human rights commitment and varied approaches to human rights mainstreaming across disconnected institutions and country offices (Oberleitner 2007).

Without a firm mandate for human rights mainstreaming in global health, institutions have sought to mainstream from within (rather than having mainstreaming imposed from outside), recognizing institution-specific ways to internalize human rights in organizational practice. Institutions have thereby sought to examine specific "essential characteristics" of human rights and then define the operational criteria that can be used to implement those characteristics, creating organizational roadmaps, plans, initiatives, funds, handbooks, and programs by which to translate international human rights obligations into public health action (Darrow and Tomas 2005). Through this "bottom-up approach" to mainstreaming, translating international treaties into internal guidelines, institutions "contribute, in essence, to human rights standard-setting and to the clarification and interpretation of human rights norms" (Oberleitner 2008, 387). These institutional policies, programs, and practices have required institutions to build human rights capacity among technical staff—in headquarters and country offices—in order to shape the work of those seeking to advance human rights in global health governance (Kędzia 2009). Requiring interactive dialogue between technical staff and human rights advisors to operationalize human rights standards within a technical sphere of influence, these mainstreaming efforts have developed a "two-way street" by which mutual learning can develop a context-specific approach to human rights implementation (Hunt 2017). By developing collaborative recommendations for how staff can understand and implement human rights (without allowing this context-specific mainstreaming to strip human rights norms and principles of their meaning), institutions are seeking a basis to monitor mainstreaming efforts in institutional programming.

Mainstreaming human rights has thus become more than simply the coordination of human rights activities but also a basis to facilitate accountability for the implementation of human rights law through global health governance. With scholars calling for "quality control" to assess institutional implementation of human rights, it has become necessary to develop criteria—at the organizational, unit, and individual levels—to determine:

- the "authenticity" of efforts to implement human rights norms and principles in institutional actions (Hunt 2017);
- the efficacy of those mainstreaming actions on institutional policies, programs, and practices (Oberleitner 2008); and
- the impact of those policies, programs, and practices on public health outcomes (Murphy 2013).

Such accountability mechanisms, developed internally and in cooperation with the human rights system, will become crucial under the Sustainable Development Goals (SDGs) (HRC 2016). With continuing support from states for human rights mainstreaming, the SDGs will provide a continuing basis for institutions to come together to advance and assess the role of human rights in global health governance (UNDG 2017).

CONCLUSION

The implementation of human rights in global health requires the dedicated involvement of an array of actors in the global health governance landscape. While decentralized institutions of global health governance are achieving human rights gains, the fragmentation of these uncoordinated human rights initiatives across a proliferation of institutions creates a need for comparative research to analyze the institutional policies, programs, and practices conducive to human rights implementation. The mainstreaming of human rights in global governance for public health is far from complete, and progress is by no means assured in the years to come, yet this tentative progress can be studied as a means to understand how human rights are translated from international treaty to institutional action. With institutions seeking to mainstream human rights in institutional policies, programs, and practices as a way of implementing human rights norms and principles through global health governance, this expansion of human rights implementation calls for scholarly attention to institutions as a basis for understanding human rights in global health.

REFERENCES

Aginam, Obijiofor. 2005. *Global Health Governance: International Law and Public Health in a Divided World*. Toronto: University of Toronto Press.

Alston, Philip. 1979. "The United Nations' Specialized Agencies and Implementation of the International Covenant on Economic, Social and Cultural Rights." *Columbia Journal of Transnational Law* 18(1): 79–118.

Alston, Philip. 1992. *The United Nations and Human Rights: A Critical Appraisal*. New York: Oxford University Press.

Alston, Philip. 2002. "Resisting the Merger and Acquisition of Human Rights by Trade Law: A Reply to Petersmann." *European Journal of International Law* 13(4): 815–842.

Alvarez, José E. 2005. *International Organizations as Law-Makers*. New York: Oxford University Press.

Ascher, Charles S. 1952. "Problems in the World Health Organization's Program." *International Organization* 6(1): 27–50.

Barkhuus, Arne. 1943. "The Dawn of International Cooperation in Medicine." *Ciba Symposia* 5: 1554–1562.

Basch, Paul F. 1978. *International Health*. New York: Oxford University Press.

Beaglehole, Robert and Ruth Bonita. 2010. "What Is Global Health?" *Global Health Action* 3: 1–2.

Birn, Anne-Emanuelle, Yogan Pillay, and Timothy Holtz. 2017. *Textbook of Global Health*. New York: Oxford University Press.

Borowy, Iris. 2009. *Coming to Terms with World Health: The League of Nations Health Organisation, 1921–1946*. Frankfurt: Peter Lang GmbH.

Brabandere, Eric De. 2009. "Non-State Actors, State-Centrism and Human Rights Obligations." *Leiden Journal of International Law* 22: 191–209.

Brown, Garrett W. and Lauren Paremoer. 2014. "Global Health Justice and the Right to Health." In *The Handbook of Global Health Policy*, edited by Garrett W. Brown, Gavin Yamey, and Sarah Wamala, 77–95. New York: Wiley.

Brown, Theodore, Marcos Cueto, and Elizabeth Fee. 2006. "The World Health Organization and the Transition from 'International' to 'Global' Public Health." *American Journal of Public Health* 96(1): 62–72.

Buergenthal, Thomas. 1997. "The Normative and Institutional Evolution of International Human Rights." *Human Rights Quarterly* 19(4): 703–723.

Burci, Gian Luca and Andrew Cassels. 2016. "Health." In *The Oxford Handbook of International Organizations*, edited by Jacob Katz Cogan, Ian Hurd, and Ian Johnstone. Oxford: Oxford University Press.

Burci, Gian Luca and Claude-Henri Vignes. 2004. *The World Health Organization.* London: Kluwer Law International.

Buse, Kent and Andrew Harmer. 2009. "Global Health Partnerships: The Mosh Pit of Global Health Governance." In *Making Sense of Global Health Governance: A Policy Perspective*, edited by Kent Buse, Wolfgang Hein, and Nick Drager. New York: Palgrave MacMillan.

Buse, Kent, Wolfgang Hein, and Nick Drager. 2009. *Making Sense of Global Health Governance: A Policy Perspective.* New York: Palgrave MacMillan.

Bustamante, Miguel E. 1955. *The Pan American Sanitary Bureau: Half a Century of Health Activities 1902–1954.* Washington: Pan American Sanitary Bureau.

CESCR (Committee on Economic, Social and Cultural Rights). 2000. "General Comment No. 14: The Right to the Highest Attainable Standard of Health (Art. 12)." 11 August. UN Doc. E/C.12/2000/4.

Clarke, Alisa. 2012. "The Potential of the Human Rights-Based Approach for the Evolution of the United Nations as a System." *Human Rights Review* 13(2): 225–248.

Clinton, Chelsea and Devi Lalita Sridhar. 2017. *Governing Global Health: Who Runs the World and Why?* New York: Oxford University Press.

Coomans, Fons. 2012. "On the Right(s) Track? United Nations (Specialized) Agencies and the Use of Human Rights Language." *Verfassung und Recht in Übersee* 45(3): 274–294.

Darrow, Mac and Louise Arbour. 2009. "The Pillar of Glass: Human Rights in the Development Operations of the United Nations." *American Journal of International Law* 103(3): 446–501.

Darrow, Mac and Amparo Tomas. 2005. "Power, Capture, and Conflict: A Call for Human Rights Accountability in Development Cooperation." *Human Rights Quarterly* 27(2): 471–538.

Davies, Sara E. 2008. "Securitizing Infectious Disease." *International Affairs* 84(2): 295–313.

Drager, Nick and Laura Sunderland. 2007. "Public Health in a Globalising World: The Perspective from the World Health Organization." In *Governing Global Health: Challenge, Response, Innovation*, edited by Andrew F. Cooper, John J. Kirton, and Ted Schrecker, 67–78. Aldershot, England: Ashgate Publishing.

ECOSOC, 49th Session. 1998. "Further Measures for the Restructuring and Revitalization of the United Nations in the Economic, Social and Related Fields." 31 July. Res. 1998/46.

Elliott, Leilani. "How Do Institutions Engage with the Idea of a Human Rights-Based Approach to Matters Involving Children?: A Case Study of UNICEF and the World Bank." PhD diss., Melbourne Law School, 2015.

FAO (UN Food and Agriculture Organization). 2005. *Voluntary Guidelines to Support the Progressive Realization of the Right to Adequate Food in the Context of National Food Security.* Rome: Chief, Publishing Management Service.

Fidler, David P. 1999. *International Law and Infectious Diseases*. New York: Clarendon Press.

Fidler, David P. 2004. "Caught Between Paradise and Power: Public Health, Pathogenic Threats, and the Axis of Illness." *McGeorge Law Review* 35(1): 45–101.

Fidler, David P. 2007. "Architecture Amidst Anarchy: Global Health's Quest for Governance." *Global Health Governance* 1: 1–17.

Frankovits, André. 2006. *The Human Rights Based Approach and the United Nations System*. Paris: UN Educational, Scientific and Cultural Organization.

Frenk, Julio, Octavio Gómez-Dantés, and Suerie Moon. 2014. "From Sovereignty to Solidarity: A Renewed Concept of Global Health for an Era of Complex Interdependence." *The Lancet* 383(9911): 94–97.

Fried, Linda P., Margaret E. Bentley, Pierre Buekens, Donald S. Burke, Julio J. Frenk, Michael J. Klag, and Harrison Spencer. 2010. "Global Health Is Public Health." *The Lancet* 375: 535–537.

Friedman, Eric A. and Lawrence O. Gostin. 2012. "Pillars for Progress on the Right to Health: Harnessing the Potential of Human Rights through a Framework Convention on Global Health." *Health and Human Rights: An International Journal* 14:1–16.

Gable, Lance. 2007. "The Proliferation of Human Rights in Global Health Governance." *The Journal of Law, Medicine and Ethics* 35(4): 534–544.

Gable, Lance and Benjamin Mason Meier. 2013. "Global Health Rights: Employing Human Rights to Develop and Implement the Framework Convention on Global Health." *Health and Human Rights* 15(1): 20–31.

Garrett, Laurie. 1994. *The Coming Plague*. New York: Penguin Publishing Group.

Goodman, Neville. 1952. *International Health Organizations and Their Work*. Philadelphia: The Blakiston Company.

Gostin, Lawrence O. 2005. "World Health Law: Toward a New Conception of Global Health Governance for the 21st Century." *Yale Journal of Health Policy, Law & Ethics* 5: 413–424.

Gostin, Lawrence O. 2008. "Meeting Basic Survival Needs of the World's Least Healthy People: Toward a Framework Convention on Global Health." *Georgetown Law Journal* 96: 331–392.

Gostin, Lawrence O. 2014. *Global Health Law*. Harvard University Press.

Gostin, Lawrence O., Eric A. Friedman, Paulo Buss, Mushtaque Chowdhury, Anand Grover, Mark Heywood, Churnrirtai Kanchanachitra [et al.]. 2016. "The Next WHO Director-General's Highest Priority: A Global Treaty on the Human Right to Health." *Lancet Global Health* 4(12): e890–e892.

Gostin, Lawrence and Zita Lazzarini. 1997. *Human Rights and Public Health in the AIDS Pandemic*. New York: Oxford University Press.

Gostin, Lawrence O. and Devi Sridhar. 2014. "Global Health and the Law." *New England Journal of Medicine* 370: 1732–1740.

Gostin, Lawrence O. and Allyn L. Taylor. 2008. "Global Health Law: A Definition and Grand Challenges." *Public Health Ethics* 1(1): 53–63.

Gruskin, Sofia, Edward J. Mills, and Daniel Tarantola. 2007. "History, Principles, and Practice of Health and Human Rights." *The Lancet* 370: 449–455.

Harman, Sophie. 2012. *Global Health Governance*. London: Routledge.

Howard-Jones, Norman. 1974. "The Scientific Background of the International Sanitary Conferences." *WHO Chronicles* 28(10): 455–470.

HRC (Human Rights Council), 31st Session. 2016. "Concept Note: The 2030 Agenda for Sustainable Development and human rights, with an emphasis on the right to development." Available at: http://www.ohchr.org/EN/HRBodies/HRC/RegularSessions/Session31/Documents/Mainstreaming.doc.

Hunt, Paul. 2015. "Is the UN Human Rights Council Delivering on Its Mandate to Mainstream Human Rights?" *Universal Rights Group*. August 24. Available at: http://www.universal-rights.org/blog/unhuman-rights-council-delivering-mandate-mainstream-human-rights/.

Hunt, Paul. 2017. "Configuring the UN Human Rights System in the 'Era of Implementation': Mainland and Archipelago." *Human Rights Quarterly*.

Hunt, Paul, Judith Bueno de Mesquita, Joo-Young Lee, and Sally-Anne Way. 2014. "Implementation of Economic, Social and Cultural Rights." In *Routledge Handbook of International Human Rights Law*, edited by Scott Sheeran and Sir Nigel Rodley. London: Taylor & Francis, Ltd.

Jacobson, Harold K. 1979. *Networks of Interdependence*. New York: Alfred L. Knopf, Inc.

JALI. 2016. *FCGH: A Right's Based Framework for the SDGs and Beyond: A Framework Convention on Global Health*. Joint Action and Learning Initiative on National and Global Responsibilities for Health. Available at: https://www.jalihealth.org/documents/a-rights-based-framework-for-the-sdgs-and-beyond.pdf.

Jenks, Clarence Wilfred. 1950. "Co-Ordination: A New Problem of International Organization." *Recueil des Cours de l'Académie de Droit International* 77: 157–301.

Jenks, Clarence Wilfred. 1969. *A New World of Law? A Study of the Creative Imagination in International Law*. London: Longmans.

Kastler, Florian. "Le role normatif de l'organisation mondiale de la sante." PhD diss., Université de Neuchâtel, 2016.

Kędzia, Zdzisław. 2009. "Mainstreaming Human Rights in the United Nations." In *International Human Rights Monitoring Mechanisms: Essays in Honour of Jakob Th. Moller*, edited by Gudmundur Alfredsson, Jonas Grimheden, and Bertrand G. Ramcharan. Leiden: Martinus Nijhoff Publishers.

Kickbusch, Ilona and Kent Buse. 2001. "Global Influences and Global Responses: International Health at the Turn of the Twenty-First Century." In *International Public Health: Diseases, Programs, Systems, and Policies*, edited by Michael H. Merson, Robert E. Black, and Anne Mills. Ann Arbor: Aspen Publishers.

Klabbers, Jan. 2015. *Advanced Introduction to the Law of International Organizations*. Cheltenham: Elgar.

Koivusalo, Meri and Eeva Ollila. 1997. *Making a Healthy World: Agencies, Actors and Policies in International Health*. New York: Zed.

Koplan, Jeffrey P., T. Christopher Bond, Michael H. Merson, K. Srinath Reddy, Mario Henry Rodriguez, Nelson K. Sewankambo, and Judith N. Wasserheit. 2009. "Towards a Common Definition of Global Health." *The Lancet* 373: 1993–1995.

Koskenniemi, Martti. 2006. "Human Rights Mainstreaming as a Project of Power." *Humanity: An International Journal of Human Rights, Humanitarianism, and Development* 1(1): 47–58.

Lee, Kelley. 2009. "Understandings of Global Health Governance: The Contested Landscape." In *Global Health Governance: Crisis, Institutions, and Political Economy*, edited by A. Kay and O. Williams. New York: Palgrave MacMillan Distribution Ltd.

Lomazzi, Marta, Christopher Jenkins, and Bettina, Borisch. 2016. "Global Public Health Today: Connecting the Dots." *Global Health Action* 9(1): 28772.

Magnusson, Roger. 2007. "Non-Communicable Diseases and Global Health Governance: Enhancing Global Processes to Improve Health Development." *Globalization and Health* 3(2): 1–16.

Mann, Jonathan M. 1999. "Medicine and Public Health, Ethics and Human Rights." In *Health and Human Rights*, edited by Jonathan M. Mann, Sofia Gruskin, Michael Grodin, and George Annas. London: Routledge.

Marks, Stephen P. 2001. "Jonathan Mann's Legacy to the 21st Century: The Human Rights Imperative for Public Health." *The Journal of Law, Medicine and Ethics* 29(2): 131–136.

McMichael, Tony and Robert Beaglehole. 2003. "The Global Context of Public Health." In *Global Public Health*, edited by Robert Beaglehole and Ruth Bonita. London: Oxford University Press.

Meier, Benjamin Mason. 2011. "Global Health Takes a Normative Turn: The Expanding Purview of International Health Law and Global Health Policy to Meet the Public Health Challenges of the 21st Century." *The Global Community: Yearbook of International Law and Jurisprudence* 1: 69–108.

Meier, Benjamin Mason and William Onzivu. 2014. "The Evolution of Human Rights in World Health Organization Policy and the Future of Human Rights Through Global Health Governance." *Public Health* 128(2): 179–187.

Mertus, Julie. 2013. "Human Rights in Global Governance." In *International Organization and Global Governance*, edited by Thomas G. Weiss and Rorden Wilkinson. New York: Routledge.

Moon, Suerie, Nicole A. Szlezák, Catherine M. Michaud, Dean T. Jaminson, Gerald T. Keusch, William C. Clark, and Barry R. Bloom. 2010. "The Global Health System: Lessons for a Stronger Institutional Framework." *PLoS Med* 7(1): e1000193.

Murphy, Thérèse. 2013. *Health and Human Rights*. Oxford: Hart.

Nyamu-Musembi, Celestine and Andrea Cornwall. 2004. *What Is the "Rights-Based Approach" All About? Perspectives from International Development Agencies.* Brighton: Institute of Development Studies.

Oberleitner, Gerd. 2007. *Global Human Rights Institutions*. Cambridge: Polity.

Oberleitner, Gerd. 2008. "A Decade of Mainstreaming Human Rights in the UN: Achievements, Failures, Challenges." *Netherlands Quarterly of Human Rights* 26: 359–390.

Oestreich, Joel E. 2007. *Power and Principle: Human Rights Programming in International Organizations*. Washington: Georgetown University Press.

O'Neill, William and Vegard Bye. 2002. *From High Principles to Operational Practice: Strengthening O.H.C.H.R. Capacity to Support U.N. Country Teams to Integrate Human Rights in Development Programming.* Consultancy report to the UN Office of High Commissioner for Human Rights.

Ottersen, Petter Ole, Jashodhara Dasgupta, Chantal Blouin, Paulo Buss, Virasakdi Chongsuvivatwong, Julio Frenk, Sakiko Fukuda-Parr [et al.]. 2014. "The Political Origins of Health Inequity: Prospects for Change." *The Lancet* 383(9197): 630–667.

Pais, Marta Santos. 1998. *A Human Rights Conceptual Framework for UNICEF.* Florence: UNICEF International Child Development Centre.

Pannenborg, Charles O. 1979. *A New International Health Order: An Inquiry into the International Relations of World Health and Medical Care.* Alphen aan den Rijn, The Netherlands: Sijthoff and Noordhoff.

Porter, Dorothy. 1998. *Health, Civilization and the State: A History of Public Health from Ancient to Modern Times.* New York: Routledge.

Robinson, Mary. 1998. "Five-year Review of the Implementation of the Vienna Declaration and Programme of Action: Interim report of the United Nations High Commissioner for Human Rights." 20 February. UN Doc. E/CN.4/1998/104.

Roemer, Milton and Ruth Roemer. 1990. "Global Health, National Development, and the Role of Government." *American Journal of Public Health* 80(10): 1188–1192.

Ruger, Jennifer Prah. 2008. "Normative Foundations of Global Health Law." *Georgetown Law Journal* 96(2): 423–443.

Sawyer Wilbur A. 1947. "Achievements of UNRRA as an International Health Organization." *American Journal of Public Health* 37(1): 41–58.

Shelton, Dinah L. 2014. "Introduction." In *The United Nations System for Protecting Human Rights*, edited by Dinah L. Shelton. London: Routledge.

Skogly, Sigrun. 2006. *Beyond National Borders: States' Human Rights Obligations in International Cooperation*. Oxford: Intersentia.

Slaughter, Anne-Marie. 1997. "The Real New World." *Foreign Affairs* 76(5): 183–197.

Szlezák, Nicole, Barry R. Bloom, Dean T. Jamison, Gerald T. Keusch, Catherine M. Michaud, Suerie Moon, and William C. Clark. 2010. "The Global Health System: Actors, Norms, and Expectations in Transition." *PLoS Medicine* 7(1): e1000183.

Taylor, Allyn L. 2004. "Governing the Globalization of Public Health." *Journal of Law, Medicine & Ethics* 32: 500–501.

UN (United Nations). 1945. "Charter of the United Nations." 24 October. UN Doc. 1 UNTS XVI.

UN (United Nations), 57th Session. 2002. "Strengthening the United Nations: An Agenda for Further Change." 9 September. UN Doc. A/57/387.

UN Secretary-General. 1997. "Renewing the United Nations: A Programme for Reform." 14 July. UN Doc. A/51/950.

UN Secretary-General. 2005. "Address to the UN Commission on Human Rights." Available at: https://www.un.org/sg/en/content/sg/statement/2005-04-07/secretary-generals-address-commission-human-rights.

UNDG (United Nations Development Group). 2003. *The Human Rights Based Approach to Development Cooperation Towards a Common Understanding Among UN Agencies*. Available at: https://undg.org/document/the-human-rights-based-approach-to-development-cooperation-towards-a-common-understanding-among-un-agencies/.

UNDG (UN Development Group). 2015. *UNDG Guidance Note on Human Rights for Resident Coordinators and Country Teams*. Available at: https://undg.org/document/undg-guidance-note-on-human-rights-for-resident-coordinators-and-un-country-teams/.

UNDG (UN Development Group). 2017. *Mainstreaming the 2030 Agenda for Sustainable Development—Reference Guide for UN Country Teams*. Available at: https://undg.org/document/mainstreaming-the-2030-agenda-for-sustainable-development-reference-guide-for-un-country-teams/.

UNDP (UN Development Programme). 1998. *Integrating Human Rights with Sustainable Human Development, a UNDP Policy Document*. New York: United Nations Development Programme.

UNDP (UN Development Programme). 2001. *Recommendations of Inter-Agency Workshop on Implementing a Human Rights Approach in the Context of the U.N. Reform*. Princeton, New Jersey.

UNDP (UN Development Programme). 2006. *Indicators for Human Rights Based Approaches to Development in UNDP Programming: A User's Guide*. New York: UN Development Programme.

White, Nigel D. 2016. "Lawmaking." In *The Oxford Handbook of International Organizations*, edited by Jacob Katz Cogan, Ian Hurd, and Ian Johnstone. Oxford: Oxford University Press.

WHO (World Health Organization). 1948. "Constitution of the World Health Organization." Available at: http://www.who.int/governance/eb/who_constitution_en.pdf.

WHO (World Health Organization). 1958. *The First Ten Years of the World Health Organization.* Geneva: World Health Organization.

World Bank. 1998. *Development and Human Rights: The Role of the World Bank.* Washington, D.C.: The World Bank.

World Conference on Human Rights. 1993. "Vienna Declaration and Programme of Action." 25 June. UN Doc. A/CONF.157/23.

Yach, Derek and Douglas Bettcher. 1998. "The Globalization of Public Health, I: Threats and Opportunities." *American Journal of Public Health* 88(5): 735–744.

Yamin, Alicia E. 2016. *Power, Suffering and the Struggle for Dignity: Human Rights Frameworks for Health and Why They Matter.* Philadelphia: University of Pennsylvania Press.

Youde, Jeremy. 2013. *Global Health Governance.* Oxford: Wiley.

4

The Future of Global Governance for Health

Putting Rights at the Center of Sustainable Development

MICHEL SIDIBÉ, HELENA NYGREN-KRUG,
BRONWYN MCBRIDE, AND KENT BUSE*

Today's volatile and unstable world—marked by conflict, climate change, a protracted global economic recession, inequality, crisis of trust in public institutions, and the greatest-ever displacement of people by war and persecution—stands in stark contrast to the transformative vision and ambition articulated in the 2030 Agenda for Sustainable Development (2030 Agenda) and its seventeen Sustainable Development Goals (SDGs). Together, the goals weave environmental, social, and economic well-being into a single, integrated global framework. As such, they can support efforts to build resilient communities and nurture a culture of prevention—critical elements in our increasingly polarized world. Moreover, they can provide stepping stones to deepen and strengthen efforts to address health in a more integrated way, recognizing the role of a range of sectors and actors.

Achieving progress on the scale and pace required to achieve the SDGs by 2030 will demand determination and structural change—between government sectors, business, international organizations, and civil society—globally, regionally, and within countries and communities. For those seeking to assure healthy lives and well-being for all, the SDGs present an opportunity to generate the reforms necessary to ensure effective global governance for health. Such reforms will entail more than working across the SDGs; they will require the engagement of a wide range of

* Thanks to Ruth Blackshaw, Laetitia Bosio, and Annemarie Hou, our UNAIDS colleagues, for input and other support in the development of this chapter.

institutions and processes of governance at all levels that may or may not have a specific health mandate, but which impact health both directly and indirectly.

The SDGs are achievable and have the potential to reach deep into the lives of people on the ground. Collectively, the global community has the resources, technical capacity, ingenuity, and power—as member states, communities, UN agencies, civil society, and, most importantly, as peoples—to generate real change and ensure that no one is left behind. Fundamentally, success will require shifting away from development approaches and funding allocations based on the interests of the most powerful actors and toward approaches that give primacy to human rights for health, ushering in equality, justice, and inclusive prosperity.

This chapter starts in Part I by exploring some of the shortcomings of the current global health agenda resulting from a failure of governance systems to put people and their rights at its center. It then focuses in Part II on seven interrelated and mutually reinforcing reform proposals to transform the agenda into a rights-based paradigm:

1. People, in particular those most affected by ill health and who are otherwise vulnerable or marginalized, must enjoy their right to participate in decision-making processes so that their needs are prioritized in implementing the SDGs.
2. The notion of health systems should be reconceptualized into overarching systems that protect people's health and human rights, no matter where people are, who they are, or what they do.
3. Data need to be disaggregated and democratized, so that people can leverage strategic information for change from the bottom up, as well as harness existing monitoring mechanisms to review progress on the health-related SDGs.
4. Access to justice must be enhanced and the rule of law strengthened in order to secure the requisite level of accountability to meet the SDGs.
5. In this interdependent world, a strong system of health protection requires safeguarding the right to health across systems, sectors, and actors.
6. To ensure the necessary support—from the UN to governments—in implementing the health-related SDGs, the formation of innovative partnerships to promote and protect the right to health should be explored.
7. To ensure that the SDGs are financed, the structural causes blocking financing for sustainable development—from a heavy debt burden on countries to illicit financial flows—must be addressed, going beyond traditional sources of aid.

In examining these reform proposals, and to inspire and catalyze action, Part II provides concrete examples of how rights-based approaches can be operationalized— from governance mechanisms to financing—drawing in particular from the AIDS response. The chapter concludes by urging the global health community to seize the unique opportunity presented by the 2030 Agenda to make the necessary changes to enable healthy lives and wellbeing for all.

I. "BUSINESS AS USUAL" IS NOT REALIZING RIGHTS FAST ENOUGH

The reality of life for most people today is exceedingly harsh. Each day, 800 million people are starving and 663 million lack clean drinking water, with 1,000 children dying due to preventable water- and sanitation-related diseases (UNDP 2016b). In war zones from Afghanistan to Syria, health facilities are being bombed in blatant disregard for the core principle of international humanitarian law: affording protection to medical personnel and facilities (ICRC 2012). Across countries, health systems are fragmented, even broken. People lack trust in governments' ability to ensure effective systems of health protection (Pew Research Center 2015; Edelman 2017). This distrust has been exacerbated by inadequate responses to recent health emergencies, including Ebola and Zika (Gostin and Ayala 2017). Moreover, other complex and pressing challenges to population health, from antimicrobial resistance (AMR) to noncommunicable diseases (NCDs), have not yet been effectively addressed—particularly due to a failure to address their structural and social determinants.

Progress on the SDGs is impeded by major contemporary barriers and historical legacies. Corporate influences challenge the global health agenda, with profound implications for population health outcomes. This is exemplified, for example, by the widening power and authority of transnational food companies, and their ability to influence trade agreements and restrict national health promotion policies, with significant consequences for the control of NCDs (Friel et al. 2013; Moodie et al. 2013). Furthermore, with strides in technological innovation, the global health community has often sought quick-fix and "vertical" solutions while shying away from addressing the structural and root causes of ill health. Many of these causes relate to poverty and inequalities, which stem from the colonial legacies that continue to determine much of our current geopolitical landscape and influence the entire enterprise of sustainable development. Of increasing concern are illicit financial flows and offshore tax havens, acting together as perhaps the greatest driver of inequality within developing countries.[1]

While the World Health Organization (WHO) has recognized that most of the determinants of health lie outside the health sector (CSDH 2008), its key organizational constituencies—ministries of health—often lack leverage and power to influence other government sectors or key stakeholders, including large transnational corporations (Moodie et al. 2013). Moreover, while the World Health Assembly (WHA), the decision-making body of the WHO, has underscored the centrality of equity through resolutions passed in recent years, these WHA resolutions have not translated into tangible WHO programmatic support to countries. To ensure gender equality and women's empowerment, for example, disaggregated data by sex is crucial, yet remains in short supply in many countries (UNDP 2016a).

Health security, another topic often debated in global health governance, too often centers around a pathogen or a virus, rather than the human person and the economic, cultural, social, physical, and political environment that can enable her to thrive or

---

1. Tax havens—where up to $32 trillion is stored, around one-sixth of world's total private wealth—are causing governments to lose $3 trillion in revenues every year (Global Financial Integrity 2016).

render her vulnerable. Another recent debate at the WHA, on the engagement of stakeholders beyond member states, has placed nonprofit groups with corporations under one framework for "non-state actors" (WHO 2016a). While this framework does differentiate between private sector entities and non-governmental organizations (NGOs), subsuming these disparate actors under a "one size fits all" policy neverthe-less fails to (1) recognize the centrality of engaging communities because they have the right to meaningfully participate in decisions that affect them and (2) seize an op-portunity to foster greater attention to equality, dignity, justice, and the right to health.

The practice of global health governance today is overly technocratic, special-ized, and inaccessible to the people it is meant to serve. Clearly, a governance gap exists between the policies and practices in global health and development and the obligations of human rights (Van de Pas et al. 2017). This failure to put people and their rights at the center of global governance perpetuates and generates structures that are out of touch and out of place (Otterson et al. 2014). Consequently, govern-ance systems and institutions are ill-equipped to respond to the diverse challenges faced today. Now is the time for the global health community to take stock, to crit-ically revisit its values, and to consider how development approaches must be re-formed to achieve the SDGs and promote the realization of human rights for global health. Experiences from the AIDS response, where people-centered governance structures have generated tangible results, can inspire wider efforts for reform.

II. SEVEN TRANSFORMATIONS IN GLOBAL GOVERNANCE FOR HEALTH TOWARD A RIGHTS-BASED DEVELOPMENT PARADIGM

The successful implementation of the 2030 Agenda will require nothing less than transforming the highly inequitable discretionary development paradigm into one that is rights-based. To achieve the SDG targets on health, and realize the broader vision of the SDGs, governance must foster the respect, protection, and fulfillment of the right to health. It must promote the notion of "global health citizenship," whereby individuals are empowered to claim health-related rights and demand action and answerability from decision makers (Sidibé 2015).

In contrast to the previous Millennium Development Goals (MDGs), the SDGs incorporate human rights-based principles—they are universal in nature, trans-formative, comprehensive, and inclusive. Based on recognition of the inherent dig-nity of every human person, rights-based approaches provide a set of performance standards against which duty-bearers at all levels of society—but especially organs of the state—can be held accountable (OHCHR 2008). In this regard, they can go further than the SDGs, triggering concrete governmental obligations (Boesen and Martin 2007).[2] The incorporation of human rights into the SDGs therefore

---

2. A discretionary development paradigm, by contrast, is rooted in the realm of charity, allowing countries to pursue development goals selectively, in an optional manner that lacks the ambition and integration of the SDGs (Hawkes and Buse 2016). This discretionary paradigm can lead to approaches that address the health symptoms of hunger, disease, and other development challenges without paying sufficient attention to root and structural causes of these harms such as harmful

provides a recognized, legitimate, and ready-made framework to underpin, operationalize, and drive accountability on the SDGs.

At the international level, health-related human rights are codified centrally in the UN Charter (UN 1945), the WHO Constitution (WHO 1948), the Universal Declaration of Human Rights (UN General Assembly 1948), and the International Covenant on Economic, Social and Cultural Rights (ICESCR) (UN General Assembly 1966). As outlined in chapters 1 and 2, these human rights form part of a universally recognized legal framework that can, as analyzed in chapter 3, frame robust governance systems for health and cross-sectoral action.

In operationalizing health-related human rights, the AIDS response provides a strong platform for action on which to build. It is one of the best examples, as discussed in chapter 13, where a rights-based approach has been effective and has empowered people most affected—in this case people living with and affected by HIV—to drive and demand change. As they were in the AIDS response, rights-based approaches will be necessary to transform the language and even the culture surrounding global health away from "expense" to "investment," from "client" to "rights-holder," from "charity" to "justice," and from "health systems" to "systems for health." Implications for action include identifying and addressing root causes of poverty, ill health, and injustice; empowering rights-holders to claim their rights; and enabling duty-bearers to meet their obligations.

It will be a challenging journey to address the world's institutional arrangements, values, priorities, and cultural norms, all of which reflect deeply embedded power structures that ultimately govern the distribution of people's opportunities and health outcomes. However, there is no other choice; there is no shortcut, and global governance must heed perhaps the most central lesson learned from the AIDS response—that a rights-based approach is a necessary ingredient for success (UNAIDS 2015a). The story of AIDS is pertinent not only to show how health-related human rights can be operationalized in a meaningful, pragmatic, and actionable way but also as a model for rights to drive action and new governance approaches across the SDGs. Lessons in global governance for health learned in the AIDS response—including but not limited to bringing many stakeholders together to crowdsource solutions and taking a multi-sectoral, rights-based, and evidence-led approach—are highly relevant for addressing the interlinked and complex challenges of health-related SDGs.

Building on this platform set by the AIDS response, a rights-based system of global governance for health will require, as indicated in Figure 4.1, striving for seven interrelated and mutually reinforcing transformations.

A. Priority-Setting by People, for People

As Amartya Sen pointed out, "progress on the SDGs is not about numbers. It requires a rich human conversation about how to reach the SDGs" (Victorero 2015). Who gets to participate in this conversation, where it takes place, and on

gender norms and discriminatory laws and policies. Of concern, a discretionary framework treats affected communities more as passive recipients rather than as active agents requiring freedom and support to effectuate meaningful and sustainable change (Ibid.).

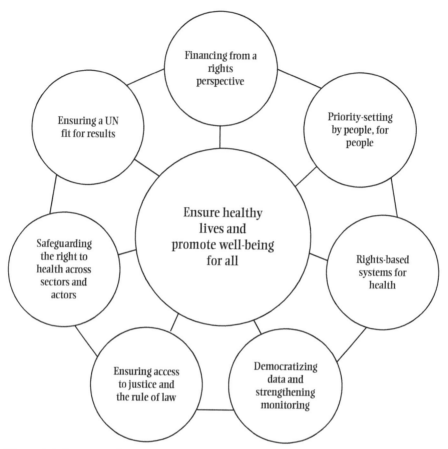

Figure 4.1 Seven transformations toward the realization of SDG 3.

what terms will be determining factors for success. To ensure that no one is being left behind, at every step of this conversation, it is necessary to engage vulnerable and marginalized groups so that priorities are set by people for people through community-led governance. As set out in SDG 16, "transparent and participatory decision-making processes, backed by accountable and inclusive institutions" are critical at all levels (UN 2015a). By effectively engaging communities, a vital exchange between civil society, policymakers, scientists, and service providers can take place that can help identify, through a transparent and participatory process, priorities that are equitable, evidence-informed, and responsive to needs on the ground. Indeed, the principle "Nothing About Us Without Us," coined by the disability rights movement during the 1990s, has been central to progress in the AIDS response, where people living with and affected by HIV have been at the forefront of breaking down the legal and social barriers to HIV prevention and treatment (UNAIDS 2016c). The right to participation, as promoted by the Joint UN Programme on HIV/AIDS (UNAIDS), is increasingly becoming operationalized in other parts of the UN system, as seen, for example, with the establishment of the UN Permanent Forum on Indigenous Issues.

The UN Permanent Forum on Indigenous Issues

More than 370 million indigenous peoples live in some seventy countries world-wide. While they represent a rich diversity of cultures, religions, traditions, languages, and histories, they are among the world's most marginalized population groups (Kirmayer and Brass 2016). To ensure greater attention to their concerns and rights, a central coordinating UN body was established: the UN Permanent Forum on Indigenous Issues (UNPFII). Composed of sixteen independent experts, the UNPFII has operationalized the right to participation by ensuring that half of its experts are nominated by indigenous organizations, with the other half nominated by governments (ECOSOC 2000). The UNPFII has helped to promote the rights-based integration and coordination of indigenous issues in countries and across the UN system.

History attests to the fact that community engagement cannot be taken for granted. It needs to be nurtured, not least among young people, who are already leading on the SDGs in their communities. This means that civil society needs sub-stantial, consistent, and predictable funding support as well as political space and freedom to act (UNAIDS 2015b). It also requires building the capacity of young people to demand their rights, starting with raising awareness of their range of health-related rights—including those governing sexual and reproductive health; education and employment; and an adequate standard of living and social security. Supporting civil society actors, ensuring a space for them at the policy table, and promoting young people's awareness of their rights represent a few of the many po-tential avenues which can enable meaningful participation in decision-making and priority-setting by people, for people.

B. Rights-Based Systems for Health

Many health systems around the world are deeply dysfunctional and mired with challenges: priorities are often skewed toward biomedical interventions and fail to address the concerns of poor, vulnerable, and marginalized communities; services are vertical and fragmented; out-of-pocket spending remains high; and corruption is rampant. As people are becoming more aware that they are rights-holders and ac-tively demanding the right to health, a surge in rights-based litigation is occurring, which has, in places like Colombia, catalyzed reform of the entire health system (Mora 2014).

Human rights should be "front-loaded" into governance, reforming and aligning systems and institutions so that they serve people from the outset rather than relying on litigation to spur health sector reform when rights are not met. Designing systems for health that are rights-based means using health-related human rights norms and principles—including the right to health and rights-based principles of equality, non-discrimination, participation, transparency, and accountability—to shape policies in the health sector and beyond (WHO 2011). Building on the history of using a human rights framework to drive accountability in the AIDS response, UNAIDS and the Global Fund to Fight AIDS, Tuberculosis and Malaria (Global Fund) are leading efforts, as discussed in chapter 19, to operationalize rights-based systems for health by supporting countries in integrating human rights principles in their HIV prevention, testing, and treatment programs. For example, UNAIDS provides actionable guidance on how human rights approaches are critical to addressing barriers to HIV services and to achieving HIV targets (UNAIDS 2017); and the Global Fund encourages grant applicants to include programs addressing human rights and gender-related barriers to HIV services and advises on the implementation and monitoring of rights-based approaches to HIV (Global Fund 2017). These coordinated efforts to integrate human rights into national HIV responses can provide inspiration for programming rights-based approaches at the national level for health and beyond to achieve the SDGs. In addition, to ensure that policies and programs enhance gender equality, harmful gender norms must be addressed and systems designed to be gender transformative (Ibid; WHO 2011). Overall, creating rights-based systems for health requires ensuring consistency in laws, policies, and practices across government so that actions undertaken by other sectors (such as finance, planning, and trade) comply with the right to health as an obligation of the government as a whole, fostering robust and comprehensive systems for health that work for all, including marginalized communities.

Practical arrangements must be made to reinforce the interface between service providers and communities to help ensure that services are accessible to all, paying particular attention to people who are being left behind due to rural residence, poverty, prejudice, or discriminatory laws. This requires investing in community-based organizations, which, as seen in the context of HIV, are often best placed to reach people (UNAIDS 2016c). Community engagement has produced health benefits across diverse countries, as shown in Figure 4.2, including improved knowledge and safer behavior, increased use of health services, and decreased incidence of HIV and other sexually transmitted infections (STIs) (Rodriguez-Garcia et al. 2013).

Evidence shows that community health workers can fill critical service gaps, particularly in low- and middle-income countries and in contexts where formal health professionals are scarce (AU 2017; UNAIDS and Stop AIDS Alliance 2015). UNAIDS shares the vision of the Global Health Workforce Alliance on the transformative potential of health workers (Campbell 2014) and advocates for increased investment into strengthening community health work and systems (UNAIDS 2016d). Supporting community health workers through budget incentives, remuneration, essential supplies, supervision, clear career pathways, and training (ideally via an accredited curriculum) are ingredients for a sustainable model that can yield gains across a range SDG targets, including SDG 3.8 on universal health coverage and SDG 8.5 on employment and decent work for all.

C. Democratizing Data and Strengthening Monitoring

One of the most powerful tools of accountability for the realization of human rights is strategic information. This was seen in the AIDS response, where the progress of UN member states has been monitored against ambitious targets set at high-level UN General Assembly meetings (Taylor et al. 2014). The Global AIDS Monitoring

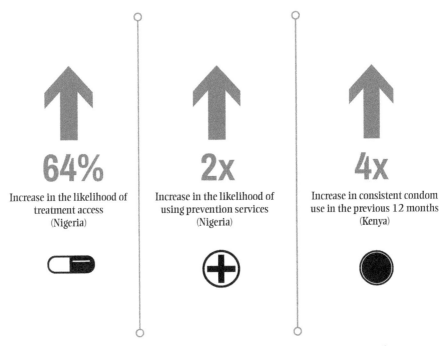

Figure 4.2 Community engagement leads to greater access to HIV treatment and prevention (increase for each community-based organization created per 100,000 people, Nigeria and Kenya).
SOURCE: Rodriguez-García 2013. Reproduced from: UNAIDS and Stop AIDS Alliance 2015, 11.

indicators and the National Commitments and Policy Instrument, an online data collection system, supports the monitoring process and enjoys one of the highest state reporting rates in global health (UNAIDS 2016b). Importantly, this tool goes beyond epidemiological data collection to include reporting on laws and policies, with civil society representatives and other nongovernmental partners completing one part of the instrument to help validate and bring critical perspective to national reports from governments (Torres et al. 2017). Another unique data collection exercise that emerged in the context of HIV is the People Living with HIV Stigma Index. Led by people living with HIV, it identifies how discrimination manifests in the social environment, such as work and access to health services, as well as the level of knowledge among communities about rights, HIV testing, and treatment (Stigma Index 2017). These data collection experiences can inspire efforts to monitor health-related rights in the SDGs in ways that are participatory and that seek to understand and address the legal and social environments that determine risk, vulnerability, and people's dignity.

The realization of human rights through the health-related SDGs will require information, monitoring, and accountability at several levels, and it is essential that national authorities are supported in collecting disaggregated data to ensure that no one is being left behind (WHO 2016b). Support should also be provided for independent monitoring, for example by investing in community-based information management systems to foster transparency and address corruption. Accountability for commitments and continuous improvement of interventions must be evaluated by stakeholders at all levels—from disadvantaged populations represented through civil society groups to parliamentary committees and international human rights institutions—often with support for data collection from academic partners (Bustreo and Hunt 2013; Hawkes and Buse 2016). Civil society has already gained experience in monitoring government budget processes to assess inclusiveness and accountability (International Budget Partnership 2014). Innovation to harness information technology must continue to be promoted in ways that can improve governance for health, for instance, in detecting and responding to outbreaks and emergencies (Making All Voices Count 2014). Underpinned by sound methodologies and innovative communications technologies, the inclusion of alternative data sources (e.g., from research institutions, think tanks, civil society, or crowdsourcing) can help fill data gaps and complement official data. Real-time data collection and reporting can help bring maximum returns on resources invested—to better prioritize and tailor programs that will have the greatest impact (UNAIDS 2016a).

While the global health agenda is relatively rich on data, it is weak on institutional mechanisms to scrutinize the performance of governments in improving the health of their peoples.[3] In contrast, the human rights system, as discussed in Section V of this volume, contains a range of international monitoring mechanisms for assessing the realization of health-related human rights. Framing the global health agenda as a human rights enterprise opens the opportunity to engage with these mechanisms to facilitate greater rights-based accountability for health, which can help boost progress on the health-related SDGs. Such mechanisms range from UN human rights treaty bodies, as described in chapter 23, to relevant supervisory bodies of the International Labor Organization (ILO), outlined in chapter 9, to the Universal Periodic Review (UPR) process of the UN Human Rights Council (HRC), as analyzed in chapter 24. With its three-stage process and regular review cycle, the UPR is proving to be an effective tool in ensuring that rights-based actions are taken by governments on health issues across countries and regions (UPR Info 2012). As seen in the issue of female genital mutilation, UPR recommendations have resulted in legal and policy reforms, prevention strategies, and program investments (Gilmore et al. 2015).

At the national level, a range of human rights mechanisms—from national human rights institutions and ombudspersons offices to parliamentary committees—can champion the right to health and help ensure that governments and other powerful actors are monitored in their efforts to realize health-related human rights. Indicators constitute a vital tool in this regard, and national human rights institutions have recently stepped up efforts to identify appropriate indicators for monitoring economic and social rights, as, for example, in the case of Nepal, where the lack of fulfillment of such rights was considered a precursor of the 1996–2006 armed conflict (OHCHR 2011b).

At the regional level, states may be more inclined to exchange experiences and subject themselves to higher levels of scrutiny, which may represent an opportunity

---

3. This is the case even in the few areas where multilateral treaties underpin monitoring, such as the WHO Framework Convention on Tobacco Control (WHO 2009).

to strengthen peer review across states for the realization of health-related human rights. For example, the African Union's (AU) African Peer Review Mechanism (APRM), established in 2003 within the framework of the New Partnership for Africa's Development (NEPAD), is a mutually agreed policy diagnostic and self-monitoring instrument among AU member states to assess conformity with shared political, socioeconomic, and corporate governance values. The APRM's inclusion of health and human rights issues provides an opportunity to further advance health-related human rights in the region (Maina 2015), particularly as this instrument is repositioned to evaluate progress on the SDG and AU Agenda 2063 targets.

D. Ensuring Access to Justice and the Rule of Law

Experience from the field of human rights demonstrates that enabling legal environments and effective national democratic institutions are critical determinants of progress on health and development (Sagasti 2013). While governments have committed to take ownership of the SDGs and to work closely on their implementation with regional and local authorities (UN 2015a), the central human rights principle of accountability demands a legal framework that enables people to challenge governments and other duty-bearers and to hold them accountable if, and when, promises are broken.

The global health community must enter what may be uncharted waters and work to create enabling legal environments to ensure healthy lives and well-being for all—from regulating the formulation and marketing of unhealthy products to ensuring both that health care providers adhere to set standards and that social safety nets are accessible and protect against all forms of discrimination (WHO 2017). To achieve this, a broad range of actors that impact health, or can impact health, but often fall outside of traditional involvement in the "health sector," must be mobilized—including community activists, judges, and parliamentarians. Future work in global health must involve training law enforcement agents, supporting law reform and legal literacy programs, and building the capacity of civil society to engage in strategic litigation. Such litigation, particularly in countries with strong constitutional provisions on the right to health, has in many instances helped reframe laws, policies, and practices to safeguard health-related human rights (KELIN 2016).

LITIGATING FOR THE PROTECTION OF THE RIGHT TO HEALTH IN KENYA

In the case of *Patricia Asero & others v. Attorney General* (eKLR 2012), the High Court of Kenya found that sections of the Anti-Counterfeit Act (2008) threatened to violate the rights to life, dignity, and health under the national constitution, given the Act's potential to limit access to affordable essential medicines, including generics.

In the case of *Daniel Ng'etich & 2 others v. Attorney General & 3 others* (eKLR 2016), the High Court of Kenya held that confining persons suffering from infectious diseases in prison (in this case, tuberculosis) was unconstitutional and unlawful. The Court further directed the government to develop a policy on the involuntary confinement of persons with tuberculosis and other infectious diseases.

SDG 16 on accountability has targets dedicated to the rule of law and access to justice, providing an opportunity for the global health community to strengthen its engagement with the legal community. Indeed, SDG 3 will not achieve its health targets with a "business-as-usual" approach or by relying on the standard public health arsenal of science and epidemiology alone. Legal and justice systems play an important role in shaping policy and social and behavioral norms in society, determining whether society strives to ensure: inclusion or exclusion; access to justice or lack thereof; and accountability or impunity. It is within this wider social construct of prevailing norms that health systems and services operate, and global health governance cannot afford to ignore law in efforts to achieve SDG 3.

E. Safeguarding the Right to Health across Sectors and Actors

In a globalized and increasingly interdependent world, the SDGs cannot be realized at the national level unless and until the right to health is recognized and operationalized across all sectors influencing human development. In aligning stakeholders on development, foreign investment, trade, and remittances are becoming more important to low-income countries than development assistance (Bhushan 2013; Lubambu 2014). Yet, a few rich countries have the power to set the rules when it comes to the debt system, structural adjustment, trade agreements, tax evasion, and tax avoidance.

Fortunately, in recent years, the right to health, in different forms and manifestations, has come to be reflected in multilateral agreements—from the Agreement on Trade-Related Aspects of Intellectual Property Rights (TRIPS) (WTO 2001) to the Paris Agreement on the UN Framework Convention on Climate Change (FCCC 2015). Anchoring the SDG-oriented global health and development efforts in the right to health can help to navigate trade and investment treaties to assure that they do not undermine development progress. At the 2017 UN High-Level Political Forum on sustainable development, major stakeholder groups—including NGOs, workers, and trade unions—called for greater attention to the intersections between trade and human rights and proposed that human rights impact and sustainability assessments be undertaken with respect to all trade and investment agreements (ECOSOC 2017a). Indeed, right-to-health impact assessments and other tools may provide critical information on how actions by corporations, investors, and government sectors may impact progress toward SDG 3 (Götzmann et al. 2016). Moreover, concrete ways to remedy policy and institutional incoherence need to be explored—as was the case between trade and intellectual property, the right to health, and public health objectives identified by the UN Secretary-General's High-Level Panel on Access to Medicines (UN 2016b).

Although the specific roles of the private sector are contested within the global health community, the private sector is encouraged to take a more active role in sustainable development under the 2030 Agenda (UN 2015a). Undoubtedly, the global health agenda is rampant with private sector interests: universal health coverage and health insurance companies; access to medicines and pharmaceutical firms; obesity and companies that formulate and market foods overly rich in sugar, trans fat, and salt; road safety and the auto manufacturing industry; and climate change, considered the leading threat to human health (Costello et al. 2009), and the entire enterprise of human consumption. When governance systems explicitly grounded in human rights are inadequate, it becomes difficult to establish effective "rules of the game" to address conflicts of interest in work with the private sector, thereby generating mistrust and inefficiency rather than robust, strong, and transparent partnerships that can help exercise the required society-wide leverage to ensure progress on the health-related SDG targets.

The Guiding Principles on Business and Human Rights provide a framework to underpin engagement with the private sector. Such Principles, directed to states and multinational corporations, aim to improve compliance based on three interdependent pillars: (1) the state duty to protect; (2) the corporate responsibility to respect; and (3) the access to remedial actions (OHCHR 2011a). Strengthening the implementation of other international legal instruments that support governments in regulating the private sector in relation to specific health issues, such as the International Code of Marketing of Breast-Milk Substitutes (WHO 1981) and the WHO Framework Convention on Tobacco Control (WHO 2009), is also critical. These international legal instruments will continue to play an important role in helping to ensure that the private sector acts in support of the achievement of SDG 3 and in synergy with the realization of human rights.

F. Ensuring a United Nations Fit for Results

Achieving the SDGs will require integrated action on a dramatically different scale than previous development targets (UN Secretary-General 2017a), demanding major shifts in work within, across, and beyond the UN system and challenging the UN to be nimble and adapt to different contexts in supporting countries. In meeting this challenge, existing silos need to be broken down and work should be performed horizontally across the organization, recognizing the interdependence and interrelatedness of rights and how the SDGs—including on health, education, food security, and nutrition—span the UN's mandate.

To truly embody the aim of leaving no one behind, national and regional development progress must be monitored through reliable disaggregated data and a stronger commitment to ending exclusion. While increased peace, resilience, and equity represent three of the many dividends that will be brought about by achieving the SDGs, it must be acknowledged that sustainable and inclusive development, grounded in human rights, is an end in itself (Ibid.). In this context, UN Secretary-General António Guterres is urging the UN system to be more focused "on people and less on process, more on results for the most poor and excluded and less on bureaucracy, more on integrated support to the 2030 Agenda and less on 'business as usual'" (UN Secretary-General 2017b).

The global health architecture, in which the UN plays an integral role, needs to be reformed so that it can better support tangible results in countries to achieve SDG 3. The global health ecosystem is extremely complex, difficult to navigate, and perhaps least accessible to the marginalized communities that stand to benefit most from global health institutions functioning effectively.

Calls have been made to streamline global health institutions to become more efficient (Sidibé and Buse 2013). While the process of reform may face resistance, institutions must rise to this challenge, as achieving progress on the SDGs demands simplification.

In considering simpler institutional models for realizing the SDGs, global governance must build upon what exists and what has been shown to work. Issue-based partnerships around a common strategy and vision, as examined in chapter 14, present a model that can foster unity of purpose and stress a focus on results for people. UNAIDS, the first and only co-sponsored program of the UN, is an example of such a partnership, uniting eleven co-sponsoring agencies in providing global leadership for the AIDS response (ECOSOC 2017b). While many called for another UN agency when establishing UNAIDS, states instead adopted an entirely new way to collaborate across the UN. As analyzed in chapter 13, AIDS was recognized as a social, and not exclusively medical or health issue, with explicit human rights and gender dimensions (Knight 2008). As a result, the skill sets of UNAIDS staff are more diverse than those of traditional public health professionals, and the organization's division of labor among co-sponsoring agencies has enabled UN support to countries and communities across a broad range of government sectors. Equally broad outreach and skill sets are needed to address not only the determinants of health but also acute health crises, which require coherent and integrated multi-sectoral action.

UNAIDS: A Unique People-Centered and Rights-Based Model

As the only co-sponsored Joint Programme in the UN, UNAIDS is a tangible example of a collaborative, multi-sectoral response to a complex and multifaceted issue. UNAIDS unites the efforts of eleven UN organizations with member states and civil society representatives (who participate in and influence the decisions of the UNAIDS Program Coordinating Board) to end the AIDS epidemic by 2030 as part of the SDGs. In 2015, ECOSOC adopted a resolution recognizing "the value of the lessons learned" from "the unique approach of the Joint Programme," reaffirming that it "offers the United Nations system a useful example, for the post-2015 period, of enhanced strategic coherence, coordination, results-based focus, inclusive governance and country-level impact, based on national contexts and priorities" (ECOSOC 2015, 20).

As learned from the AIDS experience, the global community must come together to advance the 2030 Agenda in a broad social movement that thinks and acts politically to grasp the many opportunities necessary to transform the global health agenda through a rights-based paradigm. The UN is the ultimate guardian and custodian of human rights and needs to exercise unwavering leadership for rights across global governance institutions to help make the health-related SDG ambitions a reality. With the UNAIDS model serving as an inspiration, a coordinated multi-sectoral approach to defend the right to health could be a timely initiative to spur progress on the health-related SDGs, ensuring that the UN is both fit for purpose and effective in supporting countries to reach the SDGs.

G. Financing the Health-Related SDG Targets from a Rights Perspective

Fostering inclusive economic growth, protecting the environment, and promoting social inclusion are indispensable strategies for achieving the SDGs. As part of efforts to strengthen the framework to finance sustainable development, the Addis Ababa Action Agenda (AAAA) of the Third International Conference on Financing for Development encourages countries to set national spending targets for essential public services (UN 2015b). Under human rights law, the investment of government resources to fulfill human rights is a legal obligation (OHCHR 2008). The principle of progressive realization, articulated seminally in Article 2 of the ICESCR, mandates that governments use the maximum available resources, and engage in international assistance and cooperation, to achieve progressively the full realization of rights (Ibid.). Countries such as Brazil, Mexico, and Thailand, all state parties to the ICESCR with strong constitutional and legal provisions on the right to health, have built domestic health financing systems by prioritizing general government investment in health (Oxfam 2013).

Africa now hosts ten of the twenty-five fastest growing economies in the world (IMF 2017) and has increased domestic investments in health, yet only a handful of African countries have met the Abuja Declaration (OAU 2001) target of allocating 15 percent of public expenditure toward health (UNAIDS 2013, 5).[4] Adequate government determination and strategic approaches render the Abuja target achievable. For example, domestic HIV investment nearly tripled from 2006 to 2014 (domestic sources accounted for 57 percent of all HIV investment resources in 2014) (UN General Assembly 2016, 26). As seen in the context of HIV, however, such increases can neglect to cover programs focused on key populations (UNAIDS 2015d),[5] which are critical to safeguard the protection of human rights (UN General Assembly 2016, 26). Thus, increasing investment in health is not enough; human rights approaches demand questioning how priorities are set within health budgets. Investments into equity—a principle at the heart of the SDGs—also lead to greater returns, as analyses suggest that immunization and antenatal care programs, which specifically target the impoverished, save more lives more cost-effectively (Watkins 2017). The global community can and must do better in prioritizing health, and within health, prioritize prevention and other interventions that maximize benefits for everyone, with particular attention to populations who are being left behind.

4. Health funding in AU member states has increased from 9 percent to 11 percent of public expenditures from 2001 to 2011. Six countries (Liberia, Madagascar, Malawi, Rwanda, Togo, and Zambia) have achieved the 15 percent target, and a number of other countries (e.g., Djibouti, Ethiopia, Lesotho, and Swaziland) are within reach (UNAIDS 2013).

5. UNAIDS considers the main key populations to include gay men and other men who have sex with men, sex workers, transgender people, and people who inject drugs, but it acknowledges that prisoners and other incarcerated people also are particularly vulnerable to HIV and frequently lack adequate access to services (UNAIDS 2015c).

Raising and allocating government revenue for health is an inherently political process. Populism, neoliberal orthodoxies, austerity politics, and competing priorities have hampered efforts to bolster domestic investment in health (as well as development cooperation for health). Fundamentally, there needs to be structural reforms in global governance, such as debt relief, so that indebted countries can invest in development and in tax justice to address the negative human rights implications of corporate tax avoidance (Tax Justice Network 2014). The global community must work collectively to support countries in strengthening their tax audit capacities and in taxing corporations, for example, by imposing a global minimum tax on corporate income to eliminate the incentive for corporations to use tax havens (Hickel 2017). A modest financial transactions tax among developed countries, as already implemented in 2012 in France, represents another revenue source which could help to address global health funding gaps (UNAIDS 2012).

THE TAX INSPECTORS WITHOUT BORDERS PROJECT

The Tax Inspectors Without Borders (TIWB) project, launched by the Organisation for Economic Co-operation and Development (OECD) and the UN Development Programme (UNDP), tackles widespread tax avoidance by multinational enterprises in developing countries (OECD 2016). By deploying tax experts, TIWB helps to enhance revenue recovery and local audit capacity while sending a strong global message on the need for tax compliance. The eight pilot projects developed across regions to date have recovered more than $260 million in additional tax revenues, including over $100 million in new tax revenues generated through TIWB audits in Zimbabwe (Ibid.).

Yet even with effective tax collection, the social compact envisaged in the AAAA to finance the 2030 Agenda cannot be met in many countries (Migiro 2015). Factoring in current aid levels, even if low-income countries could maximize their revenue capacity and allocate 50 percent of public spending to health, education, and social protection, these countries would still require an additional $73 billion annually to meet the social compact under the AAAA (Watson 2016). To realize the health-related SDG targets and health-related human rights, therefore, greater sums of finance (public and private; domestic and international) are needed. The SDGs, including SDG 16 on peaceful and inclusive societies and SDG 17 on means of implementation, and the indicators proposed for their monitoring, touch upon many structural issues that will make or break the realization of SDG 3 (UN 2016a). In the same way that the SDGs are indivisible and interconnected, so too must financing responses be integrated, coherent, multi-sectoral, and always focused on pursuing social justice through human rights.

CONCLUSION

To achieve the health-related SDG targets, people and their rights must be at the center of global governance for health, with "global health citizens" empowered to voice their concerns, challenge injustices, and hold decision makers to account. Too many decisions are driven by fear of what might happen, rather than a vision of what should happen. The bold vision offered by the 2030 Agenda can act as a unifying force for action among diverse stakeholders in global health. Indeed, the backbone of success achieved in the AIDS response has been a united vision and an unwavering commitment to, and operationalization of, human rights. This commitment and effort must be extended across the entire spectrum of structural determinants of health included in targets set out in the 2030 Agenda beyond SDG 3.

The ultimate measure of success is whether the poorest, the most marginalized, and the most vulnerable benefit from the SDGs. This requires acknowledging and operationalizing how health is impacted by gender equality, access to justice, multi-sectoral partnerships, and beyond. It requires going upstream and addressing the causes of exclusion and ill health, in specific contexts and for specific populations.

The onus is now on the global health community to seize the opportunity presented by the SDGs—to shift the paradigm of global health from a needs-based to a rights-based framework. This framework will allow states to hold true to universal values; enable institutions to be more effective in addressing systemic and interrelated problems of governance, power structures, and determinants of health; and shift energy and resources from managing crises to preventing them. The AIDS response provides a model for action to get there. In the age of sustainable development, the journey toward 2030 represents a new beginning to realize global governance for health that is community-led and in which people and their rights are firmly at the center.

REFERENCES

AU (African Union). 2017. *2 million African community health workers: Harnessing the demographic dividend, ending AIDS and ensuring sustainable health for all in Africa*. Report produced in partnership with UNAIDS, WHO Regional Office for Africa, Columbia University, Government of Luxembourg, International Association of Providers of AIDS Care, and the Sustainable Development Solutions Network.

Bhushan, Aniket. 2013. *Beyond Aid: Trade, Investment, and Remittances between Canada and Developing Countries*. Research Report—The North-South Institute. http://www.nsi-ins.ca/wp-content/uploads/2013/09/2013-Beyond-Aid-Trade-Investment-and-Remittances-between-Canada-and-Developing-Countries.pdf.

Boesen, Jacob Kirkemann, and Tomas Martin. 2007. *Applying a Rights-Based Approach: An Inspirational Guide for Civil Society*. Copenhagen: Danish Institute for Human Rights.

Bustreo, Flavia, and Paul Hunt. 2013. "The Right to Health Is Coming of Age: Evidence of Impact and the Importance of Leadership." *Journal of Public Health Policy* 34(4): 574–579. MEDLINE with Full Text, EBSCOhost (accessed July 18, 2017).

Campbell, Jim. 2014. *Message from the Executive Director, Global Health Workforce Alliance*. Global Health Workforce Alliance. Available at: http://www.who.int/workforcealliance/media/news/2014/jc_begins/en/.

Costello, Antony, Mustafa Abbas, Adrianna Allen, Sarah Ball, Sarah Bell, Richard Bellamy, Sharon Friel [et al.]. 2009. "Managing the Health Effects of Climate Change." *The Lancet* 373(9676): 1693–1733.

CSDH (Commission on Social Determinants of Health). 2008. *Closing the gap in a generation: health equity through action on the social determinants of health. Final report of the Commission on Social Determinants of Health.* Geneva: World Health Organization.

ECOSOC (United Nations Economic and Social Council). 2000. *Establishment of a Permanent Forum on Indigenous Issues.* E/2000/22. http://www.un.org/esa/socdev/unpfii/documents/about-us/E-RES-2000-22.pdf.

ECOSOC (United Nations Economic and Social Council). 2015. *Joint United Nations Programme on HIV/AIDS. Note by the Secretary-General.* E/2015/8. Agenda item 12g. 28 January. http://repository.un.org/bitstream/handle/11176/309519/E_2015_8-EN.pdf?sequence=3&isAllowed=y.

ECOSOC (United Nations Economic and Social Council). 2017a. "Discussion papers on the theme of the high-level political forum on sustainable development, submitted by major groups and other stakeholders. Note by the Secretariat." High-level political forum on sustainable development. 8 May. Doc. E/HLPF/2017/2.

ECOSOC (United Nations Economic and Social Council). 2017b. "Joint United Nations Programme on HIV/AIDS. Note by the Secretary-General." 27 April. Doc. E/2017/62.

Edelman. 2017. *2017 Executive Summary, 2017 Edelman Trust Barometer: Annual Global Study.* Chicago: Edelman.

eKLR (Kenya Law Reports). 2012. *Patricia Asero Ochieng and 2 Others v. Attorney General & Another. Judgement Petition No. 409 of 2009.* Nairobi: Kenya Law Reports.

eKLR (Kenya Law Reports). 2016. *Daniel Ng'etich and 2 Others v. Attorney General and 3 Others. Petition No. 329 of 2014.* Nairobi: Kenya Law Reports.

FCCC (United Nations Framework Convention on Climate Change). "Report of the Conference of the Parties on its twenty-first session, held in Paris from 30 November to 13 December 2015. Decision 1/CP.21: Adoption of the Paris Agreement." 29 January. UN Doc. FCCC/CP/2015/10/Add.1.

Friel, Sharon, Deborah Gleeson, Anne-Marie Thow, Ronald Labonte, David Stuckler, Adrian Kay, and Wendy Snowdon. 2013. "A New Generation of Trade Policy: Potential Risks to Diet-Related Health from the Trans Pacific Partnership Agreement." *Globalization and Health* 9(1): 46.

Gilmore, Kate, Luis Mora, Alfonso Barragues, and Ida Krogh Mikkelsen. 2015. "The Universal Periodic Review: A Platform for Dialogue, Accountability, and Change on Sexual and Reproductive Health and Rights." *Health and Human Rights Journal* 17(2): 167–179.

Global Financial Integrity. 2016. "New Report on Unrecorded Capital Flight Finds Developing Countries Are Net-Creditors to the Rest of the World." Last modified December 5. Available at: http://www.gfintegrity.org/press-release/new-report-on-unrecorded-capital-flight-finds-developing-countries-are-net-creditors-to-the-rest-of-the-world/.

Global Fund (The Global Fund to Fight AIDS, Tuberculosis and Malaria). 2017. *HIV, Human Rights and Gender Equality—Technical Brief.* Geneva: The Global Fund.

Gostin, Lawrence O. and Ayala, Ana. 2017. "Global Health Security in an Era of Explosive Pandemic Potential." *Georgetown Law Faculty Publications and Other Works.* 1943. Available at: http://scholarship.law.georgetown.edu/facpub/1943.

Götzmann, Nora, Tulika Bansal, Elin Wrzoncki, Cathrine Poulsen-Hansen, Jacqueline Tedaldi, and Roya Høvsgaard. 2016. *Human Rights Impact Assessment Guidance and Toolbox.* Copenhagen: Danish Institute for Human Rights.

Hawkes, Sarah, and Kent Buse. 2016. "Searching for the Right to Health in the Sustainable Development Agenda; Comment on 'Rights Language in the Sustainable Development Agenda: Has Right to Health Discourse and Norms Shaped Health Goals?'" *International Journal of Health Policy and Management* 5(5): 337–339.

Hickel, Jason. 2017. "Aid in Reverse: How Poor Countries Develop Rich Countries." *The Guardian.* January 14. Available at: https://www.theguardian.com/global-development-professionals-network/2017/jan/14/aid-in-reverse-how-poor-countries-develop-rich-countries.

International Budget Partnership. 2014. "Article 2 and Governments' Budgets." *International Budget Partnership.* Accessed March 23, 2017. Available at: http://www.internationalbudget.org/publications/escrarticle2.

ICRC (International Committee of the Red Cross). 2012. "Respecting and Protecting Health Care in Armed Conflicts and in Situations Not Covered by International Humanitarian Law." Accessed August 17, 2017. Available at: https://www.icrc.org/eng/assets/files/2012/health-care-law-factsheet-icrc-eng.pdf

IMF (International Monetary Fund). 2017. "World Economic Outlook Database—April 2017." *International Monetary Fund.* Available at: http://www.imf.org/external/pubs/ft/weo/2017/01/weodata/index.aspx.

KELIN (Kenya Legal and Ethical Issues Network on HIV/AIDS). 2016. *Monitoring the implementation of the right to health under the constitution of Kenya: A training manual.* Kenya: KELIN.

Kirmayer, Laurence J. and Gregory Brass. 2016. "Addressing Global Health Disparities among Indigenous Peoples." *The Lancet* 388(10040).

Knight, Lindsay. 2008. *UNAIDS: The First 10 Years, 1996–2006.* Geneva: Switzerland.

Lubambu, Karine M. K. 2014. *The Impacts of Remittances on Developing Countries.* Belgium: European Parliament, Directorate-General for External Policies—Policy Department.

Maina, Nyaguthii Wangui. 2015. "Report of Heads of State and Government Participating in the African Peer Review Forum before the 25th Assembly of the African Union Heads of State." *Musings of a People Blog.* June 17. Available at: https://musingsofapeople.wordpress.com/category/african-peer-review-mechanism-aprm.

Making All Voices Count. 2014. "Solutions to Boost Government Responsiveness and Effectiveness." *Making All Voices Count: A Grand Challenge for Development.* April 16. Available at: http://www.makingallvoicescount.org/news/28-cutting-edge-projects-to-boost-government-accountability-citizen-engagement.

Migiro, Katy. 2015. "Did the U.N. Financing for Development Conference Deliver?" *Reuters.* July 17. Available at: http://www.reuters.com/article/us-development-goals-finance-idUSKCN0PR1JH20150717.

Moodie, Rob, David Stuckler, Carlos Monteiro, Nick Sheron, Bruce Neal, Thaksaphon Thnmarangsi, Paul Lincoln, and Sally Casswell. 2013. "Profits and Pandemics: Prevention of Harmful Effects of Tobacco, Alcohol, and Ultra-Processed Food and Drink Industries." *The Lancet* 381(9867): 670–679.

Mora, D. A. 2014. "Health Litigation in Colombia: Have We Reached the Limit for the Judicialization of Health?" *Health and Human Rights Journal.* September 23. Available at: https://www.hhrjournal.org/2014/09/health-litigation-in-colombia-have-we-reached-the-limit-for-the-judicialization-of-health/.

OAU (Organisation of African Unity). 2001. "Abuja Declaration on HIV/AIDS, Tuberculosis and other related infectious diseases." 24–27 April. Doc. OAU/SPS/ABUJA/3.

OECD (The Organization for Economic Co-operation and Development). 2016. "Tax Inspectors Without Borders making significant progress." *OECD.* 22 November. Available at: http://www.oecd.org/tax/tax-inspectors-without-borders-making-significant-progress.htm.

OHCHR (Office of the United Nations High Commissioner for Human Rights). 2008. *Frequently Asked Questions on Economic, Social and Cultural Rights. Fact Sheet No. 33.* Geneva: OHCHR.

OHCHR (Office of the United Nations High Commissioner for Human Rights). 2011a. *Guiding principles on business and human rights: Implementing the United Nations "Protect, Respect and Remedy" framework.* New York and Geneva: OHCHR.

OHCHR (Office of the United Nations High Commissioner for Human Rights). 2011b. *Indicators for monitoring economic, social and cultural rights in Nepal: A user's guide.* Nepal: OHCHR.

Otterson, Ole Petter, Jashodhara Dasgupta, Chantal Blouin, Paulo Buss, Virasakdi Chongsuvivatwong, Julio Frenk, Sakiko Fukuda-Parr [et al.]. 2014. "The Political Origins of Health Inequity: Prospects for Change. The Lancet–University of Oslo Commission on Global Governance for Health." *The Lancet* 383(9917): 630–667.

Oxfam. 2013. *Oxfam Briefing Paper 176. Universal Health Coverage: Why health insurance schemes are leaving the poor behind.* 9 October. Oxfam: Oxford.

Pew Research Center. 2015. *Beyond Distrust: How Americans View Their Government.* November 23. Washington, D.C.: Pew Research Center.

Rodriguez-García, Rosalía, René Bonnel, David Wilson, and N'Della N'Jie. 2013. *Investing in Communities Achieves Results: Findings from an Evaluation of Community Responses to HIV and AIDS.* Washington, D.C.: International Bank for Reconstruction and Development, The World Bank.

Sagasti, Francisco. 2013. "A Human Rights Approach to Democratic Governance and Development." In OHCHR (Office of the United Nations High Commissioner for Human Rights), *Realizing the Right to Development—Essays in Commemoration of 25 Years of the United Nations Declaration on the Right to Development.* New York and Geneva: United Nations.

Sidibé, Michel. 2015. "Global Health Citizenship." In *To Save Humanity—What Matters Most for a Healthy Future,* edited by Julio Frenk and Steven J. Hoffman. Oxford: Oxford University Press.

Sidibé, Michel and Kent Buse. 2013. "AIDS Governance: Best Practices for a Post-2015 World." *The Lancet* 381(9884): 2147–2149.

Stigma Index. 2017. "The People Living with HIV Stigma Index." Accessed March 23, 2017. Available at: http://www.stigmaindex.org.

Tax Justice Network. 2014. "Human Rights." Accessed March 24, 2017. Available at: http://www.taxjustice.net/topics/inequality-democracy/human-rights.

Taylor, Allyn, Tobias Alfvén, Daniel Hougendobler, and Kent Buse. 2014. "Nonbinding Legal Instruments in Governance for Global Health: Lessons from the Global AIDS Reporting Mechanism." *Journal of Law, Medicine and Ethics* 42(2): 72–87.

Torres, Mary Ann, Sofia Gruskin, Kent Buse, Taavi Erkkola, Victoria Bendaud, and Tobias Alfvén. 2017. "Monitoring HIV-Related Laws and Policies: Lessons for AIDS and Global Health in Agenda 2030." *AIDS Behaviour* 21: 51–61.

UN (United Nations). 1945. "Charter of the United Nations." 24 October. UN Doc. 1 UNTS XVI.

UN (United Nations). 2015a. "Transforming our world: the 2030 Agenda for Sustainable Development." 21 October. UN Doc. A/RES/70/1.

UN (United Nations). 2015b. *The Addis Ababa Action Agenda of the Third International Conference on Financing for Development*. New York: United Nations.

UN (United Nations). 2016a. *Economic and Social Council: Report of the Inter-agency and Expert Group on Sustainable Development Goal Indicators*. New York: United Nations.

UN (United Nations). 2016b. *Report of the United Nations Secretary-General's High-Level Panel on access to medicines, promoting innovation and access to health technologies*. New York: United Nations.

UN General Assembly. 1948. "The Universal Declaration of Human Rights." 10 December. Res. 217 A (III).

UN General Assembly. 1966. "International Covenant on Economic, Social and Cultural Rights." 16 December. Res. 2200A (XXI).

UN General Assembly. 2016. *On the fast track to ending the AIDS epidemic. Report of the Secretary-General*. Seventeenth Session, Agenda item 11. 1 April. Geneva: United Nations.

UN Secretary-General. 2017a. *Repositioning the UN development system to deliver on the 2030 Agenda—Ensuring a Better Future for All. Report of the Secretary-General*. New York: United Nations.

UN Secretary-General. 2017b. "Secretary-General's remarks to Economic and Social Council on Repositioning the UN Development System to Deliver on the 2030 Agenda [as delivered]." 5 July. Available at: https://www.un.org/sg/en/content/sg/statement/2017-07-05/secretary-generals-remarks-economic-and-social-council-repositioning.

UNAIDS (Joint United Nations Programme on HIV/AIDS). 2012. *First meeting of the UNAIDS Executive Director with top officials in France's new government*. Geneva: UNAIDS. http://www.unaids.org/en/resources/presscentre/featurestories/2012/july/20120709france.

UNAIDS (Joint United Nations Programme on HIV/AIDS). 2013. *Abuja +12. Shaping the future of health in Africa*. Geneva: UNAIDS.

UNAIDS (Joint United Nations Programme on HIV/AIDS). 2015a. *How AIDS changed everything. MDG 6: 15 years, 15 lessons of hope from the AIDS response*. Geneva: UNAIDS.

UNAIDS (Joint United Nations Programme on HIV/AIDS). 2015b. *Sustaining the Human Rights Response to HIV: Funding landscape and community voices*. Geneva: UNAIDS.

UNAIDS (Joint United Nations Programme on HIV/AIDS). 2015c. *UNAIDS Terminology Guidelines*. Geneva: UNAIDS.

UNAIDS (Joint United Nations Programme on HIV/AIDS). 2016a. *Fast-Track update on investments needed in the AIDS response*. Geneva: UNAIDS.

UNAIDS (Joint United Nations Programme on HIV/AIDS). 2016b. *Global AIDS Monitoring 2017: Indicators for monitoring the 2016 United Nations Political Declaration on HIV and AIDS*. Geneva: UNAIDS.

UNAIDS (Joint United Nations Programme on HIV/AIDS). 2016c. *The role of UNAIDS ending AIDS by 2030*. Geneva: UNAIDS.

UNAIDS (Joint United Nations Programme on HIV/AIDS). 2016d. "UNAIDS joins forces with the One Million Community Health Workers Campaign to achieve the 90-90-90 Treatment Target." *UNAIDS*. 2 February. Available at: http://www.unaids.org/en/resources/presscentre/featurestories/2016/february/20160202_909090.

UNAIDS (Joint United Nations Programme on HIV/AIDS). 2017. *Fast-Track and human rights, Advancing human rights in efforts to accelerate the response to HIV*. Geneva: UNAIDS.

UNAIDS (Joint United Nations Programme on HIV/AIDS) and Stop AIDS Alliance. 2015. *Communities deliver: The critical role of communities in reaching global targets to end the AIDS epidemic.* Geneva: UNAIDS.

UNDP (United Nations Development Programme). 2016a. *Human Development Report 2016.* New York: United Nations Development Programme.

UNDP (United Nations Development Programme). 2016b. "Sustainable Development Goals. Goal 6: Clean Water and Sanitation. Goal 6 Targets." Accessed March 23, 2017. Available at: http://www.undp.org/content/undp/en/home/sustainable-development-goals/goal-6-clean-water-and-sanitation.html.

UPR (Universal Periodic Review) Info. 2012. *The Follow-up Programme: On the road to implementation.* Geneva: Universal Periodic Review Info.

Van de Pas, Remco, Peter S. Hill, Rachel Hammonds, Gorik Ooms, Lisa Forman, Attiya Waris, Claire E. Brolan, Martin McKee, and Devi Sridhar. 2017. "Global Health Governance in the Sustainable Development Goals: Is It Grounded in the Right to Health?" *Global Challenges* 1(1): 47–60.

Victorero, Annett. 2015. "Joseph Stiglitz and Amartya Sen on the Sustainable Development Goals." *The WIDER Angle Blog, United Nations University.* September. Available at: https://www.wider.unu.edu/publication/joseph-stiglitz-and-amartya-sen-sustainable-development-goals.

Watkins, Kevin. 2017. "Saving Lives with Equity—The Efficient Route to the SDGs." *The Lancet* 390(10092): 339–340.

Watson, Charlene. 2016. *Financing Our Shared Future: Navigating the Humanitarian, Development and Climate Finance Agendas.* London: Overseas Development Institute.

WHO (World Health Organization). 1948. "Preamble to the Constitution of the World Health Organization as adopted by the International Health Conference, New York, 19–22 June, 1946." *Official Records of the World Health Organization* 2(100).

WHO (World Health Organization). 1981. *International code of marketing of breast-milk substitutes.* Geneva: World Health Organization.

WHO (World Health Organization). 2009. *2009 Summary Report on global progress in implementation of the WHO Framework Convention on Tobacco Control.* Geneva: World Health Organization.

WHO (World Health Organization). 2011. *Human rights and gender equality in health sector strategies.* Geneva: World Health Organization.

WHO (World Health Organization). 2016a. *Framework of engagement with non-State actors: Report by the Director-General.* Resolution A69.6. Geneva: World Health Organization.

WHO (World Health Organization). 2016b. Implications of the SDGs for Health Monitoring—A Challenge and an Opportunity for all Countries. *Chapter 2, World health statistics 2016: monitoring health for the SDGs, sustainable development goals.* Geneva: World Health Organization.

WHO (World Health Organization). 2017. *Advancing the right to health: the vital role of law.* Geneva: World Health Organization.

WTO (World Trade Organization). 2001. *Declaration on the TRIPS Agreement and public health.* WT/MIN(01)/DEC/2. 20 November. Doha: World Trade Organization.

The World Health Organization

5

Development of Human Rights through WHO

BENJAMIN MASON MEIER AND FLORIAN KASTLER

Chronicling the history of human rights in global health governance, this chapter examines the World Health Organization's (WHO's) past contributions to (and, in some cases, negligence of) the rights-based approach to health. Part I presents the postwar legal debates that gave rise to both international health governance and human rights law, creating WHO's unique institutional structures and expansive public health mandate as a basis to realize a human right to health. Upon this foundation for health and human rights, Part II addresses the evolution of WHO's efforts to develop, implement, and operationalize human rights in public health, examining WHO's early neglect for the development of health-related human rights under international law, rights-based leadership to implement the right to health in its "Health for All" policy, and human rights advocacy to operationalize a rights-based HIV/AIDS response. Recognizing how WHO's past provides a basis to understand its present and situate its future in global health governance, Part III analyzes how these past struggles have continued to frame WHO's enduring challenges in: exercising its international legal authorities, collaborating with the United Nations (UN) human rights system, and mainstreaming human rights in the WHO Secretariat.

I. THE BIRTH OF A RIGHTS-BASED POSTWAR HEALTH ORDER

Out of the horrors of World War II, the development of WHO's human rights authority has been structured by the UN Charter, given meaning in the WHO Constitution, and proclaimed through the Universal Declaration of Human Rights (UDHR).

Human Rights in Global Health. Benjamin Mason Meier and Lawrence O. Gostin.
© Oxford University Press 2018. Published 2018 by Oxford University Press.

Developing international human rights law for health through the UN, the 1945 UN Charter elevated human rights as one of the principal purposes of the postwar international system. With the UN seeking to "make recommendations for the purpose of promoting respect for, and observance of, human rights and fundamental freedoms for all" (UN 1945, art. 62), states worked within the UN system to establish human rights as a formal legal basis to assess and adjudicate principles of justice (Donnelly 2003). Concurrently elevating health within the UN, state representatives established WHO as a UN specialized agency, with the WHO Constitution serving as the first international treaty to conceptualize a unique human right to health (Grad 2002, 80).

Preparing for this new postwar health organization, the UN's June–July 1946 International Health Conference in New York (Doull 1949) developed and adopted the proposed WHO Constitution pursuant to the UN Charter—thereby establishing an Interim Commission of eighteen members to subsume within WHO all of the responsibilities of the Health Organization of the League of Nations, the *Office International d'Hygiène Publique* (OIHP), and the Health Division of the UN Relief and Rehabilitation Administration (UNRRA) (WHO 1958b). To achieve these ends under an inter-governmental structure similar to those of the League of Nations and other specialized agencies of the UN, this five-week International Health Conference (drawing from a thematic outline developed by the UN's March–April 1946 Technical Preparatory Committee in Paris) established three organs through which to implement the goals of the new organization:

- The World Health Assembly, the legislative policy-making body of WHO, made up of representatives from each member state;
- The Executive Board, an executive program-developing subset of the members of the World Health Assembly; and
- The Secretariat, carrying out the decisions of the aforementioned organs through the elected Director-General and appointed staff of WHO (WHO 1946c).

Representatives of sixty-one states signed the WHO Constitution on July 22, 1946, after which it remained open for signature until it came into force on April 7, 1948.

Under the WHO Constitution, states would engage a pressing postwar imperative to facilitate international health cooperation through international health governance (UN Secretary-General 1946). WHO's first stated constitutional function would be "to act as the directing and coordinating authority on international health work" (WHO 1946a, art. 2). Whereas previous international health organizations would exist solely to prevent the spread of disease from crossing national boundaries, the WHO Secretariat would be given additional authorities to "take all necessary action" over all manner of disease prevention and health promotion, including, *inter alia*, the realization of underlying determinants of health through policy leadership and technical assistance:

- "to promote, in cooperation with other specialized agencies where necessary, the improvement of nutrition, housing, sanitation, recreation, economic or working conditions, and other aspects of environmental hygiene,"

- "to promote maternal and child health and welfare and to foster the ability to live harmoniously in a changing total environment," and
- "to study and report on ... administrative and social techniques affecting public health and medical care from preventive and curative points of view, including hospital services and social security" (Ibid.).

As states developed what would be referred to as a "Magna Carta of health" (Parran 1946, 1265), WHO was "extended from the negative aspects of public health—vaccination and other specific means of combating infection—to positive aspects, i.e. the improvement of public health by better food, physical education, medical care, health insurance, etc." (Stampar 1949, annex).

To achieve these objectives through a unique, exceptional, and strong international normative authority (Kastler 2016), WHO was given constitutional authority to propose conventions (art. 19), regulations (art. 21), and recommendations (art. 23) "with respect to any matter within its competence" (WHO 1946a). Working with states to exercise these expansive normative functions for medical care and underlying determinants of health, WHO's constitutional framework would proclaim a human rights foundation for WHO's authority to direct international action for public health.

Through the preamble of the WHO Constitution, states framed international health cooperation under the unprecedented declaration that "the enjoyment of the highest attainable standard of health is one of the fundamental rights of every human being," defining health positively to include "a state of complete physical, mental, and social well-being and not merely the absence of disease or infirmity" (Ibid., preamble). Discussions during the drafting of the Constitution show that the initial wording of the preamble explicitly recognized "the right to health as one of the fundamental rights to which every human being, without distinction of race, sex, language or religion, is entitled" (WHO 1946b, 61). The final wording of the WHO Constitution—avoiding the express phrase "right to health"—was seen as a compromise to avoid the legal and economic implications of explicitly declaring an individual right to health while states were still rebuilding after the War. Yet with state representatives recognizing that they were creating the conceptual framework for an entirely new human right, this preambular language further declared that "governments have a responsibility for the health of their peoples which can be fulfilled only by the provision of adequate health and social measures" (WHO 1946a, preamble). Under such far-reaching rights and responsibilities, even if too vague to offer any meaningful operationalization, the WHO Constitution was seen to "represent the broadest and most liberal concept of international responsibility for health ever officially promulgated" (Allen 1950, 30) and encompass the aspirations of the medical community to build a healthy world out of the ashes of the Second World War (Bok 2004).

The first World Health Assembly, with fifty-four member states, met in Geneva in June 1948 to establish WHO as the first UN specialized agency, as depicted in Figure 5.1, and to lay out WHO's mandate for realizing public health throughout the world.

WHO's human rights authority for health would be supported, as reviewed in chapter 1, by human rights obligations under the nascent UN. Drawing on the

Figure 5.1 WHO accession to the United Nations by UN Secretary General Trygvie Lie and WHO Director-General Brock Chisholm.
PHOTO CREDIT: UN Archives.

negotiations for a WHO Constitution, the UN proclaimed the 1948 UDHR, framing within it a set of interrelated social welfare rights by which:

> Everyone has the right to a standard of living adequate for the health and well-being of himself and of his family, including food, clothing, housing and medical care and necessary social services, and the right to security in the event of unemployment, sickness, disability, widow-hood, old age or other lack of livelihood in circumstances beyond his control (UN General Assembly 1948, art. 25).

Including both the fulfillment of necessary medical care and the realization of underlying determinants of health, this expansive vision of public health in the UDHR reflected budding national welfare policies and prevailing social medicine discourses as a basis for public health systems (UN 1950).

II. EVOLUTION OF HUMAN RIGHTS IN WHO GOVERNANCE

With both the WHO and UDHR coming into existence in 1948, there was great promise that these two institutions would complement each other, with WHO—like all UN specialized agencies—serving to support human rights in its policies, programs, and practices. However, in spite of this promise and early WHO support for advancing a human rights basis for its public health work, the WHO Secretariat intentionally neglected human rights discourse during crucial years in the development and implementation of health-related rights, projecting itself as a technical organization without concern for "legal rights" and squandering opportunities for WHO leadership in the evolution of rights-based approaches to health. Where WHO neglected human rights development, it did so to the detriment of public health. When WHO sought to reclaim the language of human rights in the 1970s in the pursuit of its "Health for All" strategy, its past neglect of human rights norms left it without the legal obligations necessary to implement human rights through primary health care pursuant to the Declaration of Alma-Ata. Only when faced with the dire effects of HIV/AIDS, a pandemic that laid bare the inextricable linkages between individual freedoms and public health outcomes, did WHO come to embrace human rights operationalization, viewing the rights-based approach to health as instrumental to its public health mandate.

A. WHO in the Development of the Right to Health

As states worked through the UN Commission on Human Rights to develop human rights treaty law, WHO was set to play a defining role in translating the aspirational public health language of the 1948 UDHR into the binding legal obligations of the 1966 International Covenant on Economic, Social and Cultural Rights (ICESCR). Although WHO embraced this vital human rights leadership role in the first five years of its existence, the political constraints of the Cold War led WHO to reposition itself in international health as a purely technical organization, focusing on medical intervention and disease eradication to the detriment of rights advancement.

WHO's early years were marked by the Secretariat's active role in drafting human rights treaty law and its cooperative work with other UN agencies to expand human rights frameworks for public health. Working with state representatives in the early 1950s, WHO Director-General Brock Chisholm welcomed "opportunities to co-operate with the [UN] Commission on Human Rights in drafting international conventions, recommendations and standards with a view to ensuring the enjoyment of the right to health," recognizing that "the whole programme approved by the World Health Assembly represents a concerted effort on the part of the Member States to ensure the right to health" (Chisholm 1951).

In pressing the UN Commission on Human Rights in its development of health-related obligations, the WHO Secretariat successfully suggested in 1951 that the right to health reflect state commitments in the WHO Constitution, emphasizing (1) a positive definition of health promotion, (2) the importance of social measures as underlying determinants of health, (3) governmental responsibility for health provision, and (4) the role of health ministries in creating systems for the public's health:

> Every human being shall have the right to the enjoyment of the highest standard of health obtainable, health being defined as a state of complete physical mental and social well-being.
>
> Government, having a responsibility for the health of their peoples, undertake to fulfil that responsibility by providing adequate health and social measures.

Every Party to the present Covenant shall therefore, so far as it [*sic*] means allow and with due allowance for its traditions and for local conditions, provide measures to promote and protect the health of its nationals, and in particular:

- to reduce infant mortality and provide for healthy development of the child;
- to improve nutrition, housing, sanitation, recreation, economic and working conditions and other aspects of environmental hygiene;
- to control epidemic, endemic and other diseases;
- to improve standards of medical teaching and training in the health, medical and related professions;
- to enlighten public opinion on problems of health;
- to foster activities in the field of mental health, especially those affecting the harmony of human relations (UN 1951).

While these WHO proposals survived early objections from the Cold War Superpowers, with vigorous debates among state representatives in both the WHO Executive Board and the UN Commission on Human Rights on the expansiveness of such public health commitments (Meier 2010a), the WHO Secretariat received support from its Executive Board (over the objections of the US Representative) to take a continuing leadership role in UN efforts to develop the legal language of the right to health (WHO Executive Board 1951). With the World Health Assembly supporting WHO's normative role and extending WHO's regulatory authority "to ensure the maximum security against the international spread of disease with minimum interference with world traffic," the World Health Assembly adopted the first International Sanitary Regulations in 1951 (later renamed the International Health Regulations), consolidating the previous International Sanitary Conventions and thereby coordinating infectious disease control through the WHO Secretariat (Pannenborg 1979).

The UN Commission on Human Rights continued in the ensuing year to broaden the substantive content of the right to health under WHO's leadership; however, WHO's influential contributions to the development of human rights for public health were explicitly rejected following a 1953 shift in WHO's Secretariat leadership and reform of WHO's health priorities. As the UN sought to codify a right to health in the ICESCR and extend rights to underlying determinants of health, WHO abandoned the evolution of human rights and turned its attention to technical assistance through its regional offices (van Zile Hyde 1953)—projecting itself as "technical organization" (Candau 1954, 1501), neglecting "social questions" (Kaul 1956), and finding human rights "beyond the competence of WHO" (WHO Liaison Office 1959). Under the leadership of Director-General Marcolino Gomes Candau, the WHO Secretariat repeatedly declared throughout the late 1950s and early 1960s that it was not "entrusted with safeguarding legal rights" (Candau 1957), and, as explained by WHO's chief legal officer, "a programme based on the notion of priorities has given way to one based on the needs of the countries themselves, expressed through their requests for advice and assistance" (Gutteridge 1963, 8). With this transition leading WHO to abandon its early leadership to develop expansive international legal obligations for underlying determinants of health, WHO's absence from human rights debates would enable state efforts to weaken human rights norms for health (Meier 2010a).

WHO sought throughout this period to declare its technical efforts to be "non-political," believing that avoiding engagement with human rights would prevent WHO from offending its member states while allowing it to address health solely through the purportedly objective lens of science (Aginam 2014). Drawing on the predominant medical worldview existing at WHO (Volansky 2002), this institutional conservatism toward the law (Taylor 1992) allowed WHO to justify its "timidity" toward human rights (Samson 2015, 123) even as other UN specialized agencies continued to develop human rights within their respective spheres of competence. With WHO retreating from its advancement of the right to health, the WHO Secretariat (1) declined to participate in the proceedings of the Commission on Human Rights (WHO 1958a), (2) requested that the UN Secretariat not include a section on health in its human rights summaries (Howell 1958), and (3) did not engage in the final debates on the right to health in the 1966 ICESCR (Humphrey 1957). The ICESCR would reflect this WHO neglect, with a limited codification of the right to health that abandoned language on complete health and holistic determinants of health in favor of the limited "highest attainable standard" of health (UN General Assembly 1966, art. 12). Without the legal staff to engage with international human rights law (Gutteridge 1966), the WHO Secretariat sought only to lessen its UN responsibilities to develop and implement the right to health (WHO 1972), hampering health advocates in their efforts to elaborate the scope and content of human rights (Lakin 2001).

As WHO provided little support for a rights-based approach to addressing underlying determinants of health, UN efforts would reflect WHO's neglect of public health in human rights (and human rights in public health), with the UN's 1968 review of human rights efforts enumerating the human rights activities taken by every UN specialized agency except WHO (UN Secretary-General 1968) and including only vague and perfunctory generalities on the right to health—that "[t]hrough its programme of technical assistance, WHO is helping countries achieve the objectives set forth in the preamble to its constitution, and thus the full range of its activities are relevant to human rights by assisting countries to make a reality of their people's right to health" (UN 1968).

B. Implementing the Right to Health in the Shift toward "Health for All"

Yet with WHO noting as early as 1968 that "people are beginning to ask for health, and to regard it as a right" (WHO 1968, ix), this neglect for human rights would soon turn to active engagement, returning WHO to the promise of international human rights standards as a means to realize improved standards for health. By the early 1970s, WHO came to see human rights norms as a foundation upon which to frame health policy, seeking to implement human rights for public health through "primary health care"—a long-standing undercurrent in health scholarship and advocacy that seeks to address health care in addition to the underlying social, political, and economic determinants of health (Litsios 1969). Focused on the role of weak national health systems in enabling the spread of disease, with WHO reports recognizing the limitations of medical care in preventing disease and promoting health (WHO 1973), WHO's leadership turned its attention back to the right to health as a means to improve underlying determinants of health (Evang 1973). While primary health care had long garnered technical support within WHO, only the ideological support of human rights could bring these evolving health discourses to the fore of WHO governance (Brown, Cueto, and Fee 2006).

After twenty years shunning human rights law, the WHO Secretariat sought to re-engage the right to health in the 1970s as a political catalyst upon which to advance its "Health for All" strategy. Director-General Halfdan Mahler sought to expand WHO's influence in international health by redefining its health goals to reflect human rights norms (Mahler 1973). Supported by developing nations in the World Health Assembly (WHA 1970), the WHO Secretariat engaged its legal office for the first time in human rights debates—at the Commission on Human Rights, in human rights seminars, and as a voice for policy reform (Meier 2010a). The WHO Secretariat began reporting to the Commission on Human Rights and collaborating with the UN's human rights staff, extolling human rights obligations as a clarion call to the achievement of health for all (Lambo 1974). These human rights implementation efforts would expand as states moved toward the January 1976 entry into force of the ICESCR, with WHO seeking to have a seminal role in reviewing state reports on a wide range of health-related human rights, including rights related to safe and healthy working conditions; family health, child, and mother protections; adequate standards of living; and scientific research (Sacks 1975). Notwithstanding these expansive concerns, WHO gave preeminent focus to the right to the highest attainable standard of physical and mental health in Article 12 of the ICESCR, arguing that "this provision is of primary importance from WHO's point of view, and the whole body of WHO activities is based on the right and principles contained therein" (WHO 1976, 3).

Reflected in a dramatic expansion of inter-agency studies, WHO sought to apply human rights frameworks to achieve public health ends, looking to human rights standards to govern underlying determinants of health through:

- Human Experimentation—with WHO, the World Medical Association, and CIOMS (a joint collaboration of WHO and UNESCO) advancing rights-based approaches to medical research (CIOMS 1974).
- Racism—with WHO engaging with the UN's Decade for Action to Combat Racism and Racial Discrimination to study the implications of racial discrimination and apartheid on health inequality (Jablensky 1977).
- Breastfeeding—with WHO mediating the claims of nongovernmental children's rights organizations and the infant formula industry to develop a code of conduct for the marketing of breastmilk substitutes (Sikkink 1986).

- Health Technologies—with WHO working with the UN to develop
  a study on the health benefits of human rights in light of scientific and
  technological developments (Meier 2013).
- Medical Education—with WHO working with UNESCO, United Nations
  University, the UN Division of Human Rights, and the International
  Institute of Human Rights to study programs for teaching human rights to
  health practitioners (Torelli 1980).
- Disease Prevention—with WHO working with the Special Rapporteur
  of the Commission on Human Rights to study limitations on individual
  rights to protect the public's health through mandatory vaccinations,
  disease notification, and quarantine restrictions (Daes 1981).

As international discourse developed on the policies necessary to implement human rights in public health, consensus was developing on the essential underlying determinants of health inherent in the right to health (van Boven 1979). In addressing these determinants of health through "primary health care," the WHO Secretariat would adopt human rights discourse to advocate for the national and international redistributions that would allow people to lead socially and economically satisfying lives (Evang 1973). Advancing health as a right, rather than a means to an economic end, WHO would focus on accelerating social and economic development as a basis to realize human rights for global health (Eze 1979). Grounded in human rights norms—drawn from the WHO Constitution, subsequent international treaties, and UN debates on a human right to development—this socioeconomic approach to health would form the foundation of framing what WHO officials referred to as "the onset of the health revolution" (Lambo 1979, 4). Given an expanding understanding of the coordinating role of WHO in implementing the right to health through international health governance (Vignes 1979), there was growing agreement that WHO had the constitutional authority and human rights legitimacy to elaborate international legal obligations for underlying determinants of health (Roscam Abbing 1979).

WHO's Health for All strategy would provide the central focus of its efforts to influence human rights implementation through socioeconomic development, advancing underlying determinants of health in the rights-based 1978 Declaration of Alma-Ata. This "Health for All" strategy, officially defined by the World Health Assembly in 1977 and widely regarded as WHO's "main thrust" for implementing the right to health (Taylor 1991, 14), would seek "the attainment by all citizens of the world by the year 2000 of a level of health that would permit them to lead a socially and economically productive life" (WHA 1977, para. 1). Elevating a rights-based approach to international health governance that had been wanting since the right to health was first proclaimed in the WHO Constitution, WHO and UNICEF convened the International Conference on Primary Health Care on September 6, 1978. Taking place in Alma-Ata, USSR (now Almaty, Kazakhstan), this Conference took a synoptic view of health, seeking social justice in the distribution of health resources in line with the interconnectedness of human rights in realizing public health (Mower 1985). With government representatives from 134 states, the Conference adopted the Declaration on Primary Health Care (a document that has come to be known as the 1978 Declaration of Alma-Ata), through which delegates memorialized their agreement that primary health care was the key to assuring underlying determinants of health (WHO 1978). Reaffirming the rights-based language of the WHO Constitution, Article I of the Declaration proclaimed anew that:

> health, which is a state of complete physical, mental and social well-being, and not merely the absence of disease or infirmity, is a fundamental human right and that the attainment of the highest level of health is a most important world-wide social goal whose realization requires the action of many other social and economic sectors in addition to the health sector (Ibid., art. I).

However, in spite of this rededication to human rights in global health under the Declaration of Alma-Ata, laying out WHO's programmatic vision for implementing human rights through primary health care, such obligations for distributive justice through public health never took hold in health policy discourse (Taylor 1992). While presenting a nominally rights-based framework for advancing public health (Gunn 1983), WHO's previous neglect of human rights law proved fatal to the goals of the Health for All strategy (Meier 2010b). Without UN treaty frameworks to guide primary health care, the Declaration of Alma-Ata presented no legal obligations on states (Leary 1988), with scholars noting in its aftermath that "inadequate national commitment to the 'Health for All' strategy is at some level a reflection of the ineffectiveness of WHO's strategy of securing national dedication to the right to health" (Taylor 1991, 42).

C. Operationalizing Human Rights in Responding to the HIV/AIDS Pandemic

Yet even as states stepped back from implementing the right to health through primary health care (WHO 1983), such rights-based standards endured in WHO's evolving approach to public health, reconceptualized in the international response to HIV/AIDS. With governments responding to the emergent threat of AIDS in the early 1980s through traditional public health policies—including compulsory testing, named reporting, travel restrictions, and coercive isolation or quarantine—established civil and political rights were seen by HIV-positive activists as a basis to resist intrusive public health infringements on individual liberty (Bayer 1991). In this period of rising fear and advocacy, Jonathan Mann's vocal leadership of WHO's Global Programme on AIDS (GPA) in the late 1980s, as exemplified by Figure 5.2, marked a turning point in the operationalization of individual human rights in public health policy, applying human rights to focus on the individual behaviors leading to HIV transmission (Fee and Parry 2008). With these rights-based prevention efforts grounded in individual autonomy for health, WHO's approach to AIDS found support among transnational networks of non-governmental advocates and UN human rights officers, who worked closely with the WHO Secretariat to understand the risks for transmission, educate the public on prevention, avoid

Figure 5.2 WHO Director-General Halfdan Mahler speaking with GPA Director
Johnathan Mann on World AIDS Day in 1988.
PHOTO CREDIT: WHO Archives.

stigmatization through confidentiality, and slow the spread of HIV (Gruskin, Mills,
and Tarantola 2007).

Although human rights frameworks had long recognized that infringements of
individual rights were permissible—even necessary—to protect the public's health,
the GPA viewed respect for individual rights as a precondition for public health in
the context of HIV prevention and control (Mann and Carballo 1989). The GPA
conceptualized civil and political rights protections as "inextricably linked" to the
promotion of public health, examining human rights violations as a key driver of
the spread of the disease and operationalizing human rights in WHO programming through strategies to combat HIV discrimination, promote social equity, and
encourage individual responsibility (Meier, Brugh, and Halima 2012). Through
this rights-based programming, the WHO Secretariat shifted the HIV/AIDS response away from both the biomedical framing of international health rights and
the individualistic framing of neoliberal health policy (Wolff 2012). In partnership
with the UN human rights system and with the support of Director-General Mahler,
the GPA sought to "bring together the various organizations, particularly those organizations of the UN system and related organizations involved in human rights to
discuss the relationship between AIDS, discrimination, and human rights" (Mann
1987). Confirming WHO's leadership role in applying interconnected human
rights to address intersectoral determinants of HIV, the UN General Assembly
directed all UN agencies to assist in WHO's efforts, resolving "to ensure . . . a
co-ordinated response by the United Nations system to the AIDS pandemic" (UN
General Assembly 1987, para. 6).

Tying together the efforts of international institutions, national governments, and non-governmental organizations under a universal rights-based framework for action, WHO's 1987 Global Strategy for the Prevention and Control of AIDS (Global Strategy) solidified human rights principles in preventing HIV transmission and reducing the impact of the pandemic (WHO 1987). The Global Strategy focused on principles of non-discrimination and equitable access to care, stressing the need for public health programs to respect and protect human rights as a means to achieve the individual behavior change necessary to reduce HIV transmission (Ibid.). Through this Global Strategy, civil and political rights framed the international HIV/AIDS response, serving as a normative basis for the development of international guidelines, national policies, and non-governmental action. In upholding WHO's authority through human rights to ensure global collaboration against this unprecedented threat, the World Health Assembly reaffirmed in May 1988 that "respect for human rights and dignity of HIV-infected people, people with AIDS and members of population groups is vital to the success of national AIDS prevention and control programs and of the global strategy" (WHA 1988, preamble). Although the election of Director-General Hiroshi Nakajima came to diminish the GPA's ability to promote a rights-based approach to health—leading Jonathan Mann to resign in protest, stymieing WHO authority for human rights, and leaving WHO's AIDS programs in a state of disarray (Garrett 1994)—this Secretariat focus on rights-based approaches to health would persist even as WHO lost programmatic authority for the HIV/AIDS response (Gruskin, Mills, and Tarantola 2007).

III. ENDURING HUMAN RIGHTS CHALLENGES IN THE WHO SECRETARIAT AND GLOBAL HEALTH GOVERNANCE

Moving beyond HIV/AIDS and encompassing a range of health-related human rights, WHO considered a more systematic application of civil, cultural, economic, political, and social rights to an array of public health challenges. With the end of the Cold War, a political space opened in the 1990s for human rights in international relations, as addressed in chapter 2, with the UN embracing human rights as a basis for global governance and WHO looking to women's rights in advancing reproductive health (Cook and Dickens 2001). Following from the UN Secretary-General's repeatedly reaffirmed calls to "mainstream" human rights as a cross-cutting approach to all of the UN's principal programs and activities (UN Secretary-General 1997), WHO sought to re-engage health as a human right, employing this human rights framework with mixed success to: frame state responsibilities under international legal regulation, support global health through the UN human rights system, and elevate rights-based approaches in WHO policies and programs.

A. Exercising WHO's Normative Authority through International Legal Regulation

WHO's increased use of its normative authority in the 2000s provided a basis to develop international legal instruments that contribute to the promotion of the rights-based approach. Both the Framework Convention on Tobacco Control (FCTC), adopted in 2003 through WHO's convention power (under Article 19 of the WHO Constitution), and the International Health Regulations (IHR), revised in 2005 through WHO's regulation power (under Article 21 of the WHO Constitution), recognize the importance of human rights to global health.

While not regarded as a human rights treaty (Dresler et al. 2011), the FCTC demonstrates the influence of human rights in its content and, in turn, the impact of human rights on global tobacco control (Cabrera and Gostin 2011). The FCTC Preamble begins by noting that states are determined "to give priority to their right to protect public health," recalling the right to health in both the preamble of the WHO Constitution and Article 12 of the ICESCR, with the WHO Foreword opening with the statement that the FCTC "is an evidence-based treaty that reaffirms the right of all people to the highest standard of health" (WHO 2003). Despite an absence of explicit discussion on human rights obligations during the FCTC negotiation process (Meier 2005), subsequent protocols and guidelines—implementation tools developed by the Conference of the Parties to the FCTC—have explicitly engaged fundamental human rights and freedoms, notably a rights-based duty to protect individuals from tobacco smoke and a human right to educate, communicate with, and train people to ensure a high level of public awareness of tobacco control (WHO FCTC 2007; 2010). Thus, the FCTC, by creating a rights-based minimum for tobacco control measures, has served as a normative standard to assess state parties' implementation of the right to health and a judicial standard to facilitate accountability for human rights in tobacco control efforts (Muggli et al. 2013).

Further, the 2005 revision of the IHR has provided for increased consideration of human rights in global health governance. Indeed, one key innovation of the IHR (2005) is the inclusion of explicit protections of the interests of individuals. Article 3 explicitly states that the implementation of the IHR shall be with full respect for the dignity, human rights, and fundamental freedoms of persons (WHO 2005). While framed broadly, this provision is essential, as it integrates human rights in the legal framework of the IHR and imposes an obligation on states to ensure that infectious disease control measures are compatible with human rights standards (Zidar 2015). Other IHR provisions further promote human rights—on health measures on arrival and departure (art. 23), on the treatment of travelers (art. 32), and on the treatment of personal data (art. 45) (WHO 2005). Thus the revised IHR has established for the first time in WHO a "balance" between commerce (trade and travel), public health (scientific methodologies), and human rights (Gostin and Katz 2016, 267).

By developing these legal instruments, WHO has provided the obligations and tools to advance human rights across its work in global health governance. Human rights are concretized through WHO's legal authorities, offering international legal measures to respect, protect, and fulfill rights by changing state behavior. These international legal efforts have set a precedent for future international instruments by re-engaging WHO's normative role through international law (Kastler 2016). Indeed, these advances in global health law have led to various proposals for future treaties on noncommunicable diseases (Gostin 2014; Magnusson 2010), antimicrobial resistance (Hoffman, Røttingen, and Frenk 2015), alcohol (Room

2006; Record 2007), obesity and nutrition (Basu 2012), research and development (Dentico and Ford 2005; Moon, Bermudez, and 't Hoen 2012), and global health funding (Gostin 2007). Now that WHO has exercised its constitutional authority to develop international legal regulations, it has built momentum for future efforts to implement human rights in global health (Meier and Onzivu 2014).

B. WHO's Collaboration with the Human Rights System

Building from these rights-based efforts with its member states, WHO has sought to advance health-related human rights through collaborations with the UN human rights system—developing human rights through UN human rights treaty bodies, establishing joint programming with the Office of the UN High Commissioner for Human Rights (OHCHR), and supporting the mandate of a UN special rapporteur on the right to health.

WHO has interacted with the UN human rights treaty bodies to provide input in the interpretation and monitoring of health-related human rights. This collaboration has extended across different core human rights treaty bodies, focused on the Committee on Economic, Social and Cultural Rights (CESCR), the Committee on the Elimination of Discrimination against Women (CEDAW Committee), and the Human Rights Committee (HRC). The close collaboration between WHO and the CESCR, as discussed in chapter 23, led to the adoption in 2000 of General Comment 14 on the Right to the Highest Attainable Standard of Health (CESCR 2000), which has served as an authoritative interpretation of the right to health, codifying rights-based standards that WHO first developed decades earlier in the Declaration of Alma-Ata (Riedel 2009).

Building from this technical assistance to the human rights system, WHO has worked with OHCHR to draft a Joint Work Programme that would seek to share information on health and human rights, to institutionalize a human rights approach in WHO, to collaborate on health and human rights at the country level, and to advance health as a human right (WHO 2007). This evolving WHO work with OHCHR, as addressed in detail in chapters 7 and 21, would extend to support for the state-led Human Rights Council in: establishing the Universal Periodic Review (HRC 2007), organizing informal and technical meetings between WHO and OHCHR, and jointly publishing an information sheet on "A Human Rights-Based Approach to Health" (WHO 2010).

The 2002 creation of the special procedures mandate for a special rapporteur on the right to health (UNCHR 2002) has triggered WHO collaborations to further promote a rights-based approach to health through annual reports and country missions. In his first report on the health and human rights movement, the first Special Rapporteur, Paul Hunt, argued for human rights to be mainstreamed more effectively, recognizing WHO collaborations that had supported his mandate in areas of neglected diseases, mental health, child and adolescent health, essential medicines, and sexual and reproductive health, as well as in some regional and country offices (Hunt 2007). Hunt worked closely with WHO staff, as detailed in chapter 22, to provide training on the right to health, presenting his work to WHO on right-to-health indicators and on prioritization of the right to health. Now beyond his mandate, Hunt has continued to consult on WHO's work to advance the right to health, studying the impact of human rights on global health efforts (Bustreo and Hunt et al. 2013) and advocating WHO implementation of human rights in global health (Hunt 2017).

C. Mainstreaming Human Rights within the WHO Secretariat

During the 2000s, WHO sought to promote a rights-based approach to health, contributing, as described in chapter 3, to the mainstreaming of human rights in organizational policies, programs, and practices. With Director-General Gro Harlem Brundtland seeking to re-establish WHO as "the world's health conscience" (Lee 2004, 13), this mainstreaming of human rights endeavored to increase awareness and understanding of the scope, content, and application of human rights in global health. WHO's first human rights advisor began in 1999 to draft a WHO Strategy on Health and Human Rights to solidify the place of human rights within WHO (Tarantola 2000) and to develop Informal Consultations on Health and Human Rights to build Secretariat support for human rights among WHO clusters (WHO 2000). This visible presence of human rights in WHO debates led to the 2003 creation of a small Health and Human Rights Team inside the WHO Secretariat, establishing a WHO focal point for consideration of international human rights law, re-engagement with the UN human rights system, and collaboration with organizations, academics, and advocates at the intersection of health and human rights (Nygren-Krug 2004). Building capacity for human rights within WHO, the Health and Human Rights Team began to conduct human rights training on a regular basis for WHO staff at headquarters and in country and regional offices, organizing tailored training and workshops for departments and units to ensure that WHO's programs, projects, and activities would be in line with international human rights norms and principles (WHO 2011). As mainstreaming began to take hold in the Secretariat, the Health and Human Rights Team found internal support for its rights-based efforts from human rights focal points within select program clusters and technical officer collaborations with the UN Special Rapporteur on the Right to Health (WHO 2010).

These efforts to incorporate human rights law in the work of the WHO Headquarters came to be replicated through the Secretariat's regional offices, with select regional offices strengthening rights-based governance through the mainstreaming of human rights. Within the Pan American Health Organization (PAHO), the regional human rights advisor developed a series of yearlong collaborations to mainstream human rights in various technical offices and build rights-based capacity within national offices, with PAHO member states incorporating human rights as a guiding principle of the 2008–2012 PAHO Strategic Plan and adopting a 2010 Resolution on Health and Human Rights to mainstream human rights in national health ministries and PAHO technical programs (PAHO 2010; Meier and Ayala 2014). Similarly seen in the WHO African Regional Office (AFRO), the regional human rights office sought to provide technical assistance to states to mainstream human rights in national health programs, with AFRO member states drawing on the right to health in the African Charter on Human and People's Rights to adopt a

2012 AFRO Resolution on Health and Human Rights to strengthen legal and institutional measures to promote human rights (AFRO 2012). Even where the states of the WHO Eastern Mediterranean Region (EMRO) have shown less state support for human rights, the regional human rights advisor has nevertheless held consultancies for national health ministries to build capacity to operationalize the right to health in national policies and programs (WHO 2011).

Yet despite the rise of the Health and Human Rights Unit within the Secretariat Headquarters in Geneva, the development of human rights focal points in select program clusters, and the creation of human rights officer positions in each regional secretariat and country office, human rights efforts faced reductions in budgetary allocations and isolation in the Secretariat (Meier and Onzivu 2014). With human rights de-emphasized in WHO governance in response to member state pressures, the Health and Human Rights Unit came to be disconnected from the work of Headquarters clusters and national offices, as scholars and advocates criticized WHO programs for their increasing departure from the path of human rights (Lee 2009). Given the unsteady path for human rights within WHO, Director-General Margaret Chan began to consider shifting WHO human rights staff within the institution, leading to the 2012 launch, as addressed in chapter 6, of a gender, equity, and human rights approach to health.

CONCLUSION

The long evolution of human rights in WHO—in the development, implementation, and operationalization of human rights for public health—has created an imperative for human rights in WHO's current gender, equity, and human rights mainstreaming efforts. With the WHO Executive Board calling on the Secretariat to find more effective ways to mainstream its multiple cross-cutting priorities, WHO's 2012 strategy has sought to restructure the Secretariat to be equally responsive to gender, equity, and human rights—reinforcing the conceptual interconnectedness of these priorities through the establishment of WHO's Gender, Equity, and Rights (GER) Team. Building from WHO's work to establish a rights-based approach to global health, this GER approach is testing whether WHO can learn from the political history of human rights within the Secretariat, overcome the institutional challenges to human rights mainstreaming, and revitalize its human rights authority in global health governance.

REFERENCES

AFRO (African Regional Office), World Health Organization. 2012. "Resolution: health and human rights: current situation and way forward in the African region." 20 November. WHO Doc. AFR/RC62/R6.

Aginam, Obijiofor. 2014. "Mission (Im)possible? WHO as a 'Norm Entrepreneur' in Global Health Governance." In Law and Global Health, Current Legal Issues Volume 16, edited by Michael Freeman and Sarah Hawkes. Oxford: Oxford University Press.

Allen, Charles. 1950. "World Health and World Politics." International Organization 4: 27–43.

Basu, Sanjay. 2012. "Should We Propose a Global Nutrition Treaty?" *The Health Care Blog.* July 3. Available at: http://thehealthcareblog.com/blog/2012/07/03/should-we-propose-a-global-nutrition-treaty/.

Bayer, Ronald. 1991. "Public Health Policy and the AIDS Epidemic. An End to HIV Exceptionalism?" *New England Journal of Medicine* 324(21): 1500–1504.

Bok, Sissela. 2004. "Rethinking the WHO Definition of Health (Working Paper No. 17)." *Harvard Center for Population and Development Studies* 14(7) (on file with author).

Brown, Theodore, Michael Cueto, and Elizabeth Fee. 2006. "The World Health Organization and the Transition from 'International' to 'Global' Public Health." *American Journal of Public Health* 96(1): 62–72.

Bustreo, Flavia and Paul Hunt et al. 2013. *Women's and Children's Health: Evidence of Impact of Human Rights.* Geneva: World Health Organization.

Cabrera, Oscar and Lawrence O. Gostin. 2011. "Human Rights and the Framework Convention on Tobacco Control: Mutually Reinforcing Systems." *International Journal of Law in Context* 7(3): 285–303.

Candau, Marcolina Gomes. 1954. "WHO—Prospects and Opportunities: The Road Ahead." *American Journal of Public Health* 44(12): 1499–1504.

Candau, Marcolina Gomes. 1957. "Letter from M.G. Candau, Director-General, WHO, to Martin Hill, Deputy Under-Secretary for Economic and Social Affairs, U.N." 19 February (on file with author).

CESCR (Committee on Economic, Social and Cultural Rights). 2000. "General Comment No. 14: The Right to the Highest Attainable Standard of Health (Art. 12)." 11 August. E/C.12/2000/4.

Chisholm, Brock. 1951. "Letter from Brock Chisholm, Director-General, WHO, to H. Laugier, Assistant Secretary-General, U.N." January 12 (on file with author).

CIOMS (Council for International Organization of Medical Science). 1974. *Protection of Human Rights in the Light of Scientific and Technological Progress in Biology and Medicine.* Proceedings of a Round Table Conference Organized by CIOMS with the Assistance of UNESCO and WHO at WHO Headquarters in Geneva from 14–16 November. Geneva: World Health Organization.

Cook, Rebecca and Barnard Dickens. 2001. *Advancing Safe Motherhood through Human Rights.* Geneva: World Health Organization.

Daes, Erica-Irene. 1981. "The Individual's Duties to the Community and the Limitations on Human Rights and Freedoms under Article 29 of the Universal Declaration of Human Rights, report of the Special Rapporteur." 10 March. Doc. E/CN.4/Sub.2/432/Rev.2.

Dentico, Nicoletta and Nathan Ford. 2005. "The Courage to Change the Rules: A Proposal for an Essential Health R&D Treaty." *PLOS Medicine,* 2(2): 96–99.

Donnelly, Jack. 2003. *Universal Human Rights in Theory and Practice.* Ithaca: Cornell University Press.

Doull, James A. 1949. "Nations United for Health." In *Public Health in the World Today,* edited by James S. Simmons, 317–332. Cambridge, Mass.: Harvard University Press.

Dresler, Carolyn, Harry Lando, Nick Schneider, and Hitakshi Sehgal. 2012. "Human Rights-Based Approach to Tobacco Control." *Tobacco Control* 21(2): 208–211.

Evang, Karl. 1973. "Human Rights: Health for Everyone." *World Health* 3–11.

Eze, Osita C. 1979. "Right to Health as a Human Right in Africa." In *The Right to Health as a Human Right: Workshop, The Hague, 27–29 July 1978,* edited by René-Jean Dupuy. Alphen aan den Rijn, The Netherlands: Sijthoff and Noordhoff.

Fee, Elizabeth and Manon Parry. 2008. "Jonathan Mann, HIV/AIDS, and Human Rights." *Journal of Public Health Policy* (2008): 29(1): 54–71.

Garrett, Laurie. 1994. *The Coming Plague: Newly Emerging Diseases in a World Out of Balance.* New York: Penguin.

Gostin, Lawrence O. 2007. "A Proposal for a Framework Convention on Global Health." *Journal of International Economic Law* 10(4): 989–1008.

Gostin, Lawrence O. 2014. "Non-communicable Diseases: Healthy Living Needs Global Governance." *Nature* 511(7508): 147–149.

Gostin, Lawrence O. and Rebecca Katz. 2016. "The International Health Regulations: The Governing Framework for Global Health Security." *Milbank Quarterly* 94(2): 264–313.

Grad, Frank. 2002. "The Preamble of the Constitution of the World Health Organization." *Bulletin of the World Health Organization* 80(12): 981–982.

Gruskin, Sofia, Edward Mills, and Daniel Tarantola. 2007. "History, Principles, and Practice of Health and Human Rights." *The Lancet* 370(9585): 449–455.

Gunn, S. William. 1983. "The Right to Health through International Cooperation." In *Il Diritto alla Tutela della Salute: Acts of the International Colloquium on the Right to Health Protection,* 20–21. Torino, Italy.

Gutteridge, Frank. 1963. "The World Health Organization: Its Scope and Achievements." *Temple Law Quarterly* 37(1): 1–14.

Gutteridge, Frank. 1966. "Memorandum from F. Gutteridge, Chief of the Legal Office, WHO, to Milton P. Siegel, Assistant Director-General, WHO." October 27 (on file with author).

Hoffman, Steven, John-Arne Røttingen, and Julio Frenk. 2015. "International Law Has a Role to Play in Addressing Antibiotic Resistance." *Journal of Law, Medicine and Ethics* 43(2): 65–67.

Howell, B. 1958. "Memorandum from B. Howell, WHO, to M.P. Bertrand, WHO." In *Periodic Reports on Human Rights. Notes of Conversation with Mrs. Bruce of the U.N. Department of Human Rights—4 July 1958.* Ref. N64/180/5 (on file with author).

HRC (Human Rights Council). 2007. "Institution-building of the United Nations Human Rights Council." 18 June. Res. 5/1.

Humphrey, John P. 1957. "Memorandum from John P. Humphrey, Director, Division of Human Rights, U.N., to Philippe de Seynes, Under-Secretary for Economic and Social Affairs, U.N. 747th Meeting of the Third Committee." 31 January (on file with author).

Hunt, Paul. 2007. "Report of the Special Rapporteur on the right of everyone to the enjoyment of the highest attainable standard of physical and mental health." 17 January. Doc. A/HRC/4/28.

Hunt, Paul. 2017. "Configuring the UN Human Rights System in the 'Era of Implementation': Mainland and Archipelago." *Human Rights Quarterly* 39(3): 489–538.

Jablensky, Assen. 1977. "Racism, Apartheid and Mental Health." *World Health* 16–21.

Kastler, Florian. 2016. *Le rôle normatif de l'Organisation mondiale de la santé.* Doctoral Thesis. Paris, France: Université Paris Descartes/Université de Neuchâtel.

Kaul, P. M. 1956. "Letter from WHO Director of the Division of External Relations and Technical Assistance P.M. Kaul to UN Deputy Under-Secretary for Economic and Social Affairs Martin Hill." 26 September (on file with author).

Lakin, Alison Elizabeth. 2001. *The World Health Organisation and the Right to Health.* PhD Dissertation. London, England: King's College.

Lambo, Thomas Adeoye. 1974. "Letter from WHO Deputy Director-General T.A. Lambo to UN Under-Secretary-General for Political and General Assembly Affairs Bradford Morse." 16 April (on file with author).

Lambo, Thomas Adeoye. 1979. "Towards Justice in Health." *World Health* July: 2–5.

Leary, Virginia. 1988. "Health, Human Rights and International Law." *American Society of International Law Proceedings* 82: 121–141.

Lee, Kelly. 2004. "The Pit and the Pendulum: Can Globalization Take Health Governance Forward?" *Development* 47(2): 11–17.

Lee, Kelly. 2009. "Understandings of Global Health Governance: The Contested Landscape." In *Global Health Governance: Crisis, Institutions and Political Economy*, edited by Adrian Kay and Owain David Williams, 27–42. Hampshire: Palgrave Macmillan.

Litsios, Socrates. 1969. *A Programme for Research in the Organization and Strategy of Health Services.* Paper presented at the World Health Organization Director General's Conference in Geneva, Switzerland. June 25.

Magnusson, Roger. 2010. "Global Health Governance and the Challenge of Chronic, Non-Communicable Disease." *Journal of Law, Medicine and Ethics* 38(3): 490–507.

Mahler, Halfdan. 1973. "Born to be healthy: A message from Dr. H. Mahler, Director-General of the World Health Organization." Reprinted in Secretary-General's progress report. Doc. A/9133.

Mann, Johnathan. 1987. "Memorandum from GPA Coordinator J. Mann to Director-General H. Mahler." April 2 (on file with author).

Mann, Jonathan and Manuel Carballo. 1989. "Social, Cultural and Political Aspects: Overview." *AIDS* 3: S221–S223.

Meier, Benjamin Mason. 2005. "Breathing Life into the Framework Convention on Tobacco Control: Smoking Cessation and the Right to Health." *Yale Journal of Health Policy, Law and Ethics* 5(1): 137–192.

Meier, Benjamin Mason. 2010a. "Global Health Governance and the Contentious Politics of Human Rights: Mainstreaming the Right to Health for Public Health Advancement." *Stanford Journal of International Law* 46(1): 1–50.

Meier, Benjamin Mason. 2010b. "The World Health Organization, Human Rights, and the Failure to Achieve Health for All." In *Global Health and Human Rights: Legal and Philosophical Perspectives*, edited by John Harrington and Maria Stuttaford, 163–189. Oxford: Routledge.

Meier, Benjamin Mason. 2013. "Making Health a Human Right: The World Health Organisation and the United Nations Programme on Human Rights and Scientific and Technological Developments." *Journal of the Historical Society* 13(2): 195–229.

Meier, Benjamin Mason and Ana Ayala. 2014. "The Pan American Health Organization and the Mainstreaming of Human Rights in Regional Health Governance." *Journal of Law, Medicine and Ethics* 42(3): 356–374.

Meier, Benjamin Mason, Kristen Brugh, and Yasmin Halima. 2012. "Conceptualizing a Human Right to Prevention in Global HIV/AIDS Policy." *Public Health Ethics* 5(3): 263–282.

Meier, Benjamin Mason and William Onzivu. 2014. "The Evolution of Human Rights in World Health Organization Policy and the Future of Human Rights Through Global Health Governance." *Public Health* 128: 179–187.

Moon, Suerie, Jorge Bermudez, and Ellen 't Hoen. 2012. "Innovation and Access to Medicines for Neglected Populations: Could a Treaty Address a Broken Pharmaceutical R&D System?" *PLOS Medicine* 9(5): e1001218.

Mower, Alfred Glenn. 1985. *International Cooperation for Social Justice: Global and Regional Protection of Economic/Social Rights.* Westport, Conn.: Greenwood Press.

Muggli, Monique, Annie Zheng, Johnathan Liberman, Nicholas Coxon, Liz Candler, Kaitlyn Donley, and Patricia Lambert. 2013. "Tracking the Relevance of the WHO

Framework Convention on Tobacco Control in Legislation and Litigation through the Online Resource." *Tobacco Control* 23(5): 457–460.

Nygren-Krug, Helena. 2004. "Health and Human Rights at the World Health Organization." *Saúde e Direitos Humanos* 1(7): 13–18.

PAHO (Pan American Health Organization), 50th Directing Council. 2010. "Health and human rights." 31 August. Doc. CD50/12.

Pannenborg, Charles O. 1979. *A New International Health Order: An Inquiry into the International Relations of World Health and Medical Care*. Alphen aan den Rijn, The Netherlands: Sijthoff and Noordhoff.

Parran, Thomas. 1946. "Chapter for World Health." *Public Health Reports* 61: 1265–1268.

Riedel, Eibe. 2009. "The Human Right to Health: Conceptual Foundations." In *Realizing the Right to Health*, edited by Andrew Clapham and Mary Robinson, 21–39. Zürich: Rüffer and Rub.

Record, Catherine. 2007. "A Framework Convention on Alcohol Control." *The Lancet* 370(9605): 2101–2102.

Room, Robin. 2006. "International Control of Alcohol: Alternative Paths Forward." *Drug and Alcohol Review* 25(6): 581–595.

Roscam Abbing, Henriette. 1979. *International Organizations in Europe and the Right to Health Care*. Deventer, The Netherlands: Kluwer.

Sacks, Michael R. 1975. "Letter from WHO Co-ordination with other Organizations Chief Michael R. Sacks to UN Division of Human Rights Studies and Conventions Section Chief Henri Mazaud." 23 December. Ref. 4N64/372/3 (on file with author).

Samson, Mélanie. 2015. "Réflexions sur le rôle du droit dans la gouvernance de la santé mondiale." In *Mélanges en l'honneur de Michel Belanger—Modernité du droit de la santé*, edited by Emmanuel Cadeau, Eric Mondielly, and François Vialla, 117–134. Les éditions hospitalières, coll. Mélanges.

Sikkink, Kathryn. 1986. "Codes of Conduct for Transnational Corporations: The Case of the WHO/UNICEF Code." *International Organization*. 40(4): 815–840.

Stampar, Andrija. 1949. "Suggestions relating to the Constitution of an International Health Organization." *WHO Official Records* 9(1).

Tarantola Daniel. 2000. *Building on the Synergy between Health and Human Rights: A Global Perspective (Working Paper No. 8)*. François-Xavier Bagnoud Center for Health and Human Rights.

Taylor, Allyn L. 1991. *The World Health Organization and the Right to Health*. LLM Thesis. New York, New York: Columbia Law School.

Taylor Allyn L. 1992. "Making the World Health Organization Work: A Legal Framework for Universal Access to the Conditions for Health." *American Journal of Law and Medicine* 18(4): 301–346.

Torelli, Maurice. 1980. *Le Médecin et les Droits de L'homme*. Paris: Berger-Levrault.

UN (United Nations). 1945. "Charter of the United Nations." 24 October. UN Doc. 1 UNTS XVI.

UN (United Nations). 1950. *These Rights and Freedoms*. New York: UN Department of Public Information.

UN (United Nations). 1951. "Economic and Social Council (ECOSOC). Commission on Human Rights. Seventh Session." 27 April. UN Doc. E/CN.4/AC.14/2/Add.4.

UN (United Nations). 1968. *The United Nations and Human Rights*. New York: United Nations.

UN General Assembly. 1948. "Universal Declaration of Human Rights." 10 December. Resolution 217 A(III).

UN General Assembly. 1966. "International Covenant on Economic, Social and Cultural Rights." 16 December. Resolution 2200A (XXI).

UN General Assembly. 1987. "Prevention and Control of Acquired Immune Deficiency Syndrome (AIDS)." 26 October. UN Doc. A/RES/42/8.

UN Secretary-General. 1946. "Message to the 2nd Session of the Interim Commission of the WHO in Geneva, Switzerland." 6 November.

UN Secretary-General. 1968. "Measures and Activities Undertaken in Connection with the International Year for Human Rights." 24 September. UN Doc. A/7195.

UN Secretary-General. 1997. "Renewing the United Nations: A Programme for Reform." 14 July. UN Doc. A/51/950.

UNCHR (United Nations Commission on Human Rights), Office of the High Commissioner for Human Rights. 2002. "The right of everyone to the enjoyment of the highest attainable standard of physical and mental health." 22 April. UN Res. 2002/31.

van Boven, Theodore. 1979. "The Right to Health: Paper Submitted by the United Nations Division of Human Rights." In *The Right to Health as a Human Right: Workshop, The Hague, 27–29 July 1978*, edited by René-Jean Dupuy, 54–72. Alphen aan den Rijn, The Netherlands: Sijthoff and Noordhoff.

van Zile Hyde, Henry. 1953. "The Nature of the World Health Organization." *Public Health Reports* 68(6): 601–605.

Vignes, Claude-Henri. 1979. "Droit à la santé et coordination." In *The Right to Health as a Human Right: Workshop, The Hague, 27–29 July 1978*, edited by René-Jean Dupuy, 304–311. Alphen aan den Rijn, The Netherlands: Sijthoff and Noordhoff.

Volansky, Mark J. 2002. "Achieving Global Health: A Review of the World Health Organization's Response." *Tulsa Journal of Comparative and International Law* 10(1): 223–259.

WHA (World Health Assembly). 1970. WHA Res. 23.61.

WHA. 1977. "Health for All." WHA Res. 30.43.

WHA. 1988. "Avoidance of discrimination in relation to HIV-infected people and people with AIDS." 13 May. WHA Res. 41.24.

WHO (World Health Organization). 1946a "Constitution of the World Health Organization."

WHO. 1946b. "Draft of 'preamble' to the convention of the World Health Organization (submitted by the sub-committee). Minutes of the technical preparatory committee for the International Health Conference held in Paris from March 18 to April 5." Doc. E/H/PC/W/2, Annex 10.

WHO. 1946c. "Proceedings and Final Acts of the International Health Conference." *WHO Official Records* 2(67).

WHO. 1958a. *Report on the Fourteenth Session of the Commission on Human Rights.* 10 March–3 April (on file with author).

WHO. 1958b. *The First Ten Years of the World Health Organization.* Geneva: World Health Organization.

WHO. 1968. *The Second Ten Years of the World Health Organization.* Geneva: World Health Organization.

WHO. 1972. *Notes for the Record. Meeting with Mr. Marc Schreiber, Director, United Nations Division of Human Rights—Friday, 5 May 1972.* U.N. Doc. 4N64/372/1. (May 29, 1972) (on file with author).

WHO. 1973. *Interrelationships between Health Programmes and Socioeconomic Development.* Geneva: World Health Organization.

WHO. 1976. *Working paper by WHO to the Inter-Agency Meeting on the Implementation of the Human Rights Covenants.* Geneva: World Health Organization.

WHO. 1978. "Primary Health Care: Report of the International Conference of Primary Health Care." Alma-Ata, 6–12 September. USSR.

WHO. 1983. "Progress in Primary Health Care: A Situation Report." 10 January. WHO Doc. EB71/19.

WHO. 1987. *Global Strategy for the Prevention and Control of AIDS.* Geneva: World Health Organization.

WHO. 2000. "Meeting report, Second informal consultation on health and human rights: towards a WHO health and human rights strategy." 3–4 April. WHO Doc. HSD/GCP/June 2000.

WHO. 2003. *Framework Convention on Tobacco Control.* Geneva: World Health Organization.

WHO. 2005. *International Health Regulations.* Geneva: World Health Organization.

WHO. 2007. "Draft OHRCHR-WHO Joint Work Programme." 15 May (on file with author).

WHO. 2010. *Health and human rights newsletter (No. 2).* Available at: http://www.who.int/entity/hhr/information/Newsletter2010.pdf.

WHO. 2011. *Health and human rights newsletter (No. 3).* Available at: http://www.who.int/entity/hhr/information/newsletter_2011.pdf.

WHO Executive Board. 1951. "Collaboration with the Commission on Human Rights." 2 June. WHO Doc. EB8/39.

WHO FCTC (Conference of the Parties). 2007. "Guidelines for implementation of Article 8 of the WHO FCTC on protection from exposure to tobacco smoke." 6 July. Decision FCTC/COP2(7).

WHO FCTC (Conference of the Parties). 2010. "Guidelines for implementation of Article 12 of the WHO FCTC on education, communication, training and public awareness." 19 November. Decision FCTC/COP4(7).

WHO Liaison Office. 1959. "Memorandum from WHO Liaison Office with United Nations Director to WHO Deputy-Director General. Report on the Fifteenth Session of the Commission on Human Rights." 21 April (on file with author).

Wolff, Jonathan. 2012. *The Human Right to Health.* New York: W.W. Norton.

Zidar, Andraz. 2015. "WHO International Health Regulations and Human Rights: From Allusions to Inclusion." *The International Journal of Human Rights* 19(4): 505–526.

6

Mainstreaming Human Rights across WHO

REBEKAH THOMAS AND VERONICA MAGAR[*]

The World Health Organization (WHO) has long been criticized for its human rights efforts—for failing to hold states to account due to its political member state structure and its reliance on a privileged relationship with ministries of health. With a staff composed largely of medical and public health experts, for whom the language of rights remains unfamiliar, and an organization focused on providing technical and normative support, WHO is thought to be ill-equipped to make rights a core part of its activities. However, there are signs that this is changing. This chapter describes the efforts undertaken since 2013 to mainstream gender, equity, and human rights into WHO programs, policies, and practices.

Building from the historical development of human rights through WHO in chapter 5, Part I of this chapter reviews the different institutional processes that have been introduced to mainstream human rights across WHO. Part II looks at how principles of human rights (universality, equality and non-discrimination, accountability, participation, and empowerment) and the normative attributes of a right to health (availability, accessibility, acceptability, and quality) have found an increasing

* Several colleagues from WHO provided inputs and insights into their work. Our thanks go to them. We would also like to acknowledge the contributions of former and existing WHO staff who work tirelessly to mainstream gender, equity, and human rights at WHO, in particular, to members of the global GER network: Hala Abou Taleb, Britta Baer, Anjana Bhusan, Anna Coates, Cathy Cuellar, Sandra Del Pino, Adama Diop, Evelyn Finger, Theadora Koller, Eva Lustigova, Mary Manandhar, Davison Munodawafa, Åsa Nihlen, Isabel Aguire Yordi, and Gerardo Zamora. Thanks also to Priyanka Teeluck for assistance with citations and footnotes and to Cindy Chu Hupka. Our special thanks go to Flavia Bustreo for her visionary leadership and support for human rights mainstreaming across WHO.

Human Rights in Global Health. Benjamin Mason Meier and Lawrence O. Gostin.

resonance across a wide range of WHO programs through institutional main-streaming, evidence and data collection, and country support. Exploring how these principles and norms are informing and guiding the work of WHO, Part III looks at three aspects of human rights-based approaches and how these are being applied—enabling environments, a focus on marginalized populations, and ac-countability. Part IV examines two particular drivers of mainstreaming and their im-pact on translating rights into reality: the adoption of universal health coverage (as a flagship commitment and leadership priority of WHO) and the outcomes of the WHO Commission on the Social Determinants of Health. The chapter concludes by identifying elements of mainstreaming, exploring some of the challenges faced, and considering how these challenges might be overcome to secure the future of human rights in WHO.

I. STRUCTURING THE MAINSTREAMING INITIATIVE: AN INTEGRATED APPROACH TO GENDER, EQUITY, AND HUMAN RIGHTS

As part of the organizational reform that began under the World Health Assembly (WHA) (WHA 2011), efforts to mainstream human rights were revitalized in 2011 with the announcement by WHO Director-General Margaret Chan of a new Unit to support "a WHO in which each staff member has the core values of gender, equity and human right in his/her DNA" (WHO 2012b). This Unit would catalyze attention to gender, equity, and human rights (GER), linked to the social determinants of health throughout the Organization as cross-cutting priorities (WHO 2011c). The move was aligned with the three priorities of WHO reform:

1. to maximize efficiencies (managerial reform),
2. to address complex and intersecting inequalities in a more flexible and dynamic way (programmatic reform), and
3. to provide a unifying voice for the Organization to communicate its vision to other global actors in the field, including those in gender and human rights (governance reform) (WHO 2011b).

The decision to bring gender, equity, and human rights together has had impor-tant repercussions for the way human rights mainstreaming is undertaken at WHO. Drawing from three historically distinct but complementary fields, this approach provides multiple entry points for human rights principles and norms to take hold in public health while allowing WHO staff across different programs areas to navi-gate strategically through resistance to conventional or legal "rights discourse." The composition of the Unit also supports this organization-wide leveraging role, with the appointment of a senior-level "Team Leader" (reporting directly to the Assistant Director-General for Family, Women, Children and Adolescents Health) and three full-time technical staff (covering gender, equity, and rights).[1]

---

1. By comparison, previous mainstreaming efforts had relied upon a single technical officer supported by temporary staff and interns (Meier and Onzivu 2014).

The GER Unit is supported by regional focal points and nominated staff in each department across the six WHO clusters.[2] While accountability for mainstreaming these core values has been formalized in annual performance evaluations of GER network staff, the cluster leads, regional offices, and country heads are equally expected to ensure adequate resources and time allocations to deliver on this mainstreaming mandate (WHO 2011c).

While the reinforced structure of the GER Unit marked a positive development for human rights, the capacity of the new network remained incommensurate to its mainstreaming task. Many of the newly appointed regional GER focal points have inherited these more expansive responsibilities in addition to their existing job descriptions, and for most country office staff, the GER mandate comes on top of an already overflowing job description. The seniority, expertise, and location of these staff in the regional office organigrams also varies widely, directly affecting their ability to lead and influence the mainstreaming enterprise (WHO 2016a). GER focal points in the WHO Regional Office of the Americas (AMRO/PAHO), for example, sit in several different departments (Family, Gender and Life Course; Health Equity; and Legal Counsel), providing for robust and interlinked coverage of gender, health equity, and human rights and a unique engagement of the Legal Office (Meier and Ayala 2014). In other regions, however, GER coverage relies on a smaller core of one or two staff members, jointly responsible for all (and often several other) areas.

The design of the GER Unit relies heavily on the cluster-level, regional, and country office focal points, but often these staff have neither the time, capacity, nor influence to take gender, equity, and human rights forward within their offices. Even where commitment and dedication exist, these staff may not have specific training or expertise in these areas and require support from the GER Unit at both a technical and political leadership level. This has presented a challenge to the mainstreaming work of the GER Unit, and additional efforts are needed to strengthen and sustain capacity of these focal points while acknowledging and mitigating the effects of increased staff turnover resulting from WHO's staff mobility policy.[3]

II. CHARTING A ROADMAP FOR ACTION

The early days of the integrated GER mainstreaming initiative were characterized by a period of review to: determine existing expertise and capacity; assess political opportunities and commitments through a review of global strategies, action plans, and departmental work plans; and to repurpose tools and strategies to address gender, equity, and rights in a more intersecting manner (WHO 2016e).

2. As of August 2017, WHO had six organizational clusters: (1) the Director-General's Office, (2) General Management, (3) Family, Women's, and Children's Health, (4) Health Systems and Innovation, (5) HIV/AIDS, TB, and Malaria and Neglected Tropical Diseases, and (6) Noncommunicable Diseases and Mental Health. In 2016, the Director-General established a new program for Health Emergencies that is uniquely situated between regional and headquarters levels.

3. Under the new staff mobility policy, WHO staff members are expected to move periodically between offices, locations, and functions (WHO 2016g).

Simultaneously, efforts to clarify the conceptual linkages between gender, equity, and rights were initiated to make the case for and provide guidance on why and how a more blended approach to these areas would lead to a more transformative response to health (Blas 2014). These efforts culminated in the development of an overarching strategy, the Secretariat's "GER Roadmap for Action," proposing time-bound targets and dividing the GER Unit's work into three "strategic directions": (A) institutional mainstreaming, (B) evidence and data collection, and (C) country support (WHO 2015i).

A. Institutional Mainstreaming

Strategic Direction 1 of the GER Roadmap focuses on institutional mainstreaming, weaving considerations of gender, equity, and human rights into a range of mechanisms and processes through which WHO exercises its functions and also raising staff awareness of GER concepts and tools (WHO 2011b). Anchoring GER in the heart of WHO's work is critical to the success of the mainstreaming initiative, and the mainstreaming strategy proposed "minimum standards" to be met by all health programs. The development of common minimum standards for all program areas would clarify expected results, strengthen accountability, and enhance performance management across the Organization. Drawing inspiration from the United Nations (UN) system-wide Gender Mainstreaming Action Plan (UNSWAP 2012), the GER Unit devised a set of "GER criteria" that: called for specific analyses (of laws and policies and of gender and equity-based barriers); suggested actions to mitigate gender or equity-based vulnerabilities and reduce or remove barriers to health services while actively promoting the enjoyment of the right to health; and developed mechanisms to monitor and evaluate mainstreaming (WHO 2015g). These standards are rooted normatively in the right to health and health equity, including the right-to-health attributes of availability, accessibility, acceptability, and quality (AAAQ), as well as the fundamental human rights principles of non-discrimination, accountability, and participation (CESCR 2000).

The criteria have been employed as guidance to WHO program areas to encourage them to integrate gender, equity, and human rights into their work plans as part of the overall WHO Programme Budget.[4] The GER Unit benchmarked its own performance under the 2015 operational planning process, seeking a 20 percent increase in the number of GER criteria being implemented by WHO program areas by the end of 2017 (WHO 2015f).

The distribution of guidance on how to apply the GER criteria in two consecutive Programme Budgets (2016–2017 and 2018–2019) has provided space for greater consideration of these issues at the beginning of planning processes and ensured more consistent guidance and precise benchmarks for these efforts to facilitate accountability. It has also led to closer cooperation and engagement of the GER Unit with WHO program areas. These critical relationships are instrumental to brokering

---

4. The WHO Programme Budget clusters health areas into category networks that cut across the three levels of the organization. GER activities are listed under Category 3 (on promoting health across the life course) and integrated into and across other categories and program areas.

institutional support for gender-sensitive, rights-based, and equity-oriented efforts. In early 2017, the WHO Office of Internal Oversight proposed the incorporation of the GER criteria into annual audit processes to further routinize and monitor efforts to mainstream gender, equity, and rights across the Organization.

A 2015 pilot assessment of these GER minimum standards revealed that while no program area was meeting all of the GER criteria, at least five of the seven criteria were being more frequently integrated into work planning and operations, with the criteria more likely to be met in program materials published since 2010 (WHO 2016e).[5] However, this pilot assessment also showed that understanding of the content, relevance, and applicability of key human rights principles and their normative foundations still lagged far behind those of gender and equity, and that human rights operationalization did not follow any common approach (WHO 2016b). To address this, the GER Unit began work on an addendum to the GER criteria to unpack the normative human rights standards and practices for the implementation of human rights-based approaches to health. An internal consultation with staff from headquarters and regional and country offices led to the elaboration of a set of working definitions for the content of fundamental human rights principles and core attributes of the right to health, suggesting how these principles and norms could be practically applied and measured in health programming (2015g).

This translation of complex human rights standards into guidance for health programming offers a useful bridge between public health and human rights, particularly for public health practitioners less familiar with law and international frameworks. However, human rights experts have cautioned against an overly mechanistic "checklist approach" to operationalizing complex and indivisible human rights standards (WHO 2015g). Similarly, findings from fifteen country case studies across the WHO regions showed that identifying the separate core components of human rights-based approaches tends to spur a focus on only one or two of those elements, ignoring the crucial interdependence across these principles and norms (WHO 2015g). This ongoing struggle to accurately and consistently define human rights principles and norms and operationalize them into practical guidance highlights the need for further implementation research and knowledge translation on how to apply these criteria, and in what combination, to health programming.

Institutional mainstreaming has also sought to influence other core WHO functions such as norm-setting and guideline development, evaluation processes, communications, and staff development and training. Facilitated by support and leadership from the Guideline Review Committee Secretariat,[6] considerations of gender, equity, and rights are now an integral part of WHO guideline development processes, complemented by the presence of GER focal points on the Guideline Review Committee to ensure that WHO guidance is informed by and developed in a way

5. The criteria most often incorporated included: applying a right to health framework analysis of AAAQ; addressing barriers to marginalized populations and related equity targets; promoting UN recommendations on right to health; and disaggregating data by at least two stratifiers.

6. The Guideline Review Committee was established by the WHO Director-General in 2007 to ensure that WHO guidelines are of a high methodological quality and are developed through a transparent, evidence-based decision-making process.

that is compliant with human rights standards (WHO 2014d). A growing emphasis on equity and rights in global health discourse has also led to practical innovations for human rights incorporation, as seen in greater attention to the "values and preferences" of end users for HIV interventions (WHO 2017b), the use and "grading" of qualitative evidence to strengthen the inclusion of such evidence in shaping guidance (WHO 2015e), and the elaboration of tools for conducting systematic reviews that take into account gender and other health inequities (O'Neill et al. 2014). In a milestone 2014 publication, WHO's Reproductive Health and Research Department issued guidance on a "human rights-based approach to contraception," the first ever WHO guidance to explicitly acknowledge the intersection between health interventions (contraception) and the full enjoyment of human rights (WHO 2014a). Based on the growing number of requests for GER support to guideline development, interest in applying a human rights lens to guidelines has grown, although the limited development of capacity and expertise that cuts across both public health guideline development and human rights is still a major obstacle to scaling up of these efforts.

To enhance staff capacity to mainstream gender, equity, and human rights, all new WHO staff are provided an introductory briefing on GER mainstreaming objectives and requirements, with technical training on health inequality monitoring, as well as interactive e-learning modules on GER concepts, evidence, and practice in five of the six WHO regions (WHO 2016a). These specific orientations supplement other, more detailed programmatic training and capacity programs while underscoring an organizational commitment to these GER values as cross-cutting priorities.

While all these mainstreaming efforts have helped to sustainably embed human rights norms in WHO's functions, institutionalization remains a slow, complex, and precarious process—as dependent on funding as it is on both internal and external support. Furthermore, the positive opportunities generated by these efforts have led to increased demand for GER Unit support for the integration of gender, equity, and rights, requiring far more capacity than is currently available. Where there is a risk that the current opportunities and momentum for human rights might be missed, the commitment behind these efforts will need to be reinforced through specific budget allocations to fund staff resources and capacity-building, as well as robust political leadership internally and externally.[7]

B. Evidence and Data Collection

The second pillar of the GER Roadmap focuses on gathering and disaggregating data across different health indicators and "equity stratifiers" or dimensions of inequality—to trace inequalities in health. The 2030 Agenda for Sustainable Development confirmed the importance of disaggregating data—by income, sex, age, race, ethnicity, migratory status, disability, geographic location, or other

---

7. The WHO Programme Budget—which presents the Organization's expected deliverables and budget requirements for a renewable two-year period—tends to disadvantage cross-cutting areas from receiving budget allocations by requiring WHO program areas to identify a maximum of ten priorities for funding allocations. As a result, cross-cutting areas are largely sidelined from this process.

characteristics—as a means to better understand, monitor, and address health inequalities, inform policy decisions and resource allocations, and ensure no one is left behind (UN General Assembly 2014). The disaggregation of data has also been identified as a crucial aspect of rights-based approaches (OHCHR 2016), and is routinely raised by human rights monitoring bodies, as discussed in chapter 23, as a way to assess states' fulfillment of their obligations to progressively realize the right to health, particularly in monitoring the needs of the most marginalized populations (CESCR 2000).

As part of its GER mainstreaming strategy, WHO supports national and global capacity to monitor health inequalities through the standardization of data collection—disaggregated by common dimensions of inequality, including demographic, socioeconomic, or geographical factors—and the development of health inequality monitoring tools. This information is critical to states and other stakeholders to evaluate the impact of policies, programs, and practices on disadvantaged subpopulations (Hosseinpoor et al. 2015). The WHO Global Health Observatory now includes comparable health inequality data that is updated annually across ninety-four countries on reproductive, newborn, child, and adolescent health, disaggregated by education, economic status, place of residence (rural and urban), and sex (Ibid.).[8] WHO also now publishes reports on the state of inequalities across different health areas—including reproductive, maternal, newborn, child, and adolescent health (WHO 2015k) and vaccine coverage (WHO 2016d) in low- and middle-income countries. In water and sanitation, for example, global monitoring processes now measure improvements in terms of quality, safety, affordability, and accessibility of such services, and these data (reflective of the normative attributes of the human rights to water and sanitation) can be disaggregated by health quintile as well as rural/urban location to capture subnational disparities (de Albuquerque 2012; WHO 2017g).

Health inequality monitoring is crucial to assessing who is being left behind and provides greater transparency and accountability for state obligations, monitoring gaps in services and other barriers to access. However, while such data point to patterns of inequality, they are, by themselves, insufficient to understand the determinants of such inequalities, and must be complemented by other qualitative barrier analysis to understand "why" some subpopulations are neglected (Backman et al. 2008; OHCHR 2016). Complementing human rights analysis, WHO has developed qualitative barrier analysis tools, drawing on desk reviews, supply-side interviews (with providers and district health officers), and demand-side focus groups to help uncover the barriers that subpopulations face and the supply-side bottlenecks impacting equitable coverage (WHO 2012a; WHO 2015b).

C. Country Support

Building on the two pillars described above, the third strategic direction of the GER Roadmap focuses on national-level support to integrate gender, equity, and human

---

8. These data are also now available through software that provides an interactive display of the state of health inequalities, which states themselves can use to generate an overview of the state of health inequalities using national data (Hosseinpoor et al. 2016).

rights into national health policy and programming processes. The GER Unit has developed a comprehensive package of tools to support country efforts to integrate gender, equity, and human rights. These tools seek to: (1) identify who is being missed by health services and why; (2) strengthen national health plans and health system functions to target these gaps; and (3) strengthen health programs. A key pillar of this WHO support is an eight-step national review process, Innov8, that is designed to help member states and other national partners to assess national health policies, programs, and plans (WHO 2016e). Built on a "theory of change" model, a multidisciplinary review team conducts a detailed examination of health service inequities and other shortfalls in the realization of human rights and gender equality across various points in the national policy cycle and helps to guide decision makers to identify changes in programs that would address those inequities (Ibid.). Innov8 has been piloted in the American, Eastern Mediterranean, European, and Southeast Asian regions and applied to different national and subnational health programs, strategies, and activities (Ibid.). In Indonesia, for example, the resulting WHO recommendations led to the development of rights-based targets and indicators and strengthened capacity to scale up health inequality monitoring (WHO 2016f), while in Nepal, a review of the National Adolescent Development and Health Strategy has promoted community outreach in rural, remote, and slum areas; helped to broker increased district-level funds; and triggered a commitment to strengthen work across sectors to address the causes of (and enforce laws against) early marriage (WHO 2016e).

The national assessments are conducted in parallel with efforts to reinforce the capacity of WHO country offices to understand and promote gender, equity, and human rights in their work with national stakeholders.

III. MARKERS FOR A RIGHTS-BASED APPROACH

Building from the explicit mainstreaming efforts adopted by WHO to more routinely incorporate gender, equity, and human rights into the work of the Organization, human rights have been leveraged both explicitly and implicitly in a growing and increasingly diverse number of ways. Some program areas—HIV, mental health, and sexual and reproductive health—have engaged in multiple and strategic ways for a number of years with: human rights mechanisms (as discussed in chapter 21), Special Procedures mandate-holders (as discussed in chapter 22), the human rights treaty bodies (as discussed in chapter 23), and the Human Rights Council (HRC) (as discussed in chapter 24). Buffeted by formal international legal frameworks, these WHO efforts have served to crystallize human rights norms in these areas through interpretation of legal standards[9] or elaboration of technical guidance (UNGA 2014b). Indeed, the increasing convergence of the agendas of the HRC and WHO—on issues of migrant health, disabilities, aging, sexual and reproductive health, and more—provide evidence of the ever closer engagement between these fields. There are also new and emerging areas of

9. For example, as discussed in chapter 23, WHO has worked to interpret legal standards in the development of health-related general comments through the various human rights treaty bodies.

collaboration, such as climate change and aging, where the potential of strong legal and rights-based frameworks are being explored as indispensable to addressing equitably the health impacts of these issues. Indeed, WHO's efforts to ensure the inclusion of language supporting a right to health explicitly in the preamble of the Paris Declaration signaled the first ever adoption of rights-based commitments in a global environmental agreement (Blaiklock 2015).

However, there are also an increasing number of health programs that deploy key components of the rights-based approach to health without explicit reference to the human rights system or legal normative standards. To understand this implicit operationalization of human rights, we consider three unique and interrelated "markers" for rights-based approaches: (A) enabling legal environments, (B) marginalized populations, and (C) accountability—as illustrative of how human rights are being applied in WHO programs, policies, and practices.

A. Enabling Legal Environments

The law plays a central role in determining and protecting the human rights underlying health. Beyond the provisions of international human rights law, WHO member states have entered into two multilateral treaties, the Framework Convention on Tobacco Control (FCTC)[10] and the International Health Regulations (IHR),[11] both of which, as discussed in chapter 5, have explicitly human rights foundations. In recent years, both treaties have also endorsed explicitly rights-based provisions—as seen in the decision at the recent FCTC Conference of Parties calling for states parties to collaborate with UN human rights mechanisms (WHO 2016c).

Beyond international law, national law frames the governance of health systems, including the way services are organized and financed, the way health workers are trained and the conditions in which they are employed, the quality of health service provision, and more broadly, the protections from the spread of diseases or other public health risks (Clarke 2016). Law is increasingly being used in health policy and program design to frame health interventions and improve health outcomes, as seen in the regulation of road safety (WHO 2013c), food marketing (WHO 2010), mental health (WHO 2017i), sexual and reproductive health (WHO 2015j), and communicable disease control (WHO 2017c).

These national laws give meaning to international human rights standards. As human rights norms pertaining to health have evolved and been codified and

10. The WHO FCTC is the first global public health treaty. Negotiated under the auspices of WHO, it is an evidence-based treaty that reaffirms the right of all people to the highest standard of health. It was adopted by the World Health Assembly on May 21, 2003, and entered into force on February 27, 2005. It has since become one of the most rapidly and widely embraced treaties in UN history.

11. The IHR is an international legal instrument that is binding on 196 countries around the globe, including all the member states of WHO. The aim of the IHR is to help the international community prevent and respond to acute public health risks that have the potential to cross borders and threaten people worldwide, requiring countries to report certain disease outbreaks and public health events to WHO.

interpreted under international law, national laws in turn need to be reformed and implemented to give meaning to such international legal norms and to ensure safeguards and protections for human rights (WHO 2017a). With a dynamic pro- liferation of norm-setting by the UN human rights system in recent years, including general comments by human rights treaty bodies on sexual and reproductive health and the rights of adolescents (CESCR 2016; CRC 2016), the need to monitor the corresponding national legal environment has become a primary concern for health. To support this translation of global standards to health practice, WHO has piloted toolkits and methods to undertake law and policy assessments at the country level, en- gaging in participatory multi-stakeholder dialogues to identify how and where the law acts as a barrier to public health (WHO 2014c). Inversely, the law can also positively influence the design and delivery of services within health care settings, safeguarding the quality of those services to uphold human dignity—particularly for the most vul- nerable. Operationalizing the normative standards of the Convention of the Rights of the Child, for example, tools are being piloted to review the legal environment to en- sure quality of care for children under five (WHO, forthcoming). Influencing mental health, the Convention of the Rights of Persons with Disabilities has provided the basis for benchmarks and standards of care to be applied to mental health services, in particular, in institutionalized settings such as mental health facilities (WHO 2017i).

WHO's engagement in the development, evaluation, and implementation of public health laws continues to expand (WHO 2017a), and a 2014 review showed that the vast majority of WHO action plans include reference to the legal and policy context (Sridharan et al. 2014). Not only is the law now more widely understood within WHO, but exploring the enabling legal environments for health has provided entry points for the health sector to engage with other sectors—such as housing, education, trade, and human rights. In this context, WHO has also taken new approaches to support enabling legal environments under international law, as seen in chapter 17, where WHO filed an amicus brief concerning tobacco plain packaging in response to an investment treaty claim by Philip Morris against Uruguay before the World Bank's International Centre for Settlement of Investment Disputes (ICSID 2016). Although WHO's interventions were not framed in terms of rights, these actions are unprecedented in WHO practice. Arguably, a more robust legal approach to rights within WHO could lead to similar action where international legal claims concerning human rights are at stake.

In many cases, the growing acceptance of the law's role in health policy has resulted from recognition that health services may not meet the needs of the most marginalized in society, and this marginalization often begins outside the health sector's immediate sphere of influence, necessitating a multi-sectoral response to health in all policies (WHO 2013a). However, while this growing attention to the legal environment is promising, there remains a significant knowledge gap on the current state of laws that affect health—from constitutional provisions to national and subnational laws—that would need to be filled (Clarke 2016). Such efforts are time- and resource-intensive, but—as demonstrated by the mental health MiNDbank[12] initiative (WHO 2017f)

---

12. The WHO MiNDbank is an online platform providing access to international resources and national/regional level policies, strategies, laws, and service standards for mental health, substance

and the recently launched database on abortion laws globally (WHO HRP 2017)—
they are indispensable to greater transparency and action in line with both public
health evidence and human rights standards.

B. Marginalized Populations

Prioritizing the needs of the most marginalized is a key principle of rights-based
approaches, and a primary concern of efforts to reduce health inequities (Gruskin,
Bochego, and Ferguson 2010; Gwatkin and Urgo 2010). A focus on the rights
of marginalized populations was first articulated during the HIV response, as
chronicled in chapter 1, where advocates understood that the epidemic was rooted
in discrimination and marginalization—either in law, policy, or practice—that fed
inequalities toward key populations at risk of HIV, including men who have sex
with men, sex workers, and people who use drugs (Mann 2008). This platform was
instrumental to recognizing the inextricable linkages between public health and
human rights and to putting the needs of marginalized populations at the center of
health policy and program design and delivery.

In 2010, the attention of the global health community shifted from population-based
to equity-focused responses to health, driven by attention to the social determinants of
health that are rooted in social injustice—from poverty, to education, to housing.

The language of equity has in recent years provided a bridge to overcome the often
polarized positions among member states toward certain marginalized populations,
focusing on barriers to health while providing a space for consensus around principles of non-discrimination and universality that allows programs to reach these
populations without triggering further retrenchment by recalcitrant states (WHO
2013b). While the importance of employing explicitly rights-based language remains
critical—generating a platform for social and community mobilization and legal accountability that has no equivalent in health equity—the complementarity of equity
and rights is increasingly being acknowledged (Meier 2006). Marginalization can, as
discussed above, be at least partially determined by tracking health inequalities within
and across countries, which, in turn, help to reveal discriminatory laws, practices,
and power imbalances that underlie health outcomes. Health inequality data can further be triangulated with other measures, such as national laws as well as qualitative
reports (including submissions to the human rights system), to understand who is
being missed and which populations are most in need (Meier et al., 2017).

While technical-level health programming and policy increasingly focus on the
needs of the most marginalized, this often operates in parallel with discussions in
the WHO governing bodies, where disputes among member states can paralyze
discussions and set back technical progress considerably.[13] As a result, the WHO

---

abuse, disability, general health, noncommunicable diseases, human rights and development, children and youth, and older persons.

13. In 2013, a proposed agenda item to the WHO Executive Board on the health of lesbian, gay,
bisexual, transgender, and intersex persons was debated for more than six hours before being
removed from the agenda on procedural grounds.

Secretariat has historically, as reviewed in chapter 5, sought to navigate the divided opinions of its member states by looking to health-related evidence rather than "rights" to draw attention to marginalized populations. In other instances, WHO has engaged with other partners to mark its commitment to addressing the needs of marginalized populations, developing Joint Inter-Agency statements calling for an end to, among other things, discrimination against lesbian, gay, bisexual, transgender, and intersex (LGBTI) persons (WHO 2015c) or discrimination in health care settings (WHO 2017d).

Nonetheless, recent efforts also illustrate the tendency toward this explicit articulation of rights, with non-governmental advocates for tuberculosis, leprosy, adolescent health, disabilities, and other marginalized populations actively asserting the rights of their communities as core strategic levers of their work (WHO 2015e; WHO 2016h). In a recent governing body decision in the WHA, WHO member states framed the issue of migrant health in explicitly rights-based terms (WHA 2017).

C. Accountability

Enabling legal environments and attention to marginalized populations—as proxies for human rights—are meaningless unless paired with strong and transparent accountability mechanisms. Accountability for health has traditionally focused on health outcome indicators (e.g., maternal mortality, disease incidence, or service coverage), but there is a growing trend toward more diverse sources of information as well as more independent monitoring tools that can help to ensure that processes, as well as outcomes, of these interventions respect human rights standards (Hunt 2017).

The groundbreaking Commission on Information and Accountability for Women's and Children's Health (CoIA)—founded in 2010 as a follow-up to the UN Secretary-General's "Every Woman, Every Child" initiative—recommended that all countries establish and strengthen accountability mechanisms that are transparent and inclusive of all stakeholders (WHO 2011a). This recommendation was furthered by the independent Expert Review Group (iERG), which called for strengthening national human rights oversight mechanisms to improve accountability for women's and children's health (iERG 2014).[14]

Indeed, WHO can play a role in supporting member states in more formal accountability and review processes at the national and international levels, although the Organization has a long and somewhat varied history of engagement with human rights accountability mechanisms across its different programmatic areas (Acharya and Meier 2016). Where there is a specific treaty body examining a given health topic, as reviewed in chapter 23, WHO and its regional offices have found ways to engage actively and strategically to advance health, whether through monitoring states, developing general comments, or adjudicating claims (Meier and Ayala 2014). However, this engagement has yet to become a routine

---

14. The nine-member iERG is tasked with tracking progress on the CoIA's recommendations, including specifically on the flow (and transparency) of resources and results.

and institutionalized process. The GER criteria described above have sought to make such engagement a core part of WHO's work to mainstream human rights, identifying a number of entry points at the country, regional, and global levels for such accountability support—through ministries of health, joint submissions of UN country teams, and direct technical submissions as a UN entity (WHO 2015e).

Building on the momentum generated by the recent advent of the Universal Periodic Review (UPR) process, WHO has also engaged in, as analyzed in chapter 24, a more targeted effort to identify opportunities for engagement in this state-led review, whereby states review each other's human rights records—across all UN member states across all health-related human rights. The GER Unit is currently examining the potential relevance and impact of engaging with the UPR process to advance health, assessing both the extent to which health-related human rights emerge in member states reviews and the key characteristics of recommendations that have the greatest impact on public health (WHO, forthcoming). Providing a bridge for the provision of health-related data on health inequalities and barriers into the UPR reporting process, this WHO collaboration can facilitate UN efforts to hold states accountable for their obligations to progressively realize health-related human rights.

The UN human rights system has great potential to close the existing accountability cycle for global health, providing a periodic platform for inclusive national dialogue between state, non-state, and multi-sectoral partners across justice, education, health, and gender sectors. Focusing on aspects of accountability that are left out of other health monitoring efforts—considering rights-based considerations of enabling environments, empowerment, and agency—this potential for WHO human rights engagement was reiterated recently by the High-Level Working Group on the Health and Human Rights of Women, Children and Adolescents,[15] which called on member states to more "systematically report on health and human rights," noting that such reports are dependent on the availability of good and disaggregated data on health and its determinants, as well as assessments of the enabling environment within which health is delivered (WHO 2017e). While engagement with the human rights system as a whole poses a challenge to WHO's capacity and understanding of its mandate to engender accountability for health and human rights, the UPR presents a new opportunity to assuage that concern, premised as it is on states' voluntary engagement and familiarity with the process. Given this promise of rights-based accountability for global health, it will be necessary to understand the potential relevance of the UPR to WHO's core functions and find support from staff in the UN Development Group and Office of the UN High Commissioner for Human Rights to engage WHO in human rights capacity building.

---

15. The High-Level Working Group (HLWG) was a time-bound group of eminent persons—including former heads of state, lawyers, non-governmental organization leaders, human rights activists, academics, development partners, and health experts. The HLWG's mandate was to generate political leadership and commitment among stakeholders for an explicitly rights-based approach to implementing the Global Strategy on Women's, Children's and Adolescents' Health.

IV. FROM RIGHTS TO REALITIES

In reviewing the above shifts, two particular drivers have helped to engineer a shift from implicit to explicit adoption of a rights-based approach to health (1) the adoption of universal health coverage (UHC) as a flagship commitment and leadership priority of WHO, and (2) the WHO endorsement of findings from the Commission on the Social Determinants of Health (CSDH).[16]

Building from the commitment to primary health care in the 1978 Declaration of Alma-Ata, as reviewed in chapter 5, UHC marks a commitment to expanding quality health coverage for all without discrimination, starting with those furthest behind. UHC is premised on the idea that no one should be pushed into poverty as a result of health care expenditures, and that such health care should be of adequate quality, including the availability of a trained and equipped health workforce and relevant health commodities (UN General Assembly 2012). The commitment to UHC has grown from a concept of financial governance for health into a global health movement, supported in WHO by a growing coalition of government and civil society partners that seeks to ensure accountability for this agenda (World Bank 2014; WHO 2017h). This movement, which hinges upon the notion that UHC is an entitlement and not a privilege, has drawn attention to the decisive role of the law and regulation in ensuring equitable health financing, robust governance, transparency and accountability, and efficient and quality health service delivery (WHO 2014b). Although UHC focuses on the "health system building blocks" as a lens through which to assess public health law reforms, more recent efforts have identified the broader enabling laws that affect the achievement of UHC, providing a more comprehensive understanding of multi-sectoral barriers that affect access to health (Clarke 2016). Monitoring the implementation of UHC also includes a broad range of indicators that seek to monitor inequalities over time, in line with the progressive realization of the right to health and a focus on the most marginalized.[17] As a basis for addressing health under the new 2030 Agenda for Sustainable Development, UHC has become a key priority for the new WHO Director-General, Dr. Tedros Adhanom Ghebreyesus, who, as discussed in chapter 7, has held out UHC as a vehicle to advance a more equity-oriented and rights-based approach to health, centered on reaching the most marginalized (HHRJ 2017).

As UHC was emerging, WHO endorsed the findings of the CSDH, which proposed an unprecedented emphasis on the social conditions that affect health. Underlying the four dimensions of structural inequity identified by the CSDH— political, economic, social, and cultural—legislative influences (including laws governing employment, housing, and gender equality) were understood to be crucial

16. The CSDH was established by WHO in March 2005 to draw attention to the social determinants of health and create better social conditions for health, particularly among the most vulnerable people. The CSDH delivered its report to WHO in July 2008 and subsequently ended its functions.

17. In equity, the term "progressive universalism" is used to convey the intention to ensure that people who are poor gain at least as much as those who are better off—at every step of the way toward universal coverage (Gwatkin 2010).

to ensuring preventive action to mitigate the harmful effects of these inequities on health outcomes (CSDH 2008).

The recommendations of the CSDH mirror a dramatic epidemiological shift, as health morbidities and mortalities from preventable noncommunicable diseases (NCDs) such as obesity, heart disease, and cancer outpace those from communicable diseases such as HIV, TB, and malaria (Ibid.). This new epidemiological profile is inextricably linked to domestic legal systems and the regulation of diet, physical activity, food and beverage marketing, and tobacco consumption (Clarke 2016). Framed by advocates as a human rights issue, the NCD response boasts a growing community of partners willing to support action and hold states to account to prevent NCDs, drawing from legal experts, academia, civil society, patient groups, and parliamentarians (IDLO and UNITAF 2016). This movement can now also draw from national and international instruments—including the 2013–2020 WHO Global Action Plan for the Prevention and Control of NCDs and the 2003 WHO FCTC, as well as corresponding regional commitments and action plans to hold states accountable for action (WHO 2015d). The recognized interlinkages between NCDs and the law have recently given way to calls for a new global framework (IDLO 2014), with enhanced WHO legal expertise to support member states in addressing this aspect of the law (Burris 2010; Liberman 2017) and with WHO regional office support to identify priority legal interventions for NCDs (WHO 2015d).

Lastly, human rights have acquired new significance in the recent context of public health outbreaks and emergencies. The 2005 revision of the IHR governs WHO member state commitments to monitor, report on, and strengthen their public health outbreak capacity (WHO 2008). This WHO global health security framework was roundly put to the test during the recent Zika, Ebola, and flu outbreaks of recent years (Gostin 2014). These "public health emergencies of international concern" highlighted fault lines in the capacity of member states to implement the IHR framework and protect the health-related rights of their peoples (WHO 2015h). The limitations of the WHO response have raised an imperative for reform to build country core capacities for IHR monitoring, engaging a rights-based response to infectious disease prevention, detection, and response (Gostin and Katz 2016).

These shifts have created a structural foundation that has the potential to galvanize human rights mainstreaming efforts at WHO. They provide a rationale for sustained member state commitment and investment in efforts to institutionalize human rights more firmly across the Organization and introduce a host of multisectoral partners who could be drawn into this effort. The extent to which WHO takes advantage of this moment will determine the success of mainstreaming in the years to come.

CONCLUSION

The design of the GER mainstreaming effort and its "integrated" approach to gender, equity, and human rights is unique to the UN system. Operating at the frontier of mainstreaming to chart a new course in these historically distinct approaches, this WHO mainstreaming enterprise has tried to strike a balance between strength and flexibility, using different entry points to generate greater acceptance, understanding, and application of rights-based approaches to health.

Considerations of gender and equity and a stronger articulation of human rights have increasingly filtered into WHO's health policies, programs, and practices, demonstrated by increases in the adoption of explicit rights discourse, people-centered care, greater attention to the underlying determinants of health, an emphasis on the legal and regulatory environment, and a focus on accountability toward the most marginalized. In the absence of any clearer governing body mandate for human rights at WHO, the flexibility of this approach to human rights mainstreaming has allowed for a contextualized application of human rights standards to different health issues. Indeed, the lack of a common definition of "operational" human rights programming has perhaps allowed for practical interpretations of rights to flourish in implicit and explicit ways.

However, while this diffusion of rights-based norms and principles is seemingly effective as a sustainable strategy for the institutionalization of human rights, WHO must be cautious not to allow this diffusion of principles to lead to a dilution of rights. WHO is more engaged in advocacy than ever before—and the continuing shift to make WHO more operational at the country level will need to be matched by ever-more practical and sustained efforts to operationalize rights, monitor implementation, and measure the impact of human rights-based interventions on global health. The appointment of a new Director-General—who has voiced his unequivocal support for health as a human right, to be implemented through a commitment to UHC and a global agenda that seeks to improve global health equity—sends a positive signal of this determination.

REFERENCES

Acharya, Neha and Benjamin M. Meier. 2016. "Facilitating Accountability for the Right to Health: Mainstreaming WHO Participation in Human Rights Monitoring." *Health and Human Rights Journal.* April 28. Available at: https://www.hhrjournal.org/2016/04/facilitating-accountability-for-the-right-to-health-mainstreaming-who-participation-in-human-rights-monitoring/.

Backman, Gunilla, Paul Hunt, Rajat Kholsa, Camila Jaramilla-Strouss, Belachew Mikuria Fikre, Caroline Rumble, David Pevalin [et al.]. 2008. "Health systems and the Right to Health: An Assessment of 194 Countries." *The Lancet* 372: 2047–2085.

Blaicklock, Alison. 2015. "After Paris: Hope and Fears for Justice and a Healthy Climate." *Health and Human Rights Journal.* December 22. Available at: https://www.hhrjournal.org/2015/12/after-paris-hope-and-fears-for-justice-and-a-healthy-climate/.

Blas, Erik. 2014. "Equity, Human Rights, Gender and Social Determinants Unifying Platform/Framework" (on file with author).

Burris, Scott, Alexander C. Wagenaar, Jeffrey Swanson, Jennifer K. Ibrahim, Jennifer Wood, and Michelle M. Mello. 2010. "Making the Case for Laws that Improve Health: A Framework for Public Health Law Research." *The Milbank Quarterly* 88: 169–210.

CESCR (Committee on Economic, Social, and Cultural Rights). 2000. "CESCR General Comment No. 14: The Right to the Highest Attainable Standard of Health (Art. 12)." 11 August. Doc. E/C.12/2000/4.

CESCR (Committee on Economic, Social, and Cultural Rights). 2016. "General Comment No. 22 (2016) on the right to sexual and reproductive health (article 12 of the International Covenant on Economic, Social and Cultural Rights)." UN Doc. E/C.12/GC/22. March 4. Geneva: United Nations. https://www.escr-net.org/resources/general-comment-no-22-2016-right-sexual-and-reproductive-health.

Clarke, David. 2016. "Law, Regulation and Strategizing for Health." In *Strategizing National Health in the 21st Century: A Handbook*, Chapter 10. Geneva: World Health Organization.

CRC (Committee on the Rights of the Child). 2016. "General Comment No. 20 (2016) on the Implementation of the rights of the child during adolescence." 6 December. UN Doc. CRC/C/GC/20.

CSDH (Commission on Social Determinants of Health). 2008. *Closing the gap in a generation: health equity through action on the social determinants of health, Final Report of the Commission on Social Determinants of Health.* Geneva: World Health Organization.

de Albuquerque, Catarina. 2012. *On the Right Track: Good practices in Realising the Rights to Water and Sanitation.* Geneva: United Nations. Available at: http://www.ohchr.org/Documents/Issues/Water/BookonGoodPractices_en.pdf.

Gostin, Lawrence O. 2014. *Global Health Law.* Cambridge: Harvard University Press.

Gostin, Lawrence O. and Rebecca Katz. 2016. "The International Health Regulations: The Governing Framework for Global Health Security." *The Milbank Quarterly* 94(2): 264–313.

Gruskin, Sofia, Dina Bochego, and Laura Ferguson. 2010. "'Rights-based Approaches' to Health Policies and Programmes: Articulations, Ambiguities, and Assessment." *Journal of Public Health Policy* 31(2): 129–145.

Gwatkin, Davidson R. and Alex Ergo. 2010. "Universal Health Coverage: Friend or Foe of Health Equity?" *The Lancet* 377(9784): 2160–2161.

HHRJ (Health and Human Rights Journal). 2017. "Dr. Tedros Promises WHO Reform with Human Rights at the Core." *Health and Human Rights Journal.* May 23. Available at: https://www.hhrjournal.org/2017/05/dr-tedros-promises-who-reform-with-human-rights-at-the-core/.

Hosseinpoor, Ahmad R., Nicole Bergen, and Anne Schlotheuber. 2015. "Promoting Health Equity: WHO Health Inequality Monitoring at Global and National Levels." *Global Health Action* 8 (1). Available at: https://www.ncbi.nlm.nih.gov/pmc/articles/PMC4576419/.

Hosseinpoor, Ahmed R., Devaki Nambiar, Daniel Reidpath, and Zev Ross. 2016. "Health Equity Assessment Toolkit (HEAT): Software for Exploring and Comparing Health Inequalities in Countries." *BMC Medical Research Methodology* 16: 141.

Hunt, Paul. 2017. "Configuring the UN Human Rights System in the 'Era of Implementation': Mainland and Archipelago." *Human Rights Quarterly* 39 (3): 489–538.

ICSID (International Centre for Settlement of Investment Disputes). 2016. "Philip Morris Brands SARL, Philip Morris SA and Abal Hermanos SA vs. Oriental Republic of Uruguay. Award. ICSID Case No. ARB/10/7." Available at: http://www.italaw.com/sites/default/files/case-documents/italaw7417.pdf.

IDLO (International Development Law Organization). 2014. *Human rights-based approaches and domestic legal responses to NCDs: Lessons learned, Report.* The Hague, Netherlands: International Development Law Organization.

IDLO and UNIATF (UN Inter-Agency Task Force on the Prevention and Control of Noncommunicable Diseases). 2016. *Meeting Report, Thematic session on law and the prevention and control of noncommunicable diseases.* New York: International Development Law Organization and UNITAF.

iERG (Independent Expert Review Group). 2014. *Every Woman, Every Child: A Post-2015 Vision, Third Report of the independent Expert Review Group in Information and Accountability for Women's and Children's Health*. Geneva: World Health Organization.

Liberman, Jonathan. 2017. "Building a Law and NCDs Workforce: A Necessity for Global Cancer and NCD Prevention and Control." *Journal of Cancer Policy* 12: 72–74.

Mann, Jonathan. 2008. "HIV/AIDS and Human Rights." *Journal of Public Health Policy* 29(1): 54–71.

Meier, Benjamin M. 2006. "Employing Health Rights for Global Justice: The Promise of Public Health in Response to the Insalubrious Ramifications of Globalization." *Cornell International Law Journal* 39(3): Article 13.

Meier, Benjamin M. and Ana Ayala. 2014. "The Pan American Health Organization & the Mainstreaming of Human Rights in Regional Health Governance." *Journal of Law, Medicine and Ethics* 42(3): 356–374.

Meier, Benjamin M. and William Onzivu. 2014. "The Evolution of Human Rights in World Health Organization Policy and the Future of Human Rights through Global Health Governance." *Public Health* 128(2): 179–187.

Meier, Benjamin M., Marlous De Milliano, Averi Chakrabarti and Kim Yuna. "Accountability for the Human Right to Health through Treaty Monitoring: Human Rights Treaty Bodies & the Influence of Concluding Observations", Global Public Health (2017).

OHCHR (Office of the United Nations High Commissioner for Human Rights). 2016. *A Human Rights Approach to Data, Leaving No One Behind in the 2030 Development Agenda: Guidance Note to Data Collection and Disaggregation*. Available at: http://www.ohchr.org/Documents/Issues/HRIndicators/GuidanceNoteonApproachtoData.pdf.

O'Neill, Jennifer, Hilary Tabish, Vivian Welch, Mark Petticrew, Kevin Pottie, Mike Clarke, Tim Evans [et al.]. 2014. "Applying an Equity Lens to Interventions: Using PROGRESS Ensures Consideration of Socially Stratifying Factors to Illuminate Inequities in Health." *Journal of Clinical Epidemiology* 67(1): 56–64.

Sridharan, Sanjeev, Joanna Maplazi, Apurva Shirodkar, Emma Richardson, and April Nakaima. 2016. "Incorporating Gender, Equity, and Human Rights into the Action Planning Process: Moving from Rhetoric to Action." *Global Health Action* 2014(9).

UN General Assembly. 2012. "Global health and foreign policy." 14 March. UN Doc. A/RES/67/81.

UN General Assembly. 2014. "Fundamental Principles of Official Statistics." 29 January. UN Doc. A/RES/68/261.

UN General Assembly. 2014b. "Technical guidance on the application of a human rights-based approach to the implementation of policies and programmes to reduce and eliminate preventable mortality and morbidity of children under 5 years of age." Report of the Office of the UN High Commissioner for Human Rights. June 30. A/HRC/27/31.

UNSWAP. 2012. *UN System-wide Action Plan for Implementation of the CEB United Nations System-wide Policy on Gender Equality and the Empowerment of Women*. New York: United Nations.

WHA (World Health Assembly), 64th Session. 2011. WHA64/2011/REC/1.

WHA (World Health Assembly), 70th Session. 2017. "Promoting the health of refugees and migrants." 17 May. Doc. A70/24.

WHO (World Health Organization). 2008. *International Health Regulations 2005*. Geneva: World Health Organization.

WHO. 2010. *Set of recommendations on the marketing of foods and non-alcoholic beverages to children*. Geneva: World Health Organization.

WHO. 2011a. *Keeping Promises, Measuring Results*. Commission on Information and Accountability for Women's and Children's Health.

WHO. 2011b. *Resolutions and Decisions of the Executive Board at the Sixty-Fourth World Health Assembly, in Geneva, Switzerland on May 16–24*. Geneva: World Health Organization. Available at: http://apps.who.int/gb/ebwha/pdf_files/WHA64-REC1/A64_REC1-en.pdf.

WHO. 2011c. *WHO Internal Document Mainstreaming Gender, Equity and Human Rights in the work of WHO*. Geneva: World Health Organization (on file with authors).

WHO. 2012a. *Barriers and facilitating factors in access to health services in the Republic of Moldova*. Copenhagen: WHO Regional Office for Europe.

WHO. 2012b. *World Health Assembly 2012: Gender, Equity and Human Rights at the core of the health response*. Available at: http://www.who.int/hhr/news/wha_newslr_eng.pdf.

WHO. 2013a. *The Helsinki Statement on Health in All Policies*. Available at: http://www.who.int/healthpromotion/conferences/8gchp/statement_2013/en/.

WHO. 2013b. *Provisional Agenda of the 133rd Executive Board (Annotated)*. Geneva: World Health Organization. Available at: http://apps.who.int/gb/ebwha/pdf_files/EB133/B133_1_annotated-en.pdf.

WHO. 2013c. *Strengthening Road Safety Legislation: A practice and resource manual for countries*. Geneva: World Health Organization.

WHO. 2014a. *Ensuring human rights in the provision of contraceptive information and services: Guidance and recommendations*. Geneva: World Health Organization.

WHO. 2014b. *Health Systems Governance for Universal Health Coverage: Action Plan*. Geneva: World Health Organization.

WHO. 2014c. *Reproductive, maternal, newborn and child health and human rights: A toolbox for examining laws, regulations and policies*. Geneva: World Health Organization.

WHO. 2014d. *WHO Handbook for Guideline Development—Second Edition*. Geneva: World Health Organization.

WHO. 2015a. *Applying a Human Rights Based Approach to Health Policy-making and Programming: A Draft Synthesis Report of 15 case studies*. Geneva: World Health Organization (on file with authors).

WHO. 2015b. *Barriers and facilitating factors in access to health services in Greece*. Copenhagen: WHO Regional Office for Europe.

WHO. 2015c. *Ending violence and discrimination against lesbian, gay, bisexual, transgender and intersex people*. Available at: http://www.who.int/hiv/pub/msm/mrnt_LGBTI_Statement_ENG.pdf?ua=1.

WHO. 2015d. *Framework for Action to implement the United Nations Declaration on Noncommunicable diseases including indicators to assess country progress by 2018*. Available at: http://applications.emro.who.int/docs/Framework_action_implement_UN_political_declaration_NCD_October_2015_EN.pdf?ua=1.

WHO. 2015e. *Health worker roles in providing safe abortion care and post-abortion contraception*. Geneva: World Health Organization.

WHO. 2015f. *Programme Budget 2016–2017*. Geneva: World Health Organization.

WHO. 2015g. *Report for the World Health Organization Health and Human Rights at the WHO; Expert views on draft principles and criteria* (on file with author).

WHO. 2015h. *Report of the Ebola Interim Assessment Panel.* Geneva: World Health Organization.

WHO. 2015i. *Roadmap for action, 2014–2019: Integrating equity, gender, human rights and social determinants into the work of the WHO.* Geneva: World Health Organization.

WHO. 2015j. *Sexual health, human rights and the law.* Geneva: World Health Organization.

WHO. 2015k. *State of inequality: Reproductive, maternal, newborn and child health.* Geneva: World Health Organization.

WHO. 2016a. *A Foundation to Address Equity, Gender and Human Rights in the 2030 Agenda: Progress in 2014–2015.* Geneva: Switzerland.

WHO. 2016b. *GER pilot assessment Gender, Equity and Human Rights Review of WHO Programmes (2014–15).* Geneva: World Health Organization (on file with authors).

WHO. 2016c. "International cooperation for implementation of the WHO Framework Convention on Tobacco Control (FCTC), including on human rights." Decision adopted at the Conference of Parties to the WHO FCTC, 7th Session. November 12. Doc. FCTC/COP7(26). Available at: http://www.who.int/fctc/cop/cop7/FCTC_COP7_26_EN.pdf?ua=1.

WHO. 2016d. *State of inequality: Childhood Immunization.* Geneva: World Health Organization.

WHO. 2016e. *The Innov8 approach for reviewing national health programmes to leave no one behind.* Geneva: World Health Organization.

WHO. 2016f. *The Innov8 review of the national neonatal and maternal health action plans in Indonesia.* Geneva: World Health Organization (forthcoming).

WHO. 2016g. *WHO Geography Mobility Policy.* Geneva: World Health Organization. Available at: http://www.who.int/employment/WHO-mobility-policy.pdf.

WHO. 2016h *WHO Global Leprosy Strategy 2016–2020.* Geneva: World Health Organization.

WHO. 2017a. *Advancing the right to health: the vital role of the law.* Geneva: World Health Organization.

WHO. 2017b. *Consolidated guideline on sexual and reproductive health and rights of women living with HIV.* Geneva: World Health Organization.

WHO. 2017c. "International Health Regulations." *World Health Organization.* Accessed August 9, 2017. Available at: http://www.who.int/ihr/elibrary/legal/en/.

WHO. 2017d. *Joint United Nations statement on ending discrimination in health care settings.* Available at: http://www.who.int/mediacentre/news/statements/2017/discrimination-in-health-care/en/.

WHO. 2017e. *Leading the realization of human rights to health and through health: Report of the High-Level Working Group on the Health and Human Rights of Women, Children and Adolescents.* Geneva: World Health Organization.

WHO. 2017f. "MiNDbank: More Inclusiveness Needed in Disability and Development." *World Health Organization.* July 30. Available at: http://www.emro.who.int/mental-health/mnh-news/who-mindbank.html.

WHO. 2017g. *Progress on Drinking Water, Sanitation and Hygiene: 2017 Update and SDG Baselines.* Geneva: World Health Organization and the United Nations Children's Fund (UNICEF).

WHO. 2017h. "Universal Health Coverage Partnership." Accessed August 9, 2017. Available at: http://uhcpartnership.net/.

WHO. 2017i. *WHO Quality Rights: Transforming services, promoting rights.* Available at: http://www.who.int/mental_health/policy/quality_rights/QRs_flyer_eng_2017. pdf?ua=1.

WHO. Forthcoming. "Assessment toolkit for rights-based national legal and regulatory frameworks in support of improved quality of care for children" (on file with authors).

WHO HRP (World Health Organization Human Reproduction Programme). 2017. "Global Abortion Policies Database." Accessed August 9, 2017. Available at: http://www. who.int/reproductivehealth/topics/unsafe_abortion/global-abortion-policies/en/.

World Bank. 2014. "500+ organizations launch global coalition to accelerate access to Universal Health Coverage." *The World Bank.* December 12. Available at: http:// www.worldbank.org/en/news/press-release/2014/12/12/500-organizations-global-coalition-accelerate-access-universal-health-coverage.

7

The Future of Human Rights in WHO

FLAVIA BUSTREO, VERONICA MAGAR, RAJAT KHOSLA,
MARCUS STAHLHOFER, AND REBEKAH THOMAS*

The founding Constitution of the World Health Organization (WHO) supports the right to health in its preamble. While WHO's mission is explicitly rights-based, translating this commitment into policy and programs has proven complex, with rights frequently reduced to conversations about international treaties, monographs, and normative standards that struggle to change the reality on the ground.

Two trends are emerging that set the scene for a more robust future for human rights in WHO. First, the 2030 Agenda for Sustainable Development (2030 Agenda) has ushered in an era where measuring and addressing the inequalities that undermine health, including the drivers of exclusion and inequality, is now mandated, leading to a deliberate and prioritized focus on those left behind. Second, human rights standards, processes, and principles are "coming of age" through an increasingly practical operationalization of human rights—beyond public declarations and statements and into public health policy and practice.

While encouraging, these trends will only galvanize the change they promise if WHO takes a firmer and more formal step toward a human rights-based approach to health. This chapter proposes three major shifts through which:

1. WHO formalizes its role in advancing the right to health and human rights through the adoption of a resolution on the realization of health

* The authors would like to thank the following for their indispensable expert reviews of this chapter: Pascale Allotey, Judith Bueno de Mesquita, Kate Gilmore, Paul Hunt, Lucinda O'Hanlon, and Francisco Songane. Several colleagues from WHO also provided inputs and insights into the work and future of WHO, and our thanks go to them: Christopher Dye, Shyama Kuuvilla, Mary Manandhar, Agnes Soucat, and Derek Walton. Special thanks go to Priyanka Teeluck for assistance with citations and footnotes and to WHO staff Cindy Chu Hupka for her support and patience.

as a human right and as a means to achieve human rights ("to health and through health");

2. WHO consolidates and reinforces its collaboration with the United Nations (UN) human rights system at the global and country level, its associated monitoring mechanisms, and the UN Human Rights Council (HRC); and

3. WHO generates evidence that human rights are not only fundamental, but also instrumental, to human health and well-being, challenging the perception that rights-based approaches have little or no added value.

Part I examines how, against the backdrop of the 2030 Agenda, human rights are increasingly being incorporated into WHO's work, implicitly and explicitly paving the way for a bolder endorsement and operationalization of rights in the future. In considering the ways in which human rights are being advanced at WHO, Part II identifies four "markers" of rights-based approaches: universality and attention to the most marginalized, participation and empowerment, non-discrimination, and accountability. Building from this, Part III lays out a vision for how these gains can be sustained and advanced through the adoption of a resolution on human rights, a stronger leadership role for WHO at the helm of global governance and closer partnership with human rights actors at the intersection of global public health and human rights, and the development of an evidence base to demonstrate the impact of human rights on public health.

I. THE ADVENT OF THE SUSTAINABLE DEVELOPMENT GOALS: AN AGENDA FOR HEALTH AND HUMAN RIGHTS?

Grounded in international human rights law, and principles of universality, equality, and non-discrimination, the 2030 Agenda represents a seismic shift toward a more holistic, equitable, and rights-based agenda (Donald 2016b; McInerney-Lankford 2017; Forman, Ooms, and Brolan 2015). Whereas the prior Millennium Development Goals (MDGs) focused on specific health outcomes such as maternal or child mortality or incidence of HIV, TB, or malaria, the health-related goals of the post-2015 Sustainable Development Goals (SDGs) focus on health and well-being for all, at all ages, in all settings, including humanitarian and fragile settings. The specific health goal, SDG 3, addresses all major health priorities[1] and centers around a unifying concept of "universal health coverage" (UHC), which stands as a prerequisite for all the health targets. SDG 3 is also linked to and dependent on the other goals—including climate change, gender equality, and poverty—mirroring the "indivisibility" of human rights, whereby progress toward one goal cannot be achieved or sustained without progress toward the others.[2] The SDGs are both more universal and more equity-focused than the predecessor MDGs—targeting

---

1. These health priorities in the SDGs include: sexual, reproductive, maternal, newborn, child, and adolescent health; communicable, noncommunicable, and environmental diseases and cancers; and access for all to safe, effective, quality, and affordable medicines and vaccines.

2. For example, SDG 3 links specifically to SDG targets: 2.2 (end all forms of malnutrition), 4.7 (knowledge and skills for sustainable development), 5.3 (eliminate all harmful practices, including

unfair and unjust differences across low-, middle-, and high-income settings—with a specific goal on reducing inequalities, as well as a call for more disaggregated data to ensure that "no one is left behind" (UN General Assembly 2015, para. 48).

The explicitly rights-based underpinnings of the 2030 Agenda have been re-enforced by UN agency heads in a "Statement of Commitment on equality and non-discrimination," through which UN entities have committed to tackling equality and non-discrimination through a Shared Action Framework, as well as integrated as "core programmatic principles" of UN Development Assistance Frameworks (UN 2016). WHO echoed this commitment to the equity-focused and rights-based character of the 2030 Agenda when, reporting to its own Executive Board in January 2017, the WHO Secretariat identified human rights and equity mainstreaming as one of six "instruments of change" needed to achieve the SDGs (WHO Executive Board 2016).

The ambitious, holistic, and indivisible nature of the 2030 Agenda has been recognized as having profound implications for global health. The inclusion of almost all WHO program areas under SDG 3—linked to more inclusive, people-centered health systems and UHC—acknowledges that the siloed, program-focused strategies of the past are counterproductive to achieving comprehensive health and well-being (WHO 2015b). The SDGs, as discussed in chapter 14, put health governance and multi-sectoral action at the center of health efforts, requiring closer collaboration between the health sector and other fields such as trade, migration, and income inequality. They place accountability for results squarely back with member states through a country-focused review process that looks beyond aggregate figures to examine disaggregated data on inequalities.

As the overarching directive for actors in international health and development, the SDG agenda has "radical potential" to advance health and human rights in the years to come (Donald 2016b). While some analysts have critiqued the extent of this commitment—noting that the 2030 Agenda does not adopt human rights in any substantive or consistent way across the goals and omits any formal legal obligations or accountability mechanisms beyond voluntary national reviews (Donald 2016a, Hawkes and Buse 2016; Williams and Blaiklock 2016)—WHO can play a crucial a role in ensuring that the agenda lives up to its rights-based foundations by placing human rights at the heart of its support for the health-related goals.

II. ADVANCING HUMAN RIGHTS-BASED APPROACHES AT WHO

The new 2030 Agenda for Sustainable Development comes at a time when human rights-based approaches (HRBAs) are "coming of age" (Bustreo and Hunt 2013). WHO's new Director-General, Tedros Adhanom Ghebreyesus, has argued convincingly that:

WHO's work is about serving people, about serving humanity. It's about serving people regardless of where they live, be it in developing or developed

female genital mutilation), 5.6 (universal access to sexual and reproductive health and reproductive rights), 6.1 (access to drinking water), 6.2 (access to sanitation), 7.1 (access to modern energy services), 9.5 (enhance scientific research/increase number of research and development workers), 11.6 (air quality and municipal waste), 13.1 (resilience to natural disasters), and 16.1 (reduce violence and related death rates).

countries, small islands or big nations, urban or rural settings. It's about serving people regardless of who they are. Poor or rich, displaced or disabled, elderly or the youth. Most importantly, it's about fighting to ensure the health of people as a basic human right (WHO 2017d).

The 2003 UN Common Understanding of HRBA—discussed in chapter 3 and including core principles on universality, participation, accountability, and attention to the most marginalized[3]—is increasingly guiding public health strategies at WHO through a more flexible and integrated approach to gender, equity, and rights. In 2011, the Organization officially endorsed a combined programmatic approach to mainstreaming the cross-cutting priorities of gender, equity, and human rights (GER) into all areas of its work (WHO 2011a). While this GER mainstreaming is examined in more depth in chapter 6, this integrated approach acknowledges the complex reality of health inequities and the limitations of siloed modes of inquiry and analysis that are insufficient, and even counterproductive, to WHO efforts to leave no one behind. Focusing on intersecting inequities draws on group-based inequalities (Lenhardt and Samman 2015) while exploring how different forms of marginalization overlap, layering disadvantage upon disadvantage within such groups (Mills 2015; Stuart 2016).

For WHO, this combined approach provides a pragmatic strategy to overcome the fatigue associated with a narrow emphasis on either gender or human rights mainstreaming and reduces duplication of efforts and resource expenditures. It further provides multiple entry points for human rights, whether through equity, gender equality, or social justice. The flexibility of this approach has allowed WHO program areas to more easily navigate through the political and ideological differences of WHO member states while remaining faithful to core human rights principles. The new space opened up by this GER approach is paving the way for a greater operationalization of practical rights-based approaches through adherence to fundamental human rights principles of universality and attention to the most marginalized, participation, non-discrimination and equality, and accountability.

A. Universality and Attention to the Most Marginalized

UHC is an important contributor to, albeit not synonymous with, the realization of the right to health (Ooms et al. 2014; Ooms and Hammonds 2015), seeking to ensure that health systems meet the needs of all, so that "all people have access, without discrimination, to nationally determined sets of promotive, preventive, curative, and rehabilitative basic health services and essential, safe, affordable, effective and quality medicines, without financial hardship" (UN General Assembly 2012, para. 10). A central tenet of UHC is its emphasis on the poor, vulnerable, and marginalized segments of the population. WHO's commitment to UHC was driven by a concern for greater equity across and within countries and is consistent with the notion that human rights require universal access to health.

3. The 2003 Common Understanding details the core human rights principles to include universality, non-discrimination and equality, participation, and accountability (UNDG 2003).

This determination to achieve UHC has led to increasing attention at WHO to the specific vulnerabilities of particular populations and to the multiple and intersecting barriers they face in accessing health services. Prioritizing the inequities that disadvantage these groups, "progressive universalism" has been coined as a strategy to guide the allocation of resources in line with the right to health (Gwatkin and Ergo 2010; WHA 2016a). The emphasis on equity under SDG target 17.8 requires that states improve data collection to identify those in situations of vulnerability—including older populations, women and children, people with disabilities, and migrants—and reallocate resources accordingly. To some human rights scholars, the potential of UHC to realize the right to health is so great that it has been greeted as "[o]ne of the most hopeful global health policy developments in recent years" (Chapman 2016, 283).

While initially associated only with financial arrangements to support health systems, the UHC target under SDG 3 also emphasizes the quality of care delivered by those systems, focused on more people-centered, integrated, and equitable services that put the needs of people and communities, not diseases, at the center of health systems and empower people to take charge of their own health (WHA 2016b). A people-centered framework looks beyond the way that health services are delivered, addressing the ways in which services are received, perceived, and affect human dignity (UN General Assembly 2015; WHO 2014b; WHA 2016b; WHO 2017a; WHO 2017e; Every Woman, Every Child 2017a).

Where global health and human rights scholars once critiqued "organizational resistance to legal discourse" within WHO (Meier and Onzivu 2014, 179), UHC is also galvanizing a newfound interest within WHO on the role of laws in structuring enabling environments for UHC across the building blocks of health systems[4] and through social determinants of health, including social, gender, and cultural norms that are harmful to the realization of rights (Magnusson 2017). WHO has developed legal diagnostic tools to ensure supportive legal environments for sexual and reproductive health and rights (WHO 2014a), mental health (WHO 2012), the environment (WHO 2017b), and noncommunicable disease, with indicators being developed to monitor the extent to which legislative environments provide protections and safeguards against health vulnerability (WHO 2016b; Every Woman, Every Child 2016).

B. Participation

Participation of communities and other civil society organizations is a core and fundamental principle of the rights-based approach, as articulated in the 2003 Common Understanding of HRBAs (UNDG 2003). Participation of civil society is not only a powerful vehicle to bring human rights claims into health (de Albuquerque 2012), but it is also a well-established practice in some specific program areas, such as the HIV/AIDS response, which, as discussed in chapter 13,

---

4. In 2007, WHO proposed a framework describing health systems in terms of six core components or "building blocks": (1) service delivery; (2) health workforce; (3) health information systems; (4) access to essential medicines; (5) financing; and (6) leadership/governance.

has been driven forward by social mobilization and grassroots advocacy. Such participatory approaches have contributed to some of the greatest achievements in health in recent decades, such as the scale up and provision of antiretroviral treatment. Increasingly, the participation of civil society has become more routine in other health areas—including TB, noncommunicable diseases (NCDs), mental health, emergencies, water and sanitation, and women's, children's, and adolescents' health; such participation is practiced throughout the policy cycle, expanding the previously more narrow construction of community involvement to support or supplement health service delivery (CSDH Civil Society Report 2007). With this shift toward more people-centered and integrated health care under the UHC movement, the "free, active and meaningful" participation of civil society is also understood as crucial to health system service design and delivery to make such services "more socially relevant and responsive to the changing world" (WHO 2008 ix).

Within WHO itself, innovative and dynamic consultative mechanisms and platforms are being set up to enable and facilitate civil society contributions to strategy development and policy design across global strategies—for HIV (WHO 2016a), TB (WHO 2015d), mental health (WHO 2013b), UHC (WHO 2016e), and reproductive, maternal, newborn, child, and adolescent health (WHO 2016d). Furthermore, these initiatives are expanding their reach to more grassroots levels— as seen in the "Youth Engage" initiative, ensuring participation at subnational, national, and global levels (WHO 2016f).

Empowerment is a key corollary of participation, requiring that those participating have the information, voice, and agency to engage (Potts 2008). Cognizant of this, WHO's Adolescent and Youth Constituency for women's, children's, and adolescents' health recently launched a new mentorship program for adolescents and young people to build their capacity to participate across a number of key skillsets such as advocacy, resource mobilization, and accountability (PMNCH 2017). Direct collaboration with affected communities in conducting implementation research is further helping to ensure that change is driven by the voices of those for whom programs are designed (Luckow et al. 2017).

C. Non-Discrimination and Equality

Non-discrimination and equality are fundamental principles of international human rights law and essential to the exercise and enjoyment of economic, social, and cultural rights, including health. Discrimination—be it direct, indirect, formal (in law and policy), or substantive—has been prohibited under international law, yet discrimination continues to act as a barrier to good health, whether on the basis of health, gender, ethnicity, age, or other status (CESCR 2016).

The HIV/AIDS response has catalyzed action and awareness of the linkages between discrimination and health, but efforts to redress discrimination in and around health are expanding beyond HIV, with WHO leading global movements to eliminate disrespect and abuse in maternity care (WHO 2015e), fight agism (WHA 2016c), and end discrimination in mental health (WHO 2012). In 2015, in spite of polarization among member states, the WHO Secretariat joined calls to end discrimination against lesbian, gay, bisexual, transgender, and intersex (LGBTI) persons (WHO 2015f). More recently, WHO and UNAIDS issued a joint UN statement to end discrimination toward marginalized and stigmatized populations in health care settings (WHO 2017c). Non-discrimination is also being prioritized in global and national action plans, such as the NCD Global Action Plan (WHO 2013a), the End TB Strategy (WHO 2015d), and the recently approved Global Leprosy Strategy, which includes an entire pillar dedicated to ending discrimination through the repeal of discriminatory laws and the promotion of inclusive laws and policies (WHO 2016c). Beyond these political commitments, lessons from Ebola and other disease outbreaks such as Zika have led WHO to better understand and mitigate the impact of stigma and discrimination on affected populations and to address long-term stigma toward survivors of disease through participatory intervention design, recruitment of staff specializing in anthropological and ethnographic approaches, and support for community engagement (WHO 2015a; PAHO 2017).

While these efforts are significant, there is a need for WHO to better capture and address dynamic and intersecting forms of discrimination over time and place that occur across axes of age, sex, sexual orientation, disability, ethnicity, migrant, and socioeconomic status. There are ongoing WHO efforts to understand how discrimination in health care is a sign of more systemic problems within societies—related to capacity, resources, and culture, including gender inequalities—but these are still poorly understood (WHO 2017e). WHO can bring together these efforts into a more coherent strategy to end discrimination, including through stronger evidence of patterns and manifestations through which intersecting inequalities affect health and accountability.

D. Accountability

Meaningful multi-stakeholder participation and citizen engagement is of particular importance in ensuring accountability, which is integral to rights-based approaches to development (UNDG 2003; Potts 2008). Given this rights-based imperative for accountability, SDG 16.7 calls for "responsive, inclusive, participatory, and representative decision-making at all levels" to strengthen transparency and accountability in the context of good governance (UN General Assembly 2015).

A landmark WHO initiative in recent years to conceptualize and strengthen multi-stakeholder accountability for health has been the work of the Commission on Information and Accountability for Women's and Children's Health (CoIA). Launched in 2010 under the auspices of the Every Woman, Every Child strategy, the CoIA—which included eleven current presidents, prime ministers, and ministers, as well as other prominent leaders in global health and civil society—adopted an explicitly human rights-based interpretation of accountability that recognizes three distinct components of effective accountability:

1. monitoring (providing critical and valid information on what is happening, and how much is spent, where, on what, and for whom),
2. review (analyzing data on health outcomes and whether "pledges, promises and commitments" have been kept), and

3. remedial action (taking actions to put things right, as far as possible) (WHO 2011b; Williams and Hunt 2017).

Among its ten recommendations, the CoIA called for the establishment of a nine-member independent Expert Review Group (iERG), hosted by WHO, to report to the UN Secretary-General to track progress on the CoIA's recommendations, including on the flow (and transparency) of resources and results (iERG 2012; 2013; 2014; 2015). The iERG's successor, the Independent Accountability Panel (IAP), appointed in 2015 by the UN Secretary-General, went further and, drawing explicitly on international human rights law, extended the "monitor, review, and act" accountability framework to include "remedy" though national and international mechanisms (IAP 2016). Bringing together various global and national accountability mechanisms, a Unified Accountability Framework was adopted to unite the diverse stakeholders and elements to ensure accountability at all levels (IAP 2016). This tripartite conceptualization of accountability marks a groundbreaking shift in the way accountability is understood, moving beyond monitoring to include a more structured process that includes independent review and remedial actions (Hunt 2017).

WHO also engages at times with the UN human rights system to facilitate rights-based accountability through: special procedures thematic reports or country visits (as discussed in chapter 22); human rights treaty bodies (as discussed in chapter 23); and, to a lesser extent, the Universal Periodic Review (UPR) (as discussed in chapter 24). While some WHO departments have worked with partners in the UN human rights system to provide closed public health briefings, this engagement is still largely on the margins of WHO's work. There is significant potential for WHO to more systematically initiate country dialogue and constructive engagement with member states on their obligations to realize health-related human rights, but this will require stronger support from the WHO legal office, senior management, and heads of country offices if it is to be mainstreamed across the Organization.

The incorporation of all these human rights principles into WHO's work has the potential to profoundly reframe the importance and impact of human rights in global health, yet there are also more deliberate and explicit efforts underway to bring health and human rights closer together. Building on existing and enhanced collaboration in recent years with the Office of the UN High Commissioner for Human Rights (OHCHR), including the elaboration of joint WHO/OHCHR technical guidance on maternal and under-five mortality and morbidity (HRC 2014),[5] the Director-General of WHO and the High Commissioner for Human Rights agreed in May 2016 to convene a High Level Working Group (HLWG) on the Health and Human Rights of Women, Children and Adolescents, composed of eminent persons from the Elders,[6] former heads of state, lawyers, non-governmental organizations, human rights activists and academics, development partners, and

---

5. In 2009, the HRC adopted by consensus a historic resolution on preventable maternal mortality and morbidity and human rights, triggering a process that led to the preparation of technical guidance on the application of a human rights-based approach to reduce maternal mortality and morbidity.

6. The Elders are an independent group of global leaders working together for peace and human rights (WHO 2016d).

health experts. The HLWG's mandate was to generate political leadership and commitment among stakeholders for an explicitly rights-based approach to implementing the Global Strategy on Women's, Children's and Adolescents' Health (Every Woman, Every Child 2015).

REALIZING THE RIGHT "TO HEALTH AND THROUGH HEALTH"

The HLWG was established in 2016 to deliver recommendations on how to advance the firmly rights-based Global Strategy for Women's, Children's and Adolescents' Health. The resulting report was presented to both the World Health Assembly and the HRC (the first report ever to go before both bodies). The HLWG called for the realization of rights "to health and through health" to express the idea that good health not only depends on the right to health but is also a prerequisite for realizing other rights (Every Woman, Every Child 2017a). The HLWG cautioned stakeholders that a failure to promote and protect the health and human rights of women, children, and adolescents would continue to hinder efforts to achieve the goals and targets of the SDGs (Every Woman, Every Child 2017b). In nine recommendations, the HLWG report calls for all actors—especially governments—to reaffirm their commitment to universal values of health, dignity, and human rights for all and to champion the cause of women's, children's, and adolescents' health and rights through action, advocacy, and activism:

HLWG's 9 Goals

1. Uphold the right to health in national law;
2. Establish a rights-based approach to health financing and universal health coverage;
3. Address human rights as determinants of health;
4. Remove social, gender, and cultural norms that prevent the realisation of rights;
5. Enable people to claim their rights;
6. Empower and protect those who advocate for rights;
7. Ensure accountability to the people for the people;
8. Collect rights-sensitive data; and
9. Report systematically on health and human rights (Every Woman, Every Child 2017a).

While the HLWG marks a groundbreaking moment in the history of WHO and OHCHR collaboration, translating these rights-based commitments into practice will nonetheless require significant operational shifts in the way that WHO carries out its core functions.

III. SHIFTS REQUIRED FOR THE FULL REALIZATION OF HEALTH-RELATED RIGHTS

For WHO to assume a greater role in advancing the right to health, three shifts are needed:

1. WHO needs to reaffirm its Constitutional commitment to the right to health by adopting a clear political and operational mandate, formalized in

an action-oriented resolution on the realization of human rights to health and through health.

2. WHO should use its position and leadership at the helm of global governance to pursue a more strategic collaboration with partners at the intersection of global public health and human rights—united by a shared vision, adherence to universal principles, and common strategies of application.

3. WHO must continue to demonstrate the impact of human rights on public health, providing evidence and results to policymakers on the practical reality of rights-based decision-making while reiterating the fundamental importance of human rights.

A. A Resolution on the Realization of Human Rights "to Health and through Health"

While the WHO Constitution remains the normative bedrock of the Organization and the voice of its commitment to the right to health, WHO's operational priorities are set through its five-year Global Programme of Work, biannual Programme Budget, and work plans and decisions made by the Organization's governing body at the annual World Health Assembly (WHA) of member states. More than sixty previous WHA resolutions have discussed health and human rights (Meier 2017), but the Organization has never adopted an explicit resolution endorsing WHO's role to support human rights for global health, limiting the degree to which human rights are taken up in the programmatic work of the Organization.

A WHA resolution on the realization of human rights "to health and through health" would:

1. Facilitate state accountability for the rights-based aspects of health under the SDGs,
2. Provide operational guidance and criteria on the application of rights-based approaches, and
3. Issue a clear political statement of WHO's mandate under the right to health and rights-based approaches.

1. FACILITATE STATE ACCOUNTABILITY FOR THE RIGHTS-BASED ASPECTS OF HEALTH UNDER THE SDGs

A WHA resolution would complement the existing country review mechanisms of the SDGs, enhancing accountability for the rights-related aspects of health under the 2030 Agenda. Annual reviews of progress through reports to the WHA could include specific rights-based health indicators, disaggregated by the different grounds of discrimination prohibited under international law (Hunt 2015; UN 2016). These reviews would provide interim reporting time frames on health-related SDG commitments and encompass a more detailed scope to monitor and report to the annual WHA. The resolution could also be used to report against progress toward health-related goals as part of the UPR process (Every Woman, Every Child 2017a).

2. PROVIDE OPERATIONAL GUIDANCE AND CRITERIA FOR THE APPLICATION OF RIGHTS-BASED APPROACHES

The 2003 Common Understanding of HRBA sought to provide guidance on what human rights standards mean for development programming, but the rights-based approach has struggled to find resonance among WHO's largely technical programs, leading to a divergence in the understanding and application of rights-based practices within WHO (Meier and Onzivu 2014). A resolution on the realization of human rights "to health and through health" could draw from existing technical guidance on HRBAs—particularly from the fields of sexual, reproductive, maternal, newborn, and child health, HIV/AIDS, or mental health (WHO 2012)—to translate human rights norms and principles into operational rights-based programming and WHO practice for health. The resolution could further include specific criteria for HRBAs to health, facilitating internal accountability for such practices.

3. PROVIDE A CLEAR POLITICAL STATEMENT OF WHO'S MANDATE UNDER THE RIGHT TO HEALTH AND RIGHTS-BASED APPROACHES

Although human rights principles are increasingly guiding WHO's programmatic and policy work, efforts to expand rights-based approaches are often limited by staff resistance to issues or interventions deemed political, even when the implications for health are clear and the relevant human rights standards are codified under international law. A WHA resolution would clarify WHO's role as an organization bound by, and committed to, human rights, requiring WHO to exercise its coordinating authority at the intersection of health and human rights. This would include closer cooperation on such matters with the UN human rights system—at the global and country level. It would send a strong message to WHO staff that they have both a duty and a mandate to support the realization of human rights in public health.

There is already WHO precedent for such a resolution, as noted in chapter 5, with resolutions on health and human rights having been adopted in the WHO American Regional Office (AMRO) in 2010 and African Regional Office (AFRO) in 2012 (PAHO 2010; AFRO 2012). In AMRO, the adoption of the resolution legitimized strong Pan American Health Organization (PAHO) leadership on human rights and closer collaboration with the regional human rights system, leading to documented successes across a number of technical areas (Meier and Ayala 2014) and paving the way for subsequent resolutions on the human rights of vulnerable populations, including the health-related human rights of LGBTI persons (PAHO 2013). Yet, in both regions, reviews to assess progress under these resolutions have tended to look either at structure and process reforms (e.g., the number of treaties ratified, awareness of international health frameworks, and discriminatory laws (Motari and Kirigia 2016)) or at quantifiable health outcomes, without looking at the relationship between the two. A new global resolution would do well to draw from recent experiences in exploring the intersection between health, gender, equity, and human rights, laying out specific rights-based health measures to be taken by states and introducing targeted health indicators to facilitate accountability for these measures.

Adopting a resolution explicitly endorsing a rights-based approach to health is in many ways indispensable to institutionalizing a strong and consistent human rights focus within WHO in the years to come, securing the gains of the past and acting as a bulwark against the uncertainties of the present. The enduring purview of WHA resolutions would ensure that states are bound to make progress in integrating a rights perspective regardless of the political shifts that may occur. While many might argue that the time is ill-suited to antagonize those who are uncomfortable with rights—fearing that such a resolution might further polarize and paralyze debate—now is precisely the time to create certainty for human rights in global health.

B. Leveraging Leadership and Partnership at the Intersection of Health and Human Rights

Achieving this ambitious shift requires institutionalizing closer collaboration between WHO and OHCHR to jointly leverage the full weight of existing health and human rights infrastructure and engage actors inside and outside of the UN human rights system to forge a "web of accountability" for human rights in global health (Donald and Way 2016). This collaboration will require two shifts: (1) stronger alignment and coordination between the WHA and the HRC, and (2) greater engagement by WHO with the UN human rights system's accountability mechanisms.

1. Stronger Alignment and Coordination between the WHA and HRC

In his report ten years ago, Paul Hunt, then UN Special Rapporteur on the right of everyone to the enjoyment of the highest attainable standard of physical and mental health, argued for human rights to be mainstreamed more effectively in WHO, and at the same time, stressed that the right to health must be given due attention and equal weight to other civil and political rights before the HRC (HRC 2007).

Since that time, WHO has built and sustained relationships with human rights movements and mechanisms in a variety of different thematic areas—particularly where there exist specific human rights frameworks or conventions. The WHO Director-General has addressed the HRC on multiple occasions over the past decade, underlining the importance of the rights-related aspects of maternal mortality, family planning, climate change, migration, mental health, and medicines. However, with a few notable exceptions, such as the adoption of technical guidance on the prevention of maternal and under-five mortality and morbidity (HRC 2014), the WHA and the HRC still operate largely in parallel to each another, working on different time frames, engaging different sectoral representatives (ministers of health and justice or foreign affairs, respectively), and abiding by different rules of engagement.

A resolution on human rights "to health and through health," proposed above, could provide the foundation for a more formal and strengthened partnership between the WHA and the HRC. The resolution could be submitted for endorsement by both governing bodies, cementing a unified political vision and an operational partnership across global health and human rights institutions and partners. Furthermore, it would engage a more diverse set of sectoral partners to address global health, an ambition long acknowledged as key to addressing social determinants of health (CSDH 2008). Working closely with the HRC would also allow the WHO Secretariat to support its member states in implementing their health-related human rights obligations, working under WHO's normative authority to provide guidance on what can be done to remedy and redress rights-based shortcomings in health.

2. GREATER WHO ENGAGEMENT WITH HUMAN RIGHTS MECHANISMS

The convergence between health and human rights will require more routine engagement of WHO with the broad constellation of "human rights mechanisms" in the UN human rights system—including the special procedures mandate holders, human rights treaty bodies, and the UPR.

WHO has a long history of collaboration with UN special procedures, as discussed in chapter 22, most notably with the Special Rapporteur on the right to health. Since the establishment of that mandate,[7] the Special Rapporteur has helped shape the contours of the right to health, seeking WHO counsel in examining specific health topics through the "prism" of human rights—including on neglected tropical diseases (ECOSOC 2006), access to medicines (HRC 2013), and mental health (ECOSOC 2006). The proliferation of special procedures mandates in recent years for a range of determinants of health has also led health to be regularly raised in the thematic and country reviews of UN rapporteurs and experts in areas as diverse as water and sanitation, food, the environment, as well as those covering specific countries and populations, such as independent experts on indigenous populations, migrants or displaced peoples, older persons, and people with disabilities (ECOSOC 2005). However, these special procedures mandate-holders tend to be little known outside of the human rights field, and there are too few examples of how their reports have been used effectively by WHO country staff to support health ministries in addressing the human rights issues raised (UNDG 2015). Further limiting collaborations, not once in the sixteen years of the UN special procedures mandate on health has the Special Rapporteur been invited to present to the WHA—a remarkable absence given the relevance of that UN mandate (Nolan, Freedman, and Murphy 2016).

As described in earlier sections of this book, a number of WHO program areas have engaged extensively with different UN human rights treaty bodies, supporting state monitoring and treaty interpretation, including in the milestone General Comment 14 of the UN Committee on Economic, Social and Cultural Rights that laid out the parameters of the right to health (CESCR 2000). WHO has provided inputs into country submissions to those bodies, submitted technical briefs, and delivered statements to the treaty bodies (Nygren-Krug 2013). Like the Special Procedures, the treaty bodies, as discussed in chapter 23, are an important feature of the UN human rights accountability system, and WHO has a recognized role in supporting the reporting, implementation, and follow-up on the recommendations issued by these bodies (UN General Assembly 2014).

---

7. The mandate of the Special Rapporteur on the right of everyone to the enjoyment of the highest attainable standard of physical and mental health was originally established by the Commission on Human Rights (now the Human Rights Council) in April 2002.

However, efforts to ensure more systematic WHO engagement with these treaty bodies are often thwarted by: (1) capacity and resource constraints (particularly at the country level, where staff cover multiple program areas), (2) an uncertain WHO mandate to work outside of its special relationship with ministries of health, and (3) a lack of evidence or appreciation of the value added to global health by the UN human rights system (Acharya and Meier 2016). As a result, the impact of these treaty bodies has been limited to those country offices or program areas with a demonstrated commitment or tactical interest in engaging them rather than a system-wide process of engagement.

Whereas treaty body authority is limited to those states parties that have ratified the underlying human rights treaty, the UPR applies universally to all UN member states and provides a basis, as discussed in chapter 24, to engage the range of health-related human rights. Although the UPR has tended to focus on a narrow set of health outcomes, and its recommendations are often framed in such broad terms that implementation is difficult to monitor (Hunt 2017), WHO has sought to strengthen engagement with the UPR as part of its GER mainstreaming strategy (WHO 2015c). To this end, WHO is working with the University of Essex to examine the potential of the UPR to advance global health, building an evidence base on the effective use of the UPR mechanism and raising staff awareness on the potential for supporting health through human rights (WHO, forthcoming).

These efforts to mainstream engagement in human rights monitoring processes find resonance in the recommendations of the HLWG and underlie progress toward the SDGs (Every Woman, Every Child 2017a). Only by placing a greater emphasis on health and rights at the highest levels of these different bodies, including a more deliberate effort to discuss health using human rights accountability mechanisms, will health be addressed as the pressing human rights issue that it is.

C. Demonstrating Evidence of Impact of Human Rights on Health while Reiterating the Fundamental Importance of Human Rights

Human rights offer a universal set of standards against which to assess progress in both quantitative and qualitative terms and a clear moral, political, and legal imperative to respect, protect, and fulfill these rights. But there has also been a growing interest in recent years to find and demonstrate "evidence of impact" of HRBAs—with this public health evidence thought to be the key to unlocking deeply entrenched cynicism and resistance to human rights by health practitioners and policymakers (Gruskin 2006; Meier 2017).

To address this empirical imperative, WHO and partners published a ground-breaking 2013 Monograph, in which the authors reviewed four country case studies (Nepal, Italy, Malawi, and Brazil) to assess the impact of rights-shaped approaches to women's, children's, and adolescents' health. The Monograph identified policies and interventions for women's and children's health that had been explicitly shaped by HRBAs and found in each case that the influence of human rights had contributed positively to health outcomes (Bustreo et al. 2013). Where the Monograph acknowledged the paucity of existing evidence and research in the field, and the lack of effective tools and measures to turn "plausible conclusions" into compelling evidence, the authors suggested using multidisciplinary, mixed-method research to trace causality between laws, policies, and programs and health impacts, calling for a high-level platform for policy dialogue where policymakers could share experiences and best practices in applying human rights-based approaches to health (Ibid.).

Behind this agenda, there remain divergent views around the precise application of HRBAs to different health contexts, hindering efforts to identify and measure their impact on health.[8] Furthermore, the way impact is understood and measured in public health has historically focused only on quantitative health outcomes, whereas there is increasing recognition of the importance of well-being, development, and transformative change as central to health. Addressing this latter point in a 2015 Special Issue on "Evidence of Impact" in the *Health and Human Rights Journal*, contributing authors proposed a new methodological framework to separate out different types of "impact" of significance to health (Hunt, Bustreo and Yamin, 2015). The resulting framework acknowledged that HRBAs in health are often long-term, complex, multi-sectoral, and multi-stakeholder and sought to affect change at a number different points on a "spectrum"—at individual, structural, programmatic, and societal levels (Thomas et al. 2015). It therefore followed that studies on public health impact would need to monitor changes across these different points on a scale, rather than extrapolating from health outcomes alone.

Moving ahead, these theories on the public health impact of HRBAs will need to be further tested empirically, fine-tuned, and adjusted. The recommendations from the 2013 Monograph envisaged a specific role for OHCHR and WHO to support and lead this research agenda. In so doing, however, it should be clearly and boldly stated that this research agenda does not open up for discussion the intrinsic importance of human rights. Human rights are fundamental, legally binding, and universal. Even so, by acknowledging what drives health policy and decision-making, finding evidence to speak to those instrumental processes will be crucial to making them a lived reality for everyone.

CONCLUSION

The future for human rights at WHO, and indeed globally, hangs in the balance. There have been recognized gains, such as the increased uptake of human rights standards in health programming and the recent inauguration of the HLWG on Health and Human Rights. The HLWG includes partners from all segments of society at global, regional, and national levels, draws from a robust evidence base on how to apply HRBAs to health, proposes measurable accountability tools, has a specifically rights-focused normative basis, and is aligned with the political momentum of the SDG agenda. As such, the HLWG may be a model for how to advance rights-based approaches to health at WHO. But the future is far from certain. The operationalization of human rights standards has unearthed as many challenges as it has set new precedents, not least in ensuring that the practical

---

8. The task of measuring impact is not helped by the highly fluid definitions of what constitutes a rights-based approach, even among experts in the field (Hunt 2017).

translation of human rights principles and norms into health practice retains the core values inherent in human rights. Human rights now provide a bedrock to a number of WHO health priorities and commitments, but the success of mainstreaming is still reliant on individual champion commitment and development partner support, while organizational funding and staffing—particularly at country and regional level—is woefully short of what is needed. With a new WHO Director-General expressing a strong commitment to human rights in global health, the expectations for what the Organization can and should do have never been greater. Inequalities are growing and the world is faced with globalized pandemics, population growth, humanitarian disasters, migration, climate change, conflict, and dramatic epidemiological shifts from communicable to chronic diseases. In the face of these unprecedented threats, a firm commitment to human rights by the world's "global guardian of public health" has never been more crucial. The prospects of this commitment under the new Director-General offer reasons to be optimistic. And we stand ready.

REFERENCES

Acharya, Neha and Benjamin M. Meier. 2016. "Facilitating Accountability for the Right to Health: Mainstreaming WHO Participation in Human Rights Monitoring." *Health and Human Rights Journal*. April 28. Accessed July 10, 2017. https://www.hhrjournal.org/2016/04/facilitating-accountability-for-the-right-to-health-mainstreaming-who-participation-in-human-rights-monitoring/.

AFRO (African Regional Office), World Health Organization. 2012. "Resolution: health and human rights: current situation and way forward in the African region." 20 November. WHO Doc. AFR/RC62/R6.

Bustreo, Flavia and Paul Hunt. 2013. "The Right to Health Is Coming of Age: Evidence of Impact and the Importance of Leadership." *Journal of Public Health Policy* 34(4): 574–579.

Bustreo, Flavia, Paul Hunt, Sofia Gruskin, Asbjorn Eide, Linsey McGoey, Sujatha Rao, Francisco Songane [et al.]. 2013. *Women's and Children's Health: Evidence of Impact of Human Rights*. Geneva: World Health Organization.

CESCR (Committee on Economic, Social, and Cultural Rights). 2000. "CESCR General Comment No. 14: The Right to the Highest Attainable Standard of Health (Art. 12)." 11 August. E/C.12/2000/4.

CESCR (Committee on Economic, Social, and Cultural Rights). 2016. "General Comment No. 20 on the implementation of the rights of the child during adolescence." 6 December. CRC/C/GC/20.

Chapman, Audrey R. 2016. *Global Health, Human Rights and the Challenge of Neoliberal Policies*. New York: Cambridge University Press.

CSDH (Commission on Social Determinants of Health). 2008. "Closing the Gap in a Generation: Health Equity through Action on the Social Determinants of Health." In *Final Report of the Commission on Social Determinants of Health*. Geneva: World Health Organization.

CSDH Civil Society Report. 2007. Available at: http://www.who.int/social_determinants/resources/cs_rep_2_7.pdf.

De Albuquerque, Catarina. 2012. *On the Right Track: Good Practices in Realising the Rights to Water and Sanitation*. Geneva: United Nations. Available at: http://www.ohchr.org/Documents/Issues/Water/BookonGoodPractices_en.pdf.

Donald, Kate. 2016a. "Promising the World: Accountability and the SDGs." *Health and Human Rights Journal*. January 27. Available at: https://www.hhrjournal.org/2016/01/promising-the-world-accountability-and-the-sdgs/.

Donald, Kate. 2016b. "Tackling Inequality: The Potential of the Sustainable Development Goals." *openDemocracy*. March 2. Available at: https://www.opendemocracy.net/openglobalrights/kate-donald/tackling-inequality-potential-of-sustainable-development-goals.

Donald, Kate and Sally-Anne Way. 2016. "Accountability for the Sustainable Development Goals: A Lost Opportunity?" *Ethics & International Affairs* 30(2): 201–213.

ECOSOC (UN Economic and Social Council). 2005. "The right of everyone to the enjoyment of the highest attainable standard of physical and mental health Report of the Special Rapporteur, Paul Hunt, Mission to Mozambique." 4 January. UN Doc. E/CN.4/2005/51/Add.2.

ECOSOC (UN Economic and Social Council). 2006. "Report of the Special Rapporteur on the right of everyone to the enjoyment of the highest attainable standard of physical and health, Paul Hunt, Mission to Uganda." 19 January. UN Doc. E/CN.4/2006/48/Add.2.

Every Woman, Every Child. 2015. *The Global Strategy for Women's, Children's and Adolescents' Health (2016–2030)*. Geneva: World Health Organization.

Every Woman, Every Child. 2016. *Indicator and monitoring framework for the Global Strategy for Women's, Children's and Adolescents' Health (2016–2030)*. Geneva: World Health Organization.

Every Woman, Every Child. 2017a. "Leading the realization of human rights to health and through health." In *Report of the High Level Working Group on the Health and Human Rights of Women, Children and Adolescents*. Geneva: World Health Organization.

Every Woman, Every Child. 2017b. "Statement of the first meeting of the Network for Improving Quality of Care for Maternal, Newborn and Child Health." Available at: https://www.everywomaneverychild.org/2017/02/14/quality-equity-dignity/.

Forman, Lisa, Gorik Ooms, and Claire E. Brolan. 2015. "Rights Language in the Sustainable Development Agenda: Has Right to Health Discourse and Norms Shaped Health Goals?" *International Journal of Health Policy and Management* 4(12):799–804. DOI: 10.15171/ijhpm.2015.171.

Gruskin, Sofia. 2006. "Rights-Based Approaches to Health: Something for Everyone." *Health and Human Rights* 9(2): 5–9.

Gwatkin, Davidson and Alex Ergo. 2010. "Universal Health Coverage: Friend or Foe of Health Equity?" *The Lancet* 377(9784): 2160–2161.

Hawkes, Sarah and Kent Buse. 2016. "Searching for the Right to Health in the Sustainable Development Agenda; Comment on 'Rights Language in the Sustainable Development Agenda: Has Right to Health Discourse and Norms Shaped Health Goals?'" *International Journal of Health Policy and Management* 5(5): 337–339.

HRC (Human Rights Council). 2007. The right of everyone to the enjoyment of the highest attainable standard of physical and mental health." Report of the Special Rapporteur. 14 January. UN Doc. A/HRC/4/28.

HRC. 2014. "Technical guidance on the application of a human rights-based approach to the implementation of policies and programmes to reduce and eliminate preventable mortality and morbidity of children under 5 years of age." 30 June. UN Doc. A/HRC/27/31.

HRC (Human Rights Council). 2013. "The right of everyone to the enjoyment of the highest attainable standard of physical and mental health. Report of the Special Rapporteur on the right of everyone to the enjoyment of the highest attainable standard of physical and mental health, Anand Grover, on access to medicines." 1 May. UN Doc. A/HRC/23/42.

Hunt Paul, Flavia Bustreo, and Alicia Yamin. 2015 "Making the Case: What Is the Evidence of Impact of Applying Human Rights-Based Approaches to Health?" *Health and Human Rights Journal.* December 2015. Available at: https://cdn2.sph.harvard.edu/wp-content/uploads/sites/13/2015/12/Editorial_17.2_Jan21.pdf.

Hunt, Paul. 2015. "SDGs and the Importance of Formal Independent Review: An Opportunity for Health to Lead the Way." *Health and Human Rights Journal.* September 2. Available at: https://www.hhrjournal.org/2015/09/sdg-series-sdgs-and-the-importance-of-formal-independent-review-an-opportunity-for-health-to-lead-the-way/.

Hunt, Paul. 2017. "Configuring the UN Human Rights System in the 'Era of Implementation': Mainland and Archipelago." *Human Rights Quarterly.* Available at: http://repository.essex.ac.uk/17288/1/To%20Essex%20repository%2021%20July%202016.pdf.

IAP (Independent Accountability Panel). 2016. *Old challenges, new hopes: Accountability for the Global Strategy for Women's, Children's and Adolescents' Health.* Available at: http://www.everywomaneverychild.org/wpcontent/uploads/2017/03/IAP_Report_September2016.pdf.

Independent Expert Review Group (iERG). 2012. *Every Woman, Every Child: from commitments to action.* The First Report of the independent Expert Review Group on Information and Accountability for Women's and Children's Health. Available at: http://www.who.int/woman_child_accountability/ierg/reports/2012/IERG_report_low_resolution.pdf?ua=1.

iERG. 2013. *Every Woman, Every Child: Strengthening Equity and Dignity Through Health.* Available at: http://www.who.int/woman_child_accountability/ierg/reports/2013/en/.

iERG. 2014. *Every Woman, Every Child: a Post 2015 vision.* Available at: http://www.who.int/woman_child_accountability/ierg/reports/2014/en/.

iERG. 2015. *Every Woman, Every Child, Every Adolescent: Achievements and Prospects.* Available at: http://www.who.int/woman_child_accountability/ierg/reports/2015/en/.

Lenhardt, Amanda and Emma Samman. 2015. *In Quest of Inclusive Progress: Exploring Intersecting Inequalities in Human Development.* London: Overseas Development Institute.

Luckow, Peter W., Avi Kenny, Emily White, Madeleine Ballard, Lorenzo Dorr, Kirby Erlandson, Benjamin Grant [et al.]. 2017. "Implementation Research on Community Health Workers' Provision of Maternal and Child Health Services in Rural Liberia." *Bulletin of the World Health Organization* 2017(95): 113–120.

Magnusson, Roger. 2017. *Advancing the Right to Health: The Vital Role of the Law.* Geneva: World Health Organization.

McInerney-Lankford, Siobhán. 2017. "Human Rights and the SDGs: Progress or a Missed Opportunity?" *Oxford Human Rights Hub*. January 6. Available at: http://ohrh.law. ox.ac.uk/human-rights-and-the-sdgs-progress-or-a-missed-opportunity/.

Meier, Benjamin Mason 2017. "Human Rights in the World Health Organization: Views of the Director General Candidates." *Health and Human Rights* 19(1): 293–298.

Meier, Benjamin Mason and Ana Ayala. 2014. "The Pan American Health Organization & the Mainstreaming of Human Rights in Regional Health Governance." *Journal of Law, Medicine and Ethics* 42(3): 356–374.

Meier, Benjamin Mason and William Onzivu. 2014. "The Evolution of Human Rights in World Health Organization Policy and the Future of Human Rights through Global Health Governance." *Public Health* 128(2): 179–187.

Mills, Elizabeth. 2015. "'Leave No One Behind': Gender, Sexuality and the Sustainable Development Goals." In *Brief Supporting Evidence Report 154*. Brighton: Institute of Development Studies.

Motari, Marion and J. M. Kirigia. 2016. "Realizing the Right to Health in the WHO African Region: Issues, Challenges and the Way Forward." *Health Systems and Policy Research* 3(2:11): 1–8.

Nolan, Aoife, Rosa Freedman, and Thérèse Murphy. 2016. "The United Nations Special Procedures System: Introduction." In *The United Nations Special Procedures System*. Leiden: Brill. Available at: https://ssrn.com/abstract=2830784.

Nygren-Krug, Helena. 2013. "The Right to Health, from Concept to Practice." In Gostin et al., *Advancing the Human Right to Health*, edited by José M. Zuniga, Stephen P. Marks, and Lawrence O. Gostin. Oxford: Oxford University Press.

Ooms, Gorik and Rachel Hammonds. 2015. *Anchoring Universal Health Coverage in the Right to Health: What Different Would It Make?* Geneva: World Health Organization. http://www.who.int/gender-equity-rights/knowledge/anchoring-uhc.pdf.

Ooms, Gorik, Laila A. Latif, Attiya Waris, Claire E. Brolan, Rachel Hammonds, Eric A. Friedman, Moses Mulumba, and Lisa Forman. 2014. "Is Universal Health Coverage the Practical Expression of the Right to Health Care?" *BMC International Health and Human Rights* 14:3.

PAHO (Pan American Health Organization), 50th Directing Council. 2010. "Health and human rights." 31 August. Doc. CD50/12.

PAHO (Pan American Health Organization), 65th Session. 2013. "Resolutions and Decisions of the Regional Committee." The Fifty Second Directing Council, Washington D.C., United States of America on September 30–October 4. Washington D.C.: PAHO.

PAHO. 2017. Applying Medical Anthropology to Public Health. March 2, 2017, Available at: http://www.paho.org/hq/index.php?option=com_content&view=article&id=13 007%3Amedical-anthro&catid=4717%3Afgl-news&lang=en.

PMNCH (The Partnership for Maternal, Newborn and Child Health). 2017. "Developing the AYC Mentorship Program: We Want to Hear from You!" *World Health Organization*. March 3. Available at: http://www.who.int/pmnch/media/news/2017/ayc_mentor-ship/en/.

Potts, Helen. 2008. *Accountability and the Right to the Highest Attainable Standard of Health*. University of Essex: Human Rights Centre.

Stuart, Elizabeth. 2016. "How to Leave No One Behind: A Workable Plan for Ambitious Aims." *Deliver2030*. February 3. Available at: http://deliver2030.org/?p=6723.

Thomas, Rebekah, Shyama Kuruvilla, Rachael Hinton, Steven L. B. Jensen, Veronica Magar, and Flavia Bustreo. 2015. "Assessing the Impact of a Human Rights-Based Approach across a Spectrum of Change for Women's, Children's, and Adolescent's Health." *Health and Human Rights Journal* 17(2): 11–20.

UN (United Nations). 2016. "UN System Chief Executives Board Statement of Commitment: Putting the imperative to combat inequalities and discrimination at the forefront of UN efforts to support implementation of the 2030 Agenda for Sustainable Development." 27 April. Available at: http://www.unsystem.org/CEBPublicFiles/CEB%20Jt%20Statement%20of%20Commitment_%20Combat%20inequalities%20and%20discrimination-ODS.pdf.

UN General Assembly. 2012. "Global health and foreign policy." 14 March 2013. UN Doc. A/RES/67/81.

UN General Assembly. 2014. "Strengthening and enhancing the effective functioning of the human rights treaty body system." 9 April. UN Doc. A/RES/68/268.

UN General Assembly. 2015. "Transforming our World: The 2030 Agenda for Sustainable Development." 21 October. UN Doc. A/RES/70/1.

UNDG (United Nations Development Group). 2003. *The Human Rights Based Approach to Development Cooperation Towards a Common Understanding Among UN Agencies.* Available at: https://undg.org/wp-content/uploads/2016/09/6959-The_Human_Rights_Based_Approach_to_Development_Cooperation_Towards_a_Common_Understanding_among_UN.pdf.

UNDG (United Nations Development Group). 2015. *Eight case studies on integrating the United Nations' Normative and Operational work.* Available at: https://undg.org/wp-content/uploads/2016/05/Normative-Operational-Study-FINAL.pdf.

WHA (World Health Assembly), 69th Session. 2016a. "Framework on integrated, patient-centered care services. Report by the WHO Secretariat." 15 April. Doc. A69/39.

WHA (World Health Assembly), 69th Session. 2016b. "Strengthening integrated, people-centred health services." 28 May. Doc. WHA69.24.

WHA (World Health Assembly), 69th Session. 2016c. "The Global strategy and action plan on ageing and health 2016–2020: towards a world in which everyone can live a long and healthy life." 28 May. Doc. WHA69.3.

WHO (World Health Organization). 2008. World Health Report: Primary Health Care, Now More Than Ever.

WHO. 2011a. *Keeping Promises, Measuring Results.* Commission on Information and Accountability for Women's and Children's Health.

WHO. 2011b. *Resolutions and Decisions of the Executive Board at the Sixty-Fourth World Health Assembly, in Geneva, Switzerland on May 16–24.* Geneva: World Health Organization. Available at: http://apps.who.int/gb/ebwha/pdf_files/WHA64-REC1/A64_REC1-en.pdf.

WHO. 2012. *Quality Rights Tool Kit: Assessing and improving quality and human rights in mental health and social care facilities.* Geneva: World Health Organization.

WHO. 2013a. *Global Action Plan for the Prevention and Control of Noncommunicable Diseases 2013–2020.* Geneva: World Health Organization.

WHO. 2013b. *Mental health action plan 2013–2020.* Geneva: World Health Organization

WHO. 2014a. *Reproductive, maternal, newborn and child health and human rights: A toolbox for examining laws, regulations and policies.* Geneva: World Health Organization.

WHO. 2014b. *The prevention and elimination of disrespect and abuse during facility-based childbirth.* Geneva: World Health Organization.

WHO. 2015a. *Follow up to World Health Assembly decision on Ebola virus disease outbreak and the Special Session of the Executive Board on Ebola; A Roadmap for Action.* Geneva: World Health Organization. Available at: http://www.who.int/about/who_reform/emergency-capacities/WHO-outbreasks-emergencies-Roadmap.pdf?ua=1.

WHO. 2015b. *Health in 2015: from MDGs to SDGs.* Geneva: World Health Organization

WHO. 2015c. *Programme Budget 2016–2017.* Geneva: World Health Organization.

WHO. 2015d. *Statement of Action to enhance the engagement of communities, non-governmental and other civil society organisations in the implementation of the End TB Strategy.* Geneva: World Health Organization.

WHO. 2015e. *The prevention and elimination of disrespect and abuse during facility-based childbirth, WHO Statement.* Available at: http://apps.who.int/iris/bitstream/10665/134588/1/WHO_RHR_14.23_eng.pdf.

WHO. 2015f. "UN Statement on Ending violence and discrimination against lesbian, gay, bisexual, transgender and intersex people." 29 September. Available at: http://www.who.int/gender-equity-rights/news/un-statement-on-lgbti/en/index1.html.

WHO. 2016a. "Development of the Global Health Sector Strategy on HIV/AIDS, 2016–2021." Accessed August 9, 2017. Available at: http://www.who.int/hiv/mediacentre/news/hivstrategy2016-21/en/.

WHO. 2016b. *Global consultation: monitoring system for action on the social determinants of health.* Geneva: World Health Organization.

WHO. 2016c. *Global Leprosy Strategy 2016–2020.* Geneva: World Health Organization.

WHO. 2016d. "New group to 'expand access to health and human rights' for women, children and adolescents." *World Health Organization.* 22 September. Available at: http://www.who.int/life-course/news/human-rights-working-group-for-women-children-adolescents/en/.

WHO. 2016e. *Reforming Health Service Delivery for UHC.* Geneva: World Health Organization.

WHO. 2016f. *#YouthTrackChange: Young people can shape progress towards the #WorldWeWant in 2030!* Available at: http://www.who.int/life-course/publications/youthtrackchange.pdf?ua=1.

WHO. 2017a. "Global Learning Laboratory for Quality Universal Health Coverage." *World Health Organization.* Accessed August 9, 2017. Available at: http://www.who.int/servicedeliverysafety/areas/qhc/gll/en/.

WHO. 2017b. "Health and Environment Linkages Initiative." *World Health Organization.* Accessed August 9, 2017. Available at: http://www.who.int/heli/en/.

WHO. 2017c. "Joint United Nations statement on ending discrimination in health care settings." 27 June. *World Health Organization, Media Centre.* Available at: http://www.who.int/mediacentre/news/statements/2017/discrimination-in-health-care/en/.

WHO. 2017d. "WHO Director-General Dr. Tedros takes the helm of WHO: address to WHO staff." *World Health Organization.* 3 July. Available at: http://www.who.int/dg/speeches/2017/taking-helm-who/en/?utm_source=WHO+List&utm_campaign=5e9062d53e-EMAIL_CAMPAIGN_2017_07_04&utm_medium=email&utm_term=0_823e9e35c1-5e9062d53e-266420553.

WHO. 2017e. "WHO Framework on integrated people-centred health services." *World Health Organization.* Accessed August 9, 2017. Available at: http://www.who.int/servicedeliverysafety/areas/people-centred-care/en/.

WHO. forthcoming. "Advancing the Right to Health through the UN Universal Periodic Review (UPR) Process: Opportunities and Obstacles for WHO Engagement" (on file with authors).

WHO Executive Board, 140th Session. 2016. "Progress in the implementation of the 2030 Agenda for Sustainable Development, Report by the Secretariat." 12 December. WHO Doc. EB140/32.

Williams, Carmen and Alison Blaiklock. 2016. "Human Rights Discourse in the Sustainable Development Agenda Avoids Obligations and Entitlements Comment on 'Rights Language in the Sustainable Development Agenda: Has Right to Health Discourse and Norms Shaped Health Goals?'" *International Journal of Health Policy and Management* 5(6): 387–390.

Williams, Carmel and Paul Hunt. 2017. "Neglecting Human Rights: Accountability, Data and Sustainable Development Goal 3." *International Journal of Human Rights.* 21(8): 1114–1143.

Inter-Governmental Organizations

8

The United Nations Children's Fund

Implementing Human Rights for Child Health

BENJAMIN MASON MEIER, MITRA MOTLAGH,
AND KUMANAN RASANATHAN*

The long-standing efforts of the UN Children's Fund (UNICEF) to implement human rights were reinforced by the promulgation of the 1989 Convention on the Rights of the Child (CRC), solidifying UNICEF's central institutional role in the implementation of child rights for the promotion of global health. Because children are more vulnerable to violations of their rights, and less able to protect themselves from these violations, UNICEF has sought to implement the child's right to health under the CRC's recognition of "the right of the child to the enjoyment of the highest attainable standard of health and to facilities for the treatment of illness and rehabilitation of health." Realizing the child's right to health has required UNICEF to mainstream human rights in organizational practice, translating CRC obligations into UNICEF health programming.

This chapter examines UNICEF efforts to realize the child's right to health. Part I reviews UNICEF's evolving governance to address global health, from its collaborations to prevent disease in postwar Europe to its leadership in protecting children through global policy. In protecting children under human rights law, Part II outlines how the development of the rights of the child led to the CRC, with this groundbreaking treaty specifying implementation responsibilities for UNICEF and providing normative authority for UNICEF's organization-wide approach to human rights. Shifting UNICEF from a needs-based to a rights-based approach to health, Part III examines the mainstreaming of human rights in UNICEF's work to promote the health and well-being of children—across UNICEF's health

* The authors are grateful to informants inside and outside of UNICEF for their insights on UNICEF's rights-based efforts and to Maya Kiel for her research assistance on UNICEF's institutional history and dedicated support in the finalization of this chapter.

programming, assistance to states, and work with the Committee on the Rights of the Child. Part IV analyzes the opportunities and challenges in using a rights-based approach to advance children's health, recognizing UNICEF's unique support through the CRC in implementing health-related human rights with country offices and member states. Based upon this CRC mandate and UNICEF's rights-based mission, this chapter concludes that UNICEF has cultivated the commitment and capacity to implement human rights for child health in the years to come.

I. FROM POSTWAR RECONSTRUCTION TO GLOBAL DEVELOPMENT FOR THE HEALTH OF THE CHILD

From its postwar beginnings, UNICEF focused on the emergency provision of assistance to women and children in conflict-ridden Europe, thereafter becoming a permanent institution of the United Nations (UN), enlarging its focus to address determinants of child health, and expanding its operations throughout the world. Driven by a struggling postwar economy, UNICEF shifted from postwar rehabilitation to disease prevention and concentrated on disease eradication and immunization campaigns in the context of economic development. As UNICEF increasingly sought to incorporate the needs of children in development discourses, it came to lead a series of global health policy initiatives. UNICEF's work to address child survival in development launched the "child survival revolution," positioning the organization to respond to the public health impacts of neoliberal economic policy. These evolving leadership efforts to address determinants of child health have secured UNICEF a central role in global health governance.

A. Creating a United Nations Fund for Children

The vision of an international fund for children was borne of the horrors faced by the children of Europe during World War II. With the League of Nations Health Organization dissolving in the midst of the war, the Allied Nations formed the UN Relief and Rehabilitation Administration (UNRRA) in 1943 to provide temporary aid to countries impacted by war and to meet immediate needs for food, shelter, education, and health (LaGuardia 1946). Nearing the end of its "acute crisis" operations in 1946, states sought to reallocate UNRRA's wartime responsibilities across a variety of agencies under the nascent UN system (Russell 1950). Where UNRRA had developed budding programs to feed "children-in-need" and address children's health, Ludwik Rajchman, the Polish UNRRA delegate and former head of the League of Nations Health Organization, implored nations to continue providing aid to the children affected by war (Jacobs 1950). Proposing an international children's fund to assume the remaining UNRRA resources, the UN General Assembly unanimously resolved in December 1946 to create the UN International Children's Emergency Fund (UNICEF) for the benefit of children and adolescents affected by war, for those receiving UNRRA assistance, and "for child health purposes generally" (UN General Assembly 1946). UNICEF's initial executive board, representing twenty-six national governments, would select Rajchman as the first Chairman of the Board of UNICEF, leading the organization in developing health programming to improve women's and children's health (DeForest 1950).

UNICEF collaborated closely with country officials in its early years to analyze the health problems facing women and children and develop country-specific
remedies. By December 1947, UNICEF had begun operations in six European countries, developing programs on food aid that would affect 375,000 children, a population which grew rapidly by 1950 to 5,500,000 (King 1950). Seeking to expand its
work beyond malnutrition and address communicable disease, UNICEF embarked
in 1947 on an initiative to immunize children against the diseases sweeping postwar
Europe; however, World Health Assembly delegates determined that such an infectious disease campaign was an international health issue that fell exclusively within
the mandate of the World Health Organization (WHO) (Doull and Kramer 1948).
As UNICEF still required the approval of the UNICEF-WHO Joint Committee for
all of its health programming (Beigbeder 2001), UNICEF had not yet established
its independent legitimacy in international health governance, but it was beginning
to assert itself to address determinants of health in other regions of the world. With
board members recognizing the "continuing need for an organization devoted solely
to children" ("United Nations International Children's Emergency Fund" 1950,
250), the UN renewed UNICEF's charter in 1950, and given UNICEF's unique
postwar successes in delivering food aid and controlling tuberculosis and malaria,
the UN renewed UNICEF's charter indefinitely in 1953, solidifying the permanent
role of the renamed "United Nations Children's Fund" (Fifield 1994).

B. Shifting to Global Development

UNICEF's unique role as a global advocate for children allowed it to operate
cooperatively "on both sides of the Iron Curtain" ("United Nations International
Children's Emergency Fund" 1950, 250), with UNICEF leaders recognizing this
organization-wide strength to protect children's health, safety, and well-being
throughout the world. As conditions in Europe began to improve, UNICEF's efforts
shifted from postwar rehabilitation to disease prevention. UNICEF began its first
major eradication campaign in 1950—specifically focused in Asia—and by 1956,
37 million children and mothers in ninety-eight countries had received UNICEF assistance through malarial swamp draining, treatment of trachoma and yaws, and immunization against prevalent diseases ("UNICEF Reports on Ten Years of Work for
the World's Children" 1957). With UNICEF working alongside WHO as it shifted
toward communicable disease prevention, UNICEF's local partnerships contributed
to collaborative disease eradication programs targeting yaws, trachoma, leprosy, and
malaria (Keeney 1953), and in 1960, the WHO Executive Board approved greater
autonomy for UNICEF in developing and implementing country-specific programming to address children's health ("Social, Humanitarian, and Cultural Questions"
1963). UNICEF thereafter began to expand its reach to encompass "basic maternal
and child welfare services" in an effort to provide children with "better intellectual
and emotional growth as well as improved health and nutrition," establishing national
health programs and influencing economic development efforts (Shaffer 1960, 77).

To advance public health through economic development policy, UNICEF
conceptualized the health of children and disease prevention as fundamental to
global development. UNICEF's Executive Board in 1956 recognized the challenges
facing underdeveloped regions of the world through "the mountainous obstacle of

poverty," seeking to prevent disease as a basis for economic productivity ("UNICEF Reports on Ten Years of Work for the World's Children" 1957, 211). Meeting children's basic needs as part of economic and social development programs during the first UN Development Decade (1960–1970) ("Social, Humanitarian, and Cultural Questions" 1963), UNICEF would strive to provide health services within the context of economic development programs (Marks 1968). However, with UNICEF increasingly concerned that rapid industrialization could "adversely affect the welfare of children and youth," it sought to foster a new holistic view of child well-being in the context of development, arguing that "the needs of children should be given emphasis in the national plans for developing countries" ("UNICEF Round-Table Recommends More Emphasis Be Placed on the Needs of Children in National Planning" 1964, 56). As the recipient of the 1965 Nobel Peace Prize, UNICEF's Executive Director proclaimed "that each time UNICEF contributes . . . to giving today's children a chance to grow into useful and happier citizens, it contributes to removing some of the seeds of world tension and conflicts" ("A Table for the World's Children" 1966, 90). UNICEF's Executive Board increasingly encouraged governments to establish development programming that prioritized children's health and social needs, viewing UNICEF as a "catalytic agent" to advance both children's health and a country's socioeconomic development (Marks 1968, 532).

C. Developing Policy for the Health of the Child

From this foundation in disease prevention for economic development, UNICEF came to influence international policy as a means of promoting children's health. Beginning in breastfeeding promotion in the mid-1970s, both UNICEF and WHO came to recognize the significance of formula feeding as a driver of infant malnutrition and death in the developing world, and in one of the first policy partnerships of its kind, UNICEF collaborated with WHO to regulate the formula industry through the 1981 International Code of Marketing of Breast-Milk Substitutes (Sikkink 1986). This policy collaboration with WHO continued in their co-hosting of the 1978 Alma-Ata Conference on Primary Health Care, through which UNICEF came to focus comprehensively on the health of the child through national health systems, drawing on concepts of social justice, universal access, and human rights to promote "primary health care," health care in addition to underlying determinants of health (WHO 1978). Through its extended partnership with WHO, UNICEF was able to promote its specific policy goals for child health and nutrition within the context of primary health care, taking advantage of the political advocacy of WHO to improve the health outcomes of children, as "not only a means to development" but "an end in themselves" (Mahler 1979, 225).

Even as primary health care was challenged by states at the start of the neoliberal era, UNICEF adapted the primary health care approach to drive resources toward its "Child Survival Revolution," championed by Executive Director James (Jim) Grant through a focus on GOBI (Growth monitoring, Oral rehydration, Breastfeeding, Immunization) as a means to address the select health conditions underlying the majority of infant deaths (UNICEF 1983). While critics derided the focused approach of GOBI as "selective" primary health care (Cueto 2004), UNICEF "[did] not align itself with specificity versus comprehensive primary health care" (Jolly and Taylor

1988, 973). The GOBI approach allowed UNICEF to implement inexpensive health interventions that would attract increased financial support to meet short-term measurable targets, focusing on "something easy to sell, with built-in PR appeal" that would dramatically reduce child mortality (Beigbeder 2001, 91). As development discourse in the 1980s came to be defined by neoliberal "structural adjustments" to stabilize the economies of developing countries, UNICEF focused on ameliorating the health impacts of neoliberal economic policies by the International Monetary Fund (IMF) and World Bank (Fifield 1994). UNICEF studies and publications detailed the worsening health conditions for women and children following structural adjustments, leading to a three-year partnership between UNICEF, the World Bank, and the IMF to address the "basic needs" of children and facilitate "Adjustment with a Human Face" (Cornia, Jolly, and Stewart 1998). Advocating for people-centered development that would empower the most marginalized (Jolly 1991), UNICEF created an opening to employ a rights-based approach to development as a basis to realize human rights for child health.

II. THE CONVENTION ON THE RIGHTS OF THE CHILD PROVIDES UNICEF'S HUMAN RIGHTS FOUNDATION FOR GLOBAL HEALTH

UNICEF has become central to the development and implementation of human rights to address the health of the child. Building from the 1959 Declaration on the Rights of the Child, the 1989 CRC sought to expand upon the UN human rights covenants, translating civil, cultural, economic, political, and social rights to meet the specific needs of children. By codifying child rights, the CRC would become central to UNICEF's identity and mandate, providing a legal foundation for UNICEF's organization-wide approach to human rights.

A. Declaration on the Rights of the Child

The rights of the child have long been a focus of the global community, with the wartime suffering of children garnering international interest following both the First and Second World Wars. With the non-governmental Save the Children International Union pressing nations to protect the rights of the child following World War I, the League of Nations adopted the 1924 Declaration of Geneva as a framework for national laws to give the child "the means requisite for its normal development, both materially and spiritually" (League of Nations 1924). In the aftermath of the Great Depression and World War II, the plight of children would again be brought into stark relief, giving rise to a UN Declaration on the Rights of the Child (Marshall 1999). Elaborating the proclamation that "motherhood and childhood are entitled to special care and assistance" in the 1948 Universal Declaration of Human Rights (UDHR), the 1959 UN Declaration on the Rights of the Child expanded the protections of the Declaration of Geneva, recognizing "the statutes of specialized agencies and international organizations concerned with the welfare of children" and enumerating ten principles to secure a child's need for "special safeguards and care" (UN General Assembly 1959, preamble). The resulting Declaration would seek legal protections for child health through both medical care and underlying determinants of health:

> The child shall enjoy the benefits of social security. He shall be entitled to grow and develop in health; to this end, special care and protection shall be provided both to him and to his mother, including adequate pre-natal and post-natal care. The child shall have the right to adequate nutrition, housing, recreation and medical services (UN General Assembly 1959, Principle 4).

Holding that "the best interests of the child shall be the paramount consideration" (Ibid., principle 2), the Declaration created a normative basis for codifying the health-related rights of the child under international law.

However, child rights were initially neglected in the subsequent development of international human rights law. As states sought to translate the proclamations in the UDHR into binding international covenants—through both the International Covenant on Civil and Political Rights (ICCPR) and International Covenant on Economic, Social and Cultural Rights (ICESCR)—initial proposals for an article on the rights of the child did not come to fruition (Van Bueren 1995). Without significant UNICEF participation, the ICCPR gave only brief attention to juvenile justice, and the ICESCR addressed children only briefly in clauses focused on health and nutrition (Holzscheiter 2010). While UNICEF expressed strong support for child rights, it did not prioritize these rights under international law, taking little part in the development of the 1979 UN Convention on the Elimination of All Forms of Discrimination against Women and a 1979 proposal for a binding Convention on the Rights of the Child (Cohen 1983). States were beginning work with non-governmental organizations (NGOs) to develop a treaty on the rights of the child, yet UNICEF continued to direct its efforts toward the provision of programs for children and advocacy on global social and economic policy, avoiding the Cold War politics of developing international human rights law.

B. Development of the CRC

Reflecting this pragmatic view, UNICEF did not initially engage in the development of the CRC, with UNICEF leaders believing that focusing on rights would draw it into conflict with states over treaty violations; however, UNICEF came to be an active participant in the final efforts to develop health obligations and then assure near-universal ratification of the CRC. Beginning in the 1979 International Year of the Child, the Polish delegation to the UN proposed language for a binding convention on the rights of the child (Commission on Human Rights 1979). This proposal was supported enthusiastically by a burgeoning number of child rights NGOs, which came together to develop substantive articles and implementation mechanisms to advance the drafting process in the UN Commission on Human Rights (Cohen 1990). Although UNICEF staff provided informal advice on the development of the CRC, the organization would not become officially involved until the final debates on the convention, with UNICEF then seen by states as having a specific role in CRC implementation (Smith 1998). Supporting its unanimous adoption by the UN General Assembly in November 1989, as seen in Figure 8.1, UNICEF would thereafter work with states to

Figure 8.1 Jim Grant Advocating for CRC Adoption.
PHOTO CREDIT: UNICEF Archives.

assure the CRC's rapid ratification and promulgation, leading it to become the most universally ratified human rights treaty, reaffirmed repeatedly as a legally binding basis for UNICEF's child rights work.

Where existing human rights treaties did not adequately protect the rights of the child, the CRC requires that the "best interests of the child" be addressed holistically, recognizing a specific right to the "enjoyment of the highest attainable standard of health" as part of its holistic approach to the health of the child (UN General Assembly 1989, art. 24). Article 24 of the CRC thereby frames the child's right to health to include both health care services for the treatment of illness and rehabilitation of health, as well as health systems to assure underlying determinants of health (Ibid.). More specific than any previous treaty elaboration of the right to health, CRC obligations encompass explicit measures to reduce infant and child mortality; provide primary health care; combat disease and malnutrition; ensure prenatal and postnatal care for mothers; enable access to child health, nutrition education, and breastfeeding promotion; and develop preventive health care, guidance for parents, and family planning services (Detrick 1999).

Calling for "international assistance and cooperation" in realizing the rights of the child, states would specifically authorize UNICEF to coordinate this assistance "in order to foster the effective implementation of the convention and to encourage international cooperation in the field covered by the convention" (UN General Assembly 1989, art. 45). In working with the Committee on the Rights of the Child to interpret treaty provisions and monitor state implementation, the CRC clarifies that:

The Committee may invite the specialized agencies, the United Nations Children's Fund and other competent bodies as it may consider appropriate to provide expert advice on the implementation of the Convention in areas falling within the scope of their respective mandates. (Ibid., art. 45).

The CRC is unique among treaties in its explicit delegation of implementing authority to an international organization, addressing UNICEF's specific role in supporting implementation efforts where states "request, or indicate a need, for technical advice or assistance" and in giving assistance to the new Committee on the Rights of the Child (Ibid.).

C. UNICEF's New Mission

The CRC rapidly came to transform UNICEF's mission and programming. As UNICEF's Child Rights Office came to see the influence of this new treaty to UNICEF's mission, UNICEF began a major campaign to press national governments to ratify the treaty and implement CRC obligations. The September 1990 World Summit on Children provided UNICEF with an unprecedented high-level meeting to endorse the CRC in international affairs, with heads of state from around the world heralding the CRC as a basis to create a better world for children (UNICEF 1990). With constant pressure from the UNICEF leadership to embrace human rights, near-universal ratification of the CRC among states, and rapid con-sensus on the rights of the child within the NGO community, this unique level of global agreement raised an imperative to reform UNICEF policies and practices, shifting UNICEF from a needs-based approach to health to a rights-based approach to health (Lewis 1997). Facilitating legal accountability for its health mandate, the CRC provided UNICEF with a normative basis to expand from vertical health interventions (emblematic of the GOBI approach) to include horizontal health systems for distal determinants of health (including issues of "complex causality" through malnutrition, education, and sanitation) (Jonsson 2003, 10).

Translating international legal obligations into child health programming, UNICEF would analyze its own implementation responsibilities under the CRC, revising its mission statement to mandate that the organization "advocate for the pro-tection of children's rights and strive to establish children's rights as enduring ethical principles and international standards of behaviour towards children" (UNICEF 1996). This new rights-based paradigm would expand the populations considered by UNICEF, reform UNICEF's country practices, and facilitate accountability for health programming (Jonsson 2003). While many programmatic staff already saw themselves as operating in a rights-based approach, this new organizational mission legitimized explicit reference to human rights documents in UNICEF policies and rights-based assistance to states parties in implementing the CRC. UNICEF would seek to position itself as the international coordinating body for CRC implementa-tion, appointing a human rights officer in Geneva and working with country offices to monitor CRC implementation before the Committee on the Rights of the Child (Oestreich 1998).

As the UN moved to mainstream human rights, UNICEF had already developed a basis under the CRC to make this rights-based approach a programmatic reality. Following from the UN Secretary-General's June 1997 call to "mainstream" human rights as a cross-cutting approach to all of the UN's programs and activities (UN General Assembly 1997), UNICEF's International Child Development Centre (Innocenti Centre) developed *A Human Rights Conceptual Framework for UNICEF* to clarify "UNICEF's mandate for human rights," thereby mapping UNICEF's work to implement human rights obligations, framing an organization-wide approach to human rights realization, and assessing the implications of the CRC to UNICEF country programs (Pais 1998). Through the subsequent *UNICEF Guidelines for Human Rights-Based Programming Approach*, UNICEF would outline a process to apply a human rights-based approach to development in UNICEF programming (UNICEF 1998). Defining its institutional mandate through the lens of the CRC, UNICEF came to be seen as the leading UN agency in "thinking, strategizing and experimenting on RBP [rights-based programming]" (O'Neill and Bye 2002, 4). By the time that the UN General Assembly developed a 2002 Special Session on Children, with states reviewing progress since the 1990 World Summit, UNICEF had fully reshaped its organizational mission around human rights, embracing its principal role in implementing human rights to promote the health and well-being of children (UN General Assembly 2002).

III. UNICEF'S WORK TO ADVANCE CHILD HEALTH AND HUMAN RIGHTS

The CRC has come to be seen as a "a sort of unofficial constitution of UNICEF, with almost every facet of its operations directed toward the convention's implementation" (Oestreich 1998, 187), as UNICEF has supported the implementation of human rights for children's health through its health programming, technical assistance to national governments, and work with the Committee on the Rights of the Child.

A. Human Rights in UNICEF's Health Programming

The CRC has provided a way to consider UNICEF's responsibility toward the "whole child," examining the interrelated rights that structure child health across UNICEF programs: Health; Child protection; Education; HIV and AIDS; Nutrition; Water, sanitation, and hygiene; Social inclusion and policy; and Cross-cutting issues. Grounded in UNICEF's 2003 guidebook, *Implementing a Human Rights-Based Approach to Development in the Context of UN Reform*, UNICEF has sought "to bring development theories and human rights principles together in a strategy capable of realising the rights of children" (Jonsson 2003, 6). With technical officers supported by a Human Rights Unit, the human rights-based approach supports UNICEF's health-related programming through:

(a) a programmatic focus on universality, equity, and accountability through analyses of disaggregated health indicators and training of civil society,

(b) an expanded age range, focusing on children up to the age of 18 and encouraging meaningful child participation in health policymaking, and

(c) a broadening of determinants of health analyzed and health issues addressed.

Despite these advances, the health program in UNICEF has made comparatively less use of the human rights-based approach in its explicit language and instruments. As seen in other UNICEF programs—such as the child protection and social inclusion programs (which look to national human rights institutions to facilitate accountability) and particularly the cross-cutting programs (which explicitly include human rights in work on early child development, disability, and adolescent participation)—the implementation of the rights-based approach has been instrumental to addressing underlying determinants of health. Whereas these smaller programs are more focused on advocacy and policy change, the health program (as UNICEF's largest program, with far greater responsibilities for the delivery of health services to children) has remained focused on pragmatic considerations to maximize health benefits. There remains a perception in the health program that human rights discourse needs to be grounded in practical measures and health outcomes—i.e., that its "reliance on legal measures and abstract principles . . . provide scant guidance for real-world decision making around resource allocation or programme strategies essential for supporting service delivery" (George et al. 2010, 1764). In spite of a 2012 external *Global Evaluation of the Application of the Human Rights-Based Approach to UNICEF Programming* finding the least explicit incorporation of human rights in the health program—citing a lack of human rights norms in the practical implementation of evidence-based decision-making (UNICEF 2012)—the health program has largely persisted in its pragmatic approach to achieving cost-effective health outcomes, with a focus on equity in children's health.

Yet, the health program remains informed by human rights and connected to the organization's commitment to the CRC under the umbrella of this "equity approach." Where Executive Director Anthony Lake championed a focus on equity (Lake 2012), UNICEF sought to operationalize human rights in practice by prioritizing the "worst off children" through cost-effective, equity-oriented health programming (Carrera et al. 2012). This strategic understanding has led to an institution-wide reorientation of UNICEF's work, with increased focus on data, monitoring, and social accountability, and the use of new technologies to enhance participation in decision-making (Gibbons 2015). In doing so, UNICEF has retained the principles of human rights in its health programming (enhancing universalism, non-discrimination, participation, and accountability) even as it has decreased emphasis on international human rights standards, as seen in health-related work on:

- Birth Registration—where UNICEF's health program has collaborated with the child protection program, noting that being counted is a fundamental human right, and that without birth registration data, it is not possible to analyze disaggregated health statistics and prioritize marginalized groups.
- Emergency Contexts—where UNICEF has strengthened its health programming in response to increasing numbers of children in emergency contexts, understanding that the worst off children are increasingly concentrated in such contexts and that the application of human rights can be most effective in humanitarian situations.

- Universal Health Coverage—where UNICEF has emphasized that all efforts toward universal health coverage are not equal in their impact on human rights and health equity, raising a need to implement "progressive universalism" through the prioritization of children and the worst off communities (O'Connell, Rasanathan, and Chopra 2014).

By examining the causes of rights violations in health, this pragmatic UNICEF programming has moved toward an implicit rights-based approach that analyzes the environments in which rights violations can occur and the approaches through which UNICEF can intervene to create enabling environments for health. By prioritizing the most marginalized children (Tanahashi 1978), this framework guides UNICEF's monitoring of essential health services—highlighting a focus on the availability, accessibility, acceptability, and quality of service provision that is consistent with (and, in fact, informed) the attributes of the human right to health (CESCR 2000).

To mainstream rights more explicitly under the post-2015 Sustainable Development Goals (SDGs), UNICEF has sought to map the relationship between SDG targets and CRC obligations, as outlined in Figure 8.2, highlighting where SDG targets support the child's right to health (UNICEF 2016).

As compared with the previous 2000–2015 Millennium Development Goals (MDGs), which did not reference the CRC or human rights norms (Diaz-Martinez and Gibbons 2014), the SDGs have been seen as an opportunity to engage multi-sectoral collaborations in a rights-based approach to health (Hawkes and Buse 2016) and facilitate human rights accountability through the Global Strategy for Women's, Children's and Adolescents' Health (Every Woman Every Child 2015). Building capacity for UNICEF's rights-based programming under the SDGs, UNICEF's Human Rights Unit has developed a sixty-minute voluntary "short-course" to explain the rights of the child and the rights-based approach, providing a UNICEF-specific training and an online network to complement the "Human Rights Up Front" course developed by the Office of the UN High Commissioner for Human Rights (UNICEF n.d.).

B. UNICEF Country Offices and Health Assistance to States

Human rights have thus become a principal normative framework guiding UNICEF's health assistance to states, with human rights employed to set the goals of programming, to structure the process of UNICEF's work, and to evaluate the outcomes of country planning. UNICEF's primary organizational unit is its country offices, which receive the bulk of UNICEF resources and are instrumental in delivering UNICEF's efforts to realize the rights of children. With UNICEF country offices gaining leverage in their health diplomacy through CRC obligations (UNICEF 2007), UNICEF has assisted states parties under CRC Article 24 to, among other things:

- provide healthcare to children as well as to mothers pre-natally and post-natally;
- reduce disease and malnutrition by focusing on determinants of health;

3.1	By 2030, reduce the *global maternal mortality ratio* to less than 70 per 100,000 live births
Preamble	Recognizing that the child, for the full and harmonious development of his or her personality, **should grow up in a family environment, in an atmosphere of happiness, love and understanding**
Article 1	For the purposes of the present Convention, **a child means every human being below the age of eighteen years** unless under the law applicable to the child, majority is attained earlier
Article 7.1	The child shall [have] the **right to know and be cared for by his or her parents**
Article 24.2 (d)	States Parties [...] shall take appropriate measures: To ensure appropriate **pre-natal and post-natal health care for mothers**
3.2	By 2030, *end preventable deaths of newborns and children under 5 years of age,* with all countries aiming to reduce neonatal mortality to at least as low as 12 per 1,000 live births and under-5 mortality to at least as low as 25 per 1,000 live births
3.3	By 2030, *end the epidemics of AIDS, tuberculosis, malaria and neglected tropical diseases and combat hepatitis, water-borne diseases and other communicable diseases*
Article 1	For the purposes of the present Convention, **a child means every human being below the age of eighteen years** unless under the law applicable to the child, majority is attained earlier.
Article 6	States Parties recognize that every child has the inherent right to life / States Parties shall ensure to the maximum extent possible the **survival and development of the child**
Article 24.1	the right of the child to the enjoyment of the **highest attainable standard of health** and to **facilities for the treatment of illness and rehabilitation of health**
24.2 (a)	States Parties [...] shall take appropriate measures: To **diminish infant and child mortality** /
(b)	To ensure the provision of **necessary medical assistance and health care** to all children with emphasis on the development of **primary health care** /
(c)	To **combat disease and malnutrition**, including within the framework of **primary health care.**
3.4	By 2030, reduce by one third *premature mortality from non-communicable diseases* through prevention and treatment and promote mental health and well-beings
Article 6	States Parties recognize that every child has the inherent **right to life** / States Parties shall ensure to the maximum extent possible the **survival and development of the child**
Article 24.1	the right of the child to the enjoyment of the **highest attainable standard of health** and to **facilities for the treatment of illness and rehabilitation of health**
24.2 (a)	States Parties [...] shall take appropriate measures: To **diminish infant and child mortality** /
(b)	To ensure the provision of **necessary medical assistance and health care** to all children with emphasis on the development of **primary health care** /
(c)	To **combat disease and malnutrition**, including within the framework of **primary health care** ... /
(f)	To **develop preventive health care**, guidance for parents and family planning education and services
3.5	**Strengthen the** *prevention and treatment of substance abuse*, including narcotic drug abuse and harmful use of alcohol
Article 33	protect children from the **illicit use of narcotic drugs and psychotropic substances**

Preamble ⓟ
CRC article ①
CRC article ②
CRC article ③
CRC article ④
CRC article ⑥
CRC article ⑦
CRC article ⑬
CRC article ⑰
CRC article ⑲
CRC article ㉓
CRC article ㉔
CRC article ㉕
CRC article ㉗
CRC article ㉙
CRC article ㉛
CRC article ㉜   CRC article ㉝

Click to search by:

CRC   SDG

▶ *Continued on following page*

11

Figure 8.2 Links between SDG Targets and CRC Obligations.

- increase health knowledge by educating the population about healthy practices, including family planning; and
- protect children against harmful cultural practices.

UNICEF has employed this CRC mandate in its health planning with states (as duty-bearers), its engagement with affected communities (as rights-holders), and its assistance to states in reporting to the Committee on the Rights of the Child (as a basis for rights-based accountability).

Working directly with government duty-bearers, UNICEF country offices develop a country program every five years based upon a "situation analysis" of children and women in the country. These analyses follow UNICEF's "human rights approach to programming," guided by a 2004 Programme Policy and Procedure Manual (PPPM) that frames the application of human rights by noting that:

- The aim of all Country Programmes of Cooperation is to further the realization of the rights of all children and women;
- Human rights and child rights principles guide programming in all sectors and at all phases of the programme process; and
- Programmes of Cooperation focus on developing the capacities of duty-bearers, at all levels, to meet their obligations to respect, protect and fulfil rights; as well as on developing the capacities of rights-holders to claim their rights (UNICEF 2004).

Developing UNICEF's five-year country program with government representatives, donor agencies, and other stakeholders (including local governments, civil society, and NGO representatives), the country program seeks to frame national health policy through principles of the rights-based approach and health-related rights of the CRC. This approach to examining the interconnected human rights that underlie health has allowed UNICEF health officers to expand their mandate beyond their traditional activities within the health sector, examining multi-sectoral national policy approaches to health.

UNICEF assistance to national governments has yielded programmatic successes for the implementation of health-related human rights, but it has not been without political compromise. Engaging with political stakeholders at the national level, UNICEF is often pressed to moderate its discourse on human rights, but country offices attempt to do so without compromising the obligations of human rights, employing the less-contentious language of "child rights" when discussing health programming. When addressing human rights more explicitly, UNICEF country offices have worked with independent National Human Rights Institutions (NHRIs), which, in accordance with the Paris Principles (UN General Assembly 1993), have autonomy to integrate human rights in their work and can monitor human rights in government policies. To facilitate this NHRI work, UNICEF has developed a global mapping of NHRIs, recognizing the role of these national institutions in facilitating human rights accountability (UNICEF 2013). Working directly with civil society, even if there is no common approach to civil society engagement, UNICEF looks to the country context and health issue to identify specific representatives (including indigenous rights NGOs; faith-based organizations; lesbian, gay, bisexual, transgender, and intersex (LGBTI) advocates; and youth groups) who are independent of the government, can represent constituencies affected by health programming, and will be able to facilitate "bottom-up" accountability (Nguyen 2013). To harmonize this country office approach to child rights, UNICEF's human rights and gender units have recently developed a "child rights toolkit" and online course to support country office work with national governments, highlighting strategies to integrate child rights in UNICEF development programming and providing a basis to assist states in the development of rights-based health policy (EU-UNICEF 2014).

Supporting this mainstreaming of rights in UNICEF country offices, UNICEF's Human Rights Unit works with country officers to develop capacity to apply a rights-based approach to health. Beginning in the late 1990s, UNICEF's Eastern and Southern Africa Region (ESAR) (alongside NGO partners) developed the organization's first human rights "core course," a five-day training for country office staff on the "human rights approach to programming," and this regional effort would become the basis for UNICEF Headquarters to develop its first Core Course on the Human Rights Approach to Programming. This multi-day voluntary course (with additional optional modules) provides an overview of child rights, how they relate to UNICEF's mandate, how a rights-based approach is different from a needs-based perspective, and how the organization can best assist states in implementing child rights. For experienced UNICEF staff, the Human Rights Unit has developed continuing education through human rights webinars, addressing specific issues of human rights implementation and getting practical feedback from country offices on how they have operationalized rights in their programming. Beyond these specific trainings (online and in-person at the regional level), UNICEF has established a Human Rights Intranet Page to support country officer application of human rights, providing key materials, answers to common questions, publications from the Human Rights Unit, videos of past webinars, and a roster of recommended human rights experts on thematic issues. To facilitate continuing connections between the Human Rights Unit and UNICEF country staff, UNICEF established a Human Rights Network in 2015 to connect regional human rights focal points and address gaps in country office capacity for human rights.

C. Supporting Child Health in the Human Rights System

UNICEF has also worked systematically across the international human rights system to advance children's health. Beginning through ad hoc consultations with the UN Committee on the Rights of the Child, UNICEF began in 1996 (as part of its reformed rights-based mission) to develop a permanent presence in Geneva, appointing a Geneva-based human rights "focal point" to be a liaison to the human rights treaty bodies, the then Commission on Human Rights, and the Office of the UN High Commissioner for Human Rights. With specific authority under the CRC to provide technical assistance to the Committee on the Rights of the Child, UNICEF has sought to participate in every session of the Committee and to work with the Committee in both developing general comments and monitoring states parties.

The Committee interprets CRC obligations for the health of the child through its general comments, and UNICEF has often supported the development of CRC general comments through subject matter expertise and region-specific input. While other international organizations have submitted ad hoc technical briefings to the Committee on specific general comments—e.g., UNAIDS on HIV issues and the International Labor Organization on child labor—UNICEF has contributed across all general comments. In the context of health, the Committee's fifteenth general comment interpreted Article 24 of the CRC, elucidating state obligations to realize the child's right to health holistically, defining:

> an inclusive right, extending not only to timely and appropriate prevention, health promotion, curative, rehabilitative and palliative services, but also to a right to grow and develop to their full potential and live in conditions that enable them to attain the highest standard of health through the implementation of programmes that address the underlying determinants of health (CRC 2013, para. 2).

Despite the General Comment's synoptic approach to underlying determinants of health, UNICEF's health program did not participate with the UNICEF liaison in supporting the Committee; while the resulting General Comment 15 addressed a range of stakeholders, it did little to clarify UNICEF's role in implementing the child's right to health, addressing the general comment to a range of stakeholders but not including UNICEF.

UNICEF country offices, however, have been consistently active before the Committee in monitoring state implementation of child health obligations, with the CRC requiring that states parties submit periodic reports to the Committee "on the measures they have adopted which give effect to the rights recognized" (UN General Assembly 1989, art. 44). Immediately after the promulgation of the CRC, UNICEF agreed in the first session of the Committee that it would provide data collected in accordance with the World Summit for Children and assist governments in reporting to the Committee (CRC 1991). UNICEF's participation in the treaty monitoring process has since expanded beyond the Geneva liaison and across the organization, with UNICEF country offices now engaging directly in the Committee's monitoring processes at various points and at multiple levels—in the organization of national consultations, in the development of state reports, in the submission of independent information, in the support of NGO shadow reports, and in the practice of constructive dialogue. UNICEF's Human Rights Unit has developed a monitoring toolkit to support country offices in this engagement, with this online toolkit, as shown in Figure 8.3, examining step-by-step the multiple levels of engagement with treaty bodies, providing practical information on what is required of UNICEF country offices, and highlighting illustrative case studies of national human rights implementation.

Participating throughout the monitoring process, UNICEF country offices work closely with national governments and NGOs in developing reports, attending constructive dialogue with the Committee in Geneva, and following up with states to implement the Committee's concluding observations. In preparing for

Figure 8.3 Committee on the Rights of the Child Monitoring Toolkit.

country reviews, UNICEF country offices develop a confidential report for the Committee, attend the pre-session working group to prepare questions for the state party, hold "mock constructive dialogue" sessions to prepare government representatives for constructive dialogue, and, where necessary, meet directly and confidentially with the Committee's rapporteur for the state in question (Lansdown 2000). Given this active in-person participation throughout the reporting and monitoring process, UNICEF country offices have the necessary information to follow up on the Committee's concluding observations in UNICEF's technical assistance with states, addressing Committee recommendations in subsequent situation analyses and five-year plans.

As a result of this active UNICEF country office engagement, the Committee has long focused on health obligations in monitoring the implementation of Article 24 of the CRC, consulting with UNICEF in reviewing state reports on the health of the child. This Committee interest in health has increased (in both breadth and depth), providing opportunities for the interests of individual Committee members to align with the health expertise of UNICEF on issues of adolescent health, sexual and reproductive health and rights (including teenage pregnancy), HIV/AIDS, and mental health (Doek 2001). Where UNICEF is a constant presence in monitoring health obligations, the Committee often specifically recommends in its concluding observations that states seek technical assistance from UNICEF in implementing obligations to progressively realize the highest attainable standard of health. To further expand the health policy understanding of Committee members, UNICEF has invited Committee members to visit health centers in country missions or participate in workshops on health issues, facilitating a mutually beneficial relationship between the Committee and UNICEF on issues of child health and human rights.

IV. INSTITUTIONAL DETERMINANTS OF HUMAN RIGHTS MAINSTREAMING

UNICEF is unique in having human rights obligations specifically delegated to it by a human rights treaty. Through the CRC, UNICEF has found support to frame the health-related human rights of the child—through the explicit use of legal frameworks and their implicit application in health programming. This part explores the determinants of human rights mainstreaming for children's health, analyzing the role of country offices, member states, and the Committee on the Rights of the Child.

A. Country Offices as Human Rights "Champions"

UNICEF country offices have long been key champions for the implementation of human rights in UNICEF programming. With UNICEF granting substantial autonomy to country offices, country officers have employed this agency to champion human rights implementation in national dialogues with health ministries. While other organizations have sought to implement human rights through their global health programming, no other organization has UNICEF's robust national presence, allowing country offices to work directly with states to assure implementation of child rights in national health policy. UNICEF has sought to work directly with government interests, building alliances with domestic stakeholders and offering financial assistance to implement human rights for health. To this end, UNICEF incorporates human rights principles and CRC concluding observations in each country's five-year plan, which UNICEF develops and signs alongside the national government. Despite initial post-CRC fears that UNICEF would have "little leverage to enforce compliance with the Convention" (Balton 1990, 129), UNICEF has proven itself an impactful international organization in reforming state practices, with country offices sharing best human rights practices with other country offices. Regional offices support these national efforts, providing tools and guidance to country offices to assure that human rights are operationalized in addressing the health of the most vulnerable. However, this regional office and country office autonomy "cuts both ways," with a lack of human rights harmonization across country offices leading each country health officer to pursue a distinct approach to human rights mainstreaming (Sano and Martin 2017). This ability to customize approaches to human rights has many positive qualities, but it is also associated with variability in the application of human rights in health plans, country programming, and situation analyses (Munro 2009). While this variability has narrowed with the development of e-learning modules for human rights training, there continue to be disparities in human rights capacity across regional and country offices.

B. State Support for Child Rights

UNICEF also has a privileged position in addressing human rights because of the near-universal state support for child rights obligations. The CRC rapidly came to be the UN's most universally ratified human rights treaty, creating momentum to influence national policy and UNICEF practice. This state support extended beyond the CRC, with the 1993 World Conference on Human Rights furthering the goals of 1990 World Summit for Children, recognizing that child rights were a priority across all states, and proclaiming that these rights should be regularly monitored (UN 1993). Through this international development of child rights, the child's right to health has come to be codified in national constitutions, resulting in a burgeoning implementation framework for UNICEF to provide technical support to member states on rights-based health policy. However, wading into the politics of national human rights implementation has often required context-specific compromises by UNICEF country offices to obtain government approval for UNICEF's five-year plan. As state support for human rights wanes—with the election of skeptical governments, rise of populist leaders, and pushback against human rights—greater challenges could arise for UNICEF to reconcile its commitment to human rights in programming in relation to its relationship with national governments in policymaking. Where countries (or even other international agencies and donors) have been seen to be resistant to the language of human rights (Merry 2006), UNICEF country officers have sought to implement human rights through the language of "child rights," "equity," "vulnerable populations," "gender," "human security," or "reaching the unreached," adapting their language in country-specific ways without sacrificing the universality of human rights. Although UNICEF seeks to advance human rights explicitly through its work with NHRIs, country offices have been pressed to develop alternative strategies for those governments that lack such independent human rights institutions. In building national support beyond governments, UNICEF is continuing to work with NGOs, health providers, civil society groups, and regional human rights bodies where there is a gap in national efforts, leveraging outside support to address contentious issues in national politics.

C. Relationship with the Committee on the Rights of the Child

UN specialized agencies are essential to monitoring state implementation of human rights, serving as a bridge between the health programming of national governments and the legal assessments of treaty bodies. The consistent and sustained UNICEF-CRC partnership is an unparalleled agency-treaty body relationship, with the Committee on the Rights of the Child relying on UNICEF for objective information on child health and UNICEF relying on the Committee for its recommendations to states parties (Oestreich 1998). Although other organizations submit information to treaty bodies, UNICEF is the only organization to contribute monitoring inputs directly from country offices. This "vertical integration" of UNICEF's technical advice (from country offices to Geneva institutions) provides for a credible, independent source of information on national conditions in the Committee's development of general comments and monitoring of state reports (O'Neill and Bye 2002). Because of UNICEF's systematic contributions to the Committee, UNICEF country offices hold a distinct role in assessing the progressive realization of rights across consecutive periodic reports, allowing for a dynamic dialogue with national governments over time. With a UNICEF liaison in Geneva, country offices have a permanent resource in identifying the health information most useful to the Committee in pre-sessional meetings, in translating UNICEF's country-specific health information to reflect human rights obligations, and in briefing field officers to interact directly with treaty bodies. This mutually beneficial relationship between the Committee and UNICEF has solidified over the years, and regardless of the health issue, the Committee will reach out to the UNICEF liaison on all health-related matters. Given UNICEF's targeted participation, country offices are often able to use specific recommendations in the Committee's concluding observations in their health policy efforts, with the authority of concluding observations reinforcing UNICEF recommendations to the state in implementing the CRC. Although this direct participation with treaty bodies has been limited to the Committee on the Rights of the Child, UNICEF country office contributions to consolidated UN Country Team reports hold the promise of expanding rights-based accountability for determinants of child health.

CONCLUSION

Driven by its history and galvanized by the CRC, UNICEF holds a unique position among global health agencies in its commitment and capacity to implement human rights for child health. While organizational leaders have taken varied approaches to human rights, UNICEF's mandate and the work of its country offices is informed by and reflective of the children's right to health and other health-related human rights. This rich legacy provides a foundation to consolidate disparate national approaches to human rights implementation and to integrate human rights-based approaches across its organizational efforts to achieve the child health–related SDGs. With UNICEF's continuing work guided by human rights, its 2018–2021 strategic plan incorporates health and human rights in both the narrative and the expected results, with human rights analyzed across each of UNICEF's seven programs and with UNICEF programming seeking to strengthen human rights language, mechanisms, and processes to realize health-related human rights for all children in the years to come.

REFERENCES

"A Table for the World's Children." 1966. *Social Service Review* 40(1): 90–91.

Balton, David A. 1990. "The Convention on the Rights of the Child: Prospects for International Enforcement." *Human Rights Quarterly* 12(1): 120–129.

Beigbeder, Yves. 2001. *New Challenges for UNICEF: Children, Women, and Human Rights.* Houndmills, Basingstoke, Hampshire: Palgrave.

Carrera, Carlos et al. 2012. "The Comparative Cost-Effectiveness of an Equity-Focused Approach to Child Survival, Health, and Nutrition: A Modelling Approach." *The Lancet* 380: 1341–1351.

CESCR (United Nations Committee on Economic, Social and Cultural Rights). 2000. "General Comment No. 14, The Right to the Highest Attainable Standard of Health." E/C.12/2000/4.

Cohen, Cynthia Price. 1983. "The Human Rights of Children." *Capital University Law Review* 12: 369–376.

Cohen, Cynthia Price. 1990. "The Role of Nongovernmental Organizations in the Drafting of the Convention on the Rights of the Child." *Human Rights Quarterly* 12(1): 137–147.

Commission on Human Rights, Report of the Thirty-Fifth Session, U.N. Doc. E/CN.4/ 1347 (16 March 1979).

Cornia, Giovanni Andrea, Richard Jolly, and Frances Stewart. 1998. *Adjustment with a Human Face: Country Case Studies*. London: Clarendon.

CRC (Committee on the Rights of the Child). 1991. "Summary Record of the 16th Meeting, First Session, Palais de Nations, Geneva, Switzerland, 6–9." 16 October.

CRC (Committee on the Rights of the Child). 2013. "General Comment 15 on the right of the child to the highest attainable standard of health." 17 April. CRC/C/GC/15.

Cueto, Marcos. 2004. "The ORIGINS of Primary Health Care and SELECTIVE Primary Health Care." *American Journal of Public Health* 94(11), 1864–1874.

DeForest, Walter R. 1950. "Public Health Practices in Germany Under U.S. Occupation." *American Journal of Public Health* 40:1072–1076.

Detrick, Sharon. 1999. *A Commentary on the United Nations Convention on the Rights of the Child*, 396–435. Leiden: Martinus Nijhoff Publishers.

Diaz-Martinez, Elisa and Elizabeth D. Gibbons. 2014. "The Questionable Power of the Millennium Development Goal to Reduce Child Mortality." *Journal of Human Development and Capabilities* 15(2–3): 203–216.

Doek, Jaap E. 2001. "Children and Their Right to Enjoy Health: A Brief Report on the Monitoring Activities of the Committee on the Rights of the Child." *Health and Human Rights* 5(155): 157–158.

Doull, James A. and Morton Kramer. 1948. "The First World Health Assembly." *Public Health Reports (1896–1970)* 63(43): 1379–1403.

EU-UNICEF. 2014. *Child Rights Toolkit: Integrating Child Rights in Development Cooperation.*

Every Woman Every Child. 2015. *The Global Strategy For Women's, Children's And Adolescents' Health (2016–2030).*

Fifield, Adam. 1994. *A Mighty Purpose: How Jim Grant Sold the World on Saving Its Children.* New York: Other Press.

George, Asha [et al.]. 2010. "Making Rights More Relevant for Health Professionals." *The Lancet* 375: 1764–1765.

Gibbons, Elizabeth D. 2015. *Accountability for Children's Rights: With Special Attention to Social Accountability and Its Potential to Achieve Results and Equity for Children.* New York: UNICEF.

Hawkes, Sarah and Kent Buse. 2016. "Searching for the Right to Health in the Sustainable Development Agenda: Comment on 'Rights Language in the Sustainable Development Agenda: Has Right to Health Discourse and Norms Shaped Health Goals?'" *International Journal of Health Policy and Management* 5(5): 337–339.

Holzscheiter, Anna. 2010. "Poverty Reduction Strategy in IMF Supported Programs." In *Children's Rights in International Politics*. Palgrave Macmillan.

Jacobs, Samuel K. 1950. "The United Nations International Children's Emergency Fund: An Instrument of International Social Policy. II." *Social Service Review* 24(3): 347–373.

Jolly, Richard. 1991. "Adjustment with a Human Face: A UNICEF Record and Perspective on the 1980s." *World Development* 19(12): 1807–1821.

Jolly, Richard and Carl Taylor. 1988. "The Straw Men of Primary Health Care." *Social Science and Medicine* 26(9): 971–977.

Jonsson, Urban. 2003. *Human Rights Approach to Development Programming.* Nairobi: UNICEF.

Keeney, Sam M. 1953. "Two Cooperative Projects of UNICEF and WHO." *Public Health Reports* 68(6): 606–608.

King, P. Z. 1950. "Significance of UNICEF's Role in International Child Health Activities." *American Journal of Public Health* 40: 177–182.

LaGuardia, Fiorello. 1946. United States. United Nations Relief and Rehabilitation Administration. Health Division, 1–9 (on file with author).

Lake, Anthony. 2012. "A Tipping Point for Child Survival, Health, and Nutrition." *The Lancet* 380: 1–2.

Lansdown, Gerrison. 2000. "The Reporting Process under the Convention on the Rights of the Child." *The Future of UN Human Rights Treaty Monitoring* 113–128.

League of Nations. 1924. "Geneva Declaration of the Rights of the Child."

Lewis, Stephen. 1997. "Promoting Child Health and the Convention on the Rights of the Child." *Health and Human Rights* (2): 77–82.

Mahler, Halfdan. 1979. "Action for Health." *Canadian Journal of Public Health* 70(4): 225.

Marks, Rachel B. 1968. "Review: Strategy for Children: A Study of Unicef Assistance Policies." *Social Service Review* 42(4): 531–532.

Marshall, D. 1999. "The Construction of Children as an Object of International Relations: The Declaration of Children's Rights and the Child Welfare Committee of League of Nations, 1900–1924." *International Journal of Children's Rights* 7: 103.

Merry, Sally E. 2006. "Transnational Human Rights and Local Activism: Mapping the Middle." *American Anthropologist* 108: 38–51.

Munro, Lauchlan T. 2009. "The 'Human Rights-base Approach to Programming': A Contradiction in Terms?" In *Rights-Based Approaches to Development: Exploring the Potential and Pitfalls*, edited by Sam Hickey and Diana Mitlin, 187–208. Sterling, Virginia: Kumarian Press.

Nguyen, Lena T.P. 2013. "Child-responsive Accountability: Lessons from social accountability." *UNICEF Innocenti Working Papers* 4.

Oestreich, Joel E. 1998. "UNICEF and the Implementation of the Convention on the Rights of the Child." *Global Governance* 4(2): 183–198.

O'Connell, Thomas, Kumanan Rasanathan, and Mickey Chopra. 2014. "What Does Universal Coverage Mean?" *The Lancet* 383(9913): 277–279.

O'Neill, William and Vegard Bye. 2002. *From High Principles to Operational Practice: Strengthening OHCHR Capacity to Support UN Country Teams to Integrate Human Rights in Development Programming*. Geneva: Office of the High Commissioner for Human Rights.

Pais, Marta Santos. 1998. *A Human Rights Conceptual Framework for UNICEF* (pp. 3–4, Tech.). Florence. DOI: http://www.eldis.org/vfile/upload/1/document/0708/DOC16790.pdf.

Russell, Paul F. 1950. "International Preventive Medicine." *The Scientific Monthly* 71(6): 393–400.

Sano, Hans-Otto and Tomas Max Martin. "Inside the Organization. Methods of Researching Human Rights and Organizational Dynamics." In *Research Methods in Human Rights: A Handbook*, edited by Bård A. Andreassen, Hans-Otto Sano, and Siobhán McInerney-Lankford, 253–281. Cambridge: Edward Elgar.

Shaffer, Alice C. 1960. "UNICEF in Central America." *The Annals of the American Academy of Political and Social Science* 329: 69–77.

Sikkink, Katherine. 1986. "Codes of Conduct for Transnational Corporations: The Case of the WHO/UNICEF Code." *International Organization* 40(4): 815–840.

"Social, Humanitarian, and Cultural Questions." 1963. *International Organization* 17(1): 150–171.

Smith, R. 1998. *UNICEF and the UN Convention on the Rights of the Child.* New York: UNICEF.

Tanahashi, T. 1978. "Health Service Coverage and Its Evaluation." *Bulletin of the World Health Organization* 56: 295–303.

UN General Assembly. 1946. "Establishment of an International Children's Fund. 11 December. UN Doc. A/RES/57(I).

UN General Assembly. 1959. "Declaration of the Rights of the Child." 20 November. UN Doc. A/4354.

UN General Assembly. 1989. "Convention on the Rights of the Child." 20 November. UN Doc. A/RES/44/25.

UN General Assembly. 1993. "Principles relating to the Status of National Institutions (The Paris Principles)." 20 December. Res. 48/134.

UN General Assembly. 1997. "Renewing the United Nations: A Programme for Reform, Report of the Secretary-General." 14 July. UN Doc. A/51/950.

UN General Assembly. 2002. "A World Fit for Children." 11 October. UN Doc. A/RES/S-27/2.

UNICEF. 1983. *The State of the World's Children, 1982–1983.* New York: Oxford University Press.

UNICEF. 1990. "World Summit for Children." *Population and Development Review* 16(4): 798–801.

UNICEF. 1996. "Mission Statement." 22 January. 1996/1.

UNICEF. 1998. *Guidelines for Human Rights-Based Programming Approach.* Geneva: UNICEF.

UNICEF. 2004. *Programme Policy and Procedure Manual: Programme Operations.* New York: UNICEF.

UNICEF. 2007. *Protecting the World's Children: Impact of the Convention on the Rights of the Child in Diverse Legal Systems.* Geneva: UNICEF.

UNICEF. 2012. *Global Evaluation of the Application of the Human Rights-Based Approach to UNICEF Programming.* New York: UNICEF.

UNICEF. 2013. *Championing Children's Rights: A global study of independent human rights institutions for children.* Geneva: UNICEF.

UNICEF. 2016. *Mapping the Global Goals for Sustainable Development and the Convention on the Rights of the Child.* New York: UNICEF.

UNICEF. n.d. "UN Human Rights Responsibilities." Available at: https://agora.unicef.org/course/info.php?id=2128.

"UNICEF Reports on Ten Years of Work for the World's Children." 1957. *Social Service Review* 31(2): 210–211.

"UNICEF Round-Table Recommends More Emphasis Be Placed on the Needs of Children in National Planning." 1964. *Young Children* 20(1): 56–58.

"United Nations International Children's Emergency Fund." 1950. *Social Service Review* 24(2): 247–250.

Van Bueren, Geraldine. 1995. "The International Law on the Rights of the Child." *Fordham International Law Journal* 19(2): 832–839.

WHO (World Health Organization). 1978. "Primary Health Care: Report of the International Conference of Primary Health Care Alma-Ata, USSR, 6–12 September."

9

The International Labor Organization

Human Rights to Health and Safety at Work

LEE SWEPSTON[*]

Safety and health at work is both a human right and a social and environmental issue that has long been a major concern for the International Labor Organization (ILO). Every fifteen seconds, a worker dies from a work-related accident or disease. Every fifteen seconds, 153 workers have a work-related accident. Every day, 6,300 people die as a result of occupational accidents or work-related diseases—more than 2.3 million deaths per year. Some 317 million accidents occur on the job annually, many of these resulting in extended absences from work, and millions more are permanently or temporarily disabled. This means a loss of income and social protection for workers and their families. Safety and health in the workplace is a massive problem for which serious solutions should be—and in many cases have been—put into place.

Since its establishment in 1919, the ILO has worked to improve occupational safety and health (OSH). In doing so, it has gradually evolved from approaching the problem as a purely technical issue, shifting toward a set of more rights-oriented solutions. The ILO has provided both guidance and direct assistance to promote safety and health in the workplace, helping governments respond to the consequences of gaps in protection and establishing a preventive culture in labor policy. It has also incorporated concerns about OSH into its broader standard-setting and assistance agendas. In addition to dealing with workplace diseases and injuries that underlie

* I would like to thank Benjamin Meier for inviting me to take part in this publication and for his lively interest in making the ILO's work better known, as well as for his insightful comments on the various drafts of this article. Thanks also to Professor Janice R. Bellace for her helpful and astute comments as external reviewer.

health, the ILO has tackled wider issues affecting health-related human rights, including violence at work, the situation of vulnerable workers, and social insurance.

This chapter begins in Part I by reviewing how the ILO functions, in particular its unique tripartite structure and its standard-setting role. In Part II, it goes on to examine how the ILO has gradually incorporated a human rights perspective in its work. The chapter describes the ILO's dedication to OSH as one of its most constant concerns in Part III, taking human rights into account through the adoption and supervision of dedicated international standards, practical assistance to its constituents, and coordination with other parts of the international system. The chapter concludes by reflecting on the practical and promotional approach taken by the ILO to facilitate the OSH aspects of the right to health and outlining the future challenges that lie ahead for human rights in OSH policy.

I. ILO STRUCTURE AND FUNCTIONS

The ILO is a specialized agency of the United Nations (UN) system, although it was established long before the UN existed. It was born in the aftermath of World War I, in the same Treaty of Versailles that created the League of Nations (Alcock 1971). When the League collapsed in the late 1930s, the ILO survived and became the first specialized agency of the new UN in 1946 (Shotwell 1934; Jenks 1976; Rodgers et al. 2009).

The second paragraph of the preamble to the ILO Constitution commits the ILO to protecting OSH, both directly and as it relates to the broad range of relevant ILO activities to improve labor conditions through:

> [T]he regulation of the hours of work including the establishment of a maximum working day and week, the regulation of the labour supply, the prevention of unemployment, the provision of an adequate living wage, the protection of the worker against sickness, disease and injury arising out of his employment, the protection of children, young persons and women, provision for old age and injury, protection of the interests of workers when employed in countries other than their own (ILO 1919, preamble).

OSH has come to be deeply embedded in the ILO's evolving work over the past century and continuing commitment to sustainable development, as spelled out in a recent examination of selected OSH instruments by the ILO's principal supervisory body:

> The Preamble to the ILO Constitution specifically provides that "the protection of the worker against sickness, disease and injury arising out of his employment" is a fundamental element of social justice. The obligation of the Organization to promote safe working conditions was reaffirmed in the 1944 Declaration of Philadelphia, and the 2008 Declaration on Social Justice for a Fair Globalization recognizes healthy and safe working conditions as a key element of the Decent Work Agenda.
>
> Global recognition has continued to grow that OSH is an important component of sustainable development, and the 2030 Agenda for Sustainable Development, adopted in 2015, turns the spotlight on OSH. The Sustainable Development Goal

(SDG) 8 of the 2030 Agenda is the promotion of sustained, inclusive and sustainable economic growth, full and productive employment and decent work for all. This SDG affirms that decent work is key to achieving sustainable development and that safe and secure working conditions are a fundamental part of decent work. It includes target 8.8 on protecting labour rights and promoting safe and secure working environments for all workers, including migrant workers, in particular women migrants, and those in precarious employment (ILO 2017b, 7).

In realizing this OSH mandate as part of the ILO's mission, there are two institutional features that distinguish the ILO from other inter-governmental organizations. The first is that the ILO was established with the explicit purpose of adopting international standards for the workplace, and by 2017, it has adopted 189 Conventions, six Protocols, and 205 Recommendations,[1] as well as a large number of other guidance documents (many of which relate to OSH), including codes of conduct (that are widely used as practical guidance for protecting workers and installing safety systems) and Declarations (to define ILO's orientations on, *inter alia*, human rights, apartheid, and equality). The application of ILO Conventions and Recommendations is closely monitored by a system of reporting and examination by various ILO committees, including the Committee of Experts on the Application of Conventions and Recommendations. The Committee of Experts examines nearly 2,000 reports each year from governments and from employers' and workers' organizations; evaluates compliance with these standards; and issues findings and recommendations for closer compliance (ILO 2014). Its report is reviewed each year by the tripartite Committee on the Application of Standards at the International Labor Conference, which invites selected governments to appear before it for a dialogue on the application of Conventions. Beyond the review of regular government reports, there are also various means of filing complaints of noncompliance (Ibid.).

The other distinguishing feature of the ILO is "tripartism," meaning that every state is represented at the ILO not only by governments but also by national organizations of employers and of workers (ILO 1919, Article 3; Thomann 2008). Tripartism is both an internal governance mechanism and an objective pursued by the ILO since its origins, giving non-governmental participants the right to participate fully in all ILO meetings, including the right to vote. Promoting the involvement of these "social partners" (as employers' and workers' organizations are often referred to in the ILO) in decision-making at the national level is a component of many ILO Conventions and Recommendations, beginning with those on freedom of association and collective bargaining, but also is included in many of the instruments on more technical subjects (Ibid.). One result of tripartism is a more realistic and effective standard-setting and supervisory process than is possible in purely inter-governmental organizations. Another result is the involvement of the ILO—by interventions from headquarters and through the ILO regional structure as appropriate—in providing information and assistance directly to its constituents (governments and employers' and workers'

---

1. Conventions are treaties that can be ratified and become binding, whereas Recommendations, while they cannot be ratified, contain more detailed guidance than Conventions and are most often adopted to accompany and supplement Conventions.

organizations) to target those most directly affected by OSH concerns (Rodgers et al. 2009).

II. THE ILO AND HUMAN RIGHTS

Because the ILO predates the modern human rights movement, the organization has faced difficulties in conceptualizing how it addresses human rights under international law. The drafters of the Treaty of Versailles included no reference to human rights in the founding documents of the League of Nations except for one reference in the first Constitution of the ILO, referring to the right of employers and of workers to organize for the protection of their interests (ILO 1919, preamble). As the ILO prepared for the end of World War II and the birth of what would become the UN system, it adopted the 1944 Declaration of Philadelphia (incorporated into the ILO Constitution two years later), which included the first statement of commitment to human rights ever adopted by a multilateral organization: "all human beings, irrespective of race, creed or sex, have the right to pursue both their material well-being and their spiritual development in conditions of freedom and dignity, of economic security and equal opportunity" (ILO 1944, sec. II (a)).

As the UN began to develop human rights under international law, with the adoption of the Universal Declaration of Human Rights (UDHR) in 1948 and of the two International Covenants in 1966, the international discussion of human rights focused on the UN. Driven by the ideological divisions of the Cold War, UN member states disputed whether civil and political rights or economic, social, and cultural rights were more important. The ILO did not take a position in these Cold War debates concerning the nature of human rights (Jenks 1970). ILO Conventions and Recommendations often contain elements of both categories of rights without distinguishing between them. The ILO did, however, contribute actively to the drafting of both the International Covenant on Economic, Social and Cultural Rights (ICESCR) and the International Covenant on Civil and Political Rights (ICCPR), as well as to the drafting of other UN human rights instruments (Rodgers et al. 2009).

Given these debates in international relations, most of the ILO's standard setting and supervision was not carried out with a human rights orientation, but took a more "utilitarian" approach, codifying government obligations to ensure certain outcomes (Bartolomei, von Potobsky, and Swepston 1996). This approach has persisted until the present day, with only a few Conventions and Recommendations addressing human rights directly.[2] Until the late 1990s, it might be said that the ILO's standards, like its practical activities, have implemented human rights implicitly, without citing human rights as the basis for the approaches taken (Swepston 2012). This approach has resulted in widespread international acceptance of ILO standards, with more than 8,000 ratifications of ILO Conventions (as of 2017).

---

2. The most notable exception is the 1948 Freedom of Association and Protection of the Right to Organize Convention (No. 87). Some of what are now classified as the ILO's fundamental rights instruments state in their preambles that they were adopted taking into account the UDHR, and sometimes the obligations in UN human rights instruments, but do not express themselves in terms of conferring rights directly.

Although there had been earlier references to human rights in ILO standards and deliberations, it was not until 1998 that the ILO adopted a formal commitment to human rights as a guiding philosophy, with the adoption by the International Labor Conference of the Declaration on Fundamental Principles and Rights at Work (ILO 1998). This explicit commitment to human rights followed from:

– the conclusions of the World Summit on Social Development in 1995 (UN 1995), which described specific ILO standards as human rights instruments; and
– the new UN system-wide approach in 1997 to incorporating human rights concerns in all UN activities, which sought "to enhance its [the UN's] human rights programme and fully integrate it into the broad range of the Organisation's activities" (UN Secretary-General 1997, para. 79).

The adoption of the 1998 Declaration also reflected other factors that altered the ILO's involvement in the international human rights system. With the end of the Cold War calling the ILO's *raison d'etre* into question for some,[3] the ILO Director-General launched a reflection on the ILO's future, calling for a renewed ILO mandate that included a commitment to human rights (ILO 1994). In addition, the long push for the international trading system to undertake sanctions-led enforcement of core labor standards had just collapsed with the decision by trade ministers (meeting in Singapore in 1996) to exclude labor standards from the mandate of the new World Trade Organization (WTO) (WTO 1996). Given these changes in the dynamic of international relations and the architecture of international organizations, the time had come for the ILO to move out of its relative isolation on human rights and into the evolving approach of the UN system, which was beginning to consider human rights as an integral part of economic and social development (UN Secretary-General 1997). With a push by employers' representatives to add a commitment in the ILO to general principles of human rights rather than having only binding standards available,[4] there was a growing willingness to increase the ILO's commitment to human rights without necessarily developing additional obligations on member states.

Following this 1998 Declaration on Fundamental Principles and Rights at Work, the ILO designated certain "fundamental human rights Conventions" that reflect the four fundamental human rights subjects covered by the Declaration:

– *Freedom of Association*
  – Freedom of Association and Protection of the Right to Organize Convention, 1947 (No. 87)
  – Right to Organize and Collective Bargaining Convention, 1948 (No. 98)

3. Many had come to see the ILO's work as providing a free market and democratic alternative to communism, and with the end of the Cold War, some felt that the ILO was no longer needed (Hansenne 1999). For a less optimistic (and to this writer, far overstated) view, see Langille 2016.

4. If this was indeed the intention of the employers, it has succeeded only in principle, as the adoption of the 1998 Declaration led to a push for ratification of the core human rights instruments, which now are closing in on near universal ratification.

- *Freedom from Forced Labor*
  - Forced Labor Convention, 1930 (No. 29)
  - Abolition of Forced Labor Convention, 1957 (No. 105)
- *Freedom from Discrimination*
  - Equal Remuneration Convention, 1951 (No. 100)
  - Discrimination (Employment and Occupation) Convention, 1958 (No. 111)
- *Freedom from Child Labor*
  - Minimum Age Convention, 1973 (No. 138)
  - Worst Forms of Child Labor Convention, 1999 (No. 182)

Based upon this new Declaration, some subsequent ILO standards began to take greater explicit account of human rights concerns. Whether or not the ILO itself was willing to express its human rights commitment earlier, ILO action now explicitly contributes to the implementation of human rights. In part this is achieved through the ILO's unique supervisory system for the implementation of ratified Conventions, which systematically examines the obligations that governments have undertaken against their performance in law and in practice. There is also a commitment to ensuring that the ILO's programmatic activities remain in conformity with its fundamental human rights conventions. Within a decade of the new 1998 Declaration, some scholars would find the ILO to be the preeminent organization in mainstreaming human rights in organizational practice:

> One may draw ever expanding "circles of willingness" in which the various organisations reside, depending on the seriousness with which they mainstream human rights. At the innermost circle one could place an organisation which predates the very UN human rights system and thus occupies a somewhat special place: the International Labour Organisation (ILO) (Oberleitner 2008, 364).

Applied to the ILO's health efforts, ILO action on OSH and related areas makes a significant contribution to health-related human rights, even when it does not make explicit reference to human rights standards. Since the ILO's 1998 Declaration, some OSH instruments have incorporated at least a partial rights orientation, even when not laying down human rights obligations directly. For example, the 2006 Promotional Framework for Occupational Safety and Health Convention (No. 187) contains an obligation on ratifying states to adopt a national policy to promote OSH, and defines the rights-based approach to be taken: "[e]ach Member shall promote and advance, at all relevant levels, the right of workers to a safe and healthy working environment" (ILO 2006, art. 3(2)).[5] These evolving ILO standards provide a basis to realize health-related human rights in OSH efforts.

---

5. By contrast, the earlier 1981 Occupational Safety and Health Convention (No. 155), which is considered by the ILO to be its basic modern Convention laying out OSH obligations for ratifying states, contains no reference to rights. It was instead based on a resolution concerning the working environment adopted in 1974, in which the International Labor Conference emphasized that "the improvement of the working environment should be considered a global problem in which the various factors affecting the physical and mental well-being of the worker are inter-related" (ILO 1974).

III. BASES OF INTERNATIONAL ACTION TO REALIZE RIGHTS TO OCCUPATIONAL SAFETY AND HEALTH

Nearly thirty years after the 1919 birth of the ILO, the UDHR brought OSH into the realm of human rights when it provided that "[e]veryone has the right to work, to free choice of employment, to just and favourable conditions of work and to protection against unemployment" (UN General Assembly 1948, art. 23; Swepston 2014b). Focused on the material benefits of work, this postwar Declaration went on to provide that:

> Everyone has the right to a standard of living adequate for the health and well-being of himself and of his family, including food, clothing, housing and medical care and necessary social services, and the right to security in the event of unemployment, sickness, disability, widowhood, old age or other lack of livelihood in circumstances beyond his control (UN General Assembly 1948, art. 25).

These OSH provisions under the UDHR were made more concrete in the 1966 ICESCR, which recognized "the right of everyone to the enjoyment of just and favourable conditions of work which ensure, in particular . . . safe and healthy working conditions" (UN General Assembly 1966, art. 7).

While these UN human rights treaties make general provision for rights to OSH, the ILO has given them concrete form since its earliest days. For example, the UN has adopted many human rights treaties that reinforce rights to OSH, such as the 2006 Convention on the Rights of Persons with Disabilities; yet, each of these UN human rights treaties is developed in far greater depth in ILO standards on the same subjects—as seen in this case in the 1983 Vocational Rehabilitation and Employment (Disabled Persons) Convention (No. 159), adopted by the ILO over twenty years earlier. The means of action employed by the ILO include the adoption of international labor standards (both Conventions and Recommendations), the adoption of a large number of codes of practice that provide practical guidance at the workplace level, and the implementation of these instruments through assistance to member states and to employers' and workers' organizations.

A. ILO Standard Setting and Related Action on OSH

The ILO has adopted more than forty standards dealing specifically with OSH, with nearly half of the more than 400 ILO standards touching either directly or indirectly on health issues (Wilson et al. 2006). These standards are part of the ILO's larger mission to lay down regulations, instruments, codes of practice, labor inspection, general surveys, and operational activities on work-related subjects, and they usually advance the recognition of human right for health even when they do not take a rights-based approach.

1. OSH STANDARDS

ILO standard setting on OSH has gone through several overlapping stages, and these trends in the way the ILO has addressed OSH at different times either foreshadow the broader human rights commitments arising in UN human rights instruments or develop aspects of past human rights instruments as they relate to the world of work (Swepston 2014a).

Until about 1960, the OSH standards adopted by the ILO were characterized by a piecemeal approach: standards were detailed, narrow in scope (covering a particular danger or occupation), and focused on safety and protection. The first example of this was the 1921 White Lead (Painting) Convention (No. 13), which recognized a toxic substance commonly used in construction, reviewed its dangers, and began to move toward its suppression. Subsequent standards focusing on specific substances or processes included, among others, the:

- Marking of Weight (Packages Transported by Vessels) Convention, 1929 (No. 27);
- Radiation Protection Convention, 1960 (No. 115);
- Working Environment (Air Pollution, Noise and Vibration) Convention, 1977 (No. 148);
- Asbestos Convention, 1986 (No. 162); and
- Chemicals Convention, 1990 (No. 170).

Another set of specifically focused standards drew attention to the dangers inherent in certain industries or occupations, including the:

- Plantations Convention, 1958 (No.110);
- Hygiene (Commerce and Offices) Convention, 1964 (No. 120);
- Occupational Safety and Health (Dock Work) Convention, 1979 (No. 152);
- Safety and Health in Construction Convention, 1988 (No. 167);
- Safety and Health in Mines Convention, 1995 (No. 176); and
- Safety and Health in Agriculture Convention, 2001 (No. 184).

During the long life of the ILO, there have been many individual risks, not addressed by national law in many countries, for which it was felt that international conventions could stimulate action. The ILO has sought to develop through standards a common understanding of where the greatest dangers lay (LaDou 2003). Addressing the dangers of substances and processes has meant disseminating the knowledge gained in more developed economies to developing economies that have often used dangerous materials long after they had been regulated or forbidden in industrialized countries. International law thereby becomes necessary where, for example, industrial machinery that has outlived its safe working life in developed countries, or that does not incorporate safety measures required by new legislation, is often exported to developing countries without the safeguards required in the countries exporting it, as seen in the 1963 Guarding of Machinery Convention (No. 119).

Another set of specific instruments concerns the protection of merchant seafarers and fishers, including the 1987 Health Protection and Medical Care (Seafarers) Convention (No. 164), which was adopted to respond to the particular characteristics of work aboard vessels. When the ILO adopted comprehensive standards on work in the maritime industry, it included OSH rights in the 2006 Maritime Labour Convention, detailing under "Fundamental Principles and Rights" that "[e]very seafarer has a right to health protection, medical care, welfare measures and other forms of social protection" (ILO 2006, art. IV(4)). The Convention goes on to include more than 100 references to safety and health for this special category of workers.

From 1970, ILO standards on OSH began to deal more broadly with health as well as safety, focusing on prevention and seeking to adapt the workplace to the workers rather than protect workers against existing workplaces. This represented a paradigm shift, culminating in the adoption of the 1981 Occupational Safety and Health Convention (No. 155), which calls for a dynamic, policy-based approach to OSH prevention and has the broadest possible scope—covering all workplaces and all risks (ILO 1981).

From about this time, ILO standards on safety and health began adopting what is known as a "systems approach," setting up organizational policies and ways of handling OSH questions on a more systematic basis.[6] The basic components of this systems approach are:

- Building and maintenance of a national preventative safety and health culture and the introduction of a systems approach to OSH management.
- The principle of prevention as the highest priority.
- Respect for the right to a safe and healthy working environment at all levels.
- Government, employer, and worker participation in securing a safe and healthy working environment, through a system of defined rights, responsibilities, and duties.
- Increased general awareness, knowledge, and understanding of the concepts of hazards and risks and how they may be prevented or controlled.
- A systems approach to OSH management at the enterprise level (ILO 2009).

This systems approach relies on the recognition that OSH is not only a government, employer, or trade union issue, but is a common public health concern, leading to the development of a culture of safety and health in daily life, at work, and in the home. The ILO went further into the systems approach by adopting the 2006 Promotional Framework for Occupational Safety and Health Convention (No. 187), which requires the adoption of a national policy for OSH, formulated and maintained with the participation of employers' and workers' organizations, with a view to developing "the infrastructure which provides the main framework for implementing the national policy and national programmes on occupational safety and health" (ILO 2006, art. 1).

Another approach to OSH issues is embodied in a series of instruments dealing with the treatment of workers who are affected by occupational diseases. The 1964

---

6. A full exploration of the development of ILO OSH standards and approaches is provided in ILO's General Survey of these instruments (ILO 2009).

Employment Injury Benefits Convention (No. 121) lays down the requirement that all workers who contract certain diseases after occupational exposure to factors causing them (e.g., those working with animal carcasses who contract anthrax) shall be deemed to have contracted these diseases from their work without having to prove that they are caused by work-related exposure (ILO 1964). The list of diseases and substances is periodically updated, allowing workers to receive social security benefits without having to go through a long and possibly expensive process of providing direct proof of on-the-job infection.

From this systems approach to disease, ILO standards began to be framed by human rights principles. The 2010 HIV and AIDS Recommendation (No. 200) calls for all possible measures to be taken to protect against transmission of HIV in an occupational setting, but its primary focus is on how workers who are HIV-positive (or thought to be HIV-positive) are treated in the workplace (ILO 2010). Developed with input from the Joint UN Programme on HIV/AIDS (UNAIDS) and the Office of the UN High Commissioner for Human Rights, this standard takes a firm position against mandatory testing and against revealing HIV status without the full and informed consent of the person concerned. It also deems measures taken by employers against these workers on the basis of real or presumed HIV status to be unacceptable occupational discrimination (Ibid.). Adopted as a basis to realize human rights, the Recommendation opens by:

> Noting that stigma, discrimination and the threat of job loss suffered by persons affected by HIV or AIDS are barriers to knowing one's HIV status, thus increasing the vulnerability of workers to HIV and undermining their right to social benefits, and
>
> Noting that HIV and AIDS have a more severe impact on vulnerable and at-risk groups, and
>
> Noting that HIV affects both men and women, although women and girls are at greater risk and more vulnerable to HIV infection and are disproportionately affected by the HIV pandemic compared to men as a result of gender inequality, and that women's empowerment is therefore a key factor in the global response to HIV and AIDS (Ibid., preamble).

This focus on cross-cutting human rights principles illustrates an increasing orientation of ILO standards toward human rights considerations.

2. OSH IN ILO INSTRUMENTS OF BROADER APPLICATION

Apart from Conventions and Recommendations adopted specifically to protect the health and safety of workers, there are also many provisions in instruments on other subjects that are intended to protect the health of workers as part of a more comprehensive approach to a particular problem (Takala 2013). For example, as concerns the health-related human rights of the child, the 1973 Minimum Age Convention (No. 138) covers the ages at which young people may begin to work, seeking to raise "progressively the minimum age for admission to employment or work to a level consistent with the fullest physical and mental development of young persons" (ILO 1973, art. 1), limiting the ages and conditions of undertaking more arduous and dangerous jobs, and providing that:

> The minimum age for admission to any type of employment or work which by its nature or the circumstances in which it is carried out is likely to jeopardise the health, safety or morals of young persons shall not be less than 18 years (Ibid., art. 3(1)).

While the Minimum Age Convention was not initially seen as a human rights instrument, it came to be counted as a rights-based Convention during the follow-up to the 1998 Declaration on Fundamental Principles and Rights at Work (ILO 1998).

The issue of child labor was then developed as an explicitly rights-based subject in the 1999 Worst Forms of Child Labour Convention (No. 182), which commits ratifying countries to taking "immediate and effective measures to secure the prohibition and elimination of the worst forms of child labour as a matter of urgency" (ILO 1999, art. 1). The Convention is also designated as one of the ILO's fundamental human rights Conventions, situating itself as a human rights instrument and recalling in the preamble both the 1989 Convention on the Rights of the Child and the 1998 ILO Declaration on Fundamental Principles and Rights at Work. Among the urgent measures to be taken is preventing "work which, by its nature or the circumstances in which it is carried out, is likely to harm the health, safety or morals of children" (Ibid., art. 3(d)).

Similar to issues of child labor, health-related questions beyond OSH are also dealt with in a number of other instruments that affect rights without explicitly discussing human rights, including in the 1949 Migration for Employment Convention (Revised) (No. 97), which provides for health care for migrants at departure, in transit, and on arrival (ILO 1949); and the 1989 Indigenous and Tribal Peoples Convention (No. 169), which seeks to promote and protect health and includes provisions on protecting indigenous workers from the effects of dangerous substances and processes when they work (ILO 1989). Like a number of other ILO standards that cut across organizational responsibilities, these Conventions were adopted in consultation with other UN system organizations, including the UN office responsible for human rights (now the Office of the UN High Commissioner for Human Rights).

As concerns health-related women's rights, the ILO will be developing standards on violence and harassment at the work place in the 2018 and 2019 sessions of the International Labor Conference. A September 2016 meeting on Violence against Women and Men in the World of Work (ILO 2016b) concluded, among other things, that violence and harassment at work "is a human rights issue and affects workplace relations, worker engagement, health, productivity, quality of public and private services, and enterprise reputation" (ILO 2016a, appendix 1, para. 1). As standard setting in the ILO increasingly takes human rights into account (ILO 2017b), this human rights consensus will form the basis for ILO standards in the coming years.

3. Instruments on Social Security

There is another large category of Conventions and Recommendations adopted by the ILO on social security that are intended to protect workers' safety and health. The right to social security is proclaimed as a human right in the UDHR, which states that:

> Everyone, as a member of society, has the right to social security and is entitled to realization, through national effort and international co-operation and in accordance with the organization and resources of each State, of the economic, social and cultural rights indispensable for his dignity and the free development of his personality (UN General Assembly 1948, art. 22).

This right to social security has since been elaborated and codified in a progression of UN international human rights treaties, including the:

- International Covenant on Economic, Social and Cultural Rights (arts. 9, 10(2) and 10(3));
- Convention on the Elimination of All Forms of Discrimination Against Women (arts. 11(1)(e), 11(2)(b), 14(2));
- Convention on the Rights of the Child (arts. 26, 27(1), 27(2), and 27(4));
- Convention on the Elimination of All Forms of Racial Discrimination (art. 5(e)(iv));
- International Convention on the Protection of the Rights of All Migrant Workers and Their Families (arts. 27 and 54);
- Convention on the Rights of Persons with Disabilities (art. 28);
- European Social Charter (arts. 8, 12, 13 and 16);
- American Declaration of the Rights and Duties of Man (art. XVI) (Riedel 2007).

This right is operationalized in the ILO by various instruments, including the Declaration of Philadelphia, which was incorporated in the ILO Constitution in 1946, and recognizes the ILO's "Solemn obligation to achieve ... (f) the extension of social security measures to provide a basic income to all in need of such protection and comprehensive medical care" (ILO 1944, sec. III(f)).

Among the large number of ILO standards adopted on social security, the most comprehensive is the 1952 Social Security (Minimum Aims and Standards) Convention (No. 102). These social security instruments are intended to allow workers to replace lost income when they are sick or injured for job-related reasons, or more simply when they retire for reasons of age. Supplemented by a long list of other instruments on aspects of social security, one set of ILO instruments guarantees maternity protection, calling for paid leave before and after a child is born—as seen most recently in the 2000 Maternity Protection Convention (No. 183).

B. Codes of Practice

While international Conventions and Recommendations are irreplaceable tools, they remain one step removed from working people and employers, requiring translation into action by governments at the national level. To encourage this translation through international standards, the ILO has adopted a whole series of "codes of practice" on various aspects of OSH. Adopted by expert meetings of those directly affected and approved by the ILO Governing Body, the forty-six codes adopted by the ILO touch on a range of subjects relevant to OSH, including on: Hazardous work (14), Occupational health (9), Workers' health promotion (4), Chemical safety and environment (3), Occupational safety and health (2), OSH management systems (2), HIV/AIDS in the workplace (1), Radiation protection (1), and National OSH Systems and Programmes (1) (ILO 2017a).

The most recent of these codes, the 2013 code on Safety and Health in the Use of Machinery, summarizes how the codes are to be used:

> The practical recommendations of this code of practice are intended for the use of all those who have a responsibility for safety and health in the use of machinery. The code is not intended to replace national laws, regulations or accepted standards. Its object is to provide guidance to those who may be engaged in the framing of provisions relating to the use of machinery at work, such as competent authorities and the management of companies where machinery is supplied or used. The code also offers guidelines to designers, manufacturers, suppliers and employers' and workers' organizations (ILO 2013, v–vi).

From time to time the ILO also adopts other OSH guidance to provide practical advice and information, such as the 2001 Guidelines on occupational safety and health management systems (ILO 2001).

C. Labor Administration and Governance

All the OSH measures outlined in the standards and the codes of practice described above have to be put into practice to be effective, so the ILO has adopted standards on labor administration, and in particular, labor inspection, as a basis of accountability for respecting labor law and realizing human rights. Labor inspection is an indispensable tool in a state's arsenal for enforcing human rights for OSH, and the standards on this subject are included among the ILO's priority conventions for ratification and implementation.

The basic instrument is the 1947 Labour Inspection Convention (No. 81), which outlines the responsibilities of the labor inspectorate in ways that have established a model for inspection services in almost all countries around the world:

1. The functions of the system of labour inspection shall be:
   - to secure the enforcement of the legal provisions relating to conditions of work and the protection of workers while engaged in their work, such as provisions relating to hours, wages, safety, health and welfare, the employment of children and young persons, and other connected matters, in so far as such provisions are enforceable by labour inspectors;

  – to supply technical information and advice to employers and workers concerning the most effective means of complying with the legal provisions;
  – to bring to the notice of the competent authority defects or abuses not specifically covered by existing legal provisions (ILO 1947, art. 3).[7]

Labor inspectors are therefore responsible not only for enforcing OSH laws but also for providing assistance to both workers and employers on how to implement the regulations. As the basis for law enforcement, the labor inspectorate is the basic accountability tool in most countries for the implementation of human rights in the workplace.

D. General Surveys on OSH

The ILO carries out periodic reviews of its standards and action across the range of its activities, in the form of "General Surveys," conducted each year on a selected subject by the Committee of Experts on the Application of Conventions and Recommendations. While these Surveys are intended to discuss the implementation of the instruments concerned, and any obstacles to their further ratification, the Committee of Experts has explored in some recent cases how these instruments relate to the human rights and development policies of the ILO and the broader international human rights system. A General Survey on OSH was carried out in 2009, concluding that:

> The relevance and importance of the national policy and systems approach in Convention No. 155 has been further reaffirmed through the Promotional Framework for Occupational Safety and Health Convention, 2006 (No. 187), and its Recommendation (No. 197). These instruments complement the instruments in this survey by providing further guidance on the systems approach to the management of OSH at all levels and the progressive establishment of a preventative safety and health culture based on the continuous provision of OSH information, training and education. The increasing rate of ratification of Convention No. 187 is a clear endorsement by the tripartite constituents of the ILO's timely action in the area of OSH, and indicates a renewed interest in the prevention of occupational accidents and diseases and improving working conditions and environment. In view of their close linkage, further efforts should be made to promote Convention No. 155 together with Convention No. 187. The joint support by the social partners of these efforts is an essential element in the process of achieving decent, safe and healthy working conditions and environment (ILO 2009, xii).

---

7. Convention No. 81 applies to nonagricultural workplaces and is complemented by the 1969 Labour Administration (Agriculture) Convention (No. 129), which contains similar provisions for agricultural workplaces.

The Committee of Experts also identified a number of challenges to OSH and opportunities that should be taken into account for future action.

In 2017 the ILO carried out a subsequent General Survey on OSH instruments concerning the promotional framework, construction, mines, and agriculture. In its concluding remarks the Committee of Experts stated:

> The promotion of OSH and the prevention of accidents and diseases at work is a core element of the ILO's founding mission and of the Decent Work Agenda. Moreover, the 2030 Agenda for Sustainable Development shines a light on OSH, and ILO instruments will be a key tool for countries wishing to make progress over the next 15 years towards the achievement of SDG target 8.8 in promoting safe and secure working environments for all workers. The collection, evaluation and dissemination of statistical data on OSH will be indispensable for both measuring and achieving progress (ILO 2017e).

This overview of the ILO's standard setting and supervision to address OSH illustrates the vital role of Conventions and Recommendations in expressing the Organization's policies, in setting obligations for governments, and increasingly in incorporating human rights considerations in ILO deliberations (ILO 2017c). As ILO standards become more explicitly related to the realization of health-related human rights, they also address vital development concerns that can prevent states from realizing human rights related to OSH.

E. Operational Activities

Beyond standard setting, human rights are integrated in the ILO's large program of assistance on OSH, with ILO staff working directly with governments, employers, and workers to help actors on the ground to put these policy prescriptions into practice. With ILO technical assistance regularly based on ILO standards and codes of practice, the rights-based orientation of these standards carries over into the ILO's operational programs.

Since the ILO does not have the resources to carry out all of these activities itself, the most important part of this program is training at the national and international level. With training materials available on the ILO website, examples of this training are seen most recently in the ILO's 2016–2017 Masters course in Occupational Safety and Health, which was conducted at the ILO's International Training Centre in Turin, Italy. The introduction to the course describes its "general objective" and purpose "to facilitate the knowledge and skills required for dealing effectively with safety and health management in enterprises . . . on all the topics and disciplines relevant to OSH, but also on the development of organizational, managerial and interpersonal skills" (ILO 2017d).

Beyond training, the ILO's operational programs often include OSH components, in direct or indirect implementation of the relevant ILO standards to address underlying determinants of occupational health. For example, the program on child labor includes operations for extracting children from forced labor in application of the 1999 Worst Forms of Child Labour Convention

(No. 182), reinserting children in schooling and vocational training. The same applies to indigenous and tribal peoples (in application of the 1989 Indigenous and Tribal Peoples Convention (No. 169)), whose conditions of work often subject them to unhealthy conditions. A more recent operational focus is on domestic workers, in application of the 2011 Domestic Workers Convention (No. 189), as the long hours and unhealthy conditions in which they work put their health at risk.

While operational activities evolve over time and are usually conducted in response to the needs expressed by member states, these OSH programs also take place in a context of international cooperation to achieve defined goals—whether in collaboration with the World Health Organization or within the larger UN system (WHO 2011). In September 2015, the UN General Assembly adopted the 2030 Agenda for Sustainable Development, forming a common framework for international development assistance under the SDGs (UN General Assembly 2015). This is not an exclusively human rights document, as discussed in chapter 4, but human rights are fully integrated into the goals of the international community as expressed in the SDGs. As concerns labor and associated rights, as already noted above, SDG 8.8 establishes as a common goal to "[p]rotect labour rights and promote safe and secure working environments for all workers, including migrant workers, in particular women migrants, and those in precarious employment" (ECOSOC Statistical Commission 2016, 24).

In this environment, the goals of development and human rights have become deeply intertwined for the ILO and for the UN system as a whole. The ILO OSH Plan of Action 2010–2016—adopted even before the SDGs—begins by recognizing that:

> The right to decent, safe and healthy working conditions and environment has been a central issue for the ILO since its creation, as reaffirmed in the 1944 Declaration of Philadelphia and the ILO Declaration on Social Justice for a Fair Globalization (ILO 2010).

As such, the obligations of human rights have been absorbed into the ILO agenda on OSH, among other development goals, even when the realization of human rights is not stated as the primary objective. The ILO continues to regard itself primarily as a technical resource, even as it incorporates wider visions of rights into its OSH agenda.

CONCLUSION

From its 1919 origins, the ILO has taken both a highly practical and a promotional approach to OSH policies and programs, and in this context, the role of human rights has progressively expanded. The ILO approach has evolved from regulating dangerous substances or processes, to providing for measures to be taken by specific industries, and finally to promoting a more systemic approach to the occupational aspects of the right to health. It has also stimulated coverage for health-related incapacity through social security systems, as well as encouraging countries to put into place enforcement and assistance mechanisms.

However, as the Committee of Experts noted in the 2009 General Survey, much remains to be done. The impact of the regulatory approach is limited by various factors, and additional work is needed to expand into the remaining areas where OSH approaches are limited or ineffective. The Experts have highlighted the need for multinational enterprises (MNEs) to take up OSH issues when they invest in countries that may have limited resources or capacity on the national level to regulate and enforce OSH requirements. As globalization proceeds, employers' conduct can no longer be regulated strictly on a national basis, and the value of a corporate social responsibility mindset becomes more evident.

There are other areas in which more could be, and is being, done, but the challenges remain enormous in the "informal economy." Most accidents and health risks occur in small and medium enterprises that are outside the formal economy and escape regulation and control. While in developed countries this covers only a small fragment of the population, the informal economy in some countries can occupy up to 90 percent of the workforce, who are effectively unprotected by any national safety and health laws. Similarly, ILO research shows that the social security systems put into place in compliance with ILO standards usually reach only the formal economy, and large segments of the population around the world are not protected. The ILO and the World Bank have formed a Global Partnership for Universal Social Protection to try to fill this gap in application of the 2030 Agenda for Sustainable Development, but the path here is even steeper than in other areas.

Thus while the ILO's experience shows what measures should be adopted, in OSH and the programs that underlie occupational health, it also demonstrates that measures cannot be fully effective unless they are more widely applied. The 2.5 million people who die each year of occupational disease and injury could be saved, but only if efforts continue and expand. These measures can be taken only when national economies continue to develop to the point that laws, regulations, and enforcement measures can reach the entire population. And these laws and policies are ever more closely linked to broader human rights priorities.

The ILO remains preeminent among inter-governmental organizations in mainstreaming human rights across its entire program. While the ILO itself does not always describe its actions on health as "human rights mainstreaming," it is considered to be mainstreaming rights through the commitments adopted under ILO standards, which are an integral part of the international system's human rights framework. In the end, the labels are less important than the practice.

REFERENCES

Alcock, Antony. 1971. *History of the International Labour Organisation*. London and Basingstoke: Macmillan.

Bartolomei, Hector G., Geraldo Von Potobsky, and Lee Swepston. 1996. *The International Labor Organization: The International Standards System and Basic Human Rights*. New York: Westview.

ECOSOC (UN Economic and Social Council) Statistical Commission, 48th Session. 2016. "Report of the Inter-agency and Expert Group on Sustainable Development Goal Indicators." 15 December. Doc. E/CN.3/2017/2.

Hansenne, Michel. 1999. *Un garde-fou pour la mondialisation: Le BIT dans l'après guerre froide.* Brussels and Geneva: Quorum and Zoë.

ILO (International Labor Organization). 1919. "Constitution of the International Labour Organization." Available at: http://www.ilo.org/dyn/normlex/en/f?p=1000:62:0:: NO:62:P62_LIST_ENTRIE_ID:2453907:NO.

ILO (International Labor Organization), 26th Session of the International Labor Conference. 1944. "The Declaration of Philidelphia." 10 May.

ILO, 30th Session of the International Labor Conference. 1947. "Labour Inspection Convention (Revised)." 11 July. ILO Convention No. 81.

ILO, 32nd Session of the International Labor Conference. 1949. "Migration for Employment Convention (Revised)." 1 July. ILO Convention No. 97.

ILO, 48th Session of the International Labor Conference. 1964. "Employment Injury Benefits Convention." 8 July. ILO Convention No. 121.

ILO, 58th Session of the International Labor Conference. 1973. "Minimum Age Convention." 26 June. ILO Convention No. 138.

ILO (International Labor Organization), 59th Session of the International Labor Conference. 1974. "Resolution concerning the ILO and the Working Environment."

ILO, 67th Session of the International Labor Conference. 1981. "Occupational Health and Safety Convention." 22 June. ILO Convention No. 155.

ILO, 76th Session of the International Labor Conference. 1989. "Indigenous and Tribal Peoples Convention." 27 June. ILO Convention No. 169.

ILO, 81st Session of the International Labor Conference. 1994. "Defending values, promoting change: Social justice in a global economy: an ILO agenda." Report of the Director-General (Part I).

ILO, 86th Session of the International Labor Conference. 1998. "ILO Declaration on Fundamental Principles and Rights at Work at its Follow-up." 18 June. Available at: http://www.ilo.org/declaration/info/publications/WCMS_467653/lang--en/index.htm.

ILO, 87th Session of the International Labor Conference. 1999. "Worst Forms of Child Labor Convention." 17 June. ILO Convention No. 182.

ILO. 2001. *Guidelines on occupational safety and health management system (ILO-OSH 2001).* Geneva: International Labor Office.

ILO, 95th Session of the International Labor Conference. 2006. "Promotional Framework for Occupational Safety and Health Convention." 15 June. ILO Convention No. 187.

ILO, 98th Session of the International Labor Conference. 2009. "ILO standards on occupational safety and health: Promoting a safe and healthy working environment: General Survey by the Committee of Experts." Report III (Part 1B).

ILO. 2010. *Plan of Action (2010–2016).* Geneva: International Labor Office.

ILO, 2013. Code of Practice on Safety and Health in the Use of Machinery.

ILO. 2014. *Rules of the Game: a brief introduction to International Labour Standards* (Revised edition 2014). Available at: http://www.ilo.org/wcmsp5/groups/public/--- dgreports/---dcomm/---publ/documents/publication/wcms_104643.pdf.

ILO. 2016a. *Outcomes of the Meeting on Violence against Women and Men in the World of Work.* Available at: http://www.ilo.org/gb/GBSessions/GB328/ins/WCMS_533534/lang--en/index.htm.

ILO. 2016b. *Materials relevant to violence against women.* Background paper for September 2016 ILO Meeting on Violence against Women and Men in the World of Work. Available at: http://www.ilo.org/wcmsp5/groups/public/---dgreports/---gender/documents/meetingdocument/wcms_522932.pdf.

ILO. 2017a. "Codes of Practice." Available at: http://www.ilo.org/safework/info/standards-and-instruments/codes/lang--en/index.htm.

ILO, 106th Session of the International Labor Conference. 2017b. "Employment and Decent Work for Peace and Resilience Recommendation." ILO Doc. ILC.106/V/1.

ILO. 2017c. "Report V (2B): Employment and Decent Work for Peace and Resilience." Available at: http://www.ilo.org/ilc/ILCSessions/106/reports/reports-to-the-conference/WCMS_546549/lang--en/index.htm.

ILO. 2017d. "Master in Occupational Safety and Health." Available at: http://www.ilo.org/safework/events/courses/WCMS_202133/lang--en/index.htm.

ILO, 106th Session of the International Labor Conference. 2017e. "Working together to promote a safe and healthy working environment, General Survey by the Committee of Experts on the occupational safety and health instruments concerning the promotional framework, construction, mines and agriculture." Report III (Part 1B).

Jenks, Wilfred. 1970. *Social Justice in the Law of Nations: The ILO Impact after Fifty Years.* London, Oxford, and New York: Oxford University Press.

Jenks, Wilfred. 1976. *Social Policy in a Changing World: The ILO Response.* Geneva: International Labor Organization.

LaDou, Joseph. 2003. "International Occupational Health." *International Journal of Hygiene and Environmental Health* 206(4–5): 303–313.

Langille, Brian. 2016. "Labor." In *The Oxford Handbook of International Organizations,* edited by Jacob Katz Cogan, Ian Hurd, and Ian Johnstone, 472–489. Oxford, United Kingdom: Oxford University Press.

Oberleitner, Gerd. 2008. "A Decade of Mainstreaming Human Rights in the UN: Achievements, Failures, Challenges." *Netherlands Quarterly of Human Rights* 26(3): 359–390.

Riedel, Eibe. 2007. "The Human Right to Social Security: Some Challenges." In Eibe Riedel, *Social Security as a Human Right,* 17–28. Berlin: Springer.

Rodgers, Gerry, Eddy Lee, Lee Swepston, and Jasmein Van Daele, 2009. *The International Labour Organization and the Quest for Social Justice, 1919–2009.* Geneva: International Labor Office.

Shotwell, James Thomson. 1934. *The Origins of the International Labor Organisation.* New York: Columbia University Press.

Swepston, Lee. 2012. "The International Labour Organization and Human Rights." In Catarina Krause and Martin Scheinin, *International Protection of Human Rights: A Textbook,* 2nd rev. ed. Turku/Åbo: Åbo Akademi University Institute for Human Rights.

Swepston, Lee. 2014a. "International Labour Law." In R. Blanpain, *Comparative Labour Law and Industrial Relations in Industrialized Market Economies.* Netherlands: Kluwer Law International.

Swepston, Lee. 2014b. *The Development in International Law of Articles 23 and 24 of the Universal Declaration of Human Rights: The Labor Rights Articles.* Netherlands: Brill Publishing.

Takala, Jukka. 2013. "International Agency Efforts to Protect Workers and the Environment." *International Journal of Occupational and Environmental Health* 5(1): 30–37.

Thomann, Lars. 2008. "The ILO, Tripartism, and NGOs: Do Too Many Cooks Really Spoil the Broth?" *Civil Society Participation in European and Global Governance,* 71–94. London: Palgrave Macmillan.

UN (United Nations). 1995. "Programme of Action of the World Summit for Social Development." 19 April. UN Doc. A/CONF.166/9.

UN General Assembly. 1948. "Universal Declaration of Human Rights." 10 December. UN Doc. 217 A (III).

UN General Assembly. 1996. "International Covenant on Economic, Social and Cultural Rights." 16 December. Res. 2200A (XXI).

UN General Assembly. 2015. "Transforming our world: the 2030 Agenda for Sustainable Development." 25 September. Resolution 70/1.

UN Secretary General. 1997. "Renewing the United Nations: A Programme for Reform, Report of the United Nations Secretary-General." 14 July. UN Doc. A/51/950.

Wilson, Donald J., Ken Takahashi, Derek R. Smith, Masako Yoshino, Chieko Tanaka, and Jukka Takala. 2006. "Recent Trends in ILO Conventions Related to Occupational Safety and Health." *International Journal of Occupational Safety and Ergonomics* 12(3): 255–266.

WHO (World Health Organization). 2011. "Connecting Health and Labour: Bringing Together Occupational Health and Primary Care to Improve the Health of Working People." WHO/HSE/PHE/ES/2012.1.

WTO. 1996. "Singapore Ministerial Declaration." 18 December. Doc. WT/MIN(96)/DEC.

10

The United Nations Educational, Scientific and Cultural Organization

Advancing Global Health through Human Rights in Education and Science

AUDREY R. CHAPMAN AND KONSTANTINOS TARARAS*

The United Nations Educational, Scientific and Cultural Organization (UNESCO) is the specialized agency of the United Nations (UN) dealing with education, natural sciences, social and human sciences, culture, and communication and information. The promotion of human rights is interwoven with UNESCO's purpose, as provided in Article I of its Constitution, and thus has been a component of the Organization's activities from the first years of its existence.

This chapter focuses on UNESCO's human rights work and its interconnection with initiatives relating to global health. Part I of this chapter addresses the evolution of UNESCO's human rights activities, with references wherever appropriate to global health. However, global health is not an explicit area of UNESCO interventions. Albeit not a central actor in global health governance, many of its initiatives—notably in the field of science, bioethics, and education—have contributed to the promotion of public health and the implementation of the right to health, whether directly or indirectly. These initiatives will be highlighted in Part II through an overview of UNESCO efforts on standard-setting and monitoring, rights in education, and rights in science. While the lack of a comprehensive UNESCO approach to issues in global health may be considered a weakness, Part III analyzes how this approach provides UNESCO with greater flexibility to address global health issues across the diverse areas of its mandate.

* The authors are responsible for the choice and the presentation of the facts contained in the article and for the opinions expressed therein, which are not necessarily those of UNESCO and do not commit the Organization.

The elevation of human rights and gender mainstreaming to Organization-wide priorities has been an important factor in strengthening the alignment of UNESCO activities—including those relating to global health and to human rights principles and standards. This trend was greatly influenced by the deepening commitment to the human rights priorities of the entire UN system as a result of the UN Reform process launched in 1997 by the then UN Secretary-General, through which UNESCO has been increasingly interacting on a broad array of issues. The adoption of the 2030 Agenda for Sustainable Development as a comprehensive human rights-based framework is expected to further entrench human rights in UNESCO's activities leading up to the 2018 commemoration of the seventieth anniversary of the Universal Declaration of Human Rights (UDHR).

I. EVOLUTION OF HUMAN RIGHTS THROUGH UNESCO

UNESCO was established in 1945 by thirty-seven countries "to contribute to peace and security by promoting collaboration among the nations through education, science and culture in order to further universal respect for justice, for the rule of law, and for human rights and fundamental freedoms which are affirmed for the peoples of the world, without distinction of race, sex, language or religion, by the United Nations Charter" (UNESCO 1945, art. I(1)). In the aftermath of World War II, UNESCO was founded, as noted in the preamble to its Constitution, on the belief that a peace based exclusively on the economic and political arrangements of governments would not secure the lasting support of the peoples of the world. Instead, peace had to be founded on the intellectual and moral solidarity of humankind and be driven by the mutual understanding and rapprochement among peoples (Ibid.). In building intercultural respect, UNESCO drew on the past experiences of the International Commission on Intellectual Cooperation, which dealt with similar issues within the League of Nations, to place emphasis on reaching out to the public at large and influencing decision-making (Renoliet 2005).

Based in Paris, UNESCO has 195 member states and ten associate member states. UNESCO is governed by a General Conference, which is composed of all UNESCO member states and an Executive Board. These member states meet every two years at the General Conference to determine the policies and main lines of work of the Organization (UNESCO 1945, art. IV(2)). During its two regular sessions per year, the Executive Board of fifty-eight member states examines the programmatic work of UNESCO and the corresponding budget, with the Executive Board responsible for the execution of the program adopted by the General Conference (UNESCO 1945, art. V(6)(a–c)). The Secretariat, headed by a UNESCO Director-General, implements the decisions of these two bodies. Carrying out its mandate, UNESCO currently has five major program sectors: (1) education; (2) natural sciences; (3) social and human sciences; (4) culture; and (5) communication and information (UNESCO 2013a).

A. Historical Human Rights Milestones in the Field of Global Health

Since its creation, UNESCO has engaged in the promotion of human rights, especially those rights directly linked to its mandate.[1] UNESCO was involved in the drafting of the UDHR and several of the international treaties that derived from it, in particular the International Covenant on Economic, Social and Cultural Rights (ICESCR) (UNESCO 2003a). In 1947, UNESCO created the Committee on the Philosophical Principles of the Rights of Man to explore the philosophical basis, in different cultures, of human rights as legal entitlements and thereby identify areas of possible agreement between divergent approaches to human rights (McKeon 1947). Although the UN Commission on Human Rights (now the Human Rights Council) did not formally consider the Committee's conclusions, they represented a first attempt to elucidate the different philosophical perspectives underpinning the UDHR (Oh 2005). On December 10, 1948, immediately after the proclamation of the UDHR by the UN General Assembly, UNESCO's General Conference adopted a resolution to acknowledge the importance of the UDHR for all of UNESCO's activities (UNESCO 1948). Supporting human rights far earlier than other UN specialized agencies, the resolution requested the UNESCO Director-General to disseminate information about the UDHR wherever possible—through mass communication programs, teaching materials in schools, and UNESCO's program activities (Ibid.).

In advancing human rights, countering racist doctrines has been a priority of UNESCO since the early days of the Organization. Responding to an appeal of the UN Economic and Social Council (ECOSOC) in 1948, UNESCO embarked on a research program to demonstrate the scientific fallacy of theories of racial superiority (Symonides 2001b). The findings of this research underpinned the four UNESCO statements on race and racial prejudice in the 1950s and 1960s. These statements emphasized the predominance of historical, social, and cultural factors in the explanation of differences among populations living in different geographical areas of the world (Ibid.). From these statements, UNESCO developed its 1960 Convention Against Discrimination in Education (UNESCO 1960)[2] and its 1978 Declaration on Race and Racial Prejudice (UNESCO 1978b).

Over the years, UNESCO's human rights-related activities have included the development of normative instruments; research and development of publications and tools; advocacy; awareness-raising; and knowledge exchange, notably through the organization of international meetings. Many of these initiatives, often in close cooperation with the World Health Organization (WHO), have contributed to the

---

1. The rights most relevant to UNESCO's mandate include: education; participation in cultural life; enjoyment of the benefits of scientific progress and its applications; freedom of opinion and expression, including the right to seek, receive, and impart information; and water and sanitation.

2. This Convention drew from, *inter alia*, a 1957 study by the UN Special Rapporteur on discrimination in education, who was appointed by the UN Commission on Human Rights' Sub-Commission on the Prevention of Discrimination and the Protection of Minorities (ECOSOC 1957).

promotion of global health and health-related human rights. However, this work did not lead to the elaboration of a comprehensive Organization-wide approach to global health. Rather, health-related issues have been addressed through sector-focused interventions, at times in coordination with other UN agencies. A starting point was the 1949 establishment with WHO of the Council for International Organizations of Medical Sciences (CIOMS) (Brody 1993; Bankowski et al. 1993). These two UN specialized agencies later embarked on a coordinated effort to create model programs and methodologies for teaching human rights and medical ethics in schools of medical sciences (Gelhom et al. 1977; Guilbert 1980; Torelli 1983; Vasak 1977), drawing on, *inter alia*, their interaction during the elaboration of UNESCO's 1974 "Recommendation concerning Education for International Understanding, Co-operation and Peace and Education Relating to Human Rights and Fundamental Freedoms" (Becet 1979; Fluss 1980; Fülöp 1974).[3]

UNESCO's bioethics program has been an important complement to the health and human rights-focused activities of other UN agencies, the Office of the UN High Commissioner for Human Rights (OHCHR), and the human rights monitoring bodies. A milestone in this respect was the UNESCO partnership with WHO and CIOMS to explore the ethical, social, and human rights considerations of scientific and technological progress in biology and medicine (Herzog 1972; Meier 2013).

Applied to public health, UNESCO's framework for comprehensive sexual education has reinforced HIV prevention efforts through education and worked to combat HIV-related stigma and discrimination. Its pioneering efforts on rights in science, which have sought to promote recognition of the right to secure the enjoyment of the benefits of scientific progress and its applications, have continuing importance for access to medicines. Finally, health was addressed within a two-phase analysis of poverty from a human rights perspective. The first phase examined—in the four-volume political science and economic analysis, *Freedom from Poverty as a Human Right* collection—the philosophical and legal underpinnings of a human rights approach to poverty (Sané 2010, vi). The second phase, through the *Empowering the Poor through Human Rights Litigation* manual, aimed to foster the justiciability of economic, social, and cultural rights, including the right to health, as an instrument for poverty eradication (Formisano Prada 2011).

B. Organization-Wide Strategies to Mainstream Human Rights

A key driver in the enhancement of UNESCO's human rights programs was the elaboration of Organization-wide strategic documents and the adoption of cross-cutting priorities on human rights and gender equality. The reform of the UN system to "mainstream" human rights, launched in 1997 by the UN Secretary-General and discussed further in chapter 3, placed human rights at the center of all UN activities

---

3. Extending this work on medical education for human rights, UNESCO has continued work with the World Federation for Medical Education (WFME), including as a partner in its 2003 World Conference on Medical Education, "Global Standards in Medical Education for Better Health Care" (World Federation for Medical Education n.d.).

(UN Secretary-General 1997). Drawing on an enabling internal environment, UNESCO's General Conference responded to this call for reform by adopting in 2003 the UNESCO Strategy on Human Rights and the Integrated Strategy to Combat Racism, Discrimination, Xenophobia and Related Intolerance. These strategies reaffirmed UNESCO's constitutional commitment to incorporating human rights in all programs across all its fields of competence (UNESCO 2003a). They also contextualized UNESCO's mandate in the face of new and persisting challenges and global agendas—such as the Millennium Development Goals and the Durban Declaration and Program of Action of the 2001 World Conference against Racism—building on its comparative advantage, experience, and expertise with the intention of better positioning UNESCO within the constellation of UN entities and other actors working on human rights (UNESCO 2006). These strategies provided further impetus for the mainstreaming of human rights in UNESCO. In conformity with the UN Statement of Common Understanding on Human Rights-Based Approaches (HRBAs) to Development Cooperation and Programming (UNDG 2003), this entailed that:

- all programs should further the realization of human rights;
- human rights principles and standards should guide the programming process in all fields and all stages;
- programs should contribute to the development of the capacities of "duty-bearers" to meet their obligations and of "rights-holders" to claim their rights (Ibid.).

To reach these goals, UNESCO intensified in-house coordination and invested in enhancing the knowledge and skills of UNESCO staff to apply HRBAs (UNESCO 2006).

In 2010, the UNESCO Director-General submitted a plan on human rights mainstreaming to the Executive Board for the purpose of further institutionalizing HRBAs at UNESCO and enhancing the contribution of human rights to UNESCO's inter-agency work (UNESCO 2010). One year later, the Director-General presented to the Executive Board a report on the main outcomes from the implementation of the 2003 human rights and anti-discrimination strategies (UNESCO 2011c). Regarding human rights mainstreaming, the report mentioned the human rights training of UNESCO staff—delivered since 2006 to more than 500 persons, both at headquarters and in field offices—and UN input on the design of training content (Ibid.).[4]

Efforts to mainstream a gender equality perspective served to reinforce the human rights underpinning of UNESCO programs. The Medium-Term Strategy for 2002–2007 constituted a turning point in the handling of this portfolio by the Organization, as it established gender equality as a cross-cutting priority and reinforced implementation modalities and mechanisms (UNESCO 2002);

---

4. The same report also addresses advocacy against HIV/AIDS-related discrimination through youth empowerment and collaboration with municipal authorities.

and the following medium-term strategy elevated gender equality to the status of global priority (UNESCO 2008). To operationalize this evolving commitment, UNESCO adopted the Priority Gender Equality Action Plan for 2008–2013 (UNESCO 2009b). Gender equality was preserved as one of the global priorities of UNESCO for 2014–2021 and was accompanied, as with previous medium-term strategies, by a corresponding Priority Gender Equality Action Plan (UNESCO 2014c).

C. Human Rights Inter-Agency Cooperation Affecting Global Health

Another driver for further entrenching a human rights culture within the Organization's health-related efforts was the interaction with the UN human rights system and the ever-strengthening cooperation with other UN specialized agencies, programs, and bodies, either bilaterally or within the framework of inter-agency platforms.

Recognizing shared interests and commitments with human rights treaty bodies, UNESCO has collaborated with the UN Committee on Economic, Social and Cultural Rights (CESCR), the treaty monitoring body, as discussed in chapter 23, with oversight over the rights to education, health, water and sanitation, cultural participation, and the benefits of science in the ICESCR. A main UNESCO input was its participation in CESCR deliberations when the Committee developed general comments interpreting rights that overlap with UNESCO's mandate, including in General Comments 13 (right to education, 1999), 14 (right to health, 2000), 17 (right to benefit from the protection of the moral and material interests resulting from any scientific, literary, or artistic production of which he is the author, 2005), and 21 (right of everyone to take part in cultural life, 2009) (UNESCO 2009c; UNESCO 2010; UNESCO n.d.-j).

UNESCO also contributes systematically to the Universal Periodic Review (UPR) carried out by the UN Human Rights Council (HRC), providing information within the Organization's areas of competence regarding the implementation of rights by states under review (UNESCO 2013a). Its submissions have drawn upon information made available within the framework of monitoring UNESCO's standard-setting instruments, as well as its activities with member states. UNESCO country offices also participate, as reviewed in chapter 24, in developing the UPR report prepared by the UN Country Team. Beyond the UPR, UNESCO cooperates closely with the HRC's special procedures mandate holders, as examined in chapter 22, working with the special rapporteurs on cultural rights, the right to education, freedom of opinion and expression, and anti-discrimination (Ibid.).

Finally, UNESCO participates in inter-agency platforms tasked with promoting coordination, cooperation, and coherence on human rights or on specific issues underpinned by human rights principles and standards. In particular, the Organization participates in the UN Development Group's (UNDG's) Human Rights Working Group, a platform established to mainstream human rights in the development work of the UN system, with emphasis, as discussed in chapter 3, on promoting system-wide coherence and supporting interventions at the country level (UNDG n.d.). Specific to the intersection of human rights and bioethics, UNESCO serves as the permanent secretariat to the UN Inter-Agency Committee on Bioethics (UNIACB), a platform that seeks to facilitate international engagement and dialogue in the field of bioethics, with special attention to human rights (UNESCO n.d.-i).

II. MAINSTREAMING HUMAN RIGHTS IN UNESCO PUBLIC HEALTH EFFORTS

Human rights, as per Article I of UNESCO's Constitution, underpins all of the Organization's actions across all its fields of competence. The attention to normative action derives from its centrality in the work of the Organization—from its creation and in its current functions (UNESCO 2013c)—while the emphasis on education and science is justified by the amount, diversity, and recognition of initiatives in these domains relating to public health. UNESCO mainstreams human rights in these public health efforts primarily through: (a) standard-setting and monitoring, (b) rights in education, and (c) rights in science.

A. Standard-Setting and Monitoring

The setting of standards as a means for protecting and promoting human rights has played an important role in UNESCO's activities (UNESCO n.d.-d). The normative instruments adopted by the Organization have been of two types: conventions on the one hand, and recommendations, declarations, and charters on the other (UNESCO 1945, art. IV(4)). Almost all UNESCO standard-setting instruments pertaining directly or indirectly to health are non-binding recommendations, declarations, and charters. The adoption of an international convention requires a two-thirds majority at the General Conference, while for recommendations and declarations, a simple majority suffices. As in the case of other UN human rights instruments, member states that ratify or accede to a convention are legally bound by its provisions in their national legislation, policies, and practice. While earlier UNESCO instruments contain references to human rights, it is only from the late 1990s that human rights principles and standards become more prominent in UNESCO's normative action, including several in the fields of bioethics and ethics of science and technology.[5]

1. UNESCO Bioethics Declarations

The UNESCO Bioethics Program has sponsored three health-related declarations with a strong human rights orientation:

(1) The *Universal Declaration on the Human Genome and Human Rights*, adopted by the UNESCO General Conference in 1997 and by the

5. Beyond issues of bioethics and science, UNESCO has adopted two instruments with important health implications in the area of sports and physical education: the International Convention against Doping in Sport (2005) and the Revised International Charter of Physical Education, Physical Activity and Sport (2015).

UN General Assembly in 1998. This Declaration describes the human genome as underlying the fundamental unity of all members of the human family, as well as the recognition of their inherent dignity and diversity. It recognizes that everyone has a right to respect for their dignity and for their rights regardless of their genetic characteristics. Therefore it states that no one shall be subjected to discrimination based on genetic characteristics, and practices that are contrary to human dignity, such as reproductive cloning of human beings, shall not be permitted (UNESCO 1997).

(2) The *International Declaration on Human Genetic Data*, adopted by UNESCO's General Conference in 2003:

> to ensure the respect of human dignity and the protection of human rights and fundamental freedoms in the collection, processing, use and storage of human genetic and proteomic data, and of the biological samples from which they are derived, in keeping with the requirements of equality, justice and solidarity, while giving due consideration to freedom of thought and expression, including freedom of research (UNESCO 2003b, art. 1(a)).

(3) The *Universal Declaration on Bioethics and Human Rights*, adopted by UNESCO in 2005. The aim of this Declaration is to provide guidance to individuals, corporations, institutions, and states regarding decisions and practices on ethical issues related to medicine, life sciences, and associated technologies, as well as to recognize the importance of science and the benefits from science and technological developments (UNESCO 2005). It was the first international legal document that addressed the linkages between human rights and bioethics. As such, it represents a step forward in the development of global bioethical standards. Like any declaration adopted by UN agencies, it is a soft law instrument. Given its drafting by UNESCO, the Declaration reflects a compromise between a theoretical conceptualization made by experts and the practical requirements of the governments. The Declaration's principles are not original: the goal was to integrate principles from existing international documents and to integrate them into a human rights framework in order to codify standards for responsible biomedical research and clinical practice (Andormo 2007). In terms of its content, the Declaration recognizes the importance of freedom of scientific research and the benefits derived from scientific and technological developments while stressing the need for such research and developments to occur within a framework of ethical principles and respect for human dignity, human rights, and fundamental freedoms (Andormo 2009). Using a human rights framework, the Declaration establishes normative principles in fifteen areas, including human dignity and human rights, equality, justice and equity, and protecting future generations. It states that the promotion of health

and social development is a central purpose of government that all sectors of society share. Several sections are notable in both reflecting and extending the content of general comments of the CESCR: the affirmation of the right to health as the framework for social responsibility and health; an emphasis on the broad sharing of benefits from any scientific research along with the forms it should take in giving effect to this principle; the need for the life sciences to protect future generations; the role of states in fostering international dissemination of scientific information and encouraging international cooperation; and the importance of protecting the environment, the biosphere, and biodiversity. The Declaration also stresses the importance of states establishing independent, multidisciplinary, and pluralist ethics committees to assess the relevant ethical, legal, scientific, and social issues related to human research and the need of such committees to foster debate, education, and public awareness of, and engagement in, bioethics (UNESCO 2005).

Important normative developments in the broad field of ethics of science and technology—with important implications on health and health governance—were recently accomplished in two areas.

The first concerns the revision of the 1974 Recommendation on the Status of Scientific Researchers, concluded at the thirty-ninth session of UNESCO's General Conference in November 2017. Launched in 2013, the revision sought to reflect contemporary ethical and regulatory challenges relating to the governance of science and the science-society relationship. UNESCO member states aspired to transform an insufficiently used instrument (UNESCO 2015d) into "a powerful and relevant statement of science ethics as the basis for science policies that would favour the creation of an institutional order conducive to the realization of article 27(1) of the Universal Declaration of Human Rights" (UNESCO 2013d, 43). While already an underlying consideration in the 1974 instrument, the potential benefits and possible threats to humankind (and public health in particular) from scientific discoveries and related technological developments have become more prominent in the revised text of the Recommendation on Science and Scientific Researchers (UNESCO 2017c; UNESCO 2015d; UNESCO n.d.-c).

The second area, where work initiated in 2015 after a lengthy negotiation begun in 2009, pertains to the elaboration of a declaration on ethical principles in relation to climate change. This new instrument, adopted by UNESCO's General Conference at its thirty-ninth session in November 2017, aims to reinforce ethical responses to the adverse effects of climate change on human and natural systems, in particular on certain groups that are disproportionately threatened (UNESCO 2017a). To contribute to more adequate and equitable responses at all levels, particularly in the area of adaptation and mitigation policies, this instrument proposes such principles as the prevention of harm, the precautionary principle, equity, justice and fairness, scientific knowledge, and integrity in decision-making (Ibid.).

2. UNESCO Human Rights Monitoring

The task of monitoring the implementation of UNESCO instruments—if not entrusted to a body established by the respective treaty, as is the case of most instruments in the field of culture—is handled by a permanent subsidiary body of UNESCO's Executive Board, the Committee on Conventions and Recommendations (CR). The CR, which meets in regular session twice a year, examines progress reports submitted by UNESCO member states regarding recommendations and international conventions (UNESCO 2016a). However, the monitoring procedure before the CR differs significantly from those handled by the UN treaty bodies and the HRC, with the CR: engaging in a collective, private consultation; drawing on individual country reports (rather than a country examination); and resulting in specific, confidential recommendations (Ibid.; Mukherjee 2009).

A complementary aspect of the CR mandate pertains to the examination of individual communications relating to cases and questions concerning the exercise of human rights in UNESCO's fields of competence, including the right to enjoy the benefits of scientific progress and its applications. The individual communications procedure, established by the Executive Board (UNESCO 1978a), is not adjudicatory but seeks to promote a friendly solution that improves the situation of the alleged victims whose health may be at risk (UNESCO 2016a). As a consequence, such communications take place in complete confidentiality, and the proceedings before the CR cannot be published or made accessible to the public for a period of twenty years. Until the 2013 entry into force of the Optional Protocol to the ICESCR, which established an individual complaints' procedure before the CESCR, the complaints procedure before UNESCO's CR was the only international mechanism considering individual communications in this field. Furthermore, it had the advantage of applying to all UNESCO member states, independent of ratification of a specific treaty. However, this procedure has not become sufficiently known and utilized by civil society organizations, as evidenced by the limited number of complaints received thus far.[6] Although the confidential CR mechanism preserves certain advantages, the greater appeal of the public and adjudicatory CESCR mechanism, together with the increasing ratification of the ICESCR Optional Protocol by UN member states, is expected to decrease the relevance of UNESCO's procedure. As a result, the Organization is presented with two longer-term options: either to revamp its procedure with an emphasis on raising efficiency, effectiveness, and awareness or to invest in other modalities for individual communications.

B. Rights in Education

UNESCO has had a long-standing human rights commitment to strengthening the links between education and health. Recognizing that the education of children and young people can be compromised by conditions and behaviors that undermine

---

6. Since its establishment in 1978 and until 2015, the CR had examined only 597 communications, of which 381 were settled (UNESCO 2016a; UNESCO n.d.-h).

physical and emotional well-being, the Organization has concluded that teachers and education policymakers must embrace health promotion activities to achieve their education goals, and schools must be supportive venues for the provision of essential health education and services (UNESCO 2016b). This is consistent with the language on the right to education in the UDHR, which provides that "[e]ducation shall be directed to the full development of the human personality and to the strengthening of respect for human rights and fundamental freedoms" (UN General Assembly 1948, art. 26(2)).

UNESCO has clarified this right in, *inter alia*, the 2000 Dakar World Education Forum Framework for Action and the Education for All (EFA) Goals (UNESCO 2015b). To implement the EFA Goals, UNESCO joined in 2000 with WHO, UNICEF, Education International, and the World Bank to develop the "Focusing Resources on Effective School Health (FRESH)" framework, seeking to demystify school health for governments and encourage harmonization across development partners. Based on good practices and driven by a consensus approach, this integrated framework covers considerations relating to policy, the school environment, skills education, and services (Bundy 2011). One example of the Organization's contribution in connection with the FRESH framework is a module for "Improving Learning Outcomes by Improving Health and Nutrition: Incorporating the FRESH Approach in National Action Plans for Achieving Education for All" (UNESCO 2001). The promotion of health as a core outcome of good quality education, including lifelong learning, was also pursued through the five-year Global Education First Initiative (GEFI), which was launched in September 2012 by the UN Secretary-General to accelerate progress toward the EFA goals and the education-related Millennium Development Goals (MDGs) (UN 2014).[7] UNESCO's lead position within this UN initiative is evidenced by the role of the UNESCO Director-General as Executive Secretary of the GEFI Steering Committee, the high-level body providing strategic direction and guidance to the UN Secretary-General (Killion 2013). To monitor progress on the attainment of the EFA Goals and the MDGs, UNESCO has issued an annual global report, in which the pivotal role of education and the right to education in improving people's chances of a healthier life and promoting healthy societies has been an almost constant consideration (UNESCO 2014b; UNESCO 2015b). This global education monitoring report has been extended as UNESCO's main instrument for monitoring Sustainable Development Goal (SDG) 4 on education to "[e]nsure inclusive and equitable quality education and promote lifelong learning opportunities for all" (UN 2015).

The rights-based commitment to a strengthened interconnection between education and health is particularly evidenced by UNESCO's growing investment in the promotion of comprehensive sexuality education programs and the scaling up of education sector responses to HIV. UNESCO's HIV strategy focuses on the mobilization of formal, nonformal, and informal education responses as part of a comprehensive sexual education approach. Since 1996, UNESCO has played a

---

7. While several MDGs influenced education, MDG 2 sought to "achieve universal primary education," with a target to "ensure that, by 2015, children everywhere, boys and girls alike, will be able to complete a full course of primary schooling" (UN 2000, Target 2A).

leading role within the Joint UN Programme on HIV/AIDS (UNAIDS), for which, as discussed in chapter 13, it is a co-founding co-sponsor. This co-sponsor role is showcased by UNESCO's convening role in the UNAIDS Inter-Agency Task Team (IATT) on Education and School Health, a multi-stakeholder platform created in 2002 to support accelerated and improved education sector responses to HIV (Aggleton 2011). In mainstreaming HIV/AIDS prevention in education policies and advocating for a comprehensive education response, the IATT places emphasis on monitoring and evaluation tools premised on human dignity and gender equality (Bundy 2011). Further steering global efforts to promote HIV/AIDS education, UNESCO also led EDUCAIDS, the UNAIDS Global Initiative on Education and HIV and AIDS, pushing for a comprehensive education sector response that is rights-based, gender responsive, and inclusive in order to achieve the MDGs (UNESCO 2007). These UNESCO efforts have resulted in, *inter alia*, the first global guidance on sexuality education—"International Technical Guidance on Sexuality Education: An evidence-informed approach for schools, teachers and health educators" (UNESCO 2009a)—and the reports, *Charting the Course of Education and HIV* (UNESCO 2014a) and *Comprehensive Sexuality Education: A Global Review* (UNESCO 2015a). Finally, UNESCO's HIV and Health Education Clearinghouse has proven a valuable platform for knowledge sharing, open to inputs from external partners (UNESCO n.d.-e). The converging efforts described above culminated in the development of an integrated 2016 UNESCO *Strategy on Education for Health and Well-Being: Contributing to the Sustainable Development Goals*, which addresses the broader set of skills and issues linked to the promotion of the healthy development of different learners (UNESCO 2016b). This Strategy covers a wide range of topics—from prevention of sexually transmitted infections and healthy and respectful relationships to school-related violence, good nutrition, and quality physical education—as part of the consideration of safe and inclusive learning environments. Recognizing the interconnectedness between comprehensive sexuality education and access to safe, inclusive, and health-promoting learning environments, this Strategy translates intersectional human rights and gender equality into operational priorities. It updates previous UNESCO strategies and is aligned with the new 2016–2021 UNAIDS Fast-Track Strategy and the SDGs, in particularly SDG 3 on Health, SDG 4 on Education, and SDG 5 on Gender Equality (Ibid.).

With respect to physical education, UNESCO has built over the years a global leadership role, providing technical assistance to member states on policy and capacity-building and stimulating international debate on existing and emerging challenges. Instrumental in this role has been UNESCO's work linked to the implementation of the 2015 International Charter of Physical Education, Physical Activity and Sport, which recognizes as reference points existing international instruments relating to human rights. With the revival in 2013 of the MINEPS process (the international conference of ministers and senior officials responsible for physical education and sports) as a unique multi-stakeholder global platform to take stock of developments in this field and formulate recommendations on international policy priorities (Ho et al. 2016; UNESCO n.d.-a), particular attention is paid within this framework to quality physical education that is aimed at developing the learners' physical, social, and emotional skills (UNESCO n.d.-g).

Finally, considerations relating to the realization of the right to health are an integral part of UNESCO's activities on human rights education, which is perceived by the Organization as a human right in itself and a prerequisite for the full realization of human rights and democracy, social justice, and peace (Symonides 2001a). Important drivers for these education efforts on human rights have been the UN Decade for Human Rights Education (1995–2004), co-led with the OHCHR, and its successor framework, the World Programme for Human Right Education (2005–present), within which UNESCO has maintained a central place (OHCHR. n.d.-b). With initiatives in both formal and nonformal education settings, UNESCO has provided human rights training, information, fellowships, and advisory services programs to its member states and has developed model human rights curricula, pedagogical techniques, and learning materials, such as the joint 2007 UNICEF publication on *A Human Rights-Based Approach to Education for All: A Framework for the Realization of Children's Right to Education and Rights within Education* (UNICEF 2007).

C. Rights in Science

With scientific developments central to health and human rights advancement, UNESCO is committed by its Constitution to "maintain, increase and diffuse knowledge: through conservation and protection, and cooperation in all branches of intellectual activity including international exchange" (UNESCO 1945, art. I(2)(c)). This mandate takes on special importance in an era of tremendous scientific and technological advancements in medical sciences, which have a potential to contribute to human well-being but also pose risks of harm (UNESCO 2015e). Moreover, access to applications of such advancements remains unequal—not only between countries but also within countries. Responding to these challenges was a main driver behind UNESCO's work on the right to enjoy the benefits of scientific progress and its applications and in the field of bioethics and the ethics of science and technology (Brody 1993; Schabas 2007; UNESCO 2009c).

The right to enjoy the benefits of scientific progress and its applications is expressly enumerated in both the UDHR and ICESCR,[8] but the scope and requirements of this right have received little attention until relatively recently, making it difficult to implement this right in national policy and organizational practice (Schabas 2007).

UNESCO took a leading role in the first efforts to conceptualize this right. While the importance of sharing scientific knowledge was highlighted in the report of the 2000 World Conference on Science (UNESCO 2000), the Organization's investment in clarifying the human rights underpinnings of this concept was prompted by the 2003 UNESCO Human Rights Strategy, which sought the "development of a research agenda on the content, nature of obligations, state of implementation,

8. The UDHR provides: "Everyone has the right freely to participate in the cultural life of the community, to enjoy the arts and to share in scientific advancement and its benefits" (UN General Assembly 1948, art. 27(1)). This is elaborated by the ICESCR, which provides: "The States Parties to the present Covenant recognize the right of everyone . . . to enjoy the benefits of scientific progress and its applications" (UN General Assembly 1966, art. 15(b)).

indicators and justiciability of human rights within UNESCO's fields of competence" (UNESCO 2006, para. 22). A first step toward the elucidation of this "unde-
veloped" right to the benefits of scientific progress was a "mapping" study, exploring
the rationale behind its enunciation in the UDHR and the ICESCR in light of the
travaux preparatoires (preparatory work) and also raising a set of key questions for
the clarification of the right in the 2007 publication *Human Rights in Education,
Science and Culture: Legal Developments and Challenges* (Schabas 2007). Drawing on
these findings, UNESCO sponsored three expert meetings to operationalize this
right, examining the interdependence of scientific developments with other human
rights and also exploring its interrelationship with such issues as health, intellectual property protection, climate change, and environmental protection (UNESCO
2009c). One of these expert meetings, organized in 2009 with the European Inter-
University Centre for Human Rights and Democratisation, provided an analysis of
the right to enjoy the benefits of scientific progress and its applications, with an
emphasis on conceptual challenges, normative elements, and next steps. This consensus was codified in the Venice Statement on the Right to Enjoy the Benefits of
Scientific Progress and Its Applications (Ibid.).

The Venice Statement encouraged states to use all appropriate legislative, administrative, and other means to implement this right to enjoy the benefits of scientific progress and its applications with a view to achieving progressively the full
realization of the right without discrimination of any kind (Ibid.). The document
also called upon inter-governmental organizations—including WHO, the Food
and Agricultural Organization, the World Intellectual Property Organization, and
UNESCO—to take due account of the right in implementing their activities and
programs, and it looked to human rights bodies—notably the HRC and CESCR—
to clarify its content in view of the right's operationalization. Although UNESCO
has not advanced this work on the normative clarification of all aspects of the right
to enjoy the benefits of scientific progress since the Venice conference, these rights-
based efforts have guided UNESCO's continuing work on bioethics and the ethics
of science and technology (Donders 2011; OHCHR. n.d.-a; OHCHR 2012).

Broader human rights considerations in the field of life sciences in relation to
global health have been promoted through UNESCO's work in the field of bioethics.
Building on the Organization's involvement in international debates on the ethics of
life sciences since the 1970s, the 1993 establishment of the UNESCO Bioethics
Program has provided a basis to address human rights principles for public health
(ten Have 2013).

The Bioethics Program is led by the International Bioethics Committee (IBC),
consisting of thirty-six independent experts, and the Intergovernmental Bioethics
Committee (IGBC), consisting of representatives from thirty-six member states
(UNESCO n.d.-b). They are tasked with following progress in the life sciences and
its applications and with spearheading multidisciplinary, pluralistic, and multicul-
tural reflection in order to ensure respect for human dignity and freedom (Kutukdjian
1994). A reference point for the rights-based work of the IBC is the body of relevant
UNESCO normative instruments and notably the 2005 Universal Declaration on
Bioethics and Human Rights (Andorno 2007). Meeting at least once a year to produce advice and recommendations on specific issues, health-related themes in recent

reports include: the principle of the sharing of benefits (2015), an updated reflection on the human genome and human rights (2015), non-discrimination and non-stigmatization (2014), and traditional medicine systems and their ethical implications (2013) (UNESCO n.d.-f; IBC 2015). Currently, the IBC is focusing on "big data" in health care and health research—including but not limited to issues of autonomy, consent, data protection, and governance—and is exploring the intersection between bioethics and the conditions of refugees and migrants, with emphasis on health care and considerations of equality, justice, and equity (UNESCO n.d.-f). A complementary body to the IBC is the World Commission on the Ethics of Scientific Knowledge and Technology (COMEST). Composed of eighteen independent experts, this advisory organ focuses on formulating ethical principles, including on environmental ethics (with reference, *inter alia*, to climate change), biodiversity, water and disaster prevention, and the ethics of nanotechnologies (UNESCO n.d.-k).

A core function of the Bioethics Program is to support member state efforts in addressing bioethics issues. The Bioethics Program has sponsored three non-binding international agreements that promote health-related human rights—two relating to the human genome and human rights and one on bioethics and human rights. Additionally, the Bioethics Program has pursued targeted capacity-building for the establishment of national ethics committees (through the Assisting Bioethics Committees (ABC) program) and the brokering of national and regional networking arrangements among institutions and specialists (for instance, by fostering linkages with the Network of Institutions for Medical Ethics Education (NIMED)). Finally, it promotes awareness of bioethics among a host of concerned audiences, particularly in its education efforts through the UNESCO Bioethics Core Curriculum, launched in 2008 with the aim of introducing a flexible, impartial, and minimalist approach to teaching university students the principles of the Universal Declaration on Bioethics and Human Rights.[9]

Finally, within its broader scientific mandate, UNESCO is advancing global health through its work on water security. Human rights considerations, particularly from the perspective of the human rights to water and sanitation, are an integral part of the Organization's work to address, *inter alia*, the protection of vulnerable water systems, the mitigation of water-related hazards, the integrated and equitable management of water resources, and the safeguarding of access to relevant services (UNESCO 2013b). UNESCO's action on water and sanitation is driven by its International Hydrological Program, which fosters research, education, and policy advice about a broad array of issues, including water-related disasters, water scarcity and quality, and water and human settlements (UNESCO 2009d). The interconnections with public health are central to UNESCO's initiative for water quality (UNESCO 2015c). Supporting this work, UNESCO has also developed an annual publication, the *World Water Development Report*—with the latest, released in March 2017, dedicated to the theme of "Wastewater, The Untapped Resource" (UNESCO 2017b).

---

9. To this end, UNESCO has developed a complementary Casebook Series, launched in 2011, with the two issues published thus far addressing human dignity and rights considerations and issues of benefit and harm (UNESCO 2011b; UNESCO 2011a).

III. FLEXIBILITY IN ADDRESSING GLOBAL HEALTH

An important challenge for UNESCO in discharging its work for global health relates to the diversity and reach of its mandate, which, combined with the fact that it is not a central actor in global health governance, has undoubtedly influenced its approach. These considerations offer a plausible explanation as to why there has not been so far an Organization-wide strategic document outlining a set of coherent and converging priorities in the field of global health. Although the absence of an internal policy framework could be perceived in general as a weakness, it has not weakened the development of significant activities on the part of the Organization in many health-relating domains—with bioethics and education among the most illustrative. UNESCO has in fact taken up a lead role in inter-agency platforms such as the UNAIDS IATT and the UN Inter-Agency Bioethics Committee (UNIABC)—in recognition of its experience, expertise, and contribution. Moreover, public health issues have been an integral part of UNESCO's analysis and operational responses in all relevant initiatives—for example, in relation to physical education and sports, anti-doping, water security, and anti-poverty initiatives. Perhaps the absence of a rigid reference framework on global health has allowed for greater flexibility in embarking on new initiatives motivated by necessity and relevance.

A strong feature of all these UNESCO efforts has been their increasing incorporation of human rights. This has been facilitated by the interplay of internal and external factors. Internally, UNESCO's clear constitutional commitment to human rights, combined with the strong human rights articulation of UNESCO's activities throughout the years, has facilitated the reaffirmation of the centrality of human rights for all its programs and activities, notably through the 2003 Organization-wide human rights and anti-discrimination strategies. Capacity-building on human rights mainstreaming, offered in accordance with these strategies, could also be regarded as a conducive factor. At the same time, this trend has been nurtured by an enabling international environment for human rights in UNESCO, developed since 1997 with the launching of the UN Reform to mainstream human rights and the intensification of inter-agency coordination and interaction (UN Secretary-General 1997).

CONCLUSION

The promotion of human rights has been a component of UNESCO's activities from the first years of its existence, especially in regard to those rights for which UNESCO has a particular responsibility. Albeit not a central actor in global health, many of UNESCO's human rights initiatives have had implications for public health and the realization of health-related human rights, particularly its extensive work on bioethics, scientific developments, and education. Initiatives in these domains cover a wide range of actions, from standard-setting and research to awareness-raising and advocacy. In recent years, there has been an intensification of UNESCO's normative work, with the revision of existing instruments and the elaboration of new ones to address evolving and emerging challenges.

The adoption of these strategies has demonstrated UNESCO's alignment with the UN Reform to mainstream human rights and the Organization's commitment to the collective efforts of the UN system to strengthen human rights work. This commitment has become even more critical. In the SDG era, the pursuit of holistic approaches that do justice to the complexity and interconnectedness of global challenges, as well as provide greater consistency and coherence, will be a key reference point for determining UNESCO's relevance for the years to come. Institutional relevance will be determined by the Organization's compliance with the human rights-based vision and operational commitments of the new SDG agenda. These human rights considerations are expected to guide the Organization's work, thereby allowing it to capitalize on important accomplishments thus far. With new UNESCO leadership elected in November 2017, these changes will enable UNESCO to overcome its ongoing financial and budgetary crisis, to fulfill its constitutional *raison d'être*, and to realize the "leaving no one behind" mantra of the SDGs.

REFERENCES

Aggleton, Peter, Ekua Yankah, and Mary Crewe. 2011. "Education and HIV/AIDS 30 Years On," *AIDS Education and Prevention* 23(6): 495–507.

Andorno, Roberto. 2007. "Global Bioethics at UNESCO: In Defence of the Universal Declaration on Bioethics and Human Rights." *Journal of Medical Ethics* 33(3): 150–154.

Andorno, Roberto. 2009. "Human Dignity and Human Rights as a Common Ground for a Global Bioethics." *Journal of Medicine & Philosophy* 34(3): 223–240.

Bankowski, Zenon and Robert J. Levine. 1993. *Ethics and Research on Human Subjects: International Guidelines*. Geneva: CIOMS.

Becet, Jean-Marie. 1979. "Letter to WHO Director-General Halfdan Mahler" (on file with author).

Brody, Eugene B. 1993. *Biomedical Technology and Human Rights*. Paris: UNESCO and Aldershot, Hants. Brookfield, Vermont: Dartmouth Publishing Company.

Bundy, Donald. 2011. *Rethinking School Health: A Key Component of Education for All*. Washington, D.C.: World Bank.

Donders, Yvonne. 2011. "The Right to Enjoy the Benefits of Scientific Progress: In Search of State Obligations in Relationship to Health." *Medicine, Health Care and Philosophy* 14: 371–381.

ECOSOC (Economic and Social Council). 1957. "Study of discrimination in education' by Charles D. Ammoun, Special Rapporteur of the Sub-Commission on Prevention of Discrimination and Protection of Minorities." Doc. E/CN.4/Sub.2/181/Rev.1.

Fluss, Sev S. 1980. "Note for the Record: Confidential Meeting with Mr. A.H. Zarb (formerly Director of the Legal Office in WHO) and Professor Maurice Torrelli (Institut du Droit de la Paix et du Développement, University of Nice) on 9 June 1980." Doc. N63/372/10 (on file with author).

Formisano Prada, Maritza. 2011. *Empowering the Poor Through Human Rights Litigation*. Paris: UNESCO. Available at: http://unesdoc.unesco.org/images/0021/002150/215041E.pdf.

Fülöp, Tam'as. 1974. *Special Committee of Governmental Experts to Examine the draft recommendations concerning Education for International Understanding, Co-operation and*

Peace and Education Relating to Human Rights and Fundamental Freedoms. Report on Attendance at a Meeting for UNESCO on 29 April–9 May 1974.

Gelhom, Alfred, Tam'as Fülöp, and Zbigniew Bankowski. 1977. "Health needs of society: a challenge for medical Education." 10 CIOMS Round Table Conference. Geneva: World Health Organization.

Guilbert, J. J. 1980. "Memorandum from WHO EPL/HMD to WHO Ad hoc Group Members. Coordination with UNESCO in the Field of Human Rights." Doc. N63/372/10 (on file with author).

Herzog, Marie Pierre. 1972. "Letter from UNESCO Division of Philosophy Director M.P. Herzog to CIOMS Executive Secretary S. Btesh." Doc. PH/72/283 (on file with author).

Ho, Walter King Yon, Dilzad Ahmed, Beatrice Wong, Fan Huang [et al.]. 2016. "Quality Physical Education and Global Concern—Ways Ahead and Future Development." *Actividad Física and Ciencias* 8: 60–70.

IBC (International Bioethics Committee). 2015. "Report of the International Bioethics Committee (IBC) on the Principle of the Sharing of Benefits." Available at: http://unesdoc.unesco.org/images/0023/002332/233230E.pdf.

Killion, David T. 2013. "Why UNESCO Is a Critical Tool for Twenty-First Century Diplomacy." *Fletcher Forum of World Affairs* 37(2): 7–14.

Kutukdjian, Georges B. 1994. "UNESCO International Bioethics Committee." *The Hastings Center Report* 24(2): 3–5.

McKeon, Richard P. 1947. "Report of the Meeting of the UNESCO Committee on the Philosophical Principles on the Rights of Man in Paris, 26 June–2 July." Available at: http://unesdoc.unesco.org/images/0012/001243/124347Eb.pdf.

Meier, Benjamin Mason. 2013. "Making Health a Human Right: The World Health Organization and the United Nations Programme on Human Rights and Scientific and Technological Developments." *Journal of the Historical Society* 13(2): 195–229.

Mukherjee, Bhaswati. 2009. "Role of UNESCO in Human Rights Implementation." In *International Human Rights Monitoring Mechanisms, Human Rights and Humanitarian Law*. E-Book Online: Brill Online Books and Journals.

Oh, Irene. 2005. "Le Comité des philosophes de l'UNESCO (1947–1948): À la recherche des fondements des droits de l'homme." In *60 ans de l'histoire de l'UNESCO*, Actes du colloque international, *Paris 16–18 novembre 2005*," 139–142. Available at: http://unesdoc.unesco.org/images/0015/001541/154122f.pdf.

OHCHR. n.d.-a. "The right to enjoy the benefits of scientific progress and its applications." http://www.ohchr.org/EN/Issues/CulturalRights/Pages/benefitfrom scientificprogress.aspx.

OHCHR. n.d.-b. "World Programme for Human Rights Education." http://www.ohchr.org/EN/Issues/Education/Training/Pages/Programme.aspx.

OHCHR. 2012. "Report of the Special Rapporteur in the field of cultural rights, Shaheed Farida: The right to enjoy the benefits of scientific progress and its applications." 20th Session of the UN Human Rights Council. A/HRC/20/26.

Renoliet, Jean-Jacques. 2005. "L'UNESCO oubliée: l'Organisation de Coopération Intellectuelle (1921–1946)." In *60 ans de l'histoire de l'UNESCO*, 61–66. Paris: UNESCO.

Sané, Pierre. 2010. Foreword to *Freedom from Poverty as a Human Right Law's Duty to the Poor*, edited by Geraldine Van Bueren, v–xii. Paris: UNESCO Publishing. Available at: http://unesdoc.unesco.org/images/0018/001876/187613e.pdf.

Schabas, William A. 2007. "Study of the Right to Enjoy the Benefits of Scientific and Technological Progress and Its Applications." In *Human Rights in Education, Science and Culture*, edited by Yvonne Donders and Vladimir Volodin, 273–308. Paris and Hampshire, UK: United Nations Educational, Scientific and Cultural Organization and Ashgate Publishing.

Symonides, Janusz. 2001a. "UNESCO's Contribution to the Progressive Development of Human Rights." In *Max Planck Yearbook of the United Nations Law, Volume 5*, edited by J. A. Frowei and R. Wolfrum, 307–340. The Netherlands: Kluwer Law International.

Symonides, Janusz. 2001b. "The United Nations System Standard Setting Instruments and Programmes to Combat Racism and Racial Discrimination." In *United to Combat Racism Dedicated to the World Conference against Racism, Racial Discrimination, Xenophobia and Related Intolerance in Durban, South Africa, 31 August–7 September 2001*, 3–22. Geneva: UNESCO and OHCHR.

ten Have, Henk. "Bioethics and Human Rights—Wherever the Twain Shall Meet." In *Ethik und Recht-Die Ethisierung des Rechts/Ethics and Law—The Ethicalization of Law*, 149–175. Berlin: Springer Berlin Heidelberg.

Torelli, Maurice. 1983. *Le Medecin et les Droits de L'homme*. Paris: Berger-Levrault.

UN (United Nations). 2000. Millennium Development Goals. www.un.org/millennium goals/fkgd.shtml.

UN. 2014. "Global Education First Initiative: An Initiative of the United Nations Secretary-General." Available at: https://issuu.com/globaleducationfirst/docs/gefi_ brochure_eng.

UN. 2015. "Transforming our world: the 2030 Agenda for Sustainable Development." 25 September. UN Doc. A/RES/70/1.

UN General Assembly. 1948. "Universal Declaration of Human Rights." 10 December. UN Doc. 217A (III).

UN General Assembly. 1966. "International Covenant on Economic, Social and Cultural Rights." 3 January. UN Doc. 2200A (XXI).

UN Secretary-General. 1997. "Renewing the United Nations: A Programme for Reform." 14 July. UN Doc. A/51/950.

UNDG (United Nations Development Group). n.d. "Human Rights Working Group of the UNDG." https://undg.org/human-rights/undg-human-rights-working-group/.

UNDG. 2003. *The Human Rights Based Approach to Development Cooperation Towards a Common Understanding Among UN Agencies*. Available at: https://undg.org/ document/the-human-rights-based-approach-to-development-cooperation-towards-a-common-understanding-among-un-agencies/.

UNESCO (United Nations Education, Scientific, and Cultural Organization). 1945. "Constitution of the United Nations Educational, Scientific and Cultural Organization." 19 November. Available at: http://unesdoc.unesco.org/images/0022/002269/ 226924e.pdf#page=6.

UNESCO. 1948. "Miscellaneous Resolutions, 8 UDHR." In *Records of the General Conference of UNESCO, Third session, Beirut, 1948, Volume II Resolutions*. Paris: UNESCO.

UNESCO. 1960. "Convention Against Discrimination in Education." 429 UN Treaty Series 93.

UNESCO. 1978a. *Decisions adopted by the Executive Board at its 104th Session*. Paris: UNESCO.

UNESCO. 1978b. *UNESCO Declaration on Race and Racial Prejudice*. Available at: http:// portal.unesco.org/en/ev.php-URL_ID=13161&URL_DO=DO_TOPIC&URL_ SECTION=201.html.

UNESCO. 1997. "Universal Declaration on the Human Genome and Human Rights." Available at: http://portal.unesco.org/en/ev.php-URL_ID=13177&URL_DO=DO_T.

UNESCO. 2000. *World Conference on Science, Science For The Twenty-First Century: A New Commitment*. Paris: UNESCO.

UNESCO. 2001. *Education for All: initiatives, issues and strategies*. Paris: UNESCO.

UNESCO. 2002. *Medium-Term Strategy for 2002–2007*. Paris: UNESCO. Doc. 31/C/4.

UNESCO. 2003a. *Development of an Integrated Strategy to Combat Racism, Discrimination, Xenophobia and Related Intolerance*. Paris: UNESCO.

UNESCO. 2003b. *UNESCO Declaration on Bioethics and Human Rights*. Available at: http://www.unesco.org/new/en/social-and-human-sciences/themes/bioethics/bioethics-and-human-rights/.

UNESCO. 2005. *Records of the General Conference, 33rd session, Resolutions*. Paris: UNESCO.

UNESCO. 2006. *Strategy on Human Rights*. Paris: UNESCO.

UNESCO. 2007. *EDUCAIDS: Towards a Comprehensive Education Sector Approach*. Doc. ED-2007/WS/36.

UNESCO. 2008. *Medium-Term Strategy for 2008–2013*. Paris: UNESCO.

UNESCO. 2009a. *International Technical Guidance on Sexuality Education: An evidence-informed approach for schools, teachers and health educators*. Paris: UNESCO.

UNESCO. 2009b. "Report by the Director-General on the execution of the programme adopted by the General Conference, Addendum 2." In *UNESCO Priority Gender Equality Action Plan for 2008–2013*. Paris: UNESCO.

UNESCO. 2009c. *The Right to Enjoy the Benefits of Scientific Progress and its Applications*. Paris: UNESCO.

UNESCO. 2009d. *UN World Water Development Report*. Paris: UNESCO.

UNESCO. 2010. "Reports by the Director-General on Specific Matters, Implementation of UNESCO's Strategy on Human Rights and the Integrated Strategy to Combat Racism, Discrimination, Xenophobia and Related Intolerance." 13 August. Doc. 185 EX/6 Part I.

UNESCO. 2011a. *Casebook on Benefit and Harm, Bioethics Core Curriculum*. Paris: UNESCO.

UNESCO. 2011b. *Casebook on Human Dignity and Human Rights, Bioethics Core Curriculum*. Paris: UNESCO.

UNESCO. 2011c. "Report by the Director-General on the Follow-Up to Decisions and Resolutions Adopted by the Executive Board and the General Conference at their Previous Sessions, Implementation of the UNESCO Strategy on Human Rights (2003) and the Integrated Strategy to Combat Racism, Discrimination, Xenophobia and Related Intolerance." 26 August. Doc. 187/EX/5.

UNESCO. 2013a. *Approved Programme and Budget, 2014–2017*. Paris: UNESCO.

UNESCO. 2013b. *IHP-VIII Water Security Responses to Regional and Global Challenges (2014–2021)*. Available at: http://unesdoc.unesco.org/images/0022/002251/225103e.pdf.

UNESCO. 2013c. *Medium-Term Strategy for 2014–2021*. Paris: UNESCO.

UNESCO. 2013d. *Revision of the Recommendation on the Status of Scientific Researchers, Resolution 37 C/40, Records of the General Conference, 37th session*. Paris: UNESCO.

UNESCO. 2014a. *Charting the Course of Education and HIV*. Paris: UNESCO. Available at: http://unesdoc.unesco.org/images/0022/002261/226125e.pdf.

UNESCO. 2014b. *Teaching and Learning: Achieving quality for all, EFA Global Monitoring Report 2013/4*. Paris: UNESCO. Available at: unesdoc.unesco.org/images/0022/002256/225660e.pdf.

UNESCO. 2014c. *UNESCO Gender Equality Action Plan, 2014–2021.* Paris: UNESCO.

UNESCO. 2015a. *Comprehensive Sexuality Education: A Global Review.* Paris: UNESCO.

UNESCO. 2015b. *Education for All: Achievements and Challenges, EFA Global Monitoring Report 2015.* Available at: http://unesdoc.unesco.org/images/0023/002322/232205e.pdf.

UNESCO. 2015c. *International Initiative on Water Quality.* Available at: http://unesdoc.unesco.org/images/0024/002436/243651e.pdf.

UNESCO. 2015d. "Progress Report on Preparations for Revision of the UNESCO Recommendation on the Status of Scientific Researchers (1974)." 12 August. Doc. 38 C/27.

UNESCO. 2015e. "Report of the IBC on the Principle of the Sharing of Benefits." 2 October. Doc. SHS/YES/IBC-22/15/3 Rev. 2.

UNESCO. 2016a. *Committee on Conventions and Recommendations, 2016 Edition.* Paris: UNESCO.

UNESCO. 2016b. *UNESCO Strategy on Education for Health and Well-Being: Contributing to the Sustainable Development Goals.* Paris: UNESCO.

UNESCO. 2017a. "Draft Declaration of Ethical Principles in Relation to Climate Change." 19 October. Doc. 39 C/22 Rev.

UNESCO. 2017b. *2017 UN World Water Development Report—Wastewater: The Untapped Resource.* Paris: UNESCO.

UNESCO. 2017c. "Proposal for Revision of the UNESCO Recommendation on the Status of Scientific Researchers (1974)." 8 August. Doc. 39 C/23.

UNESCO. n.d.-a. "About MINEPS." 12 August 2017. Available at: http://en.unesco.org/mineps6/about.

UNESCO. n.d.-b. "Bioethics." 12 August 2017. Available at: http://www.unesco.org/new/en/social-and-human-sciences/themes/bioethics/.

UNESCO. n.d.-c. "Call for Advice: Revision of the UNESCO Recommendation on the Status of Scientific Researchers." 12 August 2017. Available at: http://www.unesco.org/new/en/social-and-human-sciences/themes/bioethics/call-for-advice-revision-of-unesco-recommendation-on-the-status-of-scientific-researchers/.

UNESCO. n.d.-d. "General introduction to the standard-setting instruments of UNESCO." 12 August 2017. Available at: http://portal.unesco.org/en/ev.php-URL_ID=23772&URL_DO=DO_TOPIC&URL_SECTION=201.html.

UNESCO. n.d.-e. "HIV and Health Education Clearinghouse." 12 August 2017. Available at: http://hivhealthclearinghouse.unesco.org/.

UNESCO. n.d.-f. "International Bioethics Committee." 12 August 2017. Available at: http://www.unesco.org/new/en/social-and-human-sciences/themes/bioethics/international-bioethics-committee/.

UNESCO. n.d.-g. "Physical Education and Sport." 12 August 2017. Available at: http://www.unesco.org/new/en/social-and-human-sciences/themes/physical-education-and-sport/.

UNESCO. n.d.-h. "2nd aspect of the terms of reference of CR: examination of the communications relating to cases and questions concerning the exercise of human rights in UNESCO's fields of competence." Available at: http://portal.unesco.org/en/ev.php-URL_ID=15243&URL_DO=DO_TOPIC&URL_SECTION=201.html.

UNESCO. n.d.-i. "UN Interagency Committee on Bioethics." 12 August 2017. Available at: http://www.unesco.org/new/en/social-and-human-sciences/themes/bioethics/un-inter-agency-committee-on-bioethics/.

UNESCO. n.d.-j. "UN Committee on Economic, Social and Cultural Rights." 12 August 2017. Available at: http://www.unesco.org/new/en/education/themes/leading-the-international-agenda/right-to-education/monitoring/collaboration-unesco-un/un-cescr/.

UNESCO. n.d.-k. "World Commission on the Ethics of Scientific Knowledge and Technology (COMEST)." 12 August 2017. Available at: http://www.unesco.org/new/en/social-and-human-sciences/themes/comest/.

UNICEF. 2007. *A human rights-based approach to education for all: A framework for the realization of children's right to education and rights within education.* New York: UNICEF.

Vasak, Karl. 1977. "Letter to WHO Division of Health Manpower Development Director Fülöp." 6 May. Doc. SS/HR/77/234/VS (on file with author).

11

The United Nations Population Fund

An Evolving Human Rights Mission and Approach to Sexual and Reproductive Health and Reproductive Rights

EMILIE FILMER-WILSON AND LUIS MORA*

The United Nations Population Fund's (UNFPA's) approach to public health is grounded in the premise that women's sexual and reproductive health is determined not only by their access to health services but also by their ability to freely decide on all matters related to their sexual and reproductive health and rights. Accordingly, in the 150 countries where UNFPA is present, it works to strengthen sexual and reproductive health systems and care, including access to family planning, maternal health care services, HIV prevention, and sexuality education, while also advancing gender equality and empowering women to freely decide on their fertility and sexuality free of coercion and violence, including by preventing gender-based violence, female genital mutilation, and early, forced, and child marriage.

This chapter analyzes how UNFPA has evolved in its approach to public health from a human rights perspective and situates this discussion within the broader international political context on sexual and reproductive health and rights, which has both shaped and, in turn, been influenced by UNFPA. Part I provides a historical overview of UNFPA and its evolving health and human rights mission, as mainly guided by the International Conference on Population Development (ICPD) and other international agreements such as the Millennium Development Goals (MDGs) and, currently, the Sustainable Development Goals (SDGs). Part II then outlines the strategy that UNFPA has adopted to mainstream human rights within

* We would like to warmly thank the following colleagues who provided rich insights for this chapter and who have been instrumental in paving the way for human rights in UNFPA's work: Maria Jose Alcala Donegani, Ana Angarita, Hedia Belhadj, Mona Kaidbey, Luz Angela Melo, and Mari Simonen. We would particularly like to thank Alfonso Barragues for his peer review of this chapter.

Human Rights in Global Health. Benjamin Mason Meier and Lawrence O. Gostin.
© Oxford University Press 2018. Published 2018 by Oxford University Press.

its work on sexual and reproductive health and reproductive rights, and identifies key milestones in these efforts. Part III explores the distinct institutional factors that have enabled UNFPA to mainstream human rights and those that have held it back. This chapter concludes that UNFPA has played an important role in transforming the perception of sexual and reproductive health and reproductive rights—from a focus on population numbers to the realization of human rights—and has made much progress in mainstreaming human rights in its work, so that today, it is widely recognized as a human rights-based organization. Yet, it has struggled to shift its decision-making and development practice to align with the rights based vision of the ICPD. The 2030 Agenda for Sustainable Development (2030 Agenda), which is grounded in human rights, provides the organization with a policy framework that it can draw upon to accelerate and scale up these efforts.

I. ORIGINS OF UNFPA AND ITS EVOLVING PUBLIC HEALTH AND HUMAN RIGHTS MISSION

Beginning in the 1920s and 1930s, international policies on reproductive health were discussed at the League of Nations. Not framed in the language of rights, these early policies were tied to contentious debates over population growth (Skard 2008). Even after the birth of the United Nations (UN), the concern over population growth persisted. In 1962, the UN General Assembly adopted a resolution which recognized "the health and welfare of the family require special attention in areas with a relatively high rate of population growth" and that "the effective population increase during the last decade has been particularly great in many of the low-income less developed countries" (UN General Assembly 1962, preamble). This population-focused rhetoric began to shift the year prior to the establishment of UNFPA, when the General Assembly adopted a resolution in 1966 that introduced an emphasis on reproductive rights, articulating that "the size of the family should be the *free choice* of each individual family" (UN General Assembly 1966, preamble).

The creation of UNFPA, the UN's preeminent agency for population issues, reflects the increasing concerns over, on the one hand, spiraling world population growth and resource limits (Center for Global Development 2011), and on the other hand, the increasing attention to women's rights as a whole and reproductive rights—in particular, the ability of individuals to make their own reproductive decisions (Robinson 2010). These movements, combined with advances in contraceptive methods and technologies, resulted in a growing public health interest and activities in family planning (Mousky 2002). UNFPA was created in 1967 under the original name of the UN Fund for Population Activities, as a trust fund to assist countries in areas related to population. In 1969, the fund was transferred to the UN Development Programme (UNDP) and was operational by the end of the year with a staff of five and $4 million in voluntary contributions.

In 1972, UNFPA was placed under the direct authority of the UN General Assembly, ending its status as a trust fund and giving it recognition as a subsidiary body of the General Assembly. The same resolution made the governing council of UNDP the governing body for UNFPA (UN General Assembly 1972). By 1980, UNFPA had become its own autonomous UN agency, and in 1987, its name was changed to the UN Population Fund. In 1993, the General Assembly (UN General Assembly 1993) created an Executive Board for UNFPA and UNDP. Made up of thirty-six member states, the primary role of the Executive Board is to support and supervise UNFPA's work, including by reviewing and approving UNFPA's Strategic Plan, which directs the work of the whole organization and is developed every four years. It also approves all UNFPA country programs.

The 1970s and 1980s saw a huge growth in UNFPA's budget, from $4 million in 1969 to $1 billion in 1983, with half of its funding coming from the United States. During this time, the focus of UNFPA's work varied by region, with support for research and training on reproductive health in Latin America, family planning in Asia, and demographic census in Africa. UNFPA also funded the World Fertility Survey, the precursor to the Demographic and Health Surveys (Robinson 2010). In addition, it played an increasingly influential role in the organization of the global population conferences that took place in 1974, 1984, and 1994. UNFPA's role and mandate was in turn influenced by these conferences, and it was at the 1994 ICPD in Cairo that UNFPA "came fully of age" (Singh 2002, 234).

A. The International Conference on Population and Development: From Human Numbers to Human Rights

The 1994 ICPD was groundbreaking, with its outcome document—the Programme of Action, adopted by 179 governments—representing a new global consensus that individual human rights and dignity, including the equal rights of women and girls and universal access to sexual and reproductive health and reproductive rights, are a necessary precondition for sustainable development (United Nations 1994). In doing so, the ICPD reframed population and development issues from an emphasis on population numbers to one of human rights. This consensus thereby shifted the focus away from demographic targets aimed at population control and toward girls' and women's rights to bodily autonomy, integrity, and choice in relation to sexuality and reproduction. As discussed in chapter 2, this shift provided a more comprehensive approach to gender equality, women's and girls' empowerment, and sexual and reproductive health, recognizing that sexual and reproductive health services and programs—including family planning, safe abortion (where legal), maternity care, and prevention of sexually transmitted infections and HIV—must be guided by the human rights of couples and individuals (Center for Global Development 2011).

For the first time in an international consensus document, states agreed that reproductive rights were human rights, acknowledging:

> that reproductive rights embrace certain human rights that are already recognized in national laws and international human rights documents . . . and that these rights rest on the recognition of the basic right of all couples and individuals to decide freely and responsibly the number, spacing and timing of their children and to have the information and means to do so, and the right to attain the highest standard of sexual and reproductive health. It also includes their right to make decisions concerning reproduction free of discrimination, coercion and violence (United Nations 1994, para. 7.3).

UNFPA was the "driving force" behind the ICPD (Sadik 2002). Under the leadership of its Executive Director, Dr. Nafis Sadik—who also served as Secretary-General for the Conference—UNFPA galvanized wide engagement across the UN agencies, played an active role in organizing all the pre-conference events, secured funding for the conference, and worked closely with governments to formulate the conference recommendations (Robinson 2010).

UNFPA also catalyzed strong civil society participation, in particular, feminist and women's organizations from both developed and developing countries, in preparation for the conference. It was largely due to this unprecedented level of engagement at an inter-governmental conference that a broader understanding of population and development was reached (Weerakoon 2002). Civil society actors—joined by progressive voices from the family planning, health, development, and human rights research community (and backed by strong evidence and data)—were able to challenge the mainstream approaches to population and development and achieve a paradigm shift in the population agenda.

With the ICPD's comprehensive approach to reproductive health and a strong focus on women's empowerment and rights, UNFPA's mandate was considerably broadened on gender issues and women's rights (Heyzer 2002). Following the ICPD, the UN Secretary-General designated UNFPA as the lead UN organization for follow-up and implementation on the Conference's Programme of Action. In 1995, UNFPA reoriented its program activities to focus on three areas: reproductive health (including family planning and sexual health), population and data, and advocacy (Singh 2002). Empowering women and strengthening their autonomy was now an end in itself and central to UNFPA's mission. To take forward this new focus on women's rights, UNFPA created in 1996 a "Gender, Population and Development" branch (Heyzer 2002). That same year, UNFPA adopted a mission statement, which reflected its new human rights-based orientation: "All couples and individuals have the right to decide freely and responsibly the number and spacing of their children as well as the right to the information and means to do so" (Robinson 2010, 84).

B. After 1994: Changing Political Winds

The principles of the Programme of Action have been both reaffirmed and expanded through a number of subsequent inter-governmental agreements. The UN Fourth World Conference on Women in Beijing in 1995 was based on, and strongly reinforced, the reproductive rights outcomes of Cairo, with strong wording in its outcome document, the Platform for Action, specifying women's right to have control over and decide freely and responsibly on matters related to their sexuality (UN 1995). This language on reproductive rights was largely due to UNFPA's staunch advocacy for the Platform for Action, recognizing the need to empower women and to strengthen their human rights.

Progress since Cairo and Beijing, however, has not been linear for reproductive rights. A decade later, the gains of the 1990s were being significantly eroded within the UN, following a combination of the waning engagement by women's rights organizations, rising opposition to the ICDP agenda, and gaining traction of population control agendas (Girard 2009). In lights of these developments, the rights-based dimensions of the ICPD became increasingly contested. The silence on the subject of sexuality and reproduction in the 2000 MDGs reflects the attitudes of the time, and it was not until 2007 that an MDG 5 target was added on reproductive health—as a result of continuous advocacy efforts by UNFPA and its partners.

Yet, by the time of the twenty-year review of the ICPD in 2014 (ICPD +20), the political winds blew back again in support of the original vision of the ICPD. Where a series of regional and thematic based reviews were organized to feed into the global review, these reviews were notable for their progressive approach to human rights. For example, the resulting 2013 Montevideo Consensus in Latin America explicitly recognized "sexual rights" and defined those rights for the first time in a UN inter-governmental process (UNFPA 2013b). Protection of sexual rights as separate from reproductive rights in the Montevideo Consensus included a commitment to the creation of laws and policies that specifically address discrimination and violence based on sexual orientation and gender identity (Ibid.). The sixth Asia Pacific Conference on Population and Development, held in Bangkok in September 2013, similarly adopted a strongly progressive outcome document that, among other things, recognized human rights as central to all population and development programs (Ibid.). The Addis Ababa Declaration on Population and Development in Africa beyond 2014, the last of the regional ICPD review conferences, also reflected key priorities for the region, including: attention to fulfilling the sexual and reproductive rights and health of adolescents; prevention and treatment of HIV and AIDS; and an end to harmful practices that discriminate against and violate the human rights of girls and women (Ibid.). In all of these regional processes, the UNFPA regional offices had a key role in mobilizing national constituents in the region, both civil society and governments, and providing data and technical evidence to support the progressive positions reached in these reviews.

As part of the preparatory review process, a thematic-based review, entitled the ICPD Beyond 2014 International Conference on Human Rights, was organized by UNFPA in partnership with the Office of the UN High Commissioner for Human Rights (OHCHR) and the government of the Netherlands. It brought together over 300 participants from 127 countries—including civil society representatives, academics, parliamentarians, human rights defenders, young people, and service providers—and aimed to identify opportunities to strengthen the operational links between human rights and the ICPD Programme of Action, acknowledging that "far too often, human rights have been underplayed or ignored altogether in designing and implementing health and population policies and services" (UNFPA and OHCHR 2013a, 4).

The ICPD Beyond 2014 International Conference identified numerous achievements in implementing the human rights-based dimensions of the 1994 Programme of Action. These included: expanding jurisprudence and the normative framework on sexual and reproductive health and rights; removing barriers to accessing information, education, and services; and enhancing people's agency and ensuring their full participation in the development process (UN 2014). It also identified three fundamental challenges to realizing the human rights dimensions of the Programme of Action:

- Equality—making progress toward social justice and ending discrimination in all its forms.

- Quality—meeting human rights standards in sexual and reproductive health services, information, and education.
- Accountability—identifying responsibilities of key actors and enforcing rights (Ibid., 8).

By articulating the implications of these gaps and challenges to a human rights-based implementation of the ICPD Programme of Action, the ICPD +20 Review, together with the regional reviews, successfully positioned human rights in the global ICPD.

The "Framework of Actions" that came out of the ICPD +20 Review frames population and development within five thematic pillars, the first and over-arching pillar of which is dignity and human rights. The Framework of Actions focuses on the "unfinished business" of the ICPD, namely inequality. It recognizes the growing inequalities both within and across countries, and underscores that only by addressing structural poverty and human rights violations will the international community be able to close the gaps in meeting the vision of the ICPD (UNFPA 2014). Given this human rights imperative, the Framework of Actions reinforces the need for governments to work with UNFPA to identify and address discrimina-tory practices and violations of human rights and to develop reinforcing systems of accountability (Ibid.).

With this shift in political support for the rights-based dimensions of the ICPD, sexual and reproductive health and reproductive rights would be more centrally positioned within the development agenda. The Sustainable Development Goals (SDGs), which replaced the MDGs in 2015 and laid out a new development roadmap to improve the lives of people throughout the world over the next fifteen years, included specific global targets on sexual and reproductive health and repro-ductive rights. Moreover, this SDG framework recognizes that achieving these sexual and reproductive health and reproductive rights goals is critical for the achievement of all other goals, including poverty, health, and gender equality. UNFPA supported advocacy efforts to include sexual and reproductive health and reproductive rights as part of the seventeen SDGs, organizing expert group meetings with academia, civil society, and the UN, and working closely with governments to provide evi-dence and technical expertise to push this agenda forward.

II. THE EVOLUTION OF HUMAN RIGHTS IN UNFPA'S WORK TO OPERATIONALIZE SEXUAL AND REPRODUCTIVE HEALTH AND REPRODUCTIVE RIGHTS

The ICPD set a powerful normative and guiding framework for UNFPA's work on sexual and reproductive health and reproductive rights. With human rights centrally positioned in the ICPD, UNFPA was given an explicit mandate for mainstreaming human rights in its work. However, the ICPD did not prescribe how to translate this shift in approach into programming practice. A more focused effort to oper-ationalize the rights-based vision of the ICPD began in 1996 with the hiring of the first UNFPA global human rights adviser, followed in 1998 by the inclusion of "human rights" in UNFPA's Gender, Population and Development Branch (later the "Gender, Human Rights and Development Branch"), which was intended to provide global leadership for integrating human rights into UNFPA's work. Since that time, two principle strategies have been pursued in evolving efforts to operationalize the human rights based dimensions of the ICPD in UNFPA practice:

(A) Engaging with international, regional, and national human rights mechanisms to strengthen accountability for gender equality and sexual and reproductive health and reproductive rights; and

(B) Advancing operational clarity on the links between human rights, gender equality, and sexual and reproductive health and reproductive rights.

A. Engaging with International, Regional, and National Human Rights Mechanisms to Strengthen Accountability

Since the late 1990s, UNFPA has adopted a dual approach to engaging with the human rights mechanisms: (1) influencing the policy agendas of the human rights bodies in Geneva through evidence-based advocacy, and (2) bringing the work of these mechanisms to the country level, with the overall aim to strengthen accountability for gender equality, sexual and reproductive health, and reproductive rights.

1. Policy Engagement with Human Rights Mechanisms

Reproductive rights have tended to occupy a marginalized position in the international human rights landscape. This is a result of both the sensitive aspects of reproductive rights, as well as a more general marginalization of women's human rights within the broader human rights system (Gallagher 2014). To redress this gap, UNFPA has worked closely with the human rights treaty bodies (as reviewed in chapter 23) and the special procedures mandate holders (as reviewed in chapter 22) to strengthen their understanding of, and attention to, reproductive rights in their interpretation of treaties and monitoring of states. An early example of these efforts was in 1996, when UNFPA brought together the chairs of the human rights treaty bodies to discuss how reproductive rights could be better monitored in their work—the first time that treaty bodies had come together to focus on a specific issue (Heyzer 2002).

Through such examples of proactive UNFPA engagement, treaty bodies increasingly began asserting and advancing sexual and reproductive health and reproductive rights in their concluding observations and general comments (UNFPA and Center for Reproductive Rights 2013). A milestone in these efforts is the 2016 General Comment 22 of the Committee on Economic, Social and Cultural Rights (CESCR) on the Right to Sexual and Reproductive Health (CESCR 2016). This General Comment is the first authoritative interpretation of a treaty body to focus exclusively on sexual and reproductive health and rights (SRHR). The idea for General Comment 22 originated in 2008 within UNFPA. To persuade the CESCR to develop a general comment, UNFPA: provided data and evidence that highlighted the importance of sexual and reproductive health for the realization of other rights in the International Covenant on Economic, Social and Cultural Rights (ICESCR); organized expert meetings with Committee members, UN agencies, and civil society organizations; and created coalitions with civil society and UN actors to advocate for the General Comment.

UNFPA has also developed close partnerships with special procedures mandate holders, including the Special Rapporteur on the right to health and the Special Rapporteur on violence against women. Pursuant to the mandate of these Special Rapporteurs, UNFPA organized expert group meetings on specific areas of their mandate, for example, on maternal health and rights (2009) and on the political economy of the human rights of women (2008), bringing together experts from civil society, academia, and states to inform the thematic reports of the rapporteurs.

As these partnerships contributed to the strengthening of the human rights framework for reproductive rights, this strengthened, in turn, the normative foundation for UNFPA efforts to mainstream human rights and for country office efforts to support accountability of governments. The political, moral, and legal authority of the international human rights mechanisms provided an opportunity for dialogue at the country level on some of the most sensitive areas of UNFPA's mandate: adolescent reproductive health, contraception, and family structures. The recommendations from these human rights mechanisms shed light on neglected human rights issues, persistent patterns of discrimination, and legal and policy shortcomings that prevent the achievement of universal access to sexual and reproductive health and reproductive rights (Yamin 2013). In doing so, the international human rights system provides an alternative reading to conventional public health assessments, and help identify legal, social, and cultural barriers that need to be addressed (Ibid.).

2. Country-Level Engagement for Human Rights Monitoring

At the operational level, UNFPA country offices engage closely with the Committee on the Elimination of Discrimination against Women (CEDAW Committee) due to the importance of the Convention on the Elimination of All Forms of Discrimination against Women in promoting ICPD goals. Many country offices are engaged in CEDAW Committee activities related to the follow-up and implementation of recommendations and reporting by both governments and civil society. In 2008, an inter-agency group on CEDAW reporting was created—composed of UNFPA, UN Women, UNICEF, UNDP, and FAO—to ensure a more coherent, systematic, and system-wide engagement. The inter-agency group alerts "resident coordinators" (the UN lead representative in the country) when the country is to be reviewed by the CEDAW Committee and provides technical assistance to encourage UN Country Teams to submit a confidential report on national conditions. Through this proactive engagement, the UN Country Teams in the field have been better positioned to strategically engage with the CEDAW Committee, leading reproductive rights to be raised more frequently in both state party reporting to and recommendations from the CEDAW Committee (UNFPA 2011).

The opportunity for multi-stakeholder national dialogue with the human rights system has become increasingly recognized by UNFPA, in particular with the advent of the Universal Periodic Review (UPR). The UPR, as discussed in chapter 24, involves the Human Rights Council (HRC) review of the human rights records of all UN member states to assess "the fulfilment by each State of its human rights obligations and commitments in a manner which ensures universality of coverage and equal treatment" (UN General Assembly 2006). With the UPR reviewing all human rights, it provides a single human rights accountability mechanism to undertake a comprehensive review of the wide range of human rights instruments that protect reproductive rights and the equal rights of women to have control over and decide freely and responsibly on matters related to their sexuality (Gilmore et al. 2015). UNFPA seized the opportunity that the UPR provided, and initiated a concerted effort to strengthen engagement by its country offices with this mechanism (Ibid.). Following the first cycle of the UPR, a UNFPA analysis found that sexual and reproductive health and reproductive rights issues were among the most frequently cited in the first cycle of UPR recommendations (2008–2012): of the 21,956 recommendations made in the first cycle, 5,720 (26 percent) pertained to SRHR and gender equality, and of these, 77 percent were formally accepted by member states (UNFPA 2014a). To leverage the opportunity provided by this mechanism for policy dialogue, advocacy, and accountability in countries, UNFPA developed a detailed analysis of the recommendations related to sexual and reproductive health and reproductive rights for each country where UNFPA had a field office, and identified entry points where the country office could support follow-up implementation. This analysis has helped country offices better plan strategies to maximize the opportunity presented by the UPR as a platform for country dialogue on sensitive issues that otherwise could be too challenging to raise directly, bringing together state actors and a wide range of civil society groups, in particular, those representing groups that are often marginalized from national policy processes (such as adolescents).

As part of efforts to strengthen national accountability on reproductive rights, UNFPA started in 2008 to partner with National Human Rights Institutions (NHRIs) more systematically. These NHRIs—as state bodies with a constitutional or legislative mandate to protect and promote human rights—have a uniquely important role to advance national accountability for sexual and reproductive health and reproductive rights. They are also an important link between the national government and civil society, helping to bridge the "protection gap" between the rights of individuals and the responsibilities of the state (UNFPA 2014). However, the capacity of NHRIs remains uneven, as does their engagement to advance gender equality and sexual and reproductive health and reproductive rights, with studies of NHRIs revealing that the level of knowledge and understanding of the human rights dimension of sexual and reproductive health and well-being tends to be insufficient or, at best, fragmented among these institutions (Ibid.). If such rights are addressed at all, the focus of NHRIs is often narrowed to a specific issue, such as forced sterilization or sexual violence, while broader issues in the country are left unaddressed. To address this gap, UNFPA has been working at the global, regional, and country level to strengthen the attention that NHRIs give to sexual and reproductive health and reproductive rights issues and their capacity to engage. In 2012 a formal commitment was reached by NHRIs to promote and protect sexual and reproductive health and reproductive rights as a priority area in efforts to advance the rights of women. To support NHRIs to implement this commitment, UNFPA has since developed guidance for NHRIs on reproductive rights (UNFPA 2014) and, through UNFPA country offices, supported capacity-building initiatives with NHRIs in over twenty countries.

B. Advancing Operational Clarity on the Links between Human Rights, Gender Equality, and Sexual and Reproductive Health and Reproductive Rights

While the ICPD set a bold rights-based vision, it has proven complicated to translate this shift in thinking on population issues into shifts in decision-making and development practice on the ground (Yamin 2013). UNFPA policies and programs stated their commitments to human rights, but there were concerns that this was simply repacking existing programs in "rights language" without changing the underlying approaches (Ibid.). A 2002 review on the use of the rights-based approach in UNFPA programming concluded that while UNFPA country offices "are using human rights language, the conceptualisation and the linkages to UNFPA's programming areas is weak" and that "despite attempts to integrate human rights, UNFPA staff in general is not applying a human rights based approach" (UNFPA 2002, 4).

An initial barrier to the meaningful and coherent operationalization of a human rights-based approach (HRBA) throughout the work of UNFPA was the lack of a standardized conceptual framework among UN agencies on what a "rights-based approach" entailed. More problematic was resistance by a number of actors in the UN development community to recognizing that human rights were part of development work. This view gradually began to shift in the early 2000s, under the leadership of then Secretary-General Kofi Annan, whose ambitious UN reform process, as described in chapter 3, called for human rights to be integrated into all of the UN's programs, policies, and activities (UN 1997). The UN system increasingly came to recognize that human rights issues could not be left to OHCHR alone. In 2003, then High Commissioner for Human Rights Sergio de Mello addressed the UN Development Group (UNDG)—the consortium for all the UN development organizations—to call for greater efforts to mainstream human rights in the work of the UN development agencies, launching a UN Inter-agency Programme—Action 2—to support these efforts. Action 2, in which UNFPA played a leading role, provided the impetus for a wide range of efforts by the UN development system to operationalize HRBA within development programming, leading to the 2003 landmark UNDG "Common Understanding" on a Human Rights Based Approach, which provided the UN with a shared definition of a "human rights-based approach to development" (UNDG 2003). Drawing on this Common Understanding, Action 2 developed training materials for applying a HRBA to UN development programming and carried out numerous in-country HRBA training activities for the UN development system.

Based on the Common Understanding, UNFPA developed its own 2010 HRBA Manual for UNFPA staff (UNFPA 2010). The UNFPA Manual, developed in collaboration with the Harvard School of Public Health, provides a conceptual overview of the HRBA, programming guidance, and training materials (UNFPA 2010). The development of these human rights mainstreaming tools provided an important step in elaborating, both conceptually and practically, the challenge of integrating human rights into UNFPA's areas of work.

In parallel with developing these programming tools, UNFPA, in partnership with civil society and governments, worked at the global and inter-governmental level to strengthen operational clarity on the links between human rights and sexual and reproductive rights, as highlighted earlier in the ICPD Beyond 2014 International Conference on Human Rights. Another important milestone in these efforts was the work with the HRC to produce a resolution on maternal health as a human right, which provided a huge contribution in translating abstract principles of human rights into concrete policy and programming steps. The HRC's 2009 and 2010 resolutions on maternal mortality and maternal health (HRC 2009; HRC 2010) and the OHCHR's ensuing 2012 Technical Guidance on Maternal Health and HRBA (HRC 2012) sent a clear message that without paying close attention to the key principles of a human rights-based approach—accountability, participation, transparency, empowerment, and non-discrimination—attempts to reduce maternal mortality and morbidity would be insufficient. The Technical Guidance on Maternal Health and HRBA—which OHCHR developed in 2012 at the request of the HRC and with technical assistance from UNFPA—is "premised upon empowering women to claim their rights, and not merely avoiding maternal death or morbidity" (HRC 2012, principle 12). As such, it shifted thinking on maternal health from a clinical approach to a human rights approach (Yamin 2013). This Technical Guidance highlights the importance of women's agency, accountability, and non-discrimination for advancing positive maternal health outcomes, and outlines the standards that "good quality" maternal health systems should meet (HRC 2012).

Recently, gains have also been made in UNFPA's work on family planning. Where once human rights were seen only as protections against coercive family planning policies and practices (such as forced sterilization), development organizations, including UNFPA, have invested in learning how human rights principles can systematically improve the way that clinic-based family planning programs are planned, implemented, monitored, and evaluated (Newman and Feldman 2015). In 2012, UNFPA launched its 2012–2020 family planning strategy, "Choices not Chance," with HRBA as a central component (UNFPA 2013a). In support of this strategy, UNFPA worked in partnership with the World Health Organization (WHO) to develop a 2015 guide on "Ensuring Human rights within Contraceptive Service Delivery" (UNFPA and WHO 2015). This guide aims to enable UNFPA country offices to support the capacity of health systems to ensure that contraceptive services are designed and delivered in accordance with human rights, not only economic and social rights but also civil and political rights, including the right to information, the right to privacy, and the right to bodily autonomy. This guidance has provided an important contribution to UNFPA's efforts to promote human rights-based family planning and to change the mindset by which family planning is viewed: from a focus on products to a focus on empowerment and choice. The challenge for UNFPA is to equip family planning experts with the skill set to take forward the analysis, advocacy, and capacity development required to translate such an approach into practice. A 2016 internal review of UNFPA's family planning strategy found that one of the key barriers to fully implementing the strategy was a lack of clarity on applying a human rights-based approach to family planning in UNFPA and a lack of staff capacity to advocate and communicate on human rights in family planning. While UNFPA has attempted to address this need by carrying out in-country and regional trainings for staff, shrinking financial resources have hampered the ability to provide these trainings systematically and across all regions—as well as provide follow-up support to ensure that training leads to change. Moreover, the tendency for a 'siloed' approach to programming, discussed in more detail below, reduces the ability of the organization to leverage expertise across programming sectors to address the broader human rights dimensions of family planning.

III. THE DRIVERS FOR HUMAN RIGHTS MAINSTREAMING IN UNFPA

UNFPA has a number of distinct institutional features that have facilitated the mainstreaming of human rights into its public health efforts, including its human rights mandate arising out of the ICPD; its partnership with civil society, in particular women's rights organizations; and its ability to convene and engage with multiple stakeholders for policy dialogue. While much progress has been made—today there is wide acceptance among UNFPA staff and senior management that UNFPA is a rights-based organization—one would have expected that the organization would have progressed further in shifting its approach to align with the rights-based vision of the ICPD. There is still work to be done to ensure its approach matches its rhetoric. Specific challenges it faces include limitations on the international political support for its mandate; capacity of staff to engage with and advocate on human rights; and organizational structure and incentives for mainstreaming.

A. Human Rights Mandate

UNFPA is uniquely placed as a UN development agency to mainstream human rights because it is custodian of the ICPD, which explicitly and boldly affirms the centrality of human rights for population and development. Where intergovernmental agreements affirm and push further the ICPD agenda, UNFPA's leadership becomes bolder and transformative to advance sexual and reproductive health and reproductive rights. While, as illustrated earlier, the organization has struggled to fully implement the human rights based dimensions of the ICPD. The ICPD Beyond 2014 International Conference on Human Rights articulated the steps needed to accelerate these efforts, providing a roadmap for UNFPA's efforts to institutionalize human rights in its work. The focus on equality, quality and accountability are embedded in UNFPA's current (2013–2017) Strategic Plan and further strengthened in its new Strategic Plan for 2018–2021.

B. Civil Society Partnership

UNFPA's close relationship with civil society—particularly the women's rights movement, at the global and country level—has strongly influenced its rights-based agenda. Civil society has been an important partner for UNFPA in advocating the ICPD agenda and pushing the frontiers at inter-governmental processes, strengthening national accountability, and holding UNFPA accountable to its own commitments. Especially at the country level, partnerships with civil society have proved critical for UNFPA country offices to advance UNFPA's mission, ensuring the voice and participation of those groups most marginalized and excluded. The civil society organizations working with UNFPA (in areas such as female genital mutilation and child, early, and forced marriage) are in many cases human rights organizations, which have directly influenced UNFPA's way of working. These partnerships with civil society, however, are at risk in many parts of the world where many governments are working to close off civil society space, including by suppressing dissenting voices, permitting violent attacks on women's human rights defenders, and reducing resources available to civil society actors. In this context, UNFPA's role in supporting and strengthening civil society space is more relevant than ever.

C. Policy Dialogue Platform

UNFPA has played an important role in extending the limits of how sexual and reproductive health issues have been traditionally perceived and putting human rights and women's empowerment at the heart of policy discussions. As an inter-governmental agency, with strong field presence in 150 countries and technical expertise, and drawing on the UN's normative mandate, UNFPA has been uniquely placed to convene a wide range of stakeholders in dialogue, backed by solid data and evidence, in order to push the frontiers of how sexual and reproductive health are perceived and approached, creating a platform where women's rights and gender equality are at the heart of the policy debate.

D. Sensitivity of Mandate

The political salience of the ICPD is challenged by the international political environment and lack of financial support, and these political forces have an impact on UNFPA.

While the consensus on which the ICPD was built has, on the one hand, received stronger political support than ever, as reflected in the 2030 Agenda, it has, on the other hand, faced increased opposition and a contesting of the agreed language of the ICPD. The inability of the Commission on Population and Development, the UN inter-governmental body that follows up on the implementation of the Programme of Action of the ICPD, to reach consensus at two if its last three sessions (the forty-eight and fiftieth session in 2015 and 2017 respectively) on its outcome document highlights the increasing polarization of the agenda. At the country level, while the political sensitivity around UNFPA's mandate requires political acumen and tact, it is not insurmountable. Human rights standards and mechanisms can provide a valuable entry point to raise politically sensitive issues, with the UNFPA 2002 HRBA programming review concluding that "an understanding of how reproductive rights are embedded in international human rights framework could assist country offices to engage in meaningful dialogue with conservative groups, and could help to overcome opinions such as one that reproductive rights are equated with the right to abortion" (UNFPA 2002, 3). Moreover, where the rest of the UN has rallied and stood with UNFPA and spoken up with one coherent voice on some of the most politically sensitive issues that touch upon UNFPA's mandate—such as adolescent pregnancy, contraception, and sexual health—a powerful message is sent, enabling UNFPA and the UN to successfully challenge countervailing social norms and attitudes.

E. Staff Profile and Training

Looking inward, human rights mainstreaming in UNFPA is also challenged by the profile and capacity of its staff. While a large percentage of UNFPA staff have expertise in specific health sectors and demography, the organization has few staff with a background in advocacy, legal reform, or policy to support the shift required to move the organization from the delivery of services to the delivery of thinking. Raising rights-based issues—including discrimination, abuse, and violence against women, children, and adolescents—may be highly politically sensitive in a country and requires strategic tactics, political acumen, and a firm grasp of the normative basis of rights-based issues. It will be necessary for UNFPA to improve the ability of staff to engage in human rights debates, supporting UNFPA country leadership, who are on the front line of these negotiations, to navigate this complex terrain and take a bold stand when rights are violated.

F. Organizational Structures and Incentives to Support Human Rights Mainstreaming

One of the challenges to mainstreaming human rights, in any organization, is that human rights are often viewed as a "soft" agenda, supported by everyone but not viewed with the same priority as more concrete development areas. Since the early 2000s, UNFPA has supported its human rights work by drawing on human rights as both an "enabler principle" and a dedicated "outcome" of its Strategic Plan (UNFPA 2013c). This dual strategy, both targeted and mainstreamed, has been critical in keeping a focus and coherence on human rights across UNFPA, with all country offices required to report on their human rights work. This has been particularly relevant for UNFPA's work on strengthening accountability mechanisms for human rights, including engaging with international, regional, and national human rights mechanisms. However, the "mainstreaming/ enabling" part of UNFPA's work that cuts across its strategic plan has been more of a challenge to consistently and meaningfully apply and measure. One of the challenges is a "siloed" approach to UNFPA's work with vertical interventions that do not make the linkages across thematic areas—gender-based violence, adolescent health, maternal health, population data, and family planning—which are critical to effectively address the broader determinants of sexual and reproductive health—such as discriminatory norms, laws, and policies.

This tension is challenged by the UNFPA business model, where funding support to countries is calculated on the basis of a country's gross national income (GNI) and its "development needs" (e.g., maternal mortality ratio, adolescent pregnancy rate, and gender equality). While this model is one of the most nuanced business models within the UN, going beyond economic considerations and capturing issues around policies and rights, UNFPA's resources are still predominantly focused on the least developed countries. As a result, country offices operating in middle-income countries, which may have much more hostile environments for implementing the ICPD, may lack the resources to engage the policy agenda. UNFPA has recognized this challenge, particularly in light of the 2030 Agenda, which is a universal agenda, and is exploring ways to better capture these different social, cultural, and political dimensions.

CONCLUSION

UNFPA has played a catalytic role at the global, regional, and country level to transform the way that sexual and reproductive health issues have been perceived, putting human rights and women's empowerment at the heart of public health discussions. Despite the opportunities provided by international norms and commitments on reproductive rights, however, the organization has struggled to appropriate the human rights mechanisms fully in its work and move beyond speaking the language of rights to shifting its underlying approach. To do so, a more deliberate and intentional effort is required to integrate human rights into its sexual and reproductive health work and to stand firm and advocate forcefully at the national, regional, and international level when the rights-based dimensions of the ICPD are attacked. The ICPD Beyond 2014 International Conference on Human Rights provides UNFPA with a valuable compass for operationalizing human rights in its work, highlighting the importance of strengthening quality of services, addressing non-discrimination, and supporting accountability for sexual and reproductive health and rights. UNFPA's new Strategic Plan for 2018–2021, which is guided by the 2030 Agenda, an agenda grounded in human rights, provides a major opportunity to accelerate these efforts. It anchors accountability, non-discrimination and quality of care within the work of the organization over the next four years and provides an opportunity to scale up efforts to translate the rights-based dimension of the ICPD into action.

REFERENCES

Center for Global Development. 2011. *Focus UNFPA, Four Recommendations for Action: Report of the CGD Working Group on UNFPA's Leadership Transition, Co-chairs.* Available at: https://www.cgdev.org/files/1424988_file_CGD_UNFPA_FINAL_web.pdf.

CESCR (Committee on Economic, Social and Cultural Rights). 2016. "General comment No. 22 (2016) on the right to sexual and reproductive health." 1 May. E/C.12/GC/22.

Gallagher, Anne. 2014. "Promoting and Protecting the Human Rights of Women and Girls." In *A Manual for National Human Rights Institutions.* Sydney: Asia Pacific Forum on National Human Rights Institutions.

Gilmore, Kate, Luis Mora, Alfonso Barragues, and Ida Krogh Mikkelsen. 2015. "The Universal Periodic Review: A Platform for Dialogue, Accountability, and Change on Sexual and Reproductive Health and Rights." *Health and Human Rights Journal* 17(2): 167–179.

Girard, Françoise. 2009. "Advocacy for Sexuality and Women's Rights: Continuities, Discontinuities, and Strategies Since ICPD." In *Reproductive Health and Human Rights: The Way Forward,* edited by Laura Reichenbach and Mindy Jane Roseman, 167–181. Philadelphia: University of Pennsylvania Press.

Heyzer, Noeleen. 2002. "Women Are the Key to Development." In *An Agenda for the People: The UNFPA through Three Decades,* edited by Nafis Sadik, 81–94. New York: New York University Press.

HRC (Human Rights Council). 2009. "Preventable maternal mortality and morbidity and human rights." 16 June. A/HRC/11/L.16.

HRC (Human Rights Council). 2010. "Preventable maternal mortality and morbidity and human rights: follow-up to Council." 27 September. A/HRC/15/L.27.

HRC (Human Rights Council). 2012. "Technical guidance on the application of a human rights based approach to the implementation of policies and programmes to reduce preventable maternal morbidity and mortality." 2 July. A/HRC/21/22.

Mousky, Stafford. 2002. "UNFPA's Role in the Population Field." In *An Agenda for the People: The UNFPA through Three Decades,* edited by Nafis Sadik, 210–242. New York: New York University Press.

Newman, Karin and Charlotte Feldman-Jacobs. 2015. "Policy Brief: Family Planning and Human Rights—What's the Connection and Why Is It Important?" *Population Reference Bureau.* Available at: http://www.prb.org/pdf15/family-planning-rights-brief.pdf.

Robinson, Rachel Sullivan. 2010. *UNFPA in Context: An Institutional History.* Background paper prepared for the Center for Global Development Working Group on UNFPA's Leadership Transition. Available at: https://www.cgdev.org/doc/UNFPA-in-Context.pdf.

Sadik, Nafis. 2002. Preface to *An Agenda for the People: The UNFPA through Three Decades,* edited by Nafis Sadik. New York: New York University Press.

Singh, Jyoti Shankar. 2002. "UNFPA and the Global Conferences." In *An Agenda for the People: The UNFPA through Three Decades,* edited by Nafis Sadik, 152–174. New York: New York University Press.

United Nations (UN). 1994. "Report of the International Conference on Population and Development in Cairo, 5–13 September 1994." Programme of Action.

UN. 1995. "Report of the Fourth World Conference on Women, Beijing 4–15 September, 1995. A/CONF.177/20/Rev.1.

UN. 2014. "Framework of Actions for the follow-up to the Programme of Action of the ICPD Beyond 2014 of the International Conference of Population and Development Beyond." February 2014, A/69/62.

UN. 1997. "Renewing the United Nations, A Programme for Reform, Report of the Secretary General." 14 July. A/51/950.

UN General Assembly, 1962. "Population Growth and Economic Development." 1838 (XVII). 18 December.

UN General Assembly. 1966. "Population Growth and Economic Development." 2211 (XXI). 17 December.

UN General Assembly. 1972. "The United Nations Population Fund." 3019 (XXVII). 18 December.

UN General Assembly. 1993. "Further measures for the restructuring and revitalization of the United Nations in the economic, social and related fields." 20 December. A/RES/48/162.

UN General Assembly, 4th World Conference on Women. 1995. "Beijing Declaration and Platform of Action." 17 October. A/CONF.177.20.

UN General Assembly. 2006. "Resolution adopted by the General Assembly." 3 April. A/RES/60/251.

UNDG (UN Development Group). 2003. The Human Rights-Based Approach to Development Cooperation Towards a Common Understanding Among UN Agencies. Available at: https://undg.org/document/the-human-rights-based-approach-to-development-cooperation-towards-a-common-understanding-among-un-agencies/.

UNFPA (United Nations Population Fund). 2002. Report of the UNFPA Review on Use of Rights-Based Approach in Programming. Available at: http://www.unfpa.org/sites/default/files/resource-pdf/hrba_manual_in%20full.pdf.

UNFPA. 2010. A Human Rights-Based Approach to Programming, Practical Information and Training Materials. Available at: http://www.unfpa.org/resources/human-rights-based-approach-programming.

UNFPA. 2011. "Report of the Executive Director for 2010, Cumulative Analysis of Progress in Implementation of the UNFPA Strategic Plan, 2008–2013." Doc. DP/FPA/2011/3.

UNFPA. 2013a. Choices not Chance, UNFPA Family Planning Strategy 2012–2020. Available at: http://www.unfpa.org/publications/choices-not-chance.

UNFPA. 2013b. "Montevideo Consensus on Population and Development." 12–15 August. Doc. LC/L.3697.

UNFPA. 2013c. Strategic Plan 2014–2017. Available at: http://www.unfpa.org/resources/strategic-plan-2014-2017.

UNFPA. 2014a. From Commitment to Action on Sexual and Reproductive Health and Rights. Available at: http://www.unfpa.org/publications/commitment-action-sexual-and-reproductive-health-and-rights.

UNFPA. 2014. Reproductive Rights Are Human Rights, A Handbook for National Human Rights Institution. Available at: http://www.unfpa.org/publications/reproductive-rights-are-human-rights.

UNFPA and OHCHR. 2013b. ICPD Beyond 2014 International Conference on Human Rights, Netherlands, 2013. Conference Report. Available at: http://www.unfpa.org/events/icpd-beyond-2014-international-conference-human-rights.

UNFPA and WHO. 2015. Ensuring Human rights within Contraceptive Service Delivery.

Weerakoon, Bradman. 2002. "Broadening Partnerships." In An Agenda for the People: The UNFPA through Three Decades, edited by Nafis Sadik, 95–112. New York: New York University Press.

Yamin, Alicia Ely. 2013. "From Ideals to Tools: Applying Human Rights to Maternal Health." PLoS Medicine 10(11): e1001546.

12

The Food and Agriculture Organization of the United Nations

Advancing the Right to Food to Promote Public Health

CAROLIN ANTHES AND OLIVIER DE SCHUTTER*

Since its founding in 1945 as an inter-governmental organization, the Food and Agriculture Organization of the United Nations (FAO) has remained the United Nations (UN) system's foremost specialized agency working toward eradicating hunger in the world. Its three main goals include: the eradication of hunger, food insecurity, and malnutrition; the elimination of poverty; and the sustainable management and utilization of natural resources for the benefit of present and future generations. Its uptake of human rights, and of the right to food in particular, has been gradual, but it is now a key part of FAO's work.

Yet, despite an obvious shift toward a rights-based framing on normative and discursive levels, as well as palpable practical advances over the years, a gap still exists between the Organization's rhetoric and institutional practices, and this gap has been widening over recent years. This chapter argues that human rights mainstreaming within FAO's work is far from unidirectional: whereas the right to food agenda played an increasingly important role from the late 1990s to the late 2000s, FAO has

* This chapter builds on the 2013 Report of the Special Rapporteur on the right to food: "Mission to the Food and Agriculture Organization of the United Nations" and takes into account more recent developments and further considerations. During his mandate as Special Rapporteur on the right to food (2008–2014), Olivier De Schutter conducted a mission to FAO in 2012, which resulted in his report to the Human Rights Council. During that time, co-author Carolin Anthes worked as consultant in FAO's Right to Food Team on mainstreaming the right to food within FAO. The authors would like to express their gratitude to all interlocutors within and outside FAO for sharing their accounts, to the editors and external reviewers for their valuable comments and suggestions, and to Olga Perov for her excellent copy-editing support.

Human Rights in Global Health. Benjamin Mason Meier and Lawrence O. Gostin.
© Oxford University Press 2018. Published 2018 by Oxford University Press.

since witnessed a period of retrenchment. The following parts present background on FAO's development (Part I), introduce the evolution of the right to food within the Organization (Part II), assess current efforts to mainstream the right to food in FAO's operations (Part III), analyze selected factors that support or obstruct human rights mainstreaming (Part IV), and conclude with recommendations for future efforts to mainstream the right to food within FAO.

I. BIRTH, FUNCTIONS, AND WORK OF THE FAO

FAO is one of the oldest UN specialized agencies, and it has grown to become the largest (Moore 2005; Liese 2012). Dating back to, *inter alia*, the initiative of US President Franklin D. Roosevelt and the 1943 UN Conference on Food and Agriculture, the agency was founded by forty-four member states to promote common welfare by raising levels of nutrition and standards of living, securing improvements in the efficiency of production and distribution of all food and agricultural products, bettering the condition of rural populations, and thus contributing to an expanding world economy and ensuring humanity's freedom from hunger (FAO 2015a, 3).[1] Article 1 of FAO's Constitution spells out three main functions of the Organization: (1) the collection, analysis, interpretation, and dissemination of information relating to nutrition, food, and agriculture (including fisheries and forestry); (2) the promotion of various national and international efforts and activities relating to knowledge production on food, nutrition, and agriculture, to the conservation of natural resources, to the improvement of agricultural methods as well as to the processing, marketing, and distribution of food and agricultural products; and (3) the provision of technical assistance at the request of member states in the areas pertaining to FAO's mandate (FAO 2015a). Its mandate has been described as being "technical" in the provision of advice or assistance (Oberleitner 2007, 127; Moore 2005, 140) but also "comprehensive" (Shaw 2009, 68) and "extensive" (Ibid., 95).

In FAO's early years, international policy debates and the work of the Organization focused on increasing agricultural production and assuring the availability of basic foodstuffs at the international and national levels, to work toward "freedom from want of food" (Phillips 1981, 12). The deployment of FAO's field work started early; by 1951, FAO had already launched 100 projects in thirty-five developing countries, "consciously aware . . . of the prime importance of working with governments, especially in developing countries, to increase global food production" (Shaw 2009, 96). But such field presence was neither the exclusive nor even the primary function of the Organization; instead, FAO has also been described as a "knowledge organization," holding a "fundamental and unique" role regarding "knowledge management for food and agriculture," with a "mandate as a global broker of essential information and data" (Shaw 2009, 110–112).

With policy advice a key part of the Organization's mission, FAO also supports its member states in designing their food security laws, policies, and programs;

1. Today, FAO has practically universal membership, with 194 member states, two associate members, and one member organization, the European Union (FAO Legal Office 2017).

conducts programs and projects at country level; and generates knowledge that impacts vast areas of thematic debates on global food security. FAO convenes major international conferences—such as the seminal World Food Summits of 1996, 2002, and 2009—to address the state of food insecurity in the world. It is engaged in standard-setting, such as through the Codex Alimentarius, established together with the World Health Organization (WHO) in 1963, which develops harmonized international food standards to protect consumer health and promote fair practices in food trade. FAO thus plays a crucial role in the global health architecture through these various activities and programs, and over the past two decades, a fundamental shift has occurred in the way the core mandate of FAO is understood through a gradually increasing focus on the human right to adequate food.

II. FROM FOOD SECURITY TO THE RIGHT TO ADEQUATE FOOD

FAO was instrumental in codifying a human right to adequate food and developing its normative language in Article 11 of the 1966 International Covenant on Economic, Social and Cultural Rights (ICESCR) (FAO 1997; Moore 2005). However, the thirty years that followed have been described as a period of "withdrawal from human rights," mostly because of FAO's perception of itself as a technical agency at the disposal of states, providing a neutral forum for all nations, rich and poor, to improve the situation of food security (Oberleitner 2007, 128). Following this temporary withdrawal from human rights, the 1996 World Food Summit provided a path for FAO to re-engage with the human right to food.

The concept of food security was developed in the context of the world food crisis of 1973–1974, and it thereafter came to occupy public discourse for the next several decades (Mechlem 2004). In Resolution XVII, the 1974 World Food Conference described food security as the "availability at all times of adequate world supplies of basic food-stuffs . . . to sustain a steady expansion of food consumption . . . and to offset fluctuations in production and prices" (FAO 1974, 14). Although the right to food was already enshrined by that time in the ICESCR, the *individual* right to food was not mentioned in the World Food Summit Declaration (Mechlem 2004). The concept of food security became "more encompassing and multi-layered" in the 1980s (Mechlem 2004, 637), connected with an increasing focus on the individual, thus paving the way for the human right to food to re-emerge in later years (Eide 2005; Mechlem 2004; Alston and Tomaševski 1984; Eide et al. 1984).

It was not until after the 1996 World Food Summit, as depicted in Figure 12.1, when Heads of State and Government reaffirmed "the right of everyone to have access to safe and nutritious food, consistent with the right to adequate food and the fundamental right of everyone to be free from hunger" (FAO 1996), that FAO committed itself to support the UN human rights system in further clarifying the content of the right to food. Since then, the visibility of the right to food has gradually increased in the Organization's work. In 1999, the Committee on Economic, Social and Cultural Rights (CESCR) adopted General Comment 12 to interpret the right to adequate food in the ICESCR, providing an authoritative interpretation of state obligations, concretizing the scope of the right to food, and introducing a "respect,

Figure 12.1 FAO Director-General Jacques Diouf addressing the Plenary during the World Food Summit at FAO headquarters in Rome on November 13, 1996.
PHOTO CREDIT: FAO/Luigi Spaventa.

protect, fulfill" framework for all economic, social, and cultural rights (CESCR 1999). The 2002 World Food Summit—under pressure from civil society organizations (most prominently FIAN International), which had presented governments with a draft code of conduct on the realization of the right to food—provided a mandate to develop a new set of guidelines on the right to food (Oshaug 2005). After two intense years of negotiations between governments, the 2004 Voluntary Guidelines to Support the Progressive Realization of the Right to Adequate Food in the Context of National Food Security were unanimously adopted by the FAO Council (FAO 2004a; Rae et al. 2007).[2] As the only inter-governmental text clarifying the measures governments should take to implement the human right to adequate food, FAO played a crucial role in supporting these negotiations, with the resulting Guidelines marking a critical juncture for the mainstreaming of human rights and the right to food within the Organization. Upon their adoption, "many member states" called on FAO to support the implementation and mainstreaming of the Right to Food Guidelines (FAO 2004b, para. 26). This led FAO in 2006 to establish a Right to Food Unit (later renamed the Right to Food Team) within the Agricultural Development Economics Division (ESA), tasked with integrating the right to food approach and mainstreaming the Guidelines into FAO's work.

2. The Conference is FAO's major governing and deliberative body. It currently meets every two years for a regular session, where it, *inter alia*, reviews and approves the Programme of Work, decides on scales of contribution and budget, agrees on administrative matters, and deals with the election of the Director-General. The FAO Conference elects the FAO Council, consisting of forty-nine member states, which serves as the Organization's governing body between the Conference sessions (FAO 2015a; Philips 1981).

In 2009, in the aftermath of the devastating world food price crisis, the Committee on World Food Security (CFS), initially established by FAO in 1976, underwent a major reform, establishing it as the foremost inclusive international and inter-governmental platform for all stakeholders to work together to ensure food security and nutrition for all. Following the 2009 reform, the new mandate of the CFS explicitly included the right to food, and the way the CFS operates has been designed in accordance with human rights principles (e.g., meaningful participation of those most affected by hunger and malnutrition through a Civil Society Mechanism (CSM)) (Duncan 2015). Hosted by FAO in its headquarters in Rome and staffed by all three Rome-based agencies,[3] the rights-based approach of the CFS has been widely acclaimed.

In the following years, the CFS developed a series of human rights-based instruments, including the 2012 Voluntary Guidelines on Responsible Governance of Tenure of Land, Fisheries, and Forestry in the Context of National Food Security (VGGT) and the 2014 CFS Principles for Responsible Investment in Agriculture and Food Systems (RAI principles) (CFS 2012; 2014). In 2015, the CFS endorsed the Framework for Action for Food Security and Nutrition in Protracted Crises (CFS 2015). The decisions and recommendations adopted within the CFS are now collected in the Global Strategic Framework for Food Security and Nutrition (GSF), a document that is regularly updated in order to provide decision makers and policymakers with a usable template for making progress on food security and nutrition outcomes (Duncan 2015, 192–208; CFS 2016). Outside the CFS, FAO has additionally facilitated the adoption of guidelines inspired by the right to food, including the 2014 FAO Committee on Fisheries' adoption of the Voluntary Guidelines for Securing Sustainable Small-Scale Fisheries in the Context of Food Security and Poverty Eradication (SSF Guidelines) (FAO 2015e).

The right to food in FAO has seen progress since the 1990s, realized in the proliferation of rights-based instruments endorsed across the sectors in recent years. A UNESCO Chair in Human Rights and Peace sees FAO "on the road to mainstream human rights throughout the organization's activities" (Coomans 2012, 286). With leading scholars concluding that "FAO has a remarkable history in terms of human rights" (Oberleitner 2007, 127), practitioners have found that since 1996, "the Right to Adequate Food has become a rallying cry for the Organization in its attempts to raise public awareness and commitment to the goal of food security and eliminating hunger in the world" (Moore 2005, 153). According to practitioner and scholar assessments, the FAO (and the CFS in particular) is firmly anchored in and committed to human rights and the right to food in its standards, yet such assessments are insufficiently nuanced where the right to food continues to face contestation and occasional backsliding in organizational activities.

3. The FAO, the World Food Programme (WFP), and the International Fund for Agricultural Development (IFAD) comprise the three "Rome-based food agencies" of the UN system.

III. ASSESSING MAINSTREAMING OF THE RIGHT TO FOOD IN FAO

Mainstreaming the right to adequate food within FAO requires that the right to food approach permeate all core activities of FAO, including in the areas of food and agricultural policies, nutrition, land, and trade. However, despite the progressive evolution of rights-based standards, introduced by the adoption of the seminal Right to Food Guidelines in 2004, FAO has fallen short of fully mainstreaming human rights in its programs or providing for their implementation with the strong institutional support such programs require. The weaknesses of these mainstreaming efforts within the Organization's operations are seen in: (a) the rise and decline of FAO's Right to Food Unit/Team; (b) FAO's Strategic Framework; (c) cross-departmental integration of the right to food; (d) sectoral, program, and project integration; (e) country and regional policies and programs; (f) relationships between FAO and external stakeholders; and (g) policy convergence across the UN system.

A. FAO's Right to Food Unit/Team

The 2006 establishment of the Right to Food Unit allowed for a "specialist unit" (Uggla 2007, 10) to coordinate FAO's mainstreaming strategy. Through its work, the Right to Food Unit aimed to transform the "specialist unit model" into a "mainstreaming model" by trying to commit the entire organization to human rights (FAO 2017b). This multidisciplinary Unit, later renamed Team during a reform process, has been successful in disseminating information on the right to food, through which it has: provided guidance and offered training and advocacy, including the publication of toolkits and online courses; provided legal, policy, and capacity-building assistance to governments; partnered with civil society; and been involved in assessing and monitoring the right to food (FAO 2017c). In these human rights efforts, it has worked closely with other FAO divisions and provided right to food commentary to countless publications.

Since its creation, the Unit has consistently advocated for a right to food approach, arguing that the right to food offers a tool for combating hunger and malnutrition by recognizing accessible, available, and adequate food as a legal entitlement, not a form of charity or policy choice (FAO 2011). This approach has required that FAO recognize the hungry and malnourished as rights-holders—identified and empowered to claim their right to food—and that the capacity of duty-bearers (primarily states) to fulfill their obligations is strengthened (FAO 2006b). In the past years, a major focus of the Team has been carrying out projects at regional and country level: mainstreaming the right to food into subnational plans and strategies; integrating the right to adequate food and good governance in national policies, legislation, and institutions; and incorporating the right to food into global and regional food security strategies.

However, despite a positive 2015 evaluation of the Team's projects (FAO Office of Evaluation 2015), the reliance on time-bound, extrabudgetary funding for this work has proven unsustainable in the absence of regular budgetary support. Where once the Unit had eighteen people at headquarters and about twenty-four in country offices, the downgraded Team has been described by an FAO staffer as "half dead," with only a part-time Team Leader, one Project Officer, one consultant, and two part-time assistants carrying out one project in 2017. In spite of the continuously high demand for the Team's expertise, the mainstreaming of the right to food within FAO currently fails to receive adequate support and remains poorly institutionalized. Dedicated right to food staff have moved to the better funded Legal Office's Development Law Service, from which they have attempted to mainstream the right to food perspective. Compounding the lack of capacity, staff, and stable resources of the "specialist unit," no right to food focal points have been established in FAO's technical units at headquarters or in regional and national offices.

B. FAO's Reviewed Strategic Framework and Strategic Objectives

In 2012, the incoming Director-General launched a Strategic Thinking Process to review FAO's Strategic Framework 2010–2019 and Medium Term Plan 2014–2017. This resulted in realigning FAO's work along five "Strategic Objectives" (SO) and two cross-cutting themes: "gender" and "governance" (FAO 2013c). Although the right to food has not been explicitly attributed cross-cutting status, it has been argued nevertheless that the right to food—together with human rights principles (such as participation, equality, transparency, and accountability)—underpin the Strategic Objectives and the two new cross-cutting themes (Yeshanew 2014). Moreover, within FAO's Reviewed Strategic Framework, one Strategic Objective (SO 1: *Contribute to the eradication of hunger, food insecurity and malnutrition*) makes reference to the improvement of "capacities of governments and stakeholders to develop and implement legal frameworks and accountability mechanisms to realize the right to adequate food" (1.1.2). According to the Programme Implementation Report 2014–15, FAO remained active in sixteen countries to facilitate the "development and implementation of legal frameworks supportive of the right to food" (FAO 2016b).

Yet, the right to food is not mainstreamed in FAO's Strategic Framework. As compared with gender mainstreaming—which is an accepted strategy in FAO and is to be implemented under the Reviewed Strategic Framework, which features a Policy on Gender Equity and a network of gender focal points—the right to food is mostly confined to Strategic Objective 1. One rationale for establishing the new Strategic Objectives had been to break down the all-pervasive organizational "silos"[4] that inhibit a collaborative, cross-divisional work style; however, some staff in FAO find the Strategic Objectives to be new, competing silos in their own right. The current means of implementing the right to food in the work of the Organization

---

4. The term "silo" refers to a fragmented organization with entrenched obstacles to horizontal and vertical communication and collaboration. The 2007 Report of the Independent External Evaluation of the FAO (IEE) points at the Organization's "silo culture" (FAO 2007, 121) and concludes: "FAO's greatest challenge is in bringing integrated answers to interdisciplinary problems of food and agriculture . . . but as FAO is not a well joined-up organization, its shrinking budgets have tended to reinforce the silos rather than break them down" (Ibid., 38).

runs counter to the very idea of mainstreaming, where the right to food is now primarily promoted in FAO through discrete projects carried out predominantly by a single group.

Although the Reviewed Strategic Framework is undergoing the next quadrennial review in 2017 (FAO 2016c; 2017e), the new draft, firmly anchored in the 2030 Agenda for Sustainable Development, exhibits little change on the right to food, presenting another missed opportunity to elevate the right to food as a cross-cutting theme. Where rights-based governance is often perceived as too politically sensitive and confrontational in the FAO context, this choice is in line with a new FAO governance paradigm that aims at a "more modest and pragmatic agenda" away from good governance and toward "improved and more effective governance" (FAO 2016c, para. 167).

C. Cross-Departmental Integration of the Right to Food

Despite the absence of a systematic mainstreaming of the right to food within the Organization's main strategies and operations, several FAO departments and divisions have integrated cross-cutting human rights principles—including participation, cross-sectoral coordination, empowerment, or a focus on marginalized groups—in some of their projects. For example, the Forestry Department has supported national governments in the formulation of national forestry strategies to create cross-sectoral coordination and a substantive participatory process (with civil society and other stakeholders), engaging the Right to Food Team to elaborate a toolbox on the integration of the right to food in the non-wood forest product sector (FAO 2012a). The Fisheries Department has also championed the integration of a human rights-based approach (HRBA) in its work on small-scale fisheries, manifested in their collaboration with the Legal Office on a HRBA Workshop in October 2016. Although scattered, these rights-based departmental efforts may constitute building blocks from which a right to food strategy can be developed.

The newer Partnerships, Advocacy, and Capacity Development Division (OPC) is at the heart of FAO's recent efforts to strategically partner with different stakeholders, epitomized in the Director-General's widely acclaimed, participatory "open door policy" to civil society. Throughout its history, FAO has provided important strategic support for the development of the autonomous producers' movement. As seen in the FAO Policy on Indigenous and Tribal Peoples (2010)—grounded in the UN Declaration on the Rights of Indigenous Peoples, focused on a group in which the prevalence of food insecurity is particularly high—this effort contributes to the implementation of the right to food by FAO. Structured by an FAO manual, respecting indigenous Free, Prior, and Informed Consent (FPIC) is now mandatory for all FAO projects and programs (FAO 2016a). FPIC is also included in the 2015 Environmental and Social Management Guidelines, which focus on gender equality, decent work, and the avoidance of forced evictions.

While such integration often remains nonsystematic, ad hoc rather than built into the organizational culture of FAO, these examples show how the integration of right to food principles is feasible and how such integration can contribute to the fulfillment of food security objectives by FAO.

D. Sectoral Policies: Potential Mismatches

A mainstreamed right to food approach could serve as a compass for the design of sustainable sectoral policies. Yet, while the CFS-endorsed guidelines and frameworks regarding land governance and agricultural investments are the most remarkable examples of rights-based approaches to sectoral challenges, there are also instances of potential mismatches within FAO, including the support for contradictory agricultural paradigms and diverging trade-related messages.

FAO supports various agricultural paradigms that many stakeholders consider to be incompatible with each other. FAO participated in the 2008 International Assessment of Agricultural Knowledge, Science and Technology for Development (IAASTD), which called for a fundamental shift in the way agriculture is supported, but only a couple of months later, signed a Letter of Agreement with the Alliance for a Green Revolution in Africa (AGRA) without reference to IAASTD or the Right to Food Guidelines (De Schutter 2013). Similarly, FAO convened a 2010 Conference on Agricultural Biotechnologies while at the same time supporting alternate agricultural development models through its Globally Important Agricultural Heritage System (GIAHS) (Ibid.). Finally, FAO encourages national plans to subsidize chemical fertilizers, but it also convened an international symposium and regional meetings on Agroecology for Food Security and Nutrition.

In the area of trade, FAO has made valuable rights-based contributions to the field of trade negotiations and food security during the last decade. The Import Surges Project remains a landmark achievement in assessing the possible negative impacts of unregulated trade on food security, highlighting the importance for developing countries in protecting local industries and small food producers from dumping (Ibid.). FAO's report on *Agriculture, Trade Negotiations and Gender* is another example of a right to food approach to trade, assessing the possible positive and negative impacts of trade liberalization on groups particularly vulnerable to discrimination (FAO 2006a). Nonetheless, the conclusions of these efforts and reports are insufficiently reflected in the discourse promoted by FAO at the global level.

What is sometimes perceived as a mixed message from FAO is, in part, simply a reflection of the sheer complexity of its mandate and governance structure. As an inter-governmental organization, FAO aims to support governments, and in turn, state priorities affect FAO's activities. Closely connected is the influence of donors' priorities—roughly two-thirds of FAO's funding is of extrabudgetary origin, often "earmarked" for specific project use only (FAO 2007, 181). FAO must also shape consensus among its members when setting norms and defining priorities: 194 members have different views on sectoral policies. Finally, the secretariat has to interact with many governing bodies, which often creates tensions vis-à-vis management decisions. These factors lead FAO to conduct programs and provide policy advice in various, sometimes conflicting directions, and the Organization has not yet found consensus to effectively mainstream human rights to provide greater coherence across FAO policies, systematically grounding all its work on a framework based on the right to food.

E. Right to Food at Country and Regional Levels

FAO can play a key role in encouraging the national adoption of legal, institutional, and policy frameworks informed by the right to food—indeed, it has been doing so for more than a decade (Vidar et al. 2014; Blondeau 2014). Yet, although FAO leads among UN agencies in supporting the implementation of the right to food at country level, progress remains uneven across countries and regions without organization-wide guidance to ensure that human rights are systematically mainstreamed.

In country programs, FAO's 2011 Country Programming Guidelines called for adherence to the five UN Country Programming Principles, including the HRBA (FAO Programme Committee 2011), but according to FAO staff, these Guidelines no longer apply since the current Director-General, José Graziano da Silva, has taken office. The 2015 FAO Guide to the Formulation of the Country Programming Framework (CPF), by contrast, is silent on the operationalization of the right to food, making only broad reference to aligning Country Programme Frameworks (documents that define priority areas and outcomes for government collaboration over four- to five-year periods) with the UN Development Assistance Framework (UNDAF) and UN Development Group (UNDG) system-wide guidance (FAO 2015c).

In the area of project management, the 2012 Guide to the Project Cycle similarly requires FAO staff to mainstream the five UN Common Country Programming Principles, including the HRBA, into all phases of the project cycle (FAO 2012b). However, a 2015 FAO Guide and Manual to the project cycle by FAO's Technical Cooperation Programme (TCP) does not feature the HRBA or right to food prominently, appearing only in a checklist as one out of eight factors under "sustainability of results" (FAO 2015b).[5]

A newer focus of FAO's right to food activities pertains to the creation of parliamentary fronts against hunger in Asia and Africa, employing South-South Cooperation at regional and country levels (FAO 2015d). The Parliamentary Front against Hunger in Latin America serves as a blueprint of this advocacy initiative, wherein FAO's Regional Office has been instrumental to the progress made over recent decades in integrating the right to food into legal, policy, and institutional frameworks in a number of countries (De Schutter 2013; Parliamentary Front Against Hunger 2017). According to an OPC Officer, FAO also works to promote family farming policies based on the results of the successful International Year of Family Farming (2014), which has the right to food explicitly underpinning its focus on vulnerable constituencies (FAO 2017a).

F. Relationships between FAO and External Stakeholders

Despite its inter-governmental nature, FAO has moved to foster partnerships with a range of actors, including civil society, the private sector, cooperatives, academia, and nontraditional partners such as city networks. In particular, there is evidence that realization of the right to food will not be possible without the effective participation

---

5. Although the Right to Food Team was asked to participate in elaborating the new project cycle guide, it had to decline due to lack of capacity.

of organizations representing food-insecure groups (De Schutter 2010). Following the 1996 World Food Summit, a number of innovative approaches to cooperation with civil society organizations have emerged, among them a Letter of Agreement between FAO and the International Planning Committee on Food Sovereignty (IPC)[6] in 2003 and participatory negotiations within the reformed CFS since 2009. In 2013, FAO adopted a comprehensive strategy for partnerships with civil society organizations, including the right to adequate food as one of the two mutual principles for collaboration (FAO 2013a), with the Director-General receiving widespread acclaim for this "open door policy" to civil society.

FAO also interacts with the private sector in various areas—including in policy dialogue, norm- and standard-setting, technical programs, and knowledge management—as, according to the Director-General, "FAO considers the private sector to be a key ally in the fight against hunger" (FAO 2017d). However, FAO's strategy for partnerships with the private sector (FAO 2013b) is not articulated under the normative framework of the right to food, and additional guidance documents remain vague on human rights. The only human rights element that is incorporated into FAO's work with the private sector is FAO's commitment to screen proposed partners in accordance with UN Global Compact Principles, which include human and labor rights, environmental, and governance practices (FAO 2013b, 21). This differential framing of partnerships with either civil society or the private sector explains existing concerns about the influence of major corporations on the work of FAO and the possible conflicts of interest (between public and private interests) in seeking to implement the right to food.

G. Policy Convergence across the United Nations System

Finally, FAO also plays a role in shaping global governance on food and nutrition security issues, addressing the enormous problem of fragmentation across institutions. Since the world food price crises in 2007–2008, a consensus has emerged that food security cannot be dealt with separately from other areas of international cooperation (Page 2013; McKeon 2015). As a means to overcome fragmentation, the reformed CFS has emerged as an innovative site to facilitate policy convergence across the UN system (CFS 2009). Although the initial years following the CFS reform involved frequent debates on the right to food, the CFS has witnessed a significant retreat in human rights discourse in recent years. Some member states have engaged in forum shifting on right to food matters, arguing that human rights should not be dealt with in Rome and referring human rights matters altogether to the state-led Human Rights Council in Geneva.[7] Moreover, FAO has

---

6. As a platform for facilitating dialogue with FAO, the IPC is a self-managed global network of more than forty-five peoples' movements and non-governmental organizations—with at least 800 organizational members throughout the world.

7. At the forty-third CFS plenary in October 2016, the delegate of the Russian Federation stressed "that the issue of human rights in general should be dealt with by the specialized [human rights] bodies of the UN system" (FAO Webcast 2016).

not sought to replicate the CFS model of inclusiveness and active participation of civil society across its own sectoral committees. On the inter-agency level, the competitive silos among Rome-based agencies are still relatively intact, and any collaboration between FAO and the Geneva-based human rights system has been ad hoc rather than systematic.[8]

Working with other UN agencies, FAO's Right to Food Team has participated in the UNDG Human Rights Mainstreaming Mechanism (renamed in 2013 the UNDG Human Rights Working Group), which seeks to institutionalize human rights as a central part of the UN's development work through strengthening system-wide collaboration and coherence (UNDG 2014; Yeshanew 2014). In this collaborative role, FAO has contributed to the drafting of a 2011 UNDG Guidance Note to UN Country Teams, which sets out guidance on a HRBA to food security and nutrition. Due to a lack of sufficient human resources, however, the Team's current participation in inter-agency mechanisms is minimal.

As seen through this assessment, the FAO record in mainstreaming the right to food in its operations remains mixed. Since the 1990s, some important building blocks have been put in place: dedicated staff are present (although decreasing), human rights principles increasingly permeate FAO activities, and mainstreaming efforts have proven successful on a confined scale. While overall progress is palpable, the recent decline of the right to food within the Organization is undeniable. Non-governmental organizations have perceived the danger: although many of them (regrouped within the IPC) refer more frequently to food sovereignty than to the right to food, they understand the benefits of human rights—imposing requirements of accountability, participation, and non-discrimination that are binding on governments and that, by defining victims of hunger and malnutrition as rights-holders, have the potential to transform the relationships with governments. The Civil Society Mechanism—established within the CFS to allow civil society to speak with a single, coordinated voice—has taken action to set up a "Friends of the Right to Food" alliance, which would include supportive member states in an effort to revitalize the right to food focus in FAO and CFS.

IV. MAINSTREAMING THE RIGHT TO FOOD IN FAO: BETWEEN SUPPORT AND OBSTRUCTION

The period from 1996 until roughly 2010 was particularly propitious for human rights mainstreaming; however, the more recent period is one of retrenchment. Given the range of factors that may be conducive or obstructive to human rights mainstreaming in international organizations, the evolution of the right to food's trajectory within FAO reveals that—far from showing a steady, unidirectional progress—this troubled path reflects the dynamics of the contentious human rights agenda itself.

---

8. A positive example of collaboration with the Human Rights Council is seen in FAO's high-level support for the process of elaborating a UN Declaration on the Rights of Peasants and Other People Working in Rural Areas.

A. Member State Donors, Civil Society Support, and Favorable United Nations Context

Upon adopting the 2004 Right to Food Guidelines, the FAO Council requested the Secretariat to take adequate follow-up action and to seek additional extrabudgetary resources to do so. An FAO Multidonor Partnership Programme was created to provide funding for the initial five years of the Right to Food Unit's work, with this strong state support benefiting from the sense of state ownership that resulted from two years of intense and successful negotiations on the Right to Food Guidelines. Implementation of the right to food was clearly regarded as a priority for FAO by member states that were willing to invest in this line of work. This state support complemented UN system-wide efforts following Kofi Annan's call in the late 1990s to mainstream human rights across all UN work (UN General Assembly 1997; Oberleitner 2007; Kedzia 2009; Coomans 2012) and the adoption of a 2003 Common Understanding on Human Rights-Based Approaches to Development Cooperation and Programming (HRBA Portal 2017). Thus, the climate in international politics—especially after the end of the Cold War—was favorable to the rights-based development agenda, with economic, social, and cultural rights no longer regarded as a primarily "socialist" project or as an interest only to developing countries (Uvin 2004). As discussed in chapter 15, the agenda set by the work of Amartya Sen and others, defining development as the expansion of human freedoms and emphasizing the role of human rights in strengthening accountability of governments toward their populations, was one that united both rich ("donor") countries and poor ("beneficiary") countries—albeit for different reasons (Sen 1981; 1999). To rich countries, the HRBA to development meant that beneficiary governments should be closely monitored by civil society and social movements; to poorer countries, such approaches, while threatening to introduce conditionalities in development aid, nevertheless transformed aid into a duty of rich countries rather than just a matter of charity (De Schutter 2009). Civil society organizations, FIAN International most prominently, also played an indispensable role in pushing for a right to food approach in the FAO Secretariat and supporting the Right to Food Guidelines (Windfuhr 2005).

B. FAO Leadership Support

Within the Organization, the ownership and support of FAO Director-General Jacques Diouf (1994–2011) created crucial support for the rights-based approach. Although Diouf had not been known as a human rights champion, he "owned" the right to food within FAO. He showed ownership by supporting the Right to Food Unit, as seen in personally launching the Right to Food Methodological Toolbox, one of the Unit's major products (FAO 2009). Such action from the FAO leadership sent a signal throughout the Organization that the right to food was a priority area, fully supported by the leadership, which in turn created momentum for others within the Organization to become interested and open to right to food mainstreaming. Where mainstreaming human rights will necessarily meet resistance—and the right to food is no exception—support hinges upon dedicated and bold individuals who can stand up for human rights and justify their operationalization within an organization (Oestreich 2007, 6–10; Darrow and Arbour 2009; Clarke 2012; Coomans 2012; Vandenhole 2014).

C. Financial Retrenchment

Even as rhetoric on the right to food was maintained, the astounding decline of the right to food within FAO in recent years, epitomized by the withering of the once vibrant Right to Food Unit, reflects the extent to which these supportive factors can turn obstructive to human rights mainstreaming. The reliance on extrabudgetary funding and time-bound projects has not translated into a stronger regular budget commitment by FAO to the Right to Food Team. Quite the contrary, the Right to Food Team has operated exclusively on volatile project-specific funding after 2013, restricting multi-year planning as states reduced their willingness to invest further in this part of the work of FAO.[9] Other state priorities external to FAO's agenda, such as the European "refugee crisis" in recent years, also interfered with the funding of FAO's work on the right to food, as European states became less willing to provide support. FAO has thus struggled with a constant funding scarcity vis-à-vis its comprehensive and expanding mandate (FAO 2007; Shaw 2009; Liese 2012), which has led to austerity measures across most of its programs.

This waning member state support was at times specific to FAO's human rights work. The diplomats who negotiated the Right to Food Guidelines developed a vested interest in their implementation succeeding, and yet they have now been replaced, with their successors feeling far less ownership over the Guidelines and greater inclination to embrace new "cyclical fashions" in FAO and international development. Amplifying this retrenchment is the continuing opposition by powerful states to economic, social, and cultural rights—epitomized by the long-standing denial by the United States, FAO's largest financial contributor, that rights such as the right to food are truly "human rights" (FAO 2004a, Annex 2)—and the overall human rights recession in global affairs, which has recently been coined a "post–human rights world" (Strangio 2017). Reflective of this waning support, the latest version of the UNDAF guidelines, adopted in January 2017, no longer includes HRBA content, representing what a UN practitioner considers the end of the HRBA in the UN for the time being. The absence of HRBA "believers" at the highest levels of virtually all UN organizations, including FAO, has taken its toll.

D. Organizational (Silo) Culture

Within the Organization, FAO's self-perception and identity as a predominantly "technical agency," where human rights add an unnecessary additional political layer, still permeates the organization. The reproach that "you can't eat human rights after all," while caricatural, is at the same time symptomatic. This staff neglect

---

9. For example, Germany, once the largest donor of the Unit, whose bilateral trust fund had been exclusively dedicated to the Right to Food Unit, refocused its FAO investments toward the "new" VGGT process.

of human rights often translates into risk-averse "submission" to the will of member states, which have shifted away from setting the right to food as a cross-cutting FAO priority. FAO's organizational culture had already been rebuked in the 2007 IEE Report, wherein it was found to be conservative and slow to adapt, with a heavy bureaucracy creating an unhealthy and risk-averse organizational culture and silo mentality (FAO 2007, fn. 6). Despite efforts to "break down the silos" within the Organization during the past decade, the fragmentation of the work of FAO into different policy areas remains strong, inhibiting efforts to promote human rights mainstreaming. The Right to Food Unit/Team, for example, was located in a division of economists (ESA), a division with a rather distinct mindset (or "mental silo") geared toward efficiency rather than empowerment and accountability, and which may have perceived the right to food with indifference at best—at worst, as a threat to their normal way of doing things. These silos in FAO are not just unintended consequences of how the institution had evolved. On the contrary, they were at times consciously reinforced by some state and intra-organizational actors so that "they can do *their* business," with the targeted earmarking of extrabudgetary funds and volatile short-term consultancy contracts supporting this trend.

Moreover, a culture of evaluation based on the measure of short-term quantitative results (e.g., how many farmers reached, what percentage of yield productivity increased, or which acreage of land planted) does not reward field officers or program managers whose rights-based priority it is to organize farmers, build networks of civil society organizations, or establish mechanisms, which, in the name of the right to food, are meant to hold governments accountable. The strengthening of farmers' or civil society organizations and the establishment of such mechanisms may prove key in the long term to the realization of rights, and they may be seen as a condition for even short-term efforts to be sustainable (e.g., preventing corruption and the misuse of funds); however, in the short term, their "results" are difficult to see, let alone measure quantitatively.

Finally, the organizational leadership in a hierarchical organization such as FAO is of tremendous importance to human rights mainstreaming; yet, the right to food mainstreaming agenda has not been one of the priorities of the current Director-General. Where he has situated existing right to food posts in the newly created OPC division, these positions have not been filled since 2013, and it seems that the allocated regular budget funds for these right to food posts have instead been invested in other OPC priorities. An FAO staff member raised the point that it is never easy to inherit a predecessor's "baby," especially if it is a particularly troublesome one, but it must be emphasized that pushing the mainstreaming agenda forward is, after all, a political task that necessitates dedicated leadership. In the absence of strong support from the top, it is simply too risky and too costly for individuals in the system to advocate for such sweeping change.

CONCLUSION

The effort to mainstream human rights across the FAO's activities has reached a standstill. Future advocacy efforts can focus, as a matter of priority, on the lack of political will among member states and the lack of explicit human rights support from leadership, and must convincingly point to the added value of a rights-based agenda—to demonstrate the *instrumental* value of the right to food approach and how it is able to strengthen the outcomes and impact of results-based management (the prevalent programming paradigm in FAO and other UN agencies). This will require more effort and boldness by those member states that have been right to food champions in the past, as well as opposition to the current dismantling of the system-wide HRBA focus in country programming. To this end, the initiative of the Civil Society Mechanism of the CFS to revitalize and recommit those governments through a "Friends of the Right to Food" alliance could signal the start of such a countermovement.

With the future of the Right to Food Team in doubt, FAO needs to invest in a full-fledged, systematic right to food mainstreaming strategy—a powerful tool to overcome fragmentation, disconnect, and destructive "siloization." This would include, for example, integrating the right to food as a cross-cutting theme in the next Strategic Framework, right to food criteria in country programming and project cycle management, and building on successful work that has been carried out and documented by the Right to Food Team in collaboration with other divisions since 2006. Where the FAO remains hesitant to put its full weight behind specific models of support to agricultural development, it must move beyond certain fledgling rights-based regional initiatives and systematically promote food as a human right.

Treating food as a human right within FAO means adopting a normative and analytical framework that can diagnose and repair broken food systems at every level. This means instituting participatory, inclusive, multi-year political processes in national food strategies in which the voices of poor and marginalized people are heard, policies are targeted at deficits in the ability of individuals or communities to produce or procure adequate food, responsibilities and actions are defined, and mechanisms are established to hold governments to account. As the real masters of the Organization, its member states should ensure that the FAO moves toward: including such right to food criteria in program and project clearance processes, integrating the procedural requirements across FAO work, monitoring country-level outcomes with rights-based indicators, treating civil society as partners in the planning and implementation of national strategies, and reporting on the state of implementation of the right to food in its annual State of Food and Agriculture. Far from politicizing FAO, mainstreaming the right to food would provide a self-targeting device for ensuring a pro-poor approach, allowing FAO to meet its core mandate of eradicating hunger and providing a compass for the Organization to filter out policies and approaches unduly influenced by those whose interests in the reinvestment in agriculture are not purely related to tackling hunger and poverty.

REFERENCES

Alston, Philip and Katarina Tomaševski, eds. 1984. *The Right to Food*. Dordrecht: Martinus Nijhoff.

Blondeau, Simon. 2014. "Institutional Framework for the Right to Adequate Food." *Thematic Study* 2. Rome: FAO.

CESCR (Committee on Economic, Social and Cultural Rights). 1999. *General Comment 12: The Right to Adequate Food (Art.11)*. 26 April–14 May. UN Doc. E/C.12/1999/5. ECOSOC, 20th Session, Geneva.

CFS (Committee on World Food Security). 2009. Reform of the Committee on World Food Security Final Version. Rome: FAO.

CFS. 2012. *Voluntary Guidelines on the Responsible Governance of Tenure of Land, Fisheries and Forests in the Context of National Food Security*. Rome: FAO.

CFS. 2014. "Principles for Responsible Investment in Agriculture and Food Systems."

CFS. 2015. "Framework for Action for Food Security and Nutrition in Protracted Crises."

CFS. 2016. "Global Strategic Framework for Food Security & Nutrition: Fifth Version."

Clarke, Alisa. 2012. "The Potential of the Human Rights-Based Approach for the Evolution of the United Nations as a System." *Human Rights Review* 13 (2):225–248.

Coomans, Fons. 2012. "On the Right(s) Track? United Nations (Specialized) Agencies and the Use of Human Rights Language." *Verfassung und Recht in Übersee* 45 (3): 274–294.

Darrow, Mac and Louise Arbour. 2009. "The Pillar of Glass: Human Rights in the Development Operations of the United Nations." *American Journal of International Law* 103: 446–501.

De Schutter, Olivier. 2009. "Report of the Special Rapporteur on the Right to Food: The Role of Development Cooperation and Food Aid in Realizing the Right to Adequate Food: Moving from Charity to Obligation." 11 February. UN Doc. A/HRC/10/5.

De Schutter, Olivier. 2010. "Countries Tackling Hunger with a Right to Food Approach: Significant Progress in Implementing the Right to Food at National Scale in Africa, Latin America and South Asia." Briefing Note 1.

De Schutter, Olivier. 2013. "Report of the Special Rapporteur on the Right to Food: Mission to the Food and Agriculture Organization of the United Nations." 14 January. UN Doc. A/HRC/22/50/Add.3.

Duncan, Jessica. 2015. *Global Food Security Governance: Civil Society Engagement in the Reformed Committee on World Food Security*. New York: Routledge.

Eide, Asbjørn, Wenche B. Eide, Susantha Goonatilake, Joan Gussow, and Omawale. 1984. *Food as a Human Right*. Tokyo: United Nations University.

Eide, Wenche B. 2005. "From Food Security to the Right to Food." In *Food and Human Rights in Development: Legal and Institutional Dimensions and Selected Topics*, edited by Wenche B. Eide and Uwe Kracht, 67–99. Antwerpen/Oxford: Intersentia.

FAO. 1974. "Report of the World Food Conference: Rome 5–16 November 1974." World Food Conference, Rome.

FAO. 1996. "Rome Declaration on World Food Security and World Food Summit Plan of Action." Accessed June 25, 2017. Available at: http://www.fao.org/docrep/003/w3613e/w3613e00.htm.

FAO. 1997. "FAO and the Right to Food: A Background Paper for an Expert Seminar on the Right to Food held by the High Commissioner for Human Rights and for the General Discussion on the Normative Content of the Right to Food of the Committee on Economic, Social and Cultural Rights." FAO David Lubin Memorial Library Archive, Rome.

FAO. 2004a. "Intergovernmental Working Group for the Elaboration of a Set of Voluntary Guidelines to Support the Progressive Realization of the Right to Adequate Food in the Context of National Food Security." 23 September. Doc. FAO CL 127/10-Sup.1. Committee on World Food Security, 30th Session.

FAO. 2004b. "Report of the Council of FAO." 22–27 November. Doc. FAO CL 127/REP. Council, 127th Session, Rome.

FAO. 2006a. *Agriculture, Trade Negotiations and Gender*. Rome: FAO.

FAO. 2006b. *The Right to Food in Practice: Implementation at the National Level*. Rome: FAO.

FAO. 2007. "FAO: The Challenge of Renewal." Report of the Independent External Evaluation of the Food and Agriculture Organization of the United Nations. Rome: FAO.

FAO. 2009. *Right to Food Methodological Toolbox*. Rome: FAO.

FAO. 2011. *Right to Food Making it Happen: Progress and Lessons Learned through Implementation*. Rome: FAO.

FAO. 2012a. *Information Note No. 7: Toolbox on How to Integrate the Right to Food in the Central African NWFP Sector*. Rome: FAO.

FAO. 2012b. *Guide to the Project Cycle: Quality for Results*. Rome: FAO.

FAO. 2013a. *FAO Strategy for Partnerships with Civil Society Organizations*. Rome: FAO.

FAO. 2013b. *FAO Strategy for Partnerships with the Private Sector*. Rome: FAO.

FAO. 2013c. "Reviewed Strategic Framework." FAO C 2013/7. Conference, 38th Session, Rome, June 15–22, 2013. Accessed June 25, 2017. Available at: http://www.fao.org/docrep/meeting/027/mg015e.pdf.

FAO. 2015a. *Basic Texts of the Food and Agriculture Organization of the United Nations: Volumes I and II*. Rome: FAO.

FAO. 2015b. *Guide to the Project Cycle: TCP Manual: Appendix 1*. Rome: FAO.

FAO. 2015c. "Guide to the Formulation of the Country Programming Framework (CPF)." Accessed June 25, 2017. Available at: http://www.fao.org/3/a-bb020e.pdf.

FAO. 2015d. "The Director-General's Medium Term Plan (Reviewed) and Programme of Work and Budget 2016–17." 6–13 June. Doc. FAO C 2015/3. Conference, 39th Session, Rome.

FAO. 2015e. *Voluntary Guideline for Securing Sustainable Small-Scale Fisheries in the Context of Food Security and Poverty Eradication*. Rome: FAO.

FAO. 2016a. *Free Prior and Informed Consent: An Indigenous Peoples' Right and a Good Practice for Local Communities*. Rome: FAO.

FAO. 2016b. "Programme Implementation Report 2014–15." July 3–8. Doc. FAO C 2017/8. Conference, 40th Session, Rome.

FAO. 2016c. "Reviewed Strategic Framework and Outline of the Medium Term Plan 2018–21." December 5–9. FAO CL 155/3. Council, 155th Session, Rome.

FAO. 2017a. "Family Farming Knowledge Platform." Accessed June 25, 2017. Available at: http://www.fao.org/family-farming/en/.

FAO. 2017b. "Mainstreaming." Accessed March 11, 2017. Available at: http://www.fao.org/righttofood/our-work/mainstreaming/en/.

FAO. 2017c. "Our Work on the Right to Adequate Food." Accessed March 9, 2017. Available at: http://www.fao.org/righttofood/our-work/en/.

FAO. 2017d. "Private Sector." Accessed June 25, 2017. Available at: http://www.fao.org/partnerships/private-sector/en/.

FAO. 2017e. "Reviewed Strategic Framework." 3–8 July. Doc. FAO C 2017/7 Rev.1. Conference, 40th Session, Rome.

FAO Legal Office. 2017. "Membership of FAO." Accessed June 25, 2017. Available at: http://www.fao.org/legal/home/membership-of-fao/en/.

FAO Office of Evaluation. 2015. *Cluster Evaluation of Two Right to Food Projects*. Rome: FAO.

FAO Programme Committee, 108th Session. 2011. Country Programming Guidelines: Principles and Policy. 10–14 October. Doc. FAO PC 108/2.

FAO Webcast. 2016. "CFS 43: 18 October Morning Session." Accessed June 25, 2017. Available at: http://www.fao.org/webcast/home/en/item/4216/icode/.

HRBA Portal. 2017. "A Human Rights Based Approach to Development Cooperation: Towards a Common Understanding Among UN Agencies." Accessed June 25, 2017. Available at: http://hrbaportal.org/the-human-rights-based-approach-to-development-cooperation-towards-a-common-understanding-among-un-agencies.

Kedzia, Zdzislaw. 2009. "Mainstreaming Human Rights in the United Nations." In *International Human Rights Monitoring Mechanisms: Essays in Honour of Jakob Th. Möller*, edited by Gudmundur Alfredsson, Jonas Grimheden, Bertrand G. Ramcharan, and Alfred Zayas, 2nd ed., 231–238. Leiden/Boston: Martinus Nijhoff.

Liese, Andrea. 2012. "FAO." In *Handbuch Internationale Organisationen: Theoretische Grundlagen und Akteure*, edited by Katja Freistein, 113–118. Munich: Oldenbourg Wissenschaftsverlag.

McKeon, Nora. 2015. *Food Security Governance: Empowering Communities, Regulating Corporations*. Abingdon: Routledge.

Mechlem, Kerstin. 2004. "Food Security and the Right to Food in the Discourse of the United Nations." *European Law Journal* 10 (5): 631–648.

Moore, Gerald. 2005. "The Food and Agriculture Organization of the United Nations: Towards a Right to Food Approach?" In *Beyond the Nation State: Human Rights in Times of Globalization*, edited by Michael Windfuhr, 139–154. Uppsala: Global Publications Foundation.

Oberleitner, Gerd. 2007. *Global Human Rights Institutions: Between Remedy and Ritual*. Cambridge: Polity.

Oestreich, Joel E. 2007. *Power and Principle: Human Rights Programming in International Organizations*. Washington, D.C.: Georgetown University Press.

Oshaug, Arne. 2005. "Developing Voluntary Guidelines for Implementing the Right to Adequate Food: Anatomy of an Intergovernmental Process." In *Food and Human Rights in Development: Legal and Institutional Dimensions and Selected Topics*, edited by Wenche B. Eide and Uwe Kracht, 259–282. Antwerpen/Oxford: Intersentia.

Page, Hans. 2013. *Global Governance and Food Security as Global Public Good*. New York: Center on International Cooperation.

Parliamentary Front Against Hunger. 2017. "Results." Accessed June 25, 2017. Available at: http://parlamentarioscontraelhambre.org/en/results/.

Phillips, Ralph W. 1981. *FAO: Its Origins, Formation and Evolution 1945–1981*. Rome: FAO.

Rae, Isabella, Julian Thomas, and Margret Vidar. 2007. "The Right to Food as a Fundamental Human Right: FAO's Experience." In *Food Insecurity, Vulnerability and Human Rights Failure*, edited by S. S. Acharya, Benjamin Davis, and Basudeb Guha-Khasnobis, 266–285. Basingstoke: Palgrave Macmillan.

Sen, Amartya. 1981. *Poverty and Famines: An Essay on Entitlement and Deprivation*. Oxford: Clarendon.

Sen, Amartya. 1999. *Development as Freedom*. New York: Knopf.

Shaw, D. John. 2009. *Global Food and Agricultural Institutions*. London: Routledge.

Strangio, Sebastian. 2017. "Welcome to the Post-Human Rights World." *Foreign Policy*. March 7. Accessed June 25, 2017. Available at: http://foreignpolicy.com/2017/03/07/welcome-to-the-post-human-rights-world/.

Uggla, Fredrik. 2007. "Mainstreaming at Sida: A Synthesis Report." *Sida Studies in Evaluation 2007:05*. Stockholm: Sida.

UN General Assembly. 1997. Renewing the United Nations: A Programme for Reform, Report of the Secretary-General. 14 July. UN Doc. A/51/950.

UNDG. 2014. *UNDG Human Rights Working Group (HR-WG): Terms of Reference.* New York: UNDG.

Uvin, Peter. 2004. *Human Rights and Development.* Bloomfield: Kumarian.

Vandenhole, Wouter. 2014. "Overcoming the Promotion–Protection Dichotomy: Human Rights-based Approaches to Development and Organisational Change within the UN at Country Level." In *Human Rights and Development in the New Millennium: Towards a Theory of Change,* edited by Paul Gready and Wouter Vandenhole, 109–130. London: Routledge.

Vidar, Margret, Yoon J. Kim, and Luisa Cruz. 2014. "Legal Developments in the Progressive Realization of the Right to Adequate Food." *Thematic Study* 3. Rome: FAO.

Windfuhr, Michael. 2005. "Civil Society Groups Working on the Right to Adequate Food: A User's Guide to the Voluntary Guidelines." In *Closing the Gap on the Right to Adequate Food: The Voluntary Guidelines,* edited by Standing Committee on Nutrition, 21–26. Geneva: United Nations System Standing Committee on Nutrition.

Yeshanew, Sisay A. 2014. "Mainstreaming Human Rights in Development Programmes and Projects: Experience from the Work of a United Nations Agency." *Nordic Journal of Human Rights* 32 (4): 372–386.

13

The Joint United Nations Programme on HIV/AIDS

With Communities for Human Rights

HELENA NYGREN-KRUG*

From the early days of the AIDS epidemic over thirty years ago, AIDS was framed as a human rights imperative. Communities affected were at the front line, calling for urgent action to safeguard basic human rights to life, health, and dignity while caring for loved ones who were dying in the midst of denial, stigma, and neglect. The Joint United Nations Programme on HIV/AIDS (UNAIDS) was launched in 1996 to coordinate a multi-sectoral response to this unprecedented human catastrophe.

Today, we celebrate tremendous progress. In just the last couple of years, the number of people living with HIV accessing antiretroviral therapy (ART) has increased dramatically, reaching 19.5 million people; and for those people on ART, HIV has transformed into a manageable chronic disease. In the world's most affected region, Eastern and Southern Africa, AIDS-related deaths have fallen by 62 percent, since they peaked at 1.1 million in 2004. This progress has propelled the international community to commit to the target of ending AIDS by 2030 as part of the UN Sustainable Development Goals (SDGs).

Yet, as set out in UNAIDS's 2016–2021 Strategy, *On the Fast-Track to End AIDS*, efforts need to focus on reaching deeper and further into the pockets of society where populations are hardest to reach. Approximately half of the world's 36.7 million people living with HIV are currently unaware of their HIV status. To reach them with HIV

* The author is a staff member of the UNAIDS Secretariat. The author alone is responsible for the views expressed in this chapter, and they do not necessarily represent the decisions, policy, or views of UNAIDS. The author offers thanks to UNAIDS colleagues, Luisa Cabal and Peter Godrey-Faussett, for reviewing this chapter and to Bronwyn McBride and Jeremy O'Brien, interns, for help with editing and referencing.

services, efforts to address HIV-related stigma and discrimination need to be scaled up along with addressing harmful gender norms, social and economic inequalities, expensive health technologies, and unaffordable prices of treatment beyond first-line regimens. Underpinning all of these, it will be necessary to address the social and legal frameworks that discourage, and may even block, access to HIV services, particularly for key and other marginalized populations. In short, human rights advocacy, programming, movements, and approaches are more relevant than ever.

This chapter centers on the role of UNAIDS in the context of human rights and the global AIDS response. It starts, in Part I, by recalling the historical rationale for creating UNAIDS, explaining how its mandate and structure have enabled communities to remain engaged and push for human rights considerations to be addressed at the forefront of the global AIDS response. Part II explores how human rights have been embedded in the vision and strategy of UNAIDS and are supported by political commitments and monitoring efforts. Parts III–VII set out examples of UNAIDS' current priorities and past activities, illustrating how human rights are being operationalized across its vast agenda. While the chapter does not attempt to give a full picture of current work in the field of human rights, case studies illustrate how human rights norms, principles, and approaches are being operationalized in relation to different functions of UNAIDS and ways of working within and across UNAIDS. Finally, Part VIII looks at the journey ahead, taking "AIDS out of isolation" to benefit not only the AIDS response but also other health-related SDG targets, in particular universal health coverage (UHC). The chapter concludes by recognizing 2030 Agenda for Sustainable Development (2030 Agenda) as a springboard for UNAIDS to scale up efforts to support the realization of human rights, generating wider societal transformation that will ultimately determine whether the world is able to reach the end of the AIDS epidemic as a public health threat.

I. PUTTING COMMUNITIES AT THE CENTER: MANDATE, STRUCTURE, GOVERNANCE, AND FINANCING

In contrast to other UN agencies—which were introduced to the human rights discourse "late in their lives" or started out with a strong human rights mandate but drifted away from it over the years—UNAIDS emerged from an acute awareness of the profound human rights implications of HIV and AIDS. The World Health Organization (WHO) had initially taken the lead in addressing HIV, and Jonathan Mann, who headed the WHO Global Programme on AIDS during the late 1980s, was clear about HIV being more than a medical or even health issue. To Mann, HIV was fundamentally a human rights issue—as lived and experienced by affected communities in the streets and on the ground. After Mann left WHO in 1990, many considered WHO's approach "too medical" and calls were made to establish a new UN program to ensure a coordinated and intersectoral approach (Knight 2008, 18–22).

A report from the Committee of Cosponsoring Organizations (CCO) to the UN Economic and Social Council (ECOSOC) justified a new United Nations (UN) Programme by the epidemic's "urgency and magnitude, its complex socioeconomic and cultural roots, the denial and complacency still surrounding HIV and its routes of transmission, and the discrimination and human rights violations faced by those infected or threatened by HIV." Given this health and human rights imperative, "only a special United Nations system programme [was considered] capable of orchestrating a global response to a fast-growing epidemic of a feared and stigmatized disease whose roots and ramifications extend into virtually all aspects of society" (ECOSOC 1995, para. 21). In 1994, UNAIDS was established as a collective endeavor of several UN agencies to ensure a multi-sectoral and coordinated global AIDS response (ECOSOC 1994) and was launched two years later.

During this same period, the principle of GIPA (the Greater Involvement of People Living with HIV) was adopted at the 1994 Paris AIDS Summit (UNAIDS 2007). This principle recognized the critical role of communities on the ground, where people living with and affected by HIV were at the forefront of efforts to secure more funding, better care and treatment, further research, and commitment from leaders, as well as in pioneering ways of reaching out to and caring for people living with HIV (Ibid.). UNAIDS became the first (and remains the only) UN organization where civil society is formally represented on its board, the Programme Coordinating Board (PCB). The participation of civil society, represented by people living with HIV and other affected communities, opened a unique space to advance human rights issues in a UN context and has helped to anchor the global AIDS response in the lived experiences of communities. To reinforce this inclusive spirit of the PCB, it is customary for all PCB decisions to be guided by an explicit set of principles that include both GIPA and human rights (UNAIDS 2009a).[1]

HIV raises rights-based issues that in many societies are considered sensitive or taboo—around gender, sexuality, identity, exclusion, and power. The first strategic plan of UNAIDS acknowledged how "HIV tends to spread along the pre-existing fault lines of society, fueled by societal and structural factors such as poverty, disorder, discrimination and the subordinate status of women" (Timberlake 1998, 89–90). In other words, HIV disproportionately affects populations already marginalized, stigmatized, discriminated against, and even criminalized across many societies. Critical to actualizing an effective AIDS response, these groups are often referred to as "key populations" (UNAIDS 2015c). These key populations include gay men and other men who have sex with men, sex workers, transgender people, and people who inject drugs, but UNAIDS also acknowledges that prisoners and other incarcerated people are also particularly vulnerable to HIV and frequently lack adequate access to services, encouraging countries to "define the specific populations that are key to their epidemic and response, based on the epidemiological and social context" (Ibid., 31).

The PCB is not only more diverse and inclusive than most UN governing bodies because of the representation of civil society: in addition to five civil society representatives and twenty-two member states (UNAIDS 2011a), the PCB has representation

---

1. All aspects of UNAIDS work are directed by the following guiding principles:

(1) aligned to national stakeholders' priorities; (2) based on the meaningful and measurable involvement of civil society, especially people living with HIV and populations most at risk of HIV infection; (3) based on human rights and gender equality; (4) based on the best available scientific evidence and technical knowledge; (5) promoting comprehensive responses to AIDS that integrate prevention, treatment, care, and support; and (6) based on the principle of non-discrimination.

from its eleven UN co-sponsoring agencies (Cosponsors) (UNAIDS 2017a).[2] Member states, Cosponsors, and civil society (specifically people living with and affected by HIV) are all represented as board members through a constituency approach, allowing relatively flexible arrangements for participation (UNAIDS 2016a, 37). The PCB meetings, which are held in principle twice a year, consist of a decision-making segment and a thematic session (UNAIDS 2009c), the latter which provides a relatively informal forum for exchange of good practices and, at times, frank dialogue among relevant actors on critical human rights issues. Over the past few years, rights-based topics addressed during the thematic session have included *Enabling Legal Environments* (UNAIDS 2011b), *Non-discrimination* (UNAIDS 2012e), *Halving HIV transmission among people who inject drugs* (UNAIDS 2014a), and *Intellectual property related and other factors impacting the availability, affordability, and accessibility of treatment and diagnostics for HIV and co-infections* (UNAIDS 2016b).

Coordination across the broad mandate of UNAIDS is supported by a Unified Budget, Workplan and Results Framework (UBRAF) that guides the collective efforts of the Cosponsors and the Secretariat and is underpinned by an explicit division of labor (UNAIDS 2010b). While Cosponsors play a more technical role through their programmatic capacity, the UNAIDS Secretariat exercises political leadership for the global AIDS response, convenes stakeholders, provides strategic information, gives voice to people living with and affected by HIV, and supports civil society (Ibid.). The co-sponsored nature of UNAIDS allows for a diversity of staff dedicated to HIV across agencies, representing a wide range of disciplines and sector-specific expertise, which helps ensure holistic and robust support to countries, including on critical human rights issues. The UBRAF is financed through voluntary contributions, mainly from governments but also from the private sector, individuals, foundations, and other inter-governmental and non-governmental organizations. Among the top government donors are several countries (e.g., Sweden, the Netherlands, and Norway) with a strong tradition of supporting sexual and reproductive rights in relation to women and, in more recent years, also sexual and gender minorities.

II. EMBEDDING HUMAN RIGHTS IN VISION AND STRATEGY, COMMITMENTS, AND MONITORING

Success in the AIDS response is contingent upon governments adopting inclusive approaches, free from stereotyping and moralizing. Alongside "zero new HIV infections" and "zero AIDS-related deaths," "zero discrimination" forms part of the overarching vision of UNAIDS's "Three Zeros," which guides the work of the

---

2. UNAIDS brings together the efforts and resources of eleven UN organizations to unite the world against AIDS. The organizations that form UNAIDS, also called the UNAIDS Cosponsors (in no particular order), include: UNHCR (UN High Commissioner for Refugees), UNICEF (UN Children's Fund), World Bank, UNESCO (UN Educational, Scientific and Cultural Organization), UN Women (UN Entity for Gender Equality and the Empowerment of Women), UNDP (UN Development Programme), UNFPA (UN Population Fund), WHO (World Health Organization), World Food Programme, UNODC (UN Office on Drugs and Crime), and ILO (International Labor Organization).

Joint Programme (UNAIDS 2010a, 7). This vision puts non-discrimination, a fundamental human rights principle, on equal footing with more traditional public health agendas of prevention and treatment (Ibid.). It has helped to ensure the implementation of interventions aimed at addressing more upstream and structural determinants of HIV in the realms of law and policy reform.

Human rights have been explicitly embedded in the strategies adopted by the PCB for the global AIDS response. The most recent UNAIDS Strategy, 2016–2021, *On the Fast-Track to End AIDS* (UNAIDS 2015b), was adopted by the PCB in 2015 to urgently scale up the response (Piot et al. 2015). This Strategy embeds the AIDS response fully into the 2030 Agenda (Agenda 2030) (UN, 2015), recognizing how success in the AIDS response is deeply interwoven with, and interdependent on, progress in a range of sectors covered by different SDGs. Conversely, ending the AIDS epidemic by 2030 (SDG target 3.3) was recognized as a basis to accelerate progress across other SDGs, as well as across targets within SDG 3, dedicated to ensuring healthy lives (UNAIDS 2010a).

The 2016–2021 Strategy contains a number of ambitious targets and commitments significant from a human rights perspective such as removing punitive laws, policies, and practices that block access to services; ensuring access to comprehensive sexuality education for adolescents and young people; safeguarding the right to access medicines; and recognizing how HIV-related discrimination is deeply interwoven with other forms of discrimination based on gender, sexual orientation and gender identity, race, disability, drug use, immigration status, and being a sex worker, prisoner, or former prisoner (UNAIDS 2010a).[3] Moreover, the 2016–2021 Strategy has a focus on accountability, urging that people living with, at risk of, or affected by HIV know their rights and are able to access legal services and challenge violations.

The June 2016 UN High-Level Meeting on Ending AIDS (HLM) served to translate the UNAIDS Strategy into commitments negotiated and adopted by member states in a *Political Declaration on HIV and AIDS: On the Fast-Track to Accelerate the Fight against HIV and to End the AIDS Epidemic by 2030* (2016 Political Declaration) (UN General Assembly 2016a). Member states agreed that ending AIDS by 2030 requires a "Fast-Track response" to reach three milestones by 2020: (1) reduce new HIV infections to fewer than 500,000; (2) reduce AIDS-related deaths to fewer than 500,000; and (3) eliminate HIV-related stigma and discrimination. The HLM adopted commitments to:

1. Ensure that thirty million people living with HIV have access to treatment through meeting the 90-90-90 targets by 2020.[4]

---

3. Debate among member states in the PCB, during the adoption of the Strategy, featured some resistance to terminology. A particular sticking point was progressive language embracing "sexual and reproductive rights." While several states requested that the SDG-formulation of "sexual and reproductive health and reproductive rights" be reflected, a compromise was reached by using the formulation "sexual and reproductive health and rights" (SRHR) (UNAIDS 2015b).

4. This commitment sets out that by 2020, 90 percent of all people living with HIV will know their HIV status, 90 percent of all people diagnosed with HIV infection will receive sustained ART, and 90 percent of all people receiving ART will have viral suppression.

2. Eliminate new HIV infections among children by 2020 while ensuring that 1.6 million children have access to HIV treatment by 2018.
3. Ensure access to combination prevention options, including preexposure prophylaxis, voluntary medical male circumcision, harm reduction and condoms, to at least 90 percent of people by 2020, especially young women and adolescent girls in high-prevalence countries and key populations.
4. Eliminate gender inequalities and end all forms of violence and discrimination against women and girls, people living with HIV, and key populations by 2020.
5. Ensure that 90 percent of young people have the skills, knowledge, and capacity to protect themselves from HIV and have access to sexual and reproductive health services by 2020 in order to reduce the number of new HIV infections among adolescent girls and young women to below 100,000 per year.
6. Ensure that 75 percent of people living with, at risk of, and affected by HIV benefit from HIV-sensitive social protection by 2020.
7. Ensure that at least 30 percent of all service delivery is community-led by 2020.
8. Ensure that HIV investments increase to US$26 billion by 2020, including 25 percent for HIV prevention and 6 percent for social enablers.
9. Empower people living with, at risk of, and affected by HIV to know their rights and to access justice and legal services to prevent and challenge violations of human rights.
10. Commit to taking AIDS out of isolation through people-centered systems to improve universal health coverage, including treatment for tuberculosis (TB), cervical cancer, and hepatitis B and C (UNAIDS 2016c).

These commitments embedded in the 2016 Political Declaration help to operationalize a number of human rights norms and principles, including the rights to health, life, equality, information, education, and participation, as well as freedom from violence and discrimination with specific attention to marginalized populations such as gay men and other men who have sex with men, transgender people, sex workers and their clients, people who inject drugs, prisoners, children, and adolescents.

As in previous high-level meetings on HIV by the UN General Assembly, the 2016 Political Declaration contains a monitoring provision in which member states request the UN Secretary-General, with support from UNAIDS, to report to the UN General Assembly on progress achieved in realizing the commitments. Countries report annually on the AIDS response, and the reports are made available on the UNAIDS website, forming the basis of the UN Secretary-General's reports to the UN General Assembly on the Global AIDS Epidemic.[5] Relevant from a human rights perspective, this monitoring and reporting system includes

---

5. An online data collection system—the Global AIDS Monitoring (GAM) indicators, which includes the National Commitments and Policy Instrument (NCPI)—supports the monitoring of progress made by governments (UNAIDS 2016d).

information on laws and policies critical to a human rights-based AIDS response, requesting data (disaggregated on grounds such as age, sex, gender identity, sexual orientation, and HIV status) to support indicators such as avoidance of HIV services because of stigma and discrimination among key populations and prevalence of intimate partner violence (UNAIDS 2016d). This requirement for disaggregation presents challenges given the scarcity of data available, methodological differences in gathering data across countries, and safeguards to protect the right to privacy in countries where populations are criminalized (Davis et al. 2017).[6] In collecting data, UNAIDS encourages civil society to be an active partner to complement national reports submitted by government. To help ensure that communities are able to monitor what matters to them, UNAIDS supports community-based information management systems such as the People Living with HIV Stigma Index (Stigma Index 2017). Created in partnership with the International Planned Parenthood Federation, the Global Network of People Living with HIV (GNP+), and the International Community of Women Living with HIV, the Stigma Index is led by networks of people living with HIV and collects data on HIV-related stigma and discrimination. UNAIDS is also providing support for real-time monitoring of experiences of stigma and discrimination alongside stock-outs of ART and TB medicines (UNAIDS 2016e).

III. ADVANCING HUMAN RIGHTS ACROSS SECTORS THROUGH PARTNERSHIPS

The "cosponsored" nature of the Joint Programme allows UNAIDS to address HIV through a multi-sectoral approach, with a view to generating an overall enabling environment for a rights-based AIDS response (UNAIDS 2017a). For example, legal and justice systems play a critical role in shaping social and behavioral norms in society, and the UN Development Programme (UNDP), with its mandate on governance, acts as lead convener of UNAIDS in addressing punitive laws, policies, and practices that underlie stigma and discrimination (UNAIDS 2010b). Beyond the Joint Programme, the Inter Parliamentary Union has been a key partner, facilitating UNAIDS to engage parliamentarians and raise awareness and support for law reform across a range of countries to promote enabling legal environments (IPU and UNAIDS 2015).

A major milestone in galvanizing multi-sectoral action to improve the HIV-related legal environment was the Global Commission on HIV and the Law, an independent body convened by UNDP on behalf of UNAIDS, which released an action-oriented report with recommendations for countries to work in partnership with the UN, civil society, and other relevant stakeholders in addressing the legal environment relating to HIV (Global Commission on HIV and the Law 2012). One of its recommendations was the need to remedy the policy and institutional incoherence between trade and intellectual property, the right to health, and

---

6. These challenges apply to all data collection exercises, many of which now embrace "big data" and private enterprises (UNDG 2017).

public health objectives, with this Global Commission recommendation taken up by *the UN Secretary-General's High-Level Panel on Access to Medicines* (UN General Assembly 2016b).

Other recommendations being implemented by UNAIDS and its partners at country level address a range of laws underlying health, including the criminalization of HIV transmission and key populations, gender inequality and violence, rights of young people and key populations to health services, and access to medicines. Regrettably, punitive laws remain rampant across countries and continue to act as a violation of human rights and barrier to HIV services.[7]

Another human rights challenge blocking progress in the AIDS response, which requires joint efforts among a wide range of partners for coordinated multi-sectoral action, is discrimination in health care settings. While progress has been made since the early days when efforts were made to include HIV-status among the prohibited grounds of discrimination (WHA 1988), HIV-related discrimination persists within health care settings. Recent reports have documented involuntary HIV testing, involuntary disclosure of status, segregation, arbitrary additional expenses imposed due to HIV status, and medical advice against pregnancy or for sterilization on the sole basis of HIV status (Asia Catalyst 2016). To expand action to address discrimination, UNAIDS and the Global Health Workforce Alliance launched a 2016 *Agenda for Zero Discrimination in Health Care*, which aims to address the persistent challenge of HIV-related discrimination in health care by enhancing collaboration among countries, WHO, UNAIDS, other UN and inter-governmental organizations, professional health care associations, civil society, academics, and others in this field (UNAIDS 2016e). Most recently, a joint statement among UN entities was issued, committing them to working together to support states in taking coordinated multi-sectoral action to eliminate discrimination in health care settings (UNAIDS 2017b).

IV. SETTING STANDARDS AND PROVIDING NORMATIVE GUIDANCE ON HUMAN RIGHTS

From its inception, UNAIDS has engaged with the UN Commission on Human Rights (succeeded by the Human Rights Council) to address the intersection between the lack of human rights protection and vulnerability to HIV (Piot et al. 2009). In this context, the Commission on Human Rights requested guidance

---

7. Globally, only fifty-five countries accord women the same inheritance rights as men, both in law and in practice (OECD 2014); 155 nations have at least one law which limits women's economic opportunities, while 100 countries have legal restrictions on the types of work women can do (World Bank 2016). One hundred and sixteen countries criminalize some form of sex work (Global Commission on HIV and the Law 2012), and drug use remains widely criminalized across the globe. Seventy-two countries have laws in place that permit criminalization of people living with HIV—primarily involving HIV nondisclosure, exposure, or transmission (Bernard and Cameron 2016). In seventy-two countries, same-sex sexual practices are criminalized; in eight countries they are punishable by death (ILGA 2017). In addition to high rates of violence against them, transgender people are not recognized legally in most countries and are generally absent from public policy formulation and social protection programs.

for states on how to take concrete steps to protect human rights in the context of HIV. In response, the International Guidelines on HIV/AIDS and Human Rights were developed at the Second International Consultation on HIV/AIDS and Human Rights, convened by UNAIDS and the Office of the UN High Commissioner for Human Rights (OHCHR) in 1996, and updated in 2002 to recognize access to ART as fundamental to realizing the human right to health (OHCHR and UNAIDS 2006).

Over the years, moreover, specific and sector-oriented normative guidance has been issued by the Secretariat and its Cosponsors. For example, as part of its standard-setting mandate on labor rights, the International Labor Organization (ILO), as discussed in chapter 9, adopted a 2010 *Recommendation concerning HIV and AIDS and the World of Work* (No. 200), the first international labor standard on HIV and AIDS (ILO 2010). The WHO, another UNAIDS' Cosponsor, is lead for HIV treatment, care, and support, has a strong normative mandate to advance human rights, and has clearly recognized that progress in ensuring comprehensive access to health services will be limited as long as some populations fear punitive laws, violence, and harsh law enforcement practices (WHO 2013). In this context, in recent years, WHO has issued guidelines for HIV prevention, diagnosis, and treatment that specifically address key populations and are grounded in human rights principles that recognize the need for enabling legal and social environments (WHO 2014). WHO has also issued guidelines for providing comprehensive services and support for women living with HIV to support front line health care providers, program managers, and public health policymakers to effectively address the sexual and reproductive health and rights of women living with HIV (WHO 2017). These recent guidelines address: gender-based violence, which hampers women's ability to protect themselves from HIV and unwanted pregnancies; the need for sexual and reproductive health services, free of judgment and coercion, to be available and accessible to girls and women; and the need for HIV treatment and support during pregnancy and breastfeeding.

Specific legal challenges to an effective AIDS response have also been addressed in normative guidance issued by UNAIDS. For instance, UNAIDS issued guidance in 2013 on how to address overly broad criminalization of HIV nondisclosure, exposure, and transmission, explaining why such criminalization is inconsistent with human rights and good public health practice (UNAIDS 2013). In ensuring enabling legal environments for human rights, UNAIDS has developed guidance on human rights and the law as part of a resource kit for high-impact programming that addresses HIV planning and processes with simple, concise, and practical guidance on key areas of the AIDS response (UNAIDS 2014e).

V. ADVOCATING AND EXERCISING LEADERSHIP FOR HUMAN RIGHTS

For a UN agency to be in a position to take action to promote and protect human rights, the importance of political leadership cannot be overstated. The Executive Director of UNAIDS, Michel Sidibé, has been consistent in his commitment to human rights, not only with external partners but also internally with his staff, rewarding them with a "human rights prize" for taking initiatives and bold actions that have led to the protection of people's rights in countries (UNAIDS 2016f).

Moreover, to be an effective and credible human rights advocate, an organization needs to internalize and nurture a "human rights culture" as part of its institutional fabric. The UNAIDS Secretariat has been a pioneer among international organizations when it comes to aligning staffing policies with human rights. As the first UN agency to change how it categorizes staff personal status, UNAIDS has allowed same-sex couples equal access to the benefits enjoyed by their heterosexual counterparts, and pushed the rest of the UN system to follow its lead (UNAIDS 2012d). Since the launch of the UNAIDS Secretariat Gender Action Plan in 2013, UNAIDS has also demonstrated significant progress toward achieving gender equality and empowerment of women staff in the Secretariat (UNAIDS 2016f).

An important institutional mechanism that supports the wider work of UNAIDS in exercising leadership on HIV and human rights is the UNAIDS Reference Group on HIV and Human Rights. Established in 2002 to advise UNAIDS on critical human rights issues, this Reference Group can speak and act publicly on its own initiative (UNAIDS Reference Group 2011). It is instrumental in ensuring that UNAIDS maintains a strong focus on human rights across its range of functions (Clayton and Amon 2017) and in encouraging UNAIDS to consolidate human rights perspectives across Cosponsors and other relevant partners into joint positions that influence the way that policies or programs are formulated or implemented in countries. The latter is exemplified in the case of a joint statement from UN entities urging countries to close compulsory drug detention and rehabilitation centers and implement voluntary, evidence-informed, and rights-based health and social services in the community (UNAIDS 2012b).

Another critical rights-based area of work of UNAIDS is evidence-informed advocacy. As seen in the International Task Team on HIV-related Travel Restrictions, which was convened by UNAIDS in 2008 to address HIV-related discrimination in the context of freedom of movement (UNAIDS 2009b), this advocacy initiative was successful in influencing legislation on HIV and travel across the globe: between 2008 and 2015, the number of countries featuring HIV-related travel restrictions decreased from fifty-nine to thirty-five, with the United States and China among the twenty-four countries that removed their restrictions (UNAIDS 2015d). This advocacy utilized a wide range of evidence-based means and approaches, from engaging the business community with economic arguments (UNAIDS 2012a) to using the state party reporting process under relevant UN human rights treaties.

Other examples of how UNAIDS has engaged in evidence-informed advocacy include its issuance of the 2014 *GAP Report*, which explored why specific populations are being left behind and what, concretely, must be done to include them in the AIDS response (UNAIDS 2014b).[8] The same year, UNAIDS launched the international "Zero Discrimination Day," an annual celebration on March 1 by the

---

8. The twelve specific populations described in the 2014 *Gap Report* include people living with HIV, adolescent girls and young women, prisoners, migrants, people who inject drugs, sex workers, gay men and other men who have sex with men, transgender people, children and pregnant women living with HIV, displaced persons, people with disabilities, and people aged fifty years and older.

UN and other international organizations to promote equality before the law and in practice throughout all of the member countries of the UN (UNAIDS 2014f). UNAIDS also engages in high-level events to influence government policies and approaches to HIV-related challenges to become more inclusive and human rights-based. For example, at the 2016 UN General Assembly Special Session on the World Drug Problem, UNAIDS presented evidence to demonstrate an imperative to move away from laws and policies harmful to people who use drugs and increase investment in harm reduction (UNAIDS 2016g).

VI. TAKING ACTION IN RESPONSE TO HUMAN RIGHTS CRISES

Given that the UN by nature is an inter-governmental entity, the question that often haunts its leadership is to whom are they accountable: governments or their peoples? The UN Charter makes clear that it was "We the peoples" who established the UN, and that promoting and encouraging respect for human rights constitutes one of its key purposes (UN 1945, preamble). UNAIDS has sought to consistently stand with people who are suffering human rights violations, even when this means confronting governments.

In this context, UNAIDS has stepped up action to protect human rights in response to situations of egregious HIV-related human rights violations around the globe in recent years. As seen in the UNAIDS response to the passing of the Same Sex Marriage (Prohibition) Act 2013 in Nigeria, efforts were undertaken to engage in high-level advocacy for the protection of human rights. Together with the Global Fund to Fight AIDS, Tuberculosis and Malaria (Global Fund), UNAIDS called on Nigeria to reconsider its anti-homosexuality legislation (UNAIDS 2014c), and through this work, UNAIDS: engaged the Office of the President, the national AIDS authorities, and relevant ministries; assisted civil society organizations in developing crisis response mechanisms; supported those arrested and advocated for their protection and uninterrupted access to HIV services as well as to pro bono legal aid; and monitored the impact of homophobic laws on the national AIDS response (UNAIDS 2016h).

These efforts have been backed by the UN Secretary-General's 2013 launch of the *Human Rights Up Front Initiative* to ensure early and effective action to prevent or respond to large-scale violations of human rights (UN 2016). To support UNAIDS staff to respond in such situations, UNAIDS has worked with the OHCHR, the Global Fund, and others to issue guidance for UN agencies and programs on *Preventing and Responding to HIV Related Human Rights Crises* (UNDP et al. 2014).

In protecting human rights, the UNAIDS Secretariat has expanded its work to engage in judicial proceedings. As a "friend of the court," or *amicus curiae,* the Secretariat has intervened in several cases at national and international levels. For example, in *Agency for International Development et al. v. Alliance for Open Society International, Inc.* (2013), the Supreme Court of the United States struck down a federal law that required private health organizations to denounce sex work as a condition to access US global health funding (UNAIDS 2014d). The UNAIDS Secretariat had introduced evidence and arguments in support of this decision, demonstrating how sex workers were disproportionately affected by HIV and how it is crucial to engage with them to ensure an effective HIV response. Similar evidence and arguments were put forward by the UNAIDS Secretariat before the European Court of Human Rights in support of the human rights of people who use drugs in the case of *Kurmanayevskyi, Abyusheva and Anoshkin v. Russia*. The European Court found that human rights, including freedom from torture, were violated by denying access to life-saving opioid substitution therapy (International Centre on Human Rights and Drug Policy 2016).

VII. SUPPORTING HUMAN RIGHTS PROGRAMS IN COUNTRIES

To support work in countries, UNAIDS works closely with major donors such as the Global Fund and the US President's Emergency Plan for AIDS Relief (PEPFAR) to advance human rights in the context of national AIDS responses. UNAIDS provides strategic information to tailor interventions to focus on geographic areas where the most vulnerable, marginalized, or excluded populations reside (GF/UNAIDS collaboration note 2016). Using its convening functions, UNAIDS additionally supports the Global Fund in ensuring that country dialogues fully engage civil society (UNAIDS 2016i).

Civil society performs a range of essential functions to safeguard human rights in national AIDS responses, from advocate to watchdog and whistleblower, and is an important service provider given that it is often best placed to reach, and is often more trusted by, key populations (Stop AIDS Alliance and UNAIDS 2015). Indeed, the UNAIDS partnership with civil society has been a hallmark of the success of the global AIDS response. (OHCHR 2015). Lamentably, civil society's ability to operate effectively has been weakened by government barriers to registration, financing, and freedom of expression and association: over 120 new restrictive laws have been enacted across sixty countries since 2012 (Rutzen 2015). Another reason why many civil society organizations are under threat is because of insufficient funding for implementing HIV-related human rights programs (UNAIDS 2015a).

Overall, donor government funding to support AIDS responses in low- and middle-income countries has fallen (Kates 2016). As many countries shift to middle income status, so does their eligibility for external aid, which means that domestic funding needs to support the national AIDS response (Burrows et al. 2016). When this transition is made in a way consistent with human rights, paying particular attention to the right to health (OHCHR and WHO 2008), it serves to realize governmental obligations, creating sustainable HIV-responses. However, in many countries, programs that address critical human rights issues, as part of the overall national AIDS response, are discontinued during this financing transition (Burrows et al. 2016).

To ensure continued support for civil society engagement in the AIDS response, UNAIDS helped in 2012 to establish the Robert Carr civil society Networks Fund, which provides funding and other resources for civil society networks (Robert Carr Network Fund 2017). A separate LGBT Fund, recently launched by UNAIDS in partnership with PEPFAR and the Elton John Aids Foundation (EJAF), aims to support civil society efforts to enhance access to HIV and sexually transmitted infection prevention, care, and treatment information and services for lesbian, gay, bisexual, and transgender (LGBT) people through "Deep Engagement" grants (EJAF et al. 2017).[9]

UNAIDS has successfully advocated for the inclusion in country HIV plans of what are referred to as "key programmes to address stigma and discrimination and ensure access to justice in national HIV responses" (UNAIDS 2012c). The Global Fund now plays a vital role in supporting these programs (GFATM and UNAIDS 2011), requiring that all funding requests from countries, regardless of income level, include such programs and respond to key and vulnerable populations (GFATM 2017). Consequently, the Global Fund has scaled up its support, as noted in chapter 19, for promoting and protecting human rights in the context of its efforts to address HIV, TB, and malaria, pledging its commitment to human rights as "an essential means by which to increase the effectiveness of Global Fund grants" (GFATM 2016, 1). PEPFAR has also stepped up its engagement with human rights, launching the DREAMS initiative, which aims at reducing HIV infections among adolescent girls and young women by supporting interventions that address many of the structural determinants of HIV. UNAIDS has provided input to the framework development process for the DREAMS initiative, which consequently reflects the UNAIDS strategy of comprehensive prevention and recognizes how discriminatory laws and gender-based violence restrict women's equal access to decision-making, education, employment, property, and credit, thereby rendering women and girls more vulnerable to HIV and preventing them from accessing services and care (PEPFAR 2017).

VIII. INNOVATING WHILE INTEGRATING HUMAN RIGHTS BEYOND HIV

The AIDS response, with affected communities at the forefront, has paved the way for addressing complex health challenges through novel approaches, allowing for creative ideas and practices to flourish and take root. In this context, UNAIDS has been recognized as an innovative partnership, which provides useful examples to inspire and guide the implementation of the 2030 Agenda (ECOSOC 2015). Strengths of UNAIDS, recently highlighted by the Multilateral Organization Performance Assessment Network (MOPAN), include:

- its demonstrated ability to convene diverse stakeholders and form strategic partnerships, acting as a critical broker and, where needed, supporting consensus-building efforts;
- its experience in national-level coordination to ensure key stakeholders have a voice;
- its systems for mutual accountability to enable partners to monitor contributions to global targets; and
- its commitment to organizational change (MOPAN 2017).

9. Through the LGBT Fund, EJAF offers two types of funding opportunities for community-based organizations working with LGBT people—small "Rapid Response Grants" (up to $20,000) and larger "Deep Engagement Grants" (in the range of $1.5 million to $2 million, for an evidence-based program lasting two years).

An overarching theme for the 2016 Political Declaration is "taking AIDS out of isolation," and among the HLM Commitments is that of integrating HIV services into UHC, including services addressing TB, cervical cancer, and hepatitis B and C (UN 2016a). This process of integration provides an opportunity to strengthen the focus on human rights, as many of the challenges to reaching targets on UHC and HIV overlap and are rooted in the common failure of governments to live up to their obligations to respect, protect, and fulfill human rights. This failure is particularly apparent when considering barriers to access for marginalized population groups. For example, ART is available to undocumented migrants in less than half of EU/European Economic Area countries (ECDC 2017), yet only by scaling up ART coverage among this population group can states ensure sustainable progress—not only to ending AIDS but also in achieving UHC in the region. Another example is how age-of-consent laws, which pose barriers for adolescents to access sexual and reproductive health services, including HIV testing, are part of UHC (UNAIDS 2016j). In short, many of the challenges to reaching targets on UHC and HIV are profound and deep, anchored in existing power structures prevailing in our societies. As expressed by Michel Sidibé, "[f]undamentally, UHC must be about leaving no one behind which means that it will need to become political, by tackling entrenched power structures and disempowerment, marginalization, and exclusion" (Sidibé 2016, 355). Echoed by the WHO's past leaders in advancing UHC:

> A number of countries are lagging behind their peers and are either making slow progress or leaving vulnerable groups behind. What appears to be lacking in these countries is the next generation of reforms that mobilize citizens to advocate for Universal Health Coverage, articulate their needs and build political momentum and commitment from governments and all stakeholders (Chan and Brundtland 2016).

The AIDS response can serve as a pathfinder for progress on UHC, particularly in relation to the need for demand driven approaches where people are empowered to mobilize for, and claim, the right to health. As noted by the new WHO Director-General, Tedros Adhanom Ghebreyesus, "It's time to walk our talk, and the world is asking for that. Health is a rights issue" (Ghebreyesus 2017). In this context, partnerships that encourage structural changes will need to be forged—among government sectors, businesses, international organizations, and civil society and across global, regional, and national levels. In short, innovative and human rights-based approaches to advance the UHC agenda can be devised while at the same time further integrating HIV services into UHC in the move toward 2030.

CONCLUSION

Inspired by the remarkable progress made so far, the international community adopted the target, as part of the 2030 Agenda, to end the AIDS epidemic as a public health threat. From a scientific and public health perspective, the tools and knowledge needed to end AIDS as a public health threat by 2030 now exist. Nevertheless, the target is extremely ambitious, with 1.8 million people acquiring HIV each year and with the populations experiencing marginalization and discrimination continuing to be most affected and hardest to reach.

Success in reaching the end of the AIDS epidemic will ultimately be determined by the ability to deliver against an increasingly challenging human rights landscape marked by conflict, forced migration, violent extremism, exclusion, and huge inequalities between and within countries. Furthermore, a trend of discontent is fueling populism and the scapegoating of marginalized population groups in many parts of the world. Today's human rights and resource challenges are wider than the global AIDS response and too complex for the AIDS movement to tackle singlehandedly, yet success in reaching the SDG target on AIDS depends on the ability of this generation to overcome them.

UNAIDS has learned how to turn challenges into opportunities. The 2030 Agenda is essentially about generating profound structural change and societal transformation. As such, it provides momentum for UNAIDS to continue promoting and protecting human rights as part of the global AIDS response, while raising an opportunity for its further engagement with the wider global health agenda by inspiring, guiding, and pushing other global health priorities, such as UHC, to build on the lessons learned from the AIDS response. Central among these is to work with, and through, communities for the realization of human rights.

REFERENCES

Asia Catalyst. 2016. *FIRST DO NO HARM: Discrimination in Health Care Settings against People Living with HIV in Cambodia, China, Myanmar, and Viet Nam.* New York: Asia Catalyst.

Bernard, Edwin and Sally Cameron. 2016. *Advancing HIV Justice 2: Building Momentum in Global Advocacy against HIV Criminalisation.* Brighton/Amsterdam: HIV Justice Network and GNP+.

Burrows, Dave, Gemma Oberth, Danielle Parsons, and Lou McCallum. 2016. *Transitions from Donor Funding to Domestic Reliance for HIV Responses—Recommendations for Transitioning Countries.* APM Global Health and Aidspan.

Chan, Margaret and Gro Harlem Brundtland. 2016. "Universal Health Coverage: An Affordable Goal for All." *World Health Organization Media Centre.* 12 December. Available at: http://who.int/mediacentre/commentaries/2016/universal-health-coverage/en/.

Clayton, Michaela and Joseph Amon. 2017. *Global Review on the Future of the UNAIDS Joint Programme Model.* UNAIDS Reference Group on HIV and Human Rights. Available at: http://www.hivhumanrights.org/commitmenttohumanrights/wp-content/uploads/downloads/2017/02/UNAIDS-Reference-Group-on-HIV-and-Human-Rights-Submission-to-Global-Review-Panel-FINAL-14Feb2017.pdf.

Davis, Sara L. M., William C. Goedel, John Emerson, and Brooke Skartvedt Guven. 2017. "Punitive Laws, Key Population Size Estimates, and Global AIDS Response Progress Reports: An Ecological Study of 154 Countries." *Journal of the International AIDS Society* 20: 21386.

ECDC (European Center for Disease Prevention and Control). 2017. "SPECIAL REPORT HIV and migrants—Monitoring implementation of the Dublin Declaration on Partnership to Fight HIV/AIDS in Europe and Central Asia: 2017 progress report."

Available at: http://ecdc.europa.eu/en/publications/Publications/HIV%20and%20 migrants.pdf.

ECOSOC (UN Economic and Social Council). 1994. "Joint and co-sponsored United Nations programme on human immunodeficiency virus/acquired immunodeficiency syndrome (HIV/AIDS)." 26 July. Resolution 1994/24.

ECOSOC (UN Economic and Social Council). 1995. "Economic and Environmental Questions: Reports of Subsidiary Bodies, Conferences and Related Questions: Prevention and Control of Acquired Immunodeficiency Syndrome (AIDS)." 19 May. E/1995/71.

ECOSOC (UN Economic and Social Council). 2015. "Joint United Nations Programme on HIV/AIDS." 31 March. Resolution 2015/5.

EJAF (Elton John Aids Foundation), the U.S. President's Emergency Plan for AIDS Relief (PEPFAR) and UNAIDS. 2017. *LGBT Fund.* Available at: http://london.ejaf.org/ grant-listings/.

GFATM (The Global Fund to Fight AIDS, Tuberculosis and Malaria). 2016. *Scaling up programs to remove human rights barriers to health services. A strategic objective and major initiative by the Global Fund.* Last revised May 2017. Available at: https://www. theglobalfund.org/media/1212/humanrights_2016-removingbarrierspart1_qa_ en.pdf.

GFATM (The Global Fund to Fight AIDS, Tuberculosis and Malaria). 2017. "Human Rights." Available at: https://www.theglobalfund.org/en/human-rights/.

GFATM (The Global Fund to Fight AIDS, Tuberculosis and Malaria) and UNAIDS. 2011. *Analysis of the Key Human Rights Programmes in Global Fund Supported HIV Programmes.* Geneva: United Nations Development Programme.

Ghebreyesus, Tedros Adhanom. 2017. "World Health Organization Press Conference." *70th World Health Assembly.* 24 May. Geneva.

Global Commission on HIV and the Law. 2012. "Rights, Risks and Health, Final Report." Available at: https://hivlawcommission.org/report/.

ILGA (The International Lesbian, Gay, Bisexual, Trans and Intersex Association). 2017. *Sexual Orientation Laws in the World—Overview.* Geneva: Switzerland.

ILO (International Labour Organization). 2010. *Recommendation concerning HIV and AIDS and the World of Work, 2010 (No. 200).* Available at: http://ilo.org/wcmsp5/ groups/public/---ed_protect/---protrav/ilo_aids/documents/normativeinstrument/ wcms_142706.pdf.

International Centre on Human Rights and Drug Policy. 2016. *Context: Russia's hidden public health crisis, Case Information Sheet: Kurmanayevskiy et al v Russia.* Available at: http://www.hr-dp.org/files/2016/05/24/ICHRDP_Factsheet_May2016_ FINAL.pdf.

IPU (Inter-Parliamentary Union) and UNAIDS. 2015. *Fast-tracking HIV treatment: Parliamentary action and policy options.* Available at: http://www.unaids.org/sites/ default/files/media_asset/2015_IPU_HIVtreatment_en.pdf.

Kates, Jennifer, Adam Wexler, and Eric Lief. 2016. *Financing the Response to HIV in Low and Middle-Income Countries: International Assistance from Donor Governments in 2015.* The Henry J. Kaiser Foundation.

Knight, Lindsay. 2008. *UNAIDS: The First 10 Years, 1996–2006.* Geneva: Switzerland.

MOPAN (The Multilateral Organisation Performance Assessment Network). 2017. *MOPAN 2015–16 Assessments Executive Summary.* Geneva: UNAIDS.

OECD (Organisation for Economic Cooperation and Development). 2014. *Social Institutions & Gender Index—2014 Synthesis Report.* Paris, France: OECD.

OHCHR. 2015. *UNAIDS's Submission to the High Commissioner on the Creation and Maintenance of Safe and Enabling Environments for Civil Society.* A/HRC/32/20. September 2015.

OHCHR and UNAIDS. 2006. *International Guidelines on HIV/AIDS and Human Rights.* Geneva: Switzerland.

OHCHR and WHO (World Health Organization). 2008. *The Right to Health—Fact Sheet No. 31.* Geneva: Switzerland.

PEPFAR (The United States President's Emergency Plan for AIDS Relief). 2017. "Working Together for an AIDS-free Future for Girls and Women." Available at: https://www.pepfar.gov/partnerships/ppp/dreams/.

Piot, Peter, Susan Timberlake, and Jason Sigurdson. 2009. "Governance and the Response to AIDS: Lessons for Development and Human Rights." In *Realizing the Right to Health, Swiss Human Rights Book*, Volume 3 Rüffer & Rub: Zurich.

Piot, Peter, Salim S. Abdool Karim, Robert Hecht, Helena Legido-Quigley, Kent Buse, John Stover, Steven Resch [et al.]. 2015. "Defeating AIDS—Advancing Global Health." *The Lancet* 386(9989): 171–218.

Robert Carr Fund (Robert Carr Fund for Civil Society Networks). 2017. "About Us." Available at: http://www.robertcarrfund.org/.

Rutzen, Douglas. 2015. "Civil Society Under Assault." *Journal of Democracy* 26(4): 28–39.

Sidibé, Michel. 2016. "Universal Health Coverage: Political Courage to Leave No One Behind." *The Lancet* 4(6): e355–356.

Stigma Index. 2017. "The People Living with HIV Stigma Index." Retrieved June 21, 2017. Available at: http://www.stigmaindex.org.

Stop AIDS Alliance and UNAIDS. 2015. *Communities Deliver: The critical role of communities in reaching global targets to end the AIDS epidemic.* Geneva: UNAIDS.

Timberlake, Susan. 1998. "UNAIDS: Human Rights, Ethics and Law." *Health and Human Rights Journal* 3(1): 87–106.

UN (United Nations). 1945. Charter of the United Nations and the Statute of the International Court of Justice. Available at: https://treaties.un.org/doc/publication/ctc/uncharter.pdf.

UN (United Nations). 2015. "Transforming our world: The 2030 Agenda for Sustainable Development." UN Doc. A/Res/70/1.

UN (United Nations). 2016. "Human Rights up front Initiative." United Nations Secretary-General. Retrieved April 10, 2017. Available at: https://www.un.org/sg/en/content/ban-ki-moon/human-rights-front-initiative.

UN General Assembly. 2016a. *Political Declaration on HIV and AIDS: On the Fast-Track to Accelerate the Fight against HIV and to End the AIDS Epidemic by 2030.* A/70/L.52. 7 June 2016. Geneva: United Nations.

UN General Assembly. 2016b. *The United Nations Secretary-General's High Level Panel on Access to Medicines Report Promoting Innovation and Access to Health Technologies.* September 14. Geneva: United Nations.

UNAIDS. 2007. *Policy Brief: The Greater Involvement of People Living with HIV (GIPA).* Geneva: UNAIDS.

UNAIDS. 2009a. *25th Meeting of the UNAIDS Programme Coordinating Board.* Geneva: UNAIDS.

UNAIDS. 2009b. *Report of the International Task Team on HIV-related Travel Restrictions.* Geneva: UNAIDS.

UNAIDS. 2009c. *The Governance Handbook.* Geneva: UNAIDS.

UNAIDS. 2010a. *UNAIDS 2011–2015 Strategy: Getting to Zero.* Geneva: UNAIDS.

UNAIDS. 2010b. *UNAIDS Division of Labour Consolidated Guidance Note 2010.* Available at: http://www.unaids.org/sites/default/files/sub_landing/files/JC2063_DivisionOfLabour_en.pdf.

UNAIDS. 2011a. *Modus Operandi of the Programme Coordinating Board of the Joint United Nations Programme on HIV/AIDS.* Geneva: UNAIDS.

UNAIDS. 2011b. *Thematic Segment: HIV and Enabling Legal Environments.* Geneva: UNAIDS.

UNAIDS. 2012a. "Ahead of World AIDS Day CEOs call to end HIV travel restrictions." *UNAIDS Press Release.* 28 November. Available at: http://www.unaids.org/en/resources/presscentre/pressreleaseandstatementarchive/2012/november/20121128prtravel restrictions.

UNAIDS. 2012b. *Joint Statement on Compulsory drug detention and rehabilitation centres.* Geneva: UNAIDS.

UNAIDS. 2012c. *Key Programmes to Reduce Stigma and Discrimination and Increase Access to Justice in National HIV Responses.* Available at: http://www.unaids.org/sites/default/files/media_asset/Key_Human_Rights_Programmes_en_May2012_0.pdf.

UNAIDS. 2012d. "Personal Status Policy, Procedures and Guidelines." 12 February. Doc. UNAIDS—HRM/IN 2011-5.

UNAIDS. 2012e. "Thematic Segment: Non-Discrimination." 26 October. Doc. UNAIDS/PCB (31)/12.25.

UNAIDS. 2013. *Ending overly broad criminalization of HIV non-disclosure, exposure and transmission: Critical scientific, medical and legal considerations.* Geneva: UNAIDS.

UNAIDS. 2014a. "Halving HIV transmission among people who inject drugs." 25 November. Doc. UNAIDS/PCB (35)/14.27.

UNAIDS. 2014b. *The Gap Report.* Geneva: UNAIDS. Available at: http://www.unaids.org/en/resources/documents/2014/20140716_UNAIDS_gap_report.

UNAIDS. 2014c. "UNAIDS and The Global Fund express deep concern about the impact of a new law affecting the AIDS response and human rights of LGBT people in Nigeria." *UNAIDS Press Statement.* 14 January. Available at: http://www.unaids.org/en/resources/presscentre/pressreleaseandstatementarchive/2014/january/20140114nigeria.

UNAIDS. 2014d. *Update on actions to reduce stigma and discrimination in all its forms.* UNAIDS/PCB (35)/14.24. Geneva: UNAIDS.

UNAIDS (Joint United Nations Programme on HIV/AIDS). 2014e. *Human Rights and the Law, Guidance Note.* Geneva: UNAIDS.

UNAIDS. 2014f. *#Zero Discrimination—Join the Transformation.* Geneva: UNAIDS.

UNAIDS. 2015a. *Sustaining the Human Rights Response to HIV. Funding Landscape and Community Voices.* Geneva: UNAIDS.

UNAIDS. 2015b. *UNAIDS 2016–2021 Strategy: On the Fast Track to End AIDS.* Geneva: UNAIDS.

UNAIDS. 2015c. *UNAIDS Terminology Guidelines.* Geneva: UNAIDS.

UNAIDS. 2015d. *Welcome (not)—How travel restrictions have changed since 2008.* Geneva: UNAIDS. Available at: http://www.unaids.org/sites/default/files/20150526_evolution_travel_restrictions_en.pdf.

UNAIDS. 2016a. *Global Review Panel on the Future of the UNAIDS Joint Programme Model.* Available at: http://www.unaids.org/sites/default/files/media_asset/refining-reinforcing-unaids-model_en.pdf.

UNAIDS. 2016b. "Synthesis report of existing research and literature on intellectual property related and other factors impacting the availability, affordability, and accessibility of treatment and diagnostics for HIV and co-infections in low and middle-income countries." 14 November. Doc. UNAIDS/PCB (39)/16.21.

UNAIDS. 2016c. *Fast-track commitments to end AIDS by 2030.* Geneva: UNAIDS.

UNAIDS. 2016d. *Indicators for monitoring the 2016 United Nations Political Declaration on HIV and AIDS.* Geneva: UNAIDS.

UNAIDS. 2016e. *Agenda for Zero Discrimination in Health Care.* Geneva: UNAIDS.

UNAIDS. 2016f. *Update on strategic human resources management issues.* Geneva: UNAIDS.

UNAIDS. 2016g. *Do no harm: health, human rights and people who use drugs.* Geneva: UNAIDS.

UNAIDS. 2016h. *Demanding Access to Justice: UNAIDS Spearheads Establishment of the Coalition of Lawyers for Human Rights.* Geneva: UNAIDS.

UNAIDS. 2016i. *UNAIDS and the Global Fund: A life changing partnership.* Geneva: UNAIDS.

UNAIDS. 2016j. *Ending the AIDS epidemic for adolescents, with adolescents UNAIDS.* Geneva: UNAIDS.

UNAIDS. 2017a. "UNAIDS Co-sponsors." Accessed March 28, 2017. Available at: http://www.unaids.org/en/aboutunaids/unaidsco-sponsors.

UNAIDS. 2017b. *Joint United Nations Statement on Ending Discrimination in Health Care Settings.* Geneva: UNAIDS.

UNAIDS Reference Group (on HIV and Human Rights). 2011. *Terms of Reference.* Available at: http://www.hivhumanrights.org.vs2.korax.net/commitmenttohumanrights/wp-content/uploads/downloads/2012/03/TOR-ENG.pdf.

UNDG (The United Nations Development Group). 2017. *Guidance Note on Big Data for Achievement of the 2030 Agenda: Data Privacy, Ethics and Protection.* Available at: https://undg.org/wp-content/uploads/2017/03/UNDG-Big-Data-Guidance-Note.pdf.

UNDP (United Nations Development Programme), UNFPA (United Nations Population Fund), ILO (International Labour Organization), UNODC (United Nations Office on Drugs and Crime), UNICEF (United Nations Children's Fund), UNHCR (United Nations High Commissioner For Refugees), GFATM (The Global Fund to Fight Aids, Tuberculosis and Malaria), and UNAIDS. 2014. *Preventing and Responding to HIV Related Human Rights Crises. Guidance for UN Agencies and Programmes.* Available at: http://www.aidsdatahub.org/sites/default/files/publication/Preventing_and_Responding_to_HIV_related_HR_crises_2014.pdf.

WHA (World Health Assembly), 41st Meeting. 1989. "Avoidance of discrimination in relation to HIV-infected people and people with AIDS." 13 May 1988. WHA Res. 41.24.

WHO (World Health Organization). 2013. *Global and regional estimates of violence against women: prevalence and health effects of intimate partner violence and non-partner sexual violence.* Geneva: Switzerland.

WHO (World Health Organization). 2014. *Consolidated Guidelines on HIV prevention, diagnosis, treatment and care for key populations.* Geneva: WHO.

WHO (World Health Organization). 2017. *Consolidated guideline on sexual and reproductive health and rights of women living with HIV.* Geneva: WHO Department of Reproductive Health and Research.

World Bank. 2016. *Women, Business and the Law 2016—Getting to Equal.* Washington, D.C. Available at: https://www.oecd.org/dev/development-gender/BrochureSIGI2015-web.pdf.

14

The Future of Inter-Governmental Organization Partnerships for Health and Human Rights

SARAH HAWKES, JULIA KREIENKAMP, AND KENT BUSE

This chapter examines the role of partnerships involving inter-governmental organizations that act to improve health outcomes and explores the extent to which such partnerships seek to ensure the realization of human rights in their stated goals and operations. These partnerships include those that focus on specific health issues, or the health of defined populations, as well as those partnerships that address the broader structural and environmental determinants of illness, in particular the effects of climate change on human health and well-being. Many, but not all, of these partnerships include the private (for-profit) sector in "public-private partnerships."

Partnerships increasingly lie at the center of approaches to sustainable development. Within the 2030 Agenda for Sustainable Development (2030 Agenda), Sustainable Development Goal (SDG) 17 seeks to "revitalize the global partnership" and bring together a variety of institutions and sectors—including governments, civil society, inter-governmental organizations, and the private (for-profit) sector. The inter-governmental system, through the United Nations (UN), has thereby committed to achieving the SDGs, in part, through the concept of joint working, including via inclusive partnerships based on "principles and values, a shared vision, and shared goals." Moreover, the SDGs have placed human rights at their core, with the opening paragraphs of the 2030 Agenda stating that the seventeen SDGs and 169 targets "seek to realize the human rights of all."

This chapter opens in Part I by defining inter-governmental organization (IGO) partnerships, and then proceeds to review the human rights approaches of a selection of these partnerships. Part II focuses on sixteen partnerships that are defined as global public-private partnerships for health, with Part III examining four public-public partnerships addressing climate change, and Part IV examining one partnership

Human Rights in Global Health. Benjamin Mason Meier and Lawrence O. Gostin.
© Oxford University Press 2018. Published 2018 by Oxford University Press.

(involving IGOs only) that focuses on the elimination of a vertically transmitted (from mother to child) infection. The chapter analyzes a number of proposed revisions to current practice in Part V to ensure that human rights are protected, respected, and realized through the actions of these partnerships in the future.

I. INTER-GOVERNMENTAL ORGANIZATION PARTNERSHIPS: THE BROADEST OF DEFINITIONS

Research on inter-governmental organizations has been described for more than eighty years as the study of "how the modern Society of Nations governs itself" (Mower 1931, 3). However, the definition of what, exactly, constitutes an IGO has a more complex history. In 1970, Wallace and Singer identified three characteristics that had defined IGOs since the early nineteenth century: (1) consist of at least two qualified members of the international system; (2) hold regular (at least once a decade) plenary sessions to bring members together; and (3) have a permanent secretariat and headquarters (Wallace and Singer 1970). These criteria were expanded on by Pevehouse, Nordstrom, and Warnke in the early 2000s when they further defined three criteria of an IGO: (1) is a formal entity (e.g., formed by an internationally recognized treaty); (2) has states as members; and (3) possesses a permanent secretariat or indicator of institutionalization (Pevehouse et al. 2004). These definitions were further developed by Volgy and colleagues, who define IGOs as encompassing those "entities created with sufficient organizational structure and autonomy to provide formal, ongoing, multilateral processes of decision-making between states, along with the capacity to execute the collective will of their members (states)" (Volgy et al. 2008, 839). This analysis focuses on the IGOs represented within the multilateral UN system—with a particular focus on those UN-IGOs with a mandate to address health and well-being across all member states. This includes the health-specific organizations (e.g., WHO, UNAIDS), as well as those institutions that include health-related issues as a major component of their mandate or scope of work (e.g., FAO, UNDP, UNICEF, UNFPA, and inter-governmental financing organizations).

The past 20-plus years have witnessed an extraordinary growth of multi-stakeholder partnerships supported by the UN system. These have been posited as a mechanism for governance that is more "networked," offers the potential to "bridge multilateral norms and local action," and has the innovative capacity to address deficits in governance, implementation, and participation (Bäckstrand 2006, 291). The UN General Assembly first debated global partnerships in the year 2000 (UN General Assembly 2000) and has since addressed this issue biennially. According to an independent review of UN multi-stakeholder partnerships, these biennial reviews offer an opportunity to encourage agencies to "uphold the integrity of the United Nations by placing greater emphasis on impact, transparency, coherence, accountability and sustainability" (Dodds n.d., 5). The principles of partnerships have been further enhanced by the UN Economic and Social Council (ECOSOC), which has convened annual Partnership Forums since 2008. These Forums are designed to bring together a wide range of stakeholders (including UN-IGOs) and report directly to the ECOSOC Annual Ministerial

Review (UN n.d.). In 2009, ECOSOC held a special event focused on partnerships to realize the "Global Public Health Agenda," with a particular emphasis on the role of corporate and philanthropic partners in achieving public health goals, such as improving the health of women and girls and addressing neglected tropical diseases (ECOSOC 2009). Subsequent ECOSOC Partnership Forums have highlighted the role of these partnerships in "protect[ing] people against human rights abuses" and have framed "human rights frameworks and codes of conduct for corporations [as] effective mechanisms that can enhance accountability of public-private partnerships" (ECOSOC 2014, 6). Thus, the UN system has both positioned partnerships (including inter-governmental partnerships in association with the private sector) as promoting human rights and positioned human rights as integral to the aims of the partnerships themselves.

Partnerships involving UN-IGOs are, then, widely framed as a legitimate and viable way forward in achieving internationally agreed goals for development—they have been supported both under the auspices of the 2000 Millennium Development Goals, and even more widely under the successor SDGs (particularly SDG 17). Given the wide reach of UN-IGO partnerships, and the extent to which overseas development assistance is channeled through this mechanism, this chapter examines: (1) the extent to which the partnerships involving UN-IGOs focus upon both the principles and practice of human rights norms in their policies and strategies and (2) the mechanisms and specific actions that the UN-IGO partnerships take to protect, promote, and realize human rights.

This study used two methods to understand the salience accorded to human rights commitments in partnerships involving UN-IGOs: cross-sectional reviews and a case study. The first methodology involved a cross-sectional review of two different types of partnerships involving UN-IGOs. The first type of partnership has been defined as Global Public-Private Partnerships for Health (GPPPH). Inclusion was based on the definition of GPPPH as "relatively institutionalised initiatives, established to address global health problems, in which public and for-profit private sector organisations have a voice in collective decision-making" (Buse and Harmer 2007, 259). For inclusion in this analysis, the public sector within a GPPPH had to include representation of at least one UN-IGO. Websites, policy, and strategy documents of such GPPPHs were reviewed to examine evidence of specific strategies or policies on human rights. In addition, this study examined the websites and key strategy documents more generally, looking for any evidence of a human rights-based approach in the partnership's vision, mission, strategy or general policies, or strategies for implementation. For those GPPPH where there was no specific mention of human rights, this study looked for any other language addressing concepts of accountability, equity, equality, discrimination, access, or vulnerability that could serve as a proxy for concern with some elements of rights-based approaches (Yamin and Cantor 2014).

The majority of these partnerships are focused on communicable disease control and/or strengthening health services/interventions to improve maternal and/or child health (Hawkes et al. 2017). Very few GPPPH focus on addressing upstream determinants of ill-health—with the exception of GPPPH addressing clean cookstoves and road traffic accidents—despite the long history of public health evidence that addressing the social or economic determinants of risk and vulnerability is likely to yield a more sustained and equitable improvement in health outcomes for the largest proportion of the population (McKeown 1979; Marmot et al. 2008). The lack of GPPPH addressing the social, political, economic, and commercial determinants of health is likely a reflection of the political economy underlying the development of these partnerships since the 1990 (Buse and Harmer 2007, 259). Characterized as "offshoots of the neoliberal globalisation" (Languille 2017, 146), these partnerships essentially represent an approach to health improvement focused on access to technologies and products—including research and development leading to such products (Buse and Walt 2000; Buse and Walt 2002, 45). Given the underlying budget constraints of IGOs, particularly within WHO (Brown et al. 2006), it is perhaps unsurprising that partnerships have tended to focus more on short-term vertical programs with defined goals, rather than broader approaches to health determinants or health systems strengthening.

In the second cross-sectional analysis, this study focused on partnerships addressing a major (and growing) determinant of ill-health: climate change. This study reviewed four climate change/environmental partnerships that have a specific focus on health, and again reviewed their websites for any mention of human rights or associated terminologies/language. These partnerships each involved at least two UN-IGOs, although none involved the private sector, reflecting, perhaps, the more narrow focus of the private sector in partnerships—i.e., promoting access to technologies and products rather than on longer-term structural issues (Buse and Walt, 2002, 45).

These cross-sectional reviews were supplemented by a second methodology: a case study of a single partnership—involving WHO, UNAIDS, UNFPA, UNICEF, and key partners working toward the elimination of mother-to-child transmission of HIV and syphilis. This case was purposively selected as an example of a partnership where assessment of human rights principles and practice forms a core component of the work of the partnership. This partnership did not fall under the category of "public-private" (since there is no private sector involvement at a decision-making level), and it does not have a formal governing structure (unlike most GPPPH). Nonetheless, this UN-IGO program involves a partnership among different UN organizations with a strong track record of addressing human rights and may potentially yield lessons for other types of partnerships.

II. ANALYSIS OF GLOBAL PUBLIC-PRIVATE PARTNERSHIPS FOR HEALTH

This study identified GPPPH that fit the criteria established by Buse and Harmer (2007)—the inclusion of both public and private sectors in formal governance mechanisms and operating at a global level (i.e., excluding those public-private partnerships that only operate at national or regional levels). Focusing on those that include representatives from the UN system on their boards, the final human rights analysis included the sixteen GPPPH outlined in Table 14.1.

Table 14.1. References To Human Rights (HR) in GPPPHs

GPPPH	Involvement of UN-IGO	HR strategy/policy	Other references to HR	Other language in use (equity, equality, access, vulnerable, discrimination, etc.)
Drugs for Neglected Diseases initiative (DNDi) www.dndi.org	Special Programme for Research and Training in Tropical Diseases (UNICEF, UNDP, World Bank, WHO)	No	HR referenced in the context of a 2016 DNDi submission to the UN Secretary-General's High-Level Panel on Access to Medicines (Pecoul et al. 2016; DNDi 2016a; DNDi 2016b).	Reference to "the poorest and most vulnerable populations in the most neglected settings" under *Vision, Mission and Strategy*, DNDi Annual Report (DNDi 2016b).
Foundation for Innovative New Diagnostics (FIND) www.finddx.org	UNAIDS (on Board)	*Code of Conduct and Ethics* states that FIND and its partners must respect HR (FIND n.d.-a). A statement on the "protection of children and vulnerable groups" also mentions HR (FIND n.d.-b).	FIND maintains an *Ethics Hotline* where HR concerns can be reported anonymously (EthicsPoint n.d.).	
GAVI, the Vaccine Alliance www.gavi.org	WHO, UNICEF, World Bank	Referenced in the *Child Protection Statement* (GAVI 2013a) and *Gender Policy* (GAVI 2013b). HR-based approach also informs evaluation of the gender policy (GAVI 2012).	Several other references on the website, including in the 2016 *Investment Committee Chair Report* (Zinser 2016) and the 2011 *Report to the GAVI Alliance Board* (Szabó 2011).	

(Continued)

Table 14.1. (Continued)

GPPPH	Involvement of UN-IGO	HR strategy/policy	Other references to HR	Other language in use (equity, equality, access, vulnerable, discrimination, etc.)
Global Alliance for Clean Cookstoves (GACC) www.cleancookstoves.org	UNSG (Leadership Council)	No	Quote on HR included in the *2016 Progress Report* (GACC 2016).	*Strategy* document (GACC 2011) states that the GACC aims to ensure access for all, including "humanitarian, refugee, or other particularly vulnerable populations (e.g. the extreme poor and HIV/AIDS patients)."
Global Fund to Fight AIDS, Tuberculosis and Malaria (GFATM) www.theglobalfund.org	UNAIDS, WHO, and World Bank (all nonvoting members of Board)	GFATM has "made the removal of human rights barriers to health services a strategic objective" (GFATM 2016). Its *Strategy* notes that "[p]romoting and protecting human rights is essential to ensure that countries can control their epidemics, scale up where needed, and sustain their gains." (GFATM 2017).	Several relevant documents, including *Focus on Human Rights* (GFATM 2015a) and a *Human Rights Complaints Procedure* (GFATM 2015b), which provides examples of potential HR violations. In 2015, UNDP and GFATM signed a US$10.5 million grant to tackle HR barriers "faced by vulnerable communities in Africa" (UNDP 2015).	
Global Health Innovative Technology Fund (GHIT) www.ghitfund.org	UNDP (full partner)	No	HR form part of the *GHIT Cultural DNA* (GHIT n.d.-a) but are rarely referenced elsewhere.	Reference to the "world's poorest of the poor" in *Strategy* (GHIT n.d.-b).

Global Public-Private Partnership for Handwashing (PPPHW) www.globalhandwashing.org	UNICEF (on Steering Committee)	No	The *Post-2015 Hygiene Advocacy Toolkit* (PPPHW 2015a) notes that hygiene is crucial to support equity and HR. Several news articles refer to HR (PPPHW 2015b; PPPHW 2015c).
Global Road Safety Partnership (GRSP) www.grsproadsafety.org	UNECA, UNESCAP, UNECE, UNESCWA, WHO, World Bank	No	Several references on the website, including under *Global Programmes* (GRSP n.d.) and in the GRSP *Strategic Plan 2016–2020* (GRSP 2016).
International Vaccine Institute (IVI) www.ivi.int	WHO as signatory to treaty	No	IVI's *Institutional Review Board* "protect[s] the rights and welfare of human subjects recruited to participate in research activities" (IVI n.d.-a). HR is also mentioned under *Support IVI* (IVI n.d.-b).
Medicines for Malaria Venture (MMV) www.mmv.org	WHO (Director of Board)	No	MMV *Quality Policy* includes brief reference to "rights of clinical study volunteers" (MMV n.d.-a). *Mission & Vision* refers to "vulnerable and under-served populations at risk of malaria" (MMV n.d.-b).

(Continued)

Table 14.1. (Continued)

GPPPH	Involvement of UN-IGO	HR strategy/policy	Other references to HR	Other language in use (equity, equality, access, vulnerable, discrimination, etc.)
Nutrition International (formerly the Micronutrient Initiative) www.nutritionintl.org	UNICEF, World Bank, World Food Programme	No	Only short references in a few news articles (Nutrition International 2016; Nutrition International 2017a).	Mission is "to ensure the world's most vulnerable populations get the vitamins and minerals they need" (Nutrition International 2017b) and "leverage nutrition to fuel the potential of overlooked or underserved populations worldwide" (Nutrition International n.d).
Partnership for Maternal, Newborn and Child Health (PMNCH) www.who.int/pmnch	UNICEF, UNFPA, WHO, World Bank, EO of SG (institutions not individuals)	HR form integral part of strategy: "In the sphere of [HR], The Partnership works to develop health linkages for accountability to: 1. Contribute to development of tools to strengthen linkages between accountability mechanisms for [HR] and health; 2. Disseminate tools and evidence for [HR] and iERG related advocacy" (PMNCH n.d.-a).	PMNCH "has been involved in the development of and follow-up to the [2010] UN Human Rights Council (HRC) Resolution on Maternal Mortality" (PMNCH n.d.-b). HR are also referenced in the *Strategic Plan 2016–2020* (PMNCH 2016).	

Roll Back Malaria (RBM) www.rollbackmalaria.org	WHO (individual board member) and UNAIDS (on Board)	No	*Advocacy for Resource Mobilization Guide* (MAWG and JHU CCP 2014) has a section on "Defining Malaria as a Human Right." More references in *Multisectoral Action Framework* (RBM and UNDP 2013) and *Action and Investment to Defeat Malaria, 2016–2030* (WHO 2015).
Scaling Up Nutrition (SUN) www.scalingupnutrition. org	UNICEF, FAO, WFP, and WHO	"Be Rights Based" is one of the *SUN Movement Principles of Engagement* (SUN n.d.). The right to food is also referenced in SUN's *Strategy and Roadmap* (SUN 2016a).	*2016 Annual Report* refers to the right to food/right of the child and lists HR criteria for national nutrition plans (SUN 2016b). More references in *An Introduction to the Scaling Up Nutrition Movement* (SUN 2014), *Enabling Good Governance in Civil Society Alliances* (SUN 2015), and news items (Verburg 2016; SUN 2016c).

Table 14.1. (CONTINUED)

GPPPH	Involvement of UN-IGO	HR strategy/policy	Other references to HR	Other language in use (equity, equality, access, vulnerable, discrimination, etc.)
Stop TB Partnership www.stoptb.org	WHO, World Bank, UNAIDS, UNITAID, and UNOPS (on Board)	In 2010, Stop TB established a *TB and Human Rights Task Force* "to protect and promote human rights, in pursuit of universal access to TB prevention, diagnosis and treatment" (Stop TB n.d.-a; Stop TB 2010).	Several references to HR on the website, e.g., under *Communities, Human Rights and Gender* (Stop TB n.d.-b), in the 2015 *Annual Report* (Stop TB 2015a), and the *Global Plan to End TB* (Stop TB 2015b).	
TB Alliance www.tballiance.org	WHO and World Bank (on Board)	No	Only scattered references in some news articles/ Stakeholder Association meeting reports (TB Alliance n.d.-a; TB Alliance n.d.-b).	

A minority of only two GPPPH explicitly address human rights in their vision, mission, or strategy statements. The Global Fund to Fight AIDS, Tuberculosis and Malaria (Global Fund) had a specific human rights policy, while the Stop TB Partnership has established a "TB and Human Rights Task Force." The Global Fund policy, as discussed in chapter 19, focuses on removing human rights barriers that limit access to services, strengthening the participation of affected communities in health governance, and adopting rights-based policies and policymaking (GFATM 2017). This approach includes the identification of key performance indicators that reflect these goals, but there is no overt mention of sanctions that will be applied if countries do not meet these performance indicators (Ibid). The stated purpose of the Stop TB Partnership "TB and Human Rights Task Force" is to develop a policy framework and strategic agenda for a rights-based approach to TB prevention, care, and control. The Task Force brings together a diverse group of stakeholders, including representatives from affected communities or risk groups (Stop TB Partnership n.d.-a).

Four other GPPPH made mention of human rights in their overall strategy: the Foundation for Innovative Diagnostics (FIND) Code of Business Conduct and Ethics includes specific reference to human rights; the Vaccine Alliance (GAVI) mentions human rights in its Child Protection Statement as well as its Gender Policy; Scaling Up Nutrition (SUN) includes a "rights-based" commitment in its Principles of Engagement and recognizes the right to good food and nutrition in its Strategy and Roadmap; and the Partnership for Maternal, Newborn and Child Health (PMNCH) states that human rights form an integral part of its overall strategy. Overall, very few partnerships made even nominal mention of human rights in their policy and strategy documents.

For most GPPPH, there was no specific human rights strategy/policy/taskforce, or mention of human rights in their overall vision, mission, or strategy documentation; however, there was sometimes mention of human rights elsewhere within their work—for example, in advocacy documents, toolkits, or annual reports. For those GPPPH without a specific human rights policy or mention of human rights in their overall strategy, the language used by GPPPH might reflect a related concern for equity, equality, or universality. Such concepts were promoted by the Drugs for Neglected Diseases Initiative (DNDi), the Global Health Innovative Technology Fund (GHITF), the Medicines for Malaria Venture (MMV), the Global Alliance for Clean Cookstoves (GACC), and Nutrition International. In these contexts, the language used tended to reflect a concern for the "most vulnerable" (DNDi 2016b, 6; Nutrition International 2017b), "the extreme poor and HIV/AIDS patients" (GACC 2011, 18), or the "poorest of the poor" (GHIT n.d.-b).

III. ANALYSIS OF HEALTH AND CLIMATE CHANGE PARTNERSHIPS

Where "[c]limate change is the biggest global health threat of the 21st century" (Costello et al. 2009, 1693), such unprecedented planetary changes threaten to undermine the right to health both directly (e.g., by increasing the risk of heat-related diseases, injuries, and deaths) and indirectly (e.g., by changing the geographical distribution of vectors that cause infectious diseases) (Smith et al. 2014). These changes also exacerbate global and national health disparities, disproportionally affecting poor and vulnerable communities whose right to health is often already under threat (Stern 2007; Levy and Patz 2015).

Given the clear linkages between climate change and health, it is surprising that there are only a few formalized global partnerships with UN-IGO involvement that focus explicitly on the global health implications of climate change. Using a relatively broad definition of what constitutes a "health and climate change part- nership," this study identified the four partnerships outlined in Table 14.2 that were concerned about the impact of climate change and other environmental factors on health outcomes. None of these partnerships included the private sector, but all involved participation of at least two UN-IGOs.

In integrating a human rights perspective in their mission statements, policies, and other online documents, however, these partnerships performed just as poorly as the sixteen GPPPH reviewed above. Of the four, only one, the Global Initiative for Child Health and Mobility (Global Initiative), mentioned human rights in its vision and mission statement, reflecting a concern for how safe, low-carbon mobility promotes key rights of the child, namely, the right to a healthy environment and the right to education. Yet, the Global Initiative did not have any specific policies or guidelines on human rights. The other three partnerships' websites and online documents had scant mention of human rights, although they did contain several references to poor and vulnerable populations, including in strategic documents such as the Implementation Plan of the Global Framework for Climate Services.

Although the human rights implications of climate change are complex and profound (Roht-Arriaza 2010; Pedersen 2010; Humphreys 2009; HRC 2009a and 2009b), they have only recently received wide recognition within policy and research communities (Schapper and Lederer 2014; Atapattu 2016). In part, this can be explained by the fact that climate change research has long been dominated by the natural sciences (Humphreys 2009). A natural sciences approach also informs the activities of the two most prominent partnerships linking health and climate change, the Climate and Clean Air Coalition to Reduce Short-lived Climate Pollutants and the Global Framework for Climate Services.

Increasingly, however, human rights, health, and climate change are recognized as inextricably linked. This is reflected, for example, in the recent shift from "environ- mental health" to "planetary health." Whereas environmental health is concerned with how aspects of the natural and built environment affect human health, the concept of planetary health goes further, considering the complex interdependencies between human health, social well-being, and the state of the natural systems on which both depend (Whitmee et al. 2015). Importantly, human rights concerns are at the core of the planetary health agenda, which "emphasises people, not diseases" and "equity, not the creation of unjust societies" (Horton et al. 2014, 847). Planetary health, therefore, offers a promising framework for a truly integrated human rights perspective on health and the environment—one that also takes into account the rights of future generations.

On the multilateral level, the 2015 Paris Agreement is the first climate treaty that explicitly links climate action, human rights, and health by stating that "[p]arties should, when taking action to address climate change, respect, promote and con- sider their respective obligations on human rights," including "the right to health"

Table 14.2. REFERENCES TO HUMAN RIGHTS (HR) IN CLIMATE CHANGE/ENVIRONMENTAL PARTNERSHIPS WITH A SPECIFIC FOCUS ON HEALTH

Partnership	Involvement of UN-IGO	HR strategy/policy	Other references to HR	Other language in use (equity, equality, access, vulnerable, discrimination, etc.)
Climate and Clean Air Coalition to Reduce Short-lived Climate Pollutants (CCAC) www.ccacoalition.org Aims to reduce pollutants that affect both climate and health.	FAO, UNDP, UNEP, UNIDO, UN-Habitat, WB, WHO, and WMO	No	Few references in partner publications (CHRE 2015; CHRE 2016) and a news item (CACC 2016).	The 2014–15 *Annual Report* states that "[r]educing near-term warming . . . reduce[s] the exposure of vulnerable populations to climate-related extreme events" (CACC 2015). The document *Time to Act* also notes that some populations (e.g., children) are "particularly vulnerable" (CACC 2014).
Global Framework for Climate Services (GFCS) www.wmo. int/gfcs Health is one of five priority areas.	WHO, WB, UNDP, IFRC, UNISDR, WFE, UNESCO, and FAO	No	Fleeting references in a news item (GFCS 2016), a calendar entry (GFCS 2012), and a publication (WMO 2014a).	According to the *Project Criteria* (GFCS n.d.), projects "should reduce the vulnerability of society to climate-related hazards . . . , particularly poor and vulnerable groups." The GFCS *Implementation Plan* also includes references to vulnerable populations (WMO 2014b).

(Continued)

Table 14.2. (Continued)

Partnership	Involvement of UN-IGO	HR strategy/policy	Other references to HR	Other language in use (equity, equality, access, vulnerable, discrimination, etc.)
Global Initiative for Child Health and Mobility www.childhealthinitiative.org Promotes safe, low-carbon transport and a healthy journey to school for every child.	UNICEF and UNEP	Mission focuses on key rights of the child: "Safe, accessible, low-carbon mobility . . . ; Clean air and a healthy environment; [and] [t]he role of safe and healthy mobility in enabling the right to an education." (Child Health Initiative n.d.-a). There is also a sub-initiative on "promoting child rights" (Child Health Initiative n.d.-b) but no (staff) policies/guidelines on HR.	Several references throughout the website.	
Health and Environment Linkages Initiative (HELI) www.who.int/heli/ Supports action in developing countries on environmental threats to health.	WHO and UNEP	No	No	The *Review of Initial Findings* notes that environmental health risks affect disproportionally "the poor and vulnerable" (WHO and UNDP 2004). *A Toolkit for Decision-Makers* also emphasizes that these risks impact "most heavily on specific populations, including women, children, the poor or certain occupational groups" (WHO and UNDP 2008).

(UN 2015, 2). More recently, the UN Framework Convention on Climate Change (UNFCCC), the "parent treaty" of the Paris Agreement,[1] has started to engage directly with the concept of planetary health. In 2016, the UNFCCC and the Rockefeller Foundation launched a three-year project on planetary health, which aims to highlight innovative action by cities, communities, non-governmental organizations (NGOs), companies and other actors that "balance the need for healthy communities with stewardship of natural ecosystems" (UNFCCC n.d.-a).[2] While not a full-fledged partnership, this project provides an example of how UN-IGOs can engage with non-state actors (and potentially other UN-IGOs) to realize human rights under the planetary health framework.

IV. A PARTNERSHIP FOR THE ELIMINATION OF MOTHER-TO-CHILD TRANSMISSION OF HIV AND SYPHILIS

Examining a case study to guide the future of human rights in global health partnerships, a global program comprising a partnership of four UN-IGOs (UNAIDS, WHO, UNICEF, and UNFPA) working with member states, civil society representatives (including from affected communities), academia, and philanthropic foundations was launched in 2011 with a goal of eliminating mother-to-child transmission of HIV and syphilis (eMTCT-HIV/syphilis). This partnership focuses on elimination not only in terms of epidemiology but also assesses human rights in relation to sexual and reproductive health in participating countries (WHO 2014).

Every year, it is estimated that more than half a million women suffer an adverse outcome of pregnancy due to syphilis infection, including more than 200,000 stillbirths, 90,000 neonatal deaths, 65,000 preterm infants, and 150,000 infants born with syphilis infection (Newman et al. 2013). The global toll of mother-to-child transmission of HIV was similar at the start of the partnership—with over 300,000 infants infected during pregnancy, at birth, or through breastfeeding (UNICEF n.d.). Prevention of these infections is, in theory, achievable with relatively simple, low-cost, and cost-effective interventions, such as ensuring: access to contraceptive methods; available and accessible antenatal care for all women; all pregnant women are screened for infection at least once in pregnancy; and appropriate treatment is provided for the mother, father, and infant.

The overall goal of the partnership is the elimination of MTCT-HIV/syphilis to levels no longer considered a public health problem (International Task Force for Disease Eradication 1993). Validation of this elimination has, historically, been defined in epidemiological terms—the incidence of new infections or disease is reduced to nearly zero (Dowdle 1999). Infectious disease elimination programs are currently

---

1. Adopted at the 1992 UN Earth Summit in Rio de Janeiro, the UNFCCC was the first international treaty to address global warming by attempting to stabilize greenhouse gas concentrations in the atmosphere. The Paris Agreement was negotiated at the Twenty-First Conference of the Parties (COP) to the UNFCCC. Its main objective is to keep the rise in global average temperature to "well below 2 °C" above pre-industrial levels (UNFCCC, 2015).

2. The project forms part of the Momentum for Change initiative, an effort spearheaded by the UNFCCC Secretariat to showcase impactful climate action (UNFCCC n.d.-b).

in place under other partnerships for, among other diseases, polio, drancunculiasis, trachoma, onchocerciasis, and leprosy. In the case of eMTCT-HIV/syphilis, progress toward elimination is being measured not only in terms of epidemiological indicators but also in terms of human rights—a global first, where human rights are recognized as an integral and equal component of disease control activities for the purposes of achieving disease elimination (WHO 2017; UNAIDS 2016).

Focusing on the human rights implications, women who are pregnant and living with HIV or syphilis frequently report suffering stigma, discrimination, lack of service access, poor-quality care, and/or fear of violence (particularly from intimate partners) (Tam, Amzel, and Phelps 2015). These women may also report forced sterilizations or abortions. Moreover, laws in many countries criminalize the transmission of HIV, and pregnant women may avoid disclosure of their HIV status for fear of legal prosecution. For example, UNAIDS (2016) reports that:

- One in ten adults living with HIV had experienced discrimination in health care facilities in a study across Burkina Faso, Kenya, Malawi, and Uganda (Neuman et al. 2013).
- The People Living with HIV Stigma Index (Stigma Index n.d.) documented that for women living with HIV:
  - 40 percent reported being advised against having a child by a health care professional in Zimbabwe (2014);
  - 8 percent reported being coerced into having an HIV test in Germany (2011);
  - 4 percent reported being denied family planning services in Cameroon (2012);
  - 3 percent reported being denied health services in the previous twelve months at least once in Uganda (2013);
  - 2 percent reported being denied sexual and reproductive health services in the previous twelve months in Honduras (2014);
  - 6 percent reported being coerced into terminating a pregnancy in Nigeria (2010);
  - 5 percent reported being coerced into being sterilized by a health care professional in Ukraine (2010).

When the eMTCT-HIV/syphilis partnership was being established, international NGOs and civil society representatives pushed to ensure that any elimination program should act to reinforce, promote, and realize the rights of women living with HIV/syphilis, and of their infants and families (UNAIDS 2012). The fundamental rights being promoted within the elimination program include the rights to health, non-discrimination, information confidentiality, expression, privacy, association, participation, and the right to found a family (UNAIDS 2016).

When countries apply to the global eMTCT-HIV/syphilis secretariat for validation status—to prove that they have eliminated these infections—they are required to undergo validation not just on epidemiological grounds but also in terms of their adherence to the above-mentioned human rights principles (WHO 2017). Countries are reviewed (usually in person) by specialist "elimination teams," composed of human rights lawyers, members of civil society organizations, epidemiologists, clinicians, and laboratory specialists. Only if the country has met specific criteria across epidemiological, laboratory, and human rights measures is it granted "validation of elimination" status (WHO 2014).

To assess human rights, the program has developed a validation tool—a checklist focusing on measures of human rights, gender equality, and community engagement. Countries must show that they are respecting and complying with the following rights-based principles in the context of eMTCT-HIV/syphilis:

1. Non-criminalization of mother-to-child transmission;
2. No mandatory or coerced testing and treatment;
3. Informed consent for screening and treatment;
4. No forced or coerced abortion, contraception, or sterilization;
5. Confidentiality and privacy are maintained;
6. No evidence of inequality and discrimination;
7. Availability, accessibility, acceptability, and quality of services;
8. Accountability, participation, and community engagement;
9. No evidence of gender-based violence affecting women living with HIV and/or syphilis; and
10. Access to justice, remedies, and redress without discrimination (WHO 2014).

Only a handful of countries have thus far applied for validation of elimination status, which have then been validated by committee consensus. Where countries have been found in breach of any of the ten principles listed above, the committee has given strong recommendations for action and has, in at least two cases, granted a time-bound certificate of validation with an option to revoke the validation if the country does not, among other things, rescind laws criminalizing HIV transmission, close sanatoria housing people living with HIV, and ensure access to sexual and reproductive health services for young adolescents. In the event of such a conditional validation, countries are reassessed to measure progress and ensure that the certificate of validation can stay in place.

V. IGO PARTNERSHIPS UNDER THE SDGS: CURRENT STATUS AND FUTURE PROSPECTS FOR HUMAN RIGHTS

Over several decades, IGOs have been increasingly encouraged to partner both with other IGOs and with representatives from other sectors (e.g., for-profit organizations, civil society, foundations, and other donor agencies) in order to increase their global reach, coverage, and, in theory, their efficiency. This push toward partnership has been solidified under the auspices of the SDGs, with SDG 17 aiming for a "revitalized partnership for sustainable development" and a specific target (17.17) on "promot[ion of] effective public, public-private and civil society partnerships" (UN Sustainable Development Knowledge Platform 2017).

While IGO partnership with the private sector has been strongly and widely promoted since the late 1980s (Brenner et al. 2010), it is not without its critiques.

Concerns that public-private partnerships represent a global agenda of privatization and neoliberalism pervading development programs (Buse and Walt 2000a; Buse and Walt 2000b) has led to more detailed analyses of the partnerships from a number of perspectives (Lee et al. 1997; Buse and Walt 2000a; Buse and Harmer 2004; Richter 2004; Buse and Harmer 2007), including their lack of emphasis on equity (Hanefeld et al. 2007; Gideon and Porter 2016) and gender (Hawkes et al. 2017). However, such partnerships have never before been analyzed from the perspective of promoting and protecting human rights.

Reviewing the sixteen GPPPHs and the four climate change/environmental partnerships, this study has found a lamentable absence of human rights language in the partnerships' outward-facing documents. Where many of the partnerships did not use the specific terminology of human rights, they were more likely to use language confirming commitment to "poor and vulnerable groups," "neglected patients and populations," or "under-served populations." Laudable though such commitments may seem, they could be said to represent a more "discretionary" approach—whereby activities are focused on "deserving" populations rather than being universally applicable. Discretionary approaches can arise when international institutions (such as the UN institutions reviewed in this and other chapters) fail to recognize their obligations with respect to human rights in their work (Skogly 2001). Labeling some sections of a population as "deserving" while overlooking the needs of others can lead to partnerships that fail to aspire to "Health for All" and instead focus on "Health for a [Deserving] Few" (Hawkes et al. 2017).

Moving from words on paper to realizing human rights in IGO partnerships requires that partnerships develop specific strategies to uphold human rights within their programs of work. Although the entirely public sector–based program to eliminate mother-to-child-transmission of HIV and syphilis does not fit the strict definition of a "partnership," it is an example of several UN-IGOs coming together to achieve a common rights-based goal. This case study provides an example of a practical tool to hold countries to account not only for their commitment to eliminate the burden of two infections but also to ensure that this goal is achieved with full respect for human rights and human dignity. As seen in this partnership, validation teams must include representatives of affected communities (e.g., women living with HIV), using a human rights "checklist" to ensure that fundamental rights to life, health, non-discrimination, founding a family, information, confidentiality, expression, privacy, association, and participation are realized while also achieving a public health goal of preventing the onward transmission of an infection between mother and child.

The global push under SDG commitments, underscored by decades of political and economic forces promoting public-private partnership, has resulted in an inexorable rise in the partnership model. Promotion, protection, and realization of human rights in the work of these partnerships is paramount.

International obligations under health-related human rights place human rights at the center of IGO work to achieve health for all. The human right to a healthy environment as well as the right to the highest attainable standard of health underlie much of the legal position with regards to the progressive realization of the right to health care services globally (CESCR 2000). This chapter takes the position that realization of these rights should be fundamental to the work of UN-IGOs and central to their activities in all areas related to improving human health and well-being—including their advocacy to advance partnership priorities and approaches.

International organizations within the UN system bear a legal duty to respect, protect, and fulfill human rights (Skolgy 2001), and this responsibility should be at the forefront of their work—including in the partnerships they enter. The failure of the majority of the partnerships included in this review to address or recognize the fundamental importance of human rights suggests, as addressed in chapter 3, a need to "mainstream" human rights more fully through the work of the UN.

Mainstreaming an approach such as human rights, however, should not—and must not—be limited to mere words written in partnership visions, missions, or strategies. One of the partnerships reviewed (the Global Fund) had a specific human rights strategy, as detailed in chapter 19. Stop TB had established a human rights taskforce, but the small number of other partnerships that mentioned human rights used this terminology to frame their approach but did not provide any clear guidance on how to implement rights in their work. In contrast, the joint UN-IGO program to eliminate mother-to-child transmission of HIV and syphilis provided not only a detailed checklist of human rights standards for each participating country to meet but also identified specific mechanisms for holding countries to account—and for removing validation status if countries fail to meet and maintain their human rights obligations.

The onus, of course, for ensuring that these public-private partnerships adopt a human rights approach in all their work should not be limited to the UN agencies involved. For the GPPPH, the private sector partners should also be abiding by human rights under the so-called Ruggie Principles to "Protect, Respect and Remedy," which represent a framework for business and human rights (HRC 2008) and include corporate responsibility to respect human rights based on three principles: the state duty to protect against human rights abuses by third parties, including business; the corporate responsibility to respect human rights, meaning due diligence to avoid infringing on the rights of others and to address adverse impacts; and greater access by victims to effective remedies (HRC 2008).

CONCLUSION

Reviewing the work of these global health partnerships has highlighted a current deficit in the human rights-based approach. The emerging planetary health agenda offers a useful rights-based framework for future partnerships addressing the broader structural and environmental determinants of health, including climate change. In addition, other deficits could best be remedied through adopting the following approaches: As a first step, UN-IGO partnerships should seek to ensure that a human rights-based approach is mainstreamed through their vision, strategy, and policy documents. Second, translating this vision into action requires the development of tools and checklists to ensure that human rights are respected by all stakeholders (including private sector partners). Third, partnerships need to be concerned about the unintentional effects that their work might have on human rights. Staff training and policies should reflect a commitment to human rights. Fourth, mechanisms to report on potential human rights violations should be made accessible. The Global Fund, for example, has compiled a "Human Rights Complaints Procedure," and the Foundation for Innovative New Diagnostics (FIND) operates an "Ethics Hotline portal" where anonymous reports can be filed. Fifth, accountability mechanisms need to be put in place. In the case of country-level eMTCT-HIV/syphilis, for example, validation can be withdrawn if countries do not adhere to the recommendations of the human rights panelists. Sixth, partnerships need to promote procedural rights. The meaningful engagement of civil society in the development of partnership policies and consultation with local stakeholders is crucial to raise potential human rights concerns and give a voice to those most affected by the partnerships' activities. Finally, human rights policies and procedures within partnerships should be transparent and ideally be made publicly accessible.

REFERENCES

Atapattu, Sumudu. 2016. "Climate Change, Human Rights, and COP 21: One Step Forward and Two Steps Back or Vice Versa?" *Georgetown Journal of International Affairs* 17(2): 47–55. DOI: 10.1353/gia.2016.0024.

Bäckstrand, Karin. 2006. "Multi-stakeholder Partnerships for Sustainable Development: Rethinking Legitimacy, Accountability and Effectiveness." *European Environment* 16(5): 290–306. DOI:10.1002/eet.425.

Brenner, Neil, Jamie Peck, and Nik Theodore. 2010. "Variegated Neoliberalization: Geographies, Modalities, Pathways." *Global Networks* 10(2): 182–222. DOI:10.1111/j.1471-0374.2009.00277.x.

Brown, Theodore M., Marcos Cueto, and Elizabeth Fee. 2006. "The World Health Organization and the Transition From 'International' to 'Global' Public Health." *American Journal of Public Health* 96(1): 62–72. DOI:10.2105/AJPH.2004.050831.

Buse, Kent and Andrew Harmer. 2004. "Power to the Partners?: The Politics of Public-Private Health Partnerships." *Development* 47(2): 49–56. DOI:10.1057/palgrave.development.1100029.

Buse, Kent and Andrew Harmer. 2007. "Seven Habits of Highly Effective Global Public-Private Health Partnerships: Practice and Potential." *Social Science and Medicine* 64(2): 259–271. DOI:10.1016/j.socscimed.2006.09.001.

Buse, Kent and Gill Walt. 2000a. "Global Public-Private Partnerships: Part I—A New Development in Health?" *Bulletin of the World Health Organisation* 78(4): 549–561.

Buse, Kent and Gill Walt. 2000b. "Global Public-Private Health Partnerships: Part II—What Are the Issues for Global Governance?" *Bulletin of the World Health Organisation* 78(5): 699–709.

Buse, Kent and Gill Walt. 2002. "Globalisation and Multilateral Public-Private Health Partnerships: Issues for Health Policy." In *Health Policy in a Globalising World*, edited by Kelley Lee, Kent Buse, and Suzanne Fustukian. Cambridge, UK: Cambridge University Press.

CCAC (Climate and Clean Air Coalition to Reduce Short-lived Climate Pollutants). 2014. "Time to Act to Reduce Short-Lived Climate Pollutants." Available at: http://www.ccacoalition.org/en/resources/time-act.

CCAC (Climate and Clean Air Coalition to Reduce Short-lived Climate Pollutants). 2015. "Annual Report September 2014–August 2015." Available for download at: http://www.ccacoalition.org/en/resources/ccac-annual-report-2014-2015.

CCAC (Climate and Clean Air Coalition to Reduce Short-lived Climate Pollutants). 2016. "WHO Director-General: Climate Change Is the Defining Issue for Public Health in the 21st Century." Available at: http://www.ccacoalition.org/fr/node/1371.

CESCR (Committee on Economic, Social and Cultural Rights). 2000. "General Comment No. 14: The Right to the Highest Attainable Standard of Health (Art. 12 of the Covenant)." 11 August. E/C.12/2000/4.

Child Health Initiative (Global Initiative for Child Health and Mobility). n.d.-a. "Our Mission." Accessed July 6, 2017. Available at: http://www.childhealthinitiative.org/about-us/our-mission.

Child Health Initiative (Global Initiative for Child Health and Mobility). n.d.-b. "Promoting Child Rights." Accessed July 6, 2017. Available at: http://www.childhealthinitiative.org/our-work/projects/promoting-child-rights.

CHRE (Center for Human Rights and Environment). 2015. "Report and Regional Strategy: Policy Advocacy Network for Latin America for Clean Brick Production (PAN LAC)." Available at: http://center-hre.org/wp-content/uploads/Region-Strategy-and-Report-PAN-LAC.pdf.

CHRE (Center for Human Rights and Environment). 2016. "Regional Guidelines: 10 Steps for National Government Actions for SLCP Reductions through Policies, Capacity Building and/or Institutional Strengthening. Policy Advocacy Network for Latin America for Clean Brick Production (PAN LAC)." Available at: http://www.ccacoalition.org/en/resources/regional-strategy-implementation-key-policies-latin-america.

Costello, Anthony, Mustafa Abbas, Adriana Allen, Sarah Ball, Sarah Bell, Richard Bellamy, Sharon Friel [et al.]. 2009. "Managing the Health Effects of Climate Change. *Lancet* and University College London Institute for Global Health Commission." *The Lancet* 373(9676): 1693–1733.

DNDi (Drugs for Neglected Diseases initiative). 2016a. "DNDi response to the Report of the United Nations Secretary-General's High-Level Panel on Access to Medicines." Available at: http://www.dndi.org/2016/advocacy/dndi-response-unhlp-report/.

DNDi (Drugs for Neglected Diseases initiative). 2016b. "From neglected diseases to neglected patients and populations. 2015 Annual Report of the Drugs for Neglected Diseases initiative (DNDi)." Available at: http://www.dndi.org/flippable/annualreport2015/index-4.html.

Dodds, Felix. n.d. "Multistakeholder partnerships: Making them work for the post-2015 Development Agenda." Independent report commissioned by UN Department of Economic and Social Affairs. Available at: https://sustainabledevelopment.un.org/content/documents/16192015partnerships_background_note.pdf.

Dowdle, Walter R. 1999. "The Principles of Disease Elimination and Eradication." *Morbidity and Mortality Weekly Reports* 48(SU01): 23–27.

ECOSOC (UN Economic and Social Council). 2009. "Achieving the Global Public Health Agenda." New York: United Nations. Available at: http://www.un.org/en/ecosoc/docs/pdfs/achieving_global_public_health_agenda.pdf.

ECOSOC (UN Economic and Social Council). 2014. "The General Assembly and ECOSOC Joint Thematic Debate/Forum on Partnerships." Available at: http://www.un.org/en/ecosoc/partnership2014/pdf/event_summary.pdf.

EthicsPoint, Inc. n.d. "Foundation for Innovative New Diagnostics (FIND) reporting system." Accessed July 6, 2017. Available at: https://secure.ethicspoint.eu/domain/media/en/gui/102191/index.html.

FIND (Foundation for Innovative New Diagnostics). n.d.-a. "Code of Conduct and Ethics." Accessed July 6, 2017. Available at: https://secure.ethicspoint.eu/domain/media/en/gui/102191/code.pdf.

FIND (Foundation for Innovative New Diagnostics). n.d.-b. "FIND's commitment to the protection of children and vulnerable groups." Accessed July 6, 2017. Available at: https://secure.ethicspoint.eu/domain/media/en/gui/102191/child.pdf.

GACC (Global Alliance for Clean Cookstoves). 2011. "Igniting Change: A Strategy for Universal Adoption of Clean Cookstoves and Fuels." Available at: http://cleancookstoves.org/resources/272.html.

GACC (Global Alliance for Clean Cookstoves). 2016. "2016 Progress Report. Clean Cooking: Key to Achieving Global Development and Climate Goals." Available at: http://cleancookstoves.org/binary-data/RESOURCE/file/000/000/495-1.pdf.

GAVI (The Vaccine Alliance). 2012. "Evaluation of the GAVI gender policy: Final Report." Available at: http://www.gavi.org/results/evaluations/evaluation-of-the-gavi-gender-policy/.

GAVI (The Vaccine Alliance). 2013a. "GAVI Alliance child protection statement. The GAVI Alliance's contribution to building a protective environment for children." Available for download at: http://www.gavi.org/about/governance/corporate-policies/value-statements/.

GAVI (The Vaccine Alliance). 2013b. "GAVI Alliance gender policy. Version 2.0." Available at: http://www.gavi.org/about/governance/programme-policies/gender/.

GFATM (Global Fund to Fight AIDS, Tuberculosis and Malaria). 2015a. "Focus on Human Rights." Available at: https://www.theglobalfund.org/media/1224/publication_humanrights_focuson_en.pdf.

GFATM (Global Fund to Fight AIDS, Tuberculosis and Malaria). 2015b. "The Global Fund Human Rights Complaints Procedure. Responding to Community Concerns." Available at: https://www.theglobalfund.org/media/1216/humanrights_2015-complaintsprocedure_brochure_en.pdf.

GFATM (Global Fund to Fight AIDS, Tuberculosis and Malaria). 2016. "Scaling up programs to remove human rights barriers to health services. A strategic objective and major initiative by the Global Fund." Available at: https://www.theglobalfund.org/media/1212/humanrights_2016-removingbarrierspart1_qa_en.pdf.

GFATM (Global Fund to Fight AIDS, Tuberculosis and Malaria). 2017. "The Global Fund Strategy, 2017–2022: Investing to End Epidemics." Available at: https://www.theglobalfund.org/media/2531/core_globalfundstrategy2017-2022_strategy_en.pdf.

GFCS (Global Framework for Climate Services). n.d. "Project Criteria." Accessed July 6, 2017. Available at: http://www.wmo.int/gfcs/project_criteria.

GFCS (Global Framework for Climate Services). 2012. "Forum on Business and Human Rights: Public consultation on the themes and modalities." Available at: http://www.wmo.int/gfcs/node/285.

GFCS (Global Framework for Climate Services). 2016. "Conference on health and climate focuses on Paris Agreement." Available at: http://www.wmo.int/gfcs/node/947.

GHIT (Global Health Innovative Technology Fund). n.d.-a. "GHIT Cultural DNA." Accessed July 6, 2017. Available at: https://www.ghitfund.org/hww/culturaldna.

GHIT (Global Health Innovative Technology Fund). n.d.-b. "How we work: Strategy." Accessed July 6, 2017. Available at: https://www.ghitfund.org/hww/strategy.

Gideon, Jasmine and Fenella Porter. 2016. "Unpacking 'Women's Health' in the Context of PPPs: A Return to Instrumentalism in Development Policy and Practice?" *Global Social Policy* 16(1): 68–85. DOI:10.1177/1468018115594650.

GRSP (Global Road Safety Partnership). n.d. "What we do: Global programmes." Accessed July 6, 2017. Available at: http://legacy.grsproadsafety.org/what-we-do/global-programmes.

GRSP (Global Road Safety Partnership). 2016. "Global Road Safety Partnership Road Map. Strategic Plan 2016–2020." Available at: https://www.grsproadsafety.org/wp-content/uploads/2016/11/GRSP-Road-Map_Strategic-Plan-2016-2020.pdf?x96695.

Hanefeld, Johanna, Neil Spicer, Ruairi Brugha, and Gill Walt. 2007. "How have global health initiatives impacted on health equity? A literature review commissioned by the health systems knowledge network." Available at: http://www.who.int/social_determinants/resources/csdh_media/global_health_initiatives_2007_en.pdf.

Hawkes, Sarah, Kent Buse, and Anuj Kapilashrami. 2017. "Gender Blind? An Analysis of Global Public Private Partnerships for Health." *Globalization and Health* 13(26). DOI:10.1186/s12992-017-0249-1.

Horton, Richard, Robert Beaglehole, Ruth Bonita, John Raeburn, Martin McKee, and Stig Wall. 2014. "From Public to Planetary Health: A Manifesto." *The Lancet* 383(9920): 847. DOI:10.1016/S0140-6736(14)60409-8.

HRC (Human Rights Council). 2008. "Promotion and protection of all human rights, civil, political, economic, social and cultural rights, including the right to development. Report of the Special Representative of the Secretary-General on the issue of human rights and transnational corporations and other business enterprises, John Ruggie." 7 April. UN Doc. A/HRC/8/5.

HRC (Human Rights Council). 2009a. "Human rights and climate change." 25 March. UN Doc. A/HRC/RES/10/4.

HRC (Human Rights Council). 2009b. "Report of the Office of the United Nations High Commissioner for Human Rights on the relationship between climate change and human rights." 15 January. UN Doc. A/HRC/10/61.

Humphreys, Stephen. 2009. "Introduction: Human Rights and Climate Change." In *Human Rights and Climate Change*, edited by Stephen Humphreys, 1–34. Cambridge: Cambridge University Press.

International Task Force for Disease Eradication. 1993. "Recommendations and Reports: Recommendations of the International Task Force for Disease Eradication." *Morbidity and Mortality Weekly Report* 42(RR-16).

IVI (International Vaccine Institute). n.d.-a. "Vaccine Resources. Institutional Review Board." Accessed July 6, 2017. Available at: http://www.ivi.int/?page_id=12997.

IVI (International Vaccine Institute). n.d.-b. "Support IVI." Accessed July 6, 2017. Available at: http://www.ivi.int/?page_id=13046.

Languille, Sonia. 2017. "Public Private Partnerships in Education and Health in the Global South: A Literature Review." *Journal of International and Comparative Social Policy* 33(2): 142–165. DOI:10.1080/21699763.2017.1307779.

Lee, Kelley, David Humphreys, and Michael Pugh. 1997. "'Privatisation' in the United Nations System: Patterns of Influence in Three Intergovernmental Organisations." *Global Society: Journal of Interdisciplinary International Relations* 11(3): 339–357. DOI: 10.1080/13600829708443140.

Levy, Barry S. and Jonathan A. Patz. 2015. "Climate Change, Human Rights, and Social Justice." *Annals of Global Health* 81(3): 310–322. DOI: 10.1016/j.aogh.2015.08.008.

Marmot, Michael, Sharon Friel, Ruth Bell, Tanja A. J. Houweling, and Sebastian Taylor, on behalf of the Commission on Social Determinants of Health. 2008. "Closing the gap in a generation: health equity through action on the social determinants of health." *The Lancet* 372(9650): 1661–1669.

MAWG and JHU CCP (Roll Back Malaria Partnership Malaria Advocacy Working Group and Johns Hopkins Bloomberg School of Public Health, Center for Communication Programs). 2014. "Advocacy for Resource Mobilization (ARM) for Malaria Guide." Accessed July 7, 2017. Available at: http://www.rollbackmalaria.org/files/files/resources/ARMGuide.pdf.

McKeown, Thomas. 1979. *The Role of Medicine: Dream, Mirage, or Nemesis.* Oxford: Basil Blackwell.

MMV (Medicines for Malaria Venture). n.d.-a. "MMV Quality Policy." Accessed July 6, 2017. Available at: https://www.mmv.org/sites/default/files/uploads/docs/policy_documents/MMV_Quality_Policy.pdf.

MMV (Medicines for Malaria Venture). n.d.-b. "About us. Our mission & vision." Accessed July 6, 2017. Available at: https://www.mmv.org/about-us/our-mission-vision.

Mower, Edmund C. 1931. *International Government.* Boston: Heath.

Neuman, Melissa, Carla M. Obermeyer, and MATCH Study Group. 2013. "Experiences of Stigma, Discrimination, Care and Support among People Living with HIV: A Four Country Study." *AIDS and Behavior* 17(5): 1796–1808. DOI: 10.1007/s10461-013-0432-1.

Newman, Lori, Mary Kamb, Sarah Hawkes, Gabriela Gomez, Lale Say, Armando Seuc, and Nathalie Broutet. 2013. "Global Estimates of Syphilis in Pregnancy and Associated Adverse Outcomes: Analysis of Multinational Antenatal Surveillance Data." *PLOS Medicine* 10(2): e1001396. DOI: 10.1371/journal.pmed.1001396.

Nutrition International. n.d. "What we do." Accessed July 6, 2017. Available at: https://www.nutritionintl.org/what-we-do/.

Nutrition International. 2016. "It's time to prioritize nutrition as a basic human right." Available at: www.micronutrient.org/2016/10/time-prioritize-nutrition-basic-human-right/.

Nutrition International. 2017a. "MI welcomes Canada's commitment to improving sexual and reproductive health and rights for women and girls." Available at: https://www.nutritionintl.org/2017/03/mi-welcomes-canadas-commitment-improving-sexual-reproductive-health-rights-women-girls/.

Nutrition International. 2017b. "The Micronutrient Initiative is now Nutrition International." Available at: https://www.nutritionintl.org/2017/04/micronutrient-initiative-now-nutrition-international/.

Pecoul, Bernard, Rachel M. Cohen, Michelle Childs, and Jean-Francois Alesandrini. 2016. "Submission to the United Nations Secretary-General's High-Level Panel on Access to Medicines on Behalf of the Drugs for Neglected Diseases Initiative (DNDi)." Available at: http://www.unsgaccessmeds.org/inbox/2016/2/27/bernard-pecoul.

Pedersen, Ole W. 2010. "Climate Change and Human Rights: Amicable or Arrested Development?" *Journal of Human Rights and the Environment* 1(2): 236–251.

Pevehouse, Jon C., Timothy Nordstrom, and Kevin Warnke. 2004. "The Correlates of War 2 International Governmental Organizations Data Version 2.0." *Conflict Management and Peace Science* 21: 101–119.

PMNCH (Partnership for Maternal, Newborn and Child Health). n.d.-a. "Human Rights." Accessed July 6, 2017. Available at: http://www.who.int/pmnch/activities/accountability/rights/en/.

PMNCH. n.d.-b. "Human rights and maternal mortality." Accessed July 6, 2017. Available at: http://www.who.int/pmnch/activities/accountability/human_rights_and_maternal_mortality/en/.

PMNCH. 2016. "The Partnership for Maternal, Newborn & Child Health in support of Every Woman Every Child. Strategic Plan 2016–2020." Available at: http://www.who.int/pmnch/knowledge/publications/pmnch_strategic_plan_2016_2020.pdf?ua=1.

PPPHW (Global Public-Private Partnership for Handwashing). 2015a. "Post-2015 Hygiene Advocacy Toolkit." Available at: http://globalhandwashing.org/wp-content/uploads/2015/03/Hygiene-Advocacy-Toolkit-.pdf.

PPPHW. 2015b. "Lessons from Zaragoza: Indicators, Integration, and Human Rights for Hygiene Post-2015." Available at: http://globalhandwashing.org/lessons-from-zaragoza/.

PPPHW. 2015c. "Raise your hand for hygiene: A global call for a hygiene indicator in the SDGs!" Available at: http://globalhandwashing.org/raise-your-voice-for-hygiene-sign-on-to-call-for-a-global-hygiene-indicator-in-the-sdgs/.

RBM and UNDP (Roll Back Malaria Partnership and United Nations Development Program). 2013. "Multisectoral Action Framework for Malaria." Accessed July 7, 2017. Available at: http://www.rollbackmalaria.org/files/files/about/Multisectoral Approach/Multisectoral-Action-Framework-for-Malaria.pdf.

Richter, Judith. 2004. "Public–Private Partnerships for Health: A Trend with No Alternatives?" *Development* 47(2): 43–48. DOI: 10.1057/palgrave.development.1100043.

Roht-Arriaza, Naomi. 2010. "Human Rights in the Climate Change Regime." *Journal of Human Rights and the Environment* 1(2): 211–235.

Schapper, Andrea and Markus Lederer. 2014. "Introduction: Human Rights and Climate Change: Mapping Institutional Inter-linkages." *Cambridge Review of International Affairs* 27(4): 666–679. DOI: 10.1080/09557571.2014.961806.

Skogly, Sigrun. 2001. *Human Rights Obligations of the World Bank and IMF.* London: Cavendish Publishing.

Smith, Kirk R., Alistair Woodward, Diamird Campbell-Lendrum, Dave D. Chadee, Yasushi Honda, Qiyong Liu, Jane M. Olwoch, Boris Revich, and Rainer Sauerborn. 2014. "Human Health: Impacts, Adaptation, and Co-benefits." In *Climate Change 2014: Impacts, Adaptation, and Vulnerability. Part A: Global and Sectoral Aspects. Contribution of Working Group II to the Fifth Assessment Report of the Intergovernmental Panel on Climate Change,* edited by Chris B. Field et al., 709–754. Cambridge, UK and New York, NY: Cambridge University Press.

Stern, Nicholas. 2007. *The Economics of Climate Change: The Stern Review.* Cambridge, UK: Cambridge University Press.

Stigma Index. n.d. "The People Living with HIV Stigma Index." Accessed March 28, 2017. Available at: http://www.stigmaindex.org/.

Stop TB Partnership. n.d.-a. "TB and Human Rights Task Force." Accessed July 7, 2017. Available at: http://www.stoptb.org/global/hrtf/.

Stop TB Partnership. n.d.-b. "Communities, Human Rights and Gender." Accessed July 7, 2017. Available at: http://www.stoptb.org/communities/.

Stop TB Partnership. 2010. "First Meeting of the Stop TB Partnership Task Force on TB and Human Rights. Berlin, 9th–10th November 2010." Available at: http://www.stoptb.org/assets/documents/global/hrtf/Report%20on%201st%20TB%20and%20HR%20Task%20Force%20Meeting.pdf.

Stop TB Partnership. 2015a. "Stop TB Partnership Annual Report 2015." Available at: http://www.stoptb.org/assets/documents/resources/publications/annualreports/AnnualReport2015_WEB.pdf.

Stop TB Partnership. 2015b. "The Paradigm Shift. 2016–2020. Global Plan to End TB." Available at: http://www.stoptb.org/assets/documents/global/plan/GlobalPlanToEndTB_TheParadigmShift_2016-2020_StopTBPartnership.pdf.

SUN (Scaling Up Nutrition). n.d. "The vision and principles of SUN. SUN Movement Principles of Engagement." Accessed July 7, 2017. Available at: http://scalingupnutrition.org/about-sun/the-vision-and-principles-of-sun/.

SUN (Scaling Up Nutrition). 2014. "Scaling Up Nutrition in Outline. An Introduction to the Scaling Up Nutrition Movement." Available at: http://scalingupnutrition.org/wp-content/uploads/2015/06/Orange_Internal_InOutline_ENG_20140415_web.pdf.

SUN (Scaling Up Nutrition). 2015. "Working Note: Enabling Good Governance in Civil Society Alliances." Available at: http://scalingupnutrition.org/wp-content/uploads/2015/05/SUN-CSN_Enabling-Good-Governance-in-CSA_EN_FinalWeb.pdf.

SUN (Scaling Up Nutrition). 2016a. "SUN Movement. Strategy and Roadmap (2016–2020)." Available at: http://docs.scalingupnutrition.org/wp-content/uploads/2016/09/SR_20160901_ENG_web_pages.pdf.

SUN (Scaling Up Nutrition). 2016b. "The Scaling Up Nutrition (SUN) Movement. Annual Progress Report 2016." Available at: http://docs.scalingupnutrition.org/wp-content/uploads/2016/11/SUN_Report_20161129_web_All.pdf.

SUN (Scaling Up Nutrition). 2016c. "Human rights experts release joint statement calling for increased efforts to support breastfeeding." Available at: http://scalingupnutrition.org/news/joint-statement-supports-increased-efforts-to-promote-support-and-protect-breastfeeding/.

Szabó, Eelco. 2011. "Report to the GAVI Alliance Board. 16–17 November 2011. Ethics and Conflict of Interest Policies." Report of Debbie Adams, MD, Law and Governance. Available at: http://www.gavi.org/about/governance/gavi-board/minutes/2011/16-november/ (see 16c—Ethics and Conflict of Interests Policies).

Tam, Melanie, Anouk Amzel, and B. Ryan Phelps. 2015. "Disclosure of HIV serostatus among pregnant and postpartum women in sub-Saharan Africa: a systematic review." *AIDS Care* 27(4):436–450.

TB Alliance. n.d.-a. "2015 Stakeholders Association Meeting." Accessed July 7, 2017. Available at: https://www.tballiance.org/events/2015-stakeholders-association-meeting.

TB Alliance. n.d.-b. "2016 Stakeholders Association Meeting." Accessed July 7, 2017. Available at: https://www.tballiance.org/events/2016-stakeholders-association-meeting.

UN (United Nations). n.d. "ECOSOC Partnerships Forum." Accessed November 26, 2017. Available at: https://www.un.org/ecosoc/en/ecosoc-partnerships-forum.

UN. 2015. "Paris Agreement." Available at: http://unfccc.int/files/essential_background/convention/application/pdf/english_paris_agreement.pdf.

UN General Assembly, 55th Session. 2000. "Programme of Work." 21 September. UN Doc. A/INF/55/3. Available at: http://www.un.org/ga/55/orgga.htm.

UN Sustainable Development Knowledge Platform. 2017. "Sustainable Development Goal 17." Available at: https://sustainabledevelopment.un.org/sdg17.

UNAIDS (Joint United Nations Programme on HIV/AIDS). 2012. "Understanding and addressing human rights concerns in the context of the elimination of mother-to-child transmission of HIV and keeping mothers alive (eMTCT), including in the Global Plan." Available at: http://www.emtct-iatt.org/wp-content/uploads/2014/08/Human-rights-and-eMTCT13Nov2012.pdf.

UNAIDS. 2016. *Elimination Without Violation; Validation Case Study*.

UNDP (UN Development Program). 2015. "New Grant to Support Human Rights in 10 African Countries." *UNDP Press Release*. Available at: http://www.undp.org/content/undp/en/home/presscenter/pressreleases/2015/11/19/new-grant-to-support-human-rights-in-10-african-countries.html.

UNFCCC (UN Framework Convention on Climate Change). n.d.-a. "Momentum for Change: Planetary Health." Available at: http://unfccc.int/secretariat/momentum_for_change/items/10481.php .

UNFCCC. n.d.-b. "Momentum for Change." Available at: http://unfccc.int/secretariat/momentum_for_change/items/6214.php.

UNFCCC. 2015. Press Release: Historic Paris Agreement on Climate Change. Available at: https://www.unfccc.int/files/press/press_releases_advisories/application/pdf/pr20151112_cop21_final.pdf.

UNICEF (UN Children's Fund). n.d. "Monitoring the Situation of Children and Women." Accessed March 28, 2017. Available at: https://data.unicef.org/topic/hivaids/emtct/.

Verburg, Gerda. 2016. "Why I'm Standing Up for Someone's Right (To Food) Today." *Scaling Up Nutrition (SUN) Blog*. Available at: http://scalingupnutrition.org/news/why-im-standing-up-for-someones-right-to-food-today/.

Volgy, Thomas J., Elizabeth Fausett, Keith A. Grant, and Stuart Rodgers. 2008. "Identifying Formal Intergovernmental Organizations." *Journal of Peace Research* 45(6): 837–850.

Wallace, Michael and David J. Singer. 1970. "Intergovernmental Organization in the Global System, 1815–1964: A Quantitative Description." *International Organization* 24(2): 239–287.

Whitmee, Sarah, Andy Haines, Chris Beyrer, Frederick Boltz, Anthony G. Capon, Braulio Ferreira de Souza Dias, Alex Ezeh [et al.]. 2015. "Safeguarding Human Health in the Anthropocene Epoch: Report of the Rockefeller Foundation-Lancet Commission on Planetary Health." *The Lancet* 386: 1973–2028. DOI: 10.1016/S0140-6736(15)60901-1.

WHO (World Health Organization). 2014. *Global guidance on criteria and processes for validation: elimination of mother-to-child transmission (EMTCT) of HIV and syphilis*. Geneva: World Health Organization.

WHO. 2015. "Action and Investment to defeat Malaria 2016–2030 (AIM)—for a malaria-free world." Geneva: World Health Organization, on behalf of the Roll Back Malaria Partnership Secretariat.

WHO. 2017. *Human Rights, Gender Equality, and Engagement of Civil Society in the EMTCT Process*. Available at: http://www.who.int/reproductivehealth/publications/rtis/9789241505888/en/.

WHO and UNDP (World Health Organization and UN Environment Programme). 2004. "Health and environment: tools for effective decision-making: review of initial findings/the WHO-UNEP Health and Environment Linkages Initiative (HELI)." Available at: http://www.who.int/heli/publications/helirevbrochure.pdf?ua=1.

WHO and UNDP. 2008. "Health environment: managing the linkages for sustainable development. A toolkit for decision-makers. Synthesis report." Available at: http://apps.who.int/iris/bitstream/10665/43946/1/9789241563727_eng.pdf.

WMO (World Meteorological Organization). 2014a. "Health Exemplar to the User Interface Platform of the Global Framework for Climate Services." Available at: https://www.wmo.int/gfcs/sites/default/files/Priority-Areas/Health/GFCS-HEALTH-EXEMPLAR-FINAL-14152_en.pdf.

WMO. 2014b. "Implementation Plan of the Global Framework for Climate Services." Available at: http://www.wmo.int/gfcs/sites/default/files/implementation-plan//GFCS-IMPLEMENTATION-PLAN-FINAL-14211_en.pdf.

Yamin, Alicia E. and Rebecca Cantor. 2014. "Between Insurrectional Discourse and Operational Guidance: Challenges and Dilemmas in Implementing Human Rights-Based Approaches to Health." *Journal of Human Rights Practice* 6(3): 451–485. DOI: 10.1093/jhuman/huu019.

Zinser, Stephen. 2016. "Investment Committee Chair Report: Report for a GAVI Board Meeting, 22–23 June 2016 Geneva." Available at: http://www.gavi.org/about/governance/gavi-board/minutes/2016/22-june/ (see 05d–Investment Committee Chair Report).

Global Economic Governance and Global Health Funding Agencies

15

Integrating a Human Rights-Based Approach to Development and the Right to Development into Global Governance for Health

STEPHEN P. MARKS[*]

This chapter proposes a human rights framework for global economic governance and specifically for the economic and financial sources of support to health systems in the form of: (1) general principles of human rights-based development—as defined primarily in inter-agency guidance and training—and (2) the right to development—as defined in the 1986 Declaration on the Right to Development and further elaborated by various mandates reporting to the UN Human Rights Council (HRC). No institution of development financing was initially inspired by or currently has as its principal vision a rights-based approach to development or the right to development. Nevertheless, each has—in different ways—been attentive to human rights norms and principles. After first examining the general principles of human rights-based development in Part I, Part II explores the emergence and current state of the right to development, focusing on its public health dimensions. The chapter concludes by addressing obstacles to the incorporation of human rights in health funding strategies.

I. GENERAL PRINCIPLES OF HUMAN RIGHTS-BASED DEVELOPMENT

Rights-based development as applied to health governance engages three intersecting understandings of human well-being:

1. Public health concentrates on the requirements of well-being defined in terms of physical, mental, and social dimensions of human existence;

* The author wishes to express his gratitude to the editors, Benjamin Meier and Lawrence Gostin, for their wise counsel and substantive suggestions, to David K. Androff for his helpful review of the chapter, and to Hanna Huffstetler and Edith Lee for their editorial assistance.

2. Development tends to focus on well-being, defined in terms of the economic processes that improve people's material conditions; and

3. Human rights tend to deal with well-being in terms of normative constraints on power relations to ensure human dignity and the elimination of repressive and oppressive processes.

Thus, while public health, development, and human rights have "human well-being" in common—or, as philosophers would say, "flourishing," or the "good life"—each approaches this meta-goal through different frameworks—physical, mental, and social well-being; economic processes; and normative constraints, respectively.

The role of international actors with respect to human rights, public health, and human development may be explored in both (A) the theory through which human rights thinking is applied to development and (B) the practice of international actors to incorporate human rights in more technocratic approaches to health and development.

A. Human Rights-Based Approaches to Health and Development in Theory

Building on the abstract definitions above, it is possible to provide a more complete picture of how public health, development, and human rights are related by examining two theoretical approaches to understanding these interconnections: (1) the social justice approach and (2) the capabilities approach.

1. THE SOCIAL JUSTICE APPROACH

Advancing social justice by eliminating social disparities and inequalities in access to health is widely regarded as fundamental to the field of public health, defining social justice as "fair and equitable treatment of people" (Ruger 2004, 1075). The social justice approach is illustrated by a focus on inequalities, fair processes (Daniels 2005; Daniels et al. 2000; Daniels et al. 2005), and social epidemiology (Krieger 2000; 2001), in addition to the extensive research on health equity (Global Equity Gauge Alliance 2003). These studies base the concept of health equity on theories of social justice and draw attention to the failure to improve overall health status in terms of the decline in mortality and morbidity to reach some social groups, denying them equality of opportunity (Sen 2004).

Social justice thereby captures an important feature of the human rights framework for development—the emphasis on a moral imperative for eliminating glaring social inequality within societies and structurally imbedded patterns of international support for those inequalities (Kim et al. 2000). However, the human rights framework goes beyond a commitment to social justice in that it supports other dimensions of a life people value, dimensions that are not focused exclusively on reducing the suffering of the poor and vulnerable. It is also different from social justice insofar as it does not rely on a subjective sense of outrage at the suffering of the poor and excluded within society—however admirable such sentiments may be—but rather on a set of agreed standards that define what governments must do to redress social injustice.

Within the institutions of global health governance, it is sometimes easier to draw on the concept of social justice rather than on human rights to define the moral basis of setting priorities in health. The World Health Organization (WHO) uses the terms "human rights" and "social justice" in different ways. WHO's 12th General Programme of Work, adopted by the World Health Assembly "as the basis for strategic planning, monitoring and evaluation of WHO's work during the period 2014–2019" (WHA 2013), considers human rights as an "added dimension" among other "wider concerns" while "the principle of equity and social justice" is one of the "key elements" of WHO's approach, according to which "WHO will continue to give emphasis where needs are greatest" (WHO 2014, 19).[1] Thus, social justice provides a moral framework which is commonly used in the context of global health governance—as exemplified by WHO's 12th General Programme of Work—whereas human rights has a more marginal status, at least in the context of global health governance, even though it is seen as central to the rights-based approach to development.

2. The Capabilities Approach

At the abstract level, the meta-goals of public health, development, and human rights have also been analyzed in terms of "human capabilities" (Nussbaum 1988; Nussbaum 1993). Nobel Prize–winning economist Amartya Sen has articulated an approach to human rights and development that is widely endorsed by United Nations (UN) institutions and is of particular relevance to health. In *Development as Freedom*, Sen devotes a chapter to "Poverty as Capability Deprivation," in which he argues that development is not the acquisition of more goods and services but the enhanced freedom to choose, to lead the kind of life one values (Sen 1998). These enhanced choices are called "capabilities" (Crocker 1992). Poverty, Sen explains, is the deprivation of basic capabilities. He examines three features of deprivation of basic capability—premature mortality, undernourishment, and illiteracy—which have come to be the basis for the Human Development Index of the UN Development Programme (UNDP). In the capabilities discourse, "capability" is the option available to the individual to partake of some valued dimension of life; "functioning" is the exercise of that option (Sen 1999).

The application of capability emerges in development theory by incorporating a range of concepts designed to shift the focus from economic growth to human welfare, drawing on Sen's earlier writing on rational choice and commodities (Sen 1985, 2005). Sen and Sudhir Anand provided a background paper for UNDP's *Human Development Report 1990*, in which they argued that "the central issue"

---

1. In the early 2000s, as discussed in chapter 5, WHO seemed to view human rights as more directly relevant to health governance. In a joint publication with the Office of the UN High Commissioner for Human Rights (OHCHR), WHO claimed that it worked to "strengthen the capacity of WHO and its member States to integrate a human rights-based approach to health; advance the right to health in international law and international development processes; and advocate for health-related human rights," and the World Health Assembly included seven priority areas in WHO's 11th General Programme of Work (2006–2015), including "promoting universal coverage, gender equality and health-related human rights" (OHCHR 2008, 29).

was "the need for universalist attention in valuing the enhancement of human capabilities, as opposed to partisan interest in promoting aggregate growth" (Anand and Sen 1994, 16). Human development, as compared with economic growth, "directly enhances the capability of people to lead worthwhile lives" (Ibid., 34).

From the beginning of this theoretical discussion, human rights was explicitly part of thinking about human development under a capability approach. For example, UNDP established a policy in 1998 of integrating human rights into its approach to sustainable human development (UNDP 1998) and drew on these ideas in devoting the *Human Development Report 2000* to human rights (UNDP 2000). As the *Human Development Report 2001* explained,

> human development shares a common vision with human rights. The goal is human freedom. And in pursuing capabilities and realizing rights, this freedom is vital. People must be free to exercise their choices and to participate in decision-making that affects their lives. Human development and human rights are mutually reinforcing, helping to secure the well-being and dignity of all people, building self-respect and the respect of others (UNDP 2001, 9).

Martha Nussbaum has been even more forceful in relating capabilities to human rights, noting that capabilities

> include many of the entitlements that are also stressed in the human rights movement: political liberties, the freedom of association, the free choice of occupation, and a variety of economic and social rights. And capabilities, like human rights, supply a moral and humanly rich set of goals for development... Thus capabilities have a very close relationship to human rights, as understood in contemporary international discussions (Nussbaum 2003, 36; Nussbaum 1999).

Nussbaum views health as central to capabilities, exemplified by the first three capabilities of her "explicit list":

1. Life. Not dying prematurely, or before one's life is so reduced as to be not worth living.
2. Bodily Health. Being able to have good health, including reproductive health; to be adequately nourished; to have adequate shelter.
3. Bodily Integrity. Being able to move freely from place to place; to be secure against violent assault, including sexual assault and domestic violence; having opportunities for sexual satisfaction and for choice in matters of reproduction (Nussbaum 2003, 41).

Jennifer Prah Ruger applies this capabilities approach to health to the practice of global health institutions, arguing that these institutions

> have important roles in the implementation of a capability approach to health because they can help generate and disseminate the knowledge and information

required to reduce health disparities [and] can also empower individuals and groups in national and global forums. Indirectly, they can push for greater citizen participation in health-related decision-making in developing countries, both within (eg, in determining resource allocation) and outside the health sector (Ruger 2004, 1079).

She adds that global health institutions can also "give individuals and groups a greater voice in national and international forums and programmes" and, reflective of the chapters in this volume, "provide technical assistance, financial aid, and global advocacy to support the development of equitable and efficient health systems and public health programmes" (Ibid.).

In addition to these positive impacts that the capabilities approach can have on global health institutions, Ruger has systematically explored the capabilities approach to the right to health (Ruger 2006). In her analysis, capabilities are clarified by reference to "provincial globalism," a theory of global health justice that involves nine principles or features, including capabilities and global governance. Regarding capabilities, she explains that provincial globalism "holds health capabilities and more specifically central health capabilities—freedom from avoidable morbidity and premature death—as morally salient human interests in their own right and as preconditions or prerequisites for other capabilities" (Ruger 2012, 37). Regarding global health governance, her theory of provincial globalism "elaborates a multilevel governance system in which all actors have respective roles and responsibilities based on functions and needs and voluntary commitments" (Ibid., 41). Provincial globalism thus becomes "a theory of global health justice that meshes with the theory of shared health governance" (Ibid., 42), providing a basis for understanding how global health governance fits into international relations theory.

These recent efforts to expand the theoretical understanding of capability reinforce the trend of international institutions, especially UNDP, to introduce the capability approach into development practice. The grounding of this approach in development economics—and its linkages to human rights—make it the most appealing theoretical framework to move from theory to practice under a human rights-based approach to health and development.

B. Human Rights-Based Approaches to Health and Development in Practice

Human rights-based approaches to development affirm that human rights must be integrated into sustainable human development as a matter of policy. This "human rights approach to development assistance" seeks to apply human rights principles as

a comprehensive guide for appropriate official development assistance, for the manner in which it should be delivered, for the priorities that it should address, for the obligations of both donor and recipient governments and for the way that official development assistance is evaluated (HRCA 1995).

Advanced by NGO advocates (Häusermann 1998, HRCA 1998), the human rights-based approach has become policy of the principal human rights agency of the UN and has been adopted by the UN agencies responsible for health and development (UNDG 2003). It has also been endorsed by regional development agencies, such as the Organisation for Economic Co-operation and Development (OECD), which in February 2007 adopted its "Action-Oriented Policy Paper on Human Rights and Development" (OECD-DAC 2007). As addressed in chapter 18, bilateral aid institutions (such as USAID, DFID, SIDA, CIDA, DANIDA) now often have explicit human rights policies which may influence their financial assistance policies. This human rights-based approach stands in marked contrast to traditional approaches to economic development (focusing on growth in GDP) and provides direct implications for global health governance, especially under the 2030 Agenda for Sustainable Development (2030 Agenda).

1. HUMAN RIGHTS POLICIES OF INTERNATIONAL AGENCIES AFFECTING HEALTH GOVERNANCE

In recent years, the UN system has sought, as reviewed in chapter 3, to translate the commitment to human rights in development into a system-wide reform process called the "Human Rights Mainstreaming Mechanism" by the UN Development Group (UNDG) or "the human rights-based approach" (HRBA) to development. Echoing ideas expressed by then UN Secretary-General Kofi Annan, the World Conference on Human Rights, in its 1993 Vienna Declaration and Programme of Action, stated that "[t]he existence of widespread extreme poverty inhibits the full and effective enjoyment of human rights; its immediate alleviation and eventual elimination must remain a high priority for the international community" (World Conference on Human Rights 1993, para. 14). The following year, the Secretary-General issued his *Agenda for Development*, which alluded to the Vienna Declaration's affirmation of the "mutually reinforcing interrelationship of democracy, development and respect for human rights" and focused more on the importance of democracy and good governance as essential for development (UN General Assembly 1994, paras. 119–120). The momentum for human rights mainstreaming accelerated in 1997, when Secretary-General Annan stated that among the priority areas for UN reform, he proposed "[e]xtending human rights activities by reorganizing and restructuring the human rights secretariat and the integration of human rights into all principal United Nations activities and programmes" (UN General Assembly 1997, para. 78). Cutting across the UN system, human rights mainstreaming would be pursued principally through the UN's development agenda.

Responding to this call across UN agencies, an inter-agency workshop adopted in 2003 a "Common Understanding on Human Rights-Based Approaches to Development" (UNDG 2003). The following year, twenty-one heads of UN departments and agencies adopted the Action 2 Plan of Action, which was fully operational from 2006 to 2009. It supported more than sixty UN country teams, introduced HRBA in training of staff,[2] and created an "HRBA Practitioners' Portal on Human Rights Based Approaches to Programming" (OHCHR 2007).

---

2. Recently (June 2017), the UN Staff College offered a new course on "Human Rights-Based Approach to Development Programming," which aims to build "capacity to integrate human rights

The Office of the UN High Commissioner for Human Rights (OHCHR) now supports UN departments and agencies in implementing the "rights-based approach to development," which it defines as "a conceptual framework for the process of human development that is normatively based on international human rights standards and operationally directed to promoting and protecting human rights" (OHCHR 2006, 15).[3] This OHCHR approach builds on Secretary-General Annan's view in 1998:

> The rights-based approach to development describes situations not simply in terms of human needs, or of development requirements, but in terms of society's obligations to respond to the inalienable rights of individuals. It empowers people to demand justice as a right, not as charity, and gives communities a moral basis from which to claim international assistance where needed (UN General Assembly 1998).

Extending these views in 2005, Annan concluded that "[w]e will not enjoy development without security, we will not enjoy security without development, and we will not enjoy either without respect for human rights" (UN General Assembly 2005, para. 17). These positions have guided the system-wide work of OHCHR to implement a human rights-based approach to development.

2. HUMAN RIGHTS IN THE 2030 DEVELOPMENT AGENDA

Since 2000, a parallel terrain for policy discussion on the relationship between economic and human rights approaches to health governance has been the Millennium Development Goals (MDGs) (2000–2015) and the Sustainable Development Goals (SDGs) (2015–2030). After more than a decade of tension between the technocratic approach of officials promoting the MDGs and the normative approach of human rights advocates (Alston 2005; Darrow 2012), the post-2015 development agenda was adopted in the form of a resolution entitled "Transforming our world: the 2030 Agenda for Sustainable Development," enumerating seventeen SDGs and 169 targets (UN General Assembly 2015). From the human rights perspective, the 2030 Agenda represents an advance over the MDGs, beginning with an affirmation in the preamble that the SDGs "seek to build on the Millennium Development Goals and complete what they did not achieve. They seek to realize the human rights of all" (Ibid., preamble). The declaration contains several strong paragraphs affirming the importance of human rights in the post-2015 development agenda, as well as this explicit paragraph on health:

> To promote physical and mental health and well-being, and to extend life expectancy for all, we must achieve universal health coverage and access to

---

into all policy and programming processes within the context of the new 2030 Agenda for Sustainable Development."

3. Part of the earlier impetus for this commitment is General Assembly Resolution 48/141 of 1993, which called on the UN High Commissioner for Human Rights, as discussed in chapter 21, to "[r]ecognize the importance of promoting a balanced and sustainable development for all people . . ." (UN General Assembly 1993, para. 3).

quality health care. No one must be left behind. We commit to accelerating the progress made to date in reducing newborn, child and maternal mortality by ending all such preventable deaths before 2030. We are committed to ensuring universal access to sexual and reproductive health-care services, including for family planning, information and education. We will equally accelerate the pace of progress made in fighting malaria, HIV/AIDS, tuberculosis, hepatitis, Ebola and other communicable diseases and epidemics, including by addressing growing anti-microbial resistance and the problem of unattended diseases affecting developing countries. We are committed to the prevention and treatment of non-communicable diseases, including behavioural, developmental and neurological disorders, which constitute a major challenge for sustainable development (Ibid., para. 26).

The High-Level Political Forum on Sustainable Development (HLPF) will monitor the implementation of the SDGs. Indicators have been prepared by the Inter-Agency and Expert Group on SDG Indicators (IAEG-SDGs) and agreed upon by the UN Statistical Commission (ECOSOC 2016). Of particular value for achieving the vision of health in the paragraph quoted above is SDG 3, which seeks to "[e]nsure healthy lives and promote well-being for all at all ages," with related targets and indicators, including on access to affordable essential medicines and vaccines (Ibid., 19). However, beyond the general affirmation that the SDGs "seek to realize the human rights of all" (UN General Assembly 2015, preamble), only a few of the indicators refer to human rights, including those on reproductive rights under SDG 5, labor rights under SDG 8, anti-discrimination in SDG 10, and access to justice in SDG 16 (ECOSOC 2016).

II. THE RIGHT TO DEVELOPMENT

Rather than affirming that development must be pursued with due attention to human rights (the rights-based approach model), the right to development seeks to establish a right of peoples and individuals both to achieve sustainable human development and to benefit from human rights in development. The idea of a human right to development was not originally part of the catalogue of human rights in the postwar Universal Declaration of Human Rights or the international covenants, although it can trace its normative content to numerous principles of international cooperation reaffirmed in UN documents since World War II (UN 1990). The first effort to formulate a distinct right was made in a 1972 lecture by Senegalese Judge Kéba M'Baye (M'Baye 1972). Five years later, with Senegal as chair, the UN Commission on Human Rights (succeeded in 2006 by the Human Rights Council) requested a study on "the international dimensions of the right to development as a human right in relation with other human rights based on international cooperation, including the right to peace, taking into account the requirements of the New International Economic Order and fundamental human needs" (Commission on Human Rights 1977). Pursuant to that request, the UN Secretariat produced a 161-page study, conceptualizing a right to development and recognizing the major challenges to this right, including the difficulties in translating the concept of a right to development "into a notion capable of providing practical guidance and inspiration, based on international human rights standards, in the context of development activities" (ECOSOC 1979, para. 315).

When the Commission on Human Rights began formulating the right to development (Commission on Human Rights 1981), the political climate had become highly charged with ideological positioning on practically every issue. Frustrated with the Cold War rivalry dominating international relations, developing countries, functioning through the Non-Aligned Movement (NAM), supported Senegal's initiative to have the UN declare development a human right and a normative basis for the establishment of a New International Economic Order (NIEO) (OHCHR 2013). Their intention was to use the declaration on the right to development to oblige those countries that dominated the international economy to accept what they had not accepted in the NIEO—greater responsibility to eliminate the structural causes of poverty, larger payments for raw materials extracted from developing countries, additional aid, and improvements to the terms of trade in favor of developing countries (Salomon 2010).

Under pressure from North American and European delegations, however, the Commission's drafting committee agreed in 1981 that, while a general moral commitment to development was acceptable, the text would neither affirm any legal obligation to transfer resources from North to South nor codify any specific obligations regarding any of the issues contained in the declaration (Marks 2004).

The UN Declaration on the Right to Development was finally proclaimed by the UN General Assembly in December 1986 (UN General Assembly 1986).[4] As a resolution of the General Assembly, the Declaration does not create any legal obligations, although it carries moral and political authority (Marks 2010). It was a compromise document of sixteen preambular paragraphs and ten articles setting out: a core definition of development; an enumeration of rights and duties of individuals and states; a commitment to the elimination of massive human rights violations and to international peace and security; a reiteration of the principles of non-discrimination, interrelatedness of rights, and participation; and an enumeration of steps states should take at the national and international levels to realize this right.

Since the adoption of the Declaration, the idea of an internationally recognized human right to development has remained contested. The North-South tension regarding the use of human rights institutions to restrain the dominant economic powers, and especially to impose any legal obligations, continues today, and debate on the issue in international forums has even been described by the UN High Commissioner for Human Rights as "political theatre" (OHCHR 2013, iii). In order to examine this right from the perspective of global economic governance and global health funding agencies, it is necessary to (A) review how the clarification of the right to development has addressed global health funding and (B) analyze the potential of the right to development to guide global governance.

---

4. States adopted the Declaration by a vote of 146 in favor, one against (United States), and eight abstentions (Denmark, Finland, the Federal Republic of Germany, Iceland, Israel, Japan, Sweden, and the United Kingdom).

A. Health Governance in the Work of the High-Level Task Force

In addition to adopting annual resolutions stressing the importance of a right to development, the Commission on Human Rights in the 1980s and 1990s set up several working groups on the implementation of the right to development. While they did not initially accomplish much in the way of practical guidance to influence development policy and action, a breakthrough occurred in 1998, with the Commission recommending the establishment of a follow-up mechanism that would consist of an open-ended working group (OEWG) of all governments and an Independent Expert on the right to development (Commission on Human Rights 1998). The mandate of the Independent Expert was "to present to the working group at each of its sessions a study on the current state of progress in the implementation of the right to development as a basis for a focused discussion, taking into account, inter alia, the deliberations and suggestions of the working group" (Commission on Human Rights 1998, para. 10).

Dr. Arjun K. Sengupta, a prominent Indian economist, was appointed Independent Expert in 2000, and by 2004, had produced eight reports. He went on to be the Independent Expert on Human Rights and Extreme Poverty and then was elected to chair the OEWG until his passing in 2010. Sengupta brought a fresh approach to understanding the right to development, which he defined as "the right to a process that expands the capabilities or freedom of individuals to improve their well-being and to realize what they value" (Commission on Human Rights 2000, para. 22). In 2004, the Commission established the high-level task force on the implementation of the right to development (the Task Force) to assist the OEWG, providing the necessary expertise to enable the OEWG to make appropriate recommendations (Commission on Human Rights 2004a). As chair of the OEWG, Sengupta worked with the Task Force as it carried out its mandate, first to look at the implementation of the MDGs, social impact assessments, and best practices in the implementation of the right to development (Commission on Human Rights 2004b) and then, from 2005 to 2010, to focus on MDG 8 (global partnership for development), proposing right to development criteria for the periodic evaluation of global partnerships (Commission on Human Rights 2005b).

In 2006, the OEWG adopted the Task Force's right to development criteria—including seven relating to "structure/enabling environment," five relating to "process," and three relating to "outcome" (HRC 2007a)—and requested the Task Force to apply them to selected partnerships. The Task Force applied these criteria from 2007 to 2009 to ten partnerships for development, three of which were directly related to global health governance, namely (1) the Intergovernmental Working Group on Public Health, Innovation, and Intellectual Property; (2) the Special Programme for Research and Training in Tropical Diseases; and (3) the Global Fund to Fight AIDS, Tuberculosis and Malaria.[5]

---

5. The other partnerships assessed by the task force were: the New Partnership for Africa's Development (NEPAD); the Paris Declaration on Aid Effectiveness; the African Peer Review Mechanism (APRM); the Cotonou Agreement between the European Union and African, Caribbean and Pacific (ACP) countries; Debt relief provided by the Heavily Indebted Poor

1. INTERGOVERNMENTAL WORKING GROUP ON PUBLIC HEALTH, INNOVATION, AND INTELLECTUAL PROPERTY

The Task Force reviewed the creation of the Intergovernmental Working Group on Public Health, Innovation, and Intellectual Property by the World Health Assembly in 2006 and the adoption of the WHO Strategy and Plan of Action in 2008 (WHA 2008). The Task Force was attentive to the fact that the Strategy and Plan of Action not only sought to facilitate access to essential medicines among the poor and promote innovation in health products and medical devices but also that the incentive schemes aimed to delink price from research, making health products cheaper and more easily available (HRC 2009a, 2010a; Forman 2013). However, while the Strategy and Plan of Action refer to WHO's constitutional commitment to the right to health, the Task Force regretted that the drafters had deleted a reference to treaty provisions on the right to health and did not mention the right to development principles in spite of the potential synergy between the Strategy and Plan of Action and the right to development (HRC 2009a; 2010a).[6]

The Task Force additionally focused on MDG 8 and specifically Target 8.E, which calls on governments, "[i]n cooperation with pharmaceutical companies, [to] provide access to affordable essential drugs in developing countries" (UN General Assembly 2001). When the Task Force met with the WHO Secretariat in November 2008 to discuss global partnerships for access to essential medicines in developing countries, WHO agreed that the Strategy and Plan of Action could be used to explore with stakeholders the potential of the "Human Rights Guidelines for Pharmaceutical Companies in relation to Access to Medicines," which had just been presented to the UN General Assembly by the Special Rapporteur on the right to health (UN General Assembly 2008), and the right to health as a basis to meet MDG Target 8.E on access to essential medicines (HRC 2010a).

The Task Force was specifically concerned that the Strategy and Plan of Action did not discourage the adoption of Trade-Related Aspects of Intellectual Property Rights (TRIPS) Plus protection in bilateral trade agreements, as discussed in chapter 17, or refer to the impact of bilateral or regional trade agreements on access to medicines. On the other hand, it looked favorably on the reference to attributes of accessibility, affordability, and quality of medicines in developing countries and on the position that protecting intellectual property should not impede states' ability to comply with their core obligations under the rights to food, health, and education (Commission on Human Rights 2005a; HRC 2009b; 2010a). The Task Force also

Countries Initiative and the Multilateral Debt Relief Initiative; the Development Agenda of the World Intellectual Property Organization (WIPO); and the Clean Development Mechanism (CDM) under the Kyoto Protocol to the UN Framework Convention on Climate Change (HRC 2010a, paras. 20–62).

6. The Strategy and Plan of Action calls upon states to take all necessary measures to ensure equality of opportunity for all in access to health services (WHA 2008), which was consistent, in the Task Force's view, with the Declaration on the Right to Development, which resolves: "States should undertake, at the national level, all necessary measures for the realization of the right to development and shall ensure, inter alia, equality of opportunity for all in their access to . . . health services . . ." (UN General Assembly 1986, art. 8.1).

found the monitoring, evaluation, and reporting expectations of governments and industry to be consistent with right to development criteria, although it commented that improvements could be made to the WHO indicators.

2. SPECIAL PROGRAMME FOR RESEARCH AND TRAINING IN TROPICAL DISEASES

The second dimension of global health governance examined by the Task Force was the Special Programme for Research and Training in Tropical Diseases (TDR). Co-sponsored by the World Bank, UNICEF, and WHO, the TDR seeks to advance research and implement practical solutions to neglected diseases, which it called "diseases of poverty." The Task Force found that certain TDR projects were community-driven in ways that increased drug distribution, improved public services, and contributed to political empowerment and democratization, thus contributing to the realization of the right to development (HRC 2009a; HRC 2010a).[7]

The Task Force, however, noted that underfunding of the response to these neglected diseases and the high price of medicines limited the TDR's impact on innovation through research and development (HRC 2009b; HRC 2010a). The emergence of private foundations and non-governmental organizations was having considerable impact on efforts to combat infectious diseases, yet the Task Force expressed concern that the governance of these private sources of funding did not provide for adequate public accountability, in particular, accountability for the failure of private entities to disclose the pricing of the products they develop. The Task Force underscored the need to strengthen transparency and accountability in the TDR's contractual agreements with pharmaceutical companies on pricing and access to medicines and to broaden the scope of independent reviews for mutual accountability (HRC 2010a; HRC 2009b).

The Task Force concluded that the TDR's strategy was supportive of the right to development and the right to health insofar as it was rights-based, that it favored the empowerment of developing country efforts through partnerships and capacity-building, and that it focused on the needs of the most vulnerable (HRC 2010a). Referring to MDG 8, however, the Task Force noted the limited impact of the TDR on innovation with regard to infectious diseases. It supported further efforts by the TDR to introduce principles of the right to development in the design and implementation of relevant programs and to explicitly use a human right to health framework to focus on empowering developing countries and meeting needs of the most vulnerable (Ibid.).

---

7. The examined projects included community-driven interventions in Africa that increased the distribution of Ivomectin (a drug that treats river blindness) as a result of communities: deciding how the drug would be used and distributed, controlling compliance with quality and quantity standards, and ensuring record keeping. The Task Force found that these community-driven initiatives "lead to better governmental services and contribute to an atmosphere of political empowerment and democratization basing research activities on people's consent and involvement, all of which contribute to the realization of the right to development ... " (HRC 2009a, para. 25).

3. THE GLOBAL FUND TO FIGHT AIDS, TUBERCULOSIS AND MALARIA

The third mechanism of global health governance assessed by the Task Force was the Global Fund to Fight AIDS, Tuberculosis and Malaria (Global Fund). As reviewed in chapter 19, the Global Fund has a shared objective to fight major diseases afflicting the world's poorest people. The Task Force noted that, like the TDR, the Global Fund attempted to improve access to health and equitable development through procedures that were generally participatory and empowering (HRC 2009a; HRC 2010a).

Specifically, the Task Force found that the attention the Global Fund paid to equity, meaningful and active participation, and the special needs of vulnerable and marginalized groups was consistent with the right to development criteria (HRC 2009a). However, the Global Fund did not apply a rights-based approach and, according to the Task Force, did not have adequate monitoring mechanisms for mutual accountability. Nevertheless, the Global Fund's impact on national capacity to control the three diseases was especially relevant in the context of MDG 8. The Task Force felt that the Global Fund had "a vital role to play in developing a more enabling international environment for both health and development and contributing to the policy agenda for promoting public health, human rights and development" (HRC 2010a, para. 51).

In sum, the criteria developed by the Task Force on the implementation of the right to development were applied to several significant processes of global health governance in the context of its mandate to develop and apply right to development criteria to MDG 8. Beyond MDG 8, however, lie broader questions of how the normative and analytical framework of the right to development might be applied to the full range of global health governance institutions and functions.

B. Normative and Analytical Framework of the Right to Development and Global Health Governance

In the final phase of its work, the Task Force refined the methodology and structure of its evaluations, developing a full set of attributes, criteria, operational subcriteria, and indicators. The 2010 final product of the Task Force's five-year effort was designed to operationalize the right to development and, as a consequence, is relevant to global health governance insofar as its provides clear and action-oriented guidance regarding the responsibilities of decision makers in government, international institutions, and civil society for planning, implementing, monitoring, and assessing their development-related policies, projects, and processes (HRC 2010b). This framework begins with the core norm of the right to development, defined as the "right of peoples and individuals to the constant improvement of their well-being and to a national and global enabling environment conducive to just, equitable, participatory and human-centred development respectful of all human rights" (Ibid., annex). Obviously, at this abstract level, WHO and other institutions of global health governance tend to articulate some version of "constant improvement of . . . well-being" and often seek to encourage a "global enabling environment conducive to just, equitable, participatory development," but are less likely to define development as "human-centred" and "respectful of all human rights."

The challenge, however, becomes more specific when it comes to the application of the criteria and subcriteria to the three components or attributes of the right to development, which the Task Force proposed and the OEWG had accepted: (1) comprehensive human-centered development, (2) enabling environment, and (3) social justice and equity.

Under the first attribute (comprehensive and human-centered development policy), the first criterion is "[t]o promote constant improvement in socio-economic well-being," and the first of five subcriteria (that is, areas where progress can be measured) is health, with the other four relating to underlying determinants of health (education, housing and water, work and social security, and food security and nutrition). Indicators are suggested for each of these five subcriteria, as indicated in Table 15.1 below.

Table 15.1. COMPREHENSIVE AND HUMAN-CENTERED DEVELOPMENT POLICY (HRC 2010b, ANNEX)

Criteria	Subcriteria	Indicators*
1 (a) To promote constant improvement in socio-economic well-being (UN General Assembly 1986, art. 2.3)	1 (a) (i) Health	Public expenditures on primary health; life expectancy at birth; access to essential drugs; low birthweight babies; child mortality; HIV prevalence; births attended by skilled personnel
	1 (a) (ii) Education	Public spending on primary education; school enrollment rates; school completion rates; international scores for student achievement
	1 (a) (iii) Housing and water	Public expenditure on public service provision; access to improved drinking water and sanitation; homelessness rate; cost of housing relative to income; slum populations
	1 (a) (iv) Work and social security	Long-term unemployment; involuntary part-time employment; public expenditure on social security; income poverty rates below national and international lines
	1 (a) (v) Food security and nutrition	Child stunting rates

* It should be stressed that the indicators are intended to be illustrative rather than comprehensive and that they meet a recognized level of validity, reliability, and intertemporal and international comparability. As the Task Force stressed in clarifying the inclusivity of indicators, "[o]thers could have been chosen from the thousands of potentially relevant indicators, and new ones will emerge. For this reason, the indicators listed . . . should be updated, and revisions and new ones added as they become available" (HRC 2010b, para. 15).

These indicators are to be used to assess the health component of the first criterion on improvement of socioeconomic well-being of the attribute concerning development policy. Applied to health governance, the extent to which a health program would be deemed to make progress regarding the well-being criterion of the right to development would be measured by the advances made in the seven indicator areas covered by Subcriterion 1 (a) (i) on Health. Similarly, the other four subcriteria of the well-being criterion would be assessed as contributing to the right to development insofar as their respective indicators show progress.

Other attributes and criteria are also relevant to assessing global health governance from the right to development perspective. For example, a subcriterion in Attribute 1 on "health technology" appears under the criterion on "access to the benefits of science and technology," with such indicators as "aid allocations to health technologies; use of TRIPS flexibilities, and price discounts to expand access to HIV antiretroviral drugs" (Ibid., annex). Attribute 2 on "participatory human rights processes" enumerates criteria and subcriteria that could be used in reviewing the extent to which any global health governance program would be contributing to the right to development—as measured by explicit reference to human rights, prioritization of marginalized groups, measures to control corruption, genuine participation and voice of affected populations, monitoring and redressing violations of human rights, and ensuring transparency, accountability, and non-discrimination (Ibid.). Attribute 3 assesses the extent to which a health governance program contributes to social justice in development, as measured by such indicators as equality of opportunity in health, equality of access to resources and public goods, and reducing marginalization of least developed and vulnerable countries, as well as "safety nets to provide for the needs of vulnerable populations in times of natural, financial or other crisis" and "[e]limination of sexual exploitation and human trafficking, child labour, and slum housing conditions" (Ibid.).

Since the Task Force completed its work in 2010, the HRC and the UN General Assembly have adopted a series of resolutions calling for further study and refinement of the right to development criteria, and the OHCHR published a 2013 compendium of essays and analyses, *Realizing the Right to Development: Essays in Commemoration of 25 Years of the United Nations Declaration on the Right to Development* (OHCHR 2013). In a remarkably frank assessment, the then High Commissioner opened the compendium by stating:

Since the adoption of that landmark document [the 1986 UN Declaration], a debate has been raging in the halls of the United Nations and beyond. On one side, proponents of the right to development assert its relevance (or even primacy) and, on the other, sceptics (and rejectionists) relegate this right to secondary importance, or even deny its very existence. Unfortunately, while generating plenty of academic interest and stimulating political theatre, that debate has done little to free the right to development from the conceptual mud and political quicksand in which it has been mired all these years (Pillay 2013, iii).

After reviewing the history of the Declaration, its underlying principles, and the related challenges of international cooperation, this OHCHR study focused on implementing the right through indicators, the MDGs, national experiences, the African Charter on Human and Peoples' Rights, and the Task Force's assessment criteria. A chapter on the lessons learned by the Task Force from efforts to operationalize the Declaration identifies seven features that have hampered progress: (1) the absence of explicit reference to human rights in the MDGs;[8] (2) the deeper structural impediments to global economic justice, which the human rights mechanisms of the UN are unable to change; (3) the resistance from states and relevant institutions to addressing trade and lending from a right to development perspective; (4) the resistance by some states to the use of measurement tools; (5) the ambiguity of "global partnership"; (6) the lack of policy coherence and incentives to move from commitment to practice; and (7) the politicization of the necessary balancing of national and international responsibilities to realize the right to development. The OHCHR study concluded by calling "for a transformative Post-2015 Development Agenda" (OHCHR 2013, 496). When the post-2015 SDGs were passed, the Human Rights Council "[w]elcom[ed] the adoption of the 2030 Agenda for Sustainable Development, and emphasiz[ed] that the 2030 Agenda is informed by the Declaration on the Right to Development and that the right to development provides a vital enabling environment for the full realization of the Sustainable Development Goals" (HRC 2016b, preamble).

In an effort to apply the SDGs to the right to development, the Chair-Rapporteur of the OEWG submitted, at the request of OEWG, a set of "Standards for the implementation of the right to development" (HRC 2016a). While acknowledging that the report of the Task Force was "also relevant" to the preparation of standards, the OEWG proposed four new "standards for the implementation of the right to development," which utilize a different methodology from the attributes-criteria-subcriteria-indicators proposed by the Task Force.[9] Standard 4 seems the most relevant to health governance insofar as it mentions international cooperation relating to health in the context of SDG 3 and calls for such cooperation "to overcome transnational epidemics such as tuberculosis, malaria, hepatitis, AIDS and other communicable diseases" and to achieve "universal health coverage and access to quality, essential health-care services, including access to safe, effective, quality and affordable essential medicines and vaccines" (Ibid., para. 37).

The UN General Assembly thereafter instructed the OEWG to "finalize consideration of the criteria and operational subcriteria, preferably no later than

8. Despite this absence, the 2000 Millennium Declaration, on which the MDGs are based, reaffirms state commitment "to making the right to development a reality for everyone and to freeing the entire human race from want" (UN General Assembly 2000, para. 11).

9. Standard 1 relates to "the necessary political will and commitment to realize the right to development"; standard 2 to the need for states to "cooperate to create the political, economic and social environment necessary to allow the implementation of the right to development"; standard 3 to focusing on the individual and promoting the right to development "at the national level, which requires a comprehensive and inclusive approach based on good, responsible governance"; and standard 4 on addressing "the most basic or core human needs . . . : poverty, the right to food, water and sanitation, health, education, housing and gender equality" (Ibid., paras. 28–31).

the nineteenth session of the Working Group [2018]" and appointed a Special Rapporteur on the right to development, with a mandate, *inter alia*, to "contribute to the promotion, protection and fulfilment of the right to development in the context of the coherent and integrated implementation of the 2030 Agenda for Sustainable Development" (HRC 2016b, paras. 13–14).

CONCLUSION

Efforts to promote a rights-based approach to development have been more effective than those to promote the right to development. Introducing human rights into development planning, monitoring, implementation, and evaluation has made considerable strides since the 1993 Vienna Declaration and Programme of Action and the 2003 Common Understanding on Human Rights-Based Approaches to Development Cooperation and Programming. The right to development, however, has been less successful in meeting the objective, defined as early as 1979, to provide practical guidance for development activities. The emergence of the right to development in human rights diplomacy in the 1980s and subsequent efforts to translate this concept into meaningful development practice has been fraught with deep political divisions relating to aid effectiveness and national ownership, trade and investment, and lack of policy coherence and incentives to take practical steps. However, the claim that the norm is too vague to affect practice loses credibility in light of the work of the Independent Expert, the Task Force, the OHCHR Secretariat, and numerous scholars. The use of indicators and the drafting of a treaty on this right have been considered by some as obstacles to progress and by others as essential tools of its effectiveness.

Under these conditions, it is not surprising that economic institutions of significance to global health governance have not found it necessary or expedient to draw on the right to development to set priorities and guide practice and resource allocation for global health. Nevertheless, of the ten "global partnerships" the Task Force examined from the perspective of the right to development, the three relating to global health governance proved to be the most in agreement with the criteria, identifying how policy, processes, and outcomes can be improved by drawing on the right to development. Without incentives or instructions from their governing bodies, however, it is unlikely that this right will be prominent as a normative framework guiding institutions of health governance. Rather than relying on the political process of the OEWG and the UN General Assembly, those economic institutions with responsibilities for global health governance might find in the thirty years of efforts to promote this right a series of specific suggestions regarding the means and methods of translating the aspirations of the right to development into development practice, including in economic governance for global health.

REFERENCES

Alston, Philip. 2005. "Ships Passing in the Night: The Current State of the Human Rights and Development Debate Seen Through the Lens of the Millennium Development Goals." *Human Rights Quarterly* 27: 755–829.

Anand, Sudhir and Amartya K. Sen. 1994. *Sustainable Human Development: Concepts and Priorities*. New York: UNDP Human Development Office.

Commission on Human Rights. 1977. 21 February. Resolution 4 (XXXIII).

Commission on Human Rights. 1981. 11 March. Resolution 36 (XXXVII).

Commission on Human Rights. 1998. "Right to Development." 22 April. Resolution 1998/72.

Commission on Human Rights. 2000. "Report of the independent expert on the right to development, Arjun Sengupta." 17 August. Doc. E/CN.4/RES/2000/5.

Commission on Human Rights. 2004a. "Right to Development." 13 April. Resolution 2004/7.

Commission on Human Rights. 2004b. "Right to Development, Report of the Working Group on the Right to Development on its fifth session." 18 March. UN Doc. E/CN.4/2004/23.

Commission on Human Rights. 2005a. "Report of the high-level task force on the implementation of the right to development on its second meeting." 8 December. UN Doc. E/CN.4/2005/WG.18/TF/3.

Commission on Human Rights. 2005b. "Right to Development, Report of the Working Group on the Right to Development on its sixth session." 3 March. UN Doc. E/CN.4/2005/25.

Crocker, David. 1992. "Functioning and Capability: The Foundation of Sen's and Nussbaum's Development Ethics." *Political Theory* 20(4): 584–612.

Daniels, Norman. 2005. "Fair Process in Patient Selection for Antiretroviral Treatment in WHO's Goal of 3 by 5." *The Lancet* 366(9480): 169–171.

Daniels, Norman, John Bryant, R. A. Castano, Octavio Gomez-Dantes, K. S. Khan, and Supasit Pannarunothai. 2000. "Benchmarks of Fairness for Health Care Reform: A Policy Tool for Developing Countries." *Bulletin of the World Health Organization* 78(6): 740–750.

Daniels, Norman, Walter Flores, Supasit Pannarunothai, Peter Ndumbe, John Bryant, T. Ngulube, and Yuankun Wang. 2005. "An Evidence-Based Approach to Benchmarking the Fairness of Health-Sector Reform in Developing Countries." *Bulletin of the World Health Organization* 83(7): 534–541.

Darrow, Mac. 2012. "The Millennium Development Goals: Milestones or Millstones? Human Rights Priorities for the Post-2015 Development." *Yale Human Rights and Development Law Journal* 15: 55–127.

ECOSOC (UN Economic and Social Council). 1979. "The international dimensions of the right to development as a human right in relation with other human rights based on international cooperation, including the right to peace, taking into account the requirement of the New International Economic Order and the fundamental human needs, Report of the Secretary-General." 2 January. UN Doc. E.CN.4/1334.

ECOSOC. 2016. "Report of the Inter-Agency and Expert Group on Sustainable Development Goal Indicators." 15 December. UN Doc. E/CN.3/2017/2.

Forman, Lisa. 2013. "The Intergovernmental Working Group on Public Health, Innovation and Intellectual Property." In *Realizing the Right to Development: Essays in Commemoration of 25 Years of the United Nations Declaration on the Right to Development* by OHCHR, 303–319. New York and Geneva: OHCHR.

Global Equity Gauge Alliance. 2003. *The Equity Gauge: Concepts, Principles, and Guidelines, A Guide for Social Policy Change in Health.* Global Equity Gauge Alliance.

HRC (UN Human Rights Council). 2007a. "Report of the High Level Task Force on the Implementation of the Right to Development on its third session." 13 February. UN Doc. A/HRC/4/WG.2/TF/2.

HRC. 2007b. "Report of the Working Group on the Right to Development on its eighth session." 14 March. UN Doc. A/HRC/4/47.

HRC. 2009a. "High-level task force (HLTF) on the Implementation of the Right to Development, Technical Mission Report: Global Partnerships on Access to Essential Medicines." 31 March. UN Doc. A/HRC/12/WG.2/TF/CRP.1.

HRC. 2009b. "Report of the high-level task force on the implementation of the right to development on its fifth session." 17 June. UN Doc. A/HRC/12/WG.2/TF/2.

HRC. 2010a. "Consolidation of findings of the high-level task force on the implementation of the right to development." 25 March. UN Doc. A/HRC/15/WG.2/TF/2/Add.1.

HRC. 2010b. "Report of the high-level task force on the implementation of the right to development on its sixth session." 8 March. UN Doc. A/HRC/15/WG.2/TF/2.Add.2.

HRC. 2016a. "Report of the Chair-Rapporteur of the Working Group on the Right to Development, Standards for the implementation of the right to development." 16 March. UN Doc. A/HRC/WG.2/17/2.

HRC. 2016b. "The Right to Development." 29 September. Resolution 33/14.

HRCA (Human Rights Council of Australia). 1995. *The Rights Way to Development: A Human Rights Approach to Development Assistance.* Sydney: HRCA.

HRCA. 1998. *Manual for a Human Rights Approach to Development Assistance.* Sydney: HRCA.

Kim, Jim Yong, Joyce V. Millen, Alex Irwin, and John Gershman. 2000. *Dying for Growth: Global Inequality and the Health of the Poor.* Monroe, Maine: Common Courage Press.

Krieger, Nancy. 2000. "Discrimination and Health." In *Social Epidemiology*, edited by Lisa F. Berkman and Ichiro Kawachi, 36–75. Oxford: Oxford University Press.

Krieger, Nancy. 2001. "Commentary: Society, Biology, and the Logic of Social Epidemiology." *International Journal of Epidemiology* 30(1): 44–46.

Marks, Stephen P. 2004. "The Human Right to Development: Between Rhetoric and Reality." *Harvard Human Rights Journal* 17: 137–168.

Marks, Stephen P. 2010. "Obligations to Implement the Right to Development: Political, Legal, and Philosophical Rationales." In *Development as a Human Right: Legal, Political and Economic Dimensions, Second Edition*, edited by Bård Anders Andreassen and Stephen P. Marks, 73–100. Brussels: Intersentia.

M'Baye, Kéba. 1972. "Le Droit au Développement Comme un Droit de L'Homme [The Right to Development as a Human Right], Leçon inaugurale de la Troisième Session d'enseignement de l'Institut International des droits de l'Homme [Inaugural Address of the Third Teaching Session of the International Institute of Human Rights]." *Revue des droits de l'homme* 5: 503.

Nussbaum, Martha. 1988. "Nature, Function and Capability: Aristotle on Political Distribution." In *Oxford Studies in Ancient Philosophy, Supplementary Volume*, edited by Julia Annas and Robert H. Grimm, 145–184. Oxford: Clarendon Press.

Nussbaum, Martha. 1993. "Non-Relative Virtues: An Aristotelian Approach." In *The Quality of Life*, edited by Martha Nussbaum and Amartya Sen. Oxford: Clarendon Press.

Nussbaum, Martha. 1999. "Capabilities, Human Rights, and the Universal Declaration." In *The Future of International Human Rights*, edited by Burns H. Weston and Stephen P. Marks, 25–64. Transnational Publishers.

Nussbaum, Martha. 2003. "Capabilities as Fundamental Entitlements: Sen and Social Justice." *Feminist Economics* 9(2–3): 33–59.

OHCHR (Office of the High Commissioner for Human Rights). 2006. Frequently Asked Questions on a Human Rights-Based Approach to Development Cooperation. Geneva and New York: OHCHR.

OHCHR. 2007. *Annual Report 2006.* Available at: http://www.ohchr.org/Documents/ AboutUs/annualreport2006.pdf.

OHCHR. 2008. *The Right to Health, Fact Sheet No. 31.* Geneva: OHCHR.

OHCHR. 2013. *Realizing the Right to Development: Essays in Commemoration of 25 Years of the United Nations Declaration on the Right to Development.* New York and Geneva: OHCHR.

OECD-DAC (Organization for Economic Co-operation and Development—Development Assistance Committee). 2007. *Action-Oriented Policy Paper on Human Rights and Development.* Available at http://www.oecd.org/development/governance-development/ 39350774.pdf

Pillay, Navanethem. 2013. "Foreword." In *Realizing the Right to Development: Essays in Commemoration of 25 Years of the United Nations Declaration on the Right to Development* by OHCHR. New York and Geneva: OHCHR.

Ruger, Jennifer Prah. 2004. "Health and Social Justice." *The Lancet* 364(9439): 1075–1080.

Ruger, Jennifer Prah. 2006. "Toward a Theory of a Right to Health: Capability and Incompletely Theorized Agreements." *Yale Journal of Law and Humanities* 17(2): 273–326.

Ruger, Jennifer Prah. 2009. *Health and Social Justice.* Oxford University Press.

Ruger, Jennifer Prah. 2012. "Global Health Justice and Governance." *American Journal of Bioethics* 12(12): 35–54.

Salomon, Margot E. 2010. "International Human Rights Obligations in Context: Structural Obstacles and the Demands of Global Justice." In *Development as a Human Right: Legal, Political, and Economic Dimensions*, edited by Bård A. Andreassen and Stephen P. Marks, 121–148. Intersentia, Antwerp, Belgium.

Sen, Amartya. 1985. *Commodities and Capabilities.* Amsterdam: North-Holland.

Sen, Amartya. 1998. *Development as Freedom.* New York: Knopf.

Sen, Amartya. 1999. *Commodities and Capabilities.* Oxford University Press.

Sen, Amartya. 2004. Preface to *Public Health, Ethics, and Equity*, edited by Sudhir Anand and Fabienne Peter. Oxford University Press.

Sen, Amartya. 2005. "Human Rights and Capabilities." *Journal of Human Development* 6(2): 151–166.

UN (United Nations). 1990. "Annotations to the Declaration on the Right to Development and related United Nations System Instruments, Resolutions and Reports." 8–12 January. UN Doc. HR/RD/1990/CONF.l.

UN General Assembly. 1986. "Declaration on the Right to Development." 4 December. Resolution 41/128.

UN General Assembly. 1993. "High Commissioner for the promotion and protection of all human rights." 20 December. Resolution 48/141.

UN General Assembly. 1994. "An Agenda for Development, Report of the Secretary-General." 6 May. UN Doc. A/48/935.

UN General Assembly. 1997. "Renewing the United Nations: A Programme for Reform: Report of the Secretary-General." 14 July. UN Doc. A/51/950.

UN General Assembly. 1998. "Agenda Item 10, Annual Report on the Work of the Organization." 21 September. UN Doc. A/53/PV.7.

UN General Assembly. 2000. "United Nations Millennium Declaration." 18 September. UN Doc. A/RES/55/2.

UN General Assembly. 2001. Road map towards the implementation of the United Nations Millennium Declaration. Report of the Secretary-General. 6 September. UN Doc. A/56/326.

UN General Assembly. 2005. "In Larger Freedom: Towards Development, Security and Human Rights for All. Report of the Secretary-General." 21 March. UN Doc. A/59/2005.

UN General Assembly. 2008. "Report of the Special Rapporteur on the right of everyone to the enjoyment of the highest attainable standard of physical and mental health." 11 August. UN Doc. A/63/263, annex.

UN General Assembly. 2015. "Transforming our world: the 2030 Agenda for Sustainable Development." 25 September. Resolution 70/1.

UNDG. 2003. *The Human Rights Based Approach to Development Cooperation Towards a Common Understanding Among UN Agencies*. Available at: https://undg.org/document/the-human-rights-based-approach-to-development-cooperation-towards-a-common-understanding-among-un-agencies/.

UNDP (UN Development Programme). 1998. *Integrating Human Rights with Sustainable Human Development, A UNDP Policy Document*. New York: UN Development Programme.

UNDP. 2000. *Human Development Report 2000*. New York: Oxford University Press.

UNDP. 2001. *Human Development Report 2001*. New York: Oxford University Press.

WHA (World Health Assembly). 61st session. 2008. Resolution 61.21. "Global Strategy and Plan of Action on Public Health, Innovation and Intellectual Property." 24 May.

WHA. 66th Session. 2013. Resolution 66.1. "Twelfth General Programme of Work, 2014–2019." 24 May.

WHO (World Health Organization). 2014. *Twelfth General Programme of Work 2014–2019 Not merely the absence of disease*. World Health Organization. Available at: http://www.who.int/about/resources_planning/twelfth-gpw/en/.

World Conference on Human Rights. 1993. "Vienna Declaration and Programme of Action." 25 June. UN Doc. A/CONF.157/23.

16

The World Bank

Contested Institutional Progress in Rights-Based Health Discourse

YUSRA RIBHI SHAWAR AND JENNIFER PRAH RUGER

Over the last several decades, the World Bank has played a central role in global health funding and policy, and has been increasingly recognized as a prominent leader in global health governance. While the World Bank has positively impacted the health of those residing in low- and middle-income countries (LMICs), it has also attracted attention over its human rights record, with the United Nations (UN) Special Rapporteur on extreme poverty and human rights declaring the institution to be a "human rights free zone." Despite increasingly addressing human rights in its discourse—as reflected in the institution's work to end poverty and as expressed by its leadership in official reports and public speeches—the World Bank continues to deny a formal legal obligation for mitigating human rights risks and lacks any systematic examination of the potential social harm that it sponsors. Internal constraints limit the World Bank's ability to do so, where its Articles of Agreement explicitly forbid the institution from interfering in a state's internal political affairs, making it unclear if human rights is a part of the institution's mandate. This denial of human rights obligations stands in contrast to the World Bank's support of human rights, as reflected in its commitment to helping countries achieve universal health coverage and in its "twin goals" of ending extreme poverty and promoting shared prosperity—all of which fundamentally contribute to the realization of social and economic rights. The implications of this tension are especially important to examine given the World Bank's central and growing role in global health governance.

This chapter analyzes the ways in which rights-based approaches have evolved and are currently incorporated into World Bank policies and practices, examining achievements, obstacles, and opportunities for global health promotion. After discussing the creation of the World Bank and its institutional structure in Part I, this chapter examines the progression of human rights discourse in the institution in Part II, with particular attention to rights-based discourse in the World Bank's global health programs, policies, and lending. Part III assesses current efforts by the World Bank to mainstream human rights in its global health strategies and programs. Thereafter, Part IV analyzes the institutional factors that have shaped, both facilitating and inhibiting, its rights-based discourse, policies, and practice for public health advancement. This chapter concludes that recent developments may support renewed conversation about the World Bank's role in supporting human rights—a necessary precondition for overcoming entrenched institutional challenges.

I. THE WORLD BANK'S ESTABLISHMENT AND INSTITUTIONAL STRUCTURE

An independent specialized UN agency, the World Bank was created, along with the International Monetary Fund (IMF), at the Bretton Woods Conference in July 1944. Originally named the International Bank for Reconstruction and Development, the World Bank Group is an umbrella enterprise composed of five member institutions. The largest of these institutions are the International Bank for Reconstruction (IBRD), which offers loans to middle-income countries, and the International Development Association (IDA), which offers concessional loans and grants to the world's poorest developing countries (Kapur, Lewis, and Webb 1997).[1] Both institutions share the same leadership and staff, follow the same policy guidelines, adhere to similar project implementation and appraisal procedures, and have a mandate to assist development efforts in member states. Each of the World Bank organizations operate according to procedures established by the Articles of Agreement, which outline the conditions of membership and general principles of the World Bank's organization, management, and operations (World Bank 2012a).

The World Bank's 189 country shareholders are represented by a Board of Governors, which is predominately composed of member states' ministers of finance or development (World Bank 2017a). These Governors delegate specific duties to the World Bank's Board of twenty-five Executive Directors, who are responsible for selecting the President for a five-year, renewable term and approving all institutional loans and policies (World Bank 2017c). Voting power and Executive Director designations are based on member state financial contributions. Accordingly, the United States is represented by one Executive Director and holds 20 percent of the vote, while forty-seven sub-Saharan African countries hold only 7 percent of the vote and together have only two Executive Directors (Bretton Woods Project 2005).

Beginning operations in 1946, the World Bank's original mandate was to finance the postwar European country economy, focusing on large capital and infrastructure projects, but over time, the World Bank's focus has turned to addressing poverty in LMICs (Kapur, Lewis, and Webb 1997). Its mission to end poverty is fundamentally

---

1. The three other World Bank institutions are the International Finance Corporation (IFC), the Multilateral Investment Guarantee Agency (MIGA), and the International Centre for Settlement of Investment Disputes (ICSID).

connected with its mission to improve global health, and as a consequence, it has become one of the largest contributors to health-related projects. The World Bank contributes to global health by funding, generating knowledge, and providing policy and technical advice in areas including health systems strengthening (Ruger 2005a; Clinton and Sridhar 2017). It manages an active Health, Nutrition, and Population (HNP) portfolio of US$11.5 billon (World Bank, 2017a), has served as the world's largest external funder of HIV/AIDS programs and plays one of the most significant roles in global health cooperation. In fact, the World Bank distributed approximately $33.8 billion in health grants and loans from 1990 through 2011, in addition to $2.8 billion through in-kind support (Institute for Health Metrics and Evaluation 2014; Baeza 2012). Between 2014 and 2016, the institution supported essential health, nutrition, and population services for approximately 311 million people (World Bank 2016c).

II. THE EVOLUTION OF HUMAN RIGHTS WITHIN THE WORLD BANK

While the World Bank continues to maintain neutrality on a legal obligation to human rights, the institution's engagement with rights has evolved, with attention and incorporation of human rights in its policies, practices, and institutional culture oscillating over time.

A. An Ongoing Tension between Legal Obligations and an Evolving Practical Mandate

The World Bank's discourse on human rights has significantly evolved since its establishment. The institution's engagement with human rights represents a long-standing tension between its legal obligations, as set out in its foundational documents, and its evolving practical mandate, as reflected in the type of work that it has chosen to engage in over the years.

The World Bank is fundamentally opposed to embracing a legal obligation for human rights (OECD and the World Bank 2013). This opposition stems from its Articles of Agreement, which clearly forbid the World Bank from intervening in a country's internal political affairs and prohibit decision-making based on political considerations:

> The Bank, its President, officers and staff shall not interfere in the political affairs of any member, nor shall they be influenced in their decisions by the political character of the member concerned. Only economic considerations shall be relevant to their decisions. Such considerations shall be weighed impartially in order to achieve and carry out the purpose and functions of the Bank (World Bank 1945, art. VIII, sec. 5(f)).

In the 1990s, the World Bank's legal counsel interpreted this provision to mean that the institution limits its consideration of human rights only to those political issues that bring economic development (Fujita 2011).

However, despite not adopting any explicit human rights requirements, the World Bank has a *de facto* concern for human rights, as manifested in the institution's programs and initiatives that concern, among other things, anti-corruption, post-conflict stability, and public health (Kim 2016). The World Bank's concern for human rights is also evident in its recent commitments to ending extreme poverty, promoting shared prosperity, and supporting universal health coverage—all of which are inherent pillars of the realization of social and economic rights (Osamani 2010). As noted in the World Bank's report, *Development and Human Rights: The Role of the World Bank*:

> The Bank contributes directly to the fulfillment of many rights articulated in the Universal Declaration [of Human Rights]. Through its support of primary education, health care and nutrition, sanitation, housing, and the environment, the Bank has helped hundreds of millions of people attain crucial economic and social rights (Gaeta and Vasilara 1998, 3).

The World Bank's evolving engagement with human rights over the years is reflected, sometimes explicitly, in the World Bank's policies and procedures. This support for the realization of human rights is specifically reflected in several areas that directly or indirectly underlie health, including involuntary resettlement (World Bank 2016b), gender equality (World Bank 2003), as well as indigenous, disabled, and HIV/AIDS-affected populations (World Bank 2005b; WHO and World Bank 2011; World Bank 2012b). In addition, some of the World Bank's operational procedures integrate a concern for human rights in an implicit manner. For example, human rights principles are reflected in the World Bank's Social Development Strategy, which offers various protections and safeguards for people and the environment impacted by Bank-funded projects. The Social Development Strategy stresses a commitment to meaningful consultation, transparency, non-discrimination, empowerment, social inclusion, and accountability (World Bank 2005a). This concern for human rights is also exemplified in the World Bank's Inspection Panel, which investigates stakeholder grievances and has progressively included aspects of human rights. The Inspection Panel serves as an accountability mechanism, investigating—when prompted—the World Bank's compliance with its own procedures and policies as a means to protect people and the environment impacted by its projects (Inspection Panel 2017). Accordingly, the Inspection Panel enables individuals to make direct grievances in instances where they believe that a World Bank funded project had or would negatively affect them (Fox 2000).

B. A Timeline of Human Rights Discourse in the World Bank

There has been intensified discussion within the World Bank about the relationship of human rights to its health-related development work. However, the institution's engagement with the subject over the last quarter century continues to be characterized as unsystematic, unofficial, and independent of international human rights law (Zhou 2012; Clark 2002; Ball 2008). The World Bank's changing human rights discourse is seen over two time periods: between 1945 and 1990, which was characterized by a rejection of human rights considerations; and the 1990s through 2010, when the World Bank expanded its mandate to incorporate initiatives of a political nature and during which there were openings to consider human rights.

1. 1945–1990: Resistance to Consideration of Human Rights

In the first forty-five years of the World Bank's existence, there was little consideration of a rights-based discourse, if not an explicit resistance to considering human rights obligations. As stipulated in its Articles of Agreement, the World Bank saw itself as an economic development agency that did not have a role in the political affairs of the countries with which it was engaged. In fact, the World Bank ignored the Universal Declaration of Human Rights (UDHR), which countries unanimously adopted shortly after the World Bank's creation (UN General Assembly 1948). In addition, the World Bank declined an invitation from the UN Commission on Human Rights to participate in early debates on the International Covenant on Economic, Social and Cultural Rights (ICESCR) (Fujita 2011).[2] Citing the Articles of Agreement, the World Bank viewed human rights to be outside its mandate and did not see any relationship between the rights that would become part of the ICESCR and its institutional activities (UNHCR 1951). The 1960s would mark the World Bank's first consideration of human rights in its lending practices (Brodnig 2002). Despite the UN General Assembly requesting that the World Bank halt its loans to South Africa (because of its apartheid policies) and Portugal (because of its colonial policies), the World Bank decided—in defiance of a series of UN resolutions—to approve several loans to these countries, citing the institution's apolitical character (Bleicher 1970).

Under Robert McNamara's presidency (1968–1981), the World Bank formally became involved in global health with the establishment of what became known as the Health, Nutrition, and Population (HNP) Department in 1979. This period was also characterized by the Bank's shift from project- to policy-based lending and its adoption of structural adjustment policies (SAPs) in the 1980s (World Bank 1981). These developments marked the institution's growing work in social development and engagement with the political affairs of the countries to which it lent. The World Bank became centrally involved in the creation of public sector policies and institutions in order to ensure "enabling environments for economic development and make reforms politically viable" (Brodnig 2002, 4). In fact, a 1989 World Bank study on the outlook of sub-Saharan Africa development highlighted "good governance" as fundamental to development (World Bank 1989).

After decades of adhering strictly to its economics mandate, avoiding political affairs and resisting a human rights-based approach, the World Bank began to recognize its value to areas of national politics and law that were historically understood to be outside of the scope of its Articles of Agreement. The World Bank developed

2. At the time the World Bank declined, the Commission on Human Rights was debating the "International Covenant on Human Rights," as it was not until 1952 that states decided to develop two separate covenants: the International Covenant on Civil and Political Rights and the International Covenant on Economic, Social and Cultural Rights.

a set of "safeguard" policies in the 1980s—in response to considerable pressure from its own stakeholders and non-governmental organizations (NGOs)—that considered the unintended social and environmental impacts of the institution's investments (Seifman et al. 2015). Yet, the World Bank remained hesitant about formally conceding a connection between political and civil rights, economic development, and good governance (Brodnig 2002; Herbertson, Thompson, and Goodland 2010).

Highlighting the importance of economic and social rights, the World Bank's adoption of SAPs had large negative public health implications. While the World Bank anticipated that SAPs would improve debt repayments, reduce fiscal deficits, encourage private sector investment, and consequently stimulate national economic growth, with subsequent "trickle-down" benefits to poor and vulnerable populations, emergent evidence of their impact was starkly contrary (Fujita 2011). Instead, many scholars concluded that SAPs had broad, negative social impacts, increased poverty, exacerbated inequalities, and disproportionately affected the health and welfare of children and vulnerable populations (Macedo 1988; Kanji, Kanji, and Manji 1991; Loewenson 1993; Kim et al. 2002). In response to this criticism, the World Bank deflected responsibility regarding the impacts of SAPs on to the beneficiary states and the societies that implement them, insisting that "it is not . . . economic reform lending that should raise concerns about human rights, but rather, how those programs are implemented, and what measures are taken" (Gaeta and Vasilara 1988, 8).

2. 1990s–2010: OPENINGS FOR CONSIDERATION OF HUMAN RIGHTS

During the 1990s and 2000s, the World Bank became increasingly prominent in its global health work, emerging as one of the largest global health financers (Stout and Johnston 1999). In 1993, the institution's annual World Development Report was dedicated to health, and in it, the World Bank introduced the concept of the Disability-Adjusted Life Year (DALY), a measure of the difference between the current health status of the population and an ideal health situation where a population lives to an advanced age, free of disease and disability (World Bank 1993). While recognized as an innovative new measure in global health, human rights proponents have widely criticized the DALY measure for devaluing the disabled, young, and elderly, as well as women and future generations (Anand and Hanson 1997).

This time period also saw a shift in the World Bank's human rights engagement. The debate about human rights in development emerged as a new interdisciplinary field, and World Bank staff increasingly came to realize that development could not occur without consideration of the economic consequences of human rights violations (NTF and World Bank 2012; Sarfaty 2012). Much of this shift occurred under the leadership of President James Wolfensohn (1995–2005). An outspoken critic of corruption, Wolfensohn paved the way for governance initiatives and considerably expanded public sector reforms targeting civil service, public finance, and tax administration (Marouf 2010; Ruger 2005b). Perhaps most crucially, his leadership catalyzed a period of greater World Bank discussion on human rights, as reflected in the early work of the Inspection Panel, the influential legal opinions and scholarly work of the World Bank's General Counsel, and the emergence of institutional publications that would lay the groundwork for applying human rights principles in the work and mission of the World Bank.

Just prior to Wolfensohn's appointment, the World Bank created the Inspection Panel in 1993 to address growing public pressure for greater transparency and accountability at the World Bank (Bradlow 1994). For the first time, the World Bank had to confront cases that raised human rights concerns. While the Inspection Panel has seldom been requested to evaluate claims that are explicitly portrayed in human rights terms, several Panel decisions addressing underlying determinants of health have highlighted instances in which World Bank procedures and policies required the World Bank to account for human rights (Herz and Perrault 2009). For example, in its investigation of the *Chad: Petroleum Development and Pipeline Project* claim, the Inspection Panel in 2002 noted that human rights are implicitly rooted in various World Bank projects, and that the institution should consider the wider human rights implications—not just when they have a direct economic effect on the project but when they "impede the implementation of the Project in a manner compatible with the Bank's policies" (World Bank 2002, para. 215; Inspection Panel 2009). In the *China: Western Poverty Reduction Project* claim, the Inspection Panel similarly concluded that the World Bank becomes obligated to evaluate a country's general state of human rights and governance when planning and carrying out its projects (World Bank 2000). Finally, the Inspection Panel highlighted the World Bank's obligation to account for the human rights protections in a country's constitutions or laws in the *Honduras Land Administration Project* claim, noting the World Bank's need to guarantee that its funding not undermine a country's international human rights commitments (World Bank 2007).

A second key development in shaping the World Bank's human rights discourse during this time was the influential legal opinions and scholarly work of the World Bank's General Counsel. Particularly influential was General Counsel Ibrahim Shihata (1983–2000), who expanded the World Bank's scope of work in the early 1990s, recognizing the relevance of human rights in development policy (Shihata 1995; Shihata 2000; Shihata 2003). In expanding the World Bank's efforts, Shihata's scholarly work and memos created a legal space for engagement in topics that were once considered too political (i.e., anti-corruption initiatives, legal and judicial reform) (Sarfaty 2012). Applying human rights to World Bank policy, the UN Special Rapporteur on extreme poverty and human rights noted that "Shihata more than any other person in the Bank . . . shaped the institution's thinking about human rights" (Alston 2014, 3). In an interview in 1994, Shihata discussed his perspective on the World Bank's role in promoting human rights:

> In [engaging with governance issues that have direct economic effects], the Bank will be protecting human rights without getting involved in politics. If you advocate the rule of law (good civil service, accountability, transparency in financial transactions), you will be promoting the basis of political human rights. If you give a country money to improve their civil service, to review their legal system, to improve their judiciary, etc., you are in fact laying the groundwork for expanded human rights, but without exceeding your legal mandate (Becker and Milobsky 1994, 28).

Roberto Dañino, who served as the World Bank's General Counsel from 2003 until 2006, also played a crucial role in extending the space for human rights discourse inside and outside the institution, giving speeches on the importance of human rights to the institution's work and seeking to strengthen the institution's relationship with the Office of the UN High Commissioner for Human Rights (OHCHR) (Sarfaty 2009). Within a month of arriving at the World Bank, Dañino, with the support of Wolfensohn, created a committee to craft a strategy paper on the World Bank and human rights. However, the resulting paper—which recommended the adoption of human rights principles—was rejected by the Board of Directors development committee in June 2003 (Herbertson, Thompson, and Goodland 2010). After reviewing multiple drafts, senior officials, "got cold feet and began to backpedal on passing a paper on human rights" before ultimately concluding that additional analyses were needed (Sarfaty 2009, 661). On his final day as General Counsel, Dañino distributed an internal legal opinion that reflected increasing momentum to consider human rights, concluding that the "Articles of Agreement permit, and in some cases require, the Bank to recognize the human rights dimensions of its development policies and activities" (Dañino 2006, 9). Two of Dañino's points were similar to those made by Shihata: first, the World Bank may help a state realize its own human rights obligations where these commitments "have an economic impact or relevance"; and second, the World Bank should take human rights into consideration when "a country has violated or not fulfilled its obligations"—again in the instance that they have an economic impact (Ibid., 7). Dañino's third point, encapsulated in the closing statement of his legal opinion, went beyond any point that Shihata had made, advancing that, independent of economic impact, the World Bank should disengage in "egregious situations, where extensive violations of human rights reach pervasive proportions" (Ibid., 8). Where Dañino's legal opinion was not presented to the World Bank's Board of Directors, as senior World Bank staff recognized that the opinion's chance of approval was minute given the Board's disagreements on human rights (Sarfaty 2009), General Counsel Ana Palacio (2006–2008) interpreted Dañino's opinion as permitting but not requiring the World Bank to act in relation to human rights (Palacio 2006). Following the Wolfensohn era, this Palacio interpretation reflected the institution's slowing momentum for considering a systematic approach to human rights integration within the World Bank.

A third key human rights development was the emergence of two World Bank publications—*Development and Human Rights: The Role of the World Bank* (1998) and *The World Bank and Human Rights: Nordic-Baltic Working Paper* (2005)— which were solicited by President Wolfensohn from the Nordic countries. In the report on *Development and Human Rights*, the World Bank recognized that "creating the conditions for attainment of human rights is a central and irreducible goal of development" and that "the world now accepts that sustainable development is impossible without human rights" (Gaeta and Vasilara 1998, 2). Subsequent to this report, the World Bank began periodically mentioning human rights in official speeches and institutional documents, and a growing collection of research emerged from the institution that provided examples where the promotion of civil liberties and human rights led to stronger economic performance (Herbertson, Thompson, and Goodland 2010; Isham, Kaufmann, and Pritchett 1997; Kaufmann, Kray and Zoido-Lobaton 1999; Kaufmann, Kraay, and Mastruzzi 2004). Nevertheless, the Board of Directors continued to resist the formal integration of human rights into World Bank policy (Herbertson, Thompson, and Goodland 2010). Adding to this debate in 2005, *The World Bank and Human Rights* discussed the importance of social and economic rights—including the right to health—and was presented to President Paul Wolfowitz (2005–2007) in the hope of creating a unique initiative that would develop a more informed view of human rights within the World Bank (Sarfaty 2009). However, internal politics and the lack of an internal champion for human rights after Wolfensohn's departure prevented the launching of what would become in 2009 the Nordic Trust Fund (Ibid.).

Momentum for integrating human rights in the World Bank slowed after Wolfensohn's departure and in some ways has since regressed. For example, from 2009 to 2013, the World Bank invested $50 billion into projects classified as "the highest risk for irreversible or unprecedented social or environmental impacts"—more than double the preceding five-year period (ICIJ 2017). Several recent projects funded by the World Bank, such as the Uganda Transport Sector Development Project and the Kenya Natural Resource Management Project, have been shown to have major detrimental impacts on the health and human rights of affected populations (World Bank 2015; Kushner et al. 2015). It is estimated that approximately 3.4 million people were economically or physically displaced by World Bank–funded projects between 2004 and 2013 (Chavkin et al. 2015).

III. CURRENT EFFORTS TO MAINSTREAM HUMAN RIGHTS IN THE WORLD BANK

There was renewed optimism for the advancement of global health and human rights when Jim Kim was appointed World Bank President in 2012. Unlike World Bank presidents of the past, Kim is a medical doctor and anthropologist, and his humanitarian experiences and perspectives were seen as unique qualifications. A co-founder of Partners in Health, a global health organization dedicated to improving the health of poor populations, he was once a major critic of the World Bank (Kim et al. 2002). As World Bank President, Kim has overseen and spearheaded significant changes in the World Bank. For example, he transferred $56 billion in loans and other types of resources in 2015—a significant share of the institution's funds—toward areas that fell outside the World Bank's traditional mandate—including climate change, Ebola control and prevention, and the circumstances underlying the Syrian refugee crisis (Rice 2016). Yet, despite expanding the institutional boundaries of the World Bank's mandate in these areas and being outspoken in his rhetoric concerning the "right to health" (Kim 2014), human rights proponents argue that Kim has not done enough to advance human rights application in World Bank practice (New York Times Editorial Board 2016; Rice 2016). Under Kim's leadership, the World Bank has advanced rights-based discourse and practice through the revision of the safeguard policies, the growing work of the Nordic Trust Fund (NTF), and the World Bank's support for universal health coverage.

The revision of safeguard policies represented an opportunity to integrate a commitment to human rights throughout the World Bank (Zhou 2012).[3] However, the newly approved Environmental and Social Framework (ESF) (World Bank 2016a), which was made official on August 4, 2016 and is expected to take effect in 2018, fell short of initial goals and disappointed human rights proponents (World Bank 2017f; Human Rights Watch 2016; Donnan 2016; Berry 2016). Under development for four years, this new framework incorporated some important reforms to the previous ad hoc and burdensome policies, including expanded protections related to discrimination, labor and working condition protections, and community health and safety standards (World Bank 2016a). Most directly addressing rights-based norms, one of the ten Environmental and Social Standards (ESS) explicitly addresses the "health, safety, and security risks and impacts on project-affected communities" (ESS4), with special attention to vulnerable populations (World Bank 2017g). While the framework explicitly references human rights in its overarching vision statement, the language of the ESS is non-binding and presents human rights as aspirational values—excluding any human rights commitments and standards (World Bank 2016a). In addition, the new policy effectively shifts responsibility and liability for harms away from the World Bank and onto borrower countries (Berry 2016). This is a significant concern for human rights proponents because borrower countries often lack the political will, as well as the financial and technical ability, to ensure that monitoring and/or grievance mechanisms operate effectively to protect vulnerable populations that may be negatively impacted by World Bank projects (Ibid.). Furthermore, the new policy essentially shifts much of the World Bank's due diligence on projects until after they are approved, allowing, for example, for governments to delay creating relocation plans for communities impacted by an infrastructure project until after a loan's approval (Donnan 2016).

One of the most promising institutional developments for advancing human rights discourse at the World Bank has come from member countries—through the work of the NTF. The NTF was proposed in 2006 and became operational in 2009, with agreed contributions from Denmark, Iceland, Norway, Finland, Sweden, and later Germany (World Bank 2017d). It was created as an internal "knowledge and learning initiative" to assist in cultivating an up-to-date view among World Bank staff on how human rights relate to their work and goals (OECD and the World Bank 2013). The establishment of the NTF, however, was not without controversy and was initially opposed by World Bank President Robert Zoellick (2007–2012) (MacCuish 2010). In order to mitigate opposition from the World Bank's leadership, the lawyers working on the NTF's plan of action advanced an instrumental approach to rights and strategically decided on an incremental strategy that focused on individual pilot projects instead of an institution-wide human rights policy (Sarfaty 2009). As part of the compromise for its establishment and after a three-year delay, the originally proposed Justice and Human Rights Trust Fund was

---

3. Safeguard policies present an opportunity for human rights mainstreaming because they aim to help identify and minimize project-related harms to people and the environment. These policies can potentially be written in a way that prevents adverse impacts on human rights.

renamed the Nordic Trust Fund and finally launched in 2009. To date, the NTF holds $34.8 million in total funds and is currently in its second phase of operation (World Bank 2017e). The NTF achieves its objectives in two main ways: the first is a Knowledge and Partnership Program, which engages partners and human rights experts in the creation of knowledge at the intersection of human rights and development through the presentation of learning events; the second is a Grant Program, which provides World Bank teams with financial and technical support to examine the role of human rights in their work. Following a request for proposals from World Bank teams to the Grant Program, grants up to $250,000 are awarded for a two-year implementation period to explore the operational and/or analytical links between a team's work and human rights.[4] Some of these projects are explicitly health related, including, among others, examining the operationalization of gender in health, considering what a human rights-based approach can offer maternal and reproductive health projects, and producing standards of practice that add a human rights perspective in adolescent, sexual, and reproductive health projects (Ibid.). While the NTF is centrally involved in educating World Bank staff about human rights issues, NTF staff are prohibited from providing recommendations on the institution's policies (World Bank 2010).

Specific to global health, the World Bank's recent support of governments to achieve universal health coverage (UHC) is proving favorable to the advancement of human rights (World Bank 2017b), drawing on the right to health as set out in the ICESCR (Sridhar et al. 2015). In support of Sustainable Development Goal (SDG) 3, the World Bank has committed $15 billion over the next five years to undertakings fundamental to the realization of UHC (World Bank 2016c). Despite this financial commitment to UHC, there are concerns that the World Bank is undermining the human right to universal health care given its blanket promotion of public-private partnerships (PPPs) and performance-based financing in health. Given emergent evidence that these PPP approaches do not necessarily improve the practice of health workers, the performance of health facilities, or access to health services to poor communities, it is unclear whether this World Bank's strategy will lead to its intended rights-based result (Lethbridge 2017).

IV. FACTORS SHAPING HUMAN RIGHTS MAINSTREAMING

The World Bank's recent progress with respect to human rights discourse and practice has been supported by three key influences, while the institution's resistance to human rights in its global health work can be attributed to five underlying factors.

A. Facilitating Human Rights for Global Health

Three institutional factors have facilitated current human rights mainstreaming in the World Bank: (1) the work of the World Bank's NTF, (2) the advocacy of NGOs

---

4. Over the course of five grant rounds, the NTF has funded 122 grants throughout the World Bank (World Bank 2017e).

to engage the World Bank on human rights principles, and (3) a growing body of World Bank research on human rights.

1. THE NORDIC TRUST FUND

The NTF, which sidesteps the World Bank's lack of institutional policy on human rights, has been crucial to improving project-level rights protections. Although NTF cannot lobby for official World Bank policy changes, it provides an important platform to increase awareness about human rights and to showcase the application of a rights-based approach in World Bank projects (World Bank 2010). Although the impact of NTF on the World Bank has yet to be formally evaluated, NTF training and support can be an important catalyst to expand acceptance for and operationalization of human rights at the World Bank.

2. NGO ADVOCACY

NGO advocacy continues to put pressure on the World Bank to engage human rights principles in its work (Herbertson, Thompson, and Goodland 2010). Organizations such as Human Rights Watch, the International Consortium of Investigative Journalists (ICIJ), the Bretton Woods Project, and the Bank Information Center serve as important accountability mechanisms, monitoring and reporting on the negative impacts that certain World Bank projects have on the human rights of certain populations. By uncovering the adverse impacts of World Bank projects on human rights, these NGOs not only contribute to the improvement of the institution's existing accountability mechanisms (i.e., the Inspection Panel and the safeguard policies) but also help to create an evidence base for considering an alternative, more sustainable channel of accountability: an explicit institutional commitment to human rights.

3. HUMAN RIGHTS RESEARCH

Finally, the growing body of World Bank research that concerns human rights facilitates greater World Bank engagement with human rights norms. Some of this research comes out of the World Bank's Development Research Group, which has published studies on:

- rights-based and economic approaches to health care in developing countries (Gauri 2004),
- the use of legal strategies in bringing about social change and achieving economic and social rights (Brinks and Gauri 2012),
- the determinants of compliance with human rights treaties (Gauri 2011),
- the relevance of human rights indicators to development practice (McInerney-Lankford and Sano 2010), and
- the benefits, risks, and limitations of human rights-based approaches to development (Gauri and Gloppen 2012).

This research builds on past World Bank studies, which have found large, statistically significant effects of civil liberties on investment project rates of return (Kaufman 2005). Collectively, this empirical research on development outcomes provides important evidence for the institution to consider a stronger commitment to human rights in its operations.

B. Inhibiting Human Rights Mainstreaming in the World Bank

Despite these potential opportunities for raising the profile of human rights at the World Bank, there are several institutional factors that continue to fundamentally challenge commitment to human rights mainstreaming in the World Bank's global health work. These can be attributed to the World Bank's (1) unresolved legal constraints, (2) economist-dominated culture, (3) lack of staff knowledge about human rights application and policy, (4) opposition by some borrowing country stakeholders, and (5) competition with emerging development banks.

1. Unresolved Legal Constraints

A principal barrier to human rights integration in the World Bank is the Articles of Agreement. When the World Bank was established in 1945, its founding member countries purposefully restricted its mandate to economic activities as a means to protect state sovereignty (Kapur, Lewis, and Webb 1997). By explicitly prohibiting the World Bank's engagement in political activity, the Articles of Agreement have historically thwarted the institution's involvement with human rights, which have been understood as "political considerations" (Fujita 2011). Even as various legal counsels have taken no issue with the World Bank's engagement with political issues such as governance, corruption, citizen security, justice, and the rule of law, the interpretation of the Articles of Agreement—which is determined by a majority vote of the Executive Directors—has not altered the Bank's engagement with human rights issues (UN General Assembly 2015). Despite former General Counsel Dañino noting that "human rights are an intrinsic part of the Bank's mission" (Dañino 2005), human rights continues to be classified as political rather than economic, and the World Bank's leadership continues to resist interpretations that would require it to systematically consider human rights in its work (Human Rights Watch 2016).

2. Organizational Culture

The World Bank's institutional culture, which is dominated and largely influenced by an economist perspective, challenges human rights mainstreaming. Although economists do not make up the majority of World Bank employees, economists occupy most senior management positions, and their way of thinking dominates, influencing how institutional goals are crafted and justifications are articulated within the institution (Davis 2004; Sarfaty 2009; UN General Assembly 2015). As one World Bank employee noted, economists are "first-class citizens, and everybody else is a second class citizen" (Sarfaty 2009, 92). From an economist perspective, human rights are "perceived as being rigid, anti-market, and overly State-centric" (UN General Assembly 2015, 11). Applying such a rights-based approach consequently concerns many within the World Bank, as they perceive that human rights mainstreaming would lead to a drastic paradigm shift with unknown development effects (Darrow 2012). In implementing human rights in World

Bank programming, there also remains an uneasy tension in balancing the World Bank's inherent aim of efficiency (swiftly designing and implementing projects with few obstructions and impediments) and an explicit commitment to human rights (making these projects participatory, transparent, etc.). Accordingly, it has been difficult to incorporate human rights into the World Bank because doing so "forces employees into a struggle between principles and pragmatism, creating a tension between normative, intangible values and goals, and practical ways to solve problems" (Sarfaty 2009, 682).

3. Knowledge Gap

This fear of human rights is compounded by insufficient knowledge that many staff members have concerning human rights application. As reported by the NTF Progress Report:

> World Bank teams do not typically have direct contact with the main human rights bodies, are not well informed about how human rights could be applied in their work, may fail to see how the core human rights treaties could be relevant to their work, and are uncertain about how human rights can help provide better concrete answers to the hard questions facing development practitioners about how to set priorities and "what actually works" (World Bank 2010, 7).

Evidence of this lack of knowledge concerning human rights was substantiated in an internal 2009 survey, which revealed that World Bank staff see human rights as relevant to their work but are uncertain how to integrate human rights in their work. Specifically, the survey revealed a staff knowledge gap around the definitions, laws, institutions, and standards governing human rights (World Bank 2014). This lack of knowledge is not limited to employees at the lower levels—members of the Board of Directors are also not informed of human rights agreements and the rights-based approach to development (MacCuish 2010). A follow-up survey in 2013 found some improvement in staff knowledge and awareness of human rights (World Bank 2014), which is likely due to implementation of NTF program-based grants and multiple NTF learning events on human rights. The UN Special Rapporteur on extreme poverty and human rights, Philip Alston, however, has noted the persistence of this challenge: "Human rights are not well understood by a great many officials within the Bank. They have a passing acquaintance, but no real sense of the overall picture" (Alston 2014, 6).

4. Country Opposition

While key World Bank stakeholders (such as the United States and several European governments) have pushed the institution to mainstream human rights, some countries—such as China, an important World Bank stakeholder with growing influence—strongly oppose human rights in World Bank policy (Human Rights Watch 2016). While some countries oppose the World Bank's engagement with human rights on the grounds that it interferes with state sovereignty, others resist it because they are concerned that a rights-based approach at the World

Bank would expose their human rights records and require them to undertake rigorous assessments as part of the loan process (MacCuish 2010). Some member states believe that a formal World Bank endorsement of human rights could result in demands for political "democracy" that could threaten non-democratic governments and unnecessarily destabilize states lacking democratic institutions (Kim 2016). There is also an unintended fear among borrowing countries that human rights could lead to World Bank sanctions (Alston 2014). This fear was renewed after the World Bank's decision to delay health project loans to Uganda in 2014 because of the country's adoption of anti-homosexuality legislation (BBC 2014). The World Bank did not provide a convincing justification for why Uganda was singled out amid the numerous countries that outlaw homosexuality or why this issue in particular was a trigger for action. The likely, unintended impact of this development was to persuade more countries that the World Bank should not engage in human rights issues because it would put them at risk of unpredictable and ad hoc sanctions (UN General Assembly 2015). Finally, member states also resist human rights where country representatives—particularly finance ministries—are largely unfamiliar with human rights policy and do not see the value of rights-based approaches (Herbertson, Thompson, and Goodland 2010).

5. Competition with Emerging Lenders

Finally, the World Bank is confronted by emergent rivalries from other development banks that are increasingly being supported by the World Bank's traditional backers (Kopiński and Sun 2014; Perlez 2014; Flanagin 2015; Wang 2016). These new multilateral investment banks—including the Asian Infrastructure Investment Bank and the New Development Bank—and rising national development banks in countries such as Brazil, China, and India do not currently have the same social standards as the World Bank (Flanagin 2015). Accordingly, there are rising suspicions and legitimate fears that the World Bank will increasingly be pushed away from integrating human rights requirements in their lending in order to remain competitive as a lender and be perceived as most efficient, with the fastest speed of fund disbursement and least project requirements offered to country borrowers (UN General Assembly 2015).

CONCLUSION

Despite growing recognition of the relevance of human rights to its work, the World Bank continues to lack systematic and formal integration of these principles and norms into its expanding global health practice. The World Bank's evolving engagement with rights-based discourse is fundamentally shaped by a deep-seated friction between its legal obligations, as set out in the Articles of Agreement, and its changing practical mandate, as reflected in the goals and type of health-related work that it pursues.

Institutional limitations have resulted in the World Bank considering health-related human rights only as a means to development—rather than an end in itself. This has subsequently limited the World Bank's ability to support better and more sustainable health outcomes, which fundamentally necessitate addressing discriminatory practices, inequalities, and unjust power relations that are central to public health problems in development. These areas have historically not been dealt with comprehensively because of the World Bank's resistance to institutionally mainstreaming human rights. Understanding the World Bank's challenging history concerning human rights, as well as its current work, is important for the potential to advance the human rights agenda within global health governance and improve public health outcomes among the world's poorest and most vulnerable populations.

Notwithstanding these long-standing institutional challenges, there have been several developments over the institution's evolution that have resulted in significant progress in the World Bank's understanding of human rights. A number of these developments occurred under President Wolfensohn's leadership, including the early work of the Inspection Panel, the influential legal opinions and scholarly work of General Counsels Shihata and Dañino, and the emergence of important institutional publications linking human rights to development outcomes. Some developments are ongoing, including the implementation of the newly revised safeguards and the work of the NTF. While their ultimate impact on the World Bank's understanding of human rights remains to be seen, these developments will likely be instrumental to overcoming entrenched institutional challenges and facilitating a renewed conversation about the World Bank's role in supporting human rights for global health.

REFERENCES

Alston, Philip. 2014. "Rethinking the World Bank's Approach to Human Rights." *Keynote address to the Nordic Trust Fund for Human Rights and Development Annual Workshop on "The Way Forward."* 15 October. Washington, D.C.: The World Bank.

Anand, Sudhir and Kara Hanson. 1997. "Disability-Adjusted Life Years: A Critical Review." *Journal of Health Economics* 16(6): 685–702.

Baeza, Cristian. 2012. *The World Bank in Health 2012: Challenges, Priorities, and Role in the Global Health Aid Architecture.* Washington, D.C.: World Bank.

Ball, Rachel. 2008. "'Doing It Quietly': The World Bank's Engagement with Human Rights." *Monash University Law Review* 34(2): 331.

BBC. 2014. "World Bank Postpones $90m Uganda Loan over Anti-Gay Law." *BBC.* 28 February. Available at: http://www.bbc.com/news/world-africa-26378230.

Becker, William and David Milobsky. 1994. "Transcript Interview with Ibrahim Shihata." *The World Bank Group/Historian's Office, Oral History Program.* May 11. Available at: http://documents.worldbank.org/curated/en/776771468178141842/pdf/791210TRN0Shih0Box0377367B00PUBLIC0.pdf.

Berry, Gregory. 2016. "World Bank Safeguards Policy Changes: Safeguarding the Bank, Not Human Rights and Environmental Integrity." *Center for International Environmental Law.* Available at: http://www.ciel.org/world-bank-safeguards-policy-changes-safeguarding-the-bank-not-human-rights-and-environmental-integrity/.

Bleicher, Samuel A. 1970. "UN v. IBRD: A Dilemma of Functionalism." *International Organization* 24(1): 31–47.

Bradlow, Daniel. 1994. "International Organizations and Private Complaints: The Case of the World Bank Inspection Panel." *Virginia Journal of International Law* 34: 1–49.

Bretton Woods Project. 2005. "How Does the World Bank Operate?" *Bretton Woods Project.* August 23. Available at: http://www.brettonwoodsproject.org/2005/08/art-320865/.

Brinks, Daniel M. and Varun Gauri. 2012. "The Law's Majestic Equality? The Distributive Impact of Litigating Social and Economic Rights." *Policy Research Working Papers*. March. Available at: http://documents.worldbank.org/curated/en/987411468157509634/ The-laws-majestic-equality-the-distributive-impact-of-litigating-social-and-economic-rights.

Brodnig, Gernot. 2002. "The World Bank and Human Rights: Mission Impossible?" *The Fletcher Journal of Development Studies* XVII: 1–15.

Chavkin, Sasha, Ben Hallman, Michael Hudson, Cecile Schilis-Gallego, and Shane Shiffet. 2015. "How the World Bank Broke Its Promise to the Poor." *Huffington Post.* April 15. Accessed on March 1, 2017. http://projects.huffingtonpost.com/projects/ worldbank-evicted-abandoned.

Clark, D. L. 2002. "The World Bank and Human Rights: The Need for Greater Accountability." *Harvard Human Rights Journal* 15: 205–317.

Clinton, Chelsea and Devi Sridhar. 2017. *Governing Global Health: Who Runs and the World and Why?* Oxford: Oxford University Press.

Dañino, Roberto. 2005. "The Legal Aspects of the World Bank's Work on Human Rights: Some Preliminary Thoughts." In *Human Rights and Development: Towards Mutual Reinforcement*, edited by Philip Alston and Mary Robinson. Oxford: Oxford University Press.

Daniño, Robert. 2006. *Legal Opinion on Human Rights and the Work of the World Bank.* Washington, D.C.: World Bank.

Darrow, Mac. 2012. "The Millennium Development Goals: Milestones or Millstones—Human Rights Priorities for the Post-2015 Development Agenda." *Yale Human Rights & Development Law Journal* 15(1): 55–128.

Davis, Gloria. 2004. *A History of the Social Development Network in the World Bank, 1973–2002.* Social Protection discussion paper series: 56. Washington, D.C.: World Bank.

Donnan, Shawn. 2016. "World Bank Draws Fire with Changes to Lending Rules." *The Financial Times.* April 9. Available at: https://www.ft.com/content/d108d6da-5e6a-11e6-bb77-a121aa8abd95.

Flanagin, Jake. 2015. "Why Human Rights Objections to China's Version of the World Bank Ring False." *Quartz.* March 19. Available at: https://qz.com/365308/why-human-rights-objections-to-chinas-version-of-the-world-bank-ring-false/.

Fox, Jonathan A. 2000. "The World Bank Inspection Panel: Lessons from the First Five Years." *Global Governance* 6(3): 279–318.

Fujita, Sanae. 2011. "The Challenges of Mainstreaming Human Rights in the World Bank." *The International Journal of Human Rights* 15(3): 374–396.

Gaeta, Anthony and Marina Vasilara. 1998. *Development and Human Rights: The Role of the World Bank.* Washington, D.C.: The World Bank.

Gauri, Varun. 2004. "Social Rights and Economics: Claims to Health Care and Education in Developing Countries." *World Development* 32(3): 465–477.

Gauri, Varun. 2011. *The Cost of Complying with Human Rights Treaties: The Convention on the Rights of the Child and Basic Immunization.* Washington, D.C.: World Bank. Available at: https://openknowledge.worldbank.org/handle/10986/5765.

Gauri, Varun and Siri Gloppen. 2012. *Human Rights–Based Approaches to Development: Concepts, Evidence and Policy.* Policy Research Working Papers, January. Washington, D.C.: World Bank.

Herbertson, Kirk, Kim Thompson, and Robert J. A. Goodland. 2010. *A Roadmap for Integrating Human Rights into the World Bank Group.* Washington, D.C.: World Resources Institute.

Herz, Steven and Anne Perrulat. 2009. "Bringing Human Rights Claims to the World Bank Inspection Panel." Available at: http://www.bankinformationcenter.org/wp-content/uploads/2013/01/InspectionPanel_HumanRights.pdf.

Human Rights Watch. 2016. "World Bank: Human Rights All But Absent in New Policy." *Human Rights Watch News.* July 21. Available at: https://www.hrw.org/news/2016/07/21/world-bank-human-rights-all-absent-new-policy.

Inspection Panel. 2009. *Accountability at the World Bank: The Inspection Panel at 15 Years.* Washington, D.C.: World Bank.

Inspection Panel. 2017. "The Inspection Panel." Accessed March 1, 2017. Available at: http://ewebapps.worldbank.org/apps/ip/Pages/AboutUs.aspx.

Institute for Health Metrics and Evaluation. 2014. *Financing Global Health 2014: Shifts in Funding as the MDG Era Closes.* Seattle: Institute for Health Metrics and Evaluation.

International Consortium of Investigative Journalism (ICIJ). 2017. "Evicted and Abandoned: The World Bank's Broken Promise to the Poor." Accessed March 1, 2017. Available at: https://www.icij.org/project/world-bank.

Isham, Jonathan, Daniel Kaufmann, and Lant H. Pritchett. 1997. "Civil Liberties, Democracy, and the Performance of Government Projects." *The World Bank Economic Review* 11(2): 219–242.

Kanji, Najmi, Nazneen Kanji, and Firoze Manji. 1991. "From Development to Sustained Crisis: Structural Adjustment, Equity and Health." *Social Science & Medicine* 33(9): 985–993.

Kaufmann, Daniel. 2005. "10 Myths about Governance and Corruption." *Finance and Development* 42(3).

Kaufmann, Daniel, Aart Kraay, and Pablo Zoido-Lobaton. 1999. *Governance Matters.* Policy Research Working Paper, WPS 2196. Washington, D.C.: World Bank.

Kaufmann, Daniel, Aart Kraay, and Massimo Mastruzzi. 2004. "Governance Matters III: Governance Indicators for 1996, 1998, 2000, and 2002." *The World Bank Economic Review* 18(2): 253–287.

Kapur, Devesh, John P. Lewis, and Richard C. Webb. 1997. *The World Bank: Its First Half Century.* Washington, D.C.: Brookings Institution Press.

Kim, Jim Y., John Gershman, Joyce Millen, and Alec Irwin, eds. 2002. *Dying for Growth: Global Inequality and the Health of the Poor.* Monroe: Common Courage Press.

Kim, Jim. 2014. "Speech by World Bank Group President Jim Yong Kim on Universal Health Coverage in Emerging Economies." *Center for Strategic and International Studies Conference on Universal Health Coverage in Emerging Economies.* Washington, D.C., United States, 14 January.

Kim, Jim. 2016. The World Bank and Human Rights. *New York Times.* June 30. Available at: https://www.nytimes.com/2016/07/01/opinion/the-world-bank-and-human-rights.html?_r=0.

Kopiński, Dominik and Qian Sun. 2014. "New Friends, Old Friends? The World Bank and Africa When the Chinese Are Coming." *Global Governance: A Review of Multilateralism and International Organizations* 20(4): 601–623.

Kushner, Jacob, Anthony Langat, Sasha Chavkin, and Michael Hudson. 2015. "Burned Out: World Bank Projects Leave Trail of Misery Around the Globe." *Huffington Post.* April 15. Accessed March 1, 2017. http://projects.huffingtonpost.com/projects/worldbank-evicted-abandoned/worldbank-projects-leave-trail-misery-around-globe-kenya.

Lethbridge, Jane. 2017. "World Bank Undermines Right to Universal Healthcare." *Bretton Woods Project* April 6. Available at: http://www.brettonwoodsproject.org/2017/04/world-bank-undermines-right-universal-healthcare/.

Loewenson, Rene. 1993. "Structural Adjustment and Health Policy in Africa." *International Journal of Health Services* 23(4): 717–730.

MacCuish, Derek. 2010. "Efforts to Make Human Rights Matter in World Bank Are Moving Forward, Despite Reluctance of Governments." *The Upstream Journal*. July. Available at: http://www.upstreamjournal.org/2010/07/efforts-to-make-human-rights-matter-in-world-bank-are-moving-forward-despite-reluctance-of-governments/.

Macedo, Roberto. 1998. "Brazilian Children and the Economic Crisis: The Evidence from the State of Sao Paulo." In G. A. Cornia, R. Jolly, and F. Stewart, *Adjustment with a Human Face Volume II*, 28–56. Oxford: Oxford University Press and UNICEF.

Marouf, Fatma E. 2010. "Holding the World Bank Accountable for Leakage of Funds from Africa's Health Sector." *Health and Human Rights* 12: 95.

McInerney-Lankford, Siobhan and Hans-Otto Sano. 2010. *Human Rights Indicators in Development: An Introduction*. October. Washington, D.C.: World Bank.

New York Times Editorial Board. 2016. "The World Bank Should Champion Human Rights." *New York Times*. June 27. Available at: https://www.nytimes.com/2016/06/27/opinion/the-world-bank-should-champion-human-rights.html.

NTF (Nordic Trust Fund) and World Bank. 2012. *Human Rights and Economic Tensions and Positive Relationships*. Available at: http://siteresources.worldbank.org/PROJECTS/Resources/40940-1331068268558/Report_Development_Fragility_Human_Rights.pdf.

OECD and The World Bank. 2013. *Integrating Human Rights into Development, 2nd Edition: Donor Approaches, Experiences and Challenges*. Washington, D.C.: The World Bank.

OHCHR. 2015. "'The World Bank is a Human Rights-Free Zone'—UN expert on extreme poverty expresses deep concern." Accessed May 1, 2017. Available at: http://www.ohchr.org/EN/NewsEvents/Pages/DisplayNews.aspx?NewsID=16517&LangID=E.

Osamani, Siddiqur R. 2010. "The Human Rights Approach to Poverty Reduction." In *Freedom from Poverty as a Human Right (volume 3)*, edited by Bard A. Andreassen, Stephen P. Marks, and Arjun K. Sengupta. Paris: UNESCO.

Palacio, Ana. 2006. "Legal Empowerment of the Poor: An Action Agenda for the World Bank." Washington, D.C.: The World Bank.

Perlez, Jane. 2014. "U.S. Opposing China's Answer to World Bank." *New York Times*. October 9. Available at: https://www.nytimes.com/2014/10/10/world/asia/chinas-plan-for-regional-development-bank-runs-into-us-opposition.html?ref=world&_r=2.

Rice, Andrew. 2016. "Is Jim Kim Destroying the World Bank—Or Saving It from Itself?" *Foreign Policy*. April 27. Available at: http://foreignpolicy.com/2016/04/27/is-jim-yong-kim-destroying-the-world-bank-development-finance/.

Ruger, Jennifer Prah. 2005a. "The Changing Role of the World Bank in Global Health." *American Journal of Public Health* 95(1): 60–70.

Ruger, Jennifer Prah. 2005b "What Will the New World Bank Head Do for Global Health?" *The Lancet* 365(9474): 1837–1840.

Ruger, Jennifer Prah. 2007 "Global Health Governance and the World Bank." *The Lancet* 370(9597): 1471–1474.

Sarfaty, Galit. 2009. "Why Culture Matters in International Institutions: The Marginality of Human Rights at the World Bank." *American Journal of International Law*: 647–683.

Sarfaty, Galit. 2012. *Values in Translation: Human Rights and the Culture of the World Bank*. Stanford: University Press.

Seifman, Richard, Sarah Kornblet, Claire Standley, Erin Sorrell, Julie Fischer, and Rebecca Katz. 2015. "Think Big, World Bank: Time for a Public Health Safeguard." *Lancet Global Health* 3(4): e186–e187.

Shihata, Ibrahim FI. 1995. *The World Bank in a Changing World: Selected Essays and Lectures.* Vol. 2. Martinus: Nijhoff Publishers.

Shihata, Ibrahim F. I. 2000. *The World Bank Legal Papers.* Martinus: Nijhoff Publishers.

Shihata, Ibrahim FI. 2003. "Prohibition of Political Activities in the Bank's Work Legal Opinion by the Senior Vice President and General Counsel." *Transnational Dispute Management.*

Sridhar, Devi, Martin McKee, Gorik Ooms, Claudia Beiersmann, Eric Friedman, Hebe Gouda, Peter Hill, and Albrecht Jahn. 2015. "Universal Health Coverage and the Right to Health: From Legal Principle to Post-2015 Indicators." *International Journal of Health Services* 45(3): 495–506.

Stout, Susan and Timothy Johnston. 1999. *Investing in Health: Development Effectiveness in the Health, Nutrition, and Population Sector: A World Bank Operations Evaluation Study.* Washington, D.C.: The World Bank.

UN General Assembly, 3rd Session. 1948. "Universal Declaration of Human Rights." 10 December. UN Doc. A/RES/3/217A.

UN General Assembly, 70th Session. 2015. "Extreme poverty and human rights. Promotion and protection of human rights: human rights questions, including alternative approaches for improving the effective enjoyment of human rights and fundamental freedoms." UN Doc. A/70/274.

UNCHR (United Nations High Commissioner for Refugees). 1951. "Co-operation Between the Commission on Human Rights and the Special Agencies and other Organs of the United Nations in the Consideration of Economic, Social and Cultural Rights." UN Doc. E/CN.4/534.

Wang, Hongying. 2016. "New Multilateral Development Banks: Opportunities and Challenges for Global Governance." *Global Order and the New Regionalism* 8(1): 113–118.

World Bank. 1945. "International Bank for Reconstruction and Development Articles of Agreement." Opened for signature 27 December. Amended 16 February 1989. Available at: http://siteresources.worldbank.org/EXTABOUTUS/Resources/ibrd-articlesofagreement.pdf.

World Bank. 1981. *The McNamara Years at the World Bank.* Washington, D.C.: World Bank.

World Bank. 1989. *Sub-Saharan Africa from Crisis to Growth: A Long-Term Perspective Study.* Washington, D.C.: World Bank.

World Bank. 1993. *World Development Report 1993: Investing in Health.* New York: Oxford University Press.

World Bank. 2000. *China—Gansu and Inner Mongolia Poverty Reduction Project: Qinghai Component—Inspection Panel Investigation Report.* Washington, D.C.: World Bank.

World Bank. 2002. *Chad—Petroleum Development and Pipeline Project: Investigation Report.* Washington, D.C.: World Bank.

World Bank. 2003. *Gender Equality and the Millennium Development Goals.* Washington, D.C.: World Bank.

World Bank. 2005a. *Empowering People by Transforming Institutions: Social Development in World Bank Operations.* Washington, D.C.: World Bank.

World Bank. 2005b. "Indigenous Peoples." Operational Policy 4.10, July. Revised April 2013. Washington, D.C.: World Bank.

World Bank. 2007. *Honduras—Land Administration Project: Inspection Panel Investigation Report.* Washington, D.C.: World Bank.

World Bank. 2010. *Nordic Trust Fund Annual Progress Report: Knowledge and Learning for Human Rights and Development, September 2009–October 2010.* Available at:

http://siteresources.worldbank.org/PROJECTS/Resources/1171NTFReportProof8.pdf.

World Bank. 2012a. *Articles of Agreement*. Last revised 27 June. Available at: http://siteresources.worldbank.org/BODINT/Resources/278027-1215526322295/IBRDArticlesOfAgreement_English.pdf.

World Bank. 2012b. *Working for a World Free of AIDS*. Washington, D.C.: World Bank.

World Bank. 2014. *Nordic Trust Fund Annual Progress Report January–December 2014*. Available at: http://documents.worldbank.org/curated/en/670301467999134745/pdf/99232-AR-PUBLIC-Box393194B.pdf.

World Bank. 2015. "World Bank Statement on Cancellation of the Uganda Transport Sector Development Project (TSDP)." Last modified December 21. Accessed May 1, 2017. http://www.worldbank.org/en/news/press-release/2015/12/21/wb-statement-cancellation-uganda-transport-sector-development-project.

World Bank. 2016a. *Environmental and Social Framework: Setting Environmental and Social Standards*. Washington, D.C.: World Bank.

World Bank. 2016b. *Involuntary Resettlement*. Washington, D.C.: World Bank Group.

World Bank. 2016c. "Press Release: Partners Launch Framework to Accelerate Universal Health Coverage in Africa; World Bank and Global Fund Commit 24 Billion." *The World Bank*. 26 August. Available at: http://www.worldbank.org/en/news/press-release/2016/08/26/partners-launch-framework-to-accelerate-universal-health-coverage-in-africa-world-bank-and-global-fund-commit-24-billion.

World Bank. 2017a. "Governors." Accessed May 1, 2017. Available at: http://www.worldbank.org/en/about/leadership/governors.

World Bank. 2017b. "Health Overview." Accessed March 1, 2017. Available at: http://www.worldbank.org/en/topic/health/overview#1.

World Bank. 2017c. "Leadership." Accessed May 1, 2017. Available at: http://www.worldbank.org/en/about/leadership.

World Bank. 2017d. Nordic Trust Fund Progress Report 2016. Washington, D.C.: World Bank.

World Bank. 2017e. "Nordic Trust Fund Grants: July 2015–June 2017" (on file with author).

World Bank. 2017f. "Safeguard Policies." Accessed 1 March. Available at: http://www.worldbank.org/en/programs/environmental-and-social-policies-for-projects/brief/environmental-and-social-safeguards-policies#safeguards.

World Bank. 2017g. "The Environmental and Social Framework." 30 March. Available at: http://www.worldbank.org/en/programs/environmental-and-social-policies-for-projects/brief/the-environmental-and-social-framework-esf.

World Health Organization and World Bank. 2011. *World Report on Disability*. Geneva: WHO.

Zhou, Suzanne. 2012. "Reassessing the Prospects of a Human Rights Safeguard Policy at the World Bank." *Journal of International Economic Law* 15 (3): 823–841.

17

The World Trade Organization

*Carving Out the Right to Health to Promote Access
to Medicines and Tobacco Control in the Trade Arena*

SUERIE MOON AND THIRUKUMARAN BALASUBRAMANIAM[*]

The World Trade Organization (WTO) is one of the central governing institutions of the global economy, with a mandate to contribute to development and human welfare through the liberalization of trade. Unlike many multilateral agreements (including human rights treaties), WTO treaties give signatories limited flexibility to opt-out of unfavorable provisions. In addition, most of its treaties are binding on all WTO members, and backed by an adjudication mechanism and enforcement arrangements. Because the WTO is among the most powerful international institutions, it is instructive to examine the evolution of health-related human rights considerations within the institution.

Policy space for health concerns has increased at the WTO, but this space is under constant threat and remains precarious. This chapter begins in Part I with a brief history of the origins of the WTO and provides a broad overview of the health implications of various WTO agreements. Part II examines the public health implications of WTO's intellectual property rules and takes a closer look at two key health-related issues: access to medicines and tobacco control. Part III analyzes the institutional factors that promote or hinder human rights protection. The conclusion considers the prospects for institutionalization of health-related human rights within the WTO.

* We are grateful to Benjamin Mason Meier, Lawrence Gostin, Hanna Huffstetler, and Edith Lee for insightful comments received on an earlier version of this chapter and for assistance in preparing this manuscript for publication.

I. BACKGROUND

The WTO's reach into the daily lives of people around the globe is both broad and deep. As of 2016, 164 governments had joined as members (WTO 2016b), accounting for about 95 percent of global trade (WTO 2014b); nineteen states were in the accession process to join (WTO 2016c); and two additional states had observer status (signaling an interest in joining). Its rules cover a broad array of human activity, having effects far beyond trade policy's traditional remit, with implications for labor, environment, national development strategies, and health and human rights.

A. Origins of the WTO

For advocates of global trade, the birth of the WTO symbolized the achievement of a robust multilateral trading organization that had been sought since the end of the Second World War. In contrast to the creation of the United Nations (UN), World Bank, and International Monetary Fund, major powers did not agree on creating an International Trade Organization in the postwar period out of concern that such an organization would impinge too heavily on domestic economic affairs. What remained was a treaty rather than an organization—the 1947 General Agreement on Tariffs and Trade (GATT)—which focused primarily on reducing tariffs on goods. This treaty evolved to become the main arena for the negotiation of global trade rules. By the 1990s, increased global economic integration and the end of the Cold War prompted in governments a new willingness to deepen trade rules, resulting in the transformation of the GATT into the WTO in 1995, following eight years of negotiations in the Uruguay Round of trade talks.[1] The resulting WTO encompassed a revised set of GATT rules (GATT (1994)), covering trade in goods, and new rules covering services and intellectual property (IP), which reached more deeply into the domestic policies of trading partners, with significant social implications (Barton et al. 2008).

In addition to expanded subject matter, the WTO differed from its predecessor in its authority to enforce its judgments. While the GATT included a system of adjudicating complaints by one party against another, it did not have any measures to enforce them. Under GATT, "compliance or non-compliance is the choice of the nations against whom decisions have been rendered" (Reitz 1996, 570). In contrast, the WTO's dispute settlement system was given a mandate not only to adjudicate complaints but also to authorize retaliatory measures. If a WTO Panel or Appellate Body found that a member had violated an agreement and did

---

1. The Uruguay Round, an eight-year trade negotiation launched in Punta del Este, Uruguay in 1986, culminated in the establishment of the WTO on January 1, 1995. The objectives of the Uruguay Round included the reduction and elimination of tariffs, increased market access, the expansion of world trade "to the benefit of all countries," and the strengthening of the rules-based trading system "under agreed, effective and enforceable multilateral disciplines" (GATT 1986). The Uruguay Round established the WTO's rules on IP, services, goods (including agriculture and textiles), and dispute settlement.

not comply with the WTO ruling within a reasonable period of time, the WTO could authorize trade sanctions by the complainant member (WTO 1994a). Governments have made active use of the dispute settlement system—about 500 cases have been brought to the WTO since its founding, and 350 rulings have been issued ("WTO Dispute Settlement Gateway" 2017). Private actors cannot directly file complaints against governments at the WTO; they can, however, persuade a friendly government to file a complaint in their interests and cover the considerable legal costs of doing so.[2]

B. Impact of WTO Treaties on Global Health

Protecting health-related human rights often requires state action, and, in particular, state intervention in the market (Hein and Moon 2013; Ottersen et al. 2014). However, the freedom to take such public health action is constrained by the rules governing global trade (Frenk and Moon 2013, 937). The binding nature of WTO agreements is one reason they have attracted such attention among both practitioners and scholars of global health governance (Hein and Moon 2013). Various WTO agreements can have significant implications for public health policymaking across all three major areas of WTO rules: goods, intellectual property, and services (Frenk and Moon 2013).

In the area of goods, concerns have arisen regarding the potential for the GATT (1994) and the Agreement on Sanitary and Phytosanitary Measures (SPS) to restrict national efforts to regulate goods that may be dangerous or harmful for human health. The WTO explains that the SPS "seeks to strike a balance between the right of WTO members to protect health and the need to allow the smooth flow of goods across international borders" by allowing members "to adopt legitimate measures to protect food safety and animal and plant health while ensuring these measures are not applied in an unnecessary manner for protectionist purposes" (WTO 2014a). SPS seeks to strike this balance by requiring that trade-restricting regulations be justified by scientific evidence (Marceau and Trachtman 2002). The first test of these rules arose in 1996 when the United States challenged a European Union (EU) ban on the import of beef produced in the United States and Canada with certain growth hormones that were banned in the EU (Pauwelyn 1999). The case was seen as an early test of how the new WTO would handle perceived conflicts between national public health policymaking and international trade rules, with the EU seeking to apply "the precautionary principle" to ban potentially harmful products from its markets.[3] The WTO Appellate Body ultimately decided that the EU did not provide adequate scientific evidence that the hormones were harmful to human health—in essence rejecting

2. Private actors have also increasingly turned to the investment regime (a web of over 3,000 bilateral investment treaties), which allows firms to bring complaints directly against government regulations (including, but not limited to, those impacting health-related human rights) (UNCTAD 2012).

3. The precautionary principle argues that governments may regulate certain goods or services to protect human health or the environment based on the risk of harm, even in the absence of conclusive proof of such harm (Tosun 2013).

the precautionary principle in favor of free trade—and found the EU in violation of its obligations. Proponents of the precautionary principle saw the WTO ruling as an overreach into a sensitive area of culturally informed domestic public health policy, whereas proponents of freer trade saw the WTO system working as it should (Vogel 2012). The EU ultimately decided not to change its domestic policies, but rather to submit to WTO-authorized retaliatory tariffs on its goods in the US and Canadian markets. Notably, the strength of the EU economy meant that it could make the political decision to retain its hormones policy and accept trade sanctions; such decisions would have greater repercussions for smaller, weaker, or less-developed economies.

In the area of services, questions have arisen regarding the potential effect of the General Agreement on Trade in Services (GATS) on the privatization of health systems, medical tourism, migration of health workers, and provision of private health insurance. Analysis in this area has largely focused on the *potential* effects of the GATS on health, since liberalization of the health services sector has been quite limited to date, data is of varying quality, and negotiations for any further liberalization are ongoing (Blouin, Drager, and Smith 2006). In terms of health service provision, governments that liberalize could potentially expect to see an increase in the private provision of health services by foreign providers, which could offer both potential benefits and risks. This influx of foreign service providers could generate increased competition among service providers, access to and transfer of new knowledge and technologies, additional supply in situations of shortage, and investment and economic growth in the health services sector; however, such an influx also raises increased challenges for appropriate regulation of services provided (particularly for services new or unfamiliar to domestic regulators), increased incentives for health worker movement (from the public to an increasingly lucrative private sector), and increased burdens on under-resourced health systems (if medical tourism brings an influx of foreign patients) (Blouin, Drager, and Smith 2006).[4]

Finally, the area of IP is where health and human rights concerns have made the greatest mark on the WTO. The debate has largely centered on concerns that (1) patent rules allow higher medicines prices and (2) trademark rules restrict tobacco control policies. The Agreement on Trade-Related Aspects of Intellectual Property Rights (TRIPS) sets minimum levels of IP protection across all members, and covers copyright and related rights, trademarks, geographical indications, industrial design, and patents (Reichman 2008). TRIPS has been the main locus of attention and flashpoint for debates over the relationship between trade and health and has brought into stark relief the tension between international trade imperatives and international human rights obligations (Hein and Moon 2013).

---

4. For example, in Southeast Asia, which is characterized by a relatively high degree of liberalization in health services, medical tourism has generated significant new revenues but also contributed to "brain drain" of highly trained specialists from the public sector to foreigner-oriented private hospitals (Kanchanachitra et al. 2011).

II. HEALTH-RELATED HUMAN RIGHTS AT THE WTO: ACCESS TO MEDICINES AND TOBACCO CONTROL

While human rights are not the WTO's focus or mandate, maintaining the institution's legitimacy has demanded that its rules respect human rights. Strong critiques of the WTO from the labor, environmental, and public health communities have weakened its standing, and the Organization has made concerted efforts to respond to these critiques (WTO 1999). While the right to health has not been "mainstreamed" into the practice of the WTO, health considerations have become more integrated into WTO rules through:

1. informal norms, as reflected in WTO reports, press releases, debates among members, and political declarations;
2. formal norms, as reflected in treaty language; and
3. formal norms, as reflected in adjudicated cases (Hein and Moon 2013).

Taken together, these three channels have clarified that national governments do have significant legal space within WTO agreements to protect health-related human rights, even if political pressure from powerful countries or private firms can dissuade governments from actually making use of it. These changes to WTO norms have largely been driven by debates over access to medicines and tobacco control—both of which are recognized explicitly as an integral part of realizing the right to health by the UN human rights system (CESCR 2000).

A. TRIPS Negotiations and Public Health Considerations

In 1982, the *New York Times* warned that the "international patent system" would collapse if an agreement could not be reached at the World Intellectual Property Organization (WIPO) during negotiations to revise the Paris Convention for the Protection of Industrial Property, then the main international standard for national laws governing patents (Lewis 1982).[5] Several developing countries had sought to revise the Paris Convention to facilitate the transfer of technology by codifying measures such as robust compulsory licensing provisions that would allow governments to override patents to achieve certain public goals. According to the then chairman of pharmaceutical company Pfizer, "[t]he revisions to the Paris treaty being considered at the U.N. would confer international respectability on the abrogation of patents" (Lewis 1982). Far from collapsing the international patent system, the failure to revise the Paris Convention unwittingly engendered the 1994 TRIPS Agreement.

---

5. A patent is a state-granted right that allows the patent-holder to establish a monopoly by barring others from making, using, offering for sale, or selling an invention for a fixed period of time. The social bargain encapsulated within the patent system is that the inventor can reap monopoly rents for a period of time as a reward or incentive for inventing a technology that is novel and useful to society (Machlup and Penrose 1950).

In an effort to counterbalance efforts at WIPO to tailor patent rules to the development needs of developing countries, a group of Washington-based industry executives began efforts in 1986 to shift international IP policymaking into the GATT—what TRIPS historian Peter Drahos has called "a radical idea" (Drahos 2003).[6] Executives at Pfizer and IBM created an industry-based Intellectual Property Committee (IPC) that included Bristol-Myers, DuPont, General Electric, Hewlett Packard, Johnson & Johnson, Merck, and Monsanto (Ibid.). Although patent policy had largely been considered a domestic policy matter prior to the Uruguay Round of GATT negotiations, the IPC persuaded states at the start of the Uruguay Round to include IP as a subject of the ensuing negotiations (GATT 1986).

During the Uruguay Round, a core group of industrialized countries (the "Quad"— the United States, Canada, the European Communities, and Japan (Drahos 2003)) pushed for new rules on IP within the future WTO ('t Hoen 2009), while developing countries broadly opposed their inclusion (GATT 1990). Ultimately, developing countries made trade-offs on TRIPS in order to secure market access for agriculture and textiles (Taubman 2015). The post–Cold War ascendance of US economic thought, and the threat to withdraw favorable access to the US market for countries identified as denying adequate protection of IP rights, had shifted the political landscape to allow TRIPS to come to fruition (Watal and Taubman 2015).

Several provisions of TRIPS would have important implications for innovation and access to medicines. Harmonizing national patent laws for pharmaceutical products, TRIPS imposed a significant new requirement on many developing country members: that patent rights be "available for any inventions, whether products or processes, in all fields of technology" (WTO 1994b, art. 27). Prior to TRIPS, countries were not obliged by international trade rules to provide patent protection for pharmaceuticals, and at the start of the Uruguay Round, at least "50 countries did not provide patent protection on pharmaceuticals" (UN Secretary-General and others 2016, 17). TRIPS mandated that all WTO members confer a twenty-year term of patent protection for pharmaceuticals (from the date of patent filing in any country)—a rule that would have profound implications for governments' ability to guarantee access to pharmaceuticals.

This requirement to grant monopoly protection on medicines was counterbalanced, in part, by several other key articles that were included by developing countries to emphasize broader social goals beyond the protection of the interests of IP rights-holders (GATT 1990), including that IP should be managed "in a manner conducive to social and economic welfare, and to a balance of rights and obligations" (WTO 1994b, art. 7) and that members may "adopt measures necessary to protect public health and nutrition, and to promote the public interest in sectors of vital importance to their socio-economic and technological development" (Ibid., art. 8). These clauses provided a foothold for overarching public health and human rights safeguards within TRIPS and the WTO.

---

6. This was considered a "radical idea" because unlike most trade liberalization efforts, which seek to *reduce* government intervention in markets, IP rights systems require *intensified* government intervention to grant, adjudicate, and enforce rights on knowledge.

In addition to these safeguards in the overall purpose of TRIPS, specific public interest safeguards were negotiated into the text. One of the most powerful and controversial was the right of a government under certain conditions to authorize the nonvoluntary use of a patent—known as "compulsory licensing," in which "a government allows someone else to produce the patented product or process without the consent of the patent owner" (WTO 2006). However, TRIPS specified that "any such use [of compulsory licensing] shall be authorized predominantly for the supply of the domestic market," which made the use of this safeguard extremely difficult for countries that would need to import a product (e.g., because they did not have adequate domestic manufacturing capacity, a limitation that applies to most WTO members in the context of pharmaceuticals) (WTO 1994b, art. 31(f)).[7]

Finally, in implementing these sweeping IP policy changes, TRIPS allowed for transition periods for certain developing countries. For example, India had until 2005 to implement fully the treaty's requirements, which allowed Indian firms to supply generic HIV medicines for a certain period of time ('t Hoen 2016). The transition period for least developed countries (LDC) has been extended several times, from 2006 to 2016, and most recently to 2033 for pharmaceutical products (WTO 2015).[8] The transition periods for LDCs may be extended further, which is a key public health safeguard for this group of countries, although not all LDCs have made full use of them.

B. The Rise of Access to Medicines Concerns at the WTO

When TRIPS came into force in 1995, few could have predicted how quickly and forcefully its public health safeguards would be put to the test. Concerns over medicine prices prompted by TRIPS were heightened by the concurrent HIV pandemic and the 1996 discovery that a triple-combination of antiretroviral drugs (ARVs) could control the virus ('t Hoen et al. 2011). Triple-therapy, then costing $10,000–$15,000 per patient per year, would remain far out of reach for developing countries, where 95 percent of the world's HIV-positive population lived ('t Hoen 2016). Some countries hardest hit by HIV, such as Brazil and Thailand, had begun granting patents on medicines for the first time in the 1990s, just as triple-therapy was developed. The drive for worldwide patenting of medicines came face to face with a devastating epidemic for which a treatment existed but—until challenged by human rights advocacy—remained inaccessible to the vast majority of people who needed it.

1. SOUTH AFRICA

In February 1998, thirty-nine pharmaceutical companies filed a lawsuit against the Government of South Africa, targeting measures in its Medicines Act that

---

7. This issue would become the subject of the first ever amendment of any WTO Agreement, when TRIPS Article 31 was formally amended in 2017 to permit export of a predominant share of products manufactured under a compulsory license (WTO 2017).

8. The extended deadline for LDCs to implement TRIPS (measures not specific to pharmaceuticals) ends earlier and is currently scheduled for 2021 (WTO 2015).

controlled the prices of medicines, alleging that "the Medicines Act violated the TRIPS Agreement and the South African Constitution" (Velasquez, Correa, and Balasubramaniam 2005, 44). Supporting this industry lawsuit in March 1998, Sir Leon Brittan, Vice President of the European Commission, wrote a sternly worded letter to South African Vice President Thabo Mbeki, alleging that the Medicines Act appeared to be "at variance with South Africa's obligations under the TRIPS and its implementation would negatively affect the interest of the European pharmaceutical industry" ('t Hoen 2002, 31). The Medicines Act also attracted scrutiny from the US Trade Representative in its 1999 Special 301 Report,[9] which expressed concern that "South Africa's Medicines Act appears to grant the Health Minister ill defined authority to issue compulsory licenses, authorize parallel imports, and potentially otherwise abrogate patent rights" (Office of the United States Trade Representative 1999, 22). The US government viewed the Medicines Act as "inconsistent with South Africa's obligations and commitments" under TRIPS and began an "assiduous, concerted campaign to persuade" South Africa to repeal the Medicines Act (US Department of State 1999).

2. BRAZIL

Amidst the tumult in South Africa, the United States initiated WTO dispute settlement proceedings against Brazil in May 2000 over compulsory licensing provisions contained in Brazil's industrial property law, which made patented inventions, including medicines, subject to compulsory license if they were not produced in Brazil. The United States challenged the TRIPS consistency of Brazil's local working requirements, which held that exclusive patent rights could only be enjoyed through the local production—"not the importation"—of patented inventions (WTO 2000). Brazil mounted a robust defense of its industrial property legislation, framing the WTO dispute as an assault on its national AIDS program and arguing that the ability to produce ARVs locally served as a bedrock of the program, with the threat of compulsory licensing serving as a tool to achieve significant price reductions and increase access to medicines ('t Hoen 2003). In retaliation, Brazil requested WTO dispute settlement consultations with the United States in January 2001, challenging the TRIPS consistency of local manufacturing requirements of the US Patents Code, specifically in relation to Patent Rights in Inventions Made with Federal Assistance (WTO 2001c). Under siege at the WTO, Brazil garnered support for its industrial policy and public health objectives in other forums, including the Office of the UN High Commissioner for Human Rights (OHCHR) and the UN Commission on Human Rights. At the Commission, Brazil spearheaded the passage of a 2003 resolution on "Access to medication in the context of pandemics such as HIV/AIDS" (Commission on Human Rights 2003), which passed with one notable abstention, the United States. This Commission on Human Rights resolution

---

9. The US government issues annual reports, known as Special 301 reports, which assess how well US trading partners have protected IP over the preceding year. The report is a diplomatic tool the US government uses to pressure other countries to change their domestic IP practices; it can be seen as a unilateral action parallel to the multilateral system for making such assessments within the WTO (Correa 2004).

was the first to recognize access to medicines as a fundamental element of the progressive realization of the right to health, and the Commission called upon states to pursue policies that would promote, *inter alia*, "availability in sufficient quantities of pharmaceuticals and medical technologies used to treat pandemics such as HIV/AIDS or the most common opportunistic infections that accompany them" (Ibid., para. 2). This move to the Commission on Human Rights reflected a clear forum-shifting strategy by the government of Brazil, reframing the intersection of IP and access to medicines as a health and human rights issue rather than a trade issue.

3. DOHA DECLARATION

The pressure exerted by the pharmaceutical industry, the European Commission, and the United States against measures by developing countries, including Brazil and South Africa, to safeguard access to medicines provoked a robust civil society response, which manifested itself in heterogeneous ways, including protests, petition campaigns, technical briefing seminars, and media advocacy (Velasquez, Correa, and Balasubramaniam 2005; Forman 2008). In response, the pharmaceutical industry dropped its lawsuit challenging the constitutionality of the South African Medicines Act in April 2001, and the United States withdrew its WTO complaint against Brazil in June 2001. These stunning reversals of fortune for the pharmaceutical industry accorded to Brazil and South Africa a sense of moral legitimacy and foreshadowed the WTO's December 2001 Doha Declaration on the TRIPS Agreement and Public Health.

Building on and contributing to this momentum, the African group of WTO members requested in April 2001 a special session of the TRIPS Council—the WTO's body for discussing TRIPS-related issues—to seek "legal clarity in the interpretation and application of the relevant TRIPS provisions" based upon "recent legal challenges by the pharmaceutical industry" (WTO 2001a, 71). A summary of the TRIPS Council discussions underscored the threats to the WTO's legitimacy that were arising from the significant human rights concerns inherent in the HIV/AIDS medicines issue:

> As the recent upsurge of public feelings and even public outrage over AIDS medicines had shown, there was at the moment a crisis of public perception about the intellectual property system and about the role of the TRIPS Agreement, which was leading to a crisis of legitimacy for the TRIPS Agreement. Whilst this storm was raging outside the WTO, and legitimately so, Members inside the WTO could not shut their eyes and ears (Ibid.).

At the June 2001 meeting of the TRIPS Council, dedicated specifically to public health concerns, a group of developing countries underscored the importance of interpreting TRIPS to confirm that "nothing in the TRIPS Agreement will prevent Members from adopting measures to protect public health" (Ibid.).

Negotiations among governments continued through 2001, but were deadlocked due to strong opposition from the United States. However, shortly after the attacks on the World Trade Center in New York on September 11, 2001, the United States was gripped by fears of a potential bioterrorism attack when anonymous letters containing anthrax spores were sent to lawmakers and others (Rothe and Muzzatti 2004). At the time, only the patented drug ciprofloxacin was considered an effective treatment for anthrax infection, and US Health Secretary Tommy Thompson faced the possibility of high prices and shortages of the medicine as public panic spread (Bradsher and Andrews 2001). Thompson publicly threatened the patent holder, Bayer, with a compulsory license on the medicine, as did the government of Canada, if the company did not offer the public sector a reasonable price and assurances regarding supply (Ibid.).[10] Two months later, the United States softened its position at the WTO conference of trade ministers in Doha, Qatar.

In November 2001, WTO members reached consensus on the issues first raised by the African Group and issued the historic Doha Declaration on the TRIPS Agreement and Public Health to clarify that:

> the TRIPS Agreement does not and should not prevent members from taking measures to protect public health. Accordingly, while reiterating our commitment to the TRIPS Agreement, we affirm that the Agreement can and should be interpreted and implemented in a manner supportive of WTO members' right to protect public health and, in particular, to promote access to medicines for all (WTO 2001b, para. 4).

The Doha Declaration did not explicitly use the language of human rights, but in its substance, it strengthened and expanded the policy space available to governments to take measures to realize the right to health in general, and in particular the right to access to medicines (Forman 2016). Other key provisions of the Doha Declaration included explicit assurance permitting parallel importation (trade in patented products when available at different prices in different countries); clarification that members had the freedom to issue compulsory licenses and to determine the grounds on which they could be granted; and extension of the transition period for LDCs to protect pharmaceutical patents until at least 2016 (later extended to 2033) (WTO 2001b).

One piece of unfinished business at Doha was reflected in Paragraph 6 of the Declaration, which called on the TRIPS Council to find an "expeditious solution" to the problems facing countries with "insufficient or no manufacturing capacities in the pharmaceutical sector," when seeking to make effective use of compulsory licensing (WTO 2001b, para. 6). After two years of subsequent negotiations, WTO members agreed on what would be called the "Paragraph 6 system," a complex and cumbersome set of processes to make legally permissible compulsory licensing primarily for export ('t Hoen 2016). Although the Paragraph 6 system has been used only once—in 2007 when a Canadian firm exported ARVs to Rwanda—it is notable that the first amendment to *any* WTO agreement in over two decades of its existence was made to TRIPS to facilitate the realization of the right to health.

---

10. Thompson never issued the compulsory license, but US opposition to developing countries making use of this policy tool for HIV medicines became untenable in light of its own compulsory licensing threat when faced with a domestic public health crisis.

This system for compulsory licensing became a permanent amendment to TRIPS in 2017, after two-thirds of the WTO membership ratified the amendment.

The Doha Declaration remains a foundational normative text—clarifying, reaffirming, and strengthening public health prerogatives within WTO rules (Abbott 2005). Between 2001 and 2009, at least thirty-one LDCs authorized the importation of generic versions of patented HIV medicines with reference to the Doha Declaration ('t Hoen 2016). Despite political pressure on countries not to make use of the various TRIPS flexibilities, governments have also made periodic use of compulsory licensing as a negotiating tool to address high medicines prices for HIV, pandemic flu, and cancer (Shankar et al. 2013). Drawing on the public health implications of the Doha Declaration, systematic public health cooperation between the WTO, WIPO, and World Health Organization (WHO) secretariats has been institutionalized through joint studies and annual symposia (WHO, WIPO, and WTO 2013).

However, the right to access medicines has not been fully safeguarded, neither within the WTO nor in the many regional trade agreements negotiated outside the WTO. Political pressure on countries not to make use of the various TRIPS flexibilities has continued. For example, Thailand came under very strong political pressure after its decision to issue several compulsory licenses in 2006–2007 (Tantivess, Kessomboon, and Laongbua 2008), as did Colombia when it considered the same in 2016 for a cancer drug (Vaca 2016). In Colombia's case, a leaked cable revealed that an aide to a powerful US senator with ties to the pharmaceutical industry was threatening to block congressional approval of a $450 million program of aid for Colombia's peace-building process in order to punish the country for taking steps toward a compulsory license (Goodman and Johnson 2016).

The continued vulnerability of the right to health under global IP rules prompted UN Secretary-General Ban Ki-Moon to establish in 2015 a High-Level Panel on Access to Medicines (UNHLP), with the mandate to "review and assess proposals and recommend solutions for remedying the *policy incoherence* between the justifiable rights of inventors, international human rights law, trade rules and public health in the context of health technologies [emphasis added]" (UN Secretary-General et al. 2016, 3). The UNHLP published its report in September 2016, through which it upbraided governments and the pharmaceutical industry for employing threats to undermine the use of TRIPS flexibilities and recommended that WTO members "must register complaints against undue political and economic pressure including taking punitive measures against offending WTO members" (UN Secretary-General and others 2016, 9). The UNHLP also recommended that WTO members revise the Paragraph 6 amendment to make it more usable and facilitate the export of pharmaceuticals produced under compulsory licenses. Immediately upon its publication, the report was harshly criticized by the US government and a group of industry representatives, including the US Chamber of Commerce (Moon 2017).

Notably, after opposition from the United States and WHO Secretariat to discussing the report at WHO (Struver 2017), the TRIPS Council became the first multilateral forum in which the UNHLP report was formally discussed. The report garnered strong opposition from the United States and a cool reception by the EU; however, it received support from emerging powers—Brazil, China, Bangladesh, India, and South Africa (WTO 2017b). At the request of Brazil and India, various specific recommendations of the UNHLP will remain on subsequent TRIPS Council agendas. While it remains to be seen how WTO members and the institution as a whole will respond, the UNHLP report has put the spotlight back on the limited political space that members have to use TRIPS flexibilities and, in so doing, reinvigorated debates on the need to reinforce the right to health at the WTO.

4. THE UNITED NATIONS HUMAN RIGHTS COUNCIL

The Commission on Human Rights (replaced in 2006 by the UN Human Rights Council (HRC)) has periodically passed resolutions and decisions since 2001 discussing access to medicines as part of the right to health. In 2016, anticipating the report of the UN Secretary-General's UNHLP, a group of eleven HRC countries (known as the Core Group) re-invigorated the medicines debate when it tabled a resolution asking member states, UN agencies, treaty bodies, civil society, and the private sector to recognize the *"primacy* of human rights over international trade, investment and intellectual property regimes" [emphasis added] (HRC 2016, 5). The idea that human rights norms trumped trade rules met stiff opposition, most notably expressed by Australia, the EU, Japan, Switzerland, and the United States (Balasubramaniam 2016b). The United Kingdom, shortly following the "Brexit" vote, questioned whether the HRC was an appropriate arena to debate medicines issues and even rejected the widely accepted principle that states have an obligation to ensure access to medicines, stating:

> While we fully support the right of everyone to the enjoyment of highest attainable standard of physical and mental health ... we cannot support the assertion ... that creates a responsibility for states to ensure access to medicines, which is unfounded in law (Balasubramaniam 2016a).

The Core Group's proposal to elevate human rights over trade and IP rules did not survive in the final resolution adopted by consensus; however, the Core Group opened a pathway for the UNHLP's work to be taken up in the human rights system, mandating that the UNHLP report be formally presented and discussed at the HRC's March 2017 meeting (UN General Assembly 2016). During this meeting, the co-chair of the UNHLP stressed that the current system of innovation, predicated on IP rights, was inadequate to address the challenges of antimicrobial resistance, neglected tropical diseases, and the medical needs of children (Saez 2017). The HRC has proven to be an enduring forum in which access to medicines can be discussed as a human rights issue, in addition to ongoing debates at the WTO, WHO, and elsewhere. While such human rights reframing has elevated the relative importance of access to medicines vis-à-vis economic concerns, it has not been sufficient to resolve the policy incoherence that remains between IP rules and the right to health.

C. The Rise of Tobacco Control Concerns at the WTO

Tobacco control has emerged alongside access to medicines as a high-level issue at the intersection of trade and health. Concerns have centered on the extent to which

WTO (and other trade and investment) rules have restricted the policy space available to states to regulate the sale and marketing of tobacco products, undercutting state efforts to realize the right to health.[11]

Starting in 2010, Indonesia filed a complaint at the WTO against a US ban on clove cigarettes (WTO 2010). Indonesia argued that a 2009 US tobacco control law discriminated against an imported product when it banned all flavored cigarettes (on the basis that these were marketed to children) but made an exception for menthol cigarettes, which are primarily domestically produced.[12] The WTO ultimately ruled that cloves and menthols were "like products," and therefore that the US law did indeed discriminate against an import (McGrady and Jones 2013). Some saw in this decision a defeat for anti-smoking policies—and therefore, for the government obligation to regulate to protect the right to health (Campaign for Tobacco-Free Kids 2012). However, it is important to note that the decision did not question the legality of banning flavored cigarettes for public health purposes; it merely challenged the policy space of the United States to tailor a public health regulation to reflect the particularities of its domestic context. Ultimately, while Indonesia was authorized to retaliate with sanctions valued at around $55 million, the two parties resolved their differences through a separate agreement, and the United States, in the end, decided to retain its clove cigarette ban (ICTSD 2014). Much like the 1996 EU decision on hormones in US beef, this resolution underscored that wealthier countries can often withstand trade-related challenges to protect health-related human rights, while poorer countries have far fewer means to do so.

The second tobacco-related issue arose in the WTO with a series of complaints filed in 2012–2013 by Ukraine, Honduras, the Dominican Republic, Cuba, and Indonesia, challenging Australia's law requiring that tobacco be sold in "plain packaging," requiring textual and/or graphic health warnings while disallowing company logos (See sample in Figure 17.1).

The complainants argued that removing trademarked logos from tobacco packaging would violate TRIPS protections, while the Australian government justified its law by arguing that it would reduce the attractiveness of tobacco products to young people and help discourage tobacco use more broadly—both important public health objectives.

Similar cases on tobacco packaging have been brought in other forums. Tobacco company Philip Morris International directly challenged the Australia law in the Australian court system and through bilateral investment treaty (BIT) arbitration proceedings. The Australian High Court upheld the law in 2012, and the arbitration body for the BIT rejected the case in 2015 due to lack of jurisdiction (Liberman 2013; Philip Morris Asia Limited (Hong Kong) v. The Commonwealth

11. The UN Committee on Economic, Social and Cultural Rights (CESCR) has explicitly identified state failure to "discourage production, marketing and consumption of tobacco, narcotics and other harmful substances" as a violation of state obligations to protect the right to health (CESCR 2000, 14; Dresler et al. 2012).

12. In response, the United States claimed that its rationale for excluding menthols from the ban was that they were far more widely used than other flavored cigarettes, and thus a ban would have been far more difficult to enforce.

Figure 17.1 Sample of cigarettes in plain packaging with graphic warning label.
PHOTO CREDIT: David Hammond.

of Australia 2012). The UK high court upheld a similar law in 2016 after an industry challenge. Philip Morris also challenged an analogous law in Uruguay, which required that cigarette packs display graphic health warnings covering 80 percent of the package, arguing in investment treaty arbitration that its trademark rights had been violated. After a six-year process, Philip Morris lost the case in 2016, with arbitrators upholding Uruguay's tobacco packaging regulation (International Centre for Settlement of Investment Disputes 2016). In 2017, media reports indicated that the WTO Appellate Body had followed suit and upheld Australia's plain packaging law (Miles and Geller 2017).[13] This decision is expected to be an important step toward institutionalizing health-related rights within the WTO, clarifying and strengthening the policy space to protect the right to health even when doing so may limit trade or other economic activity.

III. INSTITUTIONAL FACTORS INHIBITING OR FACILITATING PUBLIC HEALTH AND HUMAN RIGHTS PROTECTION AT THE WTO

The cases of access to medicines and tobacco control have demonstrated how space for health-related human rights can be carved out within the global trade regime. However, neither health nor human rights are the core mandate of the WTO, whose purpose is to liberalize global trade flows with the broader goal of contributing to economic growth and development. The training and incentives of government

13. This decision had not yet been made public by the WTO.

trade officials are geared toward negotiating, concluding, and implementing trade agreements that provide benefits for their constituents (whether conceived of broadly as country populations, or more narrowly as businesses) (Lee, Sridhar, and Patel 2009). Trade ministries are charged with reaching deals that, on balance, offer net benefits to the country—if they did not, there would be no incentive for a country to sign them. While some provisions of a trade agreement may harm public health, these are often considered trade-offs for other benefits such as economic growth (Ottersen et al. 2014). The extent to which health considerations are taken into account will depend on the political power of those advocating for them, whether from inside government (e.g., ministries of health) or outside (e.g., civil society, WHO, and the media). As seen in the context of medicines and tobacco, it has indeed been possible to increase the importance given to health concerns. However, trade partners who see these changes as adversely affecting their economic interests may shift trade negotiations away from the WTO.

With the important but small exception of the Paragraph 6 negotiations, IP rules at the WTO have not been opened for substantive renegotiation since TRIPS was finalized; the obligations to grant patents on medicines remains largely unchanged. Furthermore, states have pursued more stringent global IP rules through bilateral and regional arenas (El Said 2012). Once adopted by a critical mass of countries outside the WTO, the adoption of such bilateral norms may become more feasible within the multilateral arena—a strategy that has been labeled a "global IP upward ratchet" (Sell 2010, 1). Thus, even if global policy space for health is expanded within the WTO in the short term, it is being restricted in countries signing onto bilateral and regional trade agreements with provisions more stringent than TRIPS (e.g., longer patent terms), and in the long term, such provisions may be reimported into the WTO. Rather than having been mainstreamed, the position of health within the WTO and the broader trade regime remains precarious.

The medicines and tobacco cases also highlight the salience of significant power asymmetries between trade and health actors, between private firms and public interest groups—and perhaps most importantly, between richer and poorer countries. In the EU beef hormones and US clove cigarette cases, both economies that lost their disputes could absorb the costs of trade sanctions in order to maintain domestic health-related policies of political importance to their constituents. For smaller or less economically robust countries, especially those heavily dependent on trade, trade sanctions (or other types of pressure) can deal a heavier blow; governments may be unwilling to accept such consequences, or even the risk that they could arise. Within the WTO and broader trade regime, it is easier to protect the right to health of people in rich countries than in poorer countries.

Yet, four important factors have facilitated and solidified health and human rights considerations at the WTO.

First, securing the political legitimacy of the WTO as an institution requires that it be seen as responsive to social concerns. This point was made most forcefully at the 1999 "Battle of Seattle," when vehement street protesters—many of them advocating for environment, health, and labor rights—shut down the scheduled WTO Ministerial Conference (Smith 2001). In subsequent years, the WTO has made concerted efforts to respond to its critics. For example, the WTO

Secretariat often points out that TRIPS flexibilities allow governments to improve access to medicines (Taubman 2011). The 2001 Doha Declaration, which clarified interpretations of TRIPS but did not amend TRIPS, can be understood in part as an effort to defend the legitimacy of the WTO against critiques that its rules run counter to human rights.

Second is the dispute settlement process, which has clarified and solidified policy space for health in the clove cigarette and tobacco plain packaging cases. Public health concerns are not necessarily elevated over trade interests, as the EU beef hormones case illustrated; however, the rules-based adjudication system offers important advantages over bilateral trade wars as a method to settle disputes. In particular, dispute settlement procedures have demonstrated that judges will take health considerations into account when weighing the merits of a decision, providing health advocates and poorer countries with a more level playing field in which to raise health concerns.

Third is the growing awareness in the public health and human rights communities that engaging in trade policy in general, and with the WTO in particular, is needed to protect health-related human rights. Health advocates in governments, intergovernmental organizations (such as WHO or UNAIDS), civil society, and academia have developed expertise, networks, and negotiating strategies on relevant trade policy issues. For example, the three UN Special Rapporteurs on the Right to Health have made trade an important focus of their analyses (UN General Assembly 2004; UN General Assembly 2008; OHCHR n.d.). Scholars have analyzed various intersections between trade and health (MacDonald and Horton 2009; Drager and Fidler 2007; Labonté, Blouin, and Forman 2009; Lee, Sridhar, and Patel 2009; Ottersen et al. 2014). Developing capacity across disputes, advocates have proven influential and adept at using diplomatic tools, such as forum-shifting to "friendlier" arenas such as the HRC to reframe IP and access to medicines as a human rights issue rather than as an exclusively trade issue.

Finally, efforts to ensure access to medicines and tobacco control as an integral part of the right to health have not always been framed within the WTO explicitly using rights language, nor have they centered on the international human rights architecture. Rather, health advocates raised these issues in many different forums—including the WHO, UN General Assembly, WTO, WIPO, and G7, in addition to the HRC—and in doing so, deployed discourse tailored to the context and audience. Arguments were framed in the language of international trade law, economics, public health, and security—in addition to human rights. Nevertheless, the substantive progress achieved and impact in carving out policy space for health at the WTO has been rooted in and will help to realize the right to health.

CONCLUSION

Efforts to strengthen policy space for health-related rights within the WTO have met with an important degree of success. Such progress in the multilateral arena, however, can be counteracted through trade rules negotiated in bilateral or regional forums, or through old-fashioned power politics between countries. If major trading powers turn their back on the multilateral system in favor of unilateral approaches, the right to health—particularly in smaller or poorer countries—is likely to suffer.

The centrality of the WTO to the global trade regime is under question. The Doha round of trade talks that was launched in 2001 remains gridlocked; whereas previous multilateral trade rounds had lasted from two to eight years, the Doha round has been ongoing for over sixteen years with no resolution in sight. Governments have increasingly shifted trade talks toward bilateral, regional, or plurilateral arenas among smaller groups of countries, where agreement is easier to reach and larger economies hold more sway. Over 400 regional trade agreements have been concluded in the two decades since the WTO came into being in 1994, compared to only 124 in the five decades prior. Each WTO member is now party to at least one regional trade agreement, which frequently contain measures that are more harmful to realizing the right to health, such as measures that require countries to adopt standards more stringent than TRIPS or place additional restrictions on public health regulation.

Respecting the right to health remains largely an exception to the regular functioning of trade rules rather than their main purpose. Although changes to the text of WTO agreements is highly unlikely—given the high threshold of unanimous consent required for such changes and the starkly opposed interests among members—the most promising path to such institutionalization may come from leveraging the powerful institutional features of the WTO dispute settlement system for human rights ends. Outside the WTO, the prospects and pathways to stronger human rights protection within trade rules are far less clear. It is likely that sustained civil society mobilization will be required. Most essential is strengthened political commitment from governments to give high priority to health-related human rights when negotiating, interpreting, implementing and enforcing trade agreements. It remains to be seen whether such prioritization will materialize.

REFERENCES

Abbott, Frederick M. 2005. "The WTO Medicines Decision: World Pharmaceutical Trade and the Protection of Public Health." *The American Journal of International Law* 99(2): 317–358.

Balasubramaniam, Thirukumaran. 2016a. "Human Rights Council Adopts Watershed Resolution on Access to Medicines." *Knowledge Ecology International.* Available at: https://www.keionline.org/node/2605.

Balasubramaniam, Thirukumaran. 2016b. "Human Rights Council Heats Up during Informal Talks on the Primacy of Human Rights over International Trade and IP Regimes." *Knowledge Ecology International.* June 18. Available at: https://www.keionline.org/node/2602.

Barton, John H., Judith L. Goldstein, Timothy E. Josling, and Richard H. Steinberg. 2008. *The Evolution of the Trade Regime: Politics, Law, and Economics of the GATT and the WTO.* Princeton: Princeton University Press.

Blouin, Chantal, Nick Drager, and Richard Smith. 2006. *International Trade in Health Services and the GATS: Current Issues and Debates.* Washington, D.C.: The World Bank.

Bradsher, Keith and Edmund L. Andrews. 2001. A Nation Challenged: Cipro; U.S. Says Bayer Will Cut Cost of Its Anthrax Drug. October 24. Available at: http://www.nytimes.com/2001/10/24/business/a-nation-challenged-cipro-us-says-bayer-will-cut-cost-of-its-anthrax-drug.html.

Campaign for Tobacco-Free Kids. 2012. "WTO Ruling on Clove Cigarettes Disregards Congress' Legitimate Authority to Protect America's Kids from Tobacco." Available at: http://www.tobaccofreekids.org/press_releases/post/2012_04_04_wto.

CESCR (Committee on Economic, Social and Cultural Rights). 2000. "General Comment No. 14: The Right to the Highest Attainable Standard of Health" 11 August. UN Doc. E/C.12/2000/4.

Correa, Carlos M. 2004. "Bilateralism in Intellectual Property: Defeating the WTO System for Access to Medicines. 36 Case W. Res." *Journal of International Law* 36: 79.

Drager, Nick and David P. Fidler. 2007. Foreign Policy, Trade and Health: At the Cutting Edge of Global Health Diplomacy. *Bulletin of the World Health Organization* 85(3): 162–162.

Drahos, Peter. 2003. *Expanding Intellectual Property's Empire: The Role of FTAs.* Geneva: GRAIN.

Dresler, Carolyn, Harry Lando, Nick Schneider, and Hitakshi Sehgal. 2012. "Human Rights-Based Approach to Tobacco Control." *Tobacco Control* 21(2): 208–211.

El Said, Mohammed. 2012. "The Morning After: TRIPS-Plus, FTAs, and Wikileaks: Fresh Insights on the Implementation and Enforcement of IP Protection in Developing Countries." *American University International Law Review* 28: 71.

Forman, Lisa. 2008. "'Rights' and Wrongs: What Utility for the Right to Health in Reforming Trade Rules on Medicines?" *Health and Human Rights* 37–52.

Forman, Lisa. 2016. "The Inadequate Global Policy Response to Trade-Related Intellectual Property Rights: Impact on Access to Medicines in Low and Middle-Income Countries." *Maryland Journal of International Law* 31: 8–20.

Frenk, Julio and Suerie Moon. 2013. "Governance Challenges in Global Health." *The New England Journal of Medicine* 368: 936–942.

GATT (General Agreement on Tariffs and Trade). 1986. "Multilateral Trade Negotiations— The Uruguay Round—Ministerial Declaration on the Uruguay Round, 20 September 1986." Available at: https://www.wto.org/gatt_docs/English/SULPDF/91240152.pdf.

GATT (General Agreement on Tariffs and Trade). 1990. "Negotiating Group on Trade-Related Aspects of Intellectual Property Rights, Including Trade in Counterfeit Goods—Communication from Argentina, Brazil, Chile, China, Colombia, Cuba, Egypt, India, Nigeria, Peru, Tanzania and Uruguay." Doc. MTN.GNG/NG11/W/71.

Goodman, J., and Johnson, L. 2016. "Colombia Battles World's Biggest Drugmaker over Cheaper Cancer Drugs." *Associated Press.* May 18. Available at: http://bigstory.ap.org/article/622371a73e3f43e197875402ce6449ab/colombia-battles-worlds-biggest-drugmaker-over-cancer-drug.

Hein, Wolfgang and Suerie Moon. 2013. *Informal Norms in Global Governance: Human Rights, Intellectual Property Rules and Access to Medicines.* Aldershot, UK: Ashgate.

HRC (UN Human Rights Council). 2016. "Access to Medicines in the Context of the Right of Everyone to the Enjoyment of the Highest Attainable Standard of Physical and Mental Health." UN Doc. A/HRC/32/L.23.

ICTSD (International Centre for Settlement of Investment Disputes). 2014. "Indonesia Announces Deal with US on Clove Cigarettes Trade Dispute." *Bridges Weekly.* Available at: http://www.ictsd.org/bridges-news/bridges/news/indonesia-announces-deal-with-us-on-clove-cigarettes-trade-dispute.

ICTSD (International Centre for Settlement of Investment Disputes). 2016. "Philip Morris Brands SARL, Philip Morris SA and Abal Hermanos SA vs. Oriental Republic of Uruguay. Award. ICTSD Case No. ARB/10/7." Available at: http://www.italaw.com/sites/default/files/case-documents/italaw7417.pdf.

Kanchanachitra, Churnrurtai, Magnus Lindelow, Timothy Johnston, Piya Hanvoravongchai, Fely Marilyn Lorenzo, Nguyen Lan Huong, Siswanto Agus Wilopo, and Jennifer Frances dela Rosa. 2011. "Human Resources for Health in Southeast Asia: Shortages, Distributional Challenges, and International Trade in Health Services." *The Lancet* 377 (9767): 769–781.

Labonté, Ronald, Chantal Blouin, and Lisa Forman. 2009. "Trade and Health." In *Global Health Governance*, 182–208. United Kingdom: Palgrave Macmillan.

Lee, Kelley, Devi Sridhar, and Mayur Patel. 2009. "Bridging the Divide: Global Governance of Trade and Health." *The Lancet* 373(9661): 416–422.

Lewis, Paul. 1982. "U.S. and the Third World at Odds over Patents." *The New York Times*. October 5. Available at: http://www.nytimes.com/1982/10/05/business/us-nd-the-third-world-at-odds-over-patents.html.

Liberman, Jonathan. 2013. "Plainly Constitutional: The Upholding of Plain Tobacco Packaging by the High Court of Australia." *American Journal of Law & Medicine* 39(2–3): 361–381.

MacDonald, Rhona and Richard Horton. 2009. "Trade and Health: Time for the Health Sector to Get Involved." *The Lancet* 373(9660): 273–274.

Machlup, Fritz and Edith Penrose. 1950. "The Patent Controversy in the Nineteenth Century." *The Journal of Economic History* 10(1): 1–29.

Marceau, Gabrielle and Joel P. Trachtman. 2002. "Technical Barriers to Trade Agreement, the Sanitary and Phytosanitary Measures Agreement, and the General Agreement on Tariffs and Trade." *The Journal of World Trade* 36:811.

McGrady, Benn and Alexandra Jones. 2013. "Tobacco Control and Beyond: The Broader Implications of United States—Clove Cigarettes for Non-communicable Diseases." *American Journal of Law & Medicine* 39(2–3): 265–289.

Miles, Tom and Geller, Martinne. 2017. "Australia Wins Landmark WTO Tobacco Packaging Case." *Reuters*. May 5. Available at: http://www.reuters.com/article/us-wto-tobacco-australia-idUSKBN1801S9.

Moon, Suerie. 2017. "Powerful Ideas for Global Access to Medicines." *New England Journal of Medicine* 376(6): 505–507.

Office of the United States Trade Representative. 1999. "Special 301 Report." Washington, D.C. http://www.keionline.org/ustr/1999special301.

OHCHR. n.d. *UN experts voice concern over adverse impact of free trade and investment agreements on human rights*. Available at: http://www.ohchr.org/en/NewsEvents/Pages/DisplayNews.aspx?NewsID=16031&LangID=E.

Ottersen, Ole Petter, Jashodhara Dasgupta, Chantal Blouin, Paulo Buss, Virasakdi Chongsuvivatwong, Julio Frenk, Sakiko Fukuda-Parr [et al.]. 2014. "The Political Origins of Health Inequity: Prospects for Change." *The Lancet* 383(9917): 630–667.

Pauwelyn, Joost. 1999. "The WTO Agreement on Sanitary and Phytosanitary (SPS) Measures as Applied in the First Three SPS Disputes: EC-Hormones, Australia-Salmon and Japan-Varietals." *Journal of International Economic Law* 2(4): 641–664.

Philip Morris Asia Limited (Hong Kong) v. The Commonwealth of Australia. 2012. PCA 2012–12. Available at: http://www.pcacases.com/web/view/5.

Reichman, Jerome H. 2008. "Universal Minimum Standards of Intellectual Property Protection under the TRIPS Component of the WTO Agreement." In *Intellectual*

Property and International Trade: The TRIPS Agreement, edited by Carlos María Correa and Abdulqawi Yusuf, 23–78. Alphen aan den Rijn: Kluwer Law International.

Reitz, Curtis. 1996. "Enforcement of the General Agreement on Tariffs and Trade." *University of Pennsylvania Journal of International Law* 17(2): 555–603.

Rothe, Dawn, and Stephen L. Muzzatti. 2004. "Enemies Everywhere: Terrorism, Moral Panic, and US Civil Society." *Critical Criminology* 12(3): 327–350.

Saez, Catherine. 2017. "UN High-Level Panel on Access to Medicines Takes Next Step at Human Rights Council." *Intellectual Property Watch,* March 9.

Sell, Susan K. 2010. "TRIPS Was Never Enough: Vertical Forum Shifting, FTAS, ACTA, and TPP." *Journal of Intellectual Property* 18(2): 447–478.

Shankar, Raja, Elizabeth Kinsey, Pete Thomas, Joel Hooper, and Sheliza Teja. 2013. "Securing IP and Access to Medicine: Is Oncology the Next HIV?" *IMS Consulting.* Available at: https://www.imshealth.com/files/web/Global/Services/Services%20 TL/IMSCG_Compulsory_Licensing.pdf.

Smith, Jackie. (2001). "Globalizing Resistance: The Battle of Seattle and the Future of Social Movements." *Mobilization: An International Quarterly* 6(1): 1–19.

Struver, Zack. 2017. "CDC FOIA Shows US, WHO Opposed Request to Discuss UNSG's High-Level Panel on Access to Medicines Report at EB." *Knowledge Ecology International.* February 28. Available at: https://www.keionline.org/node/2727.

Tantivess, Sripen, Nusaraporn Kessomboon, and Chotiros Laongbua. 2008. *Introducing Government Use of Patents on Essential Medicines in Thailand, 2006–2007: Policy Analysis with Key Lessons Learned and Recommendations.* Nonthaburi, Thailand: International Health Policy Program, Ministry of Health.

Taubman, Antony. 2011. *A Practical Guide to Working with TRIPS.* Oxford University Press.

Taubman, Antony. 2015. "Thematic Review: Negotiating 'Trade-Related Aspects' of Intellectual Property Rights." In *Making of the TRIPS Agreement,* edited by Jayashree Watal, and Antony Taubman. Geneva: WTO.

Tosun, Jale. 2013. "Perspectives on the Precautionary Principle." In *Risk Regulation in Europe, Assessing the Application of the Precautionary Principle,* 39–50. New York: Springer.

't Hoen, Ellen F. M. 2002. "TRIPS, Pharmaceutical Patents, and Access to Essential Medicines: A Long Way from Seattle to Doha." *Chicago Journal of International Law* 3(1): 27–46.

't Hoen, Ellen F. M. 2003. "TRIPS, Pharmaceutical Patents and Access to Essential Medicines: Seattle, Doha and Beyond." In *Economics of AIDS and Access to HIV/AIDS Care in Developing Countries. Issues and Challenges,* edited by Jean-Paul Moatti, Benjamin Coriat, Yves Souteyrand, Tony Barnett, Jerome Dumoulin, and Yves-Antoine Flori, 39–67. Sciences Sociales et Sida. Paris: ANRS.

't Hoen, Ellen F. M. 2009. *The Global Politics of Pharmaceutical Monopoly Power: Drug Patents, Access, Innovation, and the Application of the WTO Doha Declaration on TRIPS and Public Health.* Diemen, The Netherlands: AMB Press.

't Hoen, Ellen F. M. 2016. *Private Patents and Public Health: Changing Intellectual Property Rules for Access to Medicines.* Amsterdam: Health Action International.

't Hoen, Ellen F. M., Jonathan Berger, Alexandra Calmy, and Suerie Moon. 2011. "Driving a Decade of Change: HIV/AIDS, Patents, and Access to Medicines." *Journal of the International AIDS Society* 14(15), 1–12.

UN Commission on Human Rights. 2003. "Access to Medication in the Context of Pandemics such as HIV/AIDS." Res. 2003/29.

UN General Assembly. 2004. "Report of Paul Hunt, Special Rapporteur of the Commission on Human Rights, on the right of everyone to the enjoyment of the highest attainable standard of physical and mental health. Addendum: Mission to the World Trade Organization." UN Doc. E/CN.4/2004/49/Add.1.

UN General Assembly, 63rd Session. 2008. "Promotion and protection of human rights: human rights questions, including alternative approaches for improving the effective enjoyment of human rights and fundamental freedoms: The right to health, Note by the Secretary-General." 11 August. UN Doc. A/63/263.

UN General Assembly. 2016. "Access to medicines in the context of the right of everyone to the enjoyment of the highest attainable standard of physical and mental health." 18 July. A/HRC/RES/32/15.

UN Secretary-General and others. 2016. "The United Nations Secretary-General's High-Level Panel on Access to Medicines Report: Promoting Innovation and Access to Health Technologies." Available at: https://static1.squarespace.com/static/562094dee4b0d00c1a3ef761/t/57d9c6ebf5e231b2f02cd3d4/1473890031320/UNSG+HLP+Report+FINAL+12+Sept+2016.pdf.

UNCTAD (United Nations Conference on Trade and Development), Geneva. 2012. *World Investment Report: Towards a New Generation of Investment Policies*. New York and Geneva: United Nations.

U.S. Department of State. 1999. "U.S. Government Efforts to Negotiate the Repeal, Termination or Withdrawal of Article 15(C) of the South African Medicines and Related Substances Act of 1965, 5 February." Available at: http://www.cptech.org/ip/health/sa/stdept-feb51999.html.

Vaca, Claudia. 2016. "La Declaración de Interés Público de Imatinib (Glivec®): Entre Lo Dulce Y Lo Amargo." *Revista de La Universidad Industrial de Santander Salud* 48 (3): 273–274.

Velasquez, German, Carlos M. Correa, and Thirukumaran Balasubramaniam. 2005. "WHO in the Frontlines of the Access to Medicines Battle: The Debate on Intellectual Property Rights and Public Health." In *Intellectual Property in the Context of the TRIPS Agreement: Challenges for Public Health*, edited by Jorge Z. A. Bermudez and Maria Auxiliadora Oliveira, English: 83–98. Rio de Janeiro: National School of Public Health Sergio Arouca, Fondation Oswaldo Cruz.

Vogel, David. 2012. *The Politics of Precaution: Regulating Health, Safety, and Environmental Risks in Europe and the United States*. Princeton University Press.

Watal, Jayashree, and Antony Taubman. 2015. *The Making of the TRIPS Agreement: Personal Insights from the Uruguay Round Negotiations*. Geneva: World Trade Organization.

WHO, WIPO, and WTO. 2013. *Promoting Access to Medical Technologies and Innovation: Intersections between Public Health, Intellectual Property and Trade*. Geneva: World Health Organization (WHO); World Intellectual Property Organization (WIPO); World Trade Organization (WTO).

WTO (World Trade Organization). 1994a. "DSU, Dispute Settlement Rules: Understanding on Rules and Procedures Governing the Settlement of Disputes, Marrakesh Agreement Establishing the World Trade Organization." Doc. Annex 2, 1869 U.N.T.S. 401, 33 I.L.M. 1226.

WTO. 1994b. "TRIPS: Agreement on Trade-Related Aspects of Intellectual Property Rights, Marrakesh Agreement Establishing the World Trade Organization." 15 April. Doc. Annex 1C, 1869 U.N.T.S. 299, 33 I.L.M. 1197.

WTO. 1999. *Seattle: what's at stake? A resource booklet for the Seattle Ministerial Meeting*. Switzerland: World Trade Organization.

WTO. 2000. "'Brazil—Measures Affecting Patent Protection'—Request for Consultations by the United States." 8 June 2000. Doc. WT/DS199/. Available at: https://www.wto.org/english/tratop_e/dispu_e/cases_e/ds199_e.htm.

WTO. 2001a. "Council for Trade-Related Aspects of Intellectual Property Rights—Minutes of Meeting—Held in the Centre William Rappard on 2–5 April 2001." Doc. IP/C/M/30.

WTO. 2001b. "Declaration on the TRIPS Agreement and Public Health." Doc. WT/MIN(01)/DEC/2.

WTO. 2001c. "United States—US Patents Code"—Request for Consultations by Brazil." World Trade Organization. 31 January. Doc. WT/DS224/1. Available at: https://www.wto.org/english/tratop_e/dispu_e/cases_e/ds224_e.htm.

WTO. 2006. "TRIPS and Health: Frequently Asked Questions—Compulsory Licensing of Pharmaceuticals and TRIPS." *World Trade Organization*. Available at: https://www.wto.org/english/tratop_e/trips_e/public_health_faq_e.htm.

WTO. 2010. "WTO: Dispute Settlement: Dispute DS406: United States—Measures Affecting the Production and Sale of Clove Cigarettes." Available at: https://www.wto.org/english/tratop_e/dispu_e/cases_e/ds406_e.htm.

WTO. 2014a. *Ensuring Safe Trading without Unnecessary Restrictions: Sanitary and Phytosanitary Measures*. World Trade Organization.

WTO. 2014b. The World Trade Organization . . . in Brief. *World Trade Organization*. Available at: https://www.wto.org/english/res_e/doload_e/inbr_e.pdf.

WTO. 2015. "WTO Members Agree to Extend Drug Patent Exemption for Poorest Members." *World Trade Organization*. Available at: https://www.wto.org/english/news_e/news15_e/trip_06nov15_e.htm.

WTO. 2016a. "Regional Trade Agreements: Facts and Figures." *World Trade Organization*. Available at: https://www.wto.org/english/tratop_e/region_e/regfac_e.htm.

WTO. 2016b. "Understanding the WTO: The Organization: Members and Observers." *World Trade Organization*. Available at: https://www.wto.org/english/thewto_e/whatis_e/tif_e/org6_e.htm.

WTO. 2016c. "WTO: Summary Table of Ongoing Accessions." *World Trade Organization*. Available at: https://www.wto.org/english/thewto_e/acc_e/status_e.htm.

WTO. 2017a. "WTO IP rules amended to ease poor countries' access to affordable medicines." *World Trade Organization*. 23 January. Available at: https://www.wto.org/english/news_e/news17_e/trip_23jan17_e.htm.

WTO. 2017b. "Council for Trade-Related Aspects of Intellectual Property Rights—Minutes of Meeting—Held in the Centre William Rappard on 8–9 November 2016." Doc. IP/C/M/83/Add.1.

"WTO Dispute Settlement Gateway." 2017c. *World Trade Organization*. Accessed July 8, 2017. Available at: https://www.wto.org/english/tratop_e/dispu_e/dispu_e.htm.

18

National Foreign Assistance Programs

Advancing Health-Related Human Rights through Shared Obligations for Global Health

RACHEL HAMMONDS AND GORIK J. OOMS

This chapter provides an overview of the role of bilateral development assistance in advancing health-related international human rights obligations by examining the evolution of efforts to coordinate bilateral development assistance agencies and the international public financing dimensions of their governance and goals. The competing and complementary strands that comprise bilateral health development efforts make it difficult to assess the impact of such assistance on advancing health-related human rights at a general level. Therefore, this chapter focuses on a leading institution that coordinates bilateral foreign assistance, the Organisation for Economic Co-operation and Development's Development Assistance Committee (OECD-DAC). The OECD-DAC provides an entry point for assessment due to its leading role over five decades in shaping and coordinating the discourse and practice surrounding bilateral official development assistance (ODA) and its increasing interaction with international human rights norms and goals. Specifically, it coordinates the classification and collection of ODA-related data, brings together wealthy countries to discuss common strategies, and plays a role in advocating for increasing national ODA, monitoring ODA disbursement, and countering fragmentation to improve aid effectiveness.

This chapter opens in Part I by briefly outlining the evolution of international obligations for health-related human rights, focusing on the right to health and providing a theoretical basis for the chapter. Part II reviews the origins of the OECD-DAC and the parallel rise of national development assistance agencies. Part III examines the evolution of attention to health-related human rights, both outside and within the OECD-DAC, including the factors that facilitated and/or inhibited a coordinated approach to human rights mainstreaming in its practice and those of the development assistance agencies of OECD-DAC members. Part IV reviews the

Human Rights in Global Health. Benjamin Mason Meier and Lawrence O. Gostin.

emergence of the aid effectiveness agenda and the International Health Partnership and Related Initiatives (IHP+), which unite national foreign assistance agencies and other stakeholders to deliver on IHP+ goals that build on the efforts of the OECD-DAC to improve the coordination, alignment, additionality, reliability, and volume of public international assistance for health. Part V looks to the future, assessing upcoming challenges to the current goals and governance of rights-based bilateral assistance.

I. INTERNATIONAL OBLIGATIONS FOR HEALTH-RELATED HUMAN RIGHTS

Rights-based foreign assistance starts from the premise that international public financing for health, like that provided through bilateral and multilateral foreign assistance programs, is an international legal obligation, not a charitable or voluntary gesture. This obligation is grounded in the International Covenant on Economic, Social and Cultural Rights (ICESCR), according to which "each State Party to the present Covenant undertakes to take steps, individually and through international assistance and co-operation, especially economic and technical, to the maximum of its available resources, with a view to achieving progressively the full realization of the rights recognized in the present Covenant" (UN General Assembly 1966, art. 2.1). International assistance, therefore, is fundamental to achieving the rights "to the highest attainable standard of health" (Ibid., art. 12).

The shared international obligation for realizing human rights forms part of the bedrock of the international system that emerged at the end of World War II, when nations adopted the United Nations (UN) Charter, pledging universal respect for human rights and fundamental freedoms (art. 55) and seeking to achieve this through joint and separate action (art. 56) (UN 1945). International cooperation, including financing, is fundamental to both global development goals and the realization of international human rights objectives. Yet, the approach of both fields ran in parallel for fifty-plus years. Evidence of limited overlap emerged from the mid-1990s—exemplified by a change in discourse, a gradual infiltration of human rights language, and a multiplicity of rights-based objectives and approaches—in select bilateral foreign assistance programs. There is now a growing convergence, as detailed in chapter 15, between development and human rights, "highlighting the mutual relevance of the two spheres rather than the disconnects or tensions between them" (McInerney-Lankford and Sano 2010, 4). However, convergence between development assistance and human rights does not imply that states "in a position to assist," and indeed providing such assistance, acknowledge their legal obligations. On the contrary, donor states seem to carefully avoid any statement that would link their practice of providing international assistance with a legal obligation (Alston 2005; Tobin 2012). This reluctance stems largely from the imprecision of the legal obligation and the fear of the (potential) level of the concomitant costs, thus, underlining the importance of further research in this area and the need for ongoing advocacy to drive progress.

In parallel with a period of increasing convergence of human rights and development, global governance for health has witnessed, as described in chapter 3, a proliferation of global health actors and the fragmentation of international assistance for health modalities and objectives (Frenk and Moon 2013). By 2008, it was "estimated that there are more than 40 bilateral donors, 26 UN agencies, 20 global and regional funds, and 90 global health initiatives active at the moment" (McColl 2008, 2072). Beginning in the 1980s, the OECD-DAC members had been joined by new donors, like China and later Brazil and the United Arab Emirates (World Bank Instituto de Pesquisa Econômica Aplicada 2012, 15). The early 2000s saw the emergence of new, powerful non-state actors in global health, each with their own priorities and modalities, including wealthy foundations, foremost among them the Bill and Melinda Gates Foundation, and new global health initiatives, like the Global Alliance for Vaccines and Immunization (now Gavi, the Vaccine Alliance).

The OECD-DAC recognized the challenges fragmentation posed to the need for development assistance to produce results and has played a leading role in ensuring that "aid effectiveness" came to dominate discussion on international assistance in the early 2000s, including in the field of health (OECD 2011). This focus on results and effectiveness is not the same as advancing health-related human rights. However, to ensure continued domestic political support for international assistance to advance health-related rights, bilateral agencies need to show that international assistance can deliver results in an effective manner.

II. THE ORIGINS OF INTERNATIONAL DEVELOPMENT ASSISTANCE AGENCIES AND THE OECD-DAC

The rise of national development assistance agencies parallels post–World War II efforts to create a world order that contributed to peace, development, and human rights. However, understanding how wealthy countries came together to manage the modalities of this commitment requires looking outside the human rights field to the "rich nations club," as the OECD is often referred (Mahon and McBride 2008, 3), and its role in shaping policy and commitment on ODA. Former OECD Development Center Director, Helmut Führer, claims that the establishment of the OECD-DAC "was an integral part of the creation of a network of national and international aid agencies and programmes and related institutions" (Führer 1996, 4).

Until the early 1960s, the United States provided over 40 percent of total global development assistance, largely motivated by the strategic political goal of stopping countries from "going communist" (Ehrenfeld 2004).[1] In 1961, OECD members established the OECD-DAC largely due to US interest in sharing the development assistance burden (Hynes and Scott 2013). The OECD-DAC was mandated "to consult on the methods for making national resources available for assisting countries and areas in the process of economic development and for expanding and improving the flow of long-term funds and other development assistance to them" (Führer 1996, 10).

1. It is important to note that this is only one part of the "development story," as the story of Soviet development assistance, which greatly benefited, *inter alia*, Cuba and Angola, is not included in the OECD-DAC story (National Security Archive 2002).

In the 1960s and 1970s, the OECD-DAC was largely responsible for guiding discussion and agreement on ODA norms and definitions, which focused on improving the terms and conditions of development assistance to advance economic growth (not human rights). From its inception, the OECD-DAC was the focal point of international discussions about the volume of aid targets, which were closely tied to important questions of classification and measurement (Führer 1996). The importance of the OECD-DAC's role in both accountability (by tracking ODA) and shaping discourse on how ODA is measured (i.e., what is included and spent to advance economic growth, development, and/or advance human rights obligations) plays a role in the strength of the current aid effectiveness agenda. The influential Pearson target of 0.7 percent of gross national product (GNP) (now gross national income (GNI)) to be spent on ODA, which was agreed at the UN in 1970, was "generally accepted" by OECD-DAC members, with the notable exceptions of Switzerland and the United States, which "did not subscribe to specific targets or timetable, although it supported the more general aims of the Resolution" (OECD 1970).[2] By 1972, OECD-DAC members had agreed to a definition of ODA to include:

> those flows to countries and territories on the OECD-DAC List of ODA Recipients and to multilateral institutions which are:
>   I. provided by official agencies, including state and local governments, or by their executive agencies; and
>   II. each transaction of which
>   a. is administered with the promotion of the economic development and welfare of developing countries as its main objective; and
>   b. is concessional in character and conveys a grant element of at least 25 per cent (calculated at a rate of discount of 10 per cent). (OECD-DAC 1972).

During the deliberations about this ODA definition, the two international human rights covenants, the ICESCR and the International Covenant on Civil and Political Rights (ICCPR), were negotiated and, in 1966, opened for signature and ratification. It is striking that none of the language found in the 1948 Universal Declaration of Human Rights (UDHR) or the two covenants is reflected in the definition of ODA, even though many of the same states were engaged in both sets of negotiations.

Until the present day, improving and harmonizing the financial terms of aid has been a central focus of the OECD-DAC, both in view of the impact on developing countries' debt and of burden-sharing considerations (Führer 1996). The work on agreeing to an official definition of ODA "has provided transparency to improve policies and enabled donors to set targets for increasing their aid effort" (Hynes and Scott 2013, 2). While the principle of burden-sharing, as adopted and devised by the OECD-DAC, has become a cornerstone in discussions about the allocation of the

---

2. Parallel to development assistance debates in the OECD-DAC, the UN Pearson Commission proposed a target of 0.7 percent of donor GNP to be reached "by 1975 and in no case later than 1980" (Pearson Commission 1969).

legal obligations to provide assistance to advance human rights, it was not conceived for that purpose. OECD-DAC members willing to affirm and reaffirm the principle of burden-sharing also continue to reject the legally binding nature of that principle (Alston 2005; Tobin 2012). Yet all OECD-DAC members participated in the negotiations that agreed to the ICESCR, and a large majority have signed and ratified the ICESCR, thus voluntarily accepting to be bound by this legal obligation, while likely speculating that the latter was formulated in vague enough terms to remain ineffectual.

A. The Advent of Bilateral Development Assistance Agencies

The 1960s brought with it the establishment of many of the world's leading development assistance agencies. The top five, in terms of volume of ODA, include those delineated in Table 18.1.

Table 18.1. TOP ODA DONORS BY VOLUME (ALPHABETICAL ORDER) (OECD 2016)

Country	Year of origin	Origins	Today
France	1941	Caisse centrale de la France Libre	Agence Française de Développement (AFD) 1998
Germany	1961	Federal Ministry for Economic Cooperation and Development— with GIZ	German Corporation for International Cooperation GmbH (GIZ) 2011
Japan	1962	Overseas Technical Cooperation Agency (OTCA)	Japanese International Cooperation Agency (JICA) 2003
United Kingdom	1948	Colonial Development Corporation UK Ministry of Overseas Development Assistance (1964)	Department For International Development (DFID) 1997
United States	1950	Point Four Program (inspired by the Marshall Plan)	United States Agency for International Development (USAID) 1961

Most high-income countries have a bilateral foreign assistance program coordinated by government development agencies, like the US Agency for International Development (USAID) and the Swedish International Development Agency (SIDA), charged with administering ODA to low- and middle-income countries. Despite the recent increase in multilateral development organizations, and their proliferation in the health field, bilateral ODA remains the preferred funding channel, with the ratio of bilateral to multilateral ODA holding at approximately 70:30 (OECD 2012a). The OECD defines bilateral aid as "flows from official (government) sources directly to official sources in the recipient country" (OECD 2012a). Government development agencies were originally mandated through bilateral assistance to advance what were perceived to be "politically neutral" development objectives.[3] Yet, human rights commitments have slowly crept into their objectives, often typically lumped in with "good governance" or "aid effectiveness."

The initial impetus for these agencies was to provide technical and financial capital assistance, and much of their early collaboration with the OECD-DAC involved complex technical discussions about target-setting and defining how to classify ODA—offering evidence of early attempts to align ODA (OECD 2010). However, by the 1970s, partially in response to the demand of developing nations for a New International Economic Order, as described in chapter 15, most agencies expanded their vision to add a basic human needs approach, focusing on, *inter alia*, health and education (Führer 1996). In line with the Cold War politics of the day, the 1980s saw a shift to promoting bilateral assistance that encouraged free markets, echoing high-income country support for this agenda at the World Bank, as chronicled in chapter 16, and the International Monetary Fund. The end of the Cold War saw most OECD-DAC members shift their attention toward civil and political rights through support for democracy-building and sustainable economic growth as paths to development. However, the economic recession of the early 1990s saw net ODA fall by 16 percent between 1993 and 1997 (OECD 2012b).

The new millennium brought both an upswing in ODA levels and the UN Millennium Declaration, which reasserted a global commitment to the multilateral solidarity found in the ICESCR (World Bank IDA 2007; UN 2000). Even without any legal obligation, the Millennium Development Goal (MDG) agenda supported the shared responsibility of the right to health by focusing on the need for high-income countries to play a role in addressing the health and education needs of people in low- and middle-income countries. But the MDGs also emphasized disease-specific efforts, which can fragment progress on the right to health or health-related rights more generally. Further, the MDGs put forward non-binding targets. Thus, while bilateral development assistance, especially for health, reached new highs in the 2000s (Institute for Health Metrics and Evaluation 2010), it flowed in accordance with this limited, vertical approach to realizing health rights.

---

3. As noted above, OECD-DAC's initial mandate clarified that the goal of ODA was economic growth to promote development, a logic that guided OECD-DAC members.

III. DEVELOPMENT ASSISTANCE, HUMAN RIGHTS, AND THE OECD-DAC

Examining the evolution of attention to human rights, both in bilateral assistance agencies and within the OECD-DAC, it is necessary to analyze the factors that facilitated and/or inhibited human rights mainstreaming in development assistance. Rather than assessing the various approaches to human rights in the funding of different bilateral assistance programs (UNDP 1998; Maxwell 1999; UNDG 2003; Robinson and Alston 2004; Alston and Robinson 2005; Andersen and Sano 2006; Sano 2007; Uvin 2007; McInerney-Lankford and Sano 2010; World Bank OECD 2013; Hollander et al. 2014), this part introduces a few key challenges to integrating human rights in health assistance and highlights some outstanding conceptual issues.

A. Development Assistance and Human Rights-Based Approaches

The 1986 Declaration on the Right to Development responded to the concerns of low- and middle-income countries regarding the separation of human rights from development practice, including, as discussed in chapter 15, the absence of attention to issues of participation, accountability, non-discrimination, and transparency. However, it was not until the end of the Cold War that bilateral development assistance agencies and non-governmental organizations (NGOs) began to focus on the potential of human rights to address development shortcomings (Cornwall and Nyamu-Musembi 2004). The 1993 Vienna World Conference on Human Rights heralded the international (re-)commitment to the universality and holistic nature of human rights and the recognition that social and economic rights, including the right to health, are human rights. In the development field, the Vienna Declaration and Programme of Action called for fresh approaches to conceptualize both "human needs" and "democracy" as human rights, with the individual rights holder bringing claims against the state duty bearer for failure to realize rights (UN 1993).

With the end of the Cold War, the UN slowly began to assert its leading role in shaping the development agenda and related discourses with the objective of advancing human rights. Countries increasingly turned to the UN for guidance on human rights mainstreaming in development (Alston and Robinson 2005). During the late 1990s, the UN Committee on Economic, Social and Cultural Rights (CESCR), established in 1985 to monitor and interpret the ICESCR, started to take a more active role in clarifying the content of various rights, including the right to health, providing guidance to countries, as discussed in chapter 23, on their national and international obligations. In 2000, the CESCR issued General Comment 14, which recognized the essential role of international cooperation and aid in realizing the right to health, noting states parties' "commitment to take joint and separate action to achieve the full realization of the right to health" (CESCR 2000, para. 38).

The 2000 MDGs are often viewed as a human rights setback, as they were not formally rights-based (Alston 2005). However, the very fact that this argument was made, and taken seriously, reflects the progress made since the initial concern for "human welfare" was first espoused by many development agencies. This progress is evidenced by the robust UN human rights response to the MDGs, the 2003 *U.N. Common Understanding on a Human Rights-Based Approach to Development Cooperation* (Stamford Declaration) (UNDG 2003) and subsequent UN work, as described in chapter 3, on rights-based approaches supported by the Office of the UN High Commissioner for Human Rights (OHCHR 2003; OHCHR 2012).

From a health-related human rights perspective, the MDG agenda was limited in that it focused mainly on disease-specific objectives. However, it arguably served as a catalyst for increased ODA, strengthening OECD-DAC members' spending and contributing to what is termed "the golden age of health development assistance," which saw health development assistance grow dramatically (Institute for Health Metrics and Evaluation 2012).

To the countries receiving ODA, however, the increasing power and influence of "emerging donors" suggested an appetite for diverse approaches to assistance beyond the rights-based approach (Mutua 2001). In theory, ODA should assist countries in fulfilling their human rights obligations to their citizens. In practice, the human rights prioritized by donor countries are not necessarily those that countries receiving assistance prioritize. For example, international funding and support for policies and programs that increase access to treatment and prevention for HIV and AIDS for vulnerable, marginalized, and key populations have not always been well received by recipient countries (UNAIDS 2016).[4] When it comes to donor prioritization of communicable disease detection over health systems strengthening, resorting to human rights language of global solidarity is problematic. Discourses from OECD members about the importance of human rights, solidarity, and decreasing inequality within countries "sound shallow and hollow" when proclaimed by the same countries that benefited from rising inequality between countries and never seriously considered redistribution of significant resources across state borders (Ooms et al. 2017, 2).

The parallel integration of health-related human rights into bilateral development assistance programs has taken many forms, reflecting the unique national perspectives and objectives of the development agency. For example, the "Nordic plus" countries (Canada, Norway, Sweden, and the Netherlands) have focused attention and both bilateral and multilateral funding on sexual and reproductive health and rights (Yamey et al. 2016). The United States, which signed but did not ratify the ICESCR, made a groundbreaking commitment to bilateral international assistance for access to antiretroviral treatment, launching the US President's Emergency Plan for AIDS Relief (PEPFAR), complementing the work of USAID (PEPFAR 2016).

---

4. Recent attempts to oppress the human rights of the lesbian, gay, bisexual, transgender, and intersex (LGBTI) community in several African countries through misguided appeals to oppose "Western values," including human rights, illustrate this tension over whose and what rights are prioritized (Finerty 2012; Sexual Minorities Uganda 2016).

THE US PRESIDENT'S EMERGENCY PLAN FOR AIDS RELIEF (PEPFAR): A LIMITED RIGHTS FRAMEWORK

Matthew M. Kavanagh, Georgetown University

While the United States has not ratified the ICESCR and rejects an international right to health obligation, the PEFPAR program is nonetheless guided by a limited rights schema. The program employs an implicit framework that prioritizes health rights of marginalized people. During the mid-2000s, as the South African government was stalling rollout of HIV treatment despite a landmark Constitutional Court ruling, PEPFAR provided funding to NGOs for some of the first large treatment programs, ensuring access for thousands despite protests of interference. The decision was framed in universalist terms, on an implicit right of access for people living with HIV, even where the national government failed in its obligation. During the Obama administration, a similar framework motivated expanded HIV service provision for "key populations," including men who have sex with men and transgender people, often over the objection of discriminatory governments. Programming to counter violence against, and HIV infection among, women was explicitly framed as part of a "Human Rights Action Agenda." In recent years, the Country Operational Plan process has been opened to civil society—increasing participation and providing information about rights realization often unavailable in other settings. This framework, however, is narrow and insufficient, failing to prevent the current administration expansion of the "global gag rule," banning US-funded groups from providing or speaking about abortion.

These examples of donor country efforts highlight the heterogeneity of human rights integration into development assistance policies and programs, categorized by the OECD and World Bank in accordance with the approaches outlined in Table 18.2.

Table 18.2. DONOR APPROACHES TO INTEGRATING HUMAN RIGHTS (WORLD BANK AND OECD 2013, 4)

Implicit human rights work	Development agencies may not explicitly work on human rights issues and prefer to use other descriptors (e.g., empowerment or general good governance). The goal, content, and approach can be related to other explicit forms of human rights integration rather than "repackaging."
Human rights projects	Projects or programs directly targeted at the realization of specific rights (e.g., freedom of expression), specific vulnerable groups (e.g., children), or in support of human rights organizations (e.g., in civil society).
Human rights dialogue	Foreign policy and aid dialogues include human rights norms and principles, sometimes linked to aid conditionalities. Aid modalities and funding amounts may be affected in cases of significant human rights violations.
Human rights mainstreaming	Efforts to ensure that human rights are integrated into all sectors of existing aid interventions (e.g., water, education).
Human rights-based approaches	Human rights considered constitutive of the goal of development, leading to a new approach to aid and requiring institutional change.

The human rights-based approach is arguably the most in line with an international human rights perspective, as it affirms that engagement in development assistance and cooperation is a legal obligation. Such an approach can advance the transformational potential of human rights by focusing on the political dimensions of poverty and power dynamics within a society. These dynamics lead to patterns of exclusion, and discrimination and contribute to the denial and violation of rights, including the right to health (Salomon 2007). Some commentators, however, charge that despite their potential, rights-based efforts often amount to rhetorical "fluff" because there is no "fundamental reshuffling of the cards of power, or a redistribution of resources" that is required to advance rights (Uvin 2007, 603). Although several countries claim to apply a human rights-based approach to development programming, none, even the comparatively generous Swedish health assistance program, has acknowledged that it has a legal obligation to engage in development assistance. Such an acknowledgement of a legal obligation would suggest that the cards of power are truly being reshuffled, indicating a shift toward the realization of health-related human rights through development assistance.

SWEDISH INTERNATIONAL DEVELOPMENT AGENCY COOPERATION AND HUMAN RIGHTS

Gunilla Backman, Swedish Development Cooperation Agency

The Swedish Development Cooperation Agency (SIDA) is the implementing partner of Swedish government aid. Sweden, like many other rich states, has not formally accepted that it has a legal obligation of international assistance and cooperation. In 2017, Sweden proposed to increase its aid to SEK 46.1 billion, the equivalent of 0.99 percent of GDI (new calculation model). "Human rights and democracy" is one of four key principles that shall be mainstreamed through the work of Swedish aid. A rights perspective in SIDA is understood to include four founding principles: non-discrimination, participation, transparency, and accountability. One example where the use of a rights perspective has contributed to a positive change for people with disabilities is in the Municipality of Dura, Palestine, where people with disabilities have been empowered to change the law and practice so that a minimum of 0.7 percent of the employed staff are disabled and public transports have become accessible to people with disabilities. Sexual and reproductive health and rights (SRHR) is another priority for Swedish aid and Sweden's Feminist Foreign Policy. SRHR highlights the interrelationship between all human rights and poverty reduction. Afghanistan is one example where SRHR have been used and have contributed to improved access and quality of care for men and women through the training of midwives and access to family planning services for contraceptives and counseling.

B. The OECD-DAC and Human Rights-Based Approaches

The OECD-DAC and its members have responded to this human rights dynamism through equally diverse approaches to human rights in their health programming, with the bilateral assistance agencies of OECD-DAC members, fragmenting the human rights community. Where countries do not necessarily respect their human rights obligations in all international forums (Hammonds and Ooms 2004), the OECD-DAC since the mid-1980s took note of the rising interest in human rights in international politics and adopted a highly technical approach to rights-based assistance, focused on indicator identification, statistical analysis, and impact assessment (OECD-DAC 1997). A 2006 study, commissioned by the Network on Governance Human Rights Task Team, provided a broad outline of ways in which development practice evolved to embrace human rights considerations, the levels at which it can take place, and the myriad forms it can take (OECD-DAC 2006). This study contributed to the "Action-Oriented Policy Paper on Human Rights and Development," approved by the OECD-DAC in February 2007, including ten principles to guide human rights integration and engaging with a bottom-up approach to human rights and human rights indicators (OECD 2008).[5]

Despite the increased prominence and commitment to human rights objectives by bilateral development assistance agencies, reinforced by OECD-DAC efforts, two key issues remain: the lack of a common approach to human rights and the absence of sustained increases in ODA volume (OECD 2007). Engagement with human rights is often implemented through the prism of the national assistance agency's goals and agenda. The lack of a shared understanding of what applying a human rights-based approach entails has negative consequences. The aid effectiveness agenda may address one negative consequence, namely, the non-alignment of human rights-related objectives; however, with regard to ODA volume, despite OECD-DAC's support and tracking of ODA volume, this peer pressure has not brought about an increase in the number of OECD-DAC members meeting the 0.7 percent target for foreign assistance. The OECD-DAC has chosen to focus on an aid effectiveness agenda to contribute to advancing health-related human rights.

IV. AID EFFECTIVENESS, IHP+, AND ADVANCING HEALTH-RELATED HUMAN RIGHTS

The emergence of the OECD-driven aid effectiveness agenda and the related launch of the IHP+ united leading bilateral assistance agencies to deliver on the health-related MDGs. Examining how the IHP+ assistance hindered or facilitated progress in using ODA to advance a shared obligation to provide assistance and cooperate to advance health rights, this part employs the IHP+ Results report to assess the impact of this approach as a coordination tool for advancing global health governance in accordance with the 2005 Paris Declaration on Aid Effectiveness (Paris Declaration) (OECD 2005). From a human rights perspective, the Paris

---

5. The ten principles include: (1) Build a shared understanding of the links between human rights obligations and development priorities through dialogue. (2) Identify areas of support to partner governments on human rights. (3) Safeguard human rights in processes of state-building. (4) Support the demand side of human rights. (5) Promote non-discrimination as a basis for more inclusive and stable societies. (6) Consider human rights in decisions on alignment and aid instruments. (7) Consider mutual reinforcement between human rights and aid effectiveness principles. (8) Do no harm. (9) Take a harmonized and graduated approach to deteriorating human rights situations. (10) Ensure that the scaling-up of aid is conducive to human rights.

Declaration commits countries to improving the quality and impact of ODA by focusing on ownership, alignment, harmonization, managing for results, and mutual accountability. These principles echo key human rights principles necessary for advancing health-related human rights.

A. ODA to Advance on Human Rights Objectives

Assessing rights-based foreign assistance for health, the Paris Declaration focuses on five characteristics of health ODA that need to be addressed to ensure that assistance is effective in advancing international human rights obligations of cooperation and assistance and structured, as much as possible, around the desired qualities of aid: additionality, reliability, alignment, coordination, and volume, as outlined in Table 18.3.

Table 18.3. HUMAN RIGHTS CRITERIA FOR ODA

ODA should be	Human rights justification
Additional to domestic resources	National and international obligations to fulfill rights (shared obligation) under Article 2.1 of the ICESCR.
Reliable	Reliability allows for progressive realization of a national health plan.
Aligned with national priorities	Developing a national public health strategy is part of the core obligations under Article 12 of the ICESCR. There is also a need to look at who participates in the priority-setting process.
Coordinated to ensure both burden sharing and domestic need is met	National and international obligations to fulfill rights (shared obligation) under Article 2.1 of the Covenant.
Sufficient in volume	To ensure states receiving assistance can fulfill their core obligations under the right to health under Article 12 of the ICESCR.

1. ADDITIONALITY

Article 2.1 of the ICESCR grounds the legal obligation for wealthy countries to engage in international assistance and cooperation. However, the vagueness of this legal text (i.e., no details on preferred modalities or volume) has left a great degree of latitude to donor states with regard to how they attempt to fulfill their international obligation. This international obligation exists in addition, or in parallel, to the obligations of the primary duty-bearer, the national government, which has the principal obligation toward its inhabitants. The extent of this international obligation is not settled, but legal scholars generally agree that it applies to meeting the core obligations of the right to health (CESCR 2000; Forman et al. 2016). Thus, bilateral ODA should not replace domestic health spending; rather, as elaborated in chapter 20, it should provide the additional financing necessary for a state to realize its core health-related obligations. For example, ODA should reinforce, not undermine, the 2001 Abuja Declaration, in which African Heads of State and Government committed to spend 15 percent of their budgets on health (Organisation of African Unity 2001). Despite the global financial crisis, development assistance for health (DAH) has held steady, and the World Health Organization (WHO) estimates that in 2014, an average of 33 percent of total health expenditure (THE) in low-income countries came from external resources, reaching as high as 64.9 percent in the Gambia and 73.8 percent in Malawi (World Bank 2017). However, several studies suggest that such funding has displaced government health expenditure, which undermines the goal of foreign assistance and undercuts the advancement of health rights (Ooms et al. 2010; Dieleman and Hanlon 2014).

2. RELIABILITY

Where "[s]table financing has positive implications for projects and allows for more effective long-term planning" (Dieleman and Hanlon 2014, 137), the reliability of ODA is vital to ensuring that ODA is effective in expanding the fiscal space of receiving countries. However, if ODA is unreliable it could do exactly the opposite: encourage governments receiving ODA to reduce their domestic efforts and "save" their domestic funds as insurance for when ODA decreases (Gottret and Schieber 2006). Efforts to increase the reliability of ODA can help to ensure its additionality.

3. ALIGNMENT

In clarifying Article 12 of the ICESCR, the CESCR's General Comment 14 provides that a core obligation of the right to health is for states to "adopt and implement a national public health strategy and plan of action, on the basis of epidemiological evidence, addressing the health concerns of the whole population; the strategy and plan of action shall be devised, and periodically reviewed, on the basis of a participatory and transparent process" (CESCR 2000, para. 43f). Bilateral assistance should thus be aligned with the national plan of action, not with the goals of the states providing assistance, thereby advancing country ownership of the health system.[6] However, where the national plan of action does not align with international human rights standards, as seen where the national health system may discriminate against certain groups—like people living with HIV and AIDS, LGBTI populations, or intravenous drug users—the alignment with national objectives can be problematic. In such cases, some bilateral health assistance may be shifted to supporting civil society groups that support marginalized populations.

4. COORDINATED

One key OECD-DAC objective is to coordinate development assistance. The OECD-DAC's engagement with the aid effectiveness agenda is one example of its efforts to improve coordination between states in a position to assist and to ensure that assistance is aligned with domestic priorities. From a health-related rights

6. Without such alignment, displacement of health financing "will shift health services away from those set by ministries of health in favor of the donor's priorities" (Dieleman and Hanlon 2014, 138).

perspective, coordination of DAH is of importance to ensure that no country or disease is left behind, including with respect to financing. Medium- to long-term DAH trends demonstrate that communicable diseases, like HIV, have attracted funding, while funding for noncommunicable diseases has stagnated at 1–2 percent of total DAH since 2000 (Institute for Health Metrics and Evaluation 2016). A coordinating mechanism for health-related ODA is needed, but, as discussed in chapter 20, to be effective, such efforts need to be broader than coordinating bilateral assistance actors. Private sector and private charitable actors—like the Bill and Melinda Gates Foundation—all have increasing influence and diverse motivations, yet unlike states, are not directly bound by international human rights obligations (Vandenhole, Turkelli, and Hammonds 2014).

5. Sufficient in Volume

The non-legally binding ODA Pearson target of 0.7 percent of GNI has only been achieved by seven high-income countries (Denmark, Luxembourg, the Netherlands, Norway, Sweden, the United Arab Emirates, and the United Kingdom), six of which are OECD-DAC members (OECD 2016). The United Kingdom has enshrined this target in national legislation (UK Parliament 2015). The OECD-DAC uses the 0.7 percent goal as a standard by which to rank performance, but it has no mechanism for holding countries accountable for meeting this standard. Since the development of General Comment 14 in 2000, the CESCR has routinely cited the 0.7 percent target when reviewing wealthy states parties' reports on compliance with ICESCR obligations, including key health-related rights like health, education, and housing (Coomans 2011). The CESCR has expressed satisfaction when a state party "in a position to assist" reaches or exceeds the 0.7 percent target, as seen in concluding observations on Denmark, Luxembourg, the Netherlands, and Sweden (CESCR 2003a; CESCR 2003b; CESCR 2003c; CESCR 2003d). For those that fail to reach the 0.7 percent target, the Committee often expresses concern or regret and encourages the state to raise its ODA, as seen in concluding observations on Belgium, Canada, France, Germany, and Italy (CESCR 2001; CESCR 2004; CESCR 2008a; CESCR 2008b; CESCR 2016).

United Kingdom ODA and the Right to Health

Giorgiana Rosa, Save the Children

The United Kingdom is legally bound under national law to spend 0.7 percent of UK GNI on ODA, following legislation approved by Parliament in 2015. According to the International Development Act of 2002, the primary purpose of UK ODA must be to contribute to poverty reduction, sustainable development, and improving welfare. There is generally cross-party support for ODA, with a widespread assertion that aid spending is in the United Kingdom's national interest—contributing to increased prosperity and national security. Supporters of ODA argue that there is also a moral imperative to address poverty and injustice; however, ODA is not generally described in human rights terms, nor as an international obligation. There is no clear policy framework for a human rights-based approach to UK ODA, ensuring consistency with the right to health. Nevertheless, UK aid has historically supported some aspects of the right to health, such as sexual, reproductive, maternal, and child health services (including for marginalized populations) and efforts to strengthen national health systems through sector support. The recent decline in bilateral ODA for health, and an increasing focus on economic development and private actors, signals a shift away from this. The increase in UK ODA being channeled through other government departments also raises questions on the long-standing role and expertise of the Department for International Development (DFID) in supporting global health. The global commitment to universal health coverage and the transition from the IHP+ to UHC2030 may help align UK ODA with the right to health.

It is important to note, however, that meeting the 0.7 percent target does not, in itself, mean that a country has satisfied its obligation to engage in international cooperation and assistance enshrined in the ICESCR. The policies and programs that it chooses to advance through this assistance are also key to fulfilling this obligation. From a right to health perspective, the CESCR has clarified that the obligation to engage in economic assistance and cooperation applies, at a minimum, to core content and obligations of a comparable priority (CESCR 2000). To date, a robust methodology for approximating the cost to realize core obligations under the right to health has not yet found agreement. However, economic modeling efforts suggest, as calculated in chapter 20, that with respect to health, the DAH target of a minimum of 0.1 percent of GNI would raise US$43 billion annually (Ottersen et al. 2014). It is estimated that if high-income countries met this 0.1 percent target, when added to a domestic health spending target of 5 percent of GNI, it would provide the $86 per capita per annum necessary to ensure access to primary health care, which would be a progressive step toward achieving the minimum core obligations under the right to health (McIntyre and Meheus 2014).

B. Aid Effectiveness and the Rise of IHP+

The Paris Declaration attempts to address the problems associated with donor proliferation and fragmentation, including the diverse approaches to human rights and development that stem from a multitude of donors. Along with the 2008 Accra Agenda for Action, the Paris Declaration emphasizes country ownership and accountability, arguing for clearer targets and indicators of success, a commitment to harmonization among partners, alignment with nationally prepared country strategies, and mutual accountability for measurable outcomes (OECD 2005; OECD 2008).[7] While not grounded in legally binding commitments, some believe the Paris Declaration's emphasis on "ownership and mutual accountability may support further efforts to mainstream principles of participation and equity, particularly given the increased recognition of the mutual relevance of so-called

---

7. The Accra Agenda for Action was designed to strengthen implementation of the Paris Declaration targets on alignment and effectiveness, focusing on improvement in ownership, inclusive partnerships, delivering results, and capacity development (OECD 2008).

cross-cutting policy issues—such as gender, human rights, and environment—to aid effectiveness" (McInerney-Lankford and Sano 2010, 33).

Seeking to put the Paris Declaration's principles into action in health ODA, the IHP+ was launched in 2007 as a coordination mechanism to bring together diverse partners committed to advancing health for all in low-income countries, including countries in a position to assist, countries needing assistance, civil society organizations, and multilateral organizations. Starting from twenty-six signatories, this global compact for achieving the health MDGs rose to have sixty-six signatories (IHP+ 2016a). This compact encouraged broad cooperation across all partners for a single national health strategy or plan, a single monitoring and evaluation framework, and a strong emphasis on mutual partner accountability, with the aim of building confidence among all stakeholders whose activities affect health in a country (Conway, Shaun, and Shorten 2015).

The IHP+ Results Review (IRR), which monitored adherence with the IHP+, indicated that although this coordination mechanism sought to realize health-related human rights, it did not go far enough in resolving the challenges of coordinating bilateral health ODA through:

- Alignment—For IHP+ partners to be aligned, countries need to develop a national health plan that all partners agree to fund and that can facilitate accountability. From a right to health perspective, such plans should be developed in an inclusive, non-discriminatory, transparent, and participatory manner (CESCR 2000). Reviewing participation in the development of these plans, the IRR notes that ministries of health reported a high level of participation of civil society organizations (CSOs) in health policy and planning processes "with the exception of participation in budget development and resource allocation where a 50% decrease was recorded since the last monitoring round" (IRR 2014, 7). Clearly, this assessment is not sufficiently granular to demonstrate that the preparation of national plans complies with rights-based requirements of participation of vulnerable and marginalized groups. The IHP+ appears to enhance alignment as a shared commitment to a common goal, noting that "[d]evelopment partners increasingly align and continue to participate in accountability processes at country level. The proportion of expenditures by development partners that are aligned with the country results framework ranged from 98% by the World Bank to 34% by UNAIDS. Alignment has increased since the last monitoring round" (IRR 2014, X). However, with respect to health ODA recorded in national budgets, the percentage remained at 71 percent, down from 81 percent in the first monitoring round (IRR 2014, XI). This assessment found that progress on alignment was slow but in the right direction, as evidenced by increased civil society participation in setting health policy and alignment of health development partners with country priorities.
- Reliability—One indicator for assessing reliability of ODA is the agreement of a medium-term expenditure framework (MTEF) to govern

spending commitments. The IRR noted that nineteen of twenty-four ministries of health (MOHs) had agreed on an MTEF or a three-year rolling budget, thus moving away from short-term funding horizons. However, looking at forward planning, the IRR estimated that "MOHs had forward expenditure estimates for about 86% of development funds in the year immediately following the survey, falling to 34% in year three" (IRR 2014, XI).

- Additionality—The IRR noted both improved financing and "to some extent" financial management of the health sector. In addition, the average proportion of the national budget allocated to health increased from 8 percent to 10 percent, with two countries reaching the Abuja target of 15 percent (IRR 2014, X), which suggests increased national commitment to health-related human rights obligations.

- Sufficient in Volume—The IHP+ focuses on governance, not volume of ODA; however, several different sources have found that the volume of health ODA has increased since the start of IHP+ (Dieleman et al. 2016). However, even with the increased engagement tied to IHP+, only the United Kingdom has been added to the list of countries that reach the 0.7 percent ODA target.

V. THE FUTURE OF RIGHTS-BASED INTERNATIONAL ASSISTANCE FOR GLOBAL HEALTH

By examining how the global health community engages with the 2015 Sustainable Development Goals (SDGs), it is clear that there remain challenges and opportunities for the future of bilateral health ODA to address global health inequalities. The SDGs have one explicit health goal, SDG 3 (ensuring healthy lives and promoting the well-being for all at all ages) but express a more holistic vision of the actions beyond the health sector needed to realize the right to health for all, including through the environment and gender equality (Van de Pas et al. 2017). In addressing ODA, SDG health target 3.8 (achieve universal health coverage (UHC)) is of particular interest because the IHP+ and its political supporters have seized on this target as a vehicle for achieving greater accountability, alignment, participation, and effectiveness (IHP+ 2016). Following the SDG launch, the IHP+ evaluated how its partnership approach could best contribute to advancing the SDGs, and in particular the SDG 3. The resulting September 2016 establishment of the International Health Partnership for Universal Health Coverage 2030 (UHC2030) aims to:

1. Improve coordination of health systems strengthening (HSS) efforts for UHC at the global level, including synergies with related technical networks;
2. Strengthen multi-stakeholder policy dialogue and coordination of HSS efforts in countries, including adherence to IHP+ principles and behaviors in countries receiving external assistance;
3. Facilitate accountability for progress toward HSS for UHC that contributes to a more integrated approach to accountability for SDG 3;

4. Build political momentum around a shared global vision of HSS for UHC and advocate for sufficient, appropriate, and well-coordinated resource allocation to HSS (IHP+ 2016b).

Despite the broad coalition of supporters, it is unclear how effective UHC2030 will be in ensuring that sufficient international funds are mobilized. Given the rise of isolationist candidates among OECD-DAC members, the future prospects for wealthy nations embracing and fulfilling their legal obligation related to cooperating and providing assistance are dim. The prospect of all OECD-DAC members achieving the 0.7 percent target in the mid-term thus appears even dimmer, suggesting a challenging future for both bilateral development assistance and progress on health-related human rights, particularly in low-income countries requiring assistance.

Yet, bilateral assistance in recent years has expanded beyond the "usual suspects," looking beyond the OECD-DAC members to include "emerging donors," "South-South Cooperation," and "Arab donors" (Zimmerman and Smith 2011, 722).

BRICS BILATERAL AID IN HEALTH

Eduardo J. Gómez, King's College London

In recent years, the so-called BRICS countries (Brazil, Russia, India, China, and South Africa) have emerged as important contributors to foreign aid in health; however, the motive behind this assistance has varied, shaped by differences in domestic normative commitments to human rights in health and geopolitical interests. By the late 1990s, Brazil emerged as the first of these nations to provide bilateral and multilateral assistance for health, mainly in response to HIV/AIDS and shaped by the government's constitutional commitment to health care as a human right, rather than any effort to adhere to international legal obligations. While Russia eventually joined Brazil in providing bilateral aid, the government's geopolitical interests mainly influenced Russia's motives, viewing bilateral aid as a means to increase its reputation as an influential global power while avoiding both domestic and international human rights obligations. Foreign investment interests, prioritizing Africa, and efforts to obtain regional support, have shaped China's recent bilateral assistance, although it has never based its bilateral assistance on domestic or international human rights principles or legal obligations. In contrast to the foreign assistance of their BRICS counterparts, India and South Africa have never prioritized providing bilateral aid in health, focusing instead on strengthening their domestic health care systems.

While OECD-DAC "remains the core of the global aid system, its monopoly of world ODA is eroding with the rise of the so-called new development partners . . . Traditional donors that form the OECD/DAC can no longer claim to speak for the world's donor community" (Mawdsley 2014, 632). With emerging donors presenting heterogeneous approaches to human rights, these new development partners have not adopted the largely UN-led human rights approaches advanced by some OECD-DAC members. However, many of these new partners' assistance programs include human rights objectives, with both Brazilian cooperation on social assistance programs and the long-standing Cuban medical training program serving as examples of South-South cooperation that address social rights (Kirk and Erisman 2009; Mawdsley 2014).

CONCLUSION

The expanding number of actors engaged in development assistance and cooperation is a source of optimism even as it enlarges the fragmentation problem in global health governance. Recognizing the influence of these new donors, a global recommitment to UN human rights ideals is needed, as distinguished from the current UN model that remains gridlocked and ineffective in addressing twenty-first-century challenges. To address the challenges associated with global health inequality, the world requires fresh approaches to development assistance efforts beyond the OECD-DAC's efforts to harmonize ODA. The 1972 definition of ODA has come under increasing criticism with respect to how it is measured and the underlying politics are manifested. A new definition of ODA is needed (Lomøy, Jon. 2013). Yet, overcoming twenty-first-century challenges requires far more than a new definition of ODA. Building on the success of bilateral ODA in advancing health-related human rights, while recognizing that the current model may have gone beyond its usefulness, there is a continuing imperative for global cooperation, requiring efforts to advance new rights-based models to coordinate health-related ODA to realize health for all.

REFERENCES

Alston, Philip. 2005. "Ships Passing in the Night: The Current State of the Human Rights and Development Debate Seen through the Lens of the Millennium Development Goal." *Human Rights Quarterly* 27(3): 755–829.

Alston, Philip and Mary Robinson. 2005. "The Challenges of Ensuring the Mutuality of Human Rights and Development Endeavours." In *Human Rights and Development: Towards Mutual Reinforcement*, edited by P. Alston and M. Robinson. New York: Oxford University Press.

Andersen, Erik A. and Hans Otto Sano. 2006. *Human Rights Indicators at Programme and Project Level—Guidelines for Defining Indicators, Monitoring and Evaluation.* Copenhagen: Danish Institute for Human Rights.

CESCR (United Nations Committee on Economic, Social and Cultural Rights). 2000. "General Comment No. 14, The Right to the Highest Attainable Standard of Health." UN Doc. E/C.12/2000/4.

CESCR (United Nations Committee on Economic, Social and Cultural Rights). 2001. "Concluding Observations regarding Germany." 24 September 2001. UN Doc. E/C.12/1/Add.68.

CESCR (United Nations Committee on Economic, Social and Cultural Rights). 2003a. "Concluding Observations regarding Denmark." 14 December 2004. UN Doc. E/C.12/1/Add.102.

CESCR (United Nations Committee on Economic, Social and Cultural Rights). 2003b. "Concluding Observations regarding Luxembourg." 26 June 2003. UN Doc. E/C.12/1/Add.86.

CESCR (United Nations Committee on Economic, Social and Cultural Rights). 2003c. "Concluding Observations regarding the Netherlands." 24 November 2006, UN Doc. E/C.12/NLD/CO/3.

CESCR (United Nations Committee on Economic, Social and Cultural Rights). 2003d. "Concluding Observations regarding Sweden." 1 December 2008. UN Doc. E/C.12/SWE/CO/5.

CESCR (United Nations Committee on Economic, Social and Cultural Rights). 2004. "Concluding Observations regarding Italy." 14 December 2004. UN Doc. E/C.12/1/Add.103.

CESCR (United Nations Committee on Economic, Social and Cultural Rights). 2008a. "Concluding Observations regarding Belgium." 4 January 2008. UN Doc. E/C.12/BEL/CO/3.

CESCR (United Nations Committee on Economic, Social and Cultural Rights). 2008b. "Concluding Observations regarding France." 9 June 2008. UN Doc. E/C.12/FRA/CO/3.

CESCR (United Nations Committee on Economic, Social and Cultural Rights). 2016. "Concluding Observations regarding Canada." 4 March 2016. UN Doc. E/C.12/CAN/CO/6.

Conway, Shaun and Tim Shorten. 2015. *Improving Aid Effectiveness in Global Health, The International Health Partnership*, edited by Elvira Beracochea, 111–118. New York: Springer.

Coomans, Fons. 2011. "The Extraterritorial Scope of the International Covenant on Economic, Social and Cultural Rights in the Work of the United Nations Committee on Economic, Social and Cultural Rights." *Human Rights Law Review* 11(1): 1–35.

Cornwall, Andrea and Celestine Nyamu-Musembi. 2004. "Putting the 'Rights-Based Approach' to Development into Perspective." *Third World Quarterly* 25(8): 1415–1437.

Dieleman, Joseph L. and Michael Hanlon. 2014. "Measuring the Displacement and Replacement of Government Health Expenditure." *Health Economics* 23.2 (2014): 129–140.

Dieleman, Joseph L., Matthew T. Schneider, Annie Haalensta, Lavanya Singh, Nafis Sadat, Maxwell Birger, Alex Reynolds [et al.]. 2016. "Development Assistance for Health: Past Trends, Associations, and the Future of International Financial Flows for Health." *The Lancet* 387(10037): 2536–2544.

Ehrenfeld, Daniel. 2004. "Foreign Aid Effectiveness, Political Rights and Bilateral Distribution." *The Journal of Humanitarian Assistance*. Available at: https://sites.tufts.edu/jha/archives/75.

Finerty, Courtney E. 2012. "Being Gay in Kenya: The Implications of Kenya's New Constitution for Its Anti-Sodomy Laws." *Cornell International Law Journal* 45(2): 431–459.

Forman, Lisa, Luljeta Caroshi, Audrey R. Chapman, and Lamprea Everaldo. 2016. "Conceptualising Minimum Core Obligations under the Right to Health: How Should We Define and Implement the 'Morality of the Depths.'" *The International Journal of Human Rights* 20(1): 531–548.

Frenk, Julio and Suerie Moon. 2013. "Governance Challenges in Global Health." *The New England Journal of Medicine* 368(10): 936–942.

Führer, Helmut. 1996. *A History of the Development Assistance Committee and the Development Co-Operation Directorate in Dates, Names and Figures.* Paris: OECD.

Gottret, Pablo and George Schieber. 2006. *Health Financing Revisited: A Practitioner's Guide.* Washington, D.C.: World Bank.

Hammonds, Rachel and Gorik Ooms. 2004. "World Bank Policies and the Obligation of Its Members to Respect, Protect and Fulfill the Right to Health." *Health and Human Rights* 8(1): 26–60.

Hollander, David, Axel Marx, and Jan Wouters. 2014. "Integrating Human Rights into Development Cooperation: A Comparative Assessment of Strategies and Practices of Donors." *Paper No. 15.* Leuven: KU Leuven.

Hynes, William and Simon Scott. 2013. *The Evolution of Official Development Assistance: Achievements, Criticisms and a Way Forward, OECD Development Co-operation Working Papers, No. 12.* Paris: OECD Publishing.

IHP+ (International Health Partnership Plus). 2016a. *Development Cooperation and Health.* Available at: https://www.internationalhealthpartnership.net/en/about-ihp/.

IHP+ (International Health Partnership Plus). 2016b. *Transforming IHP+.* Available at: https://www.internationalhealthpartnership.net/en/about-ihp/transforming-ihp/.

Institute for Health Metrics and Evaluation. 2010. *Financing Global Health 2010.* Available at: http://www.healthmetricsandevaluation.org/publications/policy-report/financing_global_health_2010_IHME.

Institute for Health Metrics and Evaluation. 2012. *Financing Global Health 2012: The End of the Golden Age?* Available at: http://www.healthdata.org/sites/default/files/files/policy_report/2012/FGH/IHME_FGH2012_FullReport_MedResolution.pdf.

Institute for Health Metrics and Evaluation. 2016. *Financing Global Health 2015: development assistance steady on the path to new global goals.* Available at: http://www.healthdata.org/policy-report/financing-global-health-2015-development-assistance-steady-path-new-global-goals.

IRR (IHP+ Results Review). 2014. *The 2014 Performance Report.* Available at: https://www.internationalhealthpartnership.net/fileadmin/uploads/ihp/Documents/Results___Evidence/IHP___Results/2014_Monitoring_Round/IHP_report-ENG-WEB.PDF.

Kirk, John M. and Michael Erisman. 2009. *Cuban Medical Internationalism: Origins, Evolution, and Goals.* Basingstoke: Palgrave Macmillan.

Lomøy, Jon. 2013. "Yes, it is time to revisit the concept of Official Development Assistance." *OECD Insights Blog: 3 May 2013.* Available at: http://oecdinsights.org/2013/05/04/yes-it-is-time-to-revisit-the-concept-of-official-development-assistance/.

Mahon, Rianne and Stephen McBride. 2008. Introduction to *The OECD and Transnational Governance,* edited by Rianne Mahon and Stephen McBride. Vancouver: UBC Press.

Matua, Makau W. 2001. "Savages, Saviors and Victims: The Metaphor of Human Rights." *Harvard International Law Journal* 42 (201): 227–234.

Mawdsley, Emily. 2014. Human Rights and South-South Development Cooperation. *Human Rights Quarterly* 36 (2014): 630–652.

Maxwell, Simon. 1999. "What Can We Do with a Rights-Based Approach to Development?" *Overseas Development Institute (ODI) Briefing Paper 99.*

McColl, Karen. 2008. "Europe Told to Deliver More Aid for Health." *The Lancet* 371(9630): 2072–2073.

McInerney-Lankford, Siobahn and Hans Otto Sano. 2010. *Human Rights Indicators in Development: An Introduction, World Bank Study.* Washington, D.C.: World Bank.

McIntyre, Di and Filip Meheus. 2014. *Fiscal Space for Domestic Funding of Health and Other Social Services*. London: Chatham House. https://www.chathamhouse.org/sites/files/ chathamhouse/home/chatham/public_html/sites/default/files/20140300Domestic FundingHealthMcIntyreMeheus.pdf.

National Security Archive. 2002. "Conflicting Missions: Secret Cuban Documents on History of Africa Involvement." *National Archive Electronic Briefing Book*. 67. Available at: http://nsarchive.gwu.edu/NSAEBB/NSAEBB67/.

OECD (Organisation for Economic Cooperation and Development). 1970. *The 0.7% ODA/GNI target—a history*. Available at: http://www.oecd.org/dac/stats/ the07odagnitarget-ahistory.htm.

OECD (Organisation for Economic Cooperation and Development). 2005. *The Paris Declaration on Aid Effectiveness*. Available at: http://www.mfdr.org/sourcebook/ 2-1paris.pdf.

OECD (Organisation for Economic Cooperation and Development). 2007. *DAC Action-Oriented Policy Paper on Human Rights and Development*. Paris: OECD.

OECD. 2008. "Measuring Human Rights and Democratic Governance: Experiences and Lessons from Metagora." *OECD Journal on Development* 9(2).

OECD (Organisation for Economic Cooperation and Development). 2008. *The Paris Declaration on Aid Effectiveness and the Accra Agenda for Action*. Available at: http:// www.oecd.org/dac/effectiveness/34428351.pdf.

OECD (Organisation for Economic Cooperation and Development). 2010. *The DAC, 50 Years, 50 Highlights*. Available at: http://www.oecd.org/dac/46717535.pdf.

OECD (Organisation for Economic Cooperation and Development). 2011. *The High Level Forum on Aid Effectiveness—A History*. Available at: http://www.oecd.org/dac/ effectiveness/thehighlevelforaonaideffectivenessahistory.htm.

OECD (Organisation for Economic Cooperation and Development). 2012a. "1. Definition of ODA, 1.3 What is the difference between bilateral and multilateral aid (ODA)?" *Introduction to Official Development Assistance*. Available at: http://www.oecd.org/dac/ financing-sustainable-development/development-finance-standards/intro-to-oda.htm.

OECD (Organisation for Economic Cooperation and Development). 2012b. "3. History of ODA, 3.2 Historic levels and evolution of ODA." *Introduction to Official Development Assistance*. Available at: http://www.oecd.org/dac/financing-sustainable-development/development-finance-standards/intro-to-oda.htm.

OECD (Organisation for Economic Cooperation and Development). 2016. *Development aid rises again in 2015, spending on refugees doubles*. Available at: http://www.oecd.org/ dac/development-aid-rises-again-in-2015-spending-on-refugees-doubles.htm.

OECD-DAC. 1972. *Official development assistance—definition and coverage*. Available at: http://www.oecd.org/dac/stats/officialdevelopmentassistancedefinitionandcover age.htm.

OECD-DAC. 1997. Final Report of the Ad Hoc *Working Group on Participatory Development and Good Governance*. Paris; OECD.

OECD-DAC. 2006. "Integrating Human Rights into Development: Donor Approaches, Experiences and Challenges." *The Development Dimension Series*. Paris: OECD.

OHCHR (Office of the High Commissioner for Human Rights. 2003. *Principles and Guidelines for a Human Rights Approach to Poverty Reduction Strategies*. Geneva: Office of the United Nations High Commissioner for Human Rights.

OHCHR (Office of the High Commissioner for Human Rights). 2012. *Human Rights Indicators: A Guide to Measurement and Implementation*. Geneva: Office of the United Nations High Commissioner for Human Rights.

Ooms, Gorik, Kristof Decoster, Katabaro Miti, Sabine Rens, Luc Van Leeput, Peter Vermeiren, and Wim Van Damme. 2010. "Crowding Out: Are Relations between International Health Aid and Government Health Funding Too Complex to Be Captured in Averages Only?" *The Lancet* 375 (9723): 1403–1405.

Ooms, Gorik, Remco van de Pas, Kristof Decoster, and Rachel Hammonds. 2017. Thinking Out of the Box: A Green and Social Climate Fund: Comment on "Politics, Power, Poverty and Global Health: Systems and Frames." *International Journal of Health Policy and Management* 6(1):1–4.

Organization of African Unity. 2001. Abuja Declaration on HIV/AIDS, Tuberculosis and other related infection diseases. Doc. OAU/SPS/ABUJA 3.

Ottersen, Trygve, Amparna Kamath, Suerie Moon, and John-Arne Røttingen. 2014. *Development Assistance for Health: Quantitative Allocation Criteria and Contribution Norms.* London: Chatham House.

Pearson Commission. 1969. *Partners in Development—Report of the Commission on International Development.* New York, Washington, and London.

PEPFAR. 2016. "About PEPFAR." Available at: https://www.pepfar.gov/about/270968.htm.

Robinson, Mary and Philip Alston. 2004. *Human Rights and Development: Towards Mutual Reinforcement.* Oxford: Oxford University Press.

Salomon, Margot. 2007. *Global Responsibility for Human Rights: World Poverty and the Development of International Law.* Oxford: Oxford University Press.

Sano, Hans-Otto. 2007. "Does a Human Rights-Based Approach Make a Difference?" In *Casting the Net Wider: Human Rights, Development and New Duty-Bearer,* edited by Margot Salomon, Arne Tostensen, and Wouter Vandenhole. Antwerp: Intersentia.

Sexual Minorities Uganda. 2016. "Sexual Minorities Uganda, Justice and Equity." Available at: http://sexualminoritiesuganda.com.

Tobin, John. 2012. *The Right to Health in International Law.* Oxford: Oxford University Press.

UNAIDS. 2016. *HIV Prevention Among Key Populations.* Available at: http://www.unaids.org/en/resources/presscentre/featurestories/2016/november/20161121_keypops.

UN (United Nations). 1945. "Charter of the United Nations." 26 October. UN Doc. 1 UNTS XVI.

UN (United Nations). 1993. "World Conference on Human Rights, Vienna Declaration and Program of Action." UN Doc. A/Conf.157/23.

UN (United Nations). 2000. "The Millennium Declaration." 18 September. A/RES/55/2.

UN General Assembly. 1966. "International Covenant on Economic, Social and Cultural Rights, International Covenant on Civil and Political Rights and Optional Protocol to the International Covenant on Civil and Political Rights." 16 December. Res. 2200 (XXI).

UNDG (United Nations Development Group). 2003. *The Human Rights-Based Approach to Development Cooperation. Towards a Common Understanding among the UN Agencies.* Stamford, CT (also referred to as the *Stamford Declaration*).

UNDP (United Nations Development Programme). 1998. "Integrating Human Rights with Sustainable Development." *UNDP Policy Document 2,* New York: UNDP.

United Kingdom Parliament. 2015. International Development (Official Development Assistance Target) Act 2015 (Chapter 12). Available at: http://www.legislation.gov.uk/ukpga/2015/12/pdfs/ukpga_20150012_en.pdf.

Uvin, Peter. 2007. "From the Right to Development to the Rights-Based Approach: How 'Human Rights' Centered Development?" *Development in Practice* 17(4–5): 597–604.

Van de Pas, Remco, Peter S. Hill, Rachel Hammonds, Gorik Ooms, Lisa Forman, Attiya Waris, Claire Brolan, Martin McKee, and Devi Sridhar. 2017. "Global Health

Governance in the Sustainable Development Goals: Is It Grounded in the Right to Health?" *Global Challenges* 1: 47–60.

Vandenhole, Wouter, Gamze Erdem Türkelli, and Rachel Hammonds. 2014. "New Human Rights Duty-Bearers: Towards a Re-conceptualisation of the Human Rights Duty-Bearer Dimension." In *The SAGE Handbook of Human Rights*, edited by Anja Mihr and Mark Gibney. London: Sage.

World Bank. 2017. *External resources for health (% of total expenditure on health).* Available at: http://data.worldbank.org/indicator/SH.XPD.EXTR.ZS.

World Bank IDA (International Development Association) 2007. *Aid Architecture: An Overview Of The Main Trends In Official Development Assistance Flows.* Available at: http://siteresources.worldbank.org/IDA/Resources/Seminar%20PDFs/73449-1172525976405/3492866-1172527584498/Aidarchitecture.pdf.

World Bank Instituto de Pesquisa Econômica Aplicada. 2012. *Bridging the Atlantic: Brazil and Sub-Saharan Africa South-South Partnering for Growth.* Available at: http://siteresources.worldbank.org/AFRICAEXT/Resources/africa-brazil-bridging-final.pdf.

World Bank and OECD. 2013. *Integrating Human Rights into Development: Donor Approaches, Experiences and Challenges, 2nd Edition.* Washington, DC: World Bank. Available at: http://hdl.handle.net/10986/12800.

Yamey, Gavin, Jesper Sundewall, Helen Saxenian, Robert Hecht, Keely Jordan, Marco Schäferhoff, Christina Schrade [et al.]. 2016. "Reorienting Health Aid to Meet Post-2015 Global Health Challenges: A Case Study of Sweden as a Donor." *Oxford Review of Economic Policy* 32 (1): 122–146.

Zimmermann, Felix and Kimberly Smith. 2011. "More Actors, More Money, More Ideas for International Development Co-operation." *Journal of International Development* 23: 722–738.

The Global Fund to Fight AIDS, Tuberculosis and Malaria

Funding Basic Services and Meeting the Challenge of Rights-Based Programs

RALF JÜRGENS, JOANNE CSETE, HYEYOUNG LIM, SUSAN TIMBERLAKE, AND MATTHEW SMITH*

The Global Fund to Fight AIDS, Tuberculosis and Malaria (hereinafter "the Global Fund") is a public-private partnership that receives support from governments and private institutions and is one of the most important funders in the world in responding to HIV, tuberculosis, and malaria. Beginning its operations in 2002, it has sought to work toward the eradication of these diseases as public health problems. As of mid-2017, the Global Fund estimated that, with total disbursements of over US$30 billion, it has supported antiretroviral therapy (ART) for about ten million people with HIV, TB testing and treatment for about 16.6 million people, and the distribution of over 713 million bed nets for malaria prevention.

This chapter describes the strategies and initiatives undertaken by the Global Fund in its effort to support human rights-centered programs to address HIV, TB, and malaria. Part I gives some background on the history and basic operations of the Global Fund, exploring how country ownership has formalized rights in country programming. Recounting the way in which the Global Fund built on programmatic human rights ideas developed by other institutions, Part II describes how these Global Fund efforts led to the development of its own institutional strategic objectives on human rights. Part III elaborates on the challenges encountered in the implementation of these objectives and measures taken to overcome these challenges, including the building of technical capacity of Global Fund grant recipients to assess human rights-related barriers to services and to design and implement programs to overcome them. Parts IV and V describe an intensive ongoing effort to scale up programs to address human rights-related barriers in selected countries,

* We thank the editors and Sara L. M. Davis for helpful comments on earlier drafts.

Human Rights in Global Health. Benjamin Mason Meier and Lawrence O. Gostin.
© Oxford University Press 2018. Published 2018 by Oxford University Press.

which the Global Fund hopes will result in the acceleration of programs to overcome human rights-related impediments to health services. Within the institutional constraints specific to its foundational values and processes, this chapter concludes that the Global Fund has found progressively more active ways to assist grantees in designing, implementing, and evaluating rights-centered health programs.

I. HUMAN RIGHTS AND THE BASIC OPERATION OF THE GLOBAL FUND

The Global Fund was born into a period in which health and human rights had established itself as a distinct area of public health practice and an intellectual discipline. By 2002, the United Nations (UN) entities that were brought together as the Joint UN Programme on HIV/AIDS (UNAIDS) had a strong commitment to rights-centered approaches to HIV, however imperfectly that commitment was realized. The Global Fund faced the challenge of bringing lessons from HIV efforts to bear on programs to address tuberculosis and malaria. It was also challenged to operate in concert with agreed human rights norms of HIV programs and policies while, as a financial institution without field-based staff, operating under different circumstances from a UN agency and other traditional on-the-ground service providers.[1]

A. Origins of the Global Fund

The Global Fund was created in 2001, partly as a response to the reluctance of many traditional providers of development assistance in health to finance ART, which had been available since 1996 but was seen by some donors to be unsustainable in low-income countries (Lidén 2013). Donor-supported HIV interventions in the period before the US President's Emergency Plan for AIDS Relief (PEPFAR) initiative and the World Health Organization (WHO) and UNAIDS "3 by 5" initiatives—both dating from 2003—were largely focused on awareness-raising campaigns and health worker training ('t Hoen et al. 2011). For some years, the French government had called for a "solidarity" fund for ART (Lidén 2013).

The 2000 International AIDS Conference in Durban brought global attention to a growing movement to challenge prices and patents of ART medicines as well as the indifference of donor nations to the plight of Africans living with HIV. Major donor countries meeting as the G8 in 2000 were also inspired by the recent creation of the Global Alliance for Vaccines and Immunization (GAVI, now Gavi, the Vaccine Alliance) and the Medicines for Malaria Venture (MMV)—public-private partnerships that seemed better able to exploit efficiencies in procurement of medicines and other supplies than existing institutions (Brugha and Walt 2001; Lidén 2013). The G8, an inter-governmental political forum of highly industrialized countries, saw a similar opportunity for the dramatic expansion of support to programs addressing the three major killer diseases of the day (Brugha and Walt 2001). There was great hope in many quarters that the Global Fund's existence

---

1. The staff are all based in Geneva, as the Global Fund is not a program-implementing institution.

would not only scale up ART distribution dramatically, but in so doing, would also drive down prices of HIV medicines ('t Hoen et al. 2011).

The 2001 UN General Assembly Special Session (UNGASS) on HIV/AIDS committed member states to support for "a global HIV/AIDS and health fund to finance an urgent and expanded response to the epidemic based on an integrated approach to prevention, care, support and treatment . . . " (UN General Assembly 2001, para. 90). This resolution gave official UN member state backing to the idea of a Global Fund—state support that earlier initiatives such as GAVI and MMV did not have. A transitional working group was established soon after the 2001 UNGASS to develop basic operational plans, legal and management structures, and eligibility criteria for the grant-making of the Global Fund (Global Fund n.d.). The transitional group held regional consultations and met with a wide range of government, civil society, academic, and business leaders. By late 2001, the main constituencies of the Global Fund Board (hereinafter "the Board")—donor countries, lower-income countries, civil society, and the private sector—selected representatives to serve on the new Global Fund's governance body. The Board approved a foundational framework document, outlining the principles and purpose of the Global Fund before the first grants were made in 2002.

B. Governance and Functioning of the Global Fund

The Board of the Global Fund oversees the development of institutional strategies and policies and approves budgeting and funding decisions. The inclusion on the Board of people affected by the three diseases—along with non-governmental organizations (NGOs) from the Global North and South, governments, and private sector entities—sets the Global Fund apart from GAVI and other such initiatives and signals a commitment to meaningful involvement of people affected by the diseases in all decisions about the Global Fund and its activities (Lidén 2013). The Global Fund's framework document also pledges to "give due priority to the most affected countries and communities, and to those countries most at risk" and to "aim to eliminate stigmatization of and discrimination against those infected and affected by HIV/AIDS, especially . . . women, children and vulnerable groups" (Global Fund 2001, rev. 2012, sec. III.H.9–10).

The Global Fund also has another distinctive element with human rights importance—a commitment to "country-driven" grant-making. The framework document of the Global Fund said it would "base its work on programs that reflect national ownership and respect country-led formulation and implementation processes" (Global Fund 2001, rev. 2012, sec.III.C). Country coordination mechanisms (CCMs)—meant to include representatives of government, NGOs, other private-sector entities, UN agencies in the country (often called "technical partners"), and people living with or affected by the diseases—were created to develop and submit proposals to the Global Fund, requesting a realistic level of funding for health programs that could readily be absorbed and programmed. The framework document enjoins CCMs to ensure "equity and transparency" among members, all having important voices. Most grants have a Principle Recipient (PR), that is, a government, NGO, or UN entity, which is the chief implementer of the grant and may disburse funds to Sub-Recipients (SR) as needed (Global Fund 2007). In the first ten years of its operation, the Global Fund disbursed grants in ten "funding rounds," during which CCMs from all eligible countries could respond to calls for proposals (Global Fund 2013). Nevertheless, this country ownership effort would come to be operationalized in a different funding model in the years that followed.

C. Country Ownership

"Country ownership" and these country-driven processes may not have worked out ideally in every case, but they represented an early attempt to do business in a new way. Early independent observers of the Global Fund's work echoed the long-held concern of some donors that while the "country-driven" processes of the Global Fund had indeed put program design and implementation more squarely in the hands of recipient countries themselves, some of those programs floundered for lack of outside technical assistance (McCarthy 2007). The Global Fund defended its approach, asserting that it was necessary for infectious disease programs to be designed by the affected countries themselves, not just by experts in Geneva or Washington (Ibid.). Key actors in the field appreciated this sentiment. Médecins Sans Frontières (MSF), for example, argued that entrusting countries with the responsibility to estimate resources that could be absorbed and realistic rates of scale up of programs resulted in unprecedented progress—both in the programs themselves and in strengthening health systems (MSF 2014). While maintaining a core commitment to country-driven processes, the Global Fund had somewhat overstepped the "country ownership" line in 2004, requiring that CCMs include a person living with HIV among their members. In 2007, the Global Fund issued guidance "strongly encouraging" CCMs to include key populations affected by the three diseases among their members—beyond just people living with HIV—and to ensure their participation in decision-making (Global Fund 2007). Although inclusion and meaningful participation of key populations—especially persons affected by the criminalization of drug use, sex work, and aspects of sexual preference and gender identity—remained challenging in many places, in some countries, CCMs became the first platform in which key population groups could sit with policymakers and program managers and participate in decision-making on the programs affecting them (OSF and Canadian HIV/AIDS Legal Network 2011; Fried and Kowalski-Morton 2008).

The Global Fund's efforts to include key populations were a reflection of its foundational commitment to human rights principles and the need to advance the right to health of all persons. An indicator of this rights-based commitment in program terms, for example, is the unprecedented scale-up of HIV prevention activities for certain marginalized populations—including people who inject drugs—which was made possible by Global Fund support. In its first nine rounds of funding (through 2009), some US$180 million from the Global Fund enabled expansion of drug-related harm reduction services in forty-two countries, many of which had never been able to scale up services of this kind (Atun and Kazatchkine 2010). Much of this achievement can be attributed to civil society organizations, including those that have played an important role in services provision as well as rights-based advocacy for expanded services.

Country ownership was appealing from a human rights perspective, as development assistance was long seen as "top-down," with priorities dictated from the Global North and various political and strategic strings often attached to donor funding; however, human rights advocates over the years noted the possible negative aspect of this approach—that "ownership" of programs by countries with poor human rights records or little culture of human rights might steer programs in ways that undermine (or at least do not protect) human rights (OSF and Canadian HIV/AIDS Legal Network 2011). Some observers concluded that the Global Fund's commitment to rights-based programs was too passive. At a Global Fund "partnership" meeting in 2006, civil society organizations presented an appeal signed by over 250 health and human rights NGOs, calling on the Global Fund to

> increase funding for programs to eliminate human rights abuses against people living with and at high risk of HIV/AIDS—including sexual and gender-based violence; discrimination; and violations of the right to complete and accurate information about HIV/AIDS prevention, treatment and care (ICASO 2006, 4).

Dr. Michel Kazatchkine, director of the Global Fund from 2007 to 2012, agreed that the country ownership principle did indeed pose human rights concerns, but he noted that the Global Fund had processes to ensure that it would not fund programs that contributed to human rights violations or did not reflect sound evidence-based approaches (Kazatchkine 2010). With respect to human rights questions, the Technical Review Panel (TRP), an independent expert body that reviews Global Fund proposals and makes recommendations for funding, is tasked to consider whether proposals ensure

> that human rights-related barriers to accessing services are identified, and [the applicant] invests in and scales up programs to reduce these barriers, . . . and that key and vulnerable populations disproportionately affected by HIV/AIDS, TB and/or malaria can meaningfully engage in decisions that affect their lives at all levels (Global Fund 2010c, 5).

D. Steps toward Formalizing Human Rights in Country Programming

Although the Global Fund Board did not formally adopt human rights objectives until 2011, the Global Fund Secretariat adopted a human rights-based "Gender Equality Strategy" in 2008 that addressed rights-based principles (Global Fund 2008). Noting that gender inequalities are a "strong driver" of all three diseases in the Global Fund's mandate, the Gender Equality Strategy gives detailed guidance and examples of ways to "encourage a positive bias in funding towards programs and activities that address gender inequalities and strengthen the response for women and girls," including programs to address discrimination, gender-based violence, and other structural factors (Ibid., 4). Similarly in 2009, the Board adopted a "Sexual Orientation and Gender Identity (SOGI) Strategy" (Global Fund 2009), highlighting some programmatic responses to discrimination and marginalization (e.g., of men who have sex with men, transgender people, and sex workers) that undermine access to and utilization of health services.[2] Emphasizing the importance of meaningful participation by the populations affected by SOGI-related discrimination, these documents were disseminated to CCMs, the TRP, and Global Fund staff, all of which also benefited from training and other program guidance related to the core principles of the gender and SOGI strategies.

In about this same period, UNAIDS was working to systematize thinking about HIV-related human rights challenges and programs to address them. Following consultations with governments and civil society, UNAIDS established seven categories of programs that would reduce human rights-related barriers to HIV services and thus help to ensure that national HIV responses were inclusive, effective, and rights-based:

1. Reduction of stigma and discrimination;
2. Access to HIV-related legal services;
3. Monitoring and reform of policies, regulations, and laws that undermine HIV programs;
4. Legal literacy or "know your rights" efforts;
5. Sensitization of law-makers and law enforcement agents;
6. Training of health care providers on rights and ethics related to HIV; and
7. Reducing discrimination against women and gender-based violence (UNAIDS 2012).

The UN Development Programme (UNDP) led an investigation of whether these categories of programs were present in two Global Fund funding rounds (Rounds 6 and 7) (UNDP, UNAIDS, and the Global Fund 2010). This study found that relatively few finalized grants included programs to address human rights-related barriers and, when included, they were often of an inadequate scale to reach critical numbers of the affected populations (Ibid.). UNDP noted that stigma and discrimination reduction was the most common of the seven categories of programs to be included, and that countries with generalized epidemics were unlikely to identify program needs for key populations.

Recognizing the continuing challenge of getting funding proposals to embody human rights norms and universal access, the Global Fund established a special reserve allocation in its tenth round of funding for programs that address "most at risk populations" (MARPs) (later replaced by the term "key populations"), which were defined as:

- Men who have sex with men, transgender people, and their sexual partners;
- Female, male, and transgender sex workers and their sexual partners; and
- People who inject drugs and their sexual partners (Global Fund 2010b).

2. The SOGI Strategy is informed by the Yogyakarta Principles—a widely cited compilation of human rights norms meant to address discrimination and other abuse on SOGI grounds (Yogyakarta Principles 2006).

About one-third of the applicants to Round 10 made requests for support from the MARP reserve, requesting a total of about US$100 million in programs over two years. Almost half of that amount was finally approved (Rivers 2010), and two countries, Malaysia and Uruguay, received Global Fund support for the first time through the MARP reserve (Ibid.).

The Global Fund's recent support for what it calls "community systems strengthening" (CSS) has also been seen as an important step in encouraging rights-based programming for HIV, TB, and malaria. The CSS framework, developed by the Global Fund in 2010 (and revised in 2014) in consultation with many civil society organizations, encouraged funding applicants to see the "mobilization of key affected populations and community networks" as an essential element of effective programs (Global Fund 2010a, v). It urged applicants to include in their analyses and funding requests an emphasis on "strengthening community-based and community-led systems for prevention, treatment, care and support; advocacy; and the development of an enabling and responsive environment" (Ibid.). Thus, the Global Fund began to incorporate human rights into its program guidance and technical support activities. Drawing on programmatic approaches developed by other institutions, this experience helped to shape the programmatic human rights objectives that the Global Fund would develop as its own.

II. FORMALIZING STRATEGIC OBJECTIVES FOR HUMAN RIGHTS

As the time came to prepare an institutional strategy for 2012–2016, the Global Fund heard from civil society organizations and technical partners on the continued need for attention to human rights issues. Indeed, civil society voices were crucial at this stage, as they had been in consistently pushing the Global Fund toward a greater focus on human rights throughout its history (Davis 2014). A 2011 consultation convened by UNDP and the Open Society Foundations (OSF), which included wide civil society representation, stressed the need for the Global Fund to adopt a formal commitment to human rights goals. In a paper prepared for that consultation, representatives of OSF and the NGO Caribbean Vulnerable Communities Coalition urged the Global Fund to address explicitly the situations in which it might unwittingly undermine rights-based approaches, including:

- When health programs to benefit criminalized people who use drugs, prisoners, sex workers, or lesbian, gay, bisexual, transgender, and intersex (LGBTI) persons expose these populations to arrest, arbitrary detention, and other abuses without adequate protections of their human rights;
- When programs are carried out in closed settings such as prisons, remand centers, and drug detention centers where abusive practices are prevalent and health programs may be part of the abuse; and
- When health programs in countries with poor human rights records and weak protections of marginalized persons are carried out in ways that undermine rights, deny meaningful participation to key populations, and do not embody evidence-based health practices (Wolfe and Carr 2011).

These points partly reflected concerns about the particular case of compulsory detention of people who use drugs, ostensibly to treat their drug dependence. Human Rights Watch, among others, had for some time investigated compulsory drug "treatment" centers in East and Southeast Asia, finding that these facilities provided virtually no scientifically sound health care but rather were scenes of forced labor and physical and psychological abuse of "patients" (Human Rights Watch 2012; Ximena and Davis 2014). In 2012, a joint statement by twelve UN bodies called for the closure of these centers (ILO et al. 2012). While Global Fund Executive Director Kazatchkine also called for these centers to be shut down, he noted that, so long as they continue to operate, the Global Fund should seek out ways to provide basic care, including HIV treatment, for detainees "in an ethical manner and respectful of their rights and dignity" (Kazatchkine 2010).[3] This debate illustrated the challenges of remaining true to country ownership while also seeking to ensure the maximum impact of health services through rights-based programming.

With many explicit and implicit efforts to address human rights concerns in place but not formalized, the Global Fund Board made the decision to adopt formal strategic objectives on human rights and gender equality as part of the 2012–2016 strategy. The Global Fund strategy, approved by the Board after extensive consultation, is a multi-year roadmap for the Global Fund's work, setting out priorities for how the Global Fund can accelerate progress against HIV, TB, and malaria. The 2012–2016 strategy, unlike past strategies, included as one of five top-level strategic objectives of the Global Fund "to promote and protect human rights" (Global Fund 2011). With this strategic objective came three "strategic actions" to:

- Ensure that the Global Fund does not support programs that infringe human rights.
- Increase investments in programs that address human rights-related barriers to access.
- Integrate human rights considerations throughout the grant cycle—that is, through proposal preparation and revision and grant implementation and evaluation (Ibid.).

The 2012–2016 strategy notes that these strategic objectives and strategic actions reflect a "broad consensus" that the Global Fund could do more to address "poor and inequitable targeting of interventions, discriminatory social and legal environments, unsupportive policy settings, and sometimes severe and persistent human rights violations" that undermine programs in many countries (Ibid., 17). It also recognized that the TRP, in its review of Round 10 funding proposals, expressed its concern about "the limited inclusion in proposals of existing human rights instruments and measures to address stigma and discrimination" and other barriers to services for HIV and TB (Ibid.). At the same time, the 2012–2016 strategy recognized that the

---

3. The Global Fund would eventually adopt a policy of generally not funding "treatment" programs where there is detention without due process, "treatment" is not scientifically sound, or there is torture or cruel, inhuman, or degrading practices—unless there are exceptional circumstances (Global Fund 2014c).

Global Fund needed to balance many factors in choosing strategic priorities and actions, including "additionality, sustainability, country ownership, multi-sectoral engagement, partnership, pursuing a balanced and integrated approach in dealing with the three diseases, human rights, performance-based funding, value for money, transparency and accountability" (Ibid., 7).

III. MEETING IMPLEMENTATION CHALLENGES

Shortly after the new 2012–2016 strategy was approved, the Global Fund unveiled what it called a "New Funding Model" (NFM), through which, among other things, ceiling amounts of Global Fund grants would be determined by the Global Fund Secretariat based on policies adopted by the Board, rather than by applicants (Global Fund 2013), an important change in one of the pillars of "country owner-ship." In addition, the NFM featured a commitment by the Global Fund to focus "on those countries with the highest needs and least ability to pay, while remaining global, and supporting the highest-impact interventions" (Ibid., 1). According to the Global Fund, the NFM is a means "to re-balance and give strategic direction to the organization's portfolio of investments" and to ensure greater predictability of funding for countries (Ibid.). The NFM country-level process includes a "country dialogue," envisioned by the Global Fund not as a single event but as a continuing process by which key affected populations and others "involved in the response to the diseases," including persons not well represented in the CCM, can take part in identifying needs, developing strategies, and identifying program priorities (Global Fund 2017a). An inclusive country dialogue was thought, to some degree, to rein-force the underlying rights-based principle of meaningful participation for people in decision-making about health services affecting them.

However, a number of civil society organizations raised human rights concerns about the NFM. MSF, for example, charged that in the name of funding predicta-bility, the NFM would disempower countries and reduce the constructive capacity and ambitions that had resulted in scaled up programs and unprecedented progress on infectious disease responses (MSF 2014). Other NGOs expressed the concern that upper-middle-income countries (UMIC) with concentrated epidemics, which were likely to be phased out or receive much less funding in the NFM, were home to millions of people who use drugs and other key populations for whom programs were unlikely to be funded by governments if the Global Fund withdrew (Cook et al. 2014). In response to these concerns, the Global Fund developed a policy on "sus-tainability, transition and co-financing" that allocated resources to support transition planning and would allow for several years of funding after the end of a country's formal eligibility (Global Fund 2016d). Under this policy, UMIC in particular can apply for transitional funding for programs that address key populations. However, it has remained challenging in practice for the Global Fund (and other donors) to en-sure that much-needed programs to reduce human rights-related barriers to services and programs for key populations continue once countries are no longer eligible to receive funding and/or other donors withdraw. Without international funding, as countries transition to less and then no Global Fund support, there is little leverage to press governments to invest in programs for marginalized populations.

As the NFM was put into place, the Global Fund sought to implement the human rights objectives and actions in the 2012–2016 strategy. A Community, Rights, and Gender (CRG) Department was created in 2013 in the Global Fund Secretariat, including a senior human rights adviser (later expanded to include another human rights expert as well) and advisers on gender, key populations, and community systems strengthening (Global Fund 2016a). The CRG Department organized training sessions on human rights and gender equality for grants management and legal staff at the Secretariat, the Office of the Inspector General (an independent office), and the independent TRP experts. A CRG Advisory Group of external—mostly NGO—experts helped to steer the work and comment on the priorities of the CRG Department, as did a Human Rights Reference Group and a Harm Reduction Working Group.

In addition, a number of key human rights provisions were added to the language of Global Fund grant contracts to articulate fundamental elements of rights-based programs that would be relevant to the three diseases in all countries and assure that Global Fund–supported programs would:

1. Provide non-discriminatory services to all, including to people in the custody of the state;
2. Be based on scientifically sound and approved medicines or medical practices;
3. Not employ methods that constitute torture or that are cruel, inhuman, or degrading;
4. Be expected to respect and protect informed consent, confidentiality, and the right to privacy concerning medical testing, treatment, or health services rendered; and
5. Avoid the use of medical detention and involuntary isolation, except as measures of last resort (Global Fund 2015a).

These contract provisions were reviewed extensively in the Global Fund Secretariat, by the Human Rights Reference Group, and in consultation with human rights experts (Global Fund 2014b; Davis 2014).

The Global Fund announced the establishment in 2015 of a mechanism for reporting human rights concerns linked to Global Fund–supported programs. A "hotline" telephone number and email address were established to receive complaints, which could be made anonymously from anyone who experienced or witnessed a human rights violation linked to a Global Fund–supported program (Global Fund 2015b). Information disseminated about this procedure explained what kinds of violations might be reported, especially with respect to the five human rights points in the grant contracts. The Office of the Inspector General (OIG), reporting directly to the Global Fund Board, was charged with responding to any complaints received within forty-eight hours and determining promptly whether to conduct a full investigation (Ibid.). However, nearly two years into the working of the mechanism, only a few complaints have been considered eligible for resolution by the OIG, and an independent assessment is underway to determine why there has been such a low uptake of this human rights accountability mechanism.

Further, the Global Fund began to offer human rights technical assistance to NGOs, both to improve their participation in Global Fund processes in their countries and to support their longer-term capacity to develop and provide leadership in human rights programs (Global Fund 2016a). By early 2016, there were over 100 requests for technical assistance through this initiative, with thirty-four experts responding to them (Ibid.). This US $15 million initiative has also supported six regional "platforms" for communication with (and coordination of) civil society organizations and technical support for human rights-related program work. Collaboration with the Roll Back Malaria and the Stop TB Partnership were also formalized to provide assistance for the development of programs and situation analyses that would reflect human rights and gender equality concerns (Ibid.).

With the NFM simplifying funding applications, to be organized according to topical "modules" (Global Fund 2013), a module on "removing legal barriers" (RLB) was added to the concept note templates to reflect the place of human rights in the new strategy. Addressing UNAIDS' seven program areas—as noted above in Part I.D—for reducing human rights barriers to HIV services, applicants could include actions in the RLB module on: assessment of the legal environment; "know your rights" awareness-raising; human rights training for law enforcement officers or health care providers; community-based monitoring of human rights issues; and policy advocacy (Global Fund 2014a).[4]

It was a goal of the 2012–2016 strategy for the Global Fund to reflect on its work in "challenging operating environments" (COEs)—i.e., countries experiencing acute emergencies and those in chronic crisis with chronically weak state institutions. In these situations, the normal succession of Global Fund processes—country dialogues, regular CCM meetings, reliance on the health sector for a certain standard of functioning and care—may be compromised (Global Fund 2016b). In addition, the protection, fulfillment, and respect of human rights may be challenged, and the domestic rule of law and justice systems may be undermined. Leading up to the development of both general COE guidelines and guidance for human rights-based and gender-responsive programming in COEs, the Global Fund held a series of consultations with representatives of organizations specializing in humanitarian assistance in emergencies—to identify human rights and gender-related issues and develop guidance for human rights-based and gender-responsive programming in COEs. The resulting guidance recognizes that special efforts may be needed to reach marginalized people when the work of community-based groups and traditional means of access to justice are disrupted, emphasizing that the seven categories of programs to address HIV-related human rights barriers (and the analogous actions for TB and malaria) are as essential for uptake, effectiveness, and sustainability of health programs in COEs as in other situations (Global Fund 2017c).

In 2015 and early 2016, the CRG Department conducted an in-depth analysis of challenges that had arisen in the Global Fund's human rights work and opportunities moving forward. This analysis concluded that while substantial progress had been

---

4. The RLB module was later revised to correspond more exactly to the UNAIDS seven program areas for HIV.

made in realizing two of the strategic actions under the human rights objective (ensuring that the Global Fund does not support programs that infringe human rights and integrating human rights considerations throughout the grant cycle), investments in programs that address human rights-related barriers to access had not increased sufficiently (CRG 2016). An analysis of the RLB programs in the NFM found that there was strong recognition in many countries that addressing human rights barriers was important for successful health service outcomes, with many small-scale NGO programs undertaken to remove human rights barriers; however, scaled-up versions of these programs remained infrequently articulated as budgeted items in Global Fund grants. In the first NFM rounds of funding proposals, the CRG Department estimated that RLB represented only a tiny fraction of the total allocations—about US$33 million was spent on RLB in country grants, plus about $15 million in regional advocacy to address harmful policies (CRG 2016).[5] While the special initiative to provide technical support for design and implementation of human rights-related programs continued, the Global Fund sought to find additional means—including more direct means—to scale up the removal of human rights barriers to health services.

IV. POST-2016: REMOVING HUMAN RIGHTS BARRIERS TO GLOBAL FUND PROGRAMS

In addition to a much greater, explicit focus on gender equality and programs to support women and girls, the Global Fund strategy for 2017–2022 includes a much greater commitment to scaling up programs that remove human rights barriers to accessing HIV, TB, and malaria services. Under a core objective to "promote and protect human rights and gender equality," the 2017–2022 strategy includes a commitment to:

1. Scale up programs to support women and girls, including programs to advance sexual and reproductive health and rights.
2. Invest to reduce health inequities, including gender- and age-related disparities.
3. Introduce and scale up programs that remove human rights barriers to accessing HIV, TB, and malaria services.
4. Integrate human rights considerations throughout the grant cycle and in policies and policymaking processes.
5. Support meaningful engagement of key and vulnerable populations and networks in Global Fund–related processes (Global Fund 2016c).

5. In Latin America, it was estimated that about 2.2 percent of Global Fund support went to RLB programs, but the percentages were considerably lower in other regions (CRG 2016). Of the 119 concept notes received in the first "windows" of the NFM, 72 percent identified human rights barriers to programs, especially HIV services, but only 10 percent sought funding specifically for RLB programs (Oberth 2016).

With policies and funding allocation decisions taken to support these objectives, the Global Fund Board approved a revised Sustainability, Transition, and Co-Financing Policy that requires all funding proposals to include "appropriate focus on interventions that respond to key and vulnerable populations, human rights and gender-related barriers and vulnerabilities in all countries, regardless of income level" (Global Fund 2016d, 6). The Global Fund also launched an intensive, five-year effort to scale up programs that address human rights-related barriers to services in selected countries, accompanied by US$40 million in dedicated "matching" funds, which countries can access only if they match the funding provided by the Global Fund (Global Fund 2017e).

The objective to introduce and scale up programs that remove human rights-related barriers to services is also supported by key performance indicators that will measure, *inter alia*, "the extent to which programs to remove human rights barriers to services are implemented in 15–20 countries that will be selected for an intensive effort" (Ibid., 2). These indicators will assess the percentage of the country allocation invested in (1) programs to reduce human rights-related barriers and (2) programs targeting key populations, with a target to increase the allocation in these two areas more than fourfold. With an extensive consultation informing the selection of countries, this initiative will provide for a review of evidence on the effectiveness and cost-effectiveness of programs to reduce human rights barriers to services for HIV, TB, and malaria around the world (Ibid.).

Teams of independent researchers are currently in the process of conducting baseline assessments of human rights barriers to HIV, TB, and malaria services in a first set of the selected countries, as well as rapidly assessing existing programs to address these barriers, including an analysis of why small-scale programs have remained small-scale. These assessments include extensive consultation with civil society organizations, health care providers, key government actors, people affected by the three diseases, and others. CCM members and other key actors at the country level, informed by these baseline assessments and supported by Global Fund staff, will develop national plans to scale up programs to reduce human rights barriers (including removing policy and legal impediments). Ideally, the cost of these new or improved programs will be covered largely as part of Global Fund grants, but countries with strong plans and unfunded elements will be able to apply for supplemental matching funding that the Global Fund Board has designated for this purpose (Ibid.).

In evaluating the programs introduced and scaled up to address human rights barriers, the state of the barriers will be assessed twice by researchers in each country, at about 2.5 and 4.5 years after the national plan is developed. Detailed assessments will be made of the effectiveness, cost, and cost-effectiveness of the measures, with particular attention to how key affected populations experience the impact of these programs (Ibid.). The evidence from these assessments and lessons learned from the experiences in these selected countries will be disseminated and added to the existing evidence base on the importance of programs to reduce human rights barriers. In addition, the detailed information on scaled-up programs will form the basis for mathematical modeling and other means of estimating the impact of investments in reducing human rights barriers to uptake, sustainability, and effectiveness of HIV, TB, and malaria services (Ibid.).

The twenty selected countries include some where CCMs have already identified human rights barriers to health programs and where community-based organizations are present to ensure that key populations participate meaningfully in program design, implementation, and evaluation. However, the legal and policy environments in countries and the political unpopularity of programs may undermine the scale-up of efforts to include key populations, including criminalized populations. Additionally, there may be a lack of technical capacity to build and sustain programs to reduce human rights barriers as well as disagreements on priorities and strategies. More broadly, even if evidence shows that investing in the reduction of human rights barriers through scaled-up programs has direct benefits—including overall medium-term cost reductions linked to prevention and control of infectious disease—such evidence may still not be convincing to some policymakers. An effort such as this has not been tried on this scale, but the support of a major global health financing institution provides necessary resources to move from rhetoric to real action in removing human rights barriers to services.

This twenty-country initiative to scale up programs to reduce human rights-related barriers to HIV, TB, and malaria services is an enormously challenging initiative, but it is also much needed. There is an urgent need to achieve the health and human rights impact that results from increased access to services for people living with and experiencing enhanced risk and vulnerability to HIV, TB, and malaria when rights-related barriers are reduced. Intensive efforts appear necessary to overcome the long-standing impasse regarding insufficient inclusion and scale-up of the programs. There will be much to learn from intensive efforts undertaken in a number of countries in different regions, highlighting practical examples of improved health service outcomes because of a reduction of rights-related barriers and resulting in knowledge and experience that can inform ongoing and future efforts to address human rights-related barriers in other countries and settings.

V. OTHER RECENT HUMAN RIGHTS-RELATED EFFORTS: TECHNICAL GUIDANCE AND PARTNERSHIPS

Implementing the Global Fund's human rights objectives has also required improved collaboration with UN agencies and other partners in efforts to address HIV, TB, and malaria. With respect to HIV, the Global Fund realigned the elements of the RLB module in 2016 to correspond, as noted above, with the seven human rights categories of programs identified by UNAIDS (UNAIDS 2012). This realignment has enabled more effective Global Fund–UNAIDS coordination to promote and monitor these programs, including, among other things, emphasizing the importance of gender-based violence as a barrier to health services. Beyond gender-based violence, a 2017 technical brief for CCMs and program managers gives numerous practical examples of ways in which the impact of Global Fund–supported HIV programs can be optimized by reducing human rights-related barriers to services (Global Fund 2017b).

Similarly, with respect to TB, the Global Fund has formalized collaborations with the Stop TB Partnership, including by promoting programs to reduce human rights barriers in Global Fund–supported TB programs. Guided in part by the

Stop TB Partnership's publications on key populations affected by TB (Stop TB Partnership 2016), a TB working group convened by the Global Fund developed a technical brief on TB, gender, and human rights that is meant to guide CCMs and others seeking to design rights-based TB programs (Global Fund 2017f). In addition to concerns about key populations—including migrant workers, prisoners, people who use drugs, and others—this technical brief discusses the need for a legal framework and standard practices reflecting WHO's recommendation that involuntary isolation for the purpose to TB treatment must be a measure of last resort, only when all other efforts to ensure voluntary treatment have been exhausted (WHO 2010).

Finally, a group of experts have developed a Global Fund technical brief on malaria and human rights (Global Fund 2017d), an area that had not previously been well developed. Based on the peer-reviewed literature, program evaluations, and the experiences of the experts consulted, this technical brief considers such human rights-related barriers as subordination of women that disempowers them with respect to many health-related household decisions needed to take advantage of malaria prevention, testing, and treatment services (Ibid.). This technical brief reviews a number of examples of gender norms leading men or women to be more likely to be exposed to mosquitoes at peak infection times, as well as the particular vulnerabilities faced by mobile and migrant populations that may be exposed to malaria risk but may also face discrimination and other exclusion on linguistic, xenophobia-related, or cultural grounds. Prisoners and pretrial detainees may also face exposures beyond their control and lack access to basic services. Examples are given of programs that can address these barriers to care, including: ensuring women are included in teams conducting indoor residual spraying, assessing and addressing gender-based barriers to sleeping under an insecticide-treated bed net, bringing malaria information and screening to places where migrant workers congregate, and helping prison authorities assess and address malaria risk (Ibid.).

Facilitated by these technical briefs, direct assistance to CCMs by health and human rights experts continues under the special Global Fund initiative that began in 2016, with their elaboration of types of rights-based programs likely to be examined favorably by the TRP.

CONCLUSION

The Global Fund's commitment to human rights-centered health programs is a testament to the established understanding that HIV could not be effectively addressed without reducing rights-related barriers to health services, including for the most marginalized people affected by HIV. However, the continuing challenge of encouraging CCMs to prioritize efforts to address human rights barriers as part of health programs is a testament to the depth of political and social exclusion of those affected by HIV (and to some degree TB and malaria). It may also be the result of the virtual absence of large-scale—as opposed to small, piecemeal—human rights programs that should be a pillar of the evidence base for rights-centered health services.

Human rights advocates have criticized UNAIDS' focus on "investment frameworks" for HIV at the expense of rights advocacy—i.e., a focus on removing human rights barriers because they impede a good return on investment in HIV programs rather than because they accord with international human rights obligations (Heywood 2014). In this view, "evidence and efficiency" in an investment framework exemplifies an abandonment of the struggle for HIV treatment and other services as a central element of human rights. From the Global Fund's perspective, however, building programs to reduce human rights barriers on a scale not previously achieved is both a way to demonstrate the disease impact—and cost-effectiveness—of these programs and a tangible commitment to the human rights of affected populations (Global Fund 2017e). It is a way to address the persistent and deep underfunding of human rights-based efforts in HIV responses. In addition, the inclusion of TB and malaria in the Global Fund's efforts to reduce human rights barriers to services is pioneering and can help to concretize the impact of rights-centered approaches to health more broadly.

The Global Fund's initiatives to build, scale up, sustain, and evaluate programs addressing human rights barriers represent a programmatic shift—from the public espousal of principles to an active implementation of rights-based approaches. As the principal international funder for TB and malaria programs and one of the largest HIV funders, the Global Fund is well placed to set an example—using its leverage as a donor and its commitment of considerable resources to reinforce technical capacity to reduce rights-related barriers to care—in which human rights norms matter for the impact and sustainability of health services. In some cases, technical capacity and financial support to reduce human rights-related barriers will not be sufficient; the politics of diseases affecting marginalized and criminalized persons is complicated and entrenched. Yet, where changing unjust laws is rarely possible in a short time, the Global Fund work has the chance to show that much can be achieved in spite of a difficult legal environment. Demonstrating the effectiveness and cost-effectiveness of relying on human rights norms in health services will open doors to more accessible, respectful, and sustainable health services.

REFERENCES

Atun, Rifat and Michel Kazatchkine. 2010. "The Global Fund's Leadership on Harm Reduction: 2002–2009." *International Journal of Drug Policy* 21(2): 103–106.

Brugha, Rairí and Gill Walt. 2001. "A Global Health Fund: a Leap of Faith?" *British Medical Journal* 323(7305): 152–154.

Cook, Catherine, Jamie Bridge, Susie MacLean, Maria Phelan, and Damon Barrett. 2014. *The Funding Crisis for Harm Reduction: Donor Retreat, Government Neglect and the Way Forward.* London: International Harm Reduction Association.

CRG (Community, Rights and Gender Division of the Global Fund). 2016. Presentation to the Global Fund consultation "Scaling up programs to address human rights barriers and increasing evidence of impact." Geneva, April 2016 (on file with the authors).

Davis, Sara L. 2014. "Human Rights and the Global Fund to Fight AIDS, Tuberculosis, and Malaria." *Health and Human Rights* 16(1): 134–147.

Fried Susana T. and Shannon Kowalski-Morton. 2008. "Sex and the Global Fund: How Sex Workers, Lesbians, Gays, Bisexuals, Transgender People, and Men Who Have Sex with Men Are Benefiting from the Global Fund, or Not." *Health and Human Rights* 10(1): 1–10.

Global Fund (to Fight AIDS, Tuberculosis and Malaria). 2001 (revised 2012). *The framework document*. Geneva: The Global Fund.

Global Fund. 2007. *Guidelines on the purpose, structure, composition and funding of Country Coordinating Mechanisms*. Geneva: The Global Fund. Available at: https://www.theglobalfund.org/board-decisions/b16-dp19/.

Global Fund. 2008. *Global Fund gender equality strategy*. Geneva: The Global Fund to Fight AIDS, Tuberculosis and Malaria.

Global Fund. 2009. *The Global Fund strategy in relation to sexual orientation and gender identities*. Geneva: The Global Fund to Fight AIDS, Tuberculosis and Malaria.

Global Fund. 2010a (revised 2014). *Community systems strengthening framework*. Geneva: The Global Fund to Fight AIDS, Tuberculosis and Malaria. Available at: https://www.theglobalfund.org/media/6428/core_css_framework_en.pdf.

Global Fund. 2010b. *Dedicated reserve for Round 10 HIV/AIDS proposals for most at risk populations (MARPs): information note*. Geneva: The Global Fund to Fight AIDS, Tuberculosis and Malaria (on file with authors).

Global Fund. 2010c (updated 2016). *Terms of reference of the Technical Review Panel*. Geneva: The Global Fund to Fight AIDS, Tuberculosis and Malaria. Available at: https://www.theglobalfund.org/media/3048/trp_technicalreviewpanel_tor_en.pdf.

Global Fund. 2011. *The Global Fund strategy 2012–2016: investing for impact*. Geneva: The Global Fund to Fight AIDS, Tuberculosis and Malaria.

Global Fund. 2013. *The Global Fund's New Funding Model*. Geneva: The Global Fund to Fight AIDS, Tuberculosis and Malaria.

Global Fund. 2014a. *Local Fund Agent Manual*. Geneva: The Global Fund to Fight AIDS, Tuberculosis and Malaria.

Global Fund. 2014b. *Managing the risk of human rights violations in Global Fund-supported programs: meeting report* (Geneva, 22–23 May 2014). Geneva: The Global Fund to Fight AIDS, Tuberculosis and Malaria.

Global Fund. 2014c. "Thirty-Second Board Meeting, Strategy, Investment and Impact Committee decisions and recommendations to the Board." 20–21 November. Doc. GF/B32/27.

Global Fund. 2015a. *Focus on human rights*. Geneva: The Global Fund to Fight AIDS, Tuberculosis and Malaria. Available at: https://www.theglobalfund.org/media/1224/publication_humanrights_focuson_en.pdf.

Global Fund. 2015b. *The Global Fund human rights complaint procedure: responding to community concerns*. Geneva: The Global Fund to Fight AIDS, Tuberculosis and Malaria.

Global Fund. 2016a. "35th Board Meeting, Community, Rights and Gender Report 2016." 26–27 April. Doc. GF/B35/15.

Global Fund. 2016b. "35th Board Meeting, The challenging operating environments policy." 26–27 April. Doc. GF/B35/03.

Global Fund. 2016c. "35th Board Meeting, The Global Fund strategy 2017–2022: Investing to end epidemics." 26–27 April. Doc. GF/B35/02–Revision 1.

Global Fund. 2016d. "35th Board Meeting, The Global Fund sustainability, transition and co-financing policy." 26–27 April. Doc. GF/B35/04–Revision 1.

Global Fund. 2017a. "Funding model." *The Global Fund*. Available at: http://www.theglobalfund.org/en/fundingmodel/process/.

Global Fund. 2017b. *HIV, human rights and gender equality: technical brief*. Geneva: The Global Fund to Fight AIDS, Tuberculosis and Malaria.

Global Fund. 2017c. *Human rights and gender programming in challenging operating environments (COEs): Guidance brief.* Geneva: The Global Fund to Fight AIDS, Tuberculosis and Malaria.

Global Fund. 2017d. *Malaria, gender and human rights: technical brief.* Geneva: The Global Fund to Fight AIDS, Tuberculosis and Malaria.

Global Fund. 2017e. *Scaling up programs to reduce human rights barriers to health services— Intensified efforts in 15 to 20 countries: Questions and answers (part 1 and part 2).* Last updated May. Geneva: The Global Fund to Fight AIDS, Tuberculosis and Malaria. Available at: https://www.theglobalfund.org/media/1213/humanrights_2016-removingbarrierspart2_qa_en.pdf.

Global Fund. 2017f. *Tuberculosis, gender and human rights: technical brief.* Geneva: The Global Fund to Fight AIDS, Tuberculosis and Malaria.

Global Fund. n.d. "Transitional Working Group Archive." Accessed July 8, 2017. *The Global Fund.* Available at: https://www.theglobalfund.org/en/archive/transitional-working-group/.

Heywood, Mark. 2014. "The Unravelling of the Human Rights Response to HIV and AIDS and Why It Happened: An Activists' Perspective." In *AIDS Today: Tell No Lies, Claim No Easy Victories.* Brighton, UK: International HIV/AIDS Alliance.

Human Rights Watch. 2012. "Torture in the Name of Treatment: Human Rights Abuses in Vietnam, China, Cambodia, and Lao PDR." *Human Rights Watch.* July 24. Available at: https://www.hrw.org/report/2012/07/24/torture-name-treatment/human-rights-abuses-vietnam-china-cambodia-and-lao-pdr.

ICASO (International Council of AIDS Service Organizations). 2006. *A call for political leadership: community sector recommendations for the UN Political Declaration of HIV/AIDS.* Toronto, Canada: ICASO.

ILO (International Labour Organization), UNDP, UNAIDS, UN Office on Drugs and Crime, et al. 2012. *Joint statement: Compulsory drug detention and rehabilitation centres.* Geneva: United Nations.

Kazatchkine, Michel. 2010. "Time to Redouble Our Efforts on AIDS and Human Rights." *Canadian HIV/AIDS Legal Network 2nd annual symposium on HIV, Law, and Human Rights.* Keynote address, Toronto, 11 June.

Lidén, John. 2013. *The Grand Decade for Global Health: 1998–2008.* London: Center for Global Health Working Paper Series, Chatham House.

McCarthy, Michael. 2007. "The Global Fund: 5 Years On." *The Lancet* 370(9584): 307–308.

MSF (Médecins Sans Frontières). 2014. *Pushing the Envelope: Does the Global Fund's New Funding Model Foster Country Ambitions?* (Issue Brief). Available at: http://www.msf.org/sites/msf.org/files/msf_brief_aug_2014_pushingtheenvelope.pdf.

Oberth, Gemma. 2016. "Tracking Global Fund Investments in Human Rights Programs." *Global Fund Observer.* July 20. Available at: http://www.aidspan.org/gfo_article/tracking-global-fund-investments-human-rights-programs.

OSF (Open Society Foundations) and Canadian HIV/AIDS Legal Network. 2011. *Human Rights and the Global Fund to Fight AIDS, Tuberculosis and Malaria.* Available at: https://www.opensocietyfoundations.org/reports/human-rights-and-global-fund-fight-aids-tuberculosis-and-malaria.

Rivers, Bernard. 2010. "Global Fund Board Approves Round 10 Proposals." *Global Fund Observer.* December 16. Available at: http://www.aidspan.org/gfo_article/global-fund-board-approves-round-10-proposals.

Stop TB Partnership. 2016. "Key Populations Briefs." *Stop TB Partnership.* Available at: http://www.stoptb.org/resources/publications/.

't Hoen, Ellen, Jonathan Berger, Alexandra Calmy, and Suerie Moon. 2011. "Driving a Decade of Change: HIV/AIDS, Patents and Access to Medicines for All." *Journal of the International AIDS Society* 14(1): 15.

UN General Assembly. 2001. "Declaration of commitment on HIV/AIDS." 2 August. UN Doc. A/RES/S-26/2.

UNAIDS (Joint United Nations Programme on HIV/AIDS). 2012. *Key programmes to reduce stigma and discrimination and increase access to justice in national HIV responses.* Geneva: UNAIDS.

UNDP (UN Development Programme), UNAIDS, and the Global Fund. 2010. *Analysis of key human rights programmes in Global Fund-supported HIV programmes.* New York: UNDP.

WHO (World Health Organization). 2010. *Guidance on ethics of tuberculosis prevention, care and control.* Geneva: WHO.

Wolfe, Daniel and Robert Carr. 2011. "Strengthening Global Fund Protections Against Human Rights Abuses." In *Human Rights and the Global Fund to Fight AIDS, Tuberculosis and Malaria.* (Meeting Report, March 3–4, New York). New York: Open Society Foundations.

Ximena, Navia H. and Sara L. Davis. 2014. "Compulsory Drug Detention in East and Southeast Asia: Response from the Global Fund to Fight AIDS, Tuberculosis and Malaria." *International Journal of Drug Policy* 25(1): 21.

Yogyakarta Principles: The Application of International Human Rights Law in Relation to Sexual Orientation and Gender Identity, 2006. Available at: http://www.yogyakartaprinciples.org/principles-en/.

20

The Future of Multilateral Funding to Realize the Right to Health

GORIK OOMS AND RACHEL HAMMONDS

Where the future of multilateral funding for the realization of the right to health looks bleak—with the largest donor moving away from international assistance, multilateral cooperation, and global governance for health—a better understanding of the advantages and disadvantages of multilateral assistance and bilateral assistance would help policymakers to take appropriate decisions in the future on better grounds than inclination alone. This chapter compares two extreme options through a human rights lens. For the first option, it will be assumed that all international assistance for health is channeled via a proposed Global Fund for Health. For the other option, it will be assumed that all international assistance for health is delivered via bilateral agreements.

This chapter is divided in three sections. Part I outlines the mandate of a Global Fund for Health, based on international obligations in the International Covenant on Economic, Social and Cultural Rights (ICESCR), guidance provided by the Committee on Economic, Social and Cultural Rights (CESCR), and features of the existing Global Fund to Fight AIDS, Tuberculosis and Malaria (GFATM). It also outlines the alternative at the opposite extreme: the same volume of assistance, from the same countries to the same countries, but channeled through bilateral agreements. Part II compares the likely qualities of international funding channeled via a Global Fund for Health with the likely qualities of international assistance provided via bilateral agreements, in terms of the funding being: aligned with recipient country priorities, additional (i.e., incentivizing domestic mobilization of financial resources), reliable over time, coordinated, and sufficient. Part III explores the political feasibility of a Global Fund for Health.

Human Rights in Global Health. Benjamin Mason Meier and Lawrence O. Gostin.
© Oxford University Press 2018. Published 2018 by Oxford University Press.

I. ASSEMBLING A GLOBAL FUND FOR HEALTH AND THE ALTERNATIVE

To achieve a better understanding of the advantages and disadvantages of multilateral assistance and bilateral assistance, two extreme options will be outlined and compared—all international assistance for health channeled via a single Global Fund for Health, or all international assistance channeled via bilateral agreements— holding other variables constant.

A. "States in a Position to Assist" and How Much Assistance They Should Provide

The main textual foundation of the international obligation to provide assistance lies in Article 2(1) of the ICESCR:

> Each State Party to the present Covenant undertakes to take steps, *individually and through international assistance and co-operation*, especially economic and technical, to the maximum of its available resources, with a view to achieving progressively the full realization of the rights recognized in the present Covenant by all appropriate means ... [emphasis added] (UN General Assembly 1966).

This text does not create a hierarchy between national (each state toward the people under its jurisdiction) and international obligations. Yet most scholars agree that international obligations are "secondary" obligations, which come in addition to the primary obligation of states toward the people under their jurisdictions. The alternative interpretation—without hierarchy between primary and secondary obligations—would lead to all states being responsible for all people, and while that interpretation would fit with Shue's characterization of "basic rights," namely, "everyone's reasonable demands upon the rest of humanity" (Shue 1996, 19), this was probably not the intention of the drafters of the ICESCR.

While "several states sought to convert the moral imperative underlying the need for co-operation into a binding and specific legal obligation" under the ICESCR, "this move was resisted in equal measure by other states" (Tobin 2012, 328). Agreeing on relatively vague text for this Article 2(1) provision, the drafters left the task of further clarification to future users: individuals (or states) making claims based on texts and courts or scholars evaluating the merits of the claims and formulating rulings and opinions. In this particular case—of obligations to provide international assistance for realization of the right to health—that process is still ongoing. It is a process with many actors, including the CESCR, formulating "Concluding Observations" and "General Comments" on the ICESCR; expert panels, elaborating statements like the "Maastricht Principles on Extraterritorial Obligations of States in the Area of Economic, Social and Cultural Rights" (Experts in international law and human rights 2011); civil society groups, formulating claims and pressuring governments to live up to those claims; and United Nations (UN) agencies and programs, incorporating the obligations to provide international assistance in their guidelines and policy recommendations. According to the "Technical guidance on the application of a human rights-based approach to the implementation of policies and programmes to reduce preventable maternal morbidity and mortality," issued by the Office of the UN High Commissioner for Human Rights (OHCHR) in 2012, "[o]bligations to provide international assistance and cooperation supplement but do not displace obligations of national Governments" (OHCHR 2012, para. 84).

The consensus that this obligation of international assistance is a secondary obligation makes it difficult to estimate how much assistance is required. For the purposes of this chapter, an estimate of how much it would cost for each state to realize the right to health is needed. The amount of financial resources states can mobilize themselves also needs to be estimated. Then the gap between what states can mobilize themselves and what they need to spend can be calculated. This is the approach used in previous papers, leading the authors to a US$30 billion estimated gap in 2006 (Ooms et al. 2006) and a US $50 billion estimated gap in 2010 (Ooms and Hammonds 2010).

Others have proposed an alternative approach, based on three criteria: internationally agreed benchmarks and commitments; comparison to peer states; and progressive increase (Khalfan 2013). In 1970, high-income countries made a commitment to allocate the equivalent of 0.7 percent of their gross domestic product (GDP) to international assistance (Fürher 1996). However, this is a target for all international assistance, not only for health-related assistance. According to the Development Assistance Committee of the Organisation for Economic Co-operation and Development (OECD-DAC), about 15 percent of international assistance is allocated to the health sector (OECD 2011). The combination of 0.7 percent and 15 percent results in 0.1 percent of GDP going toward health-related issues. If this is calculated for all states "in a position to assist," i.e., those with a GDP above $12,476 per person per year—which is the threshold to be qualified as high-income country by the World Bank—a combined US $47 billion would be obtained, as illustrated in Table 20.1 below.

Table 20.1 STATES "IN A POSITION TO ASSIST" (GDP PER CAPITA > US$12,500)

Country	GDP per capita* in US$	Population*	Contribution: 0.1% of GDP
Luxembourg	101,450	569,676	57,793,612
Switzerland	80,945	8,286,976	670,789,929
Norway	74,400	5,195,921	386,578,444
Qatar	73,653	2,235,355	164,641,484
Ireland	61,134	4,640,703	283,703,217
Australia	56,311	23,781,169	1,339,140,527
United States	56,116	321,418,820	18,036,648,000
Singapore	52,889	5,535,002	292,739,308
Denmark	51,989	5,676,002	295,091,334
Sweden	50,580	9,798,871	495,623,697

(Continued)

Table 20.1. (CONTINUED)

Country	GDP per capita* in US$	Population*	Contribution: 0.1% of GDP
Iceland	50,173	330,823	16,598,495
Netherlands	44,300	16,936,520	750,283,908
United Kingdom	43,876	65,138,232	2,858,003,088
Austria	43,775	8,611,088	376,950,250
Canada	43,249	35,851,774	1,550,536,520
Finland	42,311	5,482,013	231,949,651
Germany	41,313	81,413,145	3,363,446,823
United Arab Emirates	40,439	9,156,963	370,296,256
Belgium	40,324	11,285,721	455,085,727
New Zealand	37,808	4,595,700	173,754,075
France	36,206	66,808,385	2,418,835,533
Israel	35,728	8,380,400	299,415,715
Japan	34,524	126,958,472	4,383,076,298
Brunei Darussalam	30,555	423,188	12,930,395
Italy	29,958	60,802,085	1,821,496,964
Kuwait	29,301	3,892,115	114,041,210
Korea, Rep.	27,222	50,617,045	1,377,873,108
Spain	25,832	46,418,269	1,199,057,336
Cyprus	23,243	1,165,300	27,084,882
Bahamas, The	22,817	388,019	8,853,519
Bahrain	22,600	1,377,237	31,125,851
Malta	22,596	431,333	9,746,479
Slovenia	20,727	2,063,768	42,774,770
Saudi Arabia	20,482	31,540,372	646,001,867
Portugal	19,222	10,348,648	198,923,265
Greece	18,002	10,823,732	194,851,319
Czech Republic	17,548	10,551,219	185,156,360
Trinidad and Tobago	17,322	1,360,088	23,559,287
Estonia	17,119	1,311,998	22,459,443
Slovak Republic	16,088	5,424,050	87,263,622
St. Kitts and Nevis	15,772	55,572	876,479
Uruguay	15,574	3,431,555	53,442,698
Oman	15,551	4,490,541	69,830,949
Seychelles	15,476	92,900	1,437,722
Barbados	15,429	284,215	4,385,250
Equatorial Guinea	14,440	845,060	12,202,324

(Continued)

Table 20.1. (CONTINUED)

Country	GDP per capita* in US$	Population*	Contribution: 0.1% of GDP
Lithuania	14,147	2,910,199	41,170,729
Antigua and Barbuda	13,715	91,818	1,259,259
Latvia	13,649	1,978,440	27,002,832
Palau	13,499	21,291	287,400
Argentina	13,432	43,416,755	583,168,571
Chile	13,416	17,948,141	240,796,388
Panama	13,268	3,929,141	52,132,290
Poland	12,555	37,999,494	477,066,454
Total		*1,192,414,625*	*46,839,240,911*

*SOURCE: World Development Indicators (World Bank)—extracted on February 10, 2017.

B. How a Global Fund for Health Would Distribute $47 Billion per Year

For this chapter, it is assumed that a "Global Fund for Health" would arise from a transformation of the existing GFATM and mergers with other existing global health funds while benefiting from a GDP-based mandatory replenishment mechanism: all high-income countries contributing the equivalent of 0.1 percent of GDP. It is assumed that all other features of the GFATM would be kept, except where the broadening of its mandate is required. The essential features of the GFATM, as outlined in chapter 19, include:

- International funding commitments are based on proposals developed by country coordination mechanisms (CCMs), "which are intended to bring together a range of different stakeholders at the country level—crucially including civil society as a partner in this process" (Hanefeld 2014, 55);
- Proposals are evaluated on their merits by an independent panel—the Technical Review Panel (TRP)—in accordance with guidelines developed by the World Health Organization (WHO) (Hanefeld 2014; Davis 2014);
- International funding commitments are additional to national or domestic funding commitments, also known as "co-financing requirements" (Dybul 2017); and
- A Board composed of twenty members—representing predominantly states (fifteen out of twenty voting Board members), civil society, foundations, and the private sector—makes the ultimate decisions (Ooms and Hammonds 2016).

One important feature of the GFATM that would have to be adapted is the "allocation model." Until 2012, the GFATM did not have an explicit allocation model: in principle, countries could ask for as much as they wanted or needed, as long as proposals were developed by CCMs and approved by the TRP. In 2012, the GFATM adopted a new model that "systematically accounts for two factors—countries' disease burden and 'ability to pay' for disease control programs—to partially determine potential funding levels for eligible countries" (Fan et al. 2014, 3). With a broader mandate, covering all elements of health, a Global Fund for Health would face serious difficulties in continuing to use "disease burden" as a determinant of funding levels. Thus, for the purpose of this chapter, it is assumed that "ability to contribute," or rather "inability" to contribute, would become the main (and perhaps only) factor.

In line with Article 2(1) of the ICESCR, a country's ability or inability to contribute should not be determined by real government revenue but by potential government revenue. If in some low-income countries, government revenue is merely 10 percent of GDP, while in others it is 20 percent (Besley and Persson 2014), it can be argued that the first set of countries are not generating—and, a fortiori, not allocating—"maximum available resources." Using the criteria for international assistance proposed above—i.e., internationally agreed benchmarks and commitments, comparison to peer states, and progressive increase (Khalfan 2013)—it is assumed that all countries can generate at least 20 percent of GDP as government revenue, and in line with the Abuja target, as discussed in chapter 18, can spend at least 15 percent of government revenue on health (Witter et al. 2013). The combination of assumptions here means that all countries should allocate at least the equivalent of 3 percent of GDP on domestic health spending. To estimate—very roughly—how a Global Fund for Health would allocate US $47 billion per year, based on ability to contribute, and assuming that all countries would spend at least 3 percent of GDP on health, all countries were ranked from poorest to less poor (based upon World Bank estimates) to calculate how much they could contribute from domestic resources. Then the US $47 billion was distributed in such a way that all countries would be able to spend the same amount per person per year on health. The result of this exercise, captured in Table 20.2, is that forty-nine countries—most of them low-income, some lower-middle-income—would receive assistance from the Global Fund for Health, allowing each of them to spend US $57 per person per year on health.

Table 20.2. States "needing assistance" (given US$47 billion to be distributed in accordance with ability to contribute)

	GDP per capita in US$*	Population*	3% of GDP per capita	Gap to get to US$57 per capita	Allocation model
Burundi	277	11,178,921	8	49	544,278,755
Central African Republic	323	4,900,274	10	47	231,802,315
Niger	359	19,899,120	11	46	919,961,300
Malawi	372	17,215,232	11	46	789,153,596

(Continued)

Table 20.2. (CONTINUED)

	GDP per capita in US$*	Population*	3% of GDP per capita	Gap to get to US$57 per capita	Allocation model
Madagascar	402	24,235,390	12	45	1,089,257,660
Liberia	456	4,503,438	14	43	195,105,966
Congo, Dem. Rep.	456	77,266,814	14	43	3,347,076,130
Gambia, The	472	1,990,924	14	43	85,318,826
Mozambique	529	27,977,863	16	41	1,150,525,919
Guinea	531	12,608,590	16	41	517,713,524
Somalia	549	10,787,104	16	41	437,114,928
Togo	560	7,304,578	17	40	293,723,829
Guinea-Bissau	573	1,844,325	17	40	73,423,218
Burkina Faso	590	18,105,570	18	39	711,671,432
Afghanistan	594	32,526,562	18	39	1,274,075,438
Ethiopia	619	99,390,750	19	38	3,819,081,399
Sierra Leone	653	6,453,184	20	37	241,388,094
Rwanda	697	11,609,666	21	36	418,871,562
Uganda	705	39,032,383	21	36	1,398,968,340
Comoros	717	788,474	22	35	27,972,325
Mali	724	17,599,694	22	35	620,781,889
South Sudan	731	12,339,812	22	35	432,912,651
Nepal	743	28,513,700	22	35	989,434,259
Benin	762	10,879,829	23	34	371,420,649
Chad	776	11,037,172	23	34	473,471,961
Haiti	818	10,711,067	25	32	347,570,922
Tanzania	879	53,470,420	26	31	1,637,838,898
Senegal	900	15,129,273	27	30	454,068,874
Zimbabwe	924	15,602,751	28	29	456,781,230
Tajikistan	926	8,481,855	28	29	247,862,224
Lesotho	1,067	2,135,022	32	25	53,355,120
Kyrgyz Republic	1,103	5,957,000	33	24	142,393,385
Timor-Leste	1,158	1,245,015	35	22	27,714,297
Cambodia	1,159	15,577,899	35	22	346,441,614
Myanmar	1,161	53,897,154	35	22	1,194,110,595
Bangladesh	1,212	160,995,642	36	21	3,324,391,619

(Continued)

Table 20.2. (CONTINUED)

	GDP per capita in US$*	Population*	3% of GDP per capita	Gap to get to US$57 per capita	Allocation model
Cameroon	1,217	23,344,179	37	20	478,139,674
Zambia	1,305	16,211,767	39	18	289,438,883
Ghana	1,370	27,409,893	41	16	436,063,065
Kenya	1,377	46,050,302	41	16	722,925,968
Cote d'Ivoire	1,399	22,701,556	42	15	341,211,226
Yemen, Rep.	1,406	26,832,215	42	15	397,418,657
Kiribati	1,424	112,423	43	14	1,604,453
Pakistan	1,435	188,924,874	43	14	2,637,221,218
India	1,598	1,311,050,527	48	9	11,867,929,566
Sao Tome and Principe	1,669	190,344	50	7	1,318,723
Lao PDR	1,818	6,802,023	55	2	16,642,910
Moldova	1,848	3,554,150	55	2	5,537,884
Congo, Rep.	1,851	4,620,330	56	1	6,764,175
Total		**2,533,997,350**			**45,889,251,142**

*SOURCE: World Development Indicators (World Bank)—extracted on February 10, 2017.

C. The Alternative Option: Bilateral Agreements

In spite of the exponential growth of the GFATM and other multilateral funds, bilateral assistance remains the main channel of international assistance for health (IHME 2017). To avoid comparing apples to oranges, the Global Fund for Health as outlined above will not be compared with the present situation of bilateral assistance, but some of the assumptions will be equalized in order to focus on the difference between multilateral and bilateral channels. It is therefore assumed that the same fifty-four countries mentioned in Table 20.1 will, together, try to provide the same amounts of assistance to the same forty-nine countries of Table 20.2. This means that there would potentially be 2,646 (fifty-four times forty-nine) bilateral agreements. Obviously, coordination efforts could greatly reduce the number of bilateral agreements. For example, the United States could, with its $18 billion contribution, finance the needs of the twenty poorest countries alone. Japan could finance the needs of the next five countries, and so on. However, that seems to be a rather implausible assumption in meeting this option: if states prefer bilateral agreements over a multilateral channel, it is because they want to keep control over their assistance, and therefore, to be able to decide which states receive their assistance. It will therefore be assumed that each of the forty-nine states in Table 20.2 will, on average, receive assistance from ten different states, which results in about 490 bilateral agreements.

II. COMPARING A GLOBAL FUND FOR HEALTH WITH BILATERAL AGREEMENTS

Having sketched the alternatives at opposite sides of the spectrum of possibilities, it is possible to compare the plausible qualities of both options. Both options will be "tested" with reference to a set of necessary qualities for international assistance to realize the right to health:

(a) Aligned with a national strategy, devised on the basis of a participatory and transparent process;
(b) Additional to "maximum available" domestic resources;
(c) Reliable in the long run;
(d) Coordinated between all countries contributing to and receiving international assistance;
(e) Sufficient to assist countries to fulfill at least the core obligations of the right to health.

A. Aligned with a National Strategy, Devised on the Basis of a Participatory and Transparent Process

In health, diverse forms of international cooperation existed long before the practice of development assistance started. As chronicled in chapter 3, there has long been international cooperation to address outbreaks of infectious diseases, intended to prevent the spread of infectious diseases while at the same time ensuring the continuation of trade between affected countries. The International Sanitary Conferences, which began in the 1850s, are illustrations of this form of international cooperation in health, as is the *Office International d'Hygiène Publique*, established in Paris in 1908, and the Health Section of the League of Nations, established in Geneva in 1924 (Kamradt-Scott 2015). The focus of these institutions of international cooperation was infectious disease control. In addition, "colonial medicine" has existed for a long time—the expression "international cooperation" may not be appropriate to this context—with a similar, albeit less exclusive, focus on infectious disease. It is therefore not surprising that international cooperation and assistance in health during the first decades after World War II also focused on infectious disease control (Magnussen et al. 2004). Even at present, global health governance and international financial assistance for health continue to prioritize infectious disease over noncommunicable disease.

International financial assistance for infectious disease control contributes to an important part of the realization of the right to health, but the realization of the right to health entails more than infectious disease control. While ICESCR Article 12(1) provides the broad foundation of the right to health ("The States Parties to the present Covenant recognize the right of everyone to the enjoyment of the highest attainable standard of physical and mental health"), Article 12(2) provides examples of steps to be taken (UN General Assembly 1966). These steps include the "prevention, treatment and control of epidemic, endemic, occupational and other diseases" (Ibid., art. 12(2)(c)), but they also entail "[t]he provision for the reduction of the stillbirth-rate and of infant mortality and for the healthy development of the child" (Ibid., art. 12(2)(a)); "[t]he improvement of all aspects of environmental and industrial hygiene" (Ibid., art. 12(2)(b)); and "[t]he creation of conditions which would assure to all medical service and medical attention in the event of sickness" (Ibid., art. 12(2)(d)). Furthermore, General Comment 14 of the CESCR articulated an important additional element as one of the core obligations of the right to health: states should "adopt and implement a national public health strategy and plan of action, on the basis of epidemiological evidence, addressing the health concerns of the whole population; the strategy and plan of action shall be devised, and periodically reviewed, on the basis of a participatory and transparent process" (CESCR 2000, para. 43). This participatory and transparent process is essential to ensure that the realization of the right to health does not discriminate against or exclude vulnerable and marginalized groups.

International assistance for the realization of the right to health should therefore encompass all the necessary "steps" to be taken by states at the national level, in accordance with Article 12 of the ICESCR and its interpretation in General Comment 14, and this assistance should be aligned with a national strategy and plan of action, devised and reviewed through a participatory and transparent process.

Which mechanism of international assistance for health would be better equipped to achieve this alignment with a national plan, devised and reviewed through a participatory and transparent process: a Global Fund for Health or bilateral agreements? While the GFATM currently focuses on only three infectious diseases, it has introduced—perhaps even imposed—the principle of a participatory and transparent processes, by requiring the creation of CCMs to be involved in the elaboration of proposals. Similarly, a Global Fund for Health—with a mandate encompassing all elements of the right to health—would provide assistance that is aligned with a national strategy and plan of action, devised and reviewed through a participatory and transparent process.

Bilateral assistance for health too has undertaken attempts to become more aligned with national strategies. "Sector-wide approaches" (SWAps)—which emerged in the 1990s "in response to widespread dissatisfaction with fragmented donor-sponsored projects" (Peters et al. 2013, 884)—were intended to provide "increased control to recipient governments, allowing greater domestic influence over how health aid is allocated" (Sweeney and Mortimer 2016, 559). This essentially involved a group of states providing international assistance for health agreeing with the receiving country's ministry of health on a strategy and plan of action for the health sector, aligning assistance with national priorities. However, SWAps have typically *not* involved civil society organizations. Furthermore, as discussed in greater detail in Part III, there are political economy reasons why states providing assistance will always be inclined to prioritize infectious disease control over the (broader) realization of the right to health. Even if bilateral agreements would systematically employ the SWAp methodology, each of the forty-nine countries of Table 20.2 would be alone in its partnership with about ten states providing assistance. In a Global Fund for Health, these countries would have stronger negotiating power to ensure that international assistance covers all elements of the right to health.

B. Additional to "Maximum Available" Domestic Resources

There is consensus among scholars that any international obligation is a secondary or supplementary obligation, and therefore, international assistance should incentivize—or at least not discourage—the mobilization of domestic resources. While this seems self-evident—if only because international assistance does not serve its purpose if it replaces domestic resources—it is not easy to achieve. Several studies indicate that international assistance for health often displaces domestic resources (Farag et al. 2009).

International assistance should incentivize domestic resource mobilization rather than reward states for not mobilizing domestic resources—as the latter increases the perceived need for assistance. Reliability is an important factor of international assistance, as discussed further in the next subpart, as states are reluctant to increase their overall governmental recurrent health expenditure if part of that expenditure is funded by unreliable international assistance. Yet, reliability is a necessary but insufficient condition, as some states receiving (reliable) international assistance can and may nevertheless decrease domestic resources. Ultimately, the only way to make sure that international and domestic resources are additional is through a partnership approach: a commitment from both sides. This would imply a kind of mutual "conditionality": an agreed level of domestic resources is conditioned on an agreed level of international assistance (and vice versa). While "conditionality" is a particularly unpopular expression in the practice of international assistance—where conditions have often been abused to make recipients of aid buy goods or services from the country providing assistance or, worse, to make recipient governments reduce their domestic efforts and prioritize reimbursement of debts (also known as "structural adjustment")—every real partnership entails conditions.

The GFATM has from the beginning of its existence used "counterpart financing" or "co-financing" requirements. In the beginning, these co-financing requirements existed only for middle-income countries, but since 2016, the principle has been accepted for low-income countries too. Since the April 2016 meeting of the GFATM Board, the GFATM co-financing requirement for low-income countries "expects and encourages national governments to fulfill their financial commitments to the health sector in line with recognized international declarations and national strategies," with the Abuja Declaration mentioned as an example of such international declarations (GFATM 2016, 13). The GFATM provides additional financial incentives to countries that increase domestic resources for health.

It is too soon to evaluate the impact of this broadly defined GFATM co-financing requirement, but it allows one to imagine how a Global Fund for Health could address the problem of international assistance not always being additional to domestic resources. In principle, bilateral agreements could also include similar incentives; however, if it is assumed that each of the forty-nine countries included in Table 20.2 would receive assistance from, on average, ten of the countries included in Table 20.1, this would become extremely difficult: instead of a single partnership (between the Global Fund for Health and the country receiving the assistance), a partnership between the country receiving assistance and ten countries providing assistance would be needed. Therefore, it can be concluded that when it comes to additionality of international assistance for health, a Global Fund for Health would probably perform better than a multitude of bilateral agreements.

C. Reliable in the Long Run

Closely related to the requirement of additionality, reliability becomes relevant where "donor commitments to individual countries remain short-term and highly conditional and do not come close to reflecting these global promises of increased aid, while donor disbursement performance remains volatile and unreliable," and, as a result, "governments are therefore understandably reluctant to take the risk of relying on increased aid to finance the necessary scaling up of public expenditure" (Foster 2005, 73). To ensure that international assistance is additional, it must also be reliable, otherwise recipient countries will accept international assistance without increasing domestic governmental health expenditure, or may even reduce domestic expenditure, simply replacing domestic resources with international resources and using the domestic resources for other purposes.

But the requirement of reliability is also a requirement of the right to health in its own right, not just a condition to ensure additionality. The obligation to provide international assistance for the realization of the right to health is a legal obligation because "if there is no legal obligation underpinning the human rights responsibility of international assistance and cooperation, inescapably all international assistance and cooperation is based fundamentally upon charity" (Hunt 2007, para.113). As long as the conditions for being entitled to international assistance are fulfilled, international assistance should be reliable. That does not mean that some countries will be entitled to international assistance forever; if and when countries' economies grow, their ability to finance the realization of the right to health grows as well, and at a certain point, international assistance would no longer be required. Until they have reached that point, however, poorer countries should be able to rely upon international assistance where they have met their national obligations.

Scholars have explored different theoretical approaches to pooling international assistance flows in order to make them more reliable (Foster 2005). Where research has examined the reliability of existing flows of international assistance, scholars have observed that "aid flows to the health sector are volatile in terms of observed outcomes and uncertain in terms of making and delivering future commitments," making them "poorly suited to fund recurrent costs associated with ... Primary Health Care" (Lane and Glassman 2008, 1). These scholars have concluded that pooling international assistance makes it less volatile, recognizing that "parts of the new institutional architecture, such as the [GFATM], appear to deliver stable and predictable financing" (Ibid., 23).

Given the assumptions that have been used to assemble the Global Fund for Health and the alternative option of bilateral agreements, namely, that all high-income countries would contribute the equivalent of 0.1 percent of GDP to international assistance for health, both options would be equally capable of providing reliable funding. However, these are idealized assumptions. In practice, a multilateral channel like a Global Fund for Health would provide more reliable funding than bilateral agreements because pooling of funding allows for the replacement of temporary shortfalls in assistance from one country through extra efforts from other countries.

D. Coordinated between All Countries Contributing to and Receiving International Assistance

In July 2000, at the 13th International AIDS Conference in Durban, Kenneth Roth, the Executive Director of Human Rights Watch was questioned about using the right to health as a means to mobilize an appropriate response to the HIV/AIDS pandemic, yet he was skeptical because of the nature of international obligations: "the treaty assigns responsibility for compliance more broadly—not only to the immediate national government, but also to the international community as a whole, through the duty to provide *international assistance*," and thus "[g]overnments can deflect criticism by blaming others" (Roth 2000, 94). The problem Roth identified here—at a time when the obligation to provide international assistance was more controversial than it is today—is the problem of multiple duty-bearers and multiple rights-holders. For any given individual rights-holder who lives in a poorer country, the obligation to provide assistance creates multiple duty-bearers: the state where the individual rights-holder lives, and all other states in a position to assist. For each of these duty-bearers, there are multiple rights-holders: for the poorer state, all its inhabitants are rights-holders (which is always the case), and for the states in a position to assist, all the inhabitants of all states needing assistance are rights-holders. The governments of all these states can deflect criticism by blaming other duty-bearers. The government of the state where the individual rights-holder lives can blame the wealthier states not providing as much assistance as others. The governments of the wealthier states can blame each other and also the government of the poorer state that claims a need for assistance.

Rather than looking to individual rights, it is possible that collective rights and collective duties could help to overcome this problem: "While developing states would still bear a duty to realize individual health rights, they would also hold collective health rights—where they are unable to realize public health alone—to call on the international community for cooperation and assistance," and "the duty-bearer for such collective rights would be the international community—including individual states, international organizations, and public-private partnerships" (Meier and Fox 2008, 66). This would indeed reduce some of the complexity of international obligations, but the challenge would persist to make sure that all states in a position to assist would contribute their fair share and that all states needing assistance would receive their fair share.

Roth's solution to this coordination challenge was to propose "a series of World Conferences in which all industrialized governments convene to consider a country in need, the doors are locked, and no one leaves the room until the finger-pointing and evasions stop, no one goes home until the resources are finally committed that are adequate to the emergency at hand" (Roth 2000, 95). The GFATM can be seen as an institutionalized "series of World Conferences," where representatives of all countries meet and decide which countries should contribute how much, which countries should receive how much, and under which circumstances. At least to some extent, the problem of multiple rights-holders and multiple duty-bearers has been resolved for AIDS, tuberculosis, and malaria. However, the principles that apply to HIV/AIDS (and tuberculosis and malaria) also apply to other public health issues under the right to health. A Global Fund for Health could provide the same practical solution to other public health elements of the right to health.

Bilateral agreements could not achieve a similar solution. Under the assumptions used—that the same countries of Table 20.1 would provide the same amounts of assistance to the same countries of Table 20.2—there would be no difference. But it is difficult to imagine how all these countries would coordinate their efforts in practice. As mentioned under the previous point, SWAps also provide a platform for coordination, but they are developed country by country—resulting in "donor darlings" and "aid orphans," exacerbating global health inequality—and the reasons why some end up in one or the other category are often not obvious or transparent (Schieber et al. 2006). A global coordinating mechanism, like the GFATM, is obliged to make choices in a transparent manner, and while one may agree or disagree with some of the choices made in recent years, the fact that they are made in a transparent way, and thus open for debate, is more in line with the requirements of the right to health than the outcomes arising from an opaque web of bilateral assistance.

E. Sufficient to Assist Countries to Fulfill at Least the Core Obligations of the Right to Health

Finally, international assistance that is compliant with the right to health should be sufficient to enable countries to fulfill, at the very least, the so-called "core obligations" of the right to health. The idea that every human right included in the ICESCR has a minimum obligation was introduced in General Comment 3 of the CESCR (CESCR 1990). This was a necessary clarification because some states used the principle of "progressive realization"—enshrined in Article 2(1) of the ICESCR—as an excuse to make very little or no progress. As the CESCR clarified: "If the Covenant were to be read in such a way as not to establish such a minimum core obligation, it would be largely deprived of its *raison d'être*" (CESCR 1990, para. 10).

In General Comment 14 on the right to health, the CESCR elaborated the core (and similarly important) obligations for the realization of the right to health (CESCR 2000), including:

- to ensure the right of access to health facilities, goods and services on a non-discriminatory basis, especially for vulnerable or marginalized groups;
- to ensure access to the minimum essential food which is nutritionally adequate and safe;
- to ensure access to basic shelter, housing, and sanitation, and an adequate supply of safe and potable water;

- to provide essential drugs;
- to ensure equitable distribution of all health facilities, goods, and services;
- to adopt and implement a national public health strategy and plan of action, devised and periodically reviewed on the basis of a participatory and transparent process;
- to ensure reproductive, maternal, and child health care;
- to provide immunization against the major infectious diseases occurring in the community;
- to take measures to prevent, treat, and control epidemic and endemic diseases;
- to provide education and access to information concerning the main health problems in the community; and
- to provide appropriate training for health personnel, including education on health and human rights (CESCR 2000, paras. 43 and 44).

In the next paragraph, the CESCR emphasizes that "it is particularly incumbent on States parties and other actors in a position to assist, to provide 'international assistance and cooperation, especially economic and technical,' which enable developing countries to fulfill their core and other obligations indicated in paragraphs 43 and 44 above" (CESCR 2000, para. 45). Thus, a crucial function of the obligation to provide international assistance is to enable progress on the right to health in those countries that are, without assistance, unable to fulfill their core and similarly important obligations. This supposes that poorer countries first do what they can do, after which international assistance complements domestic efforts to meet core obligations.

In calculating the cost to fulfill the core obligations of the right to health, a recent analysis has found that "it would be appropriate to use $86 as the estimate of per capita resource requirements for providing core [primary health care] services in low-income countries" (McIntyre et al. 2017, 134). Within the parameters used in this chapter, allocating $57 per person per year, this expenditure would be insufficient to provide core primary health care services. Furthermore, the core obligations of the right to health extend beyond health care, and include underlying determinants of health—e.g., food, water, housing, sanitation, and education.

Which of the alternatives—a Global Fund for Health or bilateral agreements for health—is more likely to achieve and move beyond $57 per person per year? Even scholars who are quite critical of its overall impact admit that the GFATM "succeeded beyond anyone's expectations in raising monies" (Packard 2016, 296). There are several plausible explanations for this fundraising success: "greater efficiency" (Youde 2012); the fact that "[c]ivil society organizations are central to the operations of the Global Fund" (Harman 2012, 73), which encourages civil society to advocate for more funding for the GFATM (Busby 2010); or that the transparency of the GFATM about its replenishment process and the funding it receives allows civil society organizations to find out in real time whether their governments are lagging in contributing to the GFATM, allowing targeted campaigns. While a Global Fund for Health would preserve these assets, it is hard to imagine how a patchwork of bilateral agreements could acquire them. Therefore, a Global Fund for Health is far more likely to achieve health expenditure and move beyond $57 per person per year in low-income countries than bilateral agreements for health alone.

III. EXPLORING POLITICAL FEASIBILITY

The arguments about a Global Fund for Health being far more effective in ensuring that international financial assistance for health complies with the requirements of the right to health will not suffice to convince all states whose cooperation is required to move in that direction. The main contributor of international assistance for health—the United States—has not ratified the ICESCR, and several of the other important contributors are among the states who "resisted in equal measure" attempts to transform the moral case for international assistance "into a binding and specific legal obligation" (Tobin 2012, 328).

At the same time, however, "the narrative of globalization, beginning in the 1990s, challenged perceptions of global health, leading to an increased collaboration among political, security and medical/scientific actors as infectious diseases increasingly came to be viewed as national and international security threats" (Davies et al. 2015, 138). The transformative revision of the International Health Regulations (IHR) in 2005 illustrates a "growing consensus on the importance of public health to global governance in the 21st century" (Fidler and Gostin 2006, 86).

The revised IHR, however, sparked controversy for focusing on "health risks which are primarily seen as major threats by Western developed nations," and on global responses that aim for "containment rather than prevention" (Rushton 2011, 779). Wealthier and poorer countries seem to have very different understandings of the meaning of "health security": "Policymakers in industrialized countries emphasize protection of their populations especially against external threats, for example terrorism and pandemics; while health workers and policymakers in developing countries and within the United Nations system understand the term in a broader public health context" (Aldis 2008, 369). Poorer countries expect international assistance to strengthen their health systems, not only because that makes sense as an effective strategy to control infectious diseases but also as part of a "fair deal": if they are expected to allocate scarce resources toward efforts that respond to the concerns of wealthier countries, they expect wealthier countries to provide financial support for stronger health systems.

While some scholars emphasize the risk that global responses driven by real or perceived security threats may undermine the health systems of poorer countries, others emphasize the opportunities of framing global health as a security issue: "it conceivably could still prove to be a very valuable political tool for improving the health outcomes of people all over the world due to the simple fact that security, like sex, sells" (Kamradt-Scott 2015, 187). However, as Figure 20.1 illustrates, the "prevention, treatment and control of epidemic, endemic, occupational and other diseases" (UN General Assembly 1966, art. 12(2)(c)) is only one of the elements of the right

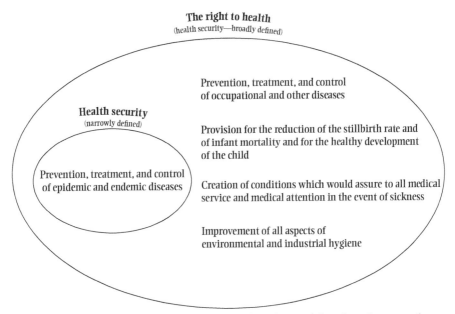

The right to health
(health security—broadly defined)

Prevention, treatment, and control
of occupational and other diseases

Health security
(narrowly defined)

Provision for the reduction of the stillbirth rate and
of infant mortality and for the healthy development
of the child

Prevention, treatment, and control
of epidemic and endemic diseases

Creation of conditions which would assure to all medical
service and medical attention in the event of sickness

Improvement of all aspects of
environmental and industrial hygiene

Figure 20.1 Health security, narrowly and broadly understood, based on elements of
Article 12(2) of the ICESCR.

to health, as defined in the ICESCR. Furthermore, international assistance driven
by health security concerns may not address "occupational and other diseases"—
perhaps not even all epidemic and endemic diseases but only those that may spread
across borders. At the same time, all elements of the right to health—including the
ones that are important for global health security—rely on efficient and effective
health systems, disease surveillance, and early intervention. If too many people
are reluctant to seek health care at the facilities where the wealthier countries have
invested in disease surveillance capacity—because they know they will have to pay
user fees they cannot afford or because they doubt that the health facility can provide
the appropriate diagnosis or treatment—the impact of the investment in disease surveillance capacity will be limited. Therefore, all elements of the right to health should
be seen as contributing to health security, if health security were broadly defined.

In order to resolve this critique of global health security, "there is the need for a
more explicit recognition of the primary beneficiaries of the current system, and of
who is bearing the costs," and that "[o]nly following such a recognition can meaningful debates be carried out about the appropriate prioritisation of global health
security in relation to other global health governance priorities" (Rushton 2011,
779). A negotiated—and repeatedly renegotiated—balance will have to be found,
between the efforts required from poorer countries to develop disease surveillance,
early warning, and rapid response capacity (to protect their own people *and* the
people of wealthier countries) and the compensation from wealthier countries for
the prioritization of health security. A Global Fund for Health would provide a platform for such negotiations.

CONCLUSION

A Global Fund for Health would be far more effective in ensuring that international financial assistance for health lives up to human rights requirements than the alternative of only bilateral agreements for health. The right to health alone would probably not suffice to convince all states whose cooperation would be required to move toward a Global Fund for Health. However, the imperatives of health security have obliged, and will continue to oblige, states to cooperate multilaterally, including through international health financing. This creates an opportunity for states needing assistance to demand from states in a position to assist that all elements of the right to health be included in multilateral financial assistance for health.

REFERENCES

Aldis, William. 2008. "Health Security as a Public Health Concept: A Critical Analysis." *Health Policy and Planning* 23(6): 369–375.

Besley, Timothy and Torsten Persson. 2014. "Why Do Developing Countries Tax so Little?" *The Journal of Economic Perspectives* 28(4): 99–120.

Busby, Joshua. 2010. *Moral Movements and Foreign Policy*. Cambridge: Cambridge University Press.

CESCR (Committee on Economic, Social, and Cultural Rights). 1990. "General Comment No. 3: The Nature of States Parties' Obligations." 14 December. E/1991/23.

CESCR. (2000). General Comment No. 14: The Right to the Highest Attainable Standard of Health. http://www.refworld.org/docid/4538838d0.html.

Davies, Sara, Adam Kamradt-Scott, and Simon Rushton. 2015. *Disease Diplomacy: International Norms and Global Health Security*. Baltimore: Johns Hopkins University Press.

Davis, Sara. 2014. "Human Rights and the Global Fund to Fight AIDS, Tuberculosis, and Malaria." *Health and Human Rights Journal* 16(1): 134–148.

Dybul, Mark. 2017. "Health Financing Seen from the Global Level: Beyond the Use of Gross National Income." *Health Economics, Policy and Law* 12(2): 117–120.

Experts in international law and human rights. 2011. *Maastricht Principles on Extraterritorial Obligations of States in the Area of Economic, Social and Cultural Rights*. http://www.etoconsortium.org/nc/en/main-navigation/library/maastricht-principles/.

Fan, Victoria, Amanda Glassman, and Rachel Silverman. 2014. "How a New Funding Model Will Shift Allocations from the Global Fund to Fight AIDS, Tuberculosis, and Malaria." *Health Affairs* 33(12): 2238–2246.

Farag, Marwa, A. K. Nandakumar, Stanley Wallack, Gary Gaumer, and Dominic Hodgkin. 2009. "Does Funding from Donors Displace Government Spending for Health in Developing Countries?" *Health Affairs* 28(4): 1045–1055.

Fidler, David and Lawrence O. Gostin. 2006. "The New International Health Regulations: An Historic Development for International Law and Public Health." *The Journal of Law, Medicine and Ethics* 34(1): 85–94.

Foster, Mick. 2005. "Fiscal Space and Sustainability: Towards a Solution for the Health Sector." In *High-Level Forum for the Health MDGs, Selected Papers 2003–2005*. Geneva: World Health Organization.

Führer, Helmut. 1996. *The Story of Official Development Assistance*. Paris: OECD. Available at: http://www.oecd.org/dac/1896816.pdf.

GFATM (Global Fund to Fight AIDS, Tuberculosis and Malaria). 2016. *The Global Fund Sustainability, Transition and Co-financing Policy.* Geneva: GFATM. GF/B35/04 Revision 1.

Hanefeld, Johanna. 2014. "The Global Fund to Fight AIDS, Tuberculosis and Malaria: 10 Years On." *Clinical Medicine* 14(1): 54–57.

Harman, Sophie. 2012. *Global Health Governance.* Abingdon: Routledge.

Hunt, Paul. 2007. "Report of the Special Rapporteur on the right of everyone to the enjoyment of the highest attainable standard of physical and mental health. Addendum: Mission to Sweden." 28 February. A/HRC/4/28/Add.2.

IHME (Institute for Health Metrics and Evaluation). 2017. Financing Global Health 2016: Development Assistance, Public and Private Health Spending for the Pursuit of Universal Health Coverage. Seattle, WA: IHME.

Kamradt-Scott, Adam. 2015. *Managing Global Health Security: The World Health Organization and Disease Outbreak Control.* Basingstoke: Palgrave MacMillan.

Khalfan, Ashfaq. 2013. "Division of Responsibility amongst States." In *Global Justice, State Duties. The Extraterritorial Scope of Economic, Social and Cultural Rights in International Law,* edited by Malcolm Langford, Wouter Vandenhole, Martin Scheinin, and William van Genugten. Cambridge: Cambridge University Press.

Lane, Chris and Amanda Glassman. 2008. *Smooth and Predictable Aid for Health: A Role for Innovative Financing?* Washington: Brookings.

Magnussen, Lesley, John Ehiri, and Pauline Jolly. 2004. "Comprehensive versus Selective Primary Health Care: Lessons for Global Health Policy." *Health Affairs* 23(3): 167–176.

McIntyre, Di, Filip Meheus, and John-Arne Røttingen. 2017. "What Level of Domestic Government Health Expenditure Should We Aspire to for Universal Health Coverage?" *Health Economics, Policy and Law* 12(2): 125–137.

Meier, Benjamin Mason and Ashley Fox. 2008. "International Obligations through Collective Rights: Moving from Foreign Health Assistance to Global Health Governance." *Health and Human Rights Journal* 12(1): 61–72.

OECD. 2011. *Aid to health.* OECD-DAC. Available at: http://www.oecd.org/dac/stats/49907438.pdf.

OHCHR (Office of the High Commissioner for Human Rights). 2012. "Technical guidance on the application of a human rights based approach to the implementation of policies and programmes to reduce preventable maternal morbidity and mortality." 2 July. A/HRC/21/22.

Ooms, Gorik, Katharine Derderian, and David Melody. 2006. "Do We Need a World Health Insurance to Realise the Right to Health?" *PLoS Medicine* 3(12): e530.

Ooms, Gorik and Rachel Hammonds. 2010. "Taking Up Daniels' Challenge: The Case for Global Health Justice." *Health and Human Rights Journal* 12(1): 29–46.

Ooms, Gorik and Rachel Hammonds. 2016. "Global Constitutionalism, Applied to Global Health Governance: Uncovering Legitimacy Deficits and Suggesting Remedies." *Globalization and Health* 12(1): 84.

Packard Randall. 2016. *A History of Global Health. Interventions into the Lives of Other Peoples.* Baltimore: Johns Hopkins Press.

Peters, David, Ligia Paina, and Finn Schleimann. 2013. "Sector-wide Approaches (SWAps) in Health: What Have We Learned?" *Health Policy and Planning* 28(8): 884–890.

Roth, Kenneth. 2000. "Human Rights and the AIDS Crisis: The Debate over Resources." *Canadian HIV/AIDS Policy and Law Review* 5(4): 93–97.

Rushton, Simon. 2011. "Global Health Security: Security for Whom? Security from What?" *Political Studies* 59(4): 779–796.

Schieber, George, Lisa Fleisher, and Paul Gottret. 2006. "Getting Real on Health Financing." *Finance and Development* 43(4).

Shue, Henry. 1996. *Basic Rights: Subsistence, Affluence, and U.S. Foreign Policy. Second Edition*. Princeton: Princeton University Press.

Sweeney, Rohan and Duncan Mortimer. 2016. "Has the Swap Influenced Aid Flows in the Health Sector?" *Health Economics* 25(5): 559–577.

Tobin, John. 2012. *The Right to Health in International Law*. Oxford: Oxford University Press.

UN General Assembly. 1966. "International Covenant on Economic, Social and Cultural Rights." 16 December. Resolution 2200A (XXI).

Witter, Sophie, Alex Jones, and Tim Ensor. 2013. "How to (or not to)...Measure Performance against the Abuja Target for Public Health Expenditure." *Health Policy and Planning* 29(4): 450–455.

Youde, Jeremy. 2012. *Global Health Governance*. Cambridge: Polity Press.

Global Health in Human Rights Governance

21

The Office of the United Nations High Commissioner for Human Rights

Mapping the Evolution of the Right to Health

GILLIAN MACNAUGHTON AND MARIAH MCGILL*

For over two decades, the Office of the UN High Commissioner for Human Rights (OHCHR) has taken a leading role in promoting human rights around the world by supporting individuals in claiming their rights, assisting governments in fulfilling their obligations, and building capacity to mainstream human rights throughout the United Nations (UN). While the OHCHR plays a vital role in supporting the UN human rights mechanisms—including the Human Rights Council (HRC), the Special Procedures, and the treaty bodies—this chapter focuses on the independent work of the OHCHR to implement the right to health. It examines the initiatives of the High Commissioner for Human Rights, who has a voice independent of the UN human rights mechanisms. It also looks at OHCHR participation in inter-agency processes—advocating for a human rights-based approach in all UN work and role as advisor to the field presences. Finally, it considers OHCHR work to convene expert meetings and carry out studies on specific health topics—often at the request of the HRC or other UN entities. In all these areas, the OHCHR has advanced the right to health and has contributed, although often on an ad hoc basis, to global health governance.

To describe and analyze the evolution of the right to health at the OHCHR, this chapter draws on (1) archival records of OHCHR publications and initiatives

* The authors would like to express their gratitude to the twenty key informants interviewed for this study during March–June 2017. As the authors assured the participants anonymity, we have not cited to these interviews despite their crucial contributions to the study. The authors would also like to thank Benjamin Mason Meier and three reviewers for their very helpful comments on an early draft. The Institutional Review Board of the University of Massachusetts Boston approved this study proposal on March 14, 2017 (#2017062).

Human Rights in Global Health. Benjamin Mason Meier and Lawrence O. Gostin.
© Oxford University Press 2018. Published 2018 by Oxford University Press.

related to health, (2) annual reports of the High Commissioners on the activities of the OHCHR, and (3) semistructured interviews with ten current and former OHCHR staff and ten external experts on the right to health (including three current and former UN Special Rapporteurs). Part I provides a brief history of the OHCHR and an overview of its current structure and capacity. Against this background, Part II traces the influence of the six High Commissioners (and one Acting High Commissioner) on the health-related rights agenda of the OHCHR, evidencing a clear trend toward greater engagement with the right to health since 1994, consistent with the growth of the OHCHR budget and staff. Following this historical account, Part III outlines recent health-related initiatives at the OHCHR. Part IV then discusses the factors that have facilitated or inhibited the mainstreaming of the right to health at the OHCHR over the past two-plus decades, focusing on the increasing acceptance of economic and social rights as "real" human rights, the importance of right-to-health champions among the OHCHR leadership, the limited capacity and resources of the OHCHR, and the challenges of moving beyond conceptualization to implementation of the right to health. The chapter concludes with reflections on the future role of the OHCHR in advancing the right to health and global health governance.

I. THE HISTORY, STRUCTURE, AND FUNCTIONS OF THE OHCHR

The UN Division of Human Rights program began in 1946 as part of the UN Secretariat in New York City. At that time, it had just a few staff with offices at Hunter College (Humphrey 1984). The Division, and its Director, John Humphrey, as shown in Figure 21.1, made a major contribution to the development of economic and social rights—including the right to health—by including these rights in the first draft of the Universal Declaration of Human Rights (UDHR) (Morsink 1999; Commission on Human Rights 1947).

The idea of a high-ranking post on human rights emerged in early discussions of the UDHR when René Cassin, a member of the Commission on Human Rights, which was responsible for drafting the document, proposed a "UN Attorney-General for Human Rights" (Mertus 2009). Uruguay raised the idea of a human rights attorney general again in the early 1950s when the International Covenant on Civil and Political Rights (ICCPR) was being drafted (Ibid.). It was not until 1965, however, that Costa Rica, with strong support from non-governmental organizations (NGOs), introduced before the Commission on Human Rights a draft proposal to establish a "High Commissioner for Human Rights" (Carey 1966). This proposal was soon approved by the Commission and subsequently by the UN Economic and Social Council (ECOSOC). However, the proposal remained stalled in the UN General Assembly throughout the Cold War (Mertus 2009).

On June 25, 1993, at the World Conference on Human Rights, 171 states adopted the Vienna Declaration and Programme of Action, which recommended to the UN General Assembly that "it begin, as a matter of priority, consideration of the question of the establishment of a High Commissioner for Human Rights for the promotion and protection of all human rights" (World Conference on Human Rights 1993, para. 18). In December 1993, the UN General Assembly followed

Figure 21.1 Mrs. Eleanor Roosevelt and Professor John P. Humphrey at the second session of the Commission on Human Rights.

up on the Vienna Declaration and Programme of Action by adopting a resolution creating the post of High Commissioner for Human Rights. This resolution established that the High Commissioner "shall be the United Nations official with principal responsibility for United Nations human rights activities under the direction and authority of the Secretary-General" (UN General Assembly 1993, para. 4). The High Commissioner is appointed by the Secretary-General and holds the rank of Under-Secretary-General, but unlike other under-secretaries, the High Commissioner appointment must be approved by the UN General Assembly (Ibid.). This requirement, as well as the mandate of the High Commissioner to engage in a wide range of activities beyond support of the UN human rights bodies, suggests that the High Commissioner, although reporting to the Secretary-General, enjoys a degree of independence (Gaer and Broecker 2013).

In 1997, UN Secretary-General Kofi Annan merged the OHCHR and the Center for Human Rights (the successor of the UN Division of Human Rights) and put them both under the direction of the High Commissioner (UN Department of Public Information 1997). Currently, the OHCHR is led by the High Commissioner for Human Rights as well as a Deputy High Commissioner in Geneva and an Assistant Secretary-General in New York. While headquartered in Geneva, the OHCHR also has an office at UN headquarters in New York, twelve regional offices and centers, and fourteen country and stand-alone offices (OHCHR 2017b). The

OHCHR also supports human rights in UN peacekeeping operations and deploys human rights advisers to work with UN Country Teams (Ibid.).

The mission of the OHCHR "is to work for the protection of all human rights for all people; to help empower people to realize their rights; and to assist those responsible for upholding such rights in ensuring that they are implemented" (OHCHR n.d.-g). The OHCHR works in four broad areas, which each support global health:

1. Providing support for the UN human rights mechanisms. The OHCHR provides both substantive and technical support to the HRC (including the Universal Periodic Review), supports the fifty-seven Special Procedures mandate holders (in legal, policy, logistical, and administrative matters), and serves as the secretariat for the ten core human rights treaty bodies (in monitoring treaty implementation and receiving individual complaints) (OHCHR 2017b).

2. Producing policies, guidelines, and tools. The OHCHR translates international human rights law into practice by providing training, advice, and support to UN member states, civil society, and national human rights institutions. Examples include the 2005 *Principles and Guidelines for a Human Rights Approach to Poverty Reduction Strategies* (OHCHR 2005), the 2008 *Human Rights, Health and Poverty Reduction Strategies* (OHCHR and WHO 2008), and the 2008 *Claiming the Millennium Development Goals: A Human Rights-Based Approach* (OHCHR 2008).

3. Ensuring that human rights are mainstreamed into all UN programs. The OHCHR participates in inter-agency initiatives to ensure that the human rights-based approach is integrated into all UN activities. For example, the OHCHR participated in the UN Task Team on the Post-2015 UN Development Agenda (OHCHR 2012) and worked to integrate accountability mechanisms for human rights into the Sustainable Development Goals (SDGs) (OHCHR and CESR 2013).

4. Collaborating with governments and other UN entities to respond to human rights challenges in context. The OHCHR operates twelve regional centers, supports sixty field presences (with permission from host governments), and also has Rapid Response Units. Through this field presence, the OHCHR carries out trainings for police and judges, helps draft legislation to implement international human rights law, provides advice to UN country teams, responds in humanitarian crises, and aids states in implementing the recommendations of treaty bodies and other human rights mechanisms (OHCHR 2017b).

From its modest beginnings in 1994, with a High Commissioner and six staff, the OHCHR had grown by December 2016 to employ 1,179 staff (UN Secretary-General 1994; OHCHR 2017b). Simultaneously, the OHCHR budget has grown from US$25 million in 1993 (to support the Center for Human Rights), which was 0.7 percent of the UN Secretariat regular budget, to US$190.5 million in 2016, 3.5 percent of the UN Secretariat regular budget (OHCHR 2017b; Gaer and Broecker 2013; OHCHR n.d.-f). On top of this budget allocation from the UN Secretariat, the High Commissioners have sought additional voluntary contributions—largely from UN member states—which in 2016 reached US$129.6 million (OHCHR 2017b).

II. THE HIGH COMMISSIONERS FOR HUMAN RIGHTS

The 1993 UN General Assembly resolution that established the position of the High Commissioner for Human Rights also set out the responsibilities of the postholder, which are to:

- Promote and protect civil, cultural, economic, political, and social rights for all;
- Carry out tasks assigned by UN bodies and make recommendations to them to improve the promotion and protection of human rights;
- Promote and protect the right to development;
- Provide technical and financial assistance to states to support action on human rights;
- Coordinate UN education and public information programs on human rights;
- Play an active role in removing obstacles to the full realization of all human rights;
- Engage in dialogue with all governments to secure respect for all human rights;
- Enhance international cooperation for the promotion and protection of all human rights;
- Coordinate human rights activities throughout the UN system;
- Strengthen the UN machinery in human rights to improve efficiency and effectiveness; and
- Supervise the Center for Human Rights (later merged with the OHCHR) (UN General Assembly 1993).

The High Commissioner for Human Rights is, therefore, the head of the OHCHR and has advocacy, diplomacy, administrative, and managerial responsibilities, which may at times be inconsistent with one another. The central function of the High Commissioner is to call attention to human rights violations around the world (Ramcharan 2009). The High Commissioner stands on the side of victims of human rights abuses in a "public role as spokesperson for universal standards" (Gaer and Broecker 2013, 2), and as such, is viewed as a moral leader for global human rights—often considered "the conscience of the world" (Koh 2004, 495). Simultaneously, the High Commissioner has a vital diplomatic role, working directly with UN member states, coordinating with governments to establish and maintain field offices, as well as providing legal, policy, and technical assistance. This dual role, condemning governments while also seeking to work with them, has made it difficult to fulfill the High Commissioner's mandate (Gaer and Broecker 2013). Although the UN General Assembly has established that the appointment of the High Commissioner is for a term of four years with a possibility for renewal for another four years, none of the six High Commissioners to date, pictured in Figures 21.2 to 21.7, has completed a full eight years in the position.

Figure 21.2 UN High Commissioner José Ayala-Lasso.

A. José Ayala-Lasso (1994–1997)

José Ayala-Lasso became the first High Commissioner for Human Rights in April 1994 and served until March 1997, when he resigned to serve as Minister of Foreign Affairs for his native country of Ecuador (OHCHR n.d.-b). While human rights advocacy organizations in the North were disappointed by Ayala-Lasso's performance because he failed to publicly criticize governments on their human rights records (Gaer and Broecker 2013), governments and activists in the South praised him for offering them technical support on human rights, building capacity in the Center for Human Rights, integrating human rights into the work of other UN entities, and establishing field presences (Mertus 2009). During his tenure as High Commissioner, Ayala-Lasso frequently expressed support for implementing the right to development and economic, social, and cultural rights that underlie public health. For example, Ayala-Lasso noted in his 1994 report that these rights "have not always received adequate attention," and that during his official country visits, he "stressed the need to promote economic, social and cultural rights" to national governments (Ayala-Lasso 1994, 7, 23). In 1995, he argued that "too often basic rights such as those to health, food, shelter and education receive insufficient protection" in the context of structural adjustment programs, and that governments should consider the impacts of their policies on the economic, social, and cultural rights of vulnerable groups (Ayala-Lasso 1995, 21). Although Ayala-Lasso's reports on the activities of the OHCHR do not evidence efforts by the OHCHR to promote the right to health specifically, he repeatedly asserted the importance of economic and social rights, which support underlying determinants of health.

B. Mary Robinson (1997–2002)

Mary Robinson, the former President of Ireland, became the second High Commissioner and served from September 1997 to September 2002 (OHCHR

Figure 21.3 UN High Commissioner Mary Robinson.

n.d.-d). In contrast to her predecessor, Robinson was known for speaking out strongly on behalf of victims of human rights abuses. She was also known to insist on the indivisibility of all civil, cultural, economic, social, and political human rights (Mertus 2009; Pillay 2013b), and during her term, the work of the OHCHR on economic and social rights expanded significantly. For example, the OHCHR engaged in consultations with both the Commission on the Status of Women and the Commission on Human Rights regarding obstacles to women's full enjoyment of economic and social rights (Robinson 1998); with UN-Habitat on the right to adequate housing (Robinson 1999); and with the Food and Agriculture Organization (FAO) on the content of the right to food (Robinson 2000). Robinson also issued a groundbreaking 1999 report documenting developments to implement economic, social, and cultural rights at the international level (Ibid.), and in 2001, the OHCHR held a workshop on the justiciability of these rights (Robinson 2001b).

Robinson also greatly expanded the OHCHR's health-related work, specifically focusing on the HIV/AIDS pandemic. For example, the OHCHR and the Joint UN Programme on HIV/AIDS (UNAIDS) jointly published the 1998 *International Guidelines on HIV/AIDS and Human Rights* (Robinson 2001a; OHCHR and UNAIDS 1998) and developed, as discussed in chapter 13, a new 2001 strategy to encourage governments, civil society, and national and international organizations to address the human rights dimensions of HIV/AIDS in their policies and activities (Robinson 2002). Supporting these efforts, Robinson created in 2001 the first OHCHR post specifically focused on health, the "Advisor on HIV/AIDS and Human Rights." During Robinson's term, the OHCHR also collaborated with other institutions on the development of the conceptual framework for the World AIDS Campaign and co-hosted with the World Health Organization (WHO) and UNAIDS a meeting with governments, NGOs, and UN agencies to discuss access to medicines for people living with HIV/AIDS under the right to health (Robinson 2002).

Figure 21.4 UN High Commissioner Sergio Vieira de Mello.

C. Sergio Vieira de Mello (2002–2003)

Sergio Vieira de Mello had worked for the UN for over thirty years, including in several high-ranking posts, when he was appointed in September 2002 to become the third High Commissioner for Human Rights. In contrast to the outspoken Robinson, human rights activists viewed the appointment of Vieira de Mello as "a more cautious approach to human rights" (Gaer and Broecker 2013, 12). Initially, Vieira de Mello indicated that the focus of his term of office would be strengthening the rule of law (Mertus 2009). In the field of health, his only report to the Commission on Human Rights declared his intention to build on the strong leadership of the OHCHR in crafting a human rights-based response to HIV/AIDS (Vieira de Mello 2003). After only eight months in the position of High Commissioner, however, Vieira de Mello took a temporary leave to serve as UN Special Representative in Iraq, where he was killed on August 19, 2003 in a suicide bombing of the UN Headquarters in Baghdad (OHCHR n.d.-h).

D. Bertrand Ramcharan (2003–2004)

Deputy High Commissioner Bertrand Ramcharan served as Acting High Commissioner when High Commissioner Vieira de Mello took the position in Iraq in May 2003, and after Vieira de Mello was killed, Ramcharan continued to serve as Acting High Commissioner until July 2004 (OHCHR n.d.-a). During Ramcharan's short term, the OHCHR continued to collaborate with FAO on the development of voluntary guidelines to support member states in progressively realizing the right to food, with UN-Habitat on indicators for the right to housing, and with WHO to identify indicators to monitor the right to health (Ramcharan 2004). Additionally, the OHCHR worked with UNAIDS on a revision of the *International Guidelines on HIV/AIDS and Human Rights* and developed user-friendly information about HIV/AIDS and human rights, including publishing, with UNAIDS and WHO,

Figure 21.5 UN High Commissioner Bertrand Ramcharan.

the cartoon booklet *HIV/AIDS: Stand Up for Human Rights* (Ibid.; OHCHR, UNAIDS, and WHO 2003).

Figure 21.6 UN High Commissioner Louise Arbour.

E. Louise Arbour (2004–2008)

Louise Arbour began her term as High Commissioner in June 2004 and served until July 2008. Previously, she had served as a Justice on the Supreme Court of Canada and as a prosecutor before the international criminal tribunals (OHCHR n.d.-c), and human rights advocates generally praised her performance as High Commissioner (Gaer and Broecker 2013). At the beginning of her term, Arbour emphasized that extreme poverty was the most widespread denial of human rights and also the cause of many conflicts and human rights abuses (Mertus 2009), and following this direction, the OHCHR embarked on a strategy to strengthen its capacity in the area of economic, social, and cultural rights, with a particular focus on providing assistance to states, UN agencies, and the treaty bodies on legal protection and advocacy for these rights (Arbour 2006). Bridging this national and international work, Arbour advocated for the UN General Assembly to adopt an Optional Protocol to the International Covenant on Economic, Social and Cultural Rights (ICESCR), establishing an individual complaints mechanism, and encouraged states to "consider how international and national jurisprudence had demonstrated that social, economic and cultural rights were not ideals, but legally enforceable entitlements" (Arbour 2005a, 10). Arbour also created "a small dedicated team of professionals" to focus on economic and social rights within the Research and Right to Development Branch, which supports the independent work of the High Commissioner (Arbour 2007, 15).

During Arbour's term, the OHCHR also continued its work to advance the right to health. For example, the OHCHR collaborated with WHO, as discussed in chapter 5, to develop indicators on the right to health (Arbour 2005b); co-authored *Health, Human Rights and Poverty Reduction Strategies* (OHCHR and WHO 2008); published *Claiming the Millennium Development Goals: A Human Rights Approach*; and developed a fact sheet on the right to health (Arbour 2008). The OHCHR also worked closely with UNAIDS, and in 2007, co-authored a *Handbook on HIV/AIDS and Human Rights for National Human Rights Institutions* (OHCHR and UNAIDS 2007). Within the OHCHR, Arbour created a new focus in the Research and Right to Development Branch on women's rights and gender (Arbour 2006), which has since played a strong role in developing the health-related work at the OHCHR, focusing first on maternal mortality and then more broadly on sexual and reproductive health.

F. Navanethem Pillay (2008–2014)

Navanethem Pillay, the longest serving High Commissioner, held the position from September 2008 to August 2014 (OHCHR n.d.-e). Pillay is a South African human rights lawyer who had served as a judge in South Africa and on international criminal tribunals, and due to her background, she was welcomed by human rights activists (Gaer and Broecker 2013). When first appointed, Pillay indicated that her focus would be on those held illegally in detention, including children, political prisoners, and those in Guantanamo Bay (Mertus 2009). During Pillay's tenure, the OHCHR continued to engage substantially on economic and social rights, including of those held in detention. Under OHCHR's thematic priority on "pursuing economic, social and cultural rights and combating inequalities and poverty," activities of the OHCHR included developing tools and training materials, as well as assisting governments, parliaments, field presences, and civil society on implementing economic, social, and cultural rights (Pillay 2010a). In her 2013 report to the HRC, Pillay noted that economic and social rights were still often neglected but remained essential, particularly as many states imposed austerity measures in response to financial and economic crises (Pillay 2013a).

Figure 21.7 UN High Commissioner Navanethem Pillay.

Under Pillay, the OHCHR furthered its engagement with health-related human rights. For example, working with the Swedish Development Agency (SIDA) and WHO, the OHCHR published a 2011 health policy assessment tool, *Human Rights and Gender Equality in Health Sector Strategies: How to Assess Policy Coherence* (Pillay 2010a; SIDA, WHO, and OHCHR 2011). Further, the OHCHR continued to advocate for a human rights-based approach to HIV/ AIDS, holding regional workshops to operationalize the joint OHCHR/UNAIDS *Handbook on HIV/AIDS and Human Rights for National Human Rights Institutions* (OHCHR and UNAIDS 2007) and organizing a side event at the Durban Review Conference on discrimination related to entry, stay, and residence of people living with HIV (Pillay 2010b). At the request of the HRC, Pillay authored a 2010 report on *Preventable Maternal Mortality and Morbidity and Human Rights* (Pillay 2010a), and subsequently issued technical guidance in 2012 on a human rights-based approach to reduce preventable maternal mortality and morbidity (Pillay 2012). Toward the end of Pillay's tenure, the OHCHR partnered with the Global Fund to Fight AIDS, Tuberculosis and Malaria (Global Fund), as reviewed in chapter 19, to integrate human rights into its operations and fund management (Pillay 2013a).

III. CURRENT OHCHR EFFORTS TO ADVANCE THE RIGHT TO HEALTH

The OHCHR is currently led by Zeid Ra'ad Al Hussein, pictured in figure 21.8, who became High Commissioner for Human Rights in September 2014 and will step down in September 2018 at the end of his first term. Zeid previously served as Jordan's Permanent Representative to the UN in New York and Jordan's Ambassador to the United States of America and has many years of experience working in international criminal law, UN peacekeeping, and international development (OHCHR n.d.-j).

Figure 21.8 UN High Commissioner Zeid Ra'ad Al Hussein.

During Zeid's term, OHCHR activities on economic, social, and cultural rights have included: (1) developing an online platform on social protection floors and human rights to assist states in implementing the right to social security; (2) publishing with UN-Habitat a factsheet on forced evictions to help stakeholders prevent and remedy human rights violations; (3) addressing the human rights implications of austerity measures; and (4) supporting ratification of the Optional Protocol to the ICESCR (Al Hussein 2014; 2015). Additionally, the OHCHR has held expert consultations on the links between armed conflict and violations of economic, social, and cultural rights and developed an analytical framework for early warnings to facilitate a rapid response to rights infringements (Al Hussein 2015; 2017a).

Much of OHCHR's recent work on the right to health has focused specifically on sexual and reproductive health and rights (SRHR). In 2015, the OHCHR launched *The Information Series on Sexual and Reproductive Health and Rights* to provide detailed guidance to policymakers, judiciaries, health service providers, and civil society "to support the adoption and effective implementation of laws, policies and programmes to respect, protect and fulfil women's sexual and reproductive health and rights" (OHCHR 2015, 1). To date, *The Information Series* has published policy briefings on HIV/AIDS, abortion, harmful practices, contraception and family planning, adolescents, women human rights defenders, violence against women, maternal mortality and morbidity, and lesbian, gay, transgender, and intersex people (OHCHR n.d.-i). Over 2015 and 2016, the OHCHR held regional and national-level workshops, meetings, and webinars on SRHR (Al Hussein 2015; 2016). Additionally, the OHCHR supported the development of training materials on SRHR for the Council of Europe (Al Hussein 2017a). At the end of 2016, the OHCHR launched a new publication, *Living Free & Equal*, a study of more than 200 initiatives in sixty-five countries aimed at protecting lesbian, gay, bisexual, transgender, and intersex (LGBTI) people from discrimination and violence (Al Hussein 2017a; UN 2016).

In a related area of work, the OHCHR led the human rights work stream in preparation for the Secretary-General's *Global Strategy for Women's, Children's and Adolescents' Health 2016–2030* (Al Hussein 2015). In collaboration with WHO, the OHCHR then established *The High-Level Working Group on the Health and Human Rights of Women, Children and Adolescents* to secure political support for implementing the *Global Strategy for Women's, Children's and Adolescents' Health 2016–2030* and the human rights-related measures in the SDGs (WHO 2017b). In May 2017, the *High-Level Working Group* presented its final report to WHO's Director-General Margaret Chan and High Commissioner Zeid (WHO 2017a). This report, also discussed in chapter 7, recognizes health care professionals as human rights defenders and stresses that achieving the right to health is a necessary prerequisite for fulfilling other human rights (WHO 2017b). It calls for sustained, focused political leadership at the national and local level to address gender-based and other forms of inequality within health care systems. Specific recommendations to states include: strengthening the legal recognition of the right to health in national constitutions and other laws, establishing a human rights-based approach to financing universal health care, empowering and protecting human rights advocates, and collecting human rights–sensitive data. Finally, the report calls on the WHO Director-General and the High Commissioner to create a joint program of work to ensure the implementation of the *High-Level Working Group*'s recommendations (Ibid.).

Following up on its work on the human rights aspects of the Millennium Development Goals (MDGs), the OHCHR is engaging in system-wide dialogue on human rights and the SDGs (Al Hussein 2017a). Prior to the adoption of the SDGs, the High Commissioner published an open letter to call upon states "to ensure that the new agenda was firmly anchored in the international human rights framework" (Al Hussein 2015, 11). That year, the OHCHR undertook preliminary consultations to compile human rights-based indicators for the SDGs, including through the Inter-Agency and Expert Group on Sustainable Development Goal Indicators (Al Hussein 2015). The OHCHR also held "an expert meeting to develop guidance on a human rights-based approach to data and statistics, with a focus on disaggregation and inclusive data collection systems" (Ibid., 11). Subsequently, the OHCHR published a 2016 guidance note on data collection and disaggregation to measure the achievement of the SDGs and began developing a methodology for compiling indicators on specific SDGs (Al Hussein 2017a; OHCHR 2016a). In June 2017, the HRC requested that the High Commissioner prepare a report detailing how a right to health framework can contribute to the effective implementation of the health-related SDGs and identifying best practices, as well as challenges and obstacles, to effective implementation of this rights-based approach to achieving those SDGs (HRC 2017).

Beyond these three key areas—sexual and reproductive health; women's, children's and adolescents' health; and the SDGs—the OHCHR is working on several other aspects of the right to health, many in response to requests from the UN General Assembly or the HRC. For example, in 2016, the OHCHR prepared a thematic report for the General Assembly on the links between violations of economic, social, and cultural rights and social unrest and conflict (OHCHR 2016b) and also prepared thematic reports for the HRC on the relationship between climate change and the right to health (OHCHR 2016c) and on universal birth registration (Al Hussein 2016). In 2017, the High Commissioner submitted reports on mental health and human rights (Al Hussein 2017c), girls' right to education (addressing the right to universal sexuality education and harmful practices such as early marriage) (Al Hussein 2017d), and state obligations to use "maximum available resources" to progressively realize economic, social, and cultural rights (Al Hussein 2017b).

In other inter-agency work, the OHCHR, for example, submitted comments to the High-Level Panel on Access to Medicines that was established by Secretary-General Ban Ki-Moon and published its final report in September 2016 (OHCHR 2017a). Currently, the OHCHR serves on the Inter-Agency Taskforce on the Prevention and Control of Non-Communicable Diseases, which was established by the Secretary-General in 2013 to support the WHO Global Plan for the Prevention and Control of Non-communicable Diseases 2013–2020 (UN Interagency Task Force 2017), as well as on the UN Inter-Agency Committee on Bioethics, established in 2003, which provides a forum for information exchange in the field of bioethics with special attention to human rights (UN Inter-Agency Committee on Bioethics n.d.). Mainstreaming rights across organizations, the OHCHR co-chairs the UN Development Group (UNDG) Human Rights Working Group, which was established in January 2015 in recognition of the increased emphasis on human rights as the foundation of the post-2015 development agenda (UN Development Group 2014). The Working Group, as discussed in chapter 3, aims to institutionalize human rights in all UN development work (Ibid.).

IV. FACTORS THAT INFLUENCE THE MAINSTREAMING OF THE RIGHT TO HEALTH AT THE OHCHR

Over the past two decades, several factors have influenced the mainstreaming of the right to health at the OHCHR. These factors fall into four broad categories: (1) recognition of economic and social rights as "real" human rights; (2) champions of the right to health among the OHCHR leadership; (3) resources and staff capacity devoted to global health challenges; and (4) the transition from conceptualization to implementation of the right to health.

A. Recognition of Economic and Social Rights as "Real" Human Rights

The idea that economic and social rights are not "real" human rights, or at least not as important as civil and political rights, dominated debates on the development of human rights throughout the Cold War (Alston 1979). Despite substantial post–Cold War progress on the recognition that all human rights are interdependent and indivisible, memorialized in the 1993 Vienna Declaration and Programme of Action, there continues to be resistance—among member states, UN staff members, and even human rights advocates—to the recognition of economic and social rights, including the right to health, as "real" and equally valuable rights

(Alston 2016; Al Hussein 2017c). As Philip Alston, UN Special Rapporteur on Extreme Poverty and Human Rights, recently reported, "[d]espite the rhetoric of indivisibility, both national and international endeavours to promote and protect economic and social rights are overshadowed by the assumption that while economic and social rights are desirable long-term social goals, they should not be treated as full-fledged human rights" (Alston 2016, 20). "[T]he biggest challenge by far is essentially ideological," he maintains, as "[t]he economic and political power of entrenched elites is best protected by policies that marginalize economic and social rights" (Ibid.).

Over the past decade and a half, the OHCHR has not consistently played a strong role in (1) ensuring that economic and social rights are an equal part of the human rights agenda and (2) educating states and human rights advocates on the interdependency and indivisibility of all human rights. Notably, the HRC, which dictates a substantial portion of the work of the OHCHR, continues to prioritize civil and political rights over economic and social rights (CESR 2016). A 2016 study on the HRC recommendations issued during the first ten years of the Universal Periodic Review, further examined in chapter 24, found that only 17 percent of the recommendations focused on economic and social rights, while 37 percent— more than double—focused on civil and political rights (Ibid.). The researchers concluded: "The fact that less than a fifth of recommendations made are focused on ESCR, despite being enshrined in roughly equal measure as CPR in the core international human rights treaties, illustrates that considerably less attention has been paid to this category of rights" (Ibid., 2–3). Among OHCHR staff members, many recognize that economic and social rights, including the right to health, are integral to the enjoyment of other human rights. Nonetheless, some staff members continue to view economic and social rights as an area of specialization, rather than interconnected with civil and political rights. As the lead UN organization on human rights continues to underserve economic and social rights, in part due to HRC priorities, it is not surprising that these rights remain marginalized globally.

B. Champions of the Right to Health among OHCHR Leadership

Strong champions of the right to health—raising the profile of the right to health, both inside the OHCHR and globally—facilitate the mainstreaming of the right to health into all areas of human rights research, policy, and implementation by recognizing that health affects the enjoyment of all human rights. As the High-Level Working Group on the Health and Human Rights of Women, Children and Adolescents maintains, "you cannot uphold rights without bold, unapologetic leadership at the highest levels" (WHO 2017b, 3). The leadership of the OHCHR, however, has not consistently championed economic and social rights generally or the right to health in particular. Although the High Commissioners have all expressed commitment to these rights, they have not all been active in promoting them.

Mary Robinson, as reflected in her foreword to this volume, stands out among the High Commissioners as a champion for economic and social rights, especially the right to health. In *A Voice for Human Rights: Mary Robinson*, editor Kevin

Boyle wrote that "[a] defining characteristic of Mary Robinson's term as High Commissioner was her commitment to change the status of economic, social and cultural rights as the neglected clauses of the Universal Declaration of Human Rights" (Boyle 2010, 114). Similarly, Julie Mertus recalls that Robinson promised "to narrow the gap between civil and political rights, on one hand, and economic and social rights, on the other" (Mertus 2009, 32). In an interview with BBC News, Robinson herself explained,

> Extreme poverty to me is the greatest denial of the exercise of human rights. You don't vote, you don't participate in any political activity, your views aren't listened to, you have no food, you have no shelter, your children are dying of preventable diseases—you don't even have the right to clean water. It's a denial of the dignity and worth of each individual which is what the universal declaration [of human rights] proclaims (*Talking Point Special* 2002).

More than a decade after Robinson's tenure, High Commissioner Pillay wrote, "[t]o this day, her [Robinson's] insistence on one of the central messages of the World Conference on Human Rights that civil and political rights and economic, social and cultural rights constitute an indivisible whole continues to resonate and inform the debate" (Pillay 2013b, 63–64).

To promote the right to health specifically, Robinson established in 2001 the first OHCHR position with a specific focus on health, the Advisor on Human Rights and HIV/AIDS. After leaving office, Robinson's deep commitment to the right to health remained evident, as she co-edited with Andrew Clapham the volume *Realizing the Right to Health* (Robinson and Clapham 2009). She also spearheaded a global campaign with Paul Hunt, then UN Special Rapporteur on the right to health, to recognize health as a human right. At the launch of this campaign in 2005, Robinson stated, "It is time for the world to come to its senses and call health a human right" (Arie 2005, 1421).

C. Resources and Staff Capacity for Global Health Challenges

No matter how committed the leadership is to promoting the right to health and mainstreaming health across OHCHR programming, the resources of the OHCHR are very limited compared to the global health and human rights challenges that need attention. The low UN budget commitment to the OHCHR—3.5 percent of the UN Secretariat regular budget—results in a lack of adequate staff to respond to the numerous demands of the ever-growing number of human rights mandates (OHCHR n.d.-f). As High Commissioner Zeid reported in 2014, "[i]n the light of the funding shortfall that OHCHR is enduring, partly due to mandated activities not funded comprehensively by the United Nations regular budget, the Office [was] compelled to reduce the level of its activities for 2015" (Al Hussein 2014, 20). By 2016, the OHCHR was eliminating positions, including national Human Rights Advisors (Al Hussein 2017a). In his most recent report, High Commissioner Zeid stated that "[w]hile there is increased demand for Human Rights Advisors, funds are insufficient, challenging both existing deployments and the ability to respond to new requests" (Al Hussein 2017a). Today, the total number of staff at the OHCHR is 1,179, with only one staff person assigned to health and a second assigned to support the UN Special Rapporteur on the right to health. A third position, the Advisor on HIV/AIDS, was eliminated in 2013. While other OHCHR staff work on health-related human rights—including, for example, those assigned to child rights, women's rights and gender, climate change, water and sanitation, and the SDGs—staff resources are incommensurate with global health needs.

The OHCHR is primarily a servicing organization. In 2016, nearly 45 percent of the total expenditures were devoted to fieldwork, 12 percent to supporting the human rights treaty bodies, and 13 percent to supporting the HRC and the Special Procedures (OHCHR 2017b). That means a total of 70 percent of expenditures were for servicing the human rights mechanisms and activities in the field. Much of the remaining expenditures were devoted to executive direction and management, resource mobilization, outreach, and program support (Ibid.). Only 10 percent of expenditures went to thematic research, human rights mainstreaming, and the development of policy, guidance, and tools (Ibid.). With such a small allocation of resources to research, staff members are often engaged in responding to issues as they arise, such as requests for studies from the General Assembly or HRC. Because the agenda is often set from the outside, the OHCHR is not generally free to undertake many substantial independent studies and become a "think tank" in the field of economic and social rights or on the right to health. At times, the mandates from the HRC are in line with OHCHR priorities, and this creates synergy for further work on an issue. Indeed, when OHCHR projects coincide with the broader international agenda, such as with the MDGs, this has provided an opportunity for the OHCHR to engage with health more deeply. At other times, mandates from the HRC make it difficult for OHCHR staff to support an independent agenda. Such HRC-mandated activities often generate short bursts of attention to an issue; however, they may lead to reports that cannot be implemented when there is not enough capacity to take them forward. Many human rights advocates would like the OHCHR to be more forward looking and develop more of an independent agenda; yet, it lacks the capacity for its current servicing responsibilities, and therefore, cannot develop a substantial independent agenda that would allow it to take a major leadership role in global health governance.

D. Transition from Conceptualization to Operationalization of the Right to Health

A final concern for mainstreaming health at the OHCHR is the difficulty in moving beyond a narrow legalistic conceptualization of the right to health to broader operationalization in the field (Hunt 2017). To date, the UN human rights mechanisms and the OHCHR have played crucial roles in developing human rights instruments, advocating for their ratification, elaborating the normative content of rights, and monitoring state implementation of human rights obligations. "Implementation" of human rights, however, requires more than laws and supervision by judicial and quasi-judicial mechanisms (Ibid.). Full implementation of the right to health requires collaboration with health professionals, including doctors, nurses, psychologists, community health workers, policymakers, economists, and administrators (Hunt 2007). It also requires recognizing that health is impacted by many social determinants, and as a result, realizing the right to health requires implementation beyond the health sector, and thus collaboration with researchers and practitioners in many additional fields as well. The need to expand beyond a narrow legalistic approach to human rights, particularly to enhance implementation of the right to health, has only recently been recognized widely.

> The law is important, but understanding human rights requires us also to understand its politics. Furthermore, law and politics do not themselves exhaust the human-rights field. The other social sciences—such as sociology, anthropology and economics are essential to our appreciation of human-rights problems and their possible solutions. In short, human rights is an interdisciplinary concept par excellence (Freeman 2011, 13).

This transition from an emphasis on law and legal mechanisms to multi-sectoral forms of implementation—such as human rights impact assessment and budget analysis—requires both an expansive understanding of public health as well as an interdisciplinary approach to human rights implementation. To some extent, both trends can be seen in the work of the OHCHR. Participation in the SDG process, for example, has helped to broaden the understanding, both within and outside the OHCHR, that public health is closely connected to many human rights and that working with people in many disciplines and sectors is necessary to implement the right to health. Further, recent interdisciplinary and multi-sectoral collaborations—with WHO, UNFPA, FAO, UN-Habitat, and other UN entities, as well as NGOs—have aided the OHCHR in developing interdisciplinary tools to implement the right to health in a variety of fields and contexts. As it is not possible for the OHCHR alone to implement the right to health, these collaborations hold the potential to expand the impact of the OHCHR on global health governance.

CONCLUSION

Against a background of growing but still weak support among states for economic and social rights, the OHCHR has managed with extremely limited resources to make a global imprint on the human right to health and health-related human rights. The credit for most of these advances is attributable to a few people who have prioritized health in their work at the OHCHR, as well as the special procedures and human rights treaty bodies (discussed in chapters 22 and 23). There remain, however, ideological challenges and budget limitations for the OHCHR, which, coupled with the growing number of mandates and assignments from the HRC, make it difficult for the OHCHR to make substantial progress in mainstreaming public health across its work and advancing human rights in global health governance. Given these limitations, the OHCHR has largely focused on a series of specific health issues, including HIV/AIDS, maternal mortality, and most recently sexual and reproductive health and rights. While the OHCHR has also engaged in many shorter term or ad hoc health issues, which often result from mandates from the HRC or other UN entities, many of these reports on specific health issues demand considerable time and yet do not generate much impact, as there are insufficient resources at the OHCHR to follow up on them. By engaging in longer-term projects that involve multiple partners (such as WHO, UNFPA, UN Women, FAO, UNAIDS, and UNICEF), the OHCHR can collaborate across UN entities, as well as with NGOs in the field, to embed human rights—and the right to health more specifically—in projects and programs. Such collaboration across institutions and disciplines will be key to the OHCHR's continuing human rights implementation in global health governance.

REFERENCES

Al Hussein, Zeid R. 2014. "Annual Report of the United Nations High Commissioner for Human Rights." 19 December. UN Doc. A/HRC/28/3.

Al Hussein, Zeid R. 2015. "Annual Report of the United Nations High Commissioner for Human Rights." 23 December. UN Doc. A/HRC/31/3.

Al Hussein, Zeid R. 2016. "Report of the High Commissioner for Human Rights: Strengthening Policies and Programmes for Universal Birth Registration." 1 July. UN Doc. A/HRC/33/22.

Al Hussein, Zeid R. 2017a. "Annual Report of the United Nations High Commissioner for Human Rights." 13 January. UN Doc. A/HRC/34/3.

Al Hussein, Zeid R. 2017b. "Report of the High Commissioner for Human Rights: Economic, Social and Cultural Rights." 16 May. UN Doc. E/2017/70.

Al Hussein, Zeid R. 2017c. "Report of the High Commissioner for Human Rights: Mental Health and Human Rights." 31 January. UN Doc. A/HRC/34/32.

Al Hussein, Zeid R. 2017d. "Report of the High Commissioner for Human Rights: Realization of the Equal Enjoyment of the Right to Education by Every Girl." 5 April. UN Doc. A/HRC/35/11.

Alston, Philip. 1979. "The United Nations' Specialized Agencies and Implementation of the International Covenant on Economic, Social and Cultural Rights." *Columbia Journal of Transnational Law* 18: 79–118.

Alston, Philip. 2016. "Report of the Special Rapporteur on Extreme Poverty and Human Rights." 28 April. UN Doc. A/HRC/32/31.

Arbour, Louise. 2005a. "Report of the United Nations High Commissioner for Human Rights to the General Assembly." UN Doc. A/60/36.

Arbour, Louise. 2005b. "The Right to Development: Report of the High Commissioner for Human Rights." 16 December. UN Doc. E/CN.4/2006/24.

Arbour, Louise. 2006. "Report of the United Nations High Commissioner for Human Rights to the General Assembly." UN Doc. A/61/36.

Arbour, Louise. 2007. "Report of the United Nations High Commissioner for Human Rights to the Human Rights Council." 2 March. UN Doc. A/HRC/4/49.

Arbour, Louise. 2008. "Report of the United Nations High Commissioner for Human Rights to the General Assembly." UN Doc. A/63/36.

Arie, Sophie. 2005. "Health Should Be Seen as a Human Right, Global Campaign Says." *BMJ* 331(7530): 1421.

Ayala-Lasso, José. 1994. "Report of the United Nations High Commissioner for Human Rights." 11 November. UN Doc. A/49/39.

Ayala-Lasso, José. 1995. "Report of the United Nations High Commissioner for Human Rights." 15 February. UN Doc. E/CN.4/1995/98.

Boyle, Kevin, ed. 2010. *A Voice for Human Rights: Mary Robinson*. Philadelphia: University of Pennsylvania Press.

Carey, John. 1966. "The UN and Human Rights; Who Should Do What?" *International and Comparative Law Bulletin* 10: 9–29.

CESR (Center for Economic and Social Rights). 2016. *The Universal Periodic Review: A Skewed Agenda, Trends Analysis of the UPR's Coverage of Economic, Social and Cultural Rights*. Available at: http://www.cesr.org/sites/default/files/CESR_ScPo_UPR_FINAL.pdf.

Commission on Human Rights. 1947. Drafting Committee: Draft Outline of the International Bill of Human Rights (prepared by the Division of Human Rights). 4 June. UN Doc. E/CN.4AC.1/3.

Freeman, Michael. 2011. *Human Rights: An Interdisciplinary Approach (2nd ed.)*. Cambridge, UK and Malden, Mass.: Polity Press.

Gaer, Felice and Christen Broecker. 2013. Introduction to *United Nations for Human Rights: Conscience for the World*, edited by Felice Gaer and Christen Broecker, 1–32. Leiden: Brill Publishing House.

HRC (Human Rights Council). 2017. The Right of Everyone to the Enjoyment of the Highest Attainable Standard of Physical and Mental Health in the Implementation of the 2030 Agenda for Sustainable Development. Draft resolution 21 June. UN Doc. A/HRC/35/L.18/Rev.1.

Humphrey, John. 1984. *Human Rights and the United Nations: A Great Adventure*. Dobbs Ferry, New York: Transnational Publishers.

Hunt, Paul. 2007. "Report of the Special Rapporteur on the Right to Health." 17 January. UN Doc. A/HRC/4/28.

Hunt, Paul. 2017. "Configuring the UN Human Rights System in the 'Era of Implementation': Mainland and Archipelago." *Human Rights Quarterly* 39: 489-538.

Koh, Harold Honju. 2004. "A Job Description for the U.N. High Commissioner for Human Rights." *Columbia Human Rights Law Review* 35: 493–502.

Mertus, Julie. 2009. "The Office of the High Commissioner for Human Rights." In *The United Nations and Human Rights: A Guide for a New Era*. Abingdon: Routledge.

Morsink, Johannes. 1999. *The Universal Declaration of Human Rights: Origins, Drafting, and Intent*. Philadelphia: University of Pennsylvania Press.

OHCHR. n.d.-a. "Bertrand Ramcharan." Available at: http://www.ohchr.org/EN/AboutUs/Pages/Ramcharan.aspx.

OHCHR. n.d.-b. "Jose Ayala Lasso." Available at: http://www.ohchr.org/EN/AboutUs/Pages/Ayala.aspx.

OHCHR. n.d.-c. "Louise Arbour." Available at: http://www.ohchr.org/EN/AboutUs/Pages/LouiseArbour.aspx.

OHCHR. n.d.-d. "Mary Robinson." Available at: http://www.ohchr.org/EN/AboutUs/Pages/Robinson.aspx.

OHCHR. n.d.-e. "Navanethem Pillay." Available at: http://www.ohchr.org/EN/AboutUs/Pages/NaviPillay.aspx.

OHCHR. n.d.-f. "OHCHR, Funding and Budget." Available at: http://www.ohchr.org/EN/AboutUs/Pages/FundingBudget.aspx.

OHCHR. n.d.-g. "OHCHR, Who We Are—Mission Statement." Available at: http://www.ohchr.org/EN/AboutUs/Pages/MissionStatement.aspx.

OHCHR. n.d.-h. "Sergio Vieira de Mello." Available at: http://www.ohchr.org/EN/AboutUs/Pages/Vieira.aspx.

OHCHR. n.d.-i. "Sexual and Reproductive Health and Rights." Available at: http://www.ohchr.org/EN/Issues/Women/WRGS/Pages/HealthRights.aspx.

OHCHR. n.d.-j. "Zeid Ra'ad Al Hussein." Available at: http://www.ohchr.org/EN/AboutUs/Pages/HighCommissioner.aspx.

OHCHR. 2005. "Principles and Guidelines for a Human Rights Approach to Poverty Reduction Strategies." UN Doc. HR/PUB/06/12.

OHCHR. 2008. "Claiming the Millennium Development Goals: A Human Rights Approach." UN Doc. HR/PUB/08/3.

OHCHR. 2012. "Towards Freedom from Fear and Want: Human Rights in the Post-2015 Agenda. Thematic Think Piece: UN System Task Team on the Post-2015 UN Development Agenda." Available at: http://www.ohchr.org/Documents/Issues/MDGs/OHCHRThinkPiece2015.pdf.

OHCHR. 2015. "Launch of the Information Series on Sexual and Reproductive Health and Rights." Available at: http://www.ohchr.org/Documents/Issues/Women/WRGS/SexualHealth/Flyer%20Launch%20Event%20Information%20Series%20SRHR%20final.pdf.

OHCHR. 2016a. "A Human Rights-Based Approach to Data: Leaving No One Behind in the 2030 Development Agenda—Guidance Note to Data Collection and Disaggregation" Available at: http://www.ohchr.org/Documents/Issues/HRIndicators/GuidanceNoteonApproachtoData.pdf.

OHCHR. 2016b. "Early Warning and Economic, Social and Cultural Rights." Available at: http://www.ohchr.org/Documents/Issues/ESCR/EarlyWarning_ESCR_2016_en.pdf.

OHCHR. 2016c. "Report of the Office of the High Commissioner for Human Rights: Analytical Study on the Relationship between Climate Change and the Human Right of Everyone to the Enjoyment of the Highest Attainable Standard of Mental Health." 6 May. UN Doc. A/HRC/32/23.

OHCHR. 2017a. "Access to Essential Medicines Is a Fundamental Element of the Right to Health." Available at: http://www.ohchr.org/EN/NewsEvents/Pages/Accessessentialmedicines.aspx.

OHCHR. 2017b. "OHCHR Report 2016." Available at: http://www2.ohchr.org/english/OHCHRreport2016/allegati/Downloads/1_The_whole_Report_2016.pdf.

OHCHR and CESR (Center for Economic and Social Rights). 2013. "Who Will Be Accountable: Human Rights and the Post-2015 Development Agenda." http://www.ohchr.org/Documents/Publications/WhoWillBeAccountable.pdf.

OHCHR and UNAIDS. 1998. "International Guidelines on HIV/AIDS and Human Rights as Adopted by the Second Consultation on HIV/AIDS and Human Rights." UN Doc. E/CN.4/1997/37, annex 1.

OHCHR and UNAIDS. 2007. "Handbook on HIV/AIDS and Human Rights for National Human Rights Institutions." UN Doc. HR/PUB/07/3.

OHCHR and WHO (World Health Organization). 2008. "Human Rights, Health and Poverty Reduction Strategies." UN Doc. HR/ PUB/08/05.

OHCHR, UNAIDS, and WHO. 2003. "HIV/AIDS: Stand Up for Human Rights." Available at: http://www.who.int/hhr/news/cartoonenglish.pdf.

Pillay, Navanethem. 2010a. "Report of the United Nations High Commissioner for Human Rights." 30 December. UN Doc. A/HRC/16/20.

Pillay, Navanethem. 2010b. "Report of the High Commissioner for Human Rights on the Question of the Realization in All Countries of Economic, Social and Culutral Rights. 6 April. UN Doc. A/HRC/14/33.

Pillay, Navanethem. 2012. "Technical Guidance on the Application of a Human Rights-Based Approach to the Implementation of Policies and Programmes to Reduce Preventable Maternal Mortality, Report of the High Commissioner for Human Rights." 2 July. UN Doc. A/HRC/21/22.

Pillay, Navanethem. 2013a. "Annual Report of the United Nations High Commissioner for Human Rights." 18 December. UN Doc. A/HRC/25/19.

Pillay, Navanethem. 2013b. "Address by the High Commissioner at the Jacob Blaustein Institute for the Advancement of Human Rights." In *United Nations for Human Rights: Conscience for the World*, edited by Felice Gaer and Christen Broecker, 63–72. Leiden: Brill Publishing House.

Ramcharan, Bertrand. 2004. "The Right to Development: Report of the High Commissioner for Human Rights." 8 January. UN Doc. E/CN.4/2004/22.

Ramcharan, Bertrand. 2009. "The Office of UN High Commissioner for Human Rights." In *International Monitoring Mechanisms: Essays in Honor of Jacob Th. Möller*, edited by Gudmundor Alfredsson, 199–204. Leiden: Brill Publishing House.

Robinson, Mary. 1998. "Report of the United Nations High Commissioner for Human Rights." 23 February. UN Doc. E/CN.4/1998/122.

Robinson, Mary. 1999. "Report of the United Nations High Commissioner for Human Rights." 29 July. UN Doc. E/1999/96.

Robinson, Mary. 2000. "The Right to Food: Report of the High Commissioner for Human Rights submitted in accordance with Commission Resolution 1999/24." 13 January. UN Doc. E/CN.4/2000/48.

Robinson, Mary. 2001a. "Report of the United Nations High Commissioner for Human Rights to the Economic and Social Council." 18 May. UN Doc. E/2001/64.

Robinson, Mary. 2001b. "Report of the United Nations High Commissioner for Human Rights, Report on the Workshop on the Justiciability of Economic, Social and Cultural Rights." 22 March. UN Doc. E/CN.4/2001/62.

Robinson, Mary. 2002. "Report of the United Nations High Commissioner for Human Rights to the Economic and Social Council." 20 May. UN Doc. E/2002/68.

Robinson, Mary and Andrew Clapham, eds. 2009. *Realizing the Right to Health: Swiss Human Rights Book Volume 3*. Zurich: rüffer & rub.

SIDA (Swedish Development Agency), WHO, and OHCHR. 2011. "Human Rights and Gender Equality in Health Sector Strategies: How to Assess Policy Coherence." Available at: http://www.ohchr.org/Documents/Publications/HRandGenderEqualit yinHealthSectorStrategies.pdf.

Talking Point Special. 2002. "Mary Robinson, UN Human Rights Chief." Presented by Zeinab Badawi. 21 November. BBC News World Edition.

UN (United Nations). 2016. *Living Free and Equal: What States Are Doing to Tackle Violence and Discrimination Against Lesbian, Gay, Bisexual, Transgender and Intersex People*. New York and Geneva: United Nations.

UN Department of Public Information. 1997. *Yearbook of the United Nations 1997*. Volume 51. New York: United Nations.

UN Development Group. 2014. "UNDG Human Rights Working Group (HR-WG): Terms of Reference." 5 December. Available at: https://undg.org/wp-content/uploads/2016/08/UNDG-Human-Rights-Working-Group-TORs-5Dec2014.pdf.

UN General Assembly. 1993. "High Commissioner For the Promotion and Protection of Human Rights." 20 December. UN Doc. A/RES/48/141.

UN Inter-Agency Committee on Bioethics. n.d. Available at: http://www.who.int/ethics/about/unintercomm/en/.

UN Interagency Task Force (on Non-Communicable Diseases). 2017. "Summary of the Eighth Meeting of the Interagency Task Force on Non-Communicable Diseases." 23 February. Available at http://www.who.int/ncds/un-task-force/events/report-8th-uniatf-meeting-feb2017.pdf.

UN Secretary-General. 1994. "Staffing and Functions of the Office of the United Nations High Commissioner for Human Rights and of the Centre for Human Rights, Report of the Secretary-General." 31 May. UN Doc. A/C.5/48/77.

Vieira de Mello, Sergio. 2003. "Report of the High Commissioner for Human Rights and Follow-Up to the World Conference on Human Rights." 26 February. UN Doc. E/CN.4/2003/14.

WHO (World Health Organization). 2017a. "High-Level Working Group on Health and Human Rights Handover their Final Report to WHO's Director General and the High Commissioner for Human Rights." Available at: http://www.who.int/life-course/news/high-level-wg-hhr-report/en/.

WHO. 2017b. *Leading the Realization of Human Rights to Health and Through Health. Report of the High-Level Working Group on the Health and Human Rights of Women, Children and Adolescents.* Geneva: World Health Organization.

High Level Working Group on the Health and Human Rights of Women, Children and Adolescents. 2017. *Leading the Realization of Human Rights to Health and Through Health.* Geneva: World Health Organization.

World Conference on Human Rights. 1993. "Vienna Declaration and Programme of Action." 25 June. UN Doc. A/CONF.157/23.

22

The United Nations Special Procedures

Peopling Human Rights, Peopling Global Health

THÉRÈSE MURPHY AND AMREI MÜLLER

This chapter examines the United Nations (UN) Special Procedures, a system of independent experts appointed to monitor and report on human rights violations, and more generally to advise and assist in promoting and protecting rights. The chapter positions the Special Procedures as a "missing population," neglected by proponents of global health and global health law, and by many human rights advocates too. It suggests that this neglect makes human rights law more vulnerable to misrepresentation, including by proponents of global health who both promote human rights law (and the human right to health in particular) and pitch it as problematic, or fail to engage with what they expect from it. The alleged problems, which are associated above all with economic and social rights, include ambiguous and imprecise standards, weak enforcement mechanisms, and general ineffectiveness arising from the focus on progressive, as opposed to immediate, realization. The centrality of states within international law is often seen as a further, more general problem. There is also a sense that law is ill suited to the grand challenges of global health, and that governance should be center stage.

To counter these criticisms and to address the broader pattern of misrepresentation, this chapter sets out to "people" human rights law; to be more precise, it sets out to people human rights law differently. It does this by adding the Special Rapporteurs and others who make up the system of Special Procedures, positioning these experts as an essential supplement to the cast of characters—courts, treaty bodies, non-governmental organizations, victims, and states—that dominate accounts of human rights law. Adding Special Procedures helps in particular to address the widespread failure to see human rights law as a deliberative and iterative process that draws in a range of actors. This failure has to be addressed if global health hopes to harness the potential of human rights law.

The chapter proceeds as follows. Part I introduces the system of Special Procedures, explaining its origins, expansion, and functioning, and pinpointing its unique role within the UN human rights machinery. Parts II and III add depth to the account: Part II focuses on the Special Rapporteur on the right to health, whereas Part III extends to other Special Procedures, paying particular attention to mandates that relate to the underlying determinants of health, such as water and sanitation, food, and housing. In describing the contribution of these Special Procedures to global health, these parts of the chapter respond to the criticisms of human rights law outlined earlier. They also explain why a human rights-based approach to global health must extend beyond the right to health. Part IV broadens the argument, emphasizing that the human rights-based approach to global health is compromised not just by global health's misrepresentations of human rights law but also by an array of problems within the system of Special Procedures.

I. THE SPECIAL PROCEDURES SYSTEM

Special Procedures of the Human Rights Council (HRC) typically take the title "Special Rapporteur," but there are also "Independent Experts," "Representatives," and "Working Groups."[1] Most examine a human rights theme of global relevance (such as violence against women, the right to education, or extreme poverty), but some cover countries or territories. Over time, the latter have become both more difficult to establish and more likely to be discontinued (Limon and Power 2014); the former, by contrast, have experienced extraordinary growth (Freedman and Mchangama 2016; Limon and Piccone 2014).

This growth has affected not just the number of thematic mandates in the Special Procedures system but also the scope of the system. Initially the thematic mandates focused on civil and political rights; today, they also include economic, social, and cultural rights and human rights issues faced by vulnerable groups. However, it is the growth in numbers that is most remarkable. In the early 1980s, there were just three thematic mandates (spanning enforced or involuntary disappearances, extrajudicial executions, and torture); in 2000, there were twenty-one; and by early 2017, there were forty-three (OHCHR 2017). Moreover, prior to 1980, there were no thematic mandates, and country-specific mandates were sparse. From 1946 to 1967, there were no mandates at all: throughout that period, the Commission on Human Rights, the predecessor to the HRC, focused on international human rights standard-setting and insisted it had "no power to take any action with regard to any complaints concerning human rights" (Commission on Human Rights 1947, para. 22; ECOSOC 1947).

The Commission's stance came under sustained pressure in the mid-1960s when a bloc of states sought a non-treaty-based, communications-type procedure as part of efforts to challenge human rights violations associated with colonialism and racism, particularly in southern Africa. Their efforts led to the appointment of the first two Special Procedures in 1967, and, later that same year, the Commission abandoned

---

1. Working groups typically include five members, one from each UN region—Africa, Asia-Pacific, Eastern Europe, Latin America and the Caribbean, and Western Europe and others.

the "no power to act" doctrine. It did so in the wake of Resolution 1235 adopted by the UN Economic and Social Council (ECOSOC), which authorized the Commission on Human Rights to examine information regarding "gross violations of human rights and fundamental freedoms," including through "a study of situations which reveal a consistent pattern of violations of human rights" (ECOSOC 1967).

Today, Special Procedures mandate-holders are appointed by, and accountable to, the HRC; however, they are independent from the HRC and act in a personal capacity (HRC 2007a, 2007b, 2007c; Pillay 2015). They are also independent from the UN High Commissioner for Human Rights (Gaer 2014), the Office of the UN High Commissioner for Human Rights (OHCHR), and the UN Secretariat more generally. Finally, they are independent from international organizations, and from states and civil society as well (HRC 2007c).

A term of office lasts for a maximum of six years in the case of a thematic mandate-holder, and generally for one year in the case of her country counterpart. Many mandate-holders, but certainly not all, have come from legal backgrounds. For example, the right to housing mandate has been held by a lawyer (and later a judge), an architect, an urban planner and architect, and the head of a non-governmental organization (NGO). The mandate on the right to health is currently held by a medical doctor; previously it was held by first, a law professor and former member of the UN Committee on Economic, Social and Cultural Rights (CESCR), and then, a practicing lawyer.

Mandate-holders are not paid for their work: they receive only travel and subsistence expenses (HRC 2007c) and administrative assistance from OHCHR. It could be said that this approach to remuneration helps to secure the independence of the Special Procedures. However, given the growth in the number of mandates and the pressures on the UN human rights budget, this approach also means either that mandate-holders work with severely limited support from OHCHR or that they engage in their own fundraising. The latter in turn creates its own issues, including how to handle the expectations of donors, how to manage such funding, and, more broadly, the risks of compromising—or seeming to compromise—one's independence (Winkler and de Albuquerque 2017).

In formal terms, the scope of each mandate depends on the HRC (formerly the Commission on Human Rights) resolution creating or extending it; however, in practice, the interpretation of the mandate—by the mandate-holder, above all—has been crucial. Typically, a mandate-holder will monitor and respond to alleged or potentially imminent violations of human rights. She will also engage in standard-setting and normative development to clarify the relevant international legal framework. And she will develop best practices in the implementation of human rights, helping to build an understanding of violations in a particular field and how to address them, and also how best to realize rights. To fulfill these functions, mandate-holders deploy a range of tools, including:

- *fact-finding missions* mostly to individual states, but occasionally to international organizations such as the World Trade Organization (WTO) or World Bank; there has also been a mission to GlaxoSmithKline, one of the world's leading research-based pharmaceutical companies.

- *communications*, principally urgent appeals and letters of allegation sent to governments through diplomatic channels,[2] but, in some cases, communications are also sent to non-state actors or inter-governmental organizations. All such communications are designed to prevent, mitigate, or seek clarification on alleged violations and to promote rights-protective measures.
- *public and press statements.*
- *annual reporting* to the HRC and, for many Special Procedures, to the UN General Assembly,[3] with provision for interactive dialogue as part of the process.

These tools were elaborated by the early mandate-holders and honed by their successors; they also continue to evolve (de Frouville 2017). Fact-finding missions, for instance, are more frequent and longer than those undertaken in the past; the terms of reference for country visits have also been updated (HRC 2017a). Other changes reflect new communications technologies: submissions to Special Procedures can be made electronically, either via an online questionnaire or via email (HRC 2017d), and a database on communications has been developed. Reports submitted by the Special Procedures are now posted relatively promptly and are available on the Internet in a number of languages. As a general rule, the content of individual reports is also richer and more detailed than in the past (HRC 2016a). Cooperation between mandate-holders—on reports, statements, urgent appeals, and letters of allegation—is more common; there is also increased cooperation between mandate-holders and the treaty bodies, and between mandate-holders and other parts of the human rights system (HRC 2017a). Follow-up to recommendations and complaints has also improved (although overall it remains problematic) (ISHR et al. 2017).

These and related enhancements can be traced at least in part to broader developments. Mandate-holders have been meeting annually since 1994; during these sessions, they also hold meetings with representatives of NGOs and UN agencies and programs. At their twelfth annual meeting, the Special Procedures established a five-person Coordination Committee, which would represent them vis-à-vis the HRC and other actors (Commission on Human Rights 2005a). They also have both a manual of operations ("Manual of Operations" 2008) and an internal advisory procedure, which is designed to review practices and working methods. More recently, they have reiterated the need for the UN human rights system to recognize the serious problem of intimidation and reprisals facing human rights defenders for engagement with Special Procedures; they have also suggested

2. Urgent action letters are used in time-sensitive situations to prevent or mitigate a violation, whereas letters of allegation are used where the alleged violation has already occurred and the impact on the victim cannot be changed. There is no obligation to exhaust domestic remedies before making contact with a mandate holder, and contact can be made either by victims of alleged violations or by individuals or organizations with direct knowledge of the violation.

3. Both the Working Group on Arbitrary Detention and the Working Group on Enforced or Involuntary Disappearances have additional tools.

actions for mandate-holders themselves, and established their own focal point on reprisals (HRC 2016c).

Paradoxically, "enhancement" has also become a clarion call for states that are keen to exert greater control over the system of Special Procedures. In 2007, a group of states secured agreement to a Code of Conduct for the Special Procedures (HRC 2007c, 2009a). That development, and related attempts to create a legal committee to enforce it, have divided opinion (Alston 2011). So, too, has the broader question of how to secure a system of Special Procedures that is independent and accountable, as well as effective in promoting and protecting human rights.

To put these questions in context and set the scene for the remainder of this chapter, the focus now shifts to what is "special" about the system of Special Procedures. Five features are examined below and developed in Parts II and III, which discuss the contributions to global health of the Special Rapporteur on the right to health and a range of other mandate-holders.

A. Unique Access to States

The first, and arguably most important, feature of the Special Procedures is that they have unique—and thus, uniquely challenging—access to states. In 2016, for instance, mandate-holders made ninety-six *country visits* to sixty-five states and territories, and submitted fifty-eight *country-visit reports* to the HRC. They also sent 526 *communications* to 119 states (and twenty-three non-state actors). Sixty-two percent of UN member states received one or more communications, and 1282 individual cases were covered. Four hundred and thirty-one replies were received, of which 313 were for communications sent in 2016 (and there was a 59 percent reply rate to communications sent in 2015). One hundred and eighty-seven communications were *followed up* by Special Procedures mandate-holders, and three *communications reports* were submitted, one to each HRC session (HRC 2017a).

These statistics do not tell the whole story, however. They do not, for instance, indicate whether any of the communications sent to state and non-state actors actually assisted individuals or groups whose rights were said to have been violated. On the other hand, they also do not indicate whether fact-finding country missions have an impact beyond the finding of facts by an individual mandate-holder. The knowledge that a country mission is imminent can galvanize not just local human rights defenders but governments too—governments may want a "heads-up" on what the mandate-holder is likely to find, or they may want to commence cover-up activities. The ways in which mandate-holders find facts is, of course, an ongoing issue: the point made here does not challenge that—it simply says that, even without any actual fact-finding, a Special Procedures mandate-holder can be a catalyst for change (Alston 2010; Piccone 2012).

B. Contributions to the Recognition and Realization of Human Rights

The second standout feature of Special Procedures is their contribution to the formal legal recognition of rights (the right to water and sanitation is an example

(Winkler and de Albuquerque 2017)) and to the development of more detailed understandings of the scope and content of particular rights and their companion responsibilities. Finding ways to operationalize human rights—ways that speak not just to courts and other legal experts but also to health workers, for instance—has also been central (Hunt and Leader 2010).

C. Agenda-Setting

Third, through their thematic reports in particular, Special Procedures mandate-holders have been agenda-setters, bringing attention and a human rights-based focus to pressing issues, both new and old. The issues range widely, from extrajudicial executions to maternal mortality, from biodiversity to stigma and discrimination, and from environmental human rights defenders to the human rights impact of trade and investment agreements.

D. Challenging Silos

Fourth, the practices of the Special Procedures challenge "silos." For example, mandate-holders traverse the international, the regional, and the national; they draw together and develop standards associated with diverse human rights instruments and international institutions; and they interact with an array of state and non-state actors (including by means of "country" reports on actors ranging from the WTO (Commission on Human Rights 2004a) to GlaxoSmithKline (HRC 2009c)). Mandate-holders also engage not just with violations but also with best practices in the field of human rights. Furthermore, their development of guiding principles as part of their best-practice efforts is a clear challenge to those who insist on drawing fixed lines between the influence of law and soft law.

E. Exercising Influence

The fifth and final standout feature is that, in doing all of the above, the Special Procedures neither accuse nor compel; they have no formal enforcement powers—they rely on cooperation and dialogue, and they do so in a vortex of politicking by states and others. They require what the first Special Rapporteur on the right to health has described as "a keen sense of strategy" (Hunt 2017, 341), and, as part of this, they have to be willing to pursue not just signaling and repeat-play but also revisions to their own approaches (Hunt and Leader 2010). They also need "coping mechanisms" when confronted by non-cooperation (Shaheed and Parris Richter 2017) or by worries that they are "selling out."

To substantiate these five claims, Parts II and III detail the work of a range of mandate-holders, beginning with the Special Rapporteur on the right to health and extending to other mandates, especially those related to underlying determinants of health. Focusing on the ways in which these mandate-holders have contributed to global health, the goal is to challenge misrepresentations of human rights law that have surfaced within the work of proponents of global health and global health law, and to pave the way for a different understanding of human rights law.

This understanding will avoid the standard refrain, which casts human rights law as thoroughly compromised by general and abstract norms, low enforceability, progressive realization, and an undue focus on states. It focuses instead on the ways in which deliberation, iteration, and inclusivity, allied with a keen sense of strategy, are at the core of this radically pluralist field of law (de Búrca 2017; McCrudden 2017; Milewicz and Goodin 2016; White and Perelman 2011). It seeks, in particular, to understand these practices and to harness their potential to meet global health's grand challenges.

II. THE SPECIAL RAPPORTEUR ON THE RIGHT TO HEALTH: ACHIEVEMENTS AND CONTRIBUTIONS TO GLOBAL HEALTH

The Commission on Human Rights established the Special Rapporteur on the right of everyone to the enjoyment of the highest attainable standard of physical and mental health (SRH) in 2002, following an initiative by the government of Brazil, which was supported by other low-income countries. The mandate has since been held by three individuals—Dainius Pūras (since August 2014); Anand Grover (August 2008–July 2014); and Paul Hunt (August 2002–July 2008).

The SRH's mandate is to support states and other relevant actors to better promote and protect the right to the highest attainable standard of physical and mental health (Commission on Human Rights 2002; HRC 2007f, 2010b, 2013b). This right is set out seminally in Article 12 of the International Covenant on Economic, Social and Cultural Rights (ICESCR), and the SRH has contributed significantly both to making it more specific and more accessible and to its operationalization by and beyond courts.

Some have disapproved of the fact that the right to health encompasses a right to enjoy underlying determinants of health (CESCR 2000, para. 11), emphasizing that this makes the right "radically 'inclusive'" (Tasioulas and Vayena 2016, 371) and threatens to overwhelm it. The first SRH appears, however, to have navigated this challenge: he acknowledged the underlying determinants as a component of the right to health (Commission on Human Rights 2005c; UN General Assembly 2005), and thereafter wrote a report on water and sanitation (UN General Assembly 2007), but the SRH has not crowded the space of mandate-holders on housing, water and sanitation, or food, for instance. The SRH has also participated in several successful coordinated efforts with fellow mandate-holders (e.g., Farha et al. 2014; Commission on Human Rights 2006a).

In so doing, the SRH has also signaled that the right to health is only one part of a human rights-based approach to health. Further evidence of this inclusive approach emerges from the SRH's "country" report on missions to Uganda, the World Bank, and the International Monetary Fund (IMF), which explored the general human rights responsibility of international assistance and cooperation (HRC 2008b). The difference between this inclusive approach (which has the potential to draw on all human rights) and its far narrower right-to-health counterpart is not always fully appreciated within global health work: this needs urgent attention if undue pressure on the right to health is to be avoided and the full capacity of human rights law is to be realized.

Intersections between the right to health and cross-cutting human rights principles such as accountability, participation, and non-discrimination and equality also need to be better understood, not least because they reinforce and concretize the call of global health advocates to promote "health equity" (Fried et al. 2010; Koplan et al. 2009) as a basis to reduce global health disparities. Here too the work of the SRH is instructive: successive mandate-holders have advocated for prioritization of the health needs of disadvantaged and marginalized groups and individuals. Country reports have consistently explored the issue (e.g., HRC 2012c (Ghana); HRC 2007d (Sweden)), further reinforcing it by a general emphasis on poverty reduction (e.g., Commission on Human Rights 2005d (Mozambique); Commission on Human Rights 2005b (Peru); HRC 2011a (Guatemala); HRC 2016b (Paraguay)). Meanwhile, thematic reports have focused on the health needs of particular vulnerable or marginalized groups, giving detailed recommendations to states and other actors on how they should meet these needs as a matter of priority. For instance, one of the SRH's first reports was dedicated to the right to health and maternal mortality (Commission on Human Rights 2004b), and the issue was revisited in two subsequent reports (UN General Assembly 2006, 2011). These reports make it clear that maternal mortality and morbidity is not simply a "tragedy"; it is a human rights issue, and root causes—including "the sharp discrepancies between men and women in their enjoyment of sexual and reproductive health rights" (UN General Assembly 2006, para. 10)—need to understood and addressed.

"Inclusivity" characterizes the work of the SRH in other ways too. Successive mandate-holders have used consultations, especially with civil society and UN bodies, to determine priorities for their terms in office and to facilitate preparation of high-quality reports. Close cooperation with health workers has brought particular benefits, including a change of course by the first SRH toward wider health system issues (HRC 2008a). It has also led to a conscious focus on writing reports that are easy to operationalize (while continuing to respect and develop the right to health framework) (Commission on Human Rights 2005b, 2006c).

The SRH's proposals on operationalizing the right to health have been agenda-setting. Challenges remain, above all in relation to the contours of a human rights-based approach to prioritization, but there have been pioneering reports spanning topics such as health financing (UN General Assembly 2012), the development of indicators and benchmarks as tools to monitor progressive realization of the right to health (Commission on Human Rights 2006b), and human rights impact assessments (UN General Assembly 2007). Relatedly, both Dainius Pūras, the current SRH, and Paul Hunt, the first SRH, have drawn a distinction between judicial and policy-oriented processes (HRC 2015b; Hunt and Leader 2010), which has helped to ensure that the SRH has contributed not just to how judges should, and can, enforce the right to health but also to more forward-looking initiatives aimed at strengthening health systems (UN General Assembly 2004, 2016d). This, in turn, has been a welcome counterweight to a tendency of human rights scholars to focus on judicial enforceability of the right to health.

Agenda-setting can be seen in other parts of the SRH's work too, and it is often allied with iterative efforts (e.g., making an issue a priority theme, or simply returning to it repeatedly). The first SRH was, for instance, the first UN expert who framed sexual and reproductive health as a human right (Commission on Human Rights 2004b). Other agenda-setting moves include the current SRH's focus on mental health (e.g., HRC 2017b), and his predecessor's direct challenge to criminalization as a key tool of international drug control (UN General Assembly 2010a).

The SRH has also challenged silos, as explained below, notably the tendency to focus either on states or on non-state actors, and the tendency to think largely in terms of legal enforceability. The SRH has regularly emphasized the *cooperation* that is required between various state and non-state actors to realize the right to health (HRC 2008b), thereby reflecting a widely held view on the need for partnerships in global health (Gostin 2014; Fried et al. 2010; Helble et al. 2009; Koplan et al. 2009). These efforts have engaged extensively with both state duties for the right to health *and* the responsibilities of non-state actors. This engagement has occurred by means of thematic and country reports and also by means of the communications system. The first SRH's first "country" report was "the first of its kind" (Hunt 2017, 342): it reported on a mission to the WTO (Commission on Human Rights 2004a), which, as also mentioned in chapter 17, presented one of the first-ever occasions on which trade experts were explicitly engaged in a discussion about the human right to health and the health implications of trade law and policies. The report highlighted how trade impacts the enjoyment of the right to health in numerous ways and called on state and non-state actors to redouble their efforts to make sure that the trade rules and policies they adopt and support are consistent with their legal obligations in relation to the right to health—in particular, that these rules and policies do not undermine the health rights of persons living in poverty or of other disadvantaged groups (Commission on Human Rights 2004a).

Taking up issues of economic governance, the second SRH, Anand Grover, discussed the unbalanced international legal regime for the protection of foreign direct investment, analyzing how investment agreements "allow transnational corporations to reduce states' policy space" with respect to public health (UN General Assembly 2014c, para. 48). Grover also engaged with the Agreement on Trade-Related Aspects of Intellectual Property (TRIPS) and free trade agreements or bilateral investment treaties containing so-called TRIPS-plus requirements (HRC 2009b).

The SRH has also produced agenda-setting thematic and "country" reports on the right of access to essential medicines. Two reports explore the primary obligations of states of jurisdiction, detailing steps (including legislation) that states shall take to ensure that individuals have access to essential medicines (UN General Assembly 2006; HRC 2013a). These reports also explore the responsibilities of pharmaceutical companies: they analyze the scope and content of pharmaceutical companies' responsibilities under the right to health in relation to state duties (UN General Assembly 2006); develop Human Rights Guidelines for Pharmaceutical Companies in relation to Access to Medicines (UN General Assembly 2008); and apply these Guidelines during a mission to GlaxoSmithKline. Concrete recommendations are also included, focusing on how pharmaceutical companies can discharge their responsibilities in the area of pricing, patents and licensing, and research and development (HRC 2009c; Grover et al. 2012; Lee and Hunt 2012).[4]

The SRH has furthermore investigated individual complaints that have been brought not only against states but also against non-state actors for alleged violations of the right to health. For example, when the first SRH received a complaint regarding the decision of the Global Fund to Fight AIDS, Tuberculosis and Malaria to terminate grants to Myanmar, he sent letters to the Global Fund, expressing his concerns that this decision would severely undermine the enjoyment of the right to health of people most vulnerable to AIDS, tuberculosis, and malaria (Commission on Human Rights 2005e; HRC 2007e; Hunt 2017).

III. BEYOND THE MANDATE ON THE RIGHT TO HEALTH: TOWARD A HUMAN RIGHTS-BASED APPROACH TO HEALTH

In "peopling" human rights law in order to "people" global health (Biehl and Petryna 2014), it is important to focus not just on the SRH but on other Special Procedures too. There are two reasons for this: first, as discussed in chapter 1, a human rights-based approach to health extends beyond the right to health and beyond human rights related to the underlying determinants of health. Second, examining the Special Procedures as a whole allows them to be assessed as a "system." This means that strengths and weaknesses of the system can be explored, both in general and in terms of whether and how the system contributes to global health. Above all, "seeing the system" paves the way for a different—improved—understanding of human rights law within global health. It demonstrates in particular that human rights law cannot—and should not—be examined through a conventional law lens. Deliberation with input from an array of actors and allied to a keen sense of strategy, is what dominates and is, thus, what needs to be drawn out and embraced. In what follows, this claim is defended using examples that show (a) how the Special Procedures persuade in the absence of formal enforcement powers; (b) how they pursue challenging issues; and (c) how they explore new terrain relevant to human rights-based approaches to health.

A. Persuasion

Persuasion has multiple dimensions. Cooperation, not surprisingly, is sought and valued. As the first Special Rapporteur on the human right to safe drinking water and sanitation pointed out, whether dealing with violations or with promotion and implementation, it is necessary to see states "primarily as partners, not as adversaries" (Winkler and de Albuquerque 2017, 203). And, while a shortfall in state cooperation continues to be a major challenge to the system, mandate-holders

---

4. A recent SRH report explores concrete responsibilities for the right to health within the food and beverage industry, aiming in particular to ensure that diet-related, noncommunicable disease burdens are significantly reduced (HRC 2014).

have shown an ability to hold their ground and seek a "workaround." One example would be the joint report on Guantánamo Bay, which was developed without an on-site visit because the five mandate-holders involved, including the SRH, refused to accept the restrictions of the United States on private interviews with detainees (Commission on Human Rights 2006a).

Sometimes a mandate-holder will be seeking to persuade states, and others too, of the need for a formal legal response. At the beginning of her mandate, the Independent Expert on human rights obligations related to access to safe drinking water and sanitation concentrated on advocacy for explicit recognition of the human right to water and sanitation by the UN General Assembly and the HRC. That recognition was achieved in 2010 (UN General Assembly 2010b; HRC 2010a), at which point the mandate-holder scaled up her focus on implementation.[5] In a similar vein, the Special Rapporteur on the right to food and the Special Rapporteur on toxic substances recently issued a joint call for a new international treaty to regulate and phase out the use of dangerous pesticides, pointing to research which shows that pesticides cause an estimated 200,000 acute poisoning deaths each year, with the vast majority of these deaths occurring in developing countries (HRC 2017c).

Special Procedures mandate-holders also seek to persuade by means of soft law, typically by developing guiding principles on a particular right or area. Earlier in this chapter, the SRH's Guiding Principles on the access-to-medicines obligations of pharmaceutical companies were discussed; other examples relevant to global health include the Guiding Principles on extreme poverty and human rights (HRC 2012a) and the Guiding Principles on human rights impact assessments of trade and investment agreements (HRC 2011b). Implementation guidance is another popular choice among the Special Procedures, in part because mandate-holders are deeply conscious of the need to make human rights "real." For example, at the end of her mandate, the first Special Rapporteur on water and sanitation published an implementation handbook, which drew on engagements with local actors such as regulators, line ministries, and national human rights institutions (de Albuquerque 2014). Elsewhere there is greater emphasis on underlying structural critique: the first three mandate-holders on housing, for instance, paid particular attention to the ways in which current socioeconomic arrangements lead inexorably to violations of the right to housing (Hohmann 2017).

It is easy to be skeptical about this focus on persuasion, but there is evidence of success. One example would be the ways in which the wide-ranging, detailed studies of the Special Rapporteur on violence against women have contributed to the recognition of violence against women as a human rights issue, imposing specific obligations on states (HRC 2009d). Moreover, the Special Procedures seem increasingly skilled at persuasion, in particular in their efforts to deploy coordination and follow-up. Coordination could involve writing a report on intersections between the right to housing and the right to life, which examines the public health implications of the right to housing (UN General Assembly 2016b). Or it could

---

5. The mandate was also extended and renamed "Special Rapporteur on the human right to safe drinking water and sanitation" (HRC 2011c).

involve writing a joint briefing note, or a report, which seeks to develop the concept of a social protection floor, as pioneered by the International Labor Organization (De Schutter and Sepúlveda 2012; UN General Assembly 2014b). It could also mean developing an idea introduced by another mandate-holder, say the 4A framework—availability, accessibility, acceptability, and adaptability—associated with Katarina Tomaševski's tenure as Special Rapporteur on the right to education (Commission on Human Rights 1999). Each of these efforts helps to strengthen the case for taking a broader human rights-based approach to particular issues, as opposed to focusing only on one particular human right—whether the right to health, life, food, housing, or water, or the right not to be subjected to cruel, inhuman, or degrading treatment.

It is also easy to be skeptical about follow-up, but there have been notable successes. A recent example emerges from mandate-holders' work on the responsibility of the UN for the 2010 cholera outbreak in Haiti, which has been traced to poor sanitation practices by a cohort of UN peacekeepers (UN General Assembly 2016c). A 2016 report from the Special Rapporteur on human rights and extreme poverty challenged the UN to do more, describing the organization's ongoing refusal to accept legal responsibility as "morally unconscionable, legally indefensible . . . politically self-defeating [and] entirely unnecessary" (Ibid., para. 3). The report was part of a series of efforts by a broader group of Special Procedures, including the SRH (Farha et al. 2014), and it was followed up in an open letter from the Special Rapporteur on human rights and extreme poverty to the Deputy Secretary-General. Shortly thereafter, the UN Secretary-General issued a belated apology and promised money to cholera victims and their families (UN General Assembly 2016a).

B. Pursuing Challenging Issues

In seeking to persuade, and thus to contribute to the recognition and realization of human rights, mandate-holders have refused to shy away from challenging issues and have developed a range of techniques for engaging with such issues. One such technique is repeat-play: taking up, for instance, issues that have been engaged with by other parts of the human rights movement—issues such as the situation of detainees at Guantánamo Bay. Another technique is strategic iteration of assumptions about human rights law. Many critics of human rights law point to a gap between the law "on the books" and the law "in practice": similarly, but with a productive aim in mind, the Special Rapporteur on housing has emphasized that it is time to address the implementation gap on the right to housing (UN General Assembly 2014a, para. 14).

Inclusivity is a further technique. This ranges from mainstreaming a gender perspective (e.g., a former Special Rapporteur on extreme poverty took up the neglected issue of unpaid care work and women's human rights (UN General Assembly 2013)), to making full use of mandates that allow scope for engagement with non-state actors. By way of example, the Special Rapporteur on the issue of human rights obligations relating to the enjoyment of a safe, clean, healthy, and sustainable environment has worked with the NGO Universal Rights Group and a range of other partners, to create a web portal with information and links for environmental human rights defenders.

The Special Procedures have also demonstrated "inclusivity" when taking to task those who fail to protect and promote human rights; there is, in other words, no sense that they see themselves as limited to criticism of states. Recently, for instance, the Special Rapporteur on extreme poverty has been critical of both the World Bank and human rights scholars. He has urged scholars to be more pragmatic, and in particular to pay more attention to the legal recognition of economic, social, and cultural rights, and to ways in which the rising sense of economic insecurity (which now affects large parts of many societies) can best be addressed (UN General Assembly 2017; HRC 2016a). And, as discussed in detail in chapter 16, he has criticized the World Bank for having an approach to human rights that is "incoherent, counterproductive and unsustainable" (UN General Assembly 2015b, para. 4).

C. Toward New Terrain

The third and final illustration concerns the ways in which mandate-holders are agenda-setters, advancing new terrain in rights-based approaches to global health. One recent example is the focus on environmental human rights defenders (UN General Assembly 2016e). Another is the exploration of the potential and challenges of using information and communications technologies to secure the right to life (HRC 2015a; McPherson and Probert 2017).

In a similar vein, a former Special Procedure in the field of cultural rights dedicated two reports to aspects of the long-neglected right to science (UN General Assembly 2015a; HRC 2012b), which may have contributed to the CESCR's current commitment to a new general comment in this area. Equally, the report on abusive practices in health care settings, which was issued by the mandate on torture (HRC 2013c), is a welcome reminder to both the global health and the health and human rights communities that the circumstances of individuals in health care facilities must not be crowded out by a public health emphasis on systems and processes (Ezer 2013; Erdman 2015).

IV. LESSONS FROM THE SPECIAL PROCEDURES SYSTEM FOR HUMAN RIGHTS IN GLOBAL HEALTH

Three global health scholars have recently insisted that "[t]he moment is ripe to revisit the idea of global health" (Frenk, Gómez-Dantés, and Moon 2014, 94). Their argument is simple but compelling: the way in which we understand global health shapes not only what we see as a problem, but how we set about addressing problems. This chapter endorses their argument; it also adds to it, suggesting that the moment is ripe to revisit the ideas of human rights law that circulate among global health proponents. Neither a human rights-based approach to health, nor a narrower approach that aims simply to use the right to health as a normative foundation for global health, will succeed unless a different understanding of human rights law emerges within global health. This different understanding needs to resist the lure of legal enforceability and precisely-worded standards, engaging instead with what can be achieved by means of deliberation, iteration, and inclusivity in a radically pluralist field of law.

This is not to say that the system of Special Procedures is challenge-free; here, too, there are factors that inhibit a human rights-based approach to health. They include the basic challenge of serving many roles at the same time: as one former mandate-holder explains, "a special rapporteur is expected simultaneously to become a human rights activist, a rallying point for human rights, an international diplomat, an academic, and a government adviser" (Subedi 2011, 212). To meet this challenge, there need to be improvements to the processes for selection and appointment of mandate-holders in order to enhance representativeness and secure high-quality candidates; there should also be improvements to the induction and integration of new appointees. Ongoing reflection on what fact-finding involves, and how to craft nonformulaic recommendations that speak to specific contexts, would help too (Alston 2010). Other essentials include: sufficient time to have substantive dialogue with the HRC following the submission of a report; continued improvements to follow-up; and improved funding. "Crowding" needs urgent attention as well; although the Special Procedures have become more adept at coordination, substantial growth in UN and other human rights mechanisms has increased the risk of unhelpful human-rights duplication and disagreement (Evans 2017).

The biggest challenge, however, arises from state non-cooperation with the system of Special Procedures. As explained earlier, states, via the HRC, create and extinguish Special Procedures: but states are also the key focus—target, even—of the Special Procedures, which means that many states are keen on control (Gaer 2017). Political and other pressures ensure that blatant, blanket non-cooperation is rare; mostly, states seek to "pick and choose" (Alston 2011, 573). Thus, they "duck and dive" in terms of which mandates they support and also in issuing invites, agreeing to a visit, and responding to a communication or a report. A range of states has engaged in *ad hominem* attacks on mandate-holders, and there is also evidence of intimidation and reprisal designed to deter cooperation with Special Procedures (Lynch 2017). The latter requires urgent and sustained attention, not least from the HRC: tackling it must not fall to the Special Procedures alone. The broader problem of state non-cooperation also requires sustained attention in a range of forums, including scholarly studies on forms of non-cooperation and on the general question of how to balance the independence and accountability of diverse international human rights actors.

CONCLUSION

The starting point for this chapter was a sense that human rights law is misrepresented by proponents of global health, either because they fail to specify what they expect from this body of law, or because they level a range of unfair criticisms. It was noted, too, that the UN Special Procedures are widely neglected both within global health scholarship and, more surprisingly, within its human rights counterpart. With this in mind, the chapter set about "peopling" human rights law, adding the UN Special Procedures in a way that would contribute, in turn, to the peopling of global health and thereby challenge misrepresentations of human rights law.

The Special Procedures are not, of course, a magic bullet. They are not flaw-free, nor is their future secure. Moreover, empirical studies, both qualitative and quantitative, are needed to test the claims in support of the Special Procedures that have been made in this chapter.

In advance of such studies, this chapter has suggested that global health's representations of human rights law are unfair. They are either impossibly general (invoking only the right to health and doing so in a way that lacks detail) or they develop a critique of human rights law that is clear and sharp—singular even— whereas the world of the Special Procedures has none of these qualities.

On the singular view, the Special Procedures are likely to be neglected, and if they are studied, they are likely to be cast as hopelessly informal, even frail. This chapter has proposed a different view, one that describes the Special Procedures via their history, their purposes and practices (including their interactions with a range of other actors), and their aspirations. In so doing, it has set aside the all-too-obvious attractions of a conventional law lens and focused instead on what has been achieved by means of deliberation, iteration, and inclusivity, allied with a keen sense of strategy. And, most importantly, it has insisted that this different understanding of human rights law has to be taken seriously if a human rights-based approach to global health is to have any chance of success.

REFERENCES

Alston, Philip. 2010. "The Challenges of Responding to Extrajudicial Executions: Interview with Philip Alston." *Journal of Human Rights Practice* 2: 355–373.

Alston, Philip. 2011. "Hobbling the Monitors: Should U.N. Human Rights Monitors Be Accountable?" *Harvard International Law Journal* 52: 561–649.

Biehl, João and Adriana Petryna. 2014. "Peopling Global Health." *Saúde Soc São Paulo* 23: 376–389.

CESCR (Committee on Economic, Social and Cultural Rights). 2000. "General Comment no. 14 on the right to the highest attainable standard of health (art. 12)." 11 August. UN Doc. E/C.12/2000/4.

Commission on Human Rights. 1947. "Report to the Economic and Social Council on the First Session of the Commission held at Lake Success, New York, from 10 January to 10 February 1947." UN Doc. E/259 Supp.

Commission on Human Rights. 1999. "Preliminary report of the Special Rapporteur on the right to education, Ms. Katarina Tomasevski, submitted in accordance with Commission on Human Rights resolution 1998/33." 13 January. UN Doc. E/CN.4/1999/49.

Commission on Human Rights. 2002. "The right of everyone to the enjoyment of the highest attainable standard of physical and mental health." 22 April. UN Doc. E/CN.4/RES/2002/31.

Commission on Human Rights. 2004a. "Report of the Special Rapporteur, Paul Hunt, Addendum, Mission to the World Trade Organization." 1 March. UN Doc. E/CN.4/2004/49/Add.1.

Commission on Human Rights. 2004b. "The right of everyone to the enjoyment of the highest attainable standard of physical and mental health Report of the Special Rapporteur, Paul Hunt." 16 February. UN Doc. E/CN.4/2004/49.

Commission on Human Rights. 2005a. "Report of the meeting of the special rapporteurs/representatives/experts and chairpersons of working groups of the special procedures of the Commission on Human Rights and of the advisory services programme 20–24 June 2005." 3 August. UN Doc. E/CN.4/2006/4.

Commission on Human Rights. 2005b. "Report submitted by the Special Rapporteur on the right of everyone to the highest attainable standard of physical and mental health, Paul Hunt, Addendum, Mission to Peru." 4 February. UN Doc. E/CN.4/2005/51/Add.3.

Commission on Human Rights. 2005c. "Report submitted by the Special Rapporteur on the right of everyone to the highest attainable standard of physical and mental health, Paul Hunt, Addendum, Mission to Romania." 21 February. UN Doc. E/CN.4/2005/51/Add.4.

Commission on Human Rights. 2005d. "The right of everyone to the enjoyment of the highest attainable standard of physical and mental health, Report of the Special Rapporteur, Paul Hunt, Addendum, Mission to Mozambique." 4 January. UN Doc. E/CN.4/2005/51/Add.2.

Commission on Human Rights. 2005e. "Report of the Special Rapporteur on the right of everyone to the enjoyment of the highest attainable standard of physical and mental health, Paul Hunt, Addendum, Summary of communications sent to and replies received from Governments and other actors, December 2004–December 2005." 22 December. UN Doc. E/CN.4/2006/48/Add.1.

Commission on Human Rights. 2006a. "Report of the Chairperson-Rapporteur of the Working Group on Arbitrary Detention, Leila Zerrougui; the Special Rapporteur on the independence of judges and lawyers, Leandro Despouy; the Special Rapporteur on torture and other cruel, inhuman or degrading treatment or punishment, Manfred Nowak; the Special Rapporteur on freedom of religion or belief, Asma Jahangir; and the Special Rapporteur on the right of everyone to the enjoyment of the highest attainable standard of physical and mental health, Paul Hunt: Situation of detainees at Guantánamo Bay." 27 February. UN Doc. E/CN.4/2006/120.

Commission on Human Rights. 2006b. "Report of the Special Rapporteur on the right of everyone to the enjoyment of the highest attainable standard of physical and mental health, Paul Hunt." 3 March. UN Doc. E/CN.4/2006/48.

Commission on Human Rights. 2006c. "Report of the Special Rapporteur on the right of everyone to the enjoyment of the highest attainable standard of physical and mental health, Paul Hunt, Addendum, Mission to Uganda." 19 January. UN Doc. E/CN.4/2006/48/Add.2.

de Albuquerque, Catarina. 2014. "Realising the Human Rights to Water and Sanitation: A Handbook by the UN Special Rapporteur." Accessed June 25, 2017. http://www.ohchr.org/EN/Issues/WaterAndSanitation/SRWater/Pages/Handbook.aspx.

de Búrca, Gráinne. 2017. "Human Rights Experimentalism." *American Journal of International Law* 117: 277–316.

de Frouville. 2017. "Working Out a Working Group: A View from a Former Working Group Member." In *The United Nations Special Procedures System*, edited by Aoife Nolan, Rosa Freedman, and Thérèse Murphy, 223–260. Leiden: Brill Nijhoff.

De Schutter, Olivier and Magdalena Sepúlveda. 2012. "Underwriting the Poor: A Global Fund for Social Protection." Briefing Note 07.

ECOSOC (Economic and Social Council). 1947. "Res 75 (V)." 5 August. UN Doc. E/RES/75 (V).

ECOSOC (Economic and Social Council). 1967. "Res 1235 (XLII)." 6 June. UN Doc. E/4393.

Erdman, Joanna N. 2015. "Bioethics, Human Rights, and Childbirth." *Health and Human Rights Journal* 17: 43–51.

Evans, Malcolm. 2017. "The UN Special Rapporteur on Torture in the Developing Architecture of UN Torture Protection." In *The United Nations Special Procedures System*, edited by Aoife Nolan, Rosa Freedman, and Thérèse Murphy, 351–384. Leiden: Brill Nijhoff.

Ezer, Tamar. 2013. "Special Issue: Human Rights in Patient Care." *Health and Human Rights Journal* 15: 5–79.

Farha, Leilani, Gustavo Gallón, Dainius Pūras, and Catarina de Albuquerque. 2014. "Letter to UN Secretary-General Ban Ki-moon (25 September 2014)." Accessed June 25, 2017. Available at: http://www.scribd.com/document/261396799/SR-Allegation-Letter-2014.

Freedman, Rosa and Jacob Mchangama. 2016. "Expanding or Diluting Human Rights? The Proliferation of United Nations Special Procedures Mandates." *Human Rights Quarterly* 38: 164–193.

Frenk Julio, Octavio Gómez-Dantés, and Suerie Moon. 2014. "From Sovereignty to Solidarity: A Renewed Concept of Global Health for an Era of Complex Interdependence." *The Lancet* 383: 94–97.

Fried, Linda P., Margaret E. Bentley, Pierre Buekens, Donald S. Burke, Julio J. Frenk, Michael J. Klag, and Harrison C. Spencer. 2010. "Global Health Is Public Health." *The Lancet* 375: 535–537.

Gaer, Felice D. 2014. "The High Commissioners and the Special Procedures: Colleagues and Competitors." In *The United Nations High Commissioner for Human Rights: Conscience for the World*, edited by Felice D. Gaer and Christen L. Broecker, 131–156. Leiden: Brill Nijhoff.

Gaer, Felice D. 2017. "Picking and Choosing? Country Visits by Thematic Special Procedures." In *The United Nations Special Procedures System*, edited by Aoife Nolan, Rosa Freedman, and Thérèse Murphy, 87–130. Leiden: Brill Nijhoff.

Gostin, Lawrence O. 2014. *Global Health Law.* Cambridge, Mass.: Harvard University Press.

Grover, Anand, Brian Citro, Mihir Kankad, and Fiona Lander. 2012. "Pharmaceutical Companies and Global Lack of Access to Medicines: Strengthening Accountability under the Right to Health." *Journal of Law, Medicine & Ethics* 40: 234–250.

Helble, Matthias, Emily Mok, Benedikte Dal, Nusaraporn Kessomboon, and Nick Drager. 2009. "International Trade and Health: Loose Governance Arrangements across Sectors." In *Making Sense of Global Health Governance: A Policy Perspective*, edited by Kent Buse, Wolfgang Hein, and Nick Drager, 164–208. Basingstoke: Palgrave Macmillan.

Hohmann, Jessie. 2017. "Principle, Politics and Practice: The Role of UN Special Rapporteurs on the Right to Adequate Housing in the Development of the Right to Housing in International Law." In *The United Nations Special Procedures System*, edited by Aoife Nolan, Rosa Freedman, and Thérèse Murphy, 271–296. Leiden: Brill Nijhoff.

HRC (Human Rights Council). 2007a. "Follow-up to Human Rights Council Resolution 5/1." 27 September. Decision 6/102.

HRC (Human Rights Council). 2007b. "Institution-building of the UN Human Rights Council." 18 June. UN Doc. A/HRC/RES/5/1, appendix.

HRC (Human Rights Council). 2007c. "Report of the Human Rights Council, 5th Sess., June 11–18, 2007, UN GAOR, 62d Sess." 18 June. UN Doc. A/HRC/RES/5/2.

HRC (Human Rights Council). 2007d. "Report of the Special Rapporteur on the right of everyone to the enjoyment of the highest attainable standard of physical and mental health, Paul Hunt, Addendum, Mission to Sweden." 28 February. UN Doc. A/HRC/4/28/Add.2.

HRC (Human Rights Council). 2007e. "Report of the Special Rapporteur on the right of everyone to the enjoyment of the highest attainable standard of physical and mental health, Paul Hunt: Summary of cases transmitted to Governments and replies received." 23 February. UN Doc. A/HRC/4/28/Add.1.

HRC (Human Rights Council). 2007f. "Right of everyone to the enjoyment of the highest attainable standard of physical and mental health." 14 December. UN Doc. A/HRC/RES/6/29.

HRC (Human Rights Council). 2008a. "Report of the Special Rapporteur on the right of everyone to the enjoyment of the highest attainable standard of physical and mental health, Paul Hunt." 31 January. UN Doc. A/HRC/7/11.

HRC (Human Rights Council). 2008b. "Report of the Special Rapporteur on the right of everyone to the enjoyment of the highest attainable standard of physical and mental health, Paul Hunt, Addendum, Missions to the World Bank and the International Monetary Fund in Washington, D.C. (20 October 2006) and Uganda (4–7 February 2007)." 5 March. UN Doc. A/HRC/7/11/Add.2.

HRC (Human Rights Council). 2009a. "Enhancement of the system of special procedures." 12 June. UN Doc. A/HRC/11/L.8.

HRC (Human Rights Council). 2009b. "Report of the Special Rapporteur on the right of everyone to the enjoyment of the highest attainable standard of physical and mental health, Anand Grover." 31 March. UN Doc. A/HRC/11/12.

HRC (Human Rights Council). 2009c. "Report of the Special Rapporteur on the right of everyone to the enjoyment of the highest attainable standard of health, Paul Hunt, Annex, Mission to GlaxoSmithKline." 5 May. UN Doc. A/HRC/11/12/Add.2.

HRC (Human Rights Council). 2009d. "Report of the Special Rapporteur on violence against women, its causes and consequences, Yakin Ertürk, Addendum, 15 Years of the United Nations Special Rapporteur on violence against women, its causes and consequences (1994–2009)—A Critical Review." 27 May. UN Doc. A/HRC/11/6/Add.5.

HRC (Human Rights Council). 2010a. Res 15/9. 6 October. UN Doc. A/HRC/RES/15/9.

HRC (Human Rights Council). 2010b. "The right of everyone to the enjoyment of the highest attainable standard of physical and mental health." 6 October. UN Doc. A/HRC/RES/15/22.

HRC (Human Rights Council). 2011a. "Report of the Special Rapporteur on the right of everyone to the enjoyment of the highest attainable standard of physical and mental health, Anand Grover, Addendum, Mission to Guatemala." 16 March. UN Doc. A/HRC/17/25/Add.2.

HRC (Human Rights Council). 2011b. "Report of the Special Rapporteur on the right to food, Olivier De Schutter, Addendum, Guiding principles on human rights impact assessments of trade and investment agreements." 19 December. UN Doc. A/HRC/19/59/Add.5.

HRC (Human Rights Council). 2011c. "Res 16/2." 8 April. UN Doc. A/HRC/RES/16/2.

HRC (Human Rights Council). 2012a. "Final draft of the guiding principles on extreme poverty and human rights, submitted by the Special Rapporteur on extreme poverty and human rights, Magdalena Sepúlveda Carmona" 18 July. UN Doc. A/HRC/21/39.

HRC (Human Rights Council). 2012b. "Report of the Special Rapporteur in the field of cultural rights, Farida Shaheed: The right to enjoy the benefits of scientific progress and its applications." 14 May. UN Doc. A/HRC/20/26.

HRC (Human Rights Council). 2012c. "Report of the Special Rapporteur on the right of everyone to the enjoyment of the highest attainable standard of physical and mental health, Anand Grover, Addendum, Mission to Ghana." 10 April. UN Doc. A/HRC/20/15/Add.1.

HRC (Human Rights Council). 2013a. "Report of the Special Rapporteur on the right of everyone to the enjoyment of the highest attainable standard of physical and mental health, Anand Grover, on access to medicines." 1 May. UN Doc. A/HRC/23/42.

HRC (Human Rights Council). 2013b. "The right of everyone to the enjoyment of the highest attainable standard of physical and mental health." 8 October. UN Doc. A/HRC/RES/24/6.

HRC (Human Rights Council). 2013c. "Report of the Special Rapporteur on torture and other cruel, inhuman or degrading treatment or punishment, Juan E. Méndez." 1 February. UN Doc. A/HRC/22/53.

HRC (Human Rights Council). 2014. "Report of the Special Rapporteur on the right of everyone to the enjoyment of the highest attainable standard of physical and mental health, Anand Grover, Unhealthy foods, non-communicable diseases and the right to health." 1 April. UN Doc. A/HRC/26/31.

HRC (Human Rights Council). 2015a. "Report of the Special Rapporteur on extrajudicial, summary or arbitrary executions, Christof Heyns." 24 April. UN Doc. A/HRC/29/37.

HRC (Human Rights Council). 2015b. "Report of the Special Rapporteur on the right of everyone to the enjoyment of the highest attainable standard of physical and mental health, Dainius Pūras." 2 April. UN Doc. A/HRC/29/33.

HRC (Human Rights Council). 2016a. "Report of the Special Rapporteur on extreme poverty and human rights." 28 April. UN Doc. A/HRC/32/31.

HRC (Human Rights Council). 2016b. "Report of the Special Rapporteur on the right of everyone to the enjoyment of the highest attainable standard of physical and mental health on his visit to Paraguay." 24 May. UN Doc. A/HRC/32/32/Add.1.

HRC (Human Rights Council). 2016c. "Report of the 22nd annual meeting of special rapporteurs/representatives, independent experts and working groups of the special procedures of the Human Rights Council (Geneva, 8–12 June 2015), including updated information on the special procedures." 23 May. UN Doc. A/HRC/31/39.

HRC (Human Rights Council). 2017a. "Facts and figures with regard to special procedures in 2016." 31 January. UN Doc. A/HRC/34/34/Add.1.

HRC (Human Rights Council). 2017b. "Report of the Special Rapporteur on the right of everyone to the enjoyment of the highest attainable standard of physical and mental health." 28 March. UN Doc. A/HRC/35/21.

HRC (Human Rights Council). 2017c. "Report of the Special Rapporteur on the right to food." 24 January. A/HRC/34/48.

HRC (Human Rights Council). 2017d. "Report on the twenty-third annual meeting of special rapporteurs/representatives, independent experts and chairpersons of working groups of the special procedures of the Human Rights Council (Geneva, 6 to 10 June 2016), including updated information on special procedures." 31 January. UN Doc. A/HRC/34/34.

Hunt, Paul. 2017. "The Challenge of Non-state Actors: The Experience of the UN Special Rapporteur on the Right to the Highest Attainable Standard of Health (2002–08)." In *The United Nations Special Procedures System*, edited by Aoife Nolan, Rosa Freedman, and Thérèse Murphy, 336–350. Leiden: Brill Nijhoff.

Hunt, Paul and Sheldon Leader. 2010. "Developing and Applying the Right to the Highest Attainable Standard of Health: The Role of the UN Special Rapporteur." In *Global Health and Human Rights: Philosophical and Legal Perspectives*, edited by John Harrington and Maria Stuttaford, 28–61. Abingdon: Routledge.

ISHR (International Service for Human Rights) et al. 2017. *The Special Procedures: Developments in Institutional Strengthening and Working Methods—A joint civil society submission to the 24th annual meeting of Special Procedures of the UN Human Rights Council*. International Service for Human Rights.

Koplan, Jeffrey P., T. Christopher Bond, Michael H. Merson, K. Srinath Reddy, Mario Henry Rodriguez, Nelson K. Sewankombo, and Judith N. Wasserheit. 2009. "Towards a Common Definition of Global Health." *The Lancet* 373: 1993–1995.

Lee, Joo-Young and Paul Hunt. 2012. "Human Rights Responsibilities of Pharmaceutical Companies in Relation to Access to Medicine." *Journal of Law, Medicine and Ethics* 40: 220–233.

Limon, Marc and Ted Piccone. 2014. "Human Rights Special Procedures: Determinants of Influence." Universal Rights Group. Accessed June 25, 2017. http://www.universal-rights.org/urg-policy-reports/special-procedures-determinants-of-influence/.

Limon, Marc and Hilary Power. 2014. "History of the United Nations Special Procedures Mechanism: Origins, Evolution and Reform." Universal Rights Group. Accessed June 25, 2017. http://www.universal-rights.org/urg-policy-reports/history-of-the-united-nations-special-procedures-mechanism-origins-evolution-and-reform/.

Lynch, Phil. 2017. "Ending Reprisals: The Role and Responsibilities of the Special Procedures of the UN Human Rights Council." In *The United Nations Special Procedures System*, edited by Aoife Nolan, Rosa Freedman, and Thérèse Murphy, 443–450. Leiden: Brill Nijhoff.

"Manual of Operations of the Special Procedures of the Human Rights Council." 2008. Accessed June 25, 2017. http://www.ohchr.org/Documents/HRBodies/SP/Manual_Operations2008.pdf.

McCrudden, Christopher. 2017. "Is the Principal Function of International Human Rights Law to Address the Pathologies of International Law? A Comment on Patrick Macklem's 'The Sovereignty of Human Rights.'" *University of Toronto Law Journal* 64: 623–636.

McPherson, Ella and Thomas Probert. 2017. "Special Procedures in the Digital Age." In *The United Nations Special Procedures System,* edited by Aoife Nolan, Rosa Freedman, and Thérèse Murphy, 261–270. Leiden: Brill Nijhoff.

Milewicz, Karolina and Robert E. Goodin. 2016. "Deliberative Capacity-Building through International Organizations: The Case of the Universal Periodic Review of Human Rights." *British Journal of Political Science* 46: 1–21.

OHCHR (Office of the High Commissioner for Human Rights). 2017. "Special Procedures of the Human Rights Council: Introduction." Accessed June 25, 2017. http://www.ohchr.org/EN/HRBodies/SP/Pages/Welcomepage.aspx.

Piccone, Ted. 2012. "Catalysts for Change: How the UN's Independent Experts Promote Human Rights." Washington D.C.: Brookings Institution Press.

Pillay, Navi. 2015. "The United Nations Human Rights Council: Remarks on Its History, Procedures, Challenges and Perspectives." In *The Special Procedures of the Human Rights Council: A Brief Look from the Inside and Perspectives from Outside,* edited by Humberto Cantú Rivera, 1–24. Cambridge: Intersentia.

Shaheed, Ahmed and Rose Parris Richter. 2017. "Coping Mechanisms for State Non-cooperation." In *The United Nations Special Procedures System,* edited by Aoife Nolan, Rosa Freedman, and Thérèse Murphy, 155–187. Leiden: Brill Nijhoff.

Subedi, Surya P. 2011. "Protection of Human Rights through the Mechanism of UN Special Rapporteurs." *Human Rights Quarterly* 33: 201–228.

Tasioulas, John and Effy Vayena. 2016. "The Place of Human Rights and the Common Good in Global Health Policy." *Theoretical Medicine & Bioethics* 37: 365–382.

UN General Assembly. 2004. "The right of everyone to the enjoyment of the highest attainable standard of physical and mental health." 8 October. UN Doc. A/59/422.

UN General Assembly. 2005. "Report of the Special Rapporteur of the Commission on Human Rights on the right of everyone to the enjoyment of the highest attainable standard of physical and mental health, Paul Hunt, submitted in accordance with Commission resolution 2005/24." 12 September. UN Doc. A/60/348.

UN General Assembly. 2006. "Report of the Special Rapporteur on the right of everyone to the enjoyment of the highest attainable standard of physical and mental health." 13 September. UN Doc. A/61/338.

UN General Assembly. 2007. "Report of the Special Rapporteur on the right of everyone to the enjoyment of the highest attainable standard of physical and mental health." 8 August. UN Doc. A/62/214.

UN General Assembly. 2008. "Report of the Special Rapporteur on the right of everyone to the enjoyment of the highest attainable standard of physical and mental health." 11 August. UN Doc. A/63/263.

UN General Assembly. 2010a. "Report of the Special Rapporteur on the right of everyone to the enjoyment of the highest attainable standard of physical and mental health." 6 August. UN Doc. A/65/255.

UN General Assembly. 2010b. "Res 64/292." 3 August. UN Doc. A/RES/64/292.

UN General Assembly. 2011. "Interim report of the Special Rapporteur on the right of everyone to the enjoyment of the highest attainable standard of physical and mental health." 3 August. UN Doc. A/66/254.

UN General Assembly. 2012. "Interim report of the Special Rapporteur on the right of everyone to the enjoyment of the highest attainable standard of physical and mental health." 13 August. UN Doc. A/67/302.

UN General Assembly. 2013. "Report of the Special Rapporteur on extreme poverty and human rights." 9 August. UN Doc. A/68/293.

UN General Assembly. 2014a. "Report of the Special Rapporteur on adequate housing as a component of the right to an adequate standard of living, and on the right to non-discrimination in this context." 7 August. UN Doc. A/69/274.

UN General Assembly. 2014b. "Report of the Special Rapporteur on extreme poverty and human rights." 11 August. UN Doc. A/69/297.

UN General Assembly. 2014c. "Report of the Special Rapporteur on the right of everyone to the enjoyment of the highest attainable standard of physical and mental health." 11 August. UN Doc. A/69/299.

UN General Assembly. 2015a. "Report of the Special Rapporteur in the field of cultural rights." 4 August. UN Doc. A/70/279.

UN General Assembly. 2015b. "Report of the Special Rapporteur on extreme poverty and human rights." 4 August. UN Doc. A/70/274.

UN General Assembly. 2016a. "A new approach to cholera in Haiti: Report by the Secretary-General." 25 November. UN Doc. A/71/620.

UN General Assembly. 2016b. "Report of the Special Rapporteur on adequate housing as a component of the right to an adequate standard of living, and on the right to non-discrimination in this context." 8 August. UN Doc. A/71/310.

UN General Assembly. 2016c. "Report of the Special Rapporteur on extreme poverty and human rights." 26 August. UN Doc. A/71/367.

UN General Assembly. 2016d. "Report of the Special Rapporteur on the right of everyone to the enjoyment of the highest attainable standard of physical and mental health." 5 August. UN Doc. A/71/304.

UN General Assembly. 2016e. "Report of the Special Rapporteur on the situation of human right defenders." 3 August. UN Doc. A/71/281.

UN General Assembly. 2017. "Report of the Special Rapporteur on extreme poverty and human rights." 22 March. UN Doc. A.HRC/35/26.

White, Lucie E. and Jeremy Perelman. 2011. *Stones of Hope: How African Activists Reclaim Human Rights to Challenge Global Poverty*. Stanford, Calif.: Stanford University Press.

Winkler, Inga T. and Catarina de Albuquerque. 2017. "Doing It All and Doing It Well? A Mandate's Challenges in Terms of Cooperation, Fundraising and Maintaining Independence." In *The United Nations Special Procedures System*, edited by Aoife Nolan, Rosa Freedman, and Thérèse Murphy, 188–222. Leiden: Brill Nijhoff.

23

Human Rights Treaty Bodies

Monitoring, Interpreting, and Adjudicating Health-Related Human Rights

BENJAMIN MASON MEIER AND VIRGÍNIA BRÁS GOMES[*]

Despite a dramatic increase in state ratification of human rights treaties, studies have continued to show an ambiguous causal relationship between treaty ratification and public health realization, leading to the conclusion that health-related human rights implementation requires independent international supervision to translate international human rights law into national public health practice. Human rights treaty bodies monitor, interpret, and adjudicate issues of state implementation under the core international human rights treaties, facilitating accountability for rights realization in health policy. Composed of independent experts, treaty bodies have an international legal mandate to supervise state implementation of human rights obligations for public health. With each core human rights treaty having its own corresponding human rights treaty body, these international institutions employ a range of distinct working methods to perform three interconnected functions:

1. monitoring state reports on the implementation of rights within their treaty purview;
2. interpreting treaty provisions through general comments, recommendations, or statements; and
3. adjudicating individual complaints relevant to their monitoring mandate.[1]

[*] The authors are grateful to Hanna Huffstetler for her dedicated research assistance throughout the development of this chapter and to Christen Broecker and Vincent Ploton for their thoughtful comments on early drafts.

1. There is also an interstate complaint system, although no state has brought a complaint against another state through the human rights treaty monitoring system. In lieu of treaty body adjudication

This human rights supervisory role has widespread influence in pressing states to take action to realize rights across a range of public health issues.

This chapter analyzes the role of human rights treaty bodies in monitoring, interpreting, and adjudicating health-related human rights obligations. As a basis for human rights accountability to promote global health, Part I chronicles the history of the treaty body system, examining the birth of treaty institutions and the creation of treaty bodies to oversee core international human rights treaties. Part II reviews both the contemporary composition and evolving functions of these treaty bodies, describing treaty body efforts to monitor state implementation, interpret treaty provisions, and adjudicate individual complaints—with case studies to highlight health-related efforts across treaty body mechanisms. Assessing the impact of this human rights governance to global health advancement, Part III looks at the effectiveness of treaty bodies in facilitating the implementation of human rights for global health, considering ongoing efforts to strengthen and streamline the work of treaty bodies. The chapter concludes by recognizing the vital role of treaty bodies in structuring the realization of health-related human rights and, given this impact on global health, advocating the expansion of public health participation in the practice of treaty bodies.

I. BIRTH OF THE TREATY BODY SYSTEM

States have always envisioned treaty bodies as a necessary part of human rights realization, developing supervisory procedures through the United Nations (UN) to facilitate accountability for human rights implementation. Prior to the adoption of the first human rights treaty, it was recognized that states party to a treaty would need "encouragement and assistance" to implement their international rights obligations (Rodley 2003). Even as their utility has been challenged by procedural backlogs and calls for reform, the underlying need to review treaty implementation, guide states parties, and facilitate accountability remains unchanged.

Influenced by the proliferation of human rights treaties over the years, as well as contentious developments in international relations following World War II, the specific functions of the treaty bodies have evolved dramatically over time. As the first treaty bodies were established throughout the 1960s, their early work was impaired by the political, ideological, and economic divides of the Cold War (Snyder 2014). Where attention to human rights was often inconsistent, across rights and throughout the world, early treaty bodies were seen as ineffective in influencing human rights implementation (Bayefsky 1996). The end of the Cold War provided the UN with an unprecedented opportunity to develop new procedures, and as a result of efforts to improve, harmonize, and streamline their working methods, treaty bodies have become more effective in both interpreting their respective underlying treaty and monitoring state implementation of human rights obligations (OHCHR 2014).

As participation in the UN treaty system has increased, the role of treaty bodies to prevent and remedy human rights violations has expanded (Bayefsky 2001). There are currently ten UN human rights treaty bodies that monitor the implementation

of interstate complaints, treaty bodies (on rare occasions) have referred interstate disputes to the International Court of Justice.

of core international human rights treaties.[2] With all UN member states having ratified at least one core international human rights treaty (with 80 percent having ratified four or more treaties), the influence of these treaty bodies is expected to grow in the years to come (OHCHR 2017). Figure 23.1 chronicles when each of the human rights treaties was adopted, when their corresponding treaty bodies were established,[3] and when specific treaty body functions were implemented.

II. COMPOSITION AND FUNCTION OF TREATY BODIES

Composed of independent experts, members of a treaty body are elected by states in their individual capacity (rather than as representatives of their states) and serve on the treaty body for fixed, renewable terms of four years.[4] Although the number of members and frequency of meetings vary by treaty body, as described in Table 23.1, treaty body members come together in Geneva to perform three main functions in assuring the realization of health-related human rights: (a) monitoring state implementation through state party reports and treaty body concluding observations; (b) interpreting treaty obligations through general comments, recommendations, and statements; and (c) adjudicating individual complaints against a state.

A. Monitoring State Implementation

The principal activity of treaty bodies is to monitor state implementation of treaty obligations, reviewing state party reports to assess progress of rights realization and allow public scrutiny of national implementation efforts (OHCHR 2012a). Providing an external check on state efforts to implement health-related human rights obligations, international monitoring assists states in assessing achievements and recommending reforms (Mechlem 2009). Such treaty body monitoring thereby serves to facilitate human rights accountability for health-related human rights through:

- Information diffusion, with treaty bodies providing for the transfer of information from national governments to civil society; and

2. The core treaties include the International Covenant on Civil and Political Rights; International Covenant on Economic, Social and Cultural Rights; International Convention on the Elimination of All Forms of Racial Discrimination; Convention on the Elimination of All Forms of Discrimination against Women; Convention against Torture and Other Cruel, Inhuman or Degrading Treatment; Convention on the Rights of the Child; International Convention on the Protection of the Rights of All Migrant Workers and Members of Their Families; International Convention on the Rights of Persons with Disabilities; and International Convention for the Protection of All Persons from Enforced Disappearance.

3. Each of the human rights treaty bodies was established by its respective underlying treaty, with the exception of the Committee on Economic, Social and Cultural Rights, which, reflecting Cold War tensions, was not created by the UN Economic and Social Council (ECOSOC) until almost twenty years after the underlying ICESCR (OHCHR 1991).

4. Nominees for treaty bodies must be recognized as (1) experts in the field of human rights and/ or the field covered by the treaty, as well as (2) be persons of high moral character. In the election of treaty body members, due consideration is given to "equitable geographical participation" and "balanced gender representation" (OHCHR 2013b, 12).

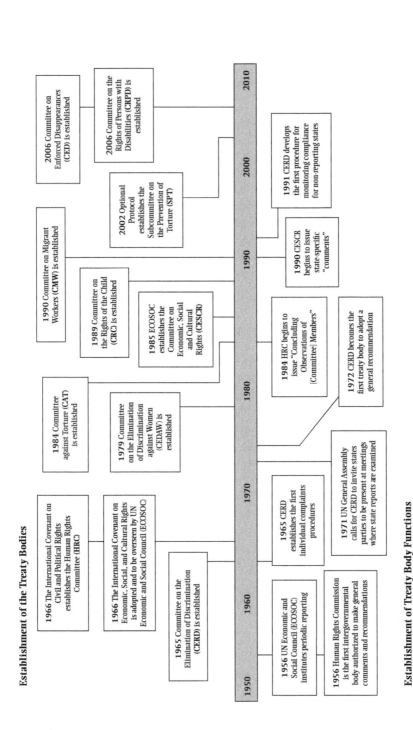

Figure 23.1 The Establishment of Treaty Bodies and Treaty Body Functions.

Table 23.1. CHARACTERISTICS OF CORE HUMAN RIGHTS TREATY BODIES

Treaty Body	Monitors	Independent Experts	Meetings/ Year
Committee on the Elimination of Racial Discrimination (CERD)	International Convention on the Elimination of All Forms of Racial Discrimination	18	3
Human Rights Committee (HRC)	International Covenant on Civil and Political Rights and the optional protocols	18	3
Committee on the Elimination of Discrimination against Women (CEDAW)	Convention on the Elimination of All Forms of Discrimination against Women and the optional protocol	23	3
Committee against Torture (CAT)	Convention against Torture and Other Cruel, Inhuman or Degrading Treatment and the optional protocol	10	3
Committee on Economic, Social and Cultural Rights (CESCR)	International Covenant on Economic, Social and Cultural Rights and the optional protocol	18	2
Committee on the Rights of the Child (CRC)	Convention on the Rights of the Child and the optional protocols	18	3
Committee on Migrant Workers (CMW)	International Convention on the Protection of the Rights of All Migrant Workers and Members of Their Families	14	2
Subcommittee on the Prevention of Torture (SPT)	Does not monitor the implementation of a particular Covenant; visits places of detention in order to prevent torture and other cruel, inhuman, or degrading treatment or punishment	25	3
Committee on the Rights of Persons with Disabilities (CRPD)	International Convention on the Rights of Persons with Disabilities	18	2
Committee on Enforced Disappearances (CED)	International Convention for the Protection of All Persons from Enforced Disappearance	10	2

- Policy persuasion, with treaty bodies influencing shifts in national public health practice (Meier and Kim 2015).

This monitoring process has particular relevance to the progressive realization of many health-related human rights (Forman et al. 2016). The principle of "progressive realization" stands as a formal recognition that the full realization of health is dependent on the state's available resources and capacity (ECOSOC 1990). Despite "core obligations" "to ensure the satisfaction of, at the very least, minimum essential levels of each of the rights" (CESCR 1990, para. 10), the principle of progressive realization gives flexibility to states in implementing health-related human rights, necessitating treaty monitoring to assess the speed of implementation efforts over time and thereby assure that states are moving as expeditiously as possible toward the full realization of health (Meier et al. 2017). Treaty bodies monitor the realization of these health-related obligations, as illustrated in Figure 23.2, by (1) reviewing periodic reports from state parties, (2) engaging in formal sessions of "constructive dialogue" with state representatives, and (3) issuing concluding observations for state response.

1. State Reporting

In order for a treaty body to monitor human rights implementation by states parties, states must report substantive information on their public health structures, processes, and outcomes. Reporting to treaty bodies constitutes a continuing obligation under international law, reaffirming state commitments to implement the rights set out in a treaty and providing an accountability mechanism to monitor compliance by states parties (UN Secretary-General 2006). To ensure that reports provide adequate information, states are required to submit both a "common core document" and a treaty body–specific document. The common core document contains general information about a state party relating to the implementation of

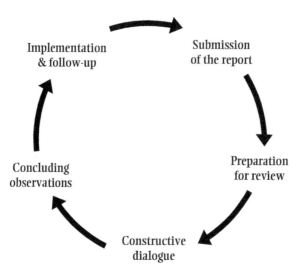

Figure 23.2 Treaty Body Monitoring Process.

human rights. Building from this common core document, which is sent to all treaty bodies, a state's treaty body–specific report contains information relating to the implementation of the specific underlying treaty (OHCHR 2012a). Each treaty body issues separate guidelines on the standard form and content of state reports—with the requested reports: chronicling the legal, administrative, and judicial measures taken by the state to implement treaty provisions, responding to specific issues raised by the treaty body, and describing the challenges faced in implementation (OHCHR 2009).

Although the UN Economic and Social Council (ECOSOC) had always requested information on state compliance with international human rights standards, it was not until 1956 that ECOSOC adopted the first resolution that called upon states to periodically report on their human rights efforts (ECOSOC 1956). States were originally requested to report every three years, describing human rights developments and processes relating to the rights proclaimed by the Universal Declaration of Human Rights; however, this system was amended in 1965 to require states to report annually in a continuous three-year cycle: reporting on civil and political rights in the first year; on economic, social, and cultural rights in the second year; and on freedom of information in the third year (ECOSOC 1965). With Cold War tensions preventing comprehensive human rights reports, this tripartite system of reporting was later devolved to individual treaty bodies through the promulgation of the UN's core human rights treaties (Sohn 1979). Beginning with the 1965 Convention on the Elimination of All Forms of Racial Discrimination, all human rights conventions since have included treaty-specific reporting requirements.[5]

A perennial challenge faced by committees over the years has been the absence, lateness, or unsatisfactory content of state reporting. Recognizing inequities in monitoring, where nonreporting states were seen to be immune from monitoring, CERD took the lead in developing the first procedure in 1991 for monitoring compliance among states whose reports were absent or long overdue, whereby the Committee's review would "be based upon the last reports submitted by the state party concerned and their consideration by the Committee" (UN General Assembly 1991, para. 27). This practice vis-à-vis late and nonreporting states was seen as successful in garnering state compliance with reporting procedures, and one year later, the UN General Assembly recommended that other treaty bodies adopt similar measures to monitor national human rights implementation in the absence of a state report (UN General Assembly 1992).

Beyond reported information from states parties, treaty bodies may also receive and consider information on health-related human rights implementation from sources independent of the state, including National Human Rights Institutions (NHRIs), UN agencies, inter-governmental organizations, and non-governmental organizations (NGOs) (OHCHR 2012a). The purpose of these public "alternative reports" (or confidential "shadow reports") is to present alternate views on state performance in implementing human rights for

5. The Subcommittee on the Prevention of Torture (SPT) is the only treaty body that does not have a reporting procedure. Instead of state reports, the SPT undertakes country missions and sends delegations to examine and report on areas that may be related to ill-treatment and torture.

public health. As states do not always provide clear or correct information on state health structures, processes, and outcomes, reporting from non-state actors can challenge select areas of a state report and highlight issues not raised by governments (Gaer 2003).

THE CENTER FOR REPRODUCTIVE RIGHTS: DEVELOPING ALTERNATIVE REPORTS TO ADVANCE SEXUAL AND REPRODUCTIVE HEALTH AND RIGHTS

Katy Mayall, The Center for Reproductive Rights

For El Salvador's 2017 periodic review by CEDAW, the Center for Reproductive Rights, local partner organization *Agrupación Ciudadana por la Despenalización del Aborto El Salvador,* and pro bono law firm Debevoise and Plimpton submitted a shadow report on the country's total criminalization of abortion, highlighting how such laws result in discrimination against women, entrench unequal access to health care, and violate women's right to reproductive freedom. During the state review, the Center facilitated in-person testimony by a Salvadoran woman who was sentenced to thirty years in prison after experiencing a miscarriage. The CEDAW review and accompanying NGO advocacy had an immediate impact on advancing law reform: at the CEDAW session, the state delegation endorsed a bill decriminalizing abortion under certain circumstances, and two days after the review, the Salvadoran Ministry of Health also endorsed the bill. The CEDAW concluding observations— which urged El Salvador to impose a moratorium on the enforcement of the current abortion law, review the detention of women under this law, and adopt the pending bill—continue to be leveraged by the Center for Reproductive Rights and its partners to advance law reforms and reproductive rights in El Salvador.

This comprehensive set of reports—from state and non-state sources—provides a basis for committees to review progress, identify obstacles, and assess prospects to implement health-related rights in constructive dialogue.

2. CONSTRUCTIVE DIALOGUE

"Constructive dialogue" is the process by which national health and human rights practices are assessed in an open, interactive dialogue between the treaty body and representatives of national governments. The value of constructive dialogue lies in the opportunity to speak directly to national governments about human rights implementation for public health promotion. This is particularly valuable for contentious health issues, where constructive dialogue allows states to reiterate, revisit, or be challenged on the value of particular norms or practices by treaty body members (Addo 2010). While the constructive dialogue has been criticized for being lengthy and poorly managed (Bayefsky 2001), treaty bodies have sought to streamline the discussion to eliminate redundancy, facilitate interaction, and focus on contentious issues.

Treaty bodies did not always engage in constructive dialogue with national governments, with the original working procedures of CERD allowing for the

Committee's concluding interpretations to be formulated immediately following the consideration of a state report (Wolfrum 1999). Where this procedure for issuing concluding observations was seen to restrict productive exchange between committee members and states parties, the UN General Assembly adopted a 1971 resolution that urged CERD to invite "State parties to be present at its meetings when their reports are examined" (UN General Assembly 1971, para. 5). This innovative decision made it possible to establish a direct dialogue between treaty bodies and states parties. The HRC, which became operational in 1976, included a similar provision for state representatives to attend its meetings (Wolfrum 1999). In the years since, all treaty bodies have included similar working methods for constructive dialogue.

Before the constructive dialogue is held with states parties, treaty bodies appoint a "task force" among their members to preexamine each state report and establish a "list of issues" that the treaty body will discuss during the constructive dialogue. When creating this list of issues, the committee takes into consideration the previous concluding observations for that state, alternative and shadow reports from NGOs, the reports from NHRIs and various UN agencies, and other relevant documents (Levin 2016). After the list of issues is developed, it is provided to the state for response—either in writing before the constructive dialogue or in person at the start of the constructive dialogue. (Under the new "simplified reporting procedure," a state may now receive this list of issues before the development of its report, allowing these treaty body issues to frame both the state report and the constructive dialogue.)

The constructive dialogue begins with a short presentation by the head of the state delegation, who outlines important human rights achievements and concerns for the state. This presentation is followed by two rounds of questions by members of the treaty body. In some treaty bodies, non-state actors also attend the hearing and have a separate opportunity to present their alternative reports and make recommendations—either in the public dialogue or in a private session (Ibid.; Faracik 2006).

UNICEF Participation in Constructive Dialogue before the CRC

Nicolette Moodie, UNICEF

UNICEF's engagement with international human rights mechanisms dates from the early days of state party reporting to the CRC, and UNICEF country offices now work closely with national governments and NGOs in reporting on child health to the CRC—from the preparation of state reports and alternative reports to support for implementation of the Committee's concluding observations. This engagement is guided closely by the UNICEF global human rights unit, which has developed an online toolkit to guide UNICEF country offices through all stages of engagement with treaty bodies and the Universal Periodic Review. In preparing for treaty monitoring, UNICEF will develop a confidential report for the CRC, attend the pre-session working group to prepare questions for the state party, and where possible, meet directly and confidentially with the CRC rapporteur for the state in question. With the CRC meeting three times per year for constructive dialogue with state delegates, UNICEF almost universally sends a country office representative to be present for constructive dialogue and respond to requests for technical assistance. To build UNICEF country office capacity for participation in constructive dialogue, the UNICEF Geneva liaison provides an in-person briefing to country officers prior to constructive dialogue—reviewing monitoring processes, sharing experiences from other countries, and raising prospective questions that may be asked by CRC members.

This constructive dialogue provides the treaty body with the detailed information necessary to assess state implementation of health-related human rights obligations.

3. Concluding Observations

Following the constructive dialogue, the treaty body's concluding observations offer specific public health recommendations for states parties. Where treaty bodies once considered state-specific recommendations to be beyond their monitoring mandate (Alston 1987), the initial concluding observations were provided generally to all member states, avoiding observations critical of any specific. The HRC first broke from this norm of generality in 1984, when it began to report on the content of constructive dialogue with specific states. In the following year, the HRC began including in its annual reports a section entitled "Concluding Observations by Individual [Committee] Members" on specific states parties (O'Flaherty 2006). The 1990s afforded greater flexibility to treaty bodies in developing state-specific observations, with the end of the Cold War lessening sensitivities regarding treaty body "interference" with the domestic proceedings of sovereign states (Fitzpatrick 2000). Providing specific recommendations on the right to health, the CESCR began in 1990 to issue country-specific "comments" from the entire Committee (Alston 1992).

Following the initial lead of both the HRC and CESCR, other treaty bodies began to issue country-specific concluding observations based on the submitted report and the constructive dialogue.[6] Over time, these assessments have evolved in length and complexity and now provide detailed recommendations for national public health practice (Pillay 2012). Concluding observations are composed of sections that assess both "positive aspects" and "principle areas of concern" in a state's human rights record. These assessments end with recommendations that seek to enhance the implementation of the health-related rights in question, offering an important interpretive tool for meeting treaty obligations (Connors 2000).

CAT and the Health-Related Human Rights of People Deprived of Their Liberty

Christen Broecker, Jacob Blaustein Institute for the Advancement of Human Rights

In interpreting the Convention against Torture and Other Cruel, Inhuman or Degrading Treatment or Punishment, CAT has found the failure of certain states to respect the right

---

6. The Subcommittee on the Prevention of Torture (SPT) does not issue concluding observations, but it does lay out its interpretation or understanding of states' obligations on specific issues in its annual reports.

to health of people deprived of their liberty to violate the obligation to prevent cruel, inhuman or degrading treatment or punishment in Article 16 of the Convention, and, in particularly severe cases, to violate the obligation to prevent torture in Article 2. The Committee's concluding observations reflect an understanding that states parties are obligated to provide prisoners with adequate health care, including timely access to qualified medical staff, medications, and specialist treatment; adequate mental health care services; and conditions of detention that are not detrimental to health, whether as a result of overcrowding or inadequate sanitation or nutrition. CAT's treatment of this issue has ensured that the health-related rights of prisoners, a particularly vulnerable group, is raised with states even if the Committee on Economic Social and Cultural Rights has not highlighted prisoners in its review of broader health-related rights compliance, and has made it clear that the right to health of prisoners is not subject to progressive realization, but is immediate, with violations requiring immediate response and redress.

While the treaty body's adoption of concluding observations brings the formal consideration of a state report to a close, a follow-up process continues in the ensuing years, with each treaty body employing distinct follow-up procedures to assess compliance with treaty body recommendations and monitor continuing state implementation (Ploton 2017).[7] The implementation of human rights for public health requires continuous effort, and after the submission of their initial reports, states are required to submit subsequent periodic reports at regular intervals (OHCHR 2012a). With each periodic report building on the one before it, this process before human rights treaty bodies forms a virtuous cycle in each round of monitoring, with these continuing health assessments building momentum for the realization of health-related human rights.

CEDAW ADDRESSES TOBACCO CONTROL TO PROTECT WOMEN'S RIGHT TO HEALTH

Belén Rios, Fundación InterAmericana del Corazón Argentina

Argentina has one of the highest rates of tobacco use in Latin America. Of about 40,600 annual tobacco-related deaths, over 11,700 of these are among women, with one in three women dying from cardiovascular diseases and twice as many women as men dying from malignant tumors. These high rates are a direct consequence of the tobacco industry's strategies to promote cigarette consumption among women and girls through targeted marketing campaigns. Responding to this harm, civil society in Argentina has submitted shadow reports before CEDAW in 2010 and 2016, exposing how—by not taking sufficient action to protect women's health from the harmful consequences of tobacco use—the Argentinian government is violating

---

7. The CRC does not have any follow-up procedure (Ploton 2017). On May 31, 2017, the CESCR announced that it would, for the first time, launch a follow-up procedure (OHCHR 2017). Beginning in its sixty-first session, the CESCR has identified specific issues requiring the urgent attention of governments and asked that states respond on follow-up actions within eighteen months.

its obligation to protect women's right to health. CEDAW has repeatedly raised its concerns regarding tobacco consumption among women during constructive dialogue and recommended that the state take further actions to protect women and girls from tobacco advertising, reduce tobacco consumption, ratify the Framework Convention on Tobacco Control (FCTC), and address the health consequences of women's tobacco use. In 2010, the Committee's recommendations were successfully used to advocate for tobacco control policy, culminating in the passage of a national tobacco control law in 2011. The Committee's recommendations from 2016 are currently being used to urge national ratification of the FCTC.

B. Interpreting Treaty Obligations

From these monitoring assessments on the health-related human rights situation of states parties, treaty bodies are further authorized to develop general comments, recommendations, or statements to interpret treaty provisions and clarify state public health obligations. Such interpretive documents allow a treaty body to publish its interpretation of thematic issues, clarifying the meaning or application of rights outlined in the underlying treaty (Johnstone 2007). These comments are not specific to the human rights situations of any individual country but are instead specific to particular treaty provisions or particular rights.

Even during the early years of treaty bodies, when there was little consensus on their authority to make country-specific recommendations, committee members did seek to provide comments of a more general nature (Rodley 2013). Prior to the creation of any treaty body, the UN General Assembly adopted a resolution in 1956 that authorized the inter-governmental Commission on Human Rights[8] to make comments, conclusions, and recommendations so long as they were not addressing any specific country or any specific situation (Keller and Grover 2012). When CERD was formed as the first independent treaty body, it was given similar authority to "make suggestions and general recommendations based on the examination of the reports and information received from the States Parties" (UN General Assembly 1965, art. 9).

Although future human rights treaties have not always given specific authorization to their respective treaty bodies to adopt general comments, treaty bodies have nevertheless seen such formal recommendations as a valuable way to orient states parties on the practical implementation of human rights obligations. For example, the 1985 Convention against Torture and Other Cruel, Inhuman or Degrading Treatment or Punishment provides CAT with a mandate only to "make such general comments *on the report* as it may consider appropriate and shall forward these

---

8. The Commission on Human Rights was an inter-governmental UN body established under ECOSOC to address human rights violations and make recommendations. It was replaced in 2006 by the Human Rights Council.

to the State Party concerned" (UN General Assembly 1984, art. 19); yet, despite the Convention not authorizing comments of a general nature—using singular language, "report" and "state party," rather than "reports" or "states parties" (Rodley 2013, 631)—CAT has issued general comments to clarify the normative content of the Convention for all states parties, beginning in General Comment 1, which clarified the intersection of Convention obligations and Committee procedures (UN General Assembly 1998, annex IX).

Although general comments have grown in length and scope to clarify public health obligations, the earliest comments, especially those adopted during the Cold War, were often short and addressed only procedural aspects of state party reports or committee practices (Keller and Grover 2012). Where it was often impossible to reach consensus on issues "touching on matters of ideological sensitivity," substantive issues in draft comments were simply omitted (Buergenthal 2001, 387). However, as states became more receptive to the work of the treaty bodies after the Cold War, treaty bodies—having then acquired experience in monitoring state reports—began to issue substantive comments, recommendations, and statements that contained significantly more normative guidance (Keller and Grover 2012). As seen in the practice of CERD, the first five general recommendations (before 1981) are all less than one page in length, focused on the reporting obligations of states party to the Convention, but the most recent general recommendations (after 2009) are now five to ten pages in length and concern specific issues such as racial discrimination against peoples of African descent and efforts to combat racist hate speech. Over the years, the proven utility of general comments, recommendations, and statements in clarifying state obligations has made their issuance common practice across treaty bodies, leading to increasing detail in treaty body guidance for health-related human rights (Rodley 2013; Marks 2016).

The current process of drafting general comments, the most common interpretive document, seeks to be both expert-driven and broadly participatory. When a general comment is first considered (based upon an internal decision by the treaty body to interpret a specific treaty provision or an outside proposal on a specific rights issue), the treaty body consults a wide range of subject matter experts about the anticipated general comment. Based upon these consultations, a designated member of the treaty body produces a draft comment. Once this draft is produced, it is then brought before the full treaty body and other interested parties for further discussion (Mechlem 2009). With a large number of actors seeking to shape the scope and content of the general comment, the treaty bodies have been described as "clearing centers" for divergent interpretations on human rights, weighing these inputs based upon the insights gained through their review of state reports. Once consensus across the treaty body has been reached on the revised draft, the general comment is formally adopted during the treaty body's plenary session (Ibid.).

With general comments implicating interconnected determinants of health, nearly all treaty bodies have issued general comments or recommendations, as shown in Table 23.2, that are tied to the realization of public health:

Table 23.2. HEALTH-RELATED GENERAL COMMENTS AND RECOMMENDATIONS

CERD	HRC	CEDAW	CESCR	CRC	CMW	CRPD
• #25 (2000) Gender-Related Dimensions of Racial Discrimination • #27 (2000) on Discrimination Against Roma • #30 (2005) on Discrimination Against Non-Citizens • #34 (2011) on Racial Discrimination Against People of African Descent	• #6 (1982) Right to Life • #20 (1992) Prohibition of Torture or Other Cruel, Inhuman or Degrading Treatment or Punishment • #28 (2000) Equality of Rights Between Men and Women • #35 (2014) on Liberty and Security of Person	• #14 (1990) Female Circumcision • #15 (1990) Avoidance of Discrimination Against Women in National Strategies for the Prevention and Control of AIDS • #18 (1991) on Disabled Women • #19 (1992) on Violence Against Women • #21 (1994) Equality in Marriage and Family Relations • #24 (1999) Women and Health • #26 (2008) on Women Migrant Workers • #27 (2010) on Older Women • #30 (2013) on Women in Conflict and Post-Conflict Situations • #31 (2014) on Harmful Practices (Joint with CRC) • #34 (2016) on the Rights of Rural Women	• #4 (1991) Right to Adequate Housing • #5 (1994) Persons with Disabilities • #6 (1995) Economic, Social, and Cultural Rights of Older Persons • #8 (1997) on the Relationship between Economic Sanctions and Economic, Social, and Cultural Rights • #12 (1999) Right to Adequate Food • #13 (1999) The Right to Education • #14 (2000) Right to the Highest Attainable Standard of Physical and Mental Health • #15 (2002) Right to Water • #16 (2005) Equal Right of Men and Women to Enjoy Economic, Social, and Cultural Rights • #19 (2007) Right to Social Security • #22 (2016) Right to Sexual and Reproductive Health	• #1 (2001) the Aims of Education • #3 (2003) HIV/AIDS and the Rights of the Child • #4 (2003) Adolescent Health and Development • #6 (2005) Treatment of Unaccompanied and Separated Children Outside Country of Origin • #7 (2006) Implementing Rights in Early Childhood • #8 (2006) Protection from Corporeal Punishment • #9 (2006) The Rights of Children with Disabilities • #10 (2007) Children's Rights in Juvenile Justice • #13 (2011) Freedom from All Forms of Violence • #15 (2013) Enjoyment of the Highest Attainable Standard of Health • #18 (2014) on Harmful Practices (Joint with CEDAW) • #20 (2016) Implementation of Rights During Adolescence	• #1 (2014) on Migrant Domestic Workers • #2 (2014) Rights of Migrant Workers in an Irregular Situation and Members of their Families	• #1 (2014) Equal Recognition Before the Law • #2 (2014) on Accessibility • #3 (2016) on Women and Girls with Disabilities • #4 (2016) Right to Inclusive Education

These interpretive documents provide a basis to expand obligations and facilitate accountability for state implementation of health-related human rights.

THE CESCR AND THE PATH FROM GENERAL COMMENT 14 TO GENERAL COMMENT 22

Jocelyn Getgen Kestenbaum, Benjamin N. Cardozo School of Law

The ability of treaty bodies to expand the normative content of human rights is exemplified by the evolving scope of CESCR general comments to address sexual and reproductive health and rights (SRHR). In 2000, the CESCR promulgated General Comment 14 on the right to health, which recognizes the SRHR of women and girls by acknowledging the right to control their health and body, identifying access to reproductive health services as essential to women's rights to non-discrimination and equality, connecting harmful social or traditional practices to violations of rights, and outlining state obligations to respect SRHR by guaranteeing access to sexual and reproductive health services, information, and education. Sixteen years later, the CESCR developed General Comment 22 specific to "the right to sexual and reproductive health," through which it offered even more detailed and comprehensive directives on SRHR for all, including lesbian, gay, bisexual, transgender, and intersex (LGBTI) persons and persons with disabilities. Expanding the normative content of SRHR, General Comment 22 recognizes the health impact of intersectional discrimination and the need for evidence-based laws, policies, and programs to protect individuals from violence, torture, criminalization, and discrimination. Building from General Comment 14, General Comment 22 reflects the CESCR's progress on SRHR and the achievements of activist movements to respond to evolving threats to public health.

C. Adjudicating Individual Complaints

Provided that the state has recognized the competence of a treaty body to receive individual complaints, that committee may, under certain conditions, receive and consider individual complaints or communications from individuals who allege that their health-related rights have been violated. When all domestic remedies have been exhausted, individual complaints mechanisms provide an opportunity to bring potential human rights violations before an international human rights body (OHCHR 2013a).[9] Such complaints may also be brought by third parties if the aggrieved individuals have given written consent or are incapable of giving such consent (OHCHR 2012a).

While the willingness of states to allow individuals to make international complaints about human rights violations was initially restrained, this mandate has steadily expanded over time (Shelton 2015). However, in contrast to the hindrances posed by the Cold War to state monitoring, the "optional" character of the individual complaints system reduced the risks of steadfast state objections, permitting treaty

---

9. Only eight treaty bodies currently provide mechanisms for individual complaints, including the HRC, CERD, CAT, CEDAW, CRPD, CED, CESCR, and CRC.

bodies greater autonomy to strengthen the individual petition system (Buergenthal 2001). CERD was the first treaty body to establish an individual complaints mechanism, with the underlying Convention on the Elimination of All Forms of Racial Discrimination allowing CERD, where states have recognized the Committee's competence to adjudicate such communications, to receive and consider complaints against a state party "from individuals or groups of individuals within its jurisdiction claiming to be victims of a violation" (UN General Assembly 1965, art. 14).

Now applied across almost all treaty bodies, a committee may undertake an independent review of health-related complaints, state their findings, and propose an appropriate remedy for a violation (Mechlem 2009). The specific procedures regarding individual complaints are authorized either by provisions in the human rights treaty or through a subsequent treaty protocol.[10] Although the consideration of individual complaints is quasi-judicial, treaty body decisions cannot be enforced directly by the committees (OHCHR 2012a). If a treaty body finds a violation, the committee indicates that the state party is under a legal obligation, by way of treaty ratification, to implement the committee's decision and grant a remedy to the complainant (Mechlem 2009).

HEALTH-RELATED INDIVIDUAL COMPLAINTS BEFORE THE HRC

Alexandra L. Phelan, O'Neill Institute for National and Global Health Law, Georgetown University Law Center

Individuals may bring complaints to the HRC against states parties under the First Optional Protocol to the International Covenant on Civil and Political Rights (ICCPR). Health-related individual complaints to the HRC primarily concern violations of:

- the right to life (art. 6)—addressing violations of states parties' negative obligation to *not* violate the right to life and their positive obligation to take steps to *protect* the right to life, as seen where there is direct responsibility to provide medical care; and/or
- the right to freedom from torture or other cruel, inhuman, or degrading treatment (art. 7)—addressing denial of access to abortion or health care, psychiatric treatment without consent, and repatriation of a refugee to a country that does not provide adequate social support services, including health care for chronic illness and maternal health care.

Where states have sought to use public health as a justification to interfere with civil and political rights, the HRC has concluded that violations must not be unlawful or arbitrary, rejecting public health justifications for the criminalization of homosexual practices as unjustified, unreasonable, and contrary to public health evidence. To assess state compliance with the HRC's concluding views on individual complaints, the HRC in 2013 adopted an A-to-E grading system as a means to maintain sustained pressure on states parties, fortify mechanisms of redress, and deter future offenses.

---

10. For procedures that are authorized by provisions in the underlying treaty, the treaty body may only consider complaints if the state party has made the necessary additional declaration accepting the complaints mechanism.

Where a number of individual complaints concerning health-related rights have been adjudicated before treaty bodies, a committee's judgment in such cases not only provides redress in individual cases of health harm but also puts pressure on states parties to implement their findings as national public health policy (Taket 2016). Deepening linkages between international treaty bodies and domestic courts, committee findings can establish legal precedent within the nation for how health-related treaty obligations should be interpreted (Ulfstein 2012).

III. THE EFFECTIVENESS OF TREATY BODIES

Treaty bodies hold promise to facilitate accountability for human rights implementation in global health; however, assessing the effectiveness of treaty bodies in securing accountability for health-related human rights remains difficult (Morjin 2011). With only limited efficacy seen in the evolving content of state reporting to treaty bodies (Meier and Kim 2015), the interconnected accountability mechanisms through treaty bodies have not been thoroughly studied (Krommendijk 2015). While treaty bodies have the legal authority to monitor, interpret, and adjudicate the human rights situation of states parties, treaty bodies lack public health capacity and legal enforcement mechanisms (Hafner-Burton and Tsutsui 2005; Hill 2010). The normative power of treaty bodies for global health advancement, therefore, lies in their ability to catalyze a process wherein multilevel and multi-sectoral stakeholders review national structures, processes, and outcomes in light of human rights obligations to realize public health. To enhance the effectiveness of this process, the UN human rights system is seeking to (a) strengthen the treaty body system by harmonizing the work of treaty bodies and (b) streamline the state reporting process through the development of human rights indicators.

A. Strengthening the Treaty Body System

Where the treaty monitoring process has long been criticized for its procedural ineffectiveness in assessing state implementation of health-related human rights (Alston 1987), a series of outside proposals have sought to strengthen the treaty body system. With the UN General Assembly repeatedly declining requests to allocate additional resources for treaty monitoring—despite a dramatic rise in treaty ratifications, treaty bodies, and treaty body operations—the treaty body system has long been pressed to address procedural redundancies (O'Flaherty and Broecker 2014). Since each committee was established separately under its respective treaty, treaty bodies have been free to develop their own unique processes and practices, and until recently, each treaty body often approached its work independently, despite an apparent overlap in treaty body procedures and no apparent benefit to human rights accountability (O'Flaherty 2006). Notwithstanding annual meetings of treaty body chairpersons to discuss the ways in which committees might better coordinate, enhance their work, and make the treaty body system as a whole more effective,[11] multiple differences continued to exist across the processes of distinct treaty bodies (Morjin 2011). While it is recognized that some variation in practice is justified—or even required in strict accordance with the relevant treaty—many remaining distinctions across treaty bodies have come to be seen as a hindrance to effectiveness (OHCHR 2012a). Responding to these limitations, treaty bodies have sought to become more effective by harmonizing their procedures—to work together as a single human rights treaty body system (Schrijver 2011).

Beginning in 2004, the UN High Commissioner for Human Rights requested that all relevant stakeholders come together to develop innovative ideas to "strengthen" the treaty body system. These stakeholders thereafter convened a series of informal consultations on treaty body strengthening, which came to be known as the "Dublin Process" (O'Flaherty 2010). The High Commissioner then published a series of reform proposals in 2012 to harmonize the work of the various treaty bodies through:

1. An overhaul of the treaty bodies' meeting procedures, restructuring the entire system around a "Comprehensive Reporting Calendar" that would make the state reporting burden more manageable;
2. The adoption of an optional "Simplified Reporting Procedure," with standardized reporting guidelines across treaty bodies that would increase the efficiency of the reporting process and limit the costs of reporting, review, and translation;
3. The expanded use of the Common Core Document alongside regular updates, focusing and reducing costs of state reports by limiting their length;
4. A streamlined constructive dialogue and concluding observations to generate more meaningful and focused feedback; and
5. A common procedure for communications among UN bodies, civil society, and individual complaints to improve accessibility and transparency of the treaty body system (UN High Commissioner 2012).

However, the High Commissioner's proposals to strengthen the treaty body system were met with criticism. Inattentive to the consultations convened through the Dublin Process, the High Commissioner's proposals were critiqued for paying scant attention to the uniqueness of each human rights treaty and the rights enshrined therein (O'Flaherty and Broecker 2014).

In anticipation of the High Commissioner's proposal, the UN General Assembly called for a separate, state-driven reform to strengthen and enhance the treaty body system. The resulting "intergovernmental process" began in July 2012, and the states that participated in this process had starkly divergent positions, seeking to

---

11. Larger Inter-Committee Meetings of treaty body representatives began in 2002 as a way to promote a unified approach to human rights monitoring, yet these gatherings of committee representatives were halted in 2009 due to their high costs and inability to make substantive decisions (Morjin 2011). Today, only the annual meeting of the chairpersons persists.

strengthen the system by expanding state oversight of treaty body work.[12] Those who participated in the Dublin Process strongly opposed these intergovernmental efforts to increase state oversight, emphasizing the importance of protecting the independent monitoring of state compliance with treaty obligations (Ibid.). Concluding this state-led process, the UN General Assembly:

1. Recognized the need for increased state compliance and full participation with the treaty body process;
2. Encouraged the streamlining of treaty body functions by simplifying the reporting procedure, limiting the length of reports, as well as limiting treaty body responses;
3. Developed a formula through which the meeting time of treaty bodies may be calculated, and financial and human resources may be allocated; and
4. Called for an increase in the transparency and accessibility of treaty bodies through webcast meetings and guidelines on translation (UN General Assembly 2014).

Drawing from these disparate reform proposals, treaty bodies have sought to simplify reporting procedures in ways that will have fundamental implications for monitoring health-related human rights. Although various treaty bodies had long adopted a "list of issues" to gather additional, focused, and updated information to clarify and/or complement state reports, the production and utilization of these lists varied by treaty body (Inter-Committee Meeting 2010). Harmonizing this process across treaty bodies, the General Assembly and the Inter-Committee of the Treaty Bodies have now both encouraged committees and states to utilize an optional "simplified reporting procedure" to strengthen and enhance the function of treaty bodies (Ibid.; UN General Assembly 2014). This new approach to state reporting, first adopted by CAT in 2007, reverses the previous order of reporting, wherein treaty bodies now adopt issue-specific questions *before* the submission of a state report, with a state responding to this list of issues in its periodic report to the treaty body. Under the simplified reporting procedure, these lists of issues are to contain two sections of questions, addressing: (1) specific issues and questions pertinent to the treaty, informed by previous concluding observations and (2) the general human rights situation of the state, informed by new measures or developments relevant to the implementation of the treaty (Inter-Committee Meeting 2010). Should states accept this simplified reporting procedure, the state's response to the treaty body's list of issues would comprise the entirety of its periodic reporting requirement. Although this optional procedure is intended to assist

12. Among those states seeking a greater role, the Russian Federation argued that "the process of strengthening or reforming the treaty bodies should primarily be subject to an interstate discussion"; Pakistan noted that "while all stakeholders have a role to play, the states parties are clearly the most important and cannot be placed on par with civil society organizations or NHRIs"; and China called for limits on the treaty bodies' use of "unverified information' from non-governmental organizations" (O'Flaherty and Broecker 2014, 14).

states in their reporting obligation—narrowing the focus of reporting, concluding observations, and follow-up—this reporting may have a detrimental effect on health-related human rights, with the list of issues unlikely to focus on health issues (which may be outside the competency of committee members) and likely to lead to periodic reports with inconsistent health data (denying the ability to assess progressive realization). With all treaty bodies now offering the simplified reporting procedure for periodic reports, often limiting the list of issues to no more than thirty questions prior to reporting (UN General Assembly 2016), it is unclear what effect this will have on public health reporting and health-related rights assessments.

The High Commissioner's proposal, the General Assembly resolution, and the simplified reporting procedure have drawn much-needed attention to the challenges facing the treaty body system (Egan 2013; O'Flaherty and Broecker 2014), but these processes to harmonize the work of treaty bodies will have widespread implications on accountability for health-related human rights. With the General Assembly resolved to review these reforms prior to 2020, the Geneva Academy of International Law and Human Rights has launched an open research project to examine and propose long-term, sustainable options for reform (Geneva Academy 2016). Given that some in this academic process seek further consolidation of the treaty body system,[13] these reform proposals may further narrow opportunities to monitor human rights across determinants of health.

B. Streamlining the State Reporting Process

In parallel with procedural efforts to strengthen the treaty body system through treaty body harmonization and simplification, there has been an ongoing effort to streamline the content of state reporting through human rights indicators. For treaty monitoring to serve its role in facilitating accountability for health-related human rights, state reports to human rights treaty bodies must present consistent public health data that accurately reflect human rights implementation (OHCHR 2012b). Identifying the specific quantitative and qualitative data reflective of human rights norms, human rights indicators can facilitate accountability under human rights law (OHCHR 2006), providing the international community with standardized, universal measurements to monitor the realization of rights (Rosga and Satterthwaite 2009). Human rights indicators provide a way to assess progress in realizing health-related human rights, and stakeholders have sought to develop and implement these indicators to monitor public health obligations before treaty bodies (Meier et al. 2014).

Debates on the operationalization of human rights indicators, including critical assessments of their use, began as early as the 1980s; yet, it is only in the past decade that stakeholders have put forward specific indicators for health-related human

13. Geneva Academy proposals include: the establishment of a single, permanent treaty body; the submission of single state reports, addressing all of the state's respective treaty commitments; and the coordination of questions, concluding observations, and follow-up among all treaty bodies (Geneva Academy 2017).

rights. While states have long included public health data in their reports to treaty bodies, they have often chosen these statistics ad hoc, thereby restricting a treaty body's ability to assess the progressive realization of health-related human rights (de Beco 2008). Where human rights monitoring seeks to compare progress to implement rights over time, such standardized monitoring of health-related human rights implementation requires consistent information in state reports. Consistent state reporting of public health data provides a basis to realize greater efficiency in treaty monitoring (focusing state reporting on targeted issues) and effectiveness in assessing progressive realization (allowing systematic monitoring across reporting cycles) (Meier and Kim 2015). In reporting consistent information to human rights treaty bodies, human rights indicators are seen to give meaning to the monitoring process by lessening the arbitrariness of narrative-based reporting, framing reports in accordance with universal standards, disclosing information to allow external scrutiny, and contextualizing reports to structure constructive dialogue and concluding observations (Rosga and Satterthwaite 2009).

While public health indicators do not fully capture the lived experiences of individuals (Merry 2011), such population-level data can provide a way to approximate the reality of the human rights situation and enhance the accountability for health-related rights. As a basis for accountability under human rights law, the health and human rights practice community has embraced universal indicators as part of a larger drive for scientific assessment of state obligations (de Beco 2008; Rosga and Satterthwaite 2009). While anecdotal and adjudicative assessments will continue to be imperative to human rights monitoring, there is particular merit in promoting the use of indicators to improve the quality of population-level assessments (Meier et al. 2014). Since no single indicator can provide a complete assessment of the national public health context, a wide range of stakeholders have developed a range of mutually supportive indicators to capture health-related human rights concerns (Gruskin and Ferguson 2009). This framework of complementary indicators contributes to the bridging of public health and human rights discourse, ultimately improving public policy measures to protect and promote human rights for health (OHCHR 2012b).

Given this promise of indicators for monitoring public health, the first UN Special Rapporteur on the Right to Health, Paul Hunt, was an early proponent of quantitative human rights indicators. Based upon the CESCR's General Comment 14 on the right to health, which invited states to develop their own indictors and benchmarks "to monitor, at the national and international levels, the State party's obligations" (CESCR 2000, para. 57), Hunt provided early justification for developing universal human rights indicators, clarifying the role of indicators as a basis to monitor the progressive realization of the right to health (UNCHR 2003). Hunt thereafter sought to delineate the types of indicators appropriate to state monitoring for the right to health, conceptualizing a specific "structure-process-outcome" framework that would soon be adopted for all human rights indicators, wherein:

- *Structural indicators* reflect the ratification of legal instruments and the existence of basic institutional mechanisms necessary for committing to the realization of the human right;

- *Process indicators* relate to state policy instruments (such as public programs, budgetary allocations, and policy interventions) and enable measurement of state efforts; and
- *Outcome indicators* capture individual and collective results that reflect the state of human rights realization in a given context (OHCHR 2006).

Illustrative of causal pathways, this methodology for assessing state commitments, efforts, and results seeks to correlate outcome measures with changes in structure and process, examining the links between policy cause and social effect (Hunt 2006). To catalyze political momentum around this evolving conceptualization of health-related human rights indicators, leaders of non-governmental organizations, international organizations, and national governments came together to declare their support for assessing implementation of the right to health through structure, process, and outcome indicators (UNCHR 2006).

In creating and adopting this broad indicator framework across treaty bodies, the UN has formalized a universal process to identify the indicators necessary for human rights assessment and implement those indicators through treaty body monitoring. A finalized set of indicators for the right to health included seventy-two indicators across fifteen attributes, which were "pilot tested" across 194 national health systems to analyze their application to the progressive realization of the right to health (Backman et al. 2008). OHCHR has drawn from this health-specific effort to identify indicators for all human rights, creating streamlined, one-page tables of illustrative indicators to define data sources reflective of the attributes of each right and guide targeted data collection for state reporting to human rights treaty bodies (OHCHR 2012b). Through these OHCHR streamlining efforts with the human rights treaty bodies, the operationalization of indicators for health-related human rights can provide a substantive foundation from which public health progress of national health systems can be monitored, information from UN specialized agencies can be incorporated, and accountability of health-related human rights can be facilitated (Acharya and Meier 2016).

CONCLUSION

The right to health and other health-related rights fall under the purview of an overlapping set of human rights treaty bodies, and the monitoring, interpretation, and adjudication of a variety of public health concerns by human rights treaty bodies has been instrumental in clarifying the interconnections between public health and human rights. Treaty bodies have served as a basis for global health, and global health stakeholders benefit public health through their engagement with these human rights treaty bodies. Complemented by the work of the Human Rights Council to interpret and monitor rights through its Special Procedures and Universal Periodic Review, the strengthening of treaty body functions and streamlining of state reports will extend the role of treaty bodies in facilitating accountability for human rights implementation, transforming multiple independent treaty bodies into a single treaty body system. Yet, there remain risks to consolidating the work of the treaty bodies where such harmonized procedures compromise the specific substance of distinct treaties. While such procedural reforms may promote efficiencies in treaty body monitoring, there remain advantages to redundancies across fragmented treaty bodies that should not be overlooked, ensuring complementary approaches to accountability for health-related human rights. As more states ratify treaties that implicate health-related human rights, the work of more effective and efficient treaty bodies to monitor, interpret, and adjudicate a diverse range of human rights issues will become increasingly relevant to global health.

REFERENCES

Acharya, Neha and Benjamin Mason Meier. 2016. "Facilitating Accountability for the Right to Health: Mainstreaming WHO Participation in Human Rights Monitoring." *Health and Human Rights Journal Blog*. April 28. Available at: https://www.hhrjournal.org/2016/04/facilitating-accountability-for-the-right-to-health-mainstreaming-who-participation-in-human-rights-monitoring/.

Addo, Michael. 2010. "Practice of United Nations Human Rights Treaty Bodies in the Reconciliation of Cultural Diversity with Universal Respect for Human Rights." *Human Rights Quarterly* 32(3): 601–664.

Alston, Philip. 1987. "Out of the Abyss: The Challenges Confronting the New U.N. Committee on Economic, Social and Cultural Rights." *Human Rights Quarterly* 9(3): 332–381.

Alston, Philip. 1992. "The Committee on Economic, Social and Cultural Rights." In *The United Nations and Human Rights: A Critical Appraisal*, edited by Philip Alston, 473–508. Oxford: Clarendon Press.

Backman, Gunilla, Paul Hunt, Rajat Khosla, Camila Jaramilo-Strouss, Belachew Mekuria Fikre, Caroline Rumble, David Pevalin [et al.]. 2008. "Health Systems and the Right to Health: An Assessment of 194 Countries." *The Lancet* 372(9655): 2047–2085.

Bayefsky, Anne. 1996. "The UN Human Rights Treaties: Facing the Implementation Crisis." *Windsor Yearbook of Access to Justice* 15: 189–201.

Bayefsky, Anne. 2001. "The UN Human Rights Treaty System: Universality at the Crossroads." Retrieved from http://www.bayefsky.com/report/finalreport.pdf.

Buergenthal, Thomas. 2001. "The U.N. Human Rights Committee." *Max Planck Yearbook of United Nations Law* 5: 341–398.

CESCR (Committee on Economic, Social and Cultural Rights). 1990. "General Comment No. 3: The Nature of States Parties' Obligations (Art. 2, Para. 1, of the Covenant)." 14 December. E/1991/23.

CESCR (Committee on Economic, Social, and Cultural Rights). 2000. "General Comment 14: The Right to the Highest Attainable Standard of Health (Art. 12)." 11 August. E/C.12/2000/4.

Connors, Jane. 2000. "An Analysis of the System of State Reporting." In *The UN Human Rights Treaty System in the 21st Century*, edited by Anne Bayefsky, 3–22. The Hague; Boston: Kluwer Law International.

De Beco, Gauthier. 2008. "Human Rights Indicators for Assessing State Compliance with International Human Rights." *Nordic Journal of International Law* 77(1–2): 23–49.

ECOSOC (UN Economic and Social Council). 1956. "Periodic Reports on Human Rights." 1 August. E/RES/624B (XXII).

ECOSOC. 1965. "Periodic Reports on Human Rights." 1 August. E/RES/1074C (XXXIX).

ECOSOC. 1990. "Comment on Economic, Social, and Cultural Rights, General Comment 3: The Nature of States Parties Obligations." E/1991/23.

Egan, Suzanne. 2013. "Strengthening the United Nations Human Rights Treaty Body System." *Human Rights Law Review* 13(2): 209–249.

Faracik, Beata. 2006. "'Constructive Dialogue' as a Cornerstone of the Human Rights Treaty Bodies Supervision." *Bracton Law Journal* 38: 39–54.

Fitzpatrick, Joan. 2000. "Human Rights Fact-Finding." In *The UN Human Rights Treaty System in the 21st Century*, edited by Anne Bayefsky, 65–96. The Hague; Boston: Kluwer Law International.

Forman, Lisa, Luljeta Caraoshi, Audrey R. Chapman, and Everaldo Lamprea. 2016. "Conceptualising Minimum Core Obligations under the Right to Health: How Should We Define and Implement the 'Morality of the Depths.'" *International Journal of Human Rights* 20(4): 531–548.

Gaer, Felice. 2003. "Implementing International Human Rights Norms: UN Treaty Bodies and NGOs." *Journal of Human Rights* 2(3): 339–357.

Geneva Academy. 2016. "Academic Platform on Treaty Body Review 2020." *UN Human Rights Mechanisms, Geneva Academy of International Humanitarian Law and Human Rights*. Retrieved from https://www.geneva-academy.ch/our-projects/our-projects/un-human-rights-mechanisms/detail/16.

Geneva Academy. 2017. "Academic Platform Project on the 2020 Review of the Human Rights Treaty Body System: Latin America Expert Regional Consultation, December 2016." Retrieved from https://www.geneva-academy.ch/joomlatools-files/docman-files/HRI%20Costa%20Rica%20TB%20Consultation%20Draft%20Outcomes%20Document%203.8.17.pdf.

Gruskin, Sofia and Laura Ferguson. 2009. "Using Indicators to Determine the Contribution of Human Rights Frameworks to Public Health Efforts." Bulletin of the World Health Organization 87: 714–719.

Hafner-Burton, Emilie and Kiyoteru Tsutsui. 2005. "Human Rights in a Globalizing World: The Paradox of Empty Promises." *American Journal of Sociology* 110(5): 1373–1411.

Hill, Daniel. 2010. "Estimating the Effects of Human Rights Treaties on State Behavior." *The Journal of Politics* 72(4): 1161–1174.

Hunt, Paul. 2006. "Human Right to the Highest Attainable Standard of Health: New Opportunities and Challenges." *Royal Society of Tropical Medicine and Hygiene* 100: 603–607.

Inter-Committee Meeting (of the Treaty Bodies), 11th Meeting. 2010. "Treaty bodies' list of issues prior to reporting (targeted/focused reports)." 19 May. HRI/ICM/2010/3.

Johnstone, Rachel. 2007. "Cynical Savings or Reasonable Reform? Reflections on a Single Unified UN Human Rights Treaty Body." *Human Rights Law Review* 7(1): 179–180.

Keller, Helen and Leena Grover. 2012. "General Comments of the Human Rights Committee and Their Legitimacy." In *UN Human Rights Treaty Bodies: Law and Legitimacy*, edited by Helen Keller and Geir Ulfstein, 121. Cambridge: Cambridge University Press.

Krommendijk, Jasper. 2015. "The Domestic Effectiveness of International Human Rights Monitoring in Established Democracies: The Case of the UN Human Rights Treaty Bodies." *Review of International Organizations* 10(4): 489–512.

Levin, Ayelet. 2016. "The Reporting Cycle to the United Nations Human Rights Treaty Bodies: Creating a Dialogue between the State and Civil Society—The Israeli Case Study." *George Washington International Law Review* 48(2): 315–376.

Marks, Stephen P. 2016. "Normative Expansion of the Right to Health and the Proliferation of Human Rights." *George Washington International Law Review* 49(1): 97–142.

Mechlem, Kerstin. 2009. "Treaty Bodies and the Interpretation of Human Rights." *Vanderbilt Journal of Transnational Law* 42(3): 905–947.

Meier, Benjamin Mason and Yuna Kim. 2015. "Human Rights Accountability through Treaty Bodies: Human Rights Treaty Monitoring for Water and Sanitation." *Duke Journal of Comparative and International Law* 26: 139–228.

Meier, Benjamin Mason, Jocelyn Kestenbaum, Georgia Kayser, Urooj Amjad, and Jamie Bartram. 2014. "Examining the Practice of Developing Human Rights Indicators to Facilitate Accountability for the Human Right to Water and Sanitation." *Journal of Human Rights Practice* 6(1): 159–181.

Meier, Benjamin Mason, Marlous De Milliano, Averi Chakrabarti, and Yuna Kim. 2017. "Accountability for the Human Right to Health through Treaty Monitoring: Human Rights Treaty Bodies and the Influence of Concluding Observations." *Global Public Health*. DOI: 10.1080/17441692.2017.1394480.

Merry, Sally. 2011. "Measuring the World: Indicators, Human Rights, and Global Governance." *Current Anthropology* 52(S3): S83–S95.

Morjin, John. 2011. "Reforming United Nations Human Rights Treaty Monitoring Reform." *Netherlands International Law Review* 58(3): 295–333.

O'Flaherty, Michael. 2006. "The Concluding Observations of United Nations Human Rights Treaty Bodies." *Human Rights Law Review* 6(1): 27–52.

O'Flaherty, Michael. 2010. "Reform of the UN Human Rights Treaty Body System: Locating the Dublin Statement." *Human Rights Law Review* 10(2): 319–335.

O'Flaherty, Michael and Christen Broecker. 2014. *The Outcome of the General Assembly's Treaty Body Strengthening Process*. Switzerland: Universal Rights Group.

OHCHR. 1991. *Fact Sheet No. 16 (Rev.1): Committee on Economic, Social and Cultural Rights*. United Nations Office of the High Commissioner for Human Rights.

OHCHR. 2006. "Report on indicators for monitoring compliance with international human rights instruments." 11 May. HRI/MC/20067.

OHCHR. 2009. "Compilation of Guidelines on the Form and Content of Reports to be Submitted by States Parties to the International Human Rights Treaties." 3 June. HRI/GEN/2/Rev.6.

OHCHR. 2012a. *Fact Sheet No. 30 (Rev. 1): The United Nations Human Rights Treaty System*. United Nations Office of the High Commissioner for Human Rights.

OHCHR. 2012b. *Human Rights Indicators: a guide to measurement and implementation*. United Nations Office of the High Commissioner for Human Rights.

OHCHR. 2013a. *Fact Sheet No. 7 (Rev. 2): Individual Complaint Procedures under the United Nations Human Rights Treaties*. United Nations Office of the High Commissioner for Human Rights.

OHCHR. 2013b. *Human Rights Treaty Bodies and Election of Treaty Body Members: A Guide for United Nations Delegates Based in New York*. United Nations Office of the High Commissioner for Human Rights.

OHCHR. 2014. "UN Strengthens Key Human Rights Reporting System." *United Nations Office of the High Commissioner, News and Events*. April 10. Available at: http://www.

ohchr.org/EN/NewsEvents/Pages/DisplayNews.aspx?NewsID=14490& LangID=E.

OHCHR. 2017. "Committee on Economic, Social, and Cultural Rights Reviews the Report of Australia." *United Nations Office of the High Commissioner, News and Events.* May 31. Available at: http://www.ohchr.org/EN/NewsEvents/Pages/DisplayNews.aspx?NewsID=21677&LangID=E.

Pillay, Nathan. 2012. *Strengthening the United Nations human rights treaty body system: A report by the United Nations High Commissioner for Human Rights.* United Nations Office of the High Commissioner for Human Rights.

Ploton, Vincent. 2017. "The Development of Grading Systems on the Implementation of UN Treaty Body Recommendations and the Potential for Replication to Other UN Human Rights Bodies." *Geneva Academy of International Humanitarian Law and Human Rights Academic Platform Project.* Available at: https://www.ishr.ch/sites/default/files/documents/tb_grading_systems_their_replicability_to_other_un_hr_bodies.pdf.

Rodley, Nigel. 2003. "United Nations Human Rights Treaty Bodies and Special Procedures of the Commission on Human Rights: Complementarity or Competition?" *Human Rights Quarterly* 25(4): 882–908.

Rodley, Nigel. 2013. "The Role and Impact of Treaty Bodies." In *The Oxford Handbook of International Human Rights Law*, edited by Dinah Shelton. Oxford University Press.

Rosga, AnnJanette and Margaret Satterthwaite. 2009. "The Trust in Indicators: Measuring Human Rights." *Berkeley Journal of International Law* 27(2): 253–315.

Schrijver, Nico. 2011. "Paving the Way Towards … One Worldwide Human Rights Treaty!" *Netherlands Quarterly of Human Rights* 29: 257–260.

Shelton, Dinah. 2015. *Remedies in International Human Rights Law.* New York: Oxford University Press.

Snyder, Sarah. 2014. "Human Rights in the Cold War." In *The Routledge Handbook of the Cold War*, edited by Artemy Kalinovsky and Craig Daigle, 237–248. New York: Routledge.

Sohn, Louis. 1979. "The Improvement of the UN Machinery on Human Rights." *International Studies Quarterly* 23(2): 186–215.

Taket, Ann. 2016. "Human Rights, Social Justice and Public Health." In *Public Health: Local and Global Perspectives*, edited by Pranee Liamputtong, 149–168. Port Melbourne: Cambridge University Press.

Ulfstein, Geir. 2012. "Individual Complaints." In *UN Human Rights Treaty Bodies: Law and Legitimacy*, edited by Helen Keller and Geir Ulfstein. Cambridge University Press.

UN General Assembly, 20th Session. 1965. "International Convention on the Elimination of All Forms of Racial Discrimination." 21 December. Res. 2106 (XX).

UN General Assembly, 26th Session. 1971. "Report of the Committee on the Elimination of Racial Discrimination." 6 December. A/RES/2783 (XXVI).

UN General Assembly, 39th Session. 1984. "Convention Against Torture and Other Cruel, Inhuman or Degrading Treatment or Punishment." 10 December.

UN General Assembly, 46th session. 1991. "Report of the Committee on the Elimination of Racial Discrimination." 25 September. A/46/18(SUPP).

UN General Assembly, 47th Session. 1992. "Effective implementation of international instruments on human rights, including reporting obligations under international instruments on human rights." 16 December. A/RES/47/111.

UN General Assembly, 53rd Session. 1998. "General Comment on the implementation of article 3 of the Convention in the context of article 22." 16 September. A/53/44, Supplement No. 44.

UN General Assembly, 68th Session. 2014. "Strengthening and enhancing the effective functioning of the human rights treaty body system." 9 April. A/RES/68/268.

UN General Assembly, 71st Session. 2016. "Status of the human rights treaty body system: Report of the Secretary General, Supplementary Information." 18 July. A/71/118.

UN High Commissioner (UN High Commissioner for Human Rights). 2012. *Strengthening the United Nations Human Rights Treaty Body System: A Report by the United Nations High Commissioner for Human Rights*. Available at: http://www2.ohchr.org/english/bodies/HRTD/docs/HCReportTBStrengthening.pdf.

UN Secretary-General. 2006. "Harmonized Guidelines on Reporting under the International Human Rights Treaties, including Guidelines on a Common Core Document and Treaty-specific Documents." 10 May. HRI/MC/2006/3.

UNCHR (UN Commission on Human Rights), 59th Session. 2003. "The Right of Everyone to the Highest Attainable Standard of Physical and Mental Health" Report of the Special Rapporteur, Paul Hunt." 13 February. E/CN.4/2003/58.

UNCHR (UN Commission on Human Rights), 62nd Session. 2006. "Report of the Special Rapporteur on the right of everyone to the enjoyment of the highest attainable standard of physical and mental health, Paul Hunt." 3 March. E/CN.4/2006/48.

Wolfrum, Rüdiger. 1999. "The Committee on the Elimination of Racial Discrimination." *Max Planck Yearbook of United Nations Law* 3: 489–519.

24

The Future of Human Rights Accountability for Global Health through the Universal Periodic Review

JUDITH R. BUENO DE MESQUITA, CONNOR FUCHS, AND DABNEY P. EVANS*

Established in 2008, the Universal Periodic Review (UPR) is the most significant recent addition to the international human rights system. A peer-review procedure, it provides scrutiny of each United Nations (UN) member state's human rights record every five years. The process consists of a review culminating in a set of recommendations issued to each "State-under-Review" (SuR). The UPR provides an unprecedented opportunity to routinely hold all states to account for their obligations under international human rights law to respect, protect, and fulfill human rights, including health-related human rights.

Accountability has been at the heart of the international human rights enterprise since its genesis in the aftermath of the Second World War, and has been increasingly prominent within the global public health agenda and commitments in more recent years. From the human rights perspective, accountability is comprised of three components: monitoring, review, and remedies and action to support correction where violations have occurred. The UPR provides an opportunity for external review of a state's human rights record, culminating in recommendations to states to improve compliance with international human rights law. Ultimately, it is primarily the responsibility of the state to implement recommendations.

* The authors wish to acknowledge the contribution of Camille Gauter, Ingrid Gjerdset, Ajeng Larasati, Tasneem Sadiq, and Rebekah Thomas, who, together with Judith Bueno de Mesquita, carried out a quantitative analysis of health recommendations in the first cycle of the Universal Periodic Review for the Human Rights Centre Clinic, University of Essex. The findings of this study, which will soon be published (Essex University and WHO forthcoming), have been used in this chapter with kind permission.

Part I of this chapter begins with an analysis of the concept of accountability in human rights and public health. From this conceptualization, Part II presents a historical overview of accountability mechanisms in the UN human rights system, leading to the birth of the Human Rights Council (HRC) and the UPR process. Part III discusses the development of the UPR process. With health-related issues of increasing relevance in the human rights system, Section IV examines the presence and prominence of health in the UPR recommendations (based on data from a range of sources), highlighting the importance of the implementation of UPR recommendations. To understand the contribution of the UPR and how public health stakeholders engage in the UPR process, it is necessary to situate the role of the UPR among the broader web of human rights and global health accountability mechanisms such as those established under the Sustainable Development Goals (SDGs). These themes are the focus of the analysis in Sections V and VI. Based on these findings and analysis, the chapter concludes that while the UPR provides a degree of global accountability for health, its potential is currently hampered by an uneven spread of recommendations across different health issues and limited engagement of the public health community with the UPR procedures.

I. ACCOUNTABILITY IN PUBLIC HEALTH AND HUMAN RIGHTS

In recent decades, there has been an unprecedented and growing preoccupation with accountability of states, specific public institutions, and private bodies exercising public functions, leading to assertions that "accountability" is "the buzzword of modern governance" (Bovens et al. 2014, 1).

In the field of health, the growth of an accountability culture has variously been attributed to critiques of health system performance, the complexity of health systems, the power of health actors to affect peoples' lives, and large budgetary expenditures on health in all countries (Brinkerhoff 2003). In the field of human rights, accountability is not a new preoccupation. The development of international human rights law in the wake of the Second World War focused first on standard-setting, but quickly moved to discussions of—and arrangements for—accountability of states through review procedures.

Although accountability is not new in the field of public health or in human rights, the arrangements for and conceptualization of accountability in these fields have differed. In the health sector, many jurisdictions examine financial performance and political/democratic accountability, focusing on: tracking and reporting of financial resources, performance in relation to agreed targets, and meeting electoral promises and societal needs (Brinkerhoff 2003). At the international level, the preoccupation with accountability in health is increasingly manifested in new oversight arrangements under, for example, the Framework Convention on Tobacco Control (FCTC), the International Health Regulations (IHR), the Global Strategy on Women's, Children's and Adolescents' Health, and the SDGs.

In contrast to health sector preoccupations, human rights-based accountability focuses on whether or not the state has upheld its human rights commitments, including those relating to health, under domestic or international human rights law. It is this human rights preoccupation that motivates the UPR, as well as other human rights review processes. Judicial, quasi-judicial, political, administrative, and social accountability mechanisms have been used to support human rights-based accountability (Potts 2008, 17).

The construct of human rights accountability has generally been understood to embody a tripartite typology of:

- monitoring—"what is happening, where and to whom" (CoIA 2011, 7),
- review—analyzing whether human rights obligations have been honored by states (Ibid.), and
- action and remedies—the expectation that the executive branch and parliament will act based on the findings of monitoring and review (IAP 2016, 10).

This chapter's assessment of the UPR and its potential as an accountability mechanism for public health focuses in particular on the review as well as the action and remedies components of accountability.

In recent years, the fields of health and human rights have become more enmeshed, and, as examined in chapters 1 and 2, human rights-based commitments in global health have proliferated. Thus it is unsurprising that the human rights-based understanding of accountability has begun to permeate select global health agendas, notably oversight of the Global Strategy on Women's, Children's and Adolescents' Health (IAP 2016). In attempts to guarantee accountability for health-related human rights, there has been increasing engagement by the public health community with human rights accountability processes through the development of the UN human rights system, most recently in the UPR.

II. THE DEVELOPMENT OF ACCOUNTABILITY FUNCTIONS WITHIN THE UNITED NATIONS CHARTER AND UNITED NATIONS TREATY BODIES

Since its foundation, the UN has tasked itself with "promoting and encouraging respect for human rights" (UN 1945, art. 1(3)). Beginning with the establishment of the UN Commission on Human Rights (the Commission) in 1946 and the adoption of the Universal Declaration of Human Rights (UDHR) in 1948, the UN has sought to define normative standards. Since then, nine core international human rights treaties, in addition to multiple optional protocols, have been adopted. These have given rise to binding obligations on states parties. During that time, the promotion of accountability for human rights realization has been a key concern of the UN through the creation of machinery to review states' human rights implementation records. To oversee compliance of states parties with their obligations under the core treaties, treaty monitoring bodies, as discussed in chapter 23, oversee the periodic review of states parties' reports.[1] However, states may avoid implementation of certain human rights or the rights of particular groups by abstaining from treaty ratification; by entering reservations that may absolve them of compliance with certain (often

---

1. In addition, eight treaty bodies currently provide mechanisms for individual complaints.

culturally sensitive) provisions; or simply by disregarding their commitments after ratification (International Institutions and Global Governance Program 2012). For example, the International Covenant on Economic, Social and Cultural Rights (ICESCR), which contains the central international protection of the right to health, has yet to be ratified by thirty-two states (OHCHR 2017c). Treaties operate according to the principle of sovereignty: states can choose which treaties they ratify, and thus choose for which treaties to be held to account. Less than full participation in treaty oversight processes amounts to the avoidance of accountability for human rights. In practice, for example, many state party reports are overdue—in May 2017, only thirty-three countries are up to date with their reporting (Al Hussein 2017). The challenge of accountability is one that has been present since the outset of the human rights system and continues today through the HRC.

A. The Commission Seeks Human Rights Accountability

The Commission was the first standard-setting organ of the UN with a human rights mandate (ECOSOC 1946). Established in 1946, the Commission, as seen in Figure 24.1, was originally composed of eighteen member states, elected by the UN Economic and Social Council (ECOSOC). By 1992, this number increased to fifty-three members (Kälin and Jimenez 2003). Each of the five regional groups[2] was allocated a set number of seats, and member states were selected for three-year terms on a regional basis (Ibid.). Between 1947 and 1966, the Commission was primarily dedicated to developing human rights through the International Bill of Human Rights, composed of the 1948 UDHR, the 1966 ICESCR, and the 1966 International Covenant on Civil and Political Rights (ICCPR). Following these initial standard-setting achievements—and allegations of human rights violations in apartheid South Africa—a need emerged for mechanisms through which the UN could respond to human rights violations in a timely manner. Two ECOSOC resolutions—1235 and 1503—were adopted in 1967 and 1970, respectively, to respond to gross violations of human rights (ECOSOC 1967). The "public" 1235 procedure allowed the Commission to establish ad hoc working groups to assess alleged human rights violations (Ibid.). Where it was presumed that confidentiality would increase state cooperation, Resolution 1503 provided for private, closed-door discussions of human rights issues (ECOSOC 1970).

Following the addition of these new procedures, the Commission entered a period of increasing politicization (Alston 2006). State attempts to avoid particular topics, in part, gave rise to the establishment and proliferation of "Special Procedures" (Surya 2011). Such Special Procedures mandates, as discussed in chapter 22, "examine, monitor, advise and publicly report on human rights situations" in a particular country or territory or on a specific human rights issue (OHCHR 2017a). Mandate-holders are either individual experts—known as Special Rapporteurs or Independent Experts—or collectives known as working groups (Nifosi 2005).

---

2. The groups are the: African group, Asia Pacific group, Eastern European group, Latin American and Caribbean group, and Western European and Others group.

Figure 24.1 During the first meeting of the UN ECOSOC Commission on Human Rights, participants included (left to right): Chair Mrs. Franklin D. Roosevelt (United States); Secretary of the Commission Prof. John P. Humphrey (Canada); Rapporteur Dr. Charles Malik (Lebanon); Charles Dukes (United Kingdom); Valentin F. Topliakov (USSR); and General Carlos P. Romulo (Philippine Republic), January 27, 1947. United Nations, Lake Success, New York.

These Special Procedures are seen as "the frontline human rights troops," as they can address situations in any country in the world without the requirement that the state has ratified a specific human rights instrument (Arbour 2006). The resulting system of complex procedures and mechanisms to monitor compliance and investigate human rights violations was critical to human rights accountability into the new millennium. In contrast to the independent treaty bodies, the Commission was thus intended to strike a balance between state sovereignty and universal accountability.

B. The Birth of the Human Rights Council

Yet, there were claims that the Commission privileged some of its own members, thereby sheltering states that abused human rights (Alston 2006). Critics repeatedly pointed to the questionable human rights records of Commission member states. The view that "[s]tates have sought membership of the Commission not to strengthen human rights but to protect themselves against criticism or to criticize others" set the stage for reforms to the UN human rights system (UN Secretary-General 2005, para. 182). To address the lack of credibility and rampant politicization of the Commission, then UN Secretary-General Kofi Annan proposed that states replace the Commission with a Council that would be able to "accord human rights a more authoritative position, corresponding to the primacy of human rights in the Charter of the United Nations" (Ibid., para. 183). At the 2005 World Summit, heads of state endorsed Annan's proposal, resolving to create a Human Rights Council (HRC) that would "be responsible for promoting universal respect for the protection of human rights and fundamental freedoms for all . . . ; address situations of human rights violations . . . and make recommendations thereon; [and] . . . promote effective coordination and mainstreaming of human rights within the United Nations system" (UN General Assembly 2005, paras. 157–159).

The constitutive document of the HRC, General Assembly Resolution 60/251, designated the HRC as a subsidiary organ of the General Assembly (UN General Assembly 2006, para. 1). This action elevated its status beyond that of the Commission—which was a subsidiary organ of ECOSOC—not only improving HRC access to the General Assembly, the UN's main deliberative organ, but also imbuing its decisions and recommendations, including UPR Working Group recommendations, with enhanced authority and legitimacy (Abebe 2013). Composed of forty-seven state representatives, based on equitable geographic distribution and elected to three-year terms by the UN General Assembly, Resolution 60/251 set out the HRC's duties, including a universal periodic review of the realization by each state of its human rights obligations and commitments (UN General Assembly 2006).

III. THE UNIVERSAL PERIODIC REVIEW

The UPR is a process intended to regularly hold all UN member states to account for their respect, protection, and fulfillment of international human rights. As a peer-review mechanism, the review of each UN member state is conducted by the UPR Working Group, composed of the forty-seven member states of the HRC. The UPR has been described as "one of the most important innovations" of the HRC (Abebe 2013, 748) and an "intriguing and ambitious development in international human rights monitoring" (Charlesworth and Larking 2014, 1).

A. Establishment and Purpose

In response to the widespread acknowledgment of the Commission's politicization and the ability of some states to avoid scrutiny, then UN Secretary-General Annan called for a process in which all UN member states' human rights record would be reviewed by other states on a periodic basis (Annan 2005). Every UN member state is reviewed in each cycle of the UPR. The UPR has now undergone two full cycles (2008–2012, 2012–2016) and is undertaking its third.[3] States are reviewed on the basis of the human rights set out in the UN Charter, the UDHR, and international human rights treaties ratified by the SuR, in addition to voluntary

---

3. The first cycle was four years, the second four and a half years, and the third cycle will be five years.

commitments and pledges (HRC 2007). This framework provides opportunities to hold states to account for health-related human rights, including the right to health, which, as noted in chapter 1, is recognized in the UDHR, the ICESCR, and various population-specific human rights treaties. Indeed, from the outset, it was envisaged that the UPR should promote the universality, interrelatedness, indivisibility, and interdependence of all human rights (Ibid.). This is important because historically the right to health and other economic, social, and cultural rights (ESC) had been neglected—as compared with civil and political (CP) rights—by the Commission and across the UN human rights system.

B. The Review Process

The UPR is carried out on the basis of information contained in three documents that must be submitted six weeks prior to the review:

- a national report by the SuR, which is meant to identify achievements, best practices, challenges, and constraints, as well as follow-up in response to the previous review (HRC 2007);
- a synthesized report of information from other UN human rights mechanisms and bodies; and
- a stakeholder report, summarizing information provided by non-governmental organizations (NGOs) and other civil society groups, academic entities, and National Human Rights Institutions (NHRIs) (Ibid.).

On the basis of this information, a constructive interactive dialogue is held between the SuR and HRC members, as well as observer states.[4] The process culminates with an outcome report, adopted by the HRC and including non-binding recommendations made to the SuR. The SuR can choose to accept or note each recommendation, with states committing to take action in response to accepted recommendations (Ibid.).

IV. HEALTH IN THE UNIVERSAL PERIODIC REVIEW

The degree to which the UPR can provide a channel for human rights accountability in global health depends on the interconnected:

- A. engagement of key public health stakeholders from government, civil society, and international organizations with the UPR prior to, during, and subsequent to the review;
- B. extent and quality of health-related recommendations made to SuRs; and
- C. degree of implementation of those recommendations.

---

4. Other stakeholders, such as NGOs and inter-governmental organizations, do not play a formal part in this dialogue.

A. Engagement of the Public Health Community

Dialogue between rights-holders and duty-bearers is an integral dimension of accountability (Potts 2008). Meaningful accountability for health within the UPR will be enhanced by the participation and engagement of relevant health-related duty-bearers from the government, organizations from civil society representing rights-holders, international organizations, and NHRIs during the periods prior to, during, and in follow-up to review. This is particularly important for a mechanism such as the UPR that involves review by peers (i.e., other states) rather than independent experts (Gujadhur and Limon 2016).

A fully consultative process—involving health and other relevant ministries, civil society, and other actors in the process of drafting national reports—supports the inclusion of reliable, impartial, and comprehensive information on the principal obstacles to and achievements in human rights realization (Ibid.). However, an analysis of seventy-four national reports from the first and second cycle of the UPR by the Universal Rights Group (URG) found that, of these, only twenty were produced on the basis of an inclusive process involving different ministries and other stakeholders.[5] These findings led to a concern that many reports could be "detached from reality and incapable of delivering tangible improvements on the ground" (Ibid., 3).

To support consultation, some countries have adopted explicitly consultative processes for the development of the national report and follow-up, including governmental structures that coordinate the preparation of reports, engagement with international and regional human rights mechanisms, and follow-up procedures (Ibid.). Such structures work "in coordination with ministries, specialized State bodies (such as the national statistics office), parliament and the judiciary, as well as in consultation with the national human rights institution(s) and civil society" (OHCHR 2016b, 2). These mechanisms may support engagement by relevant health actors, including ministries of health and civil society organizations, ensuring that the most important health-related human rights issues are included in national reports and supporting follow-up to health-related recommendations. However, state delegations to the UPR often comprise politicians, policymakers, and lawyers primarily drawn from the foreign, justice, and interior ministries, whose responsibilities tend to focus more on civil and political rights, with only limited health-related responsibilities (Hunt 2017). As a result, "it is difficult for the UPR process to promote meaningful implementation and mainstreaming of the right to health with credibility or authority" (Ibid., 506).

Civil society organizations have varied opportunities to participate, although some of these are limited in scope. In addition to engaging in national reporting processes, insofar as these are consultative, civil society can submit information to be a part of stakeholder reports, which are compiled by the Office of the UN High Commissioner for Human Rights (OHCHR) (UPR Info 2017). However, there is no guarantee that information from a given submission will be included in the

---

5. This analysis is primarily based on the first cycle of the UPR; the second cycle, finished in 2016, has yet to be subject to a full empirical analysis.

final stakeholder report. Moreover, although civil society organizations may make brief interventions after recommendations have been issued to a SuR, they cannot participate directly in the formal dialogue during the review itself. Even so, they can lobby reviewer states to raise particular issues in the review and engage in follow-up advocacy with the national government (Ibid.). Some civil society stakeholders at the intersection of health and human rights, including those working on sexual and reproductive health and rights (SRHR), have been actively involved in the UPR, including through the lobbying of HRC members to take up SRHR issues with SuRs (Gilmore et al. 2015). However, others have been discouraged by the limited impact of their health interventions, expressing disappointment that the review process either did not consider a specific health issue, or resulted in recommendations that were "too vague to be meaningful" or not followed up on by the government (Amon and Lohman 2015, 161).[6] This analysis suggests that there is a mixed picture for civil society opportunities to support accountability for health and human rights during the UPR process.

NHRIs also have an important role to play in submitting information for inclusion in the stakeholder report, as well as following up on recommendations to hold the state to account. A small number of NHRIs, including the Office of the Human Rights Commissioner in Azerbaijan (Bueno de Mesquita et al. 2015), are actively engaged in tracking UPR recommendations on health issues.

Specialized international organizations can also support human rights accountability for health advancement by providing technical support to governments and civil society as they write reports for the UPR, providing independent information on the implementation of previous recommendations through UN country team submissions, and following up on the review through dissemination and implementation of the recommendations (UNDP 2015). For example, the UN Population Fund (UNFPA) has been actively involved in monitoring and engaging with the UPR process at the global and national levels, as discussed in chapter 11, and UNFPA's Strategic Plan 2014–2017 includes an indicator that requires country offices to assess whether states have taken action on all of the accepted UPR recommendations from the previous reporting cycle (UNFPA 2013). In some UNFPA country offices, tracking and implementing recommendations by the international human rights system is an important national-level priority (Gilmore et al. 2015). Along these lines, UNFPA Azerbaijan supported the Office of the Human Rights Commissioner's (Azerbaijan's NHRI) review of the state's implementation of the Convention on the Elimination of All Forms of Discrimination against Women (CEDAW), using the UPR recommendations and the CEDAW Committee's concluding recommendations as a framework for assessment (Bueno de Mesquita et al. 2015). By contrast, the World Health Organization's (WHO's) engagement with the UPR has not been a priority in many country offices, perhaps,

---

6. These advocates have expressed frustration, in the area of palliative care, that HRC members were not decision makers in the areas of health or drug policy and often did not even know the relevant decision makers, leading them to conclude that to "advance our advocacy, we found that direct advocacy with health and drug policy makers, whether in specific countries or at UN forums, was more effective" (Amon and Lohman 2015, 162).

as discussed in chapter 7, because it is perceived as not being within the mandate of the Organization or not effective in promoting health.[7] In line with UN system-wide efforts to strengthen engagement with the human rights monitoring mechanisms, the WHO Gender, Equity, and Rights Team has been, as discussed in chapter 6, taking stock of the extent of WHO's engagement with the UPR, assessing challenges, and seeking to demonstrate the potential value of such engagement to WHO's mandate to advance health and well-being.

The UPR's potential for accountability for health is currently restricted by the inconsistent participation of key health stakeholders from civil society, national human rights institutions, and international organizations, which may inhibit an appropriate assessment of health issues brought to the attention of the UPR and implementation of recommendations following review.

B. Extent and Quality of Health-Related Recommendations

In order to assess the accountability role that the UPR can play for global health, it is also necessary to consider the extent and quality of health-related recommendations made to SuRs, including (1) the prominence of health-related recommendations, (2) the focus of these recommendations on major human rights-based obstacles to health, and (3) the extent to which these recommendations are implemented.

1. PROMINENCE OF HEALTH IN THE UPR RECOMMENDATIONS

The right to the highest attainable standard of health is considered one in a cluster of economic, social, and cultural (ESC) rights. Although the UPR process is meant to reflect the universality, interdependence, indivisibility, and interrelatedness of all human rights (HRC 2007), the most prominent analysis of ESC rights in the first cycle of the UPR found that only 17 percent of recommendations exclusively addressed ESC rights, compared to 37 percent that exclusively addressed civil and political rights, and 30 percent that addressed both sets of rights (CESR 2016). Of these ESC rights, health was the third most frequently addressed right, behind education and labor rights (Ibid.). Specific to health, research by the Human Rights Centre Clinic, University of Essex and the WHO found that 3,863 of 17,638 recommendations (22 percent) made during the first cycle were health-related (Essex University and WHO 2018).[8] Similarly, UNFPA found that 26 percent of recommendations addressed SRHR (UNFPA 2014), with analyses concluding that

---

7. As described above, the UN human rights system historically tended to focus on civil and political rights, further compounding the historical perception, as reviewed in chapter 5, that human rights are not within the remit of an organization whose focus is on providing technical and normative support to ministries of health.

8. The Essex University/WHO study focused on those health-related human rights issues that are most relevant to the mandate and operations of WHO. This includes not only health care and specific health conditions but some determinants of health, including nutrition, water and sanitation, social and economic determinants of health, as well as health security, emergencies, and disaster relief.

SRHR can be considered one of the most frequently addressed issues by the UPR (Gilmore et al. 2015).[9]

2. FOCUS OF HEALTH-RELATED RECOMMENDATIONS

Health-related recommendations focus on a range of categories of health issues. The recommendations also require different types of state implementation actions. While some recommendations are general, others are specific, and while some require new action, others encourage states to continue or deepen existing efforts.

The Essex University/WHO study found that the two most frequently addressed categories of health issues in the first cycle of the UPR were gender-based violence and harmful practices (33 percent) and maternal, child, and adolescent health (20 percent). The study found that other health issues—including nutrition, water and sanitation, communicable and noncommunicable diseases, mental health, and HIV/AIDS—were comparatively neglected, as seen in Figure 24.2.

Health systems, a vital but often neglected infrastructure, received only 10 percent of health recommendations in the first UPR cycle. Similarly, although unsafe abortion is one of the leading causes of maternal death, notably in countries with restrictive abortion laws (Sedgh et al. 2007), it was seldom raised explicitly in UPR first cycle recommendations despite a commitment by states to "deal with the health impact of unsafe abortion as a major public health concern" (UN 1994, para. 8.25). A total of twenty-eight recommendations mentioning abortion were made to thirteen countries, eleven of which were made to Nicaragua—a country with a total ban on abortion.

This uneven attention to different categories of health issues could be explained by a range of factors that merit further investigation such as, for example, the degree of familiarity with different health and human rights issues by the HRC, uneven attention to different health issues in the state reports submitted to the UPR, and political sensitivities on issues such as abortion (Essex University and WHO 2018).

The UPR clearly gives significant attention to health. However, different categories of health topics are addressed with varying frequency, meaning that while the procedure is currently providing accountability in relation to some issues (like gender-based violence or maternal, adolescent, and child health), other issues (such as water and sanitation, abortion, nutrition, and palliative care) largely pass without attention.

3. EXTENT OF IMPLEMENTATION

UPR recommendations related to health require different types of implementation actions from states, including legislative, program, or budgetary measures (Essex University and WHO 2018), reflecting the fact that under international human rights treaties, states must take a broad range of domestic and international

---

9. The differences in findings between the CESR study and the Essex University/WHO and UNFPA studies are at least partly explained by a different categorization of recommendations.

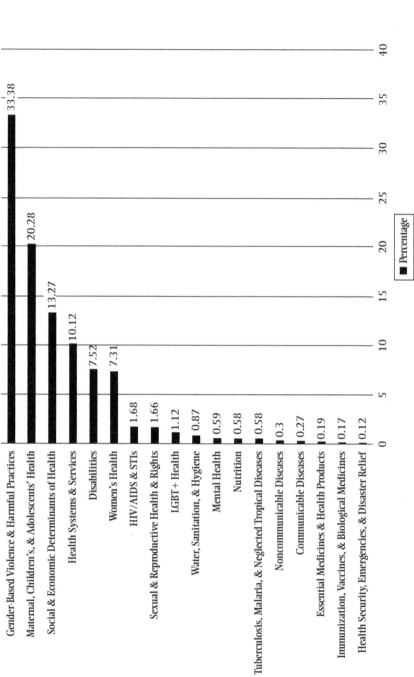

Figure 24.2 Health issues addressed by the UPR by percentage.
CREDIT: Gauter, Gjerdset, Larasati, Sadiq (Human Rights Centre Clinic, University of Essex, 2018).

measures to give effect to human rights.[10] The features of a "good quality" recommendation have been the subject of debate but not agreement. Some have
proposed that recommendations should be "Specific, Measurable, Achievable,
Relevant and Time-bound"—"SMART" recommendations that are "action-
oriented" (McMahon 2012). In considering health-related recommendations
from the first UPR cycle, some reports specified particular measures while
others were general and provided little guidance of what the state might do
in concrete "actionable" terms (Essex University and WHO 2018). However,
some have pointed out that this wider framework of reference may be required
to determine whether a recommendation is useful, including measurability, cor-
respondence to the major human rights challenges in a state, and whether a state
has the resources to implement a recommendation (or implement it in a given
time frame) (Gujadhur and Limon 2016).

C. Degree of Implementation

The implementation of recommendations corresponds to the third aspect of human
rights accountability—action and remedies. It is through the implementation of
recommendations that the state can improve its human rights record, including by
giving effect to remedies to correct human rights abuses, prevent their recurrence,
and improve the human rights record.

Although reporting under the UPR process is compulsory, implementation
of UPR recommendations is voluntary. This is reflected in two main features of
the recommendations. First, they are not legally binding. Second, states are at
liberty to accept or simply note them. In the first cycle of the UPR, 73 percent of
recommendations were accepted, according to one analysis (McMahon 2012, 13).
While the SuR commits in good faith to implement accepted recommendations,
the act of noting a recommendation is a diplomatic formulation for at least the
temporary rejection of a UPR recommendation, although a state may later accept
a noted recommendation, or even, in practice, take measures that contribute to its
fulfillment. The HRC has neither the mandate nor the machinery to pressure SuRs
to comply with accepted recommendations, although it has an opportunity to monitor the implementation of both accepted and noted recommendations in its subsequent reporting cycle (HRC 2007).

Implementation is a growing field of inquiry in the field of international human
rights, so it is surprising to find that few actors have endeavored to gauge the extent of implementation of UPR recommendations. Those studies that do exist
suggest there is a reasonable degree of implementation of UPR recommendations,
indicating that the UPR process is more than diplomatic theater, or as the UN
High Commissioner for Human Rights recently put it, "an elaborate performance
of mutual diplomatic courtesies" (Al Hussein 2017). Although it is difficult to
isolate the impact of a UPR recommendation from other possible influences on

10. Recommendations emerging from the first two cycles of the UPR devote significantly more
attention to states' domestic human rights obligations than to obligations of international cooperation and assistance (Essex University and WHO 2018).

governments, a study by UPR Info found that 48 percent of UPR recommendations made during the first cycle were either fully or partially implemented within two and a half years, including 55 percent of accepted recommendations and 19 percent of noted recommendations (UPR Info 2014). The proportion of recommendations that triggered action was highest for recommendations that focused on HIV/AIDS (78 percent), with those classified as "right to health" recommendations also considered highly implemented (64 percent) (Ibid.). While this would seem to be a positive indication of accountability for the right to health, findings on implementation should be treated cautiously. States may be more likely to report implementation of simple or imprecise recommendations, given that a range of actions may be highlighted as indicative of implementation (Gujadhur and Limon 2016).

A second concern relating to implementation focuses on how implementation is reported in the UPR process itself. The analysis by URG found that almost half of first cycle UPR recommendations were reported as fully implemented by states in their second cycle reports, with a further 20 percent reported as partially implemented (Ibid.). This study highlights that success stories might be amplified by the reporting state. The circumscribed opportunities for civil society input into the UPR process, as well as the fact that the UN report and stakeholder reports do not routinely focus on the issue of implementation of earlier recommendations, creates the potential for a one-sided information bias, limiting the accountability potential of the UPR in securing implementation. The engagement of relevant ministries—including the ministry of health, in follow-up as well as reporting—is an important basis upon which to support implementation and subsequent reporting.

V. THE UPR AS AN ACCOUNTABILITY MECHANISM FOR GLOBAL HEALTH COMMITMENTS

Where global health is addressed in the absence of human rights, accountability has historically been supported by more passive and arguably weaker oversight models, involving self-reporting and collaborative monitoring arrangements focused on globally agreed-upon goals and indicators (PMNCH 2011). This model, as discussed in chapter 1, is derived from a collaborative spirit to addressing global disease threats and a history of technical assistance that motivates global health and traces its origins to the field of tropical medicine (Birn, Pillay, and Holtz 2009). But this model has increasingly drawn criticism. Most recently, the IHR, a legally binding treaty requiring states to maintain health systems that can "detect, assess, notify and report" public health emergencies, drew criticism after the 2014–2015 Ebola Virus Disease outbreak in West Africa due to a failure of the system to hold states to account for surveillance and reporting requirements (Gostin et al. 2016). There is an emerging view in the global health community that formal institutionalized accountability is a valuable but underutilized avenue to support improvements in public health and address health inequalities through "real remedies" (IAP 2016, 7).

Human rights accountability has begun to permeate institutional agendas and arrangements in global health. Nowhere is this truer than in the 2030 Agenda for Sustainable Development (2030 Agenda), which forms the central plank of the global development agenda and is grounded in human rights, including, as discussed in chapter 4, important commitments to health-related human rights through the SDGs. The 2030 Agenda focuses on "Follow-up and Review," a form of accountability (UN General Assembly 2015). The precursor to the SDGs, the Millennium Development Goals (MDGs), did not make commitments to accountability, resulting in reporting arrangements that were described as "primitive and not especially convincing" (Alston 2005, 814). The 2030 Agenda foresees that "robust, voluntary, effective, participatory, transparent and integrated follow-up and review will make a vital contribution to implementation" that will, among other things, "promote accountability to our citizens" (UN General Assembly 2015, paras. 72–73). National processes are the lynchpin of accountability for the 2030 Agenda; however, they will be complemented by thematic reviews and voluntary national reporting and oversight at the international level by the state-led High-Level Political Forum. Another example of new accountability arrangements in the field of global health was the 2016 appointment by then UN Secretary-General Ban Ki-Moon of an Independent Accountability Panel (IAP) to provide a transparent and independent review of progress and obstacles to the implementation of the 2016–2030 Every Woman Every Child Global Strategy for Women's, Children's and Adolescents' Health (Every Woman Every Child 2015). While these efforts should be encouraged, supported, and deepened, they are in their infancy and operate with limited resources. Given their voluntary nature, the extent of state reporting remains to be seen.

There is a strong convergence between global health commitments—including the 2030 Agenda and the Global Strategy on Women's, Children's and Adolescents' Health—and the obligations of international human rights. Given this convergence, development agendas have the potential to advance health-related human rights, while the realization of human rights has both intrinsic and instrumental value to global health agendas. The UPR mechanism, as well as the other international human rights procedures reviewed in Section V of this volume, have a role to play in supporting accountability for states in relation to their global health commitments, particularly to ensure that states meet these commitments in a manner that is aligned with their human rights obligations (IAP 2016, 41). The President of the HRC has identified practical steps that the UPR can play in supporting accountability, including both (1) considering progress toward meeting the SDGs and making recommendations with reference to the SDGs in the UPR and (2) using the UPR as a comprehensive source of information that could be drawn upon by the High-Level Political Forum in its own thematic reviews of the SDGs and in the voluntary country review processes (President of the HRC 2016).

Although the UPR can support accountability of states for global health commitments, its primary framework of reference for the protection of human rights is the UN Charter, the UDHR, legally binding international human rights treaties, and other voluntary commitments. Thus, any role in relation to reviewing global health commitments should not come at the expense of HRC neglect in facilitating accountability for the full spectrum of human rights.

VI. THE UPR IS PART OF A BROADER WEB OF ACCOUNTABILITY

The UPR is only one among a range of international human rights mechanisms established to hold states to account for health-related human rights. Advocates have spoken of the importance of creating a "web of accountability" for human rights (OHCHR and CESR 2013, 18), supporting global health commitments through the UPR, the UN human rights treaty bodies (as discussed in chapter 23), and the UN special procedures (as reviewed in chapter 22). The HRC, including the UPR, was intended to reinforce, rather than duplicate the accountability functions of other procedures, and it has done that, with each accountability mechanism having comparative advantages and disadvantages in a state-by-state approach to accountability. The UPR can be an important thread in this web because of its unique features, including that all states report on the full range of human rights under the procedure, enabling the mechanism to consider all states and all determinants of health. States also report at regular intervals, and there is a formal procedure for follow-up on implementation. By contrast, although treaty bodies and special procedures also have certain unique advantages, treaty bodies only review specific sets of rights or the rights of particular groups protected by the treaty in question, they only review states parties to treaties, and many state reports are overdue (Al Hussein 2017). For their part, UN special procedures, such as the UN Special Rapporteur on the right to health, are not resourced to review the human rights situation in every country, and as a consequence, adopt a highly selective approach to accountability, usually undertaking two official country missions per year to countries that invite Special Rapporteurs to undertake official missions (Ibid.). Moreover, follow-up by UN treaty bodies and special procedures is not systematic, although efforts have been made in recent years to institutionalize follow-up mechanisms (Kalin 2014).

While independent treaty bodies are normally held up by the human rights community as the gold standard because they are less subject to political influence, there are distinct advantages to the peer-review process of the UPR. The review of states by their peers can have some drawbacks, for example, where diplomatic considerations can influence the making and acceptance of recommendations. At the same time, some SuRs reportedly feel more pressure through the UPR process due to its peer-review nature (UPR Info 2014). On this basis, it has been argued that the SuR is more likely to follow up and implement UPR recommendations than those of other human rights mechanisms, enhancing the potential for real improvements on the ground (Gujadhur and Limon 2016).

CONCLUSION

With health-related recommendations featuring prominently in the outcome documents of the first cycle of the UPR, this mechanism can and should play a role in facilitating human rights accountability for global health. At the same time, the spread of UPR recommendations across different critical health issues has been uneven, the procedure has not consistently engaged key health stakeholders, and the scope and quality of state actions to implement recommendations is not entirely clear on the basis of the available evidence. With greater engagement from the public health community—by governments, civil society, and non-governmental organizations—and a conscious attempt by the HRC to develop recommendations that address a range of critical health issues, the UPR can not only address health in a more holistic way, but it has the potential to support accountability for health under international human rights law as well as support global health commitments such as the SDGs.

REFERENCES

Abebe, Allehone M. 2013. "The Role and Future of the Human Rights Council." In *Routledge Handbook on International Human Rights Law*, edited by Scott Sheeran and Nigel Rodley, 743–760. Abingdon, Oxon: Routledge Press.

Al Hussein, Zeid Ra'ad. 2017. "Opening Statement by Zeid Ra'ad Al Hussein, United Nations High Commissioner for Human Rights, Human Rights Council 35th Session" (on file with author).

Alston, Philip. 2005. "Ships Passing in the Night: The Current State of the Human Rights and Development Debate Seen Through the Lens of the Millennium Development Goals." *Human Rights Quarterly* 27(3): 755–829.

Alston, Philip. 2006. "Reconceiving the UN Human Rights Regime: Challenges Confronting the New UN Human Rights Council." *Melbourne Journal of International Law* 7(1): 185–224.

Amon, Joseph and Diederik Lohman. 2015. "Evaluating a Human Rights-Based Advocacy Approach to Expanding Access to Pain Medicines and Palliative Care: Global Advocacy and Case Studies from India, Kenya and Ukraine." *Health and Human Rights* 17(2): 149–165.

Annan, Kofi. 2005. "UN Secretary-General's Address to the Commission on Human Rights." April 7. https://www.un.org/sg/en/content/sg/statement/2005-04-07/secretary-generals-address-commission-human-rights.

Arbour, Louise. 2006. "Statement by High Commissioner for Human Rights to Last Meeting of Commission on Human Rights." March 27. http://newsarchive.ohchr.org/EN/NewsEvents/Pages/DisplayNews.aspx?NewsID=3040&LangID=E.

Birn, Anne-Emanuelle, Yogan Pillay, and Timothy H. Holtz. 2009. *Textbook of International Health: Global Health in a Dynamic World*. New York: Oxford University Press.

Bovens, Mark, Thomas Schillermans, and Robert E. Goodin. 2014. "Public Accountability." In *The Oxford Handbook of Public Accountability*, edited by Mark Bovens, Robert Goodin, and Thomas Schillermans, 1–20. Oxford: Oxford University Press.

Brinkerhoff, Derick. 2003. *Accountability and Health Systems: Overview, Framework and Strategies*. Maryland: Partners for Health Reform*plus*.

Bueno de Mesquita, Judith, Parvana Bayramova, and Rashid Rumzade. 2015. *An Assessment of the Status of Treaty Body Recommendations on Sexual and Reproductive Rights in the Republic of Azerbaijan*. Azerbaijan: UNFPA.

Center for Economic and Social Rights. 2016. *The Universal Periodic Review: A Skewed Agenda?* New York: Center for Economic and Social Rights.

CEDAW (Committee on the Elimination of Discrimination Against Women). 1992. "General Recommendation No. 19: Violence against women." UN Doc. A/47/38.

CEDAW (Committee on the Elimination of Discrimination Against Women). 2011. "L.C. v. Peru, Communication 22/2009." 11 November. UN Doc. CEDAW/C/50/D/22/2009.

CEDAW (Committee on the Elimination of Discrimination Against Women). 2013. "General Recommendation No. 30 on women in conflict prevention, conflict and post-conflict situations." 18 October. UN Doc. CEDAW/C/GC/30.

CESCR (Committee on Economic, Social and Cultural Rights). 2003. "General Comment No. 15: The Right to Water." 20 January. UN Doc. E/C.12/2002/11.

CESCR (Committee on Economic, Social and Cultural Rights). 2016. "General Comment No. 22 on the right to sexual and reproductive health." 2 May. UN Doc. E/C.12/GC/22.

Charlesworth, Hilary and Emma Larking. 2014. "Introduction: The Regulatory Power of the Universal Periodic Review." In *Human Rights and the Universal Periodic Review: Rituals and Ritualism*, edited by Hilary Charlesworth and Emma Larking, 1–22. Cambridge: Cambridge University Press.

CoIA (Commission on Information and Accountability for Women's and Children's Health). 2011. *Keeping Promises, Measuring Results*. Geneva: United Nations.

CRC (Committee on the Rights of the Child). 2013. "General Comment No. 15 on the Right of the Child to the Highest Attainable Standard of Health." 17 April. UN Doc. CRC/C/GC/15.

ECOSOC (Economic and Social Council). 1946. "Commission on Human Rights." 21 June. UN Doc. E/RES/9(II).

ECOSOC (Economic and Social Council). 1967. "Question of the violation of human rights and fundamental freedoms, including policies of racial discrimination and segregation and of apartheid, in all countries, with particular reference to colonial and other dependent countries and territories." UN Doc. E/RES/1235(XLII).

ECOSOC (Economic and Social Council). 1970. "Procedure for dealing with communications relating to violations of human rights and fundamental freedoms." Doc. E/RES/1503(XLVIII).

Essex University Human Rights Centre Clinic and World Health Organization. 2018. *Increasing WHO-UPR Engagement on the Right to Health: Project Report*. forthcoming (on file with authors).

Every Women Every Child. 2015. *The Global Strategy for Women's, Children's and Adolescents' Health (2016–2030)*. Geneva: WHO.

Gilmore, Kate, Luis Mora, Alfonso Barragues, and Ida Krogh Mikkelsen. 2015. "The Universal Periodic Review: A Platform for Dialogue, Accountability and Change on Sexual and Reproductive Health and Rights." *Health and Human Rights* 17(2): 169–179.

Gostin, Lawrence O., Oyewale Tomori, Suwit Wibulpolprasert, Ashish K. Jha, Julio Frenk, Suerie Moon, Joy Phumaphi [et al.]. 2016. "Towards a Common Secure Future: Four Global Commissions in the Wake of Ebola." *PLOS Medicine* 13(5): e1002042.

Gujadhur, Subhas and Marc Limon. 2016. *Towards the Third Cycle of the UPR: Stick or Twist?: Lessons Learnt from the First Ten Years of the Universal Periodic Review*. New York: Universal Rights Group.

HRC (Human Rights Council), 5th Session. 2007. "Institution-building of the United Nations Human Rights Council." 7 August. Doc. A/HRC/RES/5/1.

Human Rights Committee. 2005. "K.L. v. Peru. Communication 1153/2003". 22 November. Doc. CCPR/C/85/D/1153/2003.

Hunt, Paul H. 2017. "Configuring the UN Human Rights System in the 'Era of Implementation': Mainland and Archipelago." *Human Rights Quarterly* 39(3): 489–538.

IAP (Independent Accountability Panel). 2016. *2016: Old Challenges, New Hope: Accountability for the Global Strategy for Women's, Children's and Adolescents' Health.* https://www.everywomaneverychild.org/wp-content/uploads/2017/03/IAP_Summary_September2016.pdf.

International Institutions and Global Governance Program. 2012. *The Global Human Rights Regime.* https://www.cfr.org/report/global-human-rights-regime.

Kälin, Walter. 2014. "Ritual and Ritualism at the Universal Periodic Review: A Preliminary Appraisal." In *Human Rights and the Universal Periodic Review: Rituals and Ritualism,* edited by Hilary Charlesworth and Emma Larking, 25–41. Cambridge: Cambridge University Press.

Kälin, Walter and Cecilia Jimenez. 2003. *Reform of the UN Commission on Human Rights.* Bern/Geneva, Switzerland: Institute of Public Law: University of Bern.

McMahon, Edward R. 2017. *The Universal Periodic Review: A Work in Progress.* Berlin: Friedrich Ebert Stiftung.

Nifosi, Ingrid. 2005. *The UN Special Procedures in the Field of Human Rights.* Antwerpen-Oxford: Intersentia.

OAS (Organization of American States). 1994. *Inter-American Convention on the Prevention, Punishment and Eradication of Violence against Women ("Convention of Belem do Para").* Washington, D.C.: Organization of American States.

Office of the High Commissioner for Human Rights (OHCHR). 2016a. *Information Note for UN Resident Coordinators, UN Country Teams and UN Entities regarding the Universal Periodic Review (Third Cycle) of the Human Rights Council.* Geneva: United Nations.

OHCHR. 2016b. *National Mechanisms for Reporting and Follow-up: A Practical Guide to Engagement with International Human Rights Mechanisms.* Geneva: OHCHR.

OHCHR. 2017a. "Human Rights Bodies." Accessed May 20, 2017. http://www.ohchr.org/EN/HRBodies/Pages/HumanRightsBodies.aspx.

OHCHR. 2017c. "Status of Ratification Interactive Dashboard." Last updated May 18. http://indicators.ohchr.org.

OHCHR 2017d. "Universal Periodic Review." Accessed May 20, 2017. http://www.ohchr.org/EN/HRBodies/UPR/Pages/UPRMain.aspx.

OHCHR and Center for Economic and Social Rights. 2013. *Who Will Be Accountable? Human Rights and the Post-2015 Development Agenda.* New York and Geneva: United Nations.

PMNCH (Partnership on Maternal, Newborn and Child Health). 2011. *A Review of Global Accountability Mechanisms for Women's and Children's Health.* Geneva: PMNCH.

Potts, Helen. 2008. *Accountability and the Right to the Highest Attainable Standard of Health.* Colchester: Human Rights Centre, University of Essex. http://repository.essex.ac.uk/9717/1/accountability-right-highest-attainable-standard-health.pdf.

President of the HRC (Human Rights Council). 2016. *Inputs from the President of the Human Rights Council to the 2016 HLPF: The Work of the Human Rights Council in relation to the 2030 Agenda for Sustainable Development.* Geneva: United Nations. http://www.ohchr.org/Documents/Issues/MDGs/Post2015/Contribution2016HLPF.pdf.

Sedgh, Gilda, Stanley Henshaw, Susheela Singh, Elisabeth Åhman, and Iqbal H. Shah. 2007. "Induced Abortion: Estimated Rates and Trends Worldwide." *The Lancet* 370(9595): 1338–1345.

Surya P. Subedi. 2011. "Protection of Human Rights through the Mechanism of UN Special Rapporteurs." *Human Rights Quarterly* 33(11): 201–228.

UN (United Nations). 1945. "Charter of the United Nations." 24 October. UN Doc. 1 UNTS XVI.

UN (United Nations). 1994. "Report of the International Conference on Population and Development." UN Doc. A/Conf.171/13.

UN General Assembly, 3rd Session. 1948. "Universal Declaration of Human Rights." 10 December. UN Doc. A/RES/3/217A.

UN General Assembly, 21st Session. 1966a. "International Covenant on Civil and Political Rights." 16 December. UN Doc. A/RES/21/2200.

UN General Assembly, 21st Session. 1966b. "International Covenant on Economic, Social, and Cultural Rights." 16 December. UN Doc. A/RES/21/2200A.

UN General Assembly, 85th Session. 1993. "Declaration on the Elimination of Violence Against Women." 20 December. UN Doc. A/RES/48/104.

UN General Assembly, 60th Session. 2005. "2005 World Summit Outcome." 24 October. UN Doc. A/RES/60/1.

UN General Assembly, 70th Session. 2015. "Transforming Our World: the 2030 Agenda for Sustainable Development." 25 September. UN Doc. A/RES/70/1.

UN Secretary-General. 2005. "In Larger Freedom: Towards Development, Security and Human Rights for All." 21 March. UN Doc. A/59/2005.

UNDP (UN Development Program). 2015. *Strengthening Engagement with the International Human Rights Machinery.* Oslo: United Nations Development Program.

UNFPA. 2014. *Lessons from the First Cycle of the Universal Periodic Review: From Commitment to Action on Sexual and Reproductive Health and Rights.* New York: UNFPA.

United Nations Population Fund (UNFPA). 2013. Annex of *UNFPA Strategic Plan, 2014–2017. Integrated Results Framework.* New York: UNFPA.

UPR Info (Universal Periodic Review Info). 2014. *Beyond promises: The impact of the UPR on the ground.* Geneva: UPR Info.

UPR Info. 2017. *The Civil Society Compendium: A Comprehensive Guide for Civil Society Organisations Engaging in the Universal Periodic Review.* Geneva: UPR Info.

Conclusion

Comparative Analysis of Human Rights in Global Governance for Health

BENJAMIN MASON MEIER AND LAWRENCE O. GOSTIN

Human rights are implemented in global health through a dynamic global governance system—extending across the World Health Organization's (WHO's) mandate to realize the right to health; United Nations (UN) specialized agency efforts to address a range of health-related human rights; economic governance to support rights-based priorities in public health funding; and human rights governance to advance global health. The unique context of each institution is crucial to implementing human rights for global health, with organizations often employing distinct health-related human rights to achieve institution-specific goals; however, there are generalizable themes that can be drawn from these experiences and would be broadly applicable as entry points for mainstreaming human rights in global health governance. By comparing the structures that facilitate organizational efforts to advance human rights across the contributing chapters in this volume, it becomes possible to understand the institutional determinants of the rights-based approach to health.

This concluding chapter analyzes these institutional determinants that facilitate human rights mainstreaming for global health and considers generalizable themes for the implementation of human rights through global governance for health. Drawing from across the institutions in this volume, this comparative analysis examines specific structures that shape the implementation of human rights through:

- Governance—advanced by Human Rights Leadership and Member State Support;
- Bureaucracy—engaging Human Rights Officers and Technical Units;
- Collaborations—through Human Rights System Engagement, Inter-Organizational Partnerships, and Civil Society Participation; and

Human Rights in Global Health. Benjamin Mason Meier and Lawrence O. Gostin.

- Accountability—drawing on mechanisms for Internal Monitoring and Independent Evaluation.

These themes reflect the collective analyses undertaken by the contributing chapters in this volume, which have each examined organizational structures that can either facilitate or inhibit human rights mainstreaming in global governance for health. Where these common structures highlight how institutions are advancing rights-based governance in a globalizing world—framing institutional policies, programs, and practices to implement human rights in global health—this comparative conclusion raises a research imperative to develop a field of study on human rights in global health governance.

I. GOVERNANCE

Governance for human rights in global health is grounded seminally in an organization's constitution, which provides an institutional foundation for human rights under international law. Based upon this constitutional mandate, the operationalization of human rights norms in global governance often manifests itself in the revision of the institutional mission, strategic plan, or policy framework to incorporate human rights (Oberleitner 2007). Such "institutional law" provides a basis for organizational efforts to advance human rights in global health (Alvarez 2005). This formal organizational commitment to human rights provides a basis to mainstream human rights in the strategic framework of the organization, where these political changes can be driven from the top through both secretariat leaders and member states.

A. Human Rights Leadership

Secretariat leadership has long been seen as a pivotal driver for the organizational promotion of human rights, exemplified in both UN efforts to mainstream rights (Robinson 2006) and WHO efforts to advance rights-based health reforms (Meier 2010). Drawing from UN system-wide efforts to mainstream human rights, secretariat leaders have sought to spearhead efforts to integrate human rights into their respective organizations. Where stakeholders inside and outside of the organization can be seen as cautious of the organizational implementation of human rights (Barkan 2002), secretariat leaders have the political authority to reform the practices of staff members (Chesterman 2017), overcome resistance in international relations (Chorev 2012), and implement human rights to realize their organizational mission (Oestreich 2007). These secretariat leaders are able to justify the operationalization of human rights, and this institutional imprimatur has an agenda-setting effect on the organization (Hall 2010), giving license to organizational staff who may otherwise be reluctant to advance human rights in organizational policies, programs, and practices (Darrow and Arbour 2009). Through this process, leaders transform human rights from standards under international law into mandates for organizational reforms.

Across the institutions in this volume, human rights found varied support from secretariat leaders, with organizations seen to mainstream human rights for global health where leaders expended political capital to assure human rights promotion. With this support often expressed through public statements in support of human rights, chief executives paved the way for human rights implementation. In evolving WHO efforts, former WHO Director-General Gro Harlem Brundtland prioritized human rights in the Office of the Director-General, with Director-General Margaret Chan subsequently creating a separate team dedicated to mainstreaming WHO's cross-cutting efforts on gender, equity, and human rights (GER). The UN Food and Agriculture Organization (FAO) similarly became a crucial force for implementing the right to food where former FAO Director-General Jacques Diouf facilitated support for the rights-based approach, "taking ownership and support" of human rights by personally launching human rights tools in support of the Right to Food Unit. Leading across institutions, former UN Population Fund (UNFPA) Executive Director Nafis Sadik drove support across UN agencies to advance a rights-based approach to sexual and reproductive health at the International Conference on Population and Development. Applied to economic governance, leaders of the World Bank have come to an evolving understanding that economic concerns should not take precedence over public health, recoiling from the harms of past economic policies to play a leadership role in shaping a rights-based approach to development. Similarly, there can be champions for global health among human rights leaders, as seen where former High Commissioner for Human Rights Mary Robinson raised the profile of the right to health within the Office of the UN High Commissioner for Human Rights (OHCHR) and facilitated the mainstreaming of human rights within institutions of global health governance. Where many organizations struggle to advance human rights without such rights-based leadership, bold action from the organizational leadership can send a signal throughout the organization that health-related human rights are a priority at the highest levels, creating momentum for the entire organization to embrace human rights as part of larger mainstreaming efforts.

B. Member State Support

The politics of health and human rights among member states structures the ability of an organization to implement human rights, with states seeking to influence institutions of global health governance (Chorev 2012). Where states oppose human rights, international organizations can become subject to the limitations of international relations (Coomans 2012), leading organizations either to abandon human rights mainstreaming efforts altogether or to implement human rights norms and principles *sub rosa*, without explicit reference to international human rights law (Ball 2008). Conversely, in cases where states support human rights, national efforts to realize human rights can provide a foundation to shift global governance toward human rights implementation (Bustreo and Hunt 2013), and such intergovernmental political leadership for human rights in global governance can correspondingly support the ensuing "diffusion of norms," operationalizing global norms in national policy (Brown 2014).

States have historically sought to limit efforts to advance human rights in global health, and these concerns with health-related human rights long inhibited institutions of global health governance. Seen most forcefully in the politics of the Cold War, where economic and social rights were derided by Western states as secondary to civil and political rights, WHO was pressed to restrict its efforts to develop the human right to health under international law. This political resistance to developing human rights engulfed other UN specialized agencies, each seeking to withdraw from health-related human rights as a means of presenting themselves as "non-political" organizations carrying out a technical mission. Following the Cold War, however, a political space opened for the discussion of health-related human rights in global governance—focused initially on civil and political rights but evolving to encompass economic, social, and cultural rights. The political support of states is now seen as crucial in expanding institutional mandates to implement rights underlying a wide range of determinants of health. Where institutional agendas are set by member states, acting through state-led legislative bodies, states can adopt a human rights policy to structure the work of the organization. In situations where governments have continued to be seen as obstacles in addressing the health implications of human rights violations (as seen in the political context of HIV/AIDS, abortion, and child labor), organizations have sought to implement human rights implicitly, operationalizing rights-based attributes and principles without explicit discussion of human rights or reference to international legal standards that may antagonize member states. Beyond negotiations in international relations, single states can influence an organization's approach to human rights—through governing bodies, seconded staff, or extrabudgetary support. With this influence seen in the World Bank, individual states can either shift a recalcitrant organization to mainstream rights (as seen through the Nordic Trust Fund) or oppose rights-based efforts that may scrutinize domestic practices (as seen in China's challenges to rights-based governance in the Bank). This state influence on health-related human rights is felt most directly through bilateral health assistance, with many foreign assistance programs having explicit provisions on the rights-based approach to health, and it is this rights-based assistance for health that the proposed Global Fund for Health seeks to coordinate in realizing rights to meet the health-related Sustainable Development Goals (SDGs).

II. BUREAUCRACY

Where institutions have autonomy to advance human rights in global health governance, international organization bureaucracies have independent influence over organizational programming and practice. The UN system-wide approach to human rights sought "to enhance its [the UN's] human rights programme and fully integrate it [human rights] into the broad range of the Organisation's activities" (UN Secretary-General 1997, para. 79); yet over the past two decades, this system-wide approach to human rights mainstreaming has required institution-specific bureaucratization of human rights. Rather than imposing human rights from the outside, staff must perceive the value of human rights to their organizational mission, implement rights in their global health programming, and embrace human rights as a normative basis for their efforts (Oberleitner 2007). Where this implementation of human rights requires changes in staff self-perceptions, attitudes, capacities, resources, and practices, it is necessary to understand the ways in which the organization's human rights officers seek to support the application of human rights among technical staff, reforming the organizational culture for human rights in global health governance.

A. Human Rights Officers

The application of international law in institutional programs and practices has required human rights officers to support human rights implementation. While mainstreaming should, by definition, be decentralized—with responsibility for human rights dispersed across the entire organization—specialized human rights units are necessary to build capacity and commitment for mainstreaming efforts (Uggla 2007). These specialized human rights officers provide an additional bureaucratic layer to advise technical staff in translating an organization's commitment to human rights into technical programming, assuring that an organization moves beyond the rhetoric of human rights to implement the obligations of human rights. As global health organizations with limited legal capacity have been seen as ineffective in implementing human rights law (Taylor 1992), human rights expertise is thought to play a formative role in ensuring institutional capacity to mainstream rights (Oberleitner 2007), with human rights lawyers assisting technical officers to operationalize international legal standards in rights-based programmatic actions (Oestreich 2007).

Several contributing chapters in this volume were written with the co-authorship or the review of an organization's human rights officers, providing a unique perspective into the institutional resources and structures necessary for these officers to support mainstreaming efforts. Where medical practitioners are thought to be hesitant to engage with the legal obligations of human rights, WHO's human rights advisors have sought to "demystify" the human rights paradigm, serving as a bridge between human rights standards under international law and public health agendas through WHO programming. The UN Population Fund (UNFPA) found in the late 1990s that operationalizing reproductive rights necessitated the hiring of its first human rights advisor to interpret international standards and train technical staff, with this position subsequently elevated into a "Gender, Human Rights and Development Branch" to provide guidance and develop a manual on integrating human rights into UNFPA's work. Despite these benefits of specialized human rights expertise, it is unclear where these advisors can most effectively be situated in the organization; as a result, organizations have long struggled to develop sustainable structures for human rights capacity-building and mainstreaming, often relying on short-term leadership initiatives or extrabudgetary funding to support these often-temporary positions. To institutionalize human rights advisors in the permanent structures and processes of an institution, the Global Fund to Fight AIDS, Tuberculosis and Malaria (Global Fund) created a Community, Rights, and Gender (CRG) Department to lead staff training on human rights, analyze challenges to realizing human rights objectives, and scale up human rights programming. In supporting the efforts of human rights officers, the organization's legal counsel is often seen as a key ally, shaping human rights discourse within the organization's leadership and providing influential legal opinions to recognize the relevance of human rights to the organization's mandate.

B. Technical Units

Where many institutions proclaim adherence to human rights norms and principles, this proclamation is not always translated into bureaucratic application across technical units. Beyond the work of human rights experts, mainstreaming human rights requires commitment, understanding, and application by technical professionals across disciplines and sectors, necessitating an approach to human rights beyond legal implementation (Hunt 2017). Technical unit support for human rights is seen as essential to human rights mainstreaming, where "true believers" among technical staff motivate organizational reforms and overcome internal obstacles to human rights (Oberleitner 2007); conversely, human rights mainstreaming can be blunted where technical staff resist programs that do not align with their technical training and are not seen to impact their technical mission (Oestreich 2007). Yet, the development of an institutional culture to mainstream rights is often a lengthy process, with incremental changes necessary to train staff to understand the rights-based approach (Frankovits 2006), highlight the application of human rights to technical programs (Oestreich 2007), and inspire "buy-in" from technical officers (Oberleitner 2008). As compared with human rights officers, who see the need for mainstreaming at a principled level, technical officers are often seen to require evidence that the application of human rights makes a positive difference to their technical work—improving programs, operations, and outcomes (Bustreo and Hunt 2013). Once convinced of the instrumental effects and operational feasibility of human rights, staff must then be able to understand the practical application of the rights-based approach to their programming, identifying rights-holders and duty-bearers and addressing capacity gaps in claiming rights and implementing duties (Clarke 2012).

The technical units examined across the institutions in this volume often do not fully understand either the inherent importance or the instrumental promise of human rights, and, at times, it is perceived that human rights operationalization will come at the expense of efficiency in global health programming—whether in the public health perspectives of WHO officers, the service delivery perspectives of UNFPA staff, the economics perspectives of World Bank management, or the cost-effectiveness perspectives of Global Fund support. To engender support from technical officers, human rights most clearly find technical buy-in where the implementation of human rights is seen to buttress the organization's technical mission, as seen where: WHO developed an empirical analysis of the public health impacts of the rights-based approach to health; International Labor Organization (ILO) staff saw the value of human rights in occupational safety and health efforts with vulnerable populations; FAO demonstrated the instrumental value of the right-to-food approach to overcome the retort that "you can't eat human rights"; the World Bank examined the impact of human rights promotion on development outcomes; and foreign assistance programs sought indicator identification, statistical analysis, and impact assessment for rights-based health assistance. Human rights advisors have sought to encourage these empirical assessments as a basis to provide technical validation of human rights promotion. Rather than pursuing institution-wide human rights mainstreaming, human rights officers have often pursued an incremental strategy that focuses on individual pilot projects or individual country offices that could provide evidence of the instrumental advantages of human rights. Sharing these results across technical units, human rights focal points (across units at headquarters and in regional and national offices) provide a path by which to disseminate evidence of human rights influence on public health promotion.

III. COLLABORATIONS

Rights-based collaborations can prove crucial to human rights mainstreaming in global health, enlisting allies and expanding resources to mainstream human rights across health-related sectors. Such collaborations began to spread across the UN following (1) Secretary-General Kofi Annan's system-wide call in the late 1990s to mainstream human rights across all UN work (Kędzia 2009) and (2) the UN Development Group's (UNDG's) adoption of a 2003 Common Understanding on Human Rights-based Approaches in Development Cooperation and Programming (Coomans 2012). Where rights-based collaborations can influence the substance and process of mainstreaming, these collaborations for human rights in global governance for health now encompass human rights system engagement, inter-organizational partnerships, and civil society participation.

A. Human Rights System Engagement

The human rights system can engage with other global governance institutions where those institutions seek external reinforcements for human rights mainstreaming. Global governance through the UN human rights system has arisen out of the interconnected institutions that support human rights implementation, including the UN's human rights bureaucracy in the OHCHR, independent monitoring through human rights treaty bodies, and inter-governmental policymaking under the Human Rights Council (Steiner, Alston, and Goodman 2008). Drawing on this human rights system to mainstream human rights, the effective mainstreaming of human rights in institutions of global governance can be seen as a measure of success for human rights governance, with these governing organizations developing human rights standards and implementing human rights norms (Oberleitner 2008). In operationalizing human rights at the center of global governance, the human rights system can "welcome, encourage, foster, support and scrutinize" the independent mandates of organizations of global governance in their human rights mainstreaming efforts (Hunt 2017, 529). While there are concerns that greater involvement of the human rights system will allow global governance institutions to shirk their implementation responsibilities (Mertus 2005), these complementary institutions of human rights governance can be seen as supportive (rather than redundant) in the mainstreaming of human rights in global health governance (Gilmore et al. 2015).

The UN human rights system has sought to encourage human rights main-streaming in global governance for health, clarifying institutional responsibilities for health-related human rights, providing human rights technical assistance to global health institutions, and facilitating human rights accountability for global health policy. Drawing on its human rights leadership in the global HIV/AIDS response, OHCHR now co-chairs the UNDG Human Rights Working Group to ensure that the human rights-based approach is integrated into all UN activities to meet the SDGs. Creating a formal "Framework for Cooperation" with WHO, OHCHR has established a joint program of work and high-level working groups to secure polit-ical support for implementing human rights in women's, children's, and adolescents' health. Similar OHCHR engagement has supported institutions of global health governance across the UN system, building human rights capacity among UN agencies and programs in translating their commitment to human rights into rights-based policies and programs. The political branches of the human rights system have also provided unique opportunities for organizational engagement, with the Human Rights Council proving a groundbreaking forum to advance global health in economic governance, whether in the context of shifting discussion from the WTO on access to medicines or in monitoring organizational implementation of the right to development. Where global health governance suffers from a dearth of institu-tional mechanisms to scrutinize the performance of governments in improving the health of their peoples, the human rights system provides a range of international monitoring mechanisms for assessing the realization of health-related human rights. In facilitating accountability through human rights treaty bodies, country offices of the UN Children's Fund (UNICEF) have advanced child health programming with member states through monitoring by the Committee on the Rights of the Child. UNFPA has sought to work with treaty bodies, special procedures mandate holders, and the Human Rights Council, pursuing rights-based accountability through the Universal Periodic Review (UPR) to support monitoring and follow-up on sexual and reproductive health. Ensuring that human rights are mainstreamed in global governance for health, the human rights system seeks coherence in the rights-based approach across all UN programs; however, even as global health governance is be-coming more dependent on collaborations with the human rights system, as seen under the SDGs, the recent rise of nationalist challenges may limit UN discussion of human rights, and it will be necessary to analyze how these obstacles to the human rights system will influence the rights-based approach to health.

B. Inter-Organizational Partnerships

Human rights mainstreaming in global governance also requires work across sectors that can best be facilitated through inter-organizational partnerships. Given the fragmentation, duplication, and confusion resulting from the uncoordinated initiatives of overlapping organizations, each operating under independent nor-mative frameworks and political motivations, inter-organizational partnerships provide a means to realize shared norms through human rights, contributing to a "coherent multilateralism" that can allow rights-based challenges to be addressed holistically (Oberleitner 2008, 388). Overcoming the challenges of a decentralized, "functionalist" global governance system, partnerships across organizations have arisen to address a multi-sectoral array of determinants of health (Meier and Fox 2010). Without institutional hierarchies to coordinate this crowded landscape of actors, rights-based partnerships can galvanize a disparate set of organizations to embrace a shared vision of human rights (Meier 2011). Where organizations may be reluctant to employ human rights, their work with other organizations can provide a forum for: sharing implementation experiences across organizational platforms, facilitating greater alignment with human rights norms, and raising new ways of thinking about rights-based approaches to governance (Oberleitner 2007). These decentralized partnerships lack the hierarchical structures of past efforts, yet the harmonizing force of human rights allows for positive reinforcement across multiple organizations with distributed authorities, with each organization undertaking coordinated aspects of a single global policy agenda (Szlezak et al. 2010). Facilitating collaborations across institutions, the 2030 Agenda for Sustainable Development provides a renewed basis for cooperative rights-based efforts to realize health-related targets under the SDGs (UNDG 2017).

Although WHO once had unquestioned authority over global health, the contemporary era lacks an institutional leader to coordinate global initiatives to prevent disease and promote health. Bringing together rights-based organizations in the absence of inter-organizational leadership, inter-organizational partnerships have become particularly relevant in a global health landscape of scarce resources (and increased competition for those resources among an expanding set of actors), with partnerships for specific health priorities combining the efforts of inherently limited organizations to achieve collective health goals through human rights. Beginning in the HIV/AIDS response, UNAIDS and the Global Fund have coordinated efforts to operationalize rights-based systems for HIV prevention, treatment, care, and support, with UNAIDS providing guidance on rights-based barriers to HIV services and the Global Fund encouraging country applications to address these human rights barriers. Similarly, the ILO developed its recommendations on HIV-related occupational discrimination through collaborations with both UNAIDS and OHCHR. Facilitating the public health efforts of the UN Educational, Scientific and Cultural Organization (UNESCO), its work with WHO in the development of their Council for International Organizations of Medical Sciences (CIOMS) partnership allowed for work at the intersection of human rights and bioethics that would not have been possible in isolation. Inter-organizational global health governance partnerships have evolved to embrace human rights as a normative bond, with the rights-based approach becoming the "normative glue" that binds actors together to realize shared global health goals. Implementing human rights for women's health, an inter-agency reporting group was created across UNFPA, UN Women, UNICEF, the UN Development Programme (UNDP), and FAO to ensure a more coherent, systematic, and system-wide engagement with women's rights. Bridging global health and economic governance, international financial institutions now also find themselves collaborating across sectors for the first time under shared human rights frameworks. Supported by the institutionalization of the Global Fund, proponents argue that the allocation of such independent, predictable, and sustainable funding could be a means to harmonize partnerships across global health governance and national foreign assistance. Where such partnerships necessitate coordination, the SDGs will require partnerships across a wider range of health-related institutions and governance initiatives to implement health-related human rights.

C. Civil Society Participation

The participation of civil society in global governance is a key determinant of human rights mainstreaming, assuring that human rights mainstreaming in international organizations remains attentive to communities bereft of rights. Human rights principles demand civil society participation (London and Schneider 2012), and civil society participation facilitates accountability for human rights (Weiss, Carayannis, and Jolly 2009). By taking human rights mainstreaming outside of the secretariat headquarters, organizations have engaged a bottom-up approach to human rights implementation, partnering with civil society to make human rights a reality (Silberschmidt, Matheson, and Kickbusch 2008). Recognizing the importance of civil society participation to human rights realization, organizations have worked to incorporate civil society participation into global governance structures, enlisting transnational advocacy networks in areas where domestic institutions are closed to civil society (Jönsson and Jönsson 2012). Yet, civil society participation requires organizational support and human rights training to build capacity among institutional partners, and it is not clear how organizations can support meaningful participation to encourage human rights implementation.

Global health governance institutions have been supported in the public health and human rights landscape by civil society representatives and non-governmental organizations (NGOs), which have collaborated with global institutions in their rights-based health efforts while pressuring those same institutions when they have failed to live up to their implementation obligations. Given the rise of public health issues on the global policy agenda and the political spotlight on global health inequities, civil society organizations are employing human rights advocacy to participate in global health governance—as seen in direct engagement with UNAIDS, pressure on states to support UNFPA, protests outside of WTO meetings, and inclusion on the Board of the Global Fund. Although WHO is just beginning to open space for civil society participation in strategy development, policy design, and World Health Assembly debates, other UN organizations have found mechanisms to incorporate civil society, whether through the "tripartism" of the ILO, giving non-governmental participants from workers' organizations the right to participate and vote in all ILO meetings; the "open door policy" of FAO, giving voice to food-insecure groups in the Committee on World Food Security; or the Programme Coordinating Board of UNAIDS, giving affected communities a platform to contextualize the lived experiences of those affected by AIDS. This rights-based civil society advocacy has raised awareness of the health impacts of global economic governance, with NGOs putting pressure on the World Bank to engage human rights in monitoring the health impacts of its projects and forcing the WTO to respond to protests around environmental, health, and labor rights. With human rights justifying a seat for civil society at the governance table, the Global Fund has sought to include those affected by AIDS, tuberculosis, and malaria—on its Board, in country coordination mechanisms, and through the New Funding Model—providing technical assistance to NGOs and allowing for the meaningful participation of key populations in all funding decisions. The human rights system has similarly sought to engage civil society through national human rights institutions and international monitoring mechanisms, operationalizing meaningful participation as a cross-cutting human rights principle that is instrumental to accountability for health-related human rights, with individual human rights treaty bodies and the UPR system encouraging civil society consultation in state reports and permitting alternative (or shadow) reporting from NGOs. Where civil society participation needs to be nurtured in global health governance, human rights have provided a pathway to assure support from organizations, provide opportunities for engagement, and advocate reforms to policy.

IV. ACCOUNTABILITY

Accountability for institutional action is necessary to ensure the implementation of human rights in global health. Furthering the implementation of human rights, accountability seeks responsibility, answerability, and enforceability of normative standards in global governance (OHCHR 2013). While organizations often develop accountability mechanisms to press states to realize rights in their health-related efforts (Yamin 2013), it is often unclear what accountability mechanisms exist to press the institution itself to implement rights in its governance efforts. Scholars have begun to advocate for such institutional accountability, with mechanisms to require "sustained support, constructive scrutiny and quality control of their human rights content" (Hunt 2017). In facilitating rights-based accountability in global health, institutions have looked to both internal monitoring and independent evaluation to assure the mainstreaming of human rights in instutional policies, programs, and practices.

A. Internal Monitoring

Institutions have sought to integrate human rights into organizational policies and programs, but have been less effective in changing the institutional culture guiding individual practices. Accordingly, there is a need for human rights strategies to be translated into individual-level efforts and specific practical actions that staff can take to meet key human rights norms and rights-based principles. To facilitate the implementation of human rights in organizational practice, "professionalizing" human rights implementation, organizations have sought to structure staff efforts to implement a human rights-based approach, confirming that the operationalization of human rights extends beyond self-defined values to reflect international legal obligations. Where "the mainstreaming of human rights throughout the UN system has created demand for tools that might help with that endeavour" (Murphy 2013, 129), standard management tools have been developed to assess organizational structures, processes, and outcomes to implement human rights (Hunt 2017). The UN human rights system has developed indicators to monitor state implementation of human rights; however, there is no corresponding analytic tool to assess human rights implementation in global governance. Assuring that such internal assessments become more than a technical exercise of "ticking boxes" on a checklist (Koskenniemi 2010), organizations have independently sought to develop qualitative criteria to monitor the progress of human rights mainstreaming without stifling individual creativity. These multi-disciplinary and mixed-method reviews seek to provide a basis for staff assessment, a survey of organizational strengths, a guide for program planning, a basis for support to member states, and a prioritization for capacity-building.

Internal human rights monitoring has taken various forms by different institutions of global governance for health. Seeking to mainstream human rights as part of its larger gender, equity, and human rights mainstreaming effort, WHO has developed human rights "markers" and "criteria" to assess attributes of the right to health and cross-cutting human rights principles in the practices of WHO technical programs and individual staff. Where FAO monitoring focuses on quantitative outcomes, this limited quantitative review highlights the difficulty of monitoring human rights, where measures of short-term results have not rewarded technical staff whose rights-based efforts to catalyze government human rights implementation have proven difficult to measure quantitatively. Responding to external complaints, the World Bank's Inspection Panel now investigates stakeholder grievances where noncompliance with Bank policies and procedures could bring about harms to public health or violations of human rights. Similarly, the Global Fund established an internal "hotline" telephone number and email address to receive anonymous complaints from anyone who has experienced or witnessed a human rights violation linked to a Global Fund–supported program; however, only a small number of complaints were received, of which an even smaller number were considered to be eligible for resolution. Expanding internal monitoring to assure institutional accountability, it will be necessary to look beyond process measures of human rights implementation, monitoring the outcomes of programmatic change and examining the results of rights-based programming to determine whether rights are progressively respected, protected, and fulfilled. Such an outcome assessment, to the extent that human rights implementation is amenable to measurement and correlated with public health, can serve as an evidence base to encourage technical unit application of human rights and justify the continued mainstreaming of human rights in global health governance.

B. Independent Evaluation

Independent evaluations from outside of the institution are also needed to help ensure that organizational programming applies human rights to realize public health. Grounded in a conceptual framework reflective of international human rights norms and principles, these periodic external assessments allow for: an examination of the application of human rights in organizational programming, an analysis of the enabling environment for the implementation of human rights in the organization, and a series of recommendations to overcome challenges to human rights mainstreaming (UNICEF 2012). To undertake these mixed-method reviews, institutions look to those who are outside the organization but familiar with both the human rights framework and the organization's programming. Facilitating accountability for human rights in global governance, the findings of these evaluations provide information to organizational leaders in the design of organizational programming and feedback to technical staff in the course of organizational practice.

Institutions have long looked to independent evaluations as a basis for "quality control" in the implementation of human rights in global governance for health. Commissioning outside consultancy firms, these firms have proven adept at conducting institution-wide analyses of WHO policies, programs, and practices to assess their coherence with human rights standards and UNICEF programming to understand the strengths and weaknesses of the rights-based approach. The ILO has enlisted a Committee of Experts on the Application of Conventions and Recommendations to carry out General Surveys of ILO standards and action, examining how challenges to occupational safety and health correspond with human rights obligations. Looking to other organizations, the Global Fund has turned to UNDP to investigate whether Global Fund grants sufficiently address human rights-related barriers faced by affected populations, employing inclusive consultations and key performance indicators in an initiative to assess the percentage of country allocations invested in (1) programs to reduce human rights-related barriers and (2) programs targeting key populations. Assessing the effectiveness of human rights governance, external evaluations have been undertaken through UN General Assembly reviews of OHCHR, academic analyses on the special procedures mandate holders, OHCHR reports to streamline human rights treaty bodies, and empirical research to understand the health-related focus of the UPR. Facilitating comparative empirical analysis across institutions, there is a need to develop universal indicators of human rights implementation in global governance. Human rights indicators for global health—derived from treaty language, selected with institutional actors, and sanctioned through human rights governance—can provide a basis to evaluate whether institutional implementation is in accordance with human rights obligations and thereby facilitate accountability for human rights implementation in global health governance.

CONCLUSION

Human rights provide legitimacy to global governance, and institutions of global governance have increasingly implemented human rights to advance global health. Given the evolving implementation of human rights in global governance for health, the rights-based approach is now seen as a principal normative framework for health-related policies, programs, and practices. As a result, there has been a wider sharing of human rights responsibilities beyond the human rights system, and it is crucial to recognize this larger landscape for human rights in global governance for health. While there were concerns that the proliferation of institutions of global health governance could undercut efforts to mainstream human rights, the contributing chapters in this volume tell the opposite story: an expanding number of global institutions are addressing a multisectoral array of political, economic, and social determinants of health, with the interconnectedness across these determinants of public health reflecting the inter-dependence of health-related human rights. Yet, these institutions are only beginning to develop structures to assure that organizational efforts to implement human rights are more than just rhetoric, reflecting concrete legal entitlements for public health and genuine policy efforts to effect change.

The expansion of rights-based governance for global health raises a research imperative for institutional analysis at the intersection of human rights and global health—studying universal rights frameworks and common organizational structures that reflect "good practices" for mainstreaming human rights in global governance for health. Understanding the ongoing evolution of rights-based governance in a globalizing world will require continuing research. As the first comparative survey of its kind—focusing on institutional structures conducive to human rights in global health—additional research will be necessary across a larger number of organizational approaches to implementing health-related human rights. This is the start of a larger research agenda on human rights in global health governance, analyzing why certain institutional structures facilitate human rights implementation, how the implementation of health-related human rights can be assessed, and what effects these rights-based policies, programs, and practices have on global health. By understanding the ways in which organizations realize human rights in global health, empirical analysis of these institutional structures can provide a basis to advance health as a means to a more just world.

REFERENCES

Alvarez, José E. 2005. *International Organizations as Law-Makers*. New York: Oxford University Press.

Ball, Rachel. 2008. "Doing It Quietly: The World Bank's Engagement with Human Rights." *Monash University Law Review* 34: 331–369.

Barkan, Elazar. 2002. "Human Rights Leader or Reluctant Supporter?" *International Studies Review* 4(3): 199–202.

Brown, Garrett Wallace. 2014. "Norm Diffusion and Health System Strengthening: The Persistent Relevance of National Leadership in Global Health Governance." *Review of International Studies* 40: 877–896.

Bustreo, Flavia and Paul Hunt. 2013. "The Right to Health Is Coming of Age: Evidence of Impact and the Importance of Leadership." *Journal of Public Health Policy* 34(4): 574–579.

Chesterman, Simon. 2017. "Executive Heads." In Cogan, Jacob Katz, Ian Hurd, and Ian Johnstone, *The Oxford Handbook of International Organizations*. Oxford: Oxford University Press.

Chorev, Nitsan. 2012. *The World Health Organization Between North and South*. Ithaca: Cornell University Press.

Clarke, Alisa. 2012. "The Potential of the Human Rights-Based Approach for the Evolution of the United Nations as a System." *Human Rights Review* 13: 225–248.

Coomans, Fons. 2012. "On the Right(s) Track? United Nations (Specialized) Agencies and the Use of Human Rights Language." *Verfassung und Recht in Übersee* 45(3): 274–294.

Darrow, Mac and Louise Arbour. 2009. "The Pillar of Glass: Human Rights in the Development Operations of the United Nations." *American Journal of International Law* 103: 446–501.

Frankovits, André. 2006. *The Human Rights Based Approach and the United Nations System.* Paris: UN Educational, Scientific and Cultural Organization.

Gilmore, Kate, Luis Mora, Alfonso Barragues, and Ida Krogh Mikkelsen. 2015. "The Universal Periodic Review: A Platform for Dialogue, Accountability and Change on Sexual and Reproductive Health and Rights." *Health and Human Rights* 17(2): 169–179.

Hall, Peter A. 2010. "Historical Institutionalism in Rationalist and Sociological Perspective." In *Explaining Institutional Change: Ambiguity, Agency, and Power*, edited by James A. Mahoney and Kathleen Thelen. Cambridge: Cambridge University Press.

Hunt, Paul. 2017. "Configuring the UN Human Rights System in the 'Era of Implementation': Mainland and Archipelago." *Human Rights Quarterly* 39(3): 489–538.

Jönsson, Christer and Kristina Jönsson. 2012. "Global and Local Health Governance: Civil Society, Human Rights and HIV/AIDS." *Third World Quarterly* 33(9): 1719–1734.

Kędzia, Zdzisław. 2009. "Mainstreaming Human Rights in the United Nations." In *International Human Rights Monitoring Mechanisms, Essays in Honour of Jakob Th. Möller*, edited by Gudmundur Alfredsson, Jonas Grimheden, Bertrand G. Ramcharan, and Alfred Zayas. Brill-Nijhoff. http://www.brill.com/international-human-rights-monitoring-mechanisms.

Koskenniemi, Martti. 2010. "Human Rights Mainstreaming as a Strategy for Institutional Power." *Humanity* 1(1): 47–58.

London, Leslie and Helen Schneider. 2012. "Globalisation and Health Inequalities: Can a Human Rights Paradigm Create Space for Civil Society Action?" *Social Science & Medicine* 74: 6–13.

Meier, Benjamin Mason. 2010. "Global Health Governance and the Contentious Politics of Human Rights: Mainstreaming the Right to Health for Public Health Advancement." *Stanford Journal of International Law* 46(1): 1–50.

Meier, Benjamin Mason. 2011. "Global Health Takes a Normative Turn: The Expanding Purview of International Health Law and Global Health Policy to Meet the Public Health Challenges of the 21st Century." *The Global Community: Yearbook of International Law and Jurisprudence* 69–108.

Meier, Benjamin Mason and Ashley M. Fox. 2010. "International Obligations through Collective Rights: Moving from Foreign Health Assistance to Global Health Governance." *Health and Human Rights* 12(1): 61–72.

Mertus, Julie A. 2005. *The United Nations and Human Rights: A Guide for a New Era.* New York: Routledge.

Murphy, Thérèse. 2013. *Health and Human Rights*, 129. Oxford: Hart Publishing.

Oberleitner, Gerd. 2007. *Global Human Rights Institutions.* Cambridge: Polity.

Oberleitner, Gerd. 2008. "A Decade of Mainstreaming Human Rights in the UN: Achievements, Failures, Challenges." *Netherlands Quarterly of Human Rights* 26: 359–390.

Oestreich, Joel E. 2007. *Power and Principle: Human Rights Programming in International Organizations.* Washington: Georgetown University Press.

OHCHR (UN Office of the High Commissioner for Human Rights). 2013. *Who will be accountable? Human Rights and the Post-2015 Development Agenda.* New York; Geneva: United Nations.

Robinson, Mary. 2006. *A Voice for Human Rights.* Philadelphia: University of Pennsylvania Press.

Silberschmidt, Gaudenz, Don Matheson, and Ilona Kickbusch. 2008. "Creating a Committee C of the World Health Assembly." *The Lancet* 371(9263): 1483–1486.

Steiner, Henry J., Philip Alston, and Ryan Goodman. 2008. *International Human Rights in Context: Law, Politics, Morals.* Oxford: Oxford University Press.

Szlezák, Nicole A., Barry R. Bloom, Dean T. Jamison, Gerald T. Keusch, Catherine M. Michaud, Suerie Moon, and William C. Clark. 2010. "The Global Health System: Actors, Norms, and Expectations in Transition." *PLoS Medicine* 7(1): e1000183.

Taylor, Allyn L. 1992. "Making the World Health Organization Work: A Legal Framework for Universal Access to the Conditions for Health." *American Journal of Law and Medicine* 18: 301–346.

Uggla, Fredrik. 2007. "Mainstreaming at Sida: A Synthesis Report." *Sida Studies in Evaluation 2007:05.* Stockholm: Sida.

UNICEF. 2012. *Global Evaluation of the Application of the Human Rights-Based Approach to UNICEF Programming.* New York: UNICEF.

UN Secretary-General. 1997. "Renewing the United Nations: A Programme for Reform." 14 July. UN Doc. A/51/950.

UNDG (UN Development Group). 2017. *Mainstreaming the 2030 Agenda for Sustainable Development—Reference Guide for UN Country Teams.* Available at: https://undg.org/document/mainstreaming-the-2030-agenda-for-sustainable-development-reference-guide-for-un-country-teams/.

Weiss, Thomas G., Tatiana Carayannis, and Richard Jolly. 2009. "The 'Third' United Nations." *Global Governance* 15: 123–142.

Yamin, Alicia Ely. 2013. "Applying Human Rights to Maternal Health: UN Technical Guidance on Rights-Based Approaches." *International Journal of Gynecology and Obstetrics* 121: 190–193.

Afterword

Governance for Global Health and Human Rights in a Populist Age

BENJAMIN MASON MEIER AND LAWRENCE O. GOSTIN

Out of the ashes of the Second World War, institutions of global health and human rights have brought the world together in unprecedented cooperation over the past seventy years, giving rise to the successes and opportunities detailed throughout this volume; however, the current populist age casts new doubts on many of these governance successes and raises debilitating obstacles to future progress. In challenging the shared goals of global governance in responding to a globalizing world, populism—abetted by the resurgent horrors of racism, xenophobia, anti-Semitism, and Islamophobia—seeks to retrench nations inward, with rising nationalist movements directly threatening global institutions and spurring isolationism in international affairs. Such retrenchment could lead to a rejection of both global governance and human rights as a basis for health advancement in the years to come.

The development of this edited volume began in the midst of the current populist challenges to human rights and global health. As the chapters developed, contributing authors sought to reconcile these rapidly-advancing changes in the forward-looking conclusions of their individual chapters—many contemplating for the first time the possibility of a "post–human rights" world. At the end of this comparative analysis, it is necessary to reflect on the influence of these forces across institutions, examining how this pushback is affecting institutional efforts to implement human rights for global health. The current populist age poses a direct threat to institutions of both global health governance and human rights law, and continued progress in global health and human rights should no longer be seen as inevitable. Yet, the chapters in this volume attest to the strength of global institutions and provide hope for a future in which human rights frame institutional efforts to realize the highest attainable standard of health.

Looking to universal norms as a basis for global governance, such populist threats have served not to destroy institutional approaches to human rights, but to unite institutions in their shared promotion of human rights in global health. These autonomous institutions—long working in distinct ways to implement universal rights—have come together in groundbreaking ways in recent years to examine human rights implementation as a foundation to defend global institutions from nationalist challenges. From coordination to cooperation, these institutional partnerships are envisioning governance structures that mainstream rights to strengthen institutional priorities in global health policy and ensure mutual accountability for investments in public health systems. Supported by transnational activist networks and civil society movements, such public health partnerships across non-governmental organizations and inter-governmental organizations are engaging in rights-based diplomatic advocacy as a means to buttress global governance, resisting the populist challenges facing global health and human rights.

Index

Human Rights in Global Health. Benjamin Mason Meier and Lawrence O. Gostin.
© Oxford University Press 2018. Published 2018 by Oxford University Press.